# Sixth Edition

# Essentials of Human Communication

Joseph A. DeVito

*Hunter College of the*
*City University of New York*

PEARSON

Boston   New York   San Francisco
Mexico City   Montreal   Toronto   London   Madrid   Munich   Paris
Hong Kong   Singapore   Tokyo   Cape Town   Sydney

Editor-in-Chief: Karon Bowers
Associate Editor: Deb Hanlon
Series Editorial Assistant: Jenny Lupica
Marketing Manager: Suzan Czajkowski
Editorial Production Service: Nesbitt Graphics, Inc.
Composition Buyer: Linda Cox
Manufacturing Buyer: JoAnne Sweeney
Electronic Composition: Nesbitt Graphics, Inc.
Interior Design: Nesbitt Graphics, Inc.
Photo Researcher: Nesbitt Graphics, Inc.
Cover Designer: Joel Gendron

For related titles and support materials, visit our online catalog at www.ablongman.com.

ISBN-13: 978-0-205-49146-9   ISBN-10: 0-205-49146-4

**Library of Congress Cataloging-in-Publication Data**

DeVito, Joseph A.
    Essentials of human communication/Joseph A. DeVito.—6th ed.
        p. cm.
    Includes bibliographical references and index.
    ISBN 0-205-49146-4 (pbk.)
        1. Communication. I. Title.

    P90.D483 2008
    302.2—dc22

                                                                    2005043697

# Brief Contents

## The Interviewing Guidebook

A separate book focusing on informative and employment interviews is available for packaging with this book. Some restrictions apply.

## CD-ROM Units

These sections are included on the CD-ROM with bonus units, which is available for packaging with this book. Some restrictions apply.

### The Mass Media
### Emotional Communication
### Criticism in the Public Speaking Classroom
### Developing Special Occasion Speeches

# Contents

Contents    **v**

## 9 Members and Leaders in Small Group Communication   199

## 10 Public Speaking Preparation (Steps 1–6)   217

# The Interviewing Guidebook

This separate book focuses on informative and employment interviews and is available to be packaged with the text. Some restrictions apply.

## The Nature of Interviewing
The Interview Process
General Interview Structures
Types of Interview Questions
Ethical Considerations in Interviewing

## The Information Interview
Select the Person
Secure an Appointment
Prepare Your Questions
Establish Rapport
Tape the Interview
Ask Open-Ended Questions
Close and Follow Up the Interview
Informative Interview Preparation Guide

## The Employment Interview
Prepare Yourself
Prepare Your Résumé
Prepare Answers and Questions
Make an Effective Presentation of Self
Dress for Interview Success
Arrive on Time

Demonstrate Effective Interpersonal
  Communication
Acknowledge Cultural Rules and Customs
Mentally Review the Interview
Follow Up
The Lawfulness of Questions
Employment Interview Preparation Guide
Continuing Your Study of Interviewing

## Summary of Concepts and Skills

## Interviewing Exercises
Practicing Interviewing Skills
Preparing Your Résumé
Writing the Follow-Up Letter
Responding to Unlawful Questions

## Interview for Analysis: Displaying Communication Confidence in the Employment Interview
Glossary
Bibliography
Appendix: Additional Online Help
Index

# CD-ROM Units

These sections are included on the CD-ROM with bonus units, which is available to be packaged with this book. Some restrictions apply.

## The Mass Media

The Functional and Dysfunctional Media

Becoming a Critical Consumer of Media

## Emotional Communication

Emotions and Emotional Messages

Obstacles in Communicating Emotions

Guidelines for Communicating Emotions

## Criticism in the Public Speaking Classroom

The Nature and Values of Criticism

Cultural Differences in Approaches to Criticism

Standards and Principles of Criticism

## Developing Special Occasion Speeches

The Speech of Introduction

The Speech of Presentation and Acceptance
Guidelines for Speeches of Presentation
A Sample Speech of Presentation

Guidelines for Speeches of Acceptance
Sample Speeches of Acceptance

The Speech to Secure Goodwill
Guidelines for Speeches Aimed at Securing
Goodwill
Sample Speeches to Secure Goodwill

The Speech of Tribute
Guidelines for Speeches of Tribute
A Sample Speech of Tribute

Additional Special Occasion Speeches
Dedication Speeches
Commencement Speeches
Eulogies
Farewell Speeches
Toasts

The Special Occasion Speech in Cultural
Perspective

A Sample Special Occasion Speech

# Specialized Contents

## Self-Tests

*These self-assessment tests will help you bring to awareness, analyze, and improve your communication patterns and strategies.*

## Listen to This

*These boxes provide suggestions for listening more effectively in a wide variety of communication situations. At the same time these discussions will remind you that communication can never occur without listening.*

## Communicating Ethically

*These sections examine ethical issues and dilemmas to illustrate the close connection between ethics and communication, to encourage you to think about the ethical implications of your messages, and to stimulate you to formulate your own code of ethical communication.*

## Media Literacy

*These Media Literacy boxes highlight the ways in which you can use the media more critically and logically and at the same time prevent the media from using you.*

## The Public Speaking Sample Assistant

*These sample speeches and outlines, along with their annotations, will assist you in preparing and outlining your own speeches.*

## Skill Development Experiences

*These exercises are designed to help you work actively with the skills and applications discussed in the text and to help you make these skills a part of your everyday communication behavior.*

# Welcome to
# Essentials of Human Communication

The previous editions of *Essentials of Human Communication* were all well received by students and instructors alike, largely because the book answered the need for a brief, interesting, but serious text that emphasized the essential skills of human communication, including interpersonal communication, small group communication, and public speaking. I continue to try my best to follow Einstein's directive that "things should be made as simple as possible, but not simpler." This new sixth edition remains true to that central purpose, but improves on the fifth edition in several important ways. In revising the book I have benefited from users' suggestions as well as from the rich and relevant communication research literature of recent years.

*Essentials of Human Communication* is divided into two parts. Part One, "Foundations of Human Communication," includes five chapters that cover the concepts and principles of human communication: the communication process, the self and perception, listening, verbal messages, and nonverbal messages. These chapters explain the basic principles and skills underlying all forms of communication—the way communication works, the key principles of effective self-disclosure, the strategies for achieving more accurate perception, ways to listen more effectively, and guidelines for using language and the numerous nonverbal channels to best communicate your meaning.

Part Two, "The Contexts of Human Communication," includes eight chapters that cover the concepts and skills of interpersonal communication, conversation, relationships, and managing interpersonal conflict (Chapters 6 and 7); small group interaction (Chapters 8 and 9); and public speaking (Chapters 10 through 13). These chapters explain the nature of these communication forms and emphasize the skills that make possible more effective interpersonal conversation and relationships, small group participation and leadership, and informative and persuasive public speaking. A separate book, *The Interviewing Guidebook,* is available with this text and covers the important skills of interviewing for information and for employment.

## Major Themes

Integrated throughout the book are several major themes that personalize the material and make it more relevant to your everyday communication encounters. With a focus on the knowledge and abilities you need to develop to become a competent communicator, these themes include communication skills, media literacy, computer-mediated communication, listening skills, cultural sensitivity, ethical principles, workplace communication, the expression of power, and critical thinking. These themes will prove central to your personal and work-related communication, whether in face-to-face interaction or in computer-mediated communication.

# Communication Skills

*Essentials of Human Communication* provides you with the skills you need to communicate successfully in your personal, social, and workplace interactions. These skills are integrated in several ways. Most important, communication skills are interwoven throughout the text. Additionally, the **What Do You Say?** marginal items ask you to analyze specific communication situations and apply the skills you're reading about, and the **Skill Development Experiences** provide for more focused practice on selected skills. A list of these 28 exercises appears in the Specialized Contents on page xiii. Additional exercises are available on the text's website, www.mycommunicationlab.com (access code required). These skills include:

- *perceptual and listening effectiveness*—how to make more accurate judgments of people and how to really hear what people say and mean
- *verbal and nonverbal message construction and reception*—and how to use words and all the nonverbal elements to best achieve your purposes
- *interpersonal communication*—how to manage conversation, interpersonal conflicts, and interpersonal relationships with friends, romantic partners, family, and colleagues at work
- *interviewing*—how to interview someone for information, how to make the right impression in an employment interview, and how to write your employment résumé and the letters that are a part of the job interviewing process to maximize your chances of getting the job you want (presented in *The Interiewing Guidebook*)
- *small group communication*—how to participate in and lead small groups for generating ideas, sharing information, and solving problems
- *public speaking*—how to effectively inform and persuade a wide variety of different audiences
- *media literacy*—how to analyze and not be duped by the media

# Media Literacy

New to this edition is an emphasis on media literacy. This important topic is presented in a series of **Media Literacy** boxes, which highlight ways you can use the media more logically and critically. The boxes cover such topics as "What Is Media Literacy?," "Who Are the Media?," "Hate Speech," "Product Placement," and "Reversing Media's Influence." A list of these Media Literacy boxes appears in the Specialized Contents on page xii.

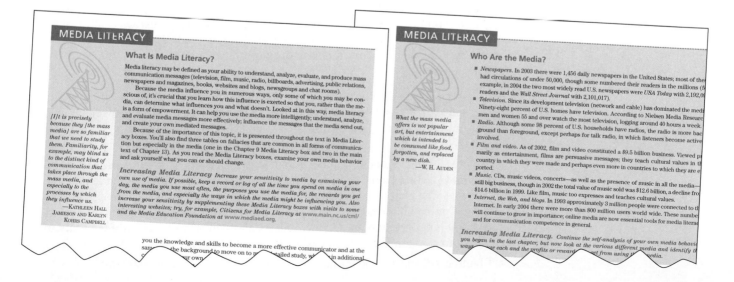

## Computer-Mediated Communication

Computer-mediated communication—the communication between people that takes place through some computer connection (for example, through e-mail, instant messaging, interactive websites, or blogs)—is a part of everyone's everyday communication and is now fully integrated into the text. In addition, new marginal features titled **E-Talk** (several per chapter) consider the similarities and differences between computer-mediated and face-to-face communication.

## Listening

Effective listening is crucial to all forms of human communication. *Essentials* gives listening a central role in human communication in two ways. First, Chapter 4 is devoted entirely to listening: the stages of listening, the styles of effective listening, and the influences of culture and gender on listening. In addition, each chapter contains a **Listen to This** box that highlights the role of listening in relation to the topics discussed in the chapter. Listen to This boxes discuss, for example, listening to yourself, listening to other perspectives, listening so as to empower, and listening to complaints. Each Listen to This box ends with a case that asks you to interact with the principles of listening (instead of just reading about them) and to develop listening guidelines to help resolve specific problems. A list of these Listen to This boxes appears in the Specialized Contents on page xi.

## Cultural Awareness and Sensitivity

You're living in a world defined by cultural diversity, a world where you interact and become friends and romantic partners, join together in families, chat online, and work together with people differing in affectional orientation, socioeconomic position, race, religion, and nationality. Culture and cultural differences are always influential in communication. For this reason, this text fully integrates culture into the discussions of all forms of communication. In fact, each chapter of *Essentials of Human Communication* contains discussions of culture as it relates to the chapter topics:

- Chapter 1 discusses culture and competence, the relevance of culture, the aim of a cultural perspective, and ethnocentrism; the chapter also provides a self-test on cultural beliefs and values and an exercise on understanding cultural beliefs.

- Chapter 2 considers cultural teachings in self-concept formation, intercultural openness, culture and gender in self-disclosure, and masculine and feminine cultures. The chapter also explores the influence of culture on perceptual judgments, personality theory and culture, the role of stereotypes in perception, cultural influences on uncertainty and its avoidance, and cultural sensitivity in perceptual accuracy.

- Chapter 3 discusses the influences of culture and gender on listening.

- Chapter 4 covers gender and cultural differences in directness and politeness; cultural rules in verbal communication; sexism, heterosexism, racism, and ageism; and cultural identifiers.

- Chapter 5 considers cultural differences in nonverbal communication throughout the text. Several areas, however, receive more extended consideration: facial expressions, colors, touch, silence, and time (including differences between monochronism and polychronism and the role of the social clock).

- Chapter 6 takes a detailed look at the role of culture and gender in interpersonal relationships, and particularly in friendship and love.

- Chapter 7 investigates cultural context and conflict, face-enhancing and face-detracting strategies, and the relevance of cultural sensitivity (including differences between high- and low-context cultures) in conversation and conflict.

- Chapter 8 addresses the nature and importance of cultural norms in small group communication.

- Chapter 9 puts membership and leadership roles into cultural perspective and discusses differences between individual and collective orientations and high and low power distances.

- Chapter 10 offers guidelines to help public speakers avoid taboo topics when addressing culturally varied audiences as well as guidance for analyzing multicultural audiences.

- Chapter 11 considers cultural considerations in the language of public speaking, culture shock, and cultural sensitivity in speech criticism.

- Chapter 12 examines cultural variations in language usage.

- Chapter 13 covers cultural differences in approaches to the use of logical, motivational, and credibility appeals.

**Economic Interdependence** Today, most countries are economically dependent on one another. Our economic lives depend on our ability to communicate effectively across cultures. Similarly, our political well-being depends in great part on that of other cultures. Political unrest in any part of the world—Africa, Eastern Europe, or the Middle East, to take a few examples—affects our own security. Intercultural communication and understanding now seem more crucial than ever.

**Communication Technology** The rapid spread of communication technology has brought foreign and sometimes very different cultures right into our living rooms. News from foreign countries is commonplace. You see nightly—in vivid color—what is going on in remote countries. Technology has made intercultural communication easy, practical, and inevitable. Daily, the media bombard you with evidence of racial tensions, religious disagreements, sexual bias, and, in general, the problems caused when intercultural communication fails. And, of course, the Internet has made intercultural communication as easy as writing a note on your computer. You can now communicate by e-mail just as easily with someone in Europe or Asia, for example, as with someone in another city or state.

**Dimensions of Culture**

Because of its importance in all forms of human communication, culture is given a prominent place in this text. Throughout this text I'll discuss theories and research findings that bear on culture and communication. Prominent among these discussions are the five major dimensions of culture. By way of a brief preview, these dimensions are:

- *Uncertainty avoidance:* The degree to which a culture values predictability. In high-uncertainty-avoidance cultures, predictability and order are extremely

# Ethics

*Essentials of Human Communication* follows in the tradition established by Aristotle, Cicero, and Quintilian—the three great theorists of the ancient world—who viewed ethics as an integral part of communication instruction. This text, too, regards ethics as central; and **Communicating Ethically** boxes highlight ethical issues as they relate to concepts and skills presented throughout the book. Each Communicating Ethically box contains an ethical dilemma—a case that asks, "What would you do?" in the situation described. These cases are designed to stimulate you to interact with the material on a more personal level. A list of these Communicating Ethically boxes appears in the Specialized Contents on page xii.

avoid noxious people, who make you feel negatively about yourself. At the same time, seek to become more nourishing yourself so that you each build up the other's self-esteem.

**Work on Projects That Will Result in Success** Some people want to fail, or so it seems. Often, they select projects that will result in failure simply be-

## COMMUNICATING ETHICALLY

### Information Ethics

One approach to ethics revolves around the notion of choice and argues that people have the right to information relevant to the choices they make. In this view, communication is ethical when it facilitates people's freedom of choice by presenting them with accurate information. Communication is unethical when it interferes with people's freedom of choice by preventing them from securing information that will help them make choices. Communications also is unethical when it gives people false or misleading information that will lead them to make choices they would not make if they had accurate and truthful information.

In this ethical system, you have the right to information about yourself that others possess and that influences the choices you will make. Thus, for example, in court you have the right to face your accusers and to know the witnesses who will be called to testify against you; you also have the right to see your credit ratings and to know what Social Security benefits you will receive. On the other hand, people do not have the right to information that is none of their business, such as information about whether you and your partner are happy or argue a lot or receive food stamps.

*All virtue is summed up in dealing justly.*
—ARISTOTLE,
NICHOMACHEAN ETHICS

*What would you do?* You are aware that your best friend's husband is having an extramarital affair with a 17-year-old girl. Your friend, suspecting this, asks if you know anything about it. Would it be ethical for you to lie and say you know nothing, or are you obligated to tell your friend what you know? Are you obligated to tell the police? What would you do?

## Communication in the Workplace

Because communication is a practical subject, with applications in all aspects of life, this book makes a special effort to illustrate the uses of communication skills in the real world, particularly in the world of work. Among the topics covered here that have special application to the workplace are office romance, small groups in the workplace, interpersonal conflict, and the varied uses of power. In addition, numerous examples of workplace situations that call for the application of communication skills appear throughout the text.

As you work through this text and the course, you'll find it useful to ask yourself how you can apply this material to the workplace—how you can use this material to function more effectively on the job and achieve your professional goals.

## Power and Empowerment

The previous edition contained Communicating with Power boxes that identified several important principles of communication power. In this new edition these boxes have been replaced by discussions integrated into the basal text. For example, types of power are discussed in Chapter 1; the ways power can be communicated verbally and nonverbally are discussed in Chapters 4 and 5; and the topic of empowering others is integrated with the functions of leadership in Chapter 9.

## Critical Thinking

Critical thinking enriches all human communication experiences, so this book gives special prominence to this subject. First, the text integrates principles of critical thinking at the points at which they are most relevant. For example, distinguishing facts from inferences, avoiding either/or thinking and allness, and discriminating among rather than against others are discussed in the chapter on verbal messages (Chapter 4); the techniques of solving a problem are discussed in the chapter dealing with small group communication (Chapter 8); techniques for listening to new ideas are presented in the context of the speech of information (Chapter 12); and guidelines for avoiding the pitfalls in reasoning from evidence to a conclusion are considered in the discussion of persuasion (Chapter 13).

Second, three tables in this edition address the issue of fallacies in reasoning: "Fallacies of Language" in Chapter 11 and "Fallacies of Pseudo-Argument" and "Fallacies of Personal Attacks" in Chapter 13.

Third, the new feature on Media Literacy is focused on thinking critically in using the mass media.

In addition, What Do You Say? marginal items, self-tests, and scenarios presented in boxed features throughout the book ask for the application of the principles of critical thinking and communication effectiveness to specific situations.

# What's New in the Sixth Edition?

This sixth edition contains a variety of new features and topics and an expansion, clarification, and improved organization of other material. For those who have used the previous editions of *Essentials*, here, in brief, is a summary of some structural changes and chapter-by-chapter changes in this edition.

## Structural Changes

The book's basic structure has been changed slightly. Instead of 14 chapters, this edition contains 13. Chapters 2 and 3 of the previous edition have been combined into one chapter (Chapter 2, "The Self and Perception") to enable the course to progress more quickly to and have more time to cover the major forms of communication: interpersonal, small group, and public speaking. The previous edition contained one chapter on conversation and conflict and one on relationships. This edition covers both conversation and relationships in Chapter 6 and devotes another chapter (Chapter 7) exclusively to "Managing Interpersonal Conflict."

As mentioned earlier, the Communicating with Power boxes have been dropped, and their most important content has been integrated into the basal text as appropriate.

New **Media Literacy** boxes appear in every chapter and identify the nature and skills of media literacy. These boxes—covering such topics as gatekeeping, the third person effect, the spiral of silence, and advertising and public relations—contribute further to the critical thinking theme of this text and also extend this treatment of human communication to include media literacy.

Also new to this edition and as already noted, computer-mediated communication is now discussed throughout the text; in addition, marginal **E-Talk** features probe the similarities and differences between computer-mediated and face-to-face communication.

New to this edition, as well, is a series of discussion questions—**Five for Discussion**—presented at the end of each chapter, designed to raise a variety of issues in human communication that may be suitable for class discussion, journal writing, or essay writing.

A somewhat different photo program was chosen for this edition. Instead of linking a question to each photo, as in the previous edition, here I have accompanied each photo by a quotation. The purpose is to provide a more open-ended and creative way of looking at the photos and at their relationship to the text material. The most relevant questions that appeared as photo ViewPoints in the previous edition can be found in the What Do You Say? marginal notes or in the Five for Discussion questions at the end of the chapters.

The quotations used in the margins of the previous edition are now integrated with the photos and with the Media Literacy, Communicating Ethically, and Listen to This boxes.

## Chapter-by-Chapter Changes

**Chapter 1** ("The Essentials of Human Communication") now covers computer-mediated communication and includes an extensive table comparing face-to-face and computer-mediated communication. The five dimensions of culture are introduced here and elaborated on in different chapters. The discussion of power identifies the nature and types of power and how it may be expressed in verbal or nonverbal messages. In addition, there is an expanded explanation of communication ambiguity, and a clearer delineation in the chapter opening material into the skills, forms, and beliefs about human communication.

**Chapter 2** ("Perception and the Self"), combining the self and perception chapters of the previous edition, now includes self-esteem.

**Chapter 3** ("Listening") includes implications of the listening model and a clarification of the importance of listening in terms of task and relationship benefits.

**Chapter 4** ("Verbal Messages") contains a rewritten discusssion of racism, heterosexism, ageism, and sexism and distingishes between individual and institutionalized forms of these -isms.

**Chapter 5** ("Nonverbal Messages") offers expanded and updated coverage of culture and color, culture and gesture, and body art and piercings.

**Chapter 6** ("Interpersonal Communication, Conversation, and Relationships") now contains major discussions of theories of interpersonal relationships (attraction, rules, social penetration and social exchange and equity), and types of relationships (friends, lovers, family). The conversation material now covers the principles of immediacy, dialogue, and turn taking.

**Chapter 7** ("Managing Interpersonal Conflict") contains an expanded discussion of conflict strategies, especially of verbal aggressiveness and argumentativeness.

**Chapter 8** ("Small Group Communication") contains a totally revised discussion of online groups as well as new sections on relationship and task groups and reference and membership groups.

**Chapter 9** ("Members and Leaders in Group Communication") now contains expanded discussions of styles of leadership and of high and low power distances.

**Chapter 10** ("Public Speaking Preparation, Steps 1–6") has a more focused discussion of public speaking and culture and a totally revised research section.

**Chapter 11** ("Public Speaking Preparation and Delivery, Steps 7–10") contains a discussion of language fallacies. The concept of abstraction, formerly discussed in the chapter on verbal messages, has been integrated here as an aid to clarity.

**Chapter 12** ("The Informative Speech") has been totally rewritten; each of the major types of informative speech is now discussed in terms of thesis and main points, support, and organization. A new annotated informative speech is included as a model of excellence.

**Chapter 13** ("The Persuasive Speech") has been totally revised. Persuasive speeches are now broken down into speeches of fact, value, and policy; and, as in the chapter on the informative speech, each type of speech is discussed in terms of thesis and main points, support, and organization. There is a new section on the goals of persuasion and a consideration of fallacies of pseudo-argument and the fallacies of personal attacks. Another new section, "Supporting Materials in Cultural Perspective," returns to the five cultural dimensions introduced in Chapter 1 and elaborated on throughout the text. A new annotated persuasive speech is included as a model of an effective speech.

## Glossary

The glossary in this edition continues to be extensive and is again divided in two parts: concepts and skills.

## Additional Units

An accompanying CD-ROM, available on request with a new textbook, offers four complete units not available in the printed text: Mass Media, Emotional Communication, Criticism in the Public Speaking Classroom, and Developing Special Occasion Speeches.

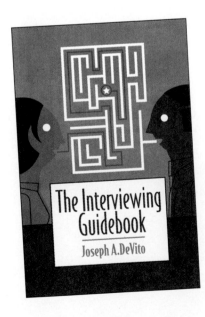

## The Interviewing Guidebook

A separate 112-page book on interviewing has been totally revised and expanded. Now titled *The Interviewing Guidebook*, this book is available packaged with a new copy of the text (some restrictions apply) and is also sold separately. The *Guidebook* discusses both the informative interview and the employment interview, along with the various types of résumés and the letters that are a part of the job interview.

# The Pedagogy

As in previous editions of *Essentials*, the pedagogy here is highly interactive. Here are some of the more important pedagogical features.

## What Do You Say? Scenarios

The **What Do You Say?** feature presents situational dilemmas—points at which you have to make a communication choice. The objective of these brief marginal items, around four to eight per chapter, is to give you opportunities to apply principles and skills to real-world situations. For example, after reading about ambiguity, you're asked how you would reduce ambiguity by finding out how your dating partner views your relationship. After reading about group leadership, you're asked how you'd deal with a group in which a few members monopolize the discussion. After reading about the principles of persuasive speaking, you're asked how you'd establish your own credibility with a specific audience.

There is no one right answer to any What Do You Say? question. Your objective in responding is to think of as many communication options as you can and, based on your understanding of how communication works, to estimate which options are likely to be most effective for you.

Facial management techniques help you display emotions in socially acceptable ways. For example, if someone gets bad news in which you secretly take pleasure, the social display rule dictates that you frown and otherwise nonverbally signal sorrow. If you place first in a race and your best friend barely finishes, the display rule requires that you minimize your expression of happiness—and certainly avoid any signs of gloating. If you violate these display rules, you'll appear insensitive. So, although facial management techniques may be deceptive, they're expected and even required by the rules for polite interaction.

***The Facial Feedback Hypothesis.*** According to the **facial feedback hypothesis**, your facial expression influences your level of physiological arousal. People who exaggerate their facial expressions show higher physiological arousal than those who suppress these expressions. In research studies, those who neither exaggerated nor suppressed their expressions had arousal levels between these two extremes (Lanzetta, Cartwright-Smith, & Kleck, 1976; Zuckerman, Klorman, Larrance, & Spiegel, 1981). In one interesting study, subjects held a pen in their teeth in such a way as to simulate a sad expression. They were then asked to rate the degree of sadness the subjects reported feeling when viewing the photographs (Larsen, Kasimatis, & Frey, 1992). So not only does your facial expression influence the judgments and impressions others have of you; it also influences your own level of emotional arousal (Cappella, 1993).

**Eye Communication** The messages communicated by the eyes vary depending on the duration, direction, and quality of the eye behavior. For example, every culture has rather strict, though unstated, rules for the proper duration of eye contact. In one study conducted in England, the average length of gaze is 2.95 seconds. The average length of mutual gaze (two persons gazing at each other) is 1.18 seconds

**WHAT DO YOU SAY?**
**Smiling**
Sally smiles almost all the time. Even when she criticizes or reprimands a subordinate, she ends with a smile and this dilutes the strength of her message. As Sally's supervisor, you need her to realize what she's doing and to change her nonverbals. *What do you say? Through what channel? In what context?*

## E-Talk Notes

**E-Talk** marginal items, as noted above, contribute further to the interactivity of this text's pedagogy, asking you to analyze your thinking about and your experiences with computer-mediated communication.

## Chapter Openers (Concepts and Skills)

The chapter openers are new and address directly your very reasonable question, "Why should I read this chapter?" For each chapter there are two answers. The first previews what you'll learn in the chapter; that is, the chapter's cognitive objectives

*Why Read* This Chapter?

Because you'll **learn about:**
■ listening and the ways in which you listen.
■ how different cultures as well as men and women view listening.

Because you'll **learn to:**
■ listen more effectively during each of the five listening stages.
■ adjust your listening so that it's most effective for the specific situation.
■ listen with an awareness of cultural and gender differences.

or the content—the concepts, theories, and research in human communication. The second answer outlines what you'll be able to do after studying the chapter; that is, the skill or behavioral objectives you should achieve.

## Listening and Ethics Boxes

The **Listen to This** and **Communicating Ethically** boxes not only connect the crucial topics of listening and ethics to the chapter topics but also present interactive cases to stimulate discussion and to encourage you to apply the material to your own communication interactions and experiences.

## Self-Tests

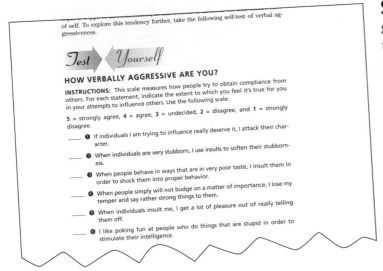

Seventeen **Test Yourself** features appear in this edition. Some of these self-tests include standard research instruments, such as measures of ethnocentrism, apprehension, love styles, time orientation, verbal aggressiveness, and argumentativeness. Others are more pedagogical and are designed to involve you in concepts discussed in the chapter. These self-tests focus on your self-esteem, your accuracy in perceiving other people, your willingness to self-disclose, and the kind of leader you are. Each self-test ends with two questions: (1) "How did you do?" gives you instructions for scoring your responses, and (2) "What will you do?" asks you to think about any action you may want to take in light of how you performed.

## Summaries of Concepts and Skills

Each chapter-end summary includes both a conceptual summary and a skills summary. The conceptual summary provides a brief paragraph thumbnailing the chapter's topic and a list of propositions that captures the essential content of the chapter. The skills summary presents the major skills covered in the chapter in a checklist format to allow you to check those skills you want to work on most.

## Key Word Quiz

A brief 10-item **Key Word Quiz** at the end of each chapter will help you review significant vocabulary terms introduced in the chapter. All quizzes have been totally revised for this edition. Key terms and their definitions are now presented as matching-columns tests.

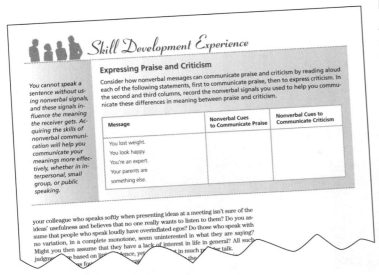

## Skill Development Experiences

This edition contains 28 **Skill Development Experiences** integrated into the text. Many are new to this edition and have been rewritten to emphasize *practical* communication skills. These exercises promote the mastery of specific communication skills in an enjoyable way and in a supportive atmosphere.

Added to this edition is a summary statement at the end of each Skill Development Experience with the implicit suggestion that you develop your own summary of what the experience means to you.

## Public Speaking Sample Assistant

In Chapters 10 through 13 of this edition, four sample annotated speeches and three outlines (preparation, template, and delivery) are presented in **Public Speaking Sample Assistant** boxes that are designed to illustrate further the principles of public speaking and outlining.

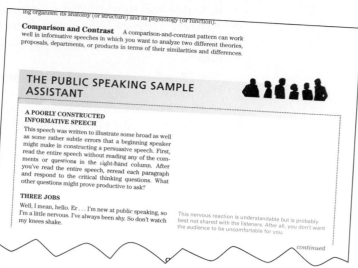

ing organism: its anatomy (or structure) and its physiology (or function).

**Comparison and Contrast**  A comparison-and-contrast pattern can work well in informative speeches in which you want to analyze two different theories, proposals, departments, or products in terms of their similarities and differences.

### THE PUBLIC SPEAKING SAMPLE ASSISTANT

**A POORLY CONSTRUCTED INFORMATIVE SPEECH**

This speech was written to illustrate some broad as well as some rather subtle errors that a beginning speaker might make in constructing a persuasive speech. First, read the entire speech without reading any of the comments or questions in the right-hand column. After you've read the entire speech, reread each paragraph and respond to the critical thinking questions. What other questions might prove productive to ask?

**THREE JOBS**

Well, I mean, hello. Er . . . I'm new at public speaking, so I'm a little nervous. I've always been shy. So don't watch my knees shake.

This nervous reaction is understandable but is probably best not shared with the listeners. After all, you don't want the audience to be uncomfortable for you.

*continued*

## The Website

Included on the book's website (www.mycommunicationlab.com) and prepared by the author of the text are more than 100 exercises and self-tests, as well as detailed explanations of concepts discussed more briefly in the text. These items are organized by chapter and are all referred to in the **Log On! MyCommunicationLab** section at the end of each chapter.

An access code is required for this website. Contact your Allyn and Bacon representative for details.

## The Communication Blog

The author maintains **The Communication Blog**, which provides a forum for users of *Essentials of Human Communication*. Brief items are posted regularly to update, expand, or somehow provide a different perspective than that presented in the textbook (http://tcbdevito.blogspot.com).

## Supplementary Materials

### Instructor's Resources

### Print Supplements

**Instructor's Manual and Test Bank with Transparency Masters**, by Christina Standerfer of the University of Central Arkansas. This detailed Instructor's Manual and Test Bank contains learning objectives for each chapter, chapter outlines, discussion questions, and skills development activities to illustrate the concepts, principles, and skills of human communication. The Instructor's Manual includes "Asides" created by Joseph A. DeVito. In addition, the Test Bank portion of the manual contains numerous multiple choice, true/false, fill-in-the-blank, and essay questions. The manual also includes transparency masters that frame key concepts and skills.

**A Guide for New Teachers of Introduction to Communication, 2/e**, by Susanna G. Porter of Kennesaw State University. This instructor's guide is designed to help new teachers effectively teach the introductory communication course.

**New Teachers Guide to Public Speaking, 3/e**, by Calvin Troup of Duquesne University. This guide helps new teachers teach the introductory course effectively. It covers such topics as preparing for the term, planning and structuring your course, evaluating speeches, utilizing the textbook, integrating technology into the classroom, and much more.

**The Blockbuster Approach: A Guide to Teaching Interpersonal Communication with Video, 3/e**, by Thomas E. Jewell of Marymount College. This guide provides lists and descriptions of commercial videos that can be used in the classroom to illustrate interpersonal concepts and complex interpersonal relationships. Sample activities are also included.

**A&B Public Speaking Transparency Package, Version II**. Includes 100 full-color transparencies created with PowerPoint™ software to provide visual support for classroom lectures and discussions.

**Great Ideas for Teaching Speech (GIFTS), 3/e**, by Raymond Zeuschner of California Polytechnic State University. This instructional booklet provides descriptions of and guidelines for assignments successfully used by experienced public speaking instructors in their classrooms.

## Electronic Supplements

**TestGen EQ: Computerized Test Bank**. The user-friendly interface enables instructors to view, edit, and add questions, transfer questions to tests, and print tests in a variety of fonts. Search and sort features allow instructors to locate questions quickly and arrange them in preferred order.

**PowerPoint Presentation Package**. This text-specific package consists of a collection of lecture outlines and graphic images keyed to every chapter in the text. Available on the Web at www.ablongman.com/irc.

**The Communication Blog** (http://tcbdevito.blogspot.com). Maintained by the author, this site offers a forum for people teaching basic courses in interpersonal communication, as well as the hybrid and public speaking courses. Regular posts by the author update the text material and share ideas for teaching.

**VideoWorkshop for Introduction to Communication, Version 2.0, Instructor's Teaching Guide**, by Kathryn Dindia of the University of Wisconsin. This guide provides teaching suggestions, quiz questions and answers, and discussion starters that will help you use the VideoWorkshop for Introduction to Communication CD-ROM in class. A correlation guide helps you relate the materials to your text. The complete CD-ROM and Student Learning Guide are included in this guide. Go to www.ablongman.com/html/videoworkshop for more details.

**Allyn & Bacon's Digital Media Archive for Communication, Version 3.0.** The Digital Media Archive CD-ROM contains electronic images of charts, graphs, maps, tables, and figures, along with media elements such as video, audio clips, and related Web links. These media assets are fully customizable to use with our pre-formatted PowerPoint™ outlines or to import into instructor's own lectures. (For Windows and Mac.)

**Allyn & Bacon Interpersonal Communication Video**. The interpersonal video contains three scenarios that illustrate key concepts in interpersonal communication. A faculty User's Guide featured transcripts and teaching activities. For adopters only. Restrictions apply. See your Allyn & Bacon/Longman representative for details.

**The Allyn & Bacon Communication Video Library**. A collection of communication videos produced by Films for the Humanities and Social Sciences. Topics include, but are not limited to: Business Presentations, Great American Speeches, and Conflict Resolution. Contact your Allyn & Bacon sales representative for ordering information. Some restrictions apply.

**A&B Contemporary Classic Speeches DVD**. This exciting supplement includes over 120 minutes of video footage in an easy-to-use DVD format. Each speech is accompanied by a biographical and historical summary that helps students understand the context and motivation behind each speech. Sold separately or packaged with participating A&B texts. Please contact your Allyn & Bacon representative for details and restrictions.

**A&B Student Speeches Video Library**. This collection of communication videos includes videos from the American Forensic Association highlighting award-winning student speeches as well as classroom-based student speeches. Please contact your Allyn & Bacon representative for details and restrictions.

**InterWrite PRS (Personal Response System)**. Assess your students' progress with the Personal Response System—an easy-to-use wireless polling system that enables you to pose questions, record results, and display those results instantly in your classrooom.

Designed by teachers, for teachers, PRS is easy to integrate into your lectures:

- Students use a cell-phone-sized transmitter which they bring to class.
- You ask multiple-choice, numerical-answer, or matching questions during class; students simply click their answer into their transmitter.
- A classroom receiver (portable or mounted) connected to your computer tabulates all answers and displays them graphically in class.
- Results can be recorded for grading, attendance, or simply used as a discussion point.

Our partnership with PRS allows us to offer student rebate cards bundled with any Allyn & Bacon/Longman text. The rebate card has a direct value of $20.00 and can be redeemed for the purchase of a new PRS student transmitter.

**Sandbox**. With Sandbox Custom Publishing from Allyn & Bacon, you can build your own textbook—one designed specifically around the course you teach, with the material relevant specifically to your course. Using texts from Allyn & Bacon, you can:

- Develop a book with a single look and feel throughout.
- Provide your students with a book that has consistent internal referencing, with updated table of contents, index, glossary, and figure numbering.
- Revise and print on demand.
- See previews within two days.
- Upon request, review a downloadable, printable evaluation copy.

You can choose how your textbook looks both inside and out, with all the chapters you want, in the order you want them. With Sandbox, you can include your own class notes. You can remove chapters from one book and add chapters from another. And you can do it without having to sacrifice quality. Create a custom book as seamless as the original products used to construct it. Imagine the possibilities when you build your book in Sandbox!

There is a minimum of 25 units and 150 pages for an order. For adoptions under 2,500 units, the book will be printed in black and white.

**For more information, contact your local Allyn & Bacon representative or go to** www.ablongmancustom.com.

# Student Resources

## Print Supplements

**The Interviewing Guidebook**, by Joseph A. DeVito, focuses on the skills needed for the information-gathering and (especially) the employment interview (along with the job résumé and the letters that are a part of the interview process). Preparation worksheets, exercises, guides to online help, and scenarios for applying these skills make this brief and user-friendly text an extremely practical supplement to any communication course.

**Brainstorms**, by Joseph A. DeVito. A guide to thinking more creatively about communication, or anything else; a perfect complement to the text's unique emphasis on critical thinking. Students find 19 practical, easy-to-use creative thinking techniques along with insights into the creative thinking process.

**ResearchNavigator.com Guide: Speech Communication**. This updated booklet, by Steven L. Epstein of Suffolk County Community College, includes tips, resources, and URLs to aid students conducting research on Pearson Education's research website, www.researchnavigator.com. The guide contains a student access code for the Research Navigator database, offering students unlimited access to a collection of more than 25,000 discipline specific articles from top-tier academic publications and peer-reviewed journals, as well as the *New York Times* and popular news publications. The guide introduces students to the basics of the Internet and the World Wide Web, and includes tips for searching for articles on the site, and a list of journals useful for research in their discipline. Also included are hundreds of Web resources for the discipline, as well as information on how to correctly cite research. The guide is available packaged with new copies of the text.

**Preparing Visual Aids for Presentations, 4/e**, by Dan Cavanaugh. This brief booklet provides a host of ideas for using today's multimedia tools to improve presentations, including suggestions for how to plan a presentation, guidelines for designing visual aids and storyboarding, and a walkthrough that shows how to prepare a visual display using PowerPoint™. Sold separately or packaged with participating A&B texts.

**The Speech Outline: Outlining to Plan, Organize, and Deliver a Speech: Activities and Exercises**, by Reeze L. Hanson and Sharon Condon of Haskell Indian Nations University. This brief workbook includes activities, exercises, and answers to help students develop and master the critical skill of outlining. Sold separately or packaged with participating A&B texts.

**Speech Preparation Workbook** by Jennifer Dreyer and Gregory H. Patton of San Diego State University. This workbook takes students through the stages of speech creation—from audience analysis to writing the speech—and includes guidelines, tips, and easy to fill-in pages. Sold separately or packaged with participating A&B texts.

**Public Speaking in the Multicultural Environment, 2/e**, by Devorah Lieberman of Portland State University. This two-chapter essay focuses on speaking and listening to a culturally diverse audience and emphasizes preparation, delivery, and how speeches are perceived. Sold separately or packaged with participating A&B texts.

**Study Card for Introduction to Speech Communication**. Colorful, affordable, and packed with useful information, Allyn & Bacon's Study Cards make studying easier, more efficient, and more enjoyable. Course information is distilled down to the basics, helping you quickly master the fundamentals, review a subject for understanding, or prepare for an exam. Because they're laminated for durability, you can keep these Study Cards for years to come and pull them out whenever you need a quick review.

## Electronic Supplements

**VideoWorkshop for Introduction to Communication, Version 2.0, Student Learning Guide**, by Kathryn Dindia of the University of Wisconsin. VideoWorkshop for Introduction to Communication is more than just video footage you can watch. It's a total learning system. Our complete program includes quality video footage on an easy-to-use CD-ROM plus a Student Learning Guide with textbook-specific correlation grids. The result? A program that brings textbook concepts to life with ease and helps you understand, analyze, and apply the objectives of the course.

**Allyn & Bacon Introduction to Communication Study Site**, by Lauren L. Breslin of the University of Phoenix, accessed at www.abintrocomm.com. This website features communication study materials for students, including flashcards and a complete set of practice tests for all major topics. Students also will find Web links to sites with speeches in texts, audio, and video formats, as well as links to other valuable sites.

**Allyn & Bacon Communication Studies Website**, by Terrence Doyle of Northern Virginia Community College, and Tim Borchers of Minnesota State University at Moorhead, and updated by Nan Peck of Northern Virginia Community College. This site includes modules on interpersonal, small group communication, and public speaking, and includes Web links, enrichment materials, and interactive activities to enhance students' understanding of key concepts. Access this site at www.ablongman.com/commstudies.

**Speech Writer's Workshop CD-ROM, Version 2.0**. This speechwriting software includes a *Speech Handbook* with tips for researching and preparing speeches, a *Speech Workshop* which guides students step-by-step through the speech writing process, a *Topics Dictionary* which gives students hundreds of ideas for speeches, and the *Documentor* citation database that helps them to format bibliographic entries in either MLA or APA style. Sold separately or packaged with participating A&B texts.

**MyCommuncationLab** is an interactive and instructive online solution for introductory communication courses. Designed to be used as a supplement to a traditional lecture course, or completely administer an online course, MyCommunicationLab combines multimedia, video, research support, tests, and quizzes to make teaching and learning fun! Students benefit from a wealth of video clips, many of which are accompanied by activities, questions to consider, and helpful tips—all geared to help students learn to communicate more effectively. Accessed at www.mycommuncationlab.com. An access code is required for this website. Contact your Allyn & Bacon representative for details.

# Acknowledgments
----------------------------------------------------------------------

I would like to thank the many reviewers who critically analyzed the previous edition. They gave graciously of their time and expertise and offered a variety of useful and insightful suggestions for this new edition. I thank you all; your comments have resulted in many improvements. Thank you to Nader H. Chaaban, Montgomery College; John Chetro-Szivos, Fitchburg State College; Eileen F. Eisen, Mesa Community College; David R. Johnson, Vol State Community College; and Richard K. Olsen Jr., University of North Carolina, Wilmington.

I also owe a great debt to the people at Allyn & Bacon who took such excellent care of this manuscript. I especially wish to thank Karon Bowers, Editor-in-Chief, who, as always, guided the process efficiently and effectively, with good spirit and good will, working well beyond what any author has a right to expect; Kristen Desmond LeFevre who served admirably as developmental editor, offering excellent advice and guidelines for revision; Jay Howland who has done extraordinary copy editing, making textbook prose easy to read and always clear; Tom Conville, project editor, who guided the process from manuscript to book with amazing efficiency, making the entire undertaking always pleasant; Suzan Czajkowski, marketing manager, also made helpful suggestions; and Jenny Lupica, editorial assistant, who always makes revisions as easy and as comfortable as possible.

Joseph A. DeVito

jadevito@earthlink.net

http://tcbdevito.blogspot.com

www.ablongman.com/devito

# Chapter

# 1

# The Essentials of Human Communication

## Why Read This Chapter?

Because you'll **learn about:**

- communication: its nature and skills.
- the essential concepts and principles of human communication.
- the role of culture in communication.

Because you'll **learn to:**

- use the essential elements and principles of human communication in your daily interactions.
- acknowledge the role of culture in all forms of human communication.

*O*f all the knowledge and skills you have, those concerning communication are among your most important and useful. Your communication ability will influence how effectively you live your personal and professional life; it will influence your effectiveness as a friend and lover, as a member and leader of small groups (both social and business), and as a public speaker, communicating information and influencing the attitudes and behaviors of others.

This first section introduces human communication, beginning with the skills and forms of human communication and some of the popular but erroneous beliefs that can get in the way of effective communication.

# Human Communication

**Human communication** consists of the sending and receiving of verbal and non-verbal messages between two or more people. This seemingly simple (but in reality quite complex) process is the subject of this book, to which this chapter provides a foundation. Let's begin by looking at the skills you'll learn as you progress through this book and this course.

## The Skills of Human Communication

Among the skills you'll learn through your study of human communication are these:

- *Self-presentation skills* enable you to present yourself as (and just for starters) a confident, likable, approachable, and credible person. It is also largely through your communication skills (or lack of them) that you display negative qualities as well.
- *Relationship skills* help you build friendships, enter into love relationships, work with colleagues, and interact with family members. These are the skills for initiating, maintaining, repairing, and sometimes dissolving relationships of all kinds.
- *Interviewing skills* enable you to interact to gain information, to successfully present yourself to get the job you want, and to participate effectively in a wide variety of other interview types. (This topic is covered in a separate supplement, *The Interviewing Guidebook.*)
- *Group interaction and leadership skills* help you participate effectively in relationship and task groups—informative, problem-solving, and brainstorming groups, at home or at work—as a member and as a leader.
- *Presentation skills* let you communicate information to and influence the attitudes and behaviors of small and large audiences.
- *Media literacy skills* enable you to become a critical user of the varied mass media you encounter on a daily basis.

## The Forms of Human Communication

You'll accomplish these objectives and acquire these skills as you engage in and master a variety of communication forms. **Intrapersonal communication** is the communication you have with yourself. Through intrapersonal communication you talk with, learn about, and judge yourself. You persuade yourself of this or that, reason about possible decisions to make, and rehearse messages that you plan to send to others. In intrapersonal communication you might, for example, wonder how you did in an interview and what you could have done differently. You might conclude you

**WHAT DO YOU SAY?**
**Communication Choice Points**
Throughout this text you'll find marginal What Do You Say? items that identify a communication choice point, a point at which you need to make a decision to say something (or, of course, to remain silent). These items are designed to encourage you to apply the skills discussed in the text to a wide variety of communication situations.

did a pretty good job but tell yourself you need to be more assertive when discussing salary.

**Interpersonal communication** occurs when you interact with a person with whom you have some kind of relationship; it can take place face-to-face as well as through electronic channels (as in e-mail or instant messaging, for example) or even in traditional letter writing. For example, you e-mail your friends or family about your plans for the weekend, ask someone in class for a date, or confront a colleague's racist remarks at the water cooler. Through interpersonal communication, you interact with others, learn about them and yourself, and reveal yourself to others. Whether with new acquaintances, old friends, lovers, family members, or colleagues at work, it's through interpersonal communication that you establish, maintain, sometimes destroy, and sometimes repair personal relationships.

**Interviewing** is communication that proceeds by question and answer. Through interviewing you learn about others and what they know, counsel or get counseling from others, and get or don't get the job you want. Today much interviewing (especially initial interviews) takes place through e-mail and (video) phone conferencing.

**Small group communication** is communication among groups of say 5 to 10 people. Small group communication serves *relationship needs* such as those for companionship, affection, or support and *task needs* such as balancing the family budget, electing a new chairperson, or designing a new ad campaign. Through small group communication you interact with others, solve problems, develop new ideas, and share knowledge and experiences. You live your work and social life largely in groups, from school orientation meetings to executive board meetings, from informal social groups to formal meetings discussing issues of local or international concern. You also may live a good part of your life in chat rooms, where you may interact with people from different cultures living thousands of miles away, and in social network chat (for example, MyFace, MySpace, Xanga) in which you learn about and communicate with others.

**Public communication** is communication between a speaker and an audience. Audiences range in size from several people to hundreds, thousands, and even millions. Through public communication others inform and persuade you. And you, in turn, inform and persuade others—to act, to buy, or to think in a particular way. Much as you can address large audiences face-to-face, you also can address such audiences electronically. Through newsgroups, blogs, or social networks, for example, you can post your "speech" for anyone to read and then read their reactions to your message. And with the help of the more traditional mass media of radio and television, you can address audiences in the hundreds of millions as they sit alone or in small groups scattered throughout the world.

**Computer-mediated communication** is communication between people that takes place through some computer connection. E-mail, chat room, newsgroup, instant messaging, website, and blog communication all are examples of computer-mediated communication, often abbreviated CMC. Throughout this text we'll examine computer-mediated communication along with face-to-face communication and will consider similarities and differences between the two.

The term **mass communication** refers to communication from one source to many receivers who may be scattered throughout the world. Newspapers, magazines, radio, television, and film are the major mass media. The coverage of mass communication in this book focuses on media literacy, helping you to become a wiser, more critical user of the media.

As you can see if you glance through your college catalogue, each of these forms of communication is likely to be covered in separate and more detailed courses. For example, most communication departments offer separate courses in public speaking, small group communication, mass communication, and so on. This course and this text introduce the essentials of these communication forms, giving

▼ E-TALK

**Computer-Mediated Communication**
Throughout this text you'll find E-Talk marginal items designed to draw your attention to the similarities and differences between computer-mediated and face-to-face communication. A definition from TheFreeDictionary.com will serve us well to begin: "Computer-mediated communication (CMC) is any form of communication between two or more individual people who interact and/or influence each other via separate computers," and the term CMC generally refers to "e-mail, video, audio or text conferencing, bulletin boards, listservs, instant messaging, and multi-player video games."

### What Is Media Literacy?

Media literacy may be defined as your ability to understand, analyze, evaluate, and produce mass communication messages (television, film, music, radio, billboards, advertising, public relations, newspapers and magazines, books, websites and blogs, newsgroups and chat rooms).

Because the media influence you in numerous ways, only some of which you may be conscious of, it's crucial that you learn how this influence is exerted so that you, rather than the media, can determine what influences you and what doesn't. Looked at in this way, media literacy is a form of empowerment. It can help you use the media more intelligently; understand, analyze, and evaluate media messages more effectively; influence the messages that the media send out, and create your own mediated messages.

Because of the importance of this topic, it is presented throughout the text in Media Literacy boxes. You'll also find three tables on fallacies that are common in all forms of communication but especially in the media (one in the Chapter 9 Media Literacy box and two in the main text of Chapter 13). As you read the Media Literacy boxes, examine your own media behavior and ask yourself what you can or should change.

*Increasing Media Literacy Increase your sensitivity to media by examining your own use of media. If possible, keep a record or log of all the time you spend on media in one day, the media you use most often, the purposes you use the media for, the rewards you get from the media, and especially the ways in which the media might be influencing you. Also increase your sensitivity by supplementing these Media Literacy boxes with visits to some interesting websites; try, for example, Citizens for Media Literacy at* www.main.nc.us/cml/ *and the Media Education Foundation at* www.mediaed.org.

*[I]t is precisely because they [the mass media] are so familiar that we need to study them. Familiarity, for example, may blind us to the distinct kind of communication that takes place through the mass media, and especially to the processes by which they influence us.*

—KATHLEEN HALL
JAMIESON AND KARLYN
KOHRS CAMPBELL

you the knowledge and skills to become a more effective communicator and at the same time the background to move on to more detailed study, whether in additional courses or in your own reading.

This book, then, focuses on all these forms of communication—and on you as both message sender and message receiver. It has three major purposes:

- It aims to explain the *concepts and principles*, the *theory and research* in human communication, so that you'll have a firm understanding of what communication is and how it works.

- It seeks to provide you with *skills* in human communication that will help you increase your own communication competence and effectiveness in the real world. Lots of social interaction and workplace examples throughout the book present useful and practical techniques that you'll take with you when you leave the college classroom.

- It endeavors to help you increase your *critical thinking* ability, both in general and about communication in particular—so as to know what your communication options are and to have the knowledge to select the right ones.

## Popular Beliefs about Human Communication

A good way to begin your study of human communication is to examine just a few of the popular but erroneous beliefs about communication. Many such popular beliefs are unfounded and are actually contradicted by research and theory. Understanding these beliefs and why they are false will help eliminate potential barriers and pave the way for more effective and efficient learning about communication.

***The more you communicate, the better your communication will be.***
Although this proposition seems logical—the same idea lies behind the popular belief

that practice makes perfect—it actually is at the heart of much faulty learning. Practice may help make perfect if you practice the right habits. But if you practice bad habits, you're likely to grow less rather than more effective. Consequently, it's important to learn and practice the principles of effectiveness.

***When two people are in a close relationship, neither person should have to explicitly communicate needs and wants; the other person should know what these are.*** This assumption is at the heart of many interpersonal difficulties—people aren't mind readers, and to assume that they are merely sets up barriers to open and honest communication.

***Interpersonal or group conflict is a reliable sign that the relationship or group is in trouble.*** Conflict is inevitable in relationships and in groups. As famed author William Ellery Channing put it: "Difficulties are meant to rouse, not discourage. The human spirit is to grow strong by conflict." In fact, if the conflict is approached effectively, it may actually benefit the individuals and the relationship.

***Like good communicators, leaders are born, not made.*** Leadership, like communication and listening, is a learned skill. You'll develop leadership abilities as you learn the principles of human communication and those unique to group communication and group leadership.

***Fear of speaking in public is detrimental and must be eliminated.*** Most speakers are nervous—and, to be perfectly honest, you're probably not going to learn from this book or this course to eliminate what is commonly called stage fright or communication apprehension. But you will learn to *manage* your fear, making it work for you rather than against you; you'll learn to become a more effective speaker regardless of your current level of anxiety.

## Communication Models and Concepts

In early **models** (representations) or theories, the communication process was seen as linear. According to this *linear* view of communication, the speaker spoke and the listener listened. Communication was seen as proceeding in a relatively straight line. Speaking and listening were seen as taking place at different times; when you spoke, you didn't listen, and when you listened, you didn't speak (Figure 1.1).

The linear view was soon replaced with an *interactional* view, in which the speaker and listener were seen as exchanging turns at speaking and listening. For example, A spoke while B listened; then B spoke in response while A listened (Figure 1.2). The interactional model still viewed speaking and listening as separate acts that did not overlap and that were not performed at the same time by the same person.

A more satisfying view, the one held currently, sees communication as a *transactional* process in which each person serves simultaneously as speaker and listener. At the same time that you send messages, you're also receiving messages from your own communications and from the reactions of the other person (see Figure 1.3 on page 6).

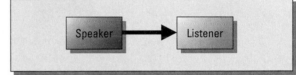

**Figure *1.1***

**The Linear View of Human Communication**

Communication researchers Paul Nelson and Judy Pearson (1996) suggest that you think of the speaker as passing a ball to the listener, who either catches it or fumbles it. Can you think of another analogy or metaphor for this linear view of communication?

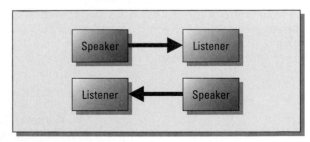

**Figure *1.2***

**The Interactional View of Human Communication**

In the interactional view, continuing with the ball-passing analogy, the speaker passes the ball to the listener, who then either passes the ball back or fumbles it (Nelson & Pearson, 1996). What other analogy would work here?

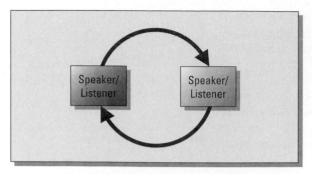

**Figure** *1.3*

**The Transactional View of Human Communication**

In the transactional view, a complex ball game is under way. Each player can send and receive any number of balls at any time. Players are able to throw and catch balls at the same time (Nelson & Pearson, 1996). Can you think of other analogies for this view?

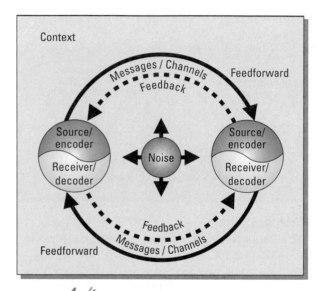

**Figure** *1.4*

**The Essentials of Human Communication**

This is a general model of communication between two people and most accurately depicts interpersonal communication. It puts into visual form the various elements of the communication process. How would you revise this model to depict small group interaction? To depict public speaking?

The transactional viewpoint sees each person as both speaker and listener, as simultaneously communicating and receiving messages (Watzlawick, Beavin, & Jackson, 1967; Watzlawick, 1977, 1978; Barnlund, 1970). Also, the transactional view sees the elements of communication as interdependent (never independent). This means that each element exists in relation to the others. A change in any one element of the process produces changes in the other elements. For example, if you're having a meeting with a group of your coworkers and your boss enters the room, this change in "audience" will lead to other changes. Perhaps you'll change what you're saying or how you're saying it. Regardless of what change is introduced, other changes will occur as a result.

In communication people act and react on the basis of the present situation as well as on the basis of their histories, past experiences, attitudes, cultural beliefs, and a host of related factors. Because of this, actions and reactions in communication are determined not only by what is said, but also by the way the person interprets what is said. Your responses to a movie, for example, don't depend solely on the words and pictures in the film; they also depend on your previous experiences, present emotions, knowledge, physical well-being, and lots more. Another implication is that two people listening to the same message will often derive two very different meanings. Although the words and symbols are the same, each person interprets them differently.

Communication occurs when you send or receive messages and when you assign meaning to another person's signals. All human communication is distorted by noise, occurs within a context, has some effect, and involves some opportunity for feedback. We can expand the basic transactional model of communication by adding these essential elements, as shown in Figure 1.4.

## Communication Context

Communication exists in a context—the physical, cultural, sociopsychological, and temporal environment—which determines, to a large extent, the meaning of any verbal or nonverbal message. The same words or behaviors may have totally different meanings when they occur in different contexts. For example, the greeting "How are you?" means "Hello" to someone you pass regularly on the street but "Is your health improving?" to a friend in the hospital. A wink to an attractive person on a bus means something completely different from a wink that signifies a put-on or a lie. Divorced from the context, it's impossible to tell what meaning was intended from just examining the signals.

The context will also influence what you say and how you say it. You communicate differently depending on the specific context you're in.

Contexts have at least four aspects: physical, cultural, social-psychological, and temporal or time.

- The *physical context* is the tangible or concrete environment, the room, park, or auditorium; you don't talk the same way at a noisy football game as you do at a quiet funeral.
- The *cultural context* involves the lifestyles, beliefs, values, behavior, and communication of a group; it is the rules of a group of people for considering something right or wrong.

- The *social-psychological context* has to do with the status relationships among speakers, the formality of the situation, the norms of a group or organization; you don't talk the same way in the cafeteria as you would at a formal dinner at your boss's house.
- The *temporal context* is a message's position within a sequence of events; you don't talk the same way after someone tells you about the death of a close relative as you do after someone reveals they've won the lottery.

These four contexts interact—each influences and is influenced by the others. For example, arriving late for a date (temporal context) may lead to changes in the degree of friendliness (social–psychological context), which would depend on the cultures of you and your date (cultural context) and may lead to changes in where you go on the date (physical context).

## Sources–Receivers

Each person involved in communication is both a **source** (speaker) and a **receiver** (listener); hence the term *sources–receivers*. You send messages when you speak, write, gesture, or smile. You receive messages in listening, reading, seeing, smelling, and so on. At the same time that you send messages, you're also receiving messages: You're receiving your own messages (you hear yourself, you feel your own movements, you see many of your own gestures), and, at least in face-to-face communication, you're receiving the messages of the other person—visually, auditorily, or even through touch or smell. As you speak, you look at the person for responses—for approval, understanding, sympathy, agreement, and so on. As you decipher these nonverbal signals, you're performing receiver functions.

When you put your ideas into speech, you're putting them into a code, hence **encoding**. When you translate the sound waves (the speech signals) that impinge on your ears into ideas, you take them out of the code they're in, hence **decoding**. Thus, speakers or writers are referred to as **encoders** and listeners or readers as **decoders.** The linked term *encoding–decoding* emphasizes the fact that you perform these functions simultaneously.

Usually, you encode an idea into a code that the other person understands—for example, English, Spanish, or Indonesian, depending on the shared knowledge that you and your listener possess. At times, however, you may want to exclude others by speaking in a language that only one of your listeners knows or using jargon. Adults, when speaking of things they don't want children to understand, may spell out key words—a code that the young children don't yet understand. Computer communication enables you to do a similar thing. For example, when sending your credit card number to a vendor, you might send it in encrypted form, coded into a symbol system that others will not be able to understand (decode). Similarly, in chat groups you might write in a language that only certain of your readers will understand. The use of jargon in texting—in instant messaging, among teens, for example—is another example of how people communicate in a secret code.

## Messages

Communication **messages** take many forms and are transmitted or received through one or a combination of sensory organs. You communicate verbally (with words) and nonverbally (without words). Your meanings or intentions are conveyed with words (Chapter 4) and with the clothes you wear, the way you walk, and the way you smile (Chapter 5). Everything about you communicates a message.

**Feedforward Messages** **Feedforward** is information you provide before sending your primary messages (Richards, 1951). Feedforward reveals something about the messages to come and includes, for example, the preface or table of contents of a book, the opening paragraph of a chapter, movie previews, magazine covers, and introductions in public speeches.

Feedforward may be verbal ("Wait until you hear this one") or nonverbal (a prolonged pause or hands motioning for silence to signal that an important message is about to be spoken). Or, as is most often the case, it is some combination of verbal and nonverbal. Feedforward may refer to the content of the message to follow ("I'll tell you exactly what they said to each other") or to the form ("I won't spare you the gory details"). In e-mail, feedforward is given in the header, where the name of the sender, the date, and the subject of the message are identified. Caller ID is another good example of feedforward.

Another type of feedforward is **phatic communication,** or "small talk" that opens the way for "big talk." It includes the "How are you" and "Nice weather" greetings that are designed to maintain rapport and friendly relationships (Placencia, 2004; Burnard, 2003). Similarly, listeners' short comments that are unrelated to the content of the conversation but that indicate interest and attention also may be considered phatic communication (McCarthy, 2003).

**Feedback Messages** When you send a message—say, in speaking to another person—you also hear yourself. That is, you get **feedback** from your own messages; you hear what you say, you feel the way you move, you see what you write. In addition to this self-feedback, you also get feedback from others. This feedback can take many forms. A frown or a smile, a yea or a nay, a pat on the back or a punch in the mouth are all types of feedback.

Feedback tells the speaker what effect he or she is having on listeners. On the basis of feedback, the speaker may adjust, modify, strengthen, deemphasize, or change the content or form of the messages. So, for example, if someone laughs at your joke (giving you positive feedback), it may influence you to tell another one. If the feedback is negative—no laughing, just blank stares—then you may resist relaying another "humorous" story.

**Metamessages** A **metamessage** is a message that refers to another message; it is communication about communication. For example, remarks such as "This statement is false" or "Do you understand what I am trying to tell you?" refer to communication and are therefore "metacommunicational."

Nonverbal behavior may also be metacommunicational. Obvious examples include crossing your fingers behind your back or winking when telling a lie. On a less obvious level, consider the blind date. As you say, "I had a really nice time," your nonverbal messages—the lack of a smile, the failure to maintain eye contact, the extra long pauses—metacommunicate and contradict the verbal "really nice time," suggesting that you did not enjoy the evening. Nonverbal messages may also metacommunicate about other nonverbal messages. The individual who, on meeting a stranger, both smiles and extends a totally lifeless hand shows how one nonverbal behavior may contradict another.

**Message Overload** Message overload, often called **information overload,** is one of the greatest obstacles to communication efficiency and has even been linked to health problems in corporate managers (Lee, 2000). The ease with which people can copy or forward e-mail and Internet messages to large numbers of recipients with a few taps of the keyboard has obviously contributed to message overload, as have the junk mail and spam that seem to multiply every day. Invariably, you must select certain messages to attend to and other messages to ignore. And research shows that under conditions of message overload, you're more likely to respond to the simpler messages and to generate simpler responses (Jones, Ravid, & Rafaeli, 2004). Today, for example, the American worker is exposed to more messages in one year than a person living in 1900 was in an entire lifetime. Today the av-

**WHAT DO YOU SAY?**
**Message Overload**
Several relatives have developed chain e-mail lists and send you virtually everything they come upon as they surf the Internet. You need to stop this e-mail overload. *What do you say? To whom? Through what channel?*

erage employee receives more than 50 e-mails daily. In one day the average manager sends and receives more than 100 documents.

One of the reasons message overload is a problem is that it absorbs an enormous amount of time. The more messages you have to deal with, the less time you have for the messages or tasks that are central to your purpose. Similarly, under conditions of message overload, errors are more likely—simply because you cannot devote the needed time to any one item. The more rushed you are, the more likely you are to make mistakes. Another problem is that message overload makes it difficult for you to determine efficiently which messages need immediate attention and which don't, which messages may be discarded and which must be retained.

## Channel

The communication **channel** is the vehicle or medium through which messages pass. Communication rarely takes place over only one channel. Rather, two, three, or four channels may be used simultaneously. In face-to-face conversations, for example, you speak and listen (vocal channel), but you also gesture and receive signals visually (visual channel). You also emit and smell odors (olfactory channel) and often touch one another; this tactile channel, too, is communication.

Another way to classify channels is by the means of communication. Thus, face-to-face contact, telephones, e-mail, movies, television, smoke signals, and telegraph all are types of channels.

At times one or more channels may be damaged. For example, in individuals who are blind, the visual channel is impaired and adjustments have to be made. Table 1.1 on page 10 gives you an idea of how such adjustments between blind and sighted persons can make communication more effective.

**Face-to-Face and Computer-Mediated Communication** Perhaps the most important channel distinction to be made today is between *face-to-face* and *computer-mediated communication*. Often, communication takes place face-to-face, as when you talk with other students or with family or friends over dinner, trade secrets with intimates, solve a problem in a group, or deliver a public speech. But, as you well know, much of today's communication is computer mediated. Online communication, or what is now called computer-mediated communication, is now a major part of people's experience throughout the world. Such communication is important personally, socially, and professionally.

E-mail is today the most common use of the Internet. Unlike face-to-face communication, traditional e-mail does not take place in real time. You may send your message today, but the receiver may not read it for a week and may take another week to respond. Consequently, much of the spontaneity created by real-time communication is lost. You may, for example, be very enthusiastic about a topic when you send your e-mail but practically forget it by the time someone responds. Also, e-mail is more like a postcard than a letter in that it can be read by others along the route. It's also virtually unerasable, a feature that has important consequences and that is discussed later in this section.

The listserv or mailing-list group consists of a group of people interested in a particular topic who communicate with one another through e-mail. Generally, you subscribe to a list and communicate with all other members by addressing your mail to the group e-mail address. Any message you send to this address will be sent to each member who subscribes to the list. Your message is sent to all members at the same time; there are no asides to the person sitting next to you (as in face-to-face groups).

Instant messaging (often abbreviated IM) is an Internet text-based system that allows you to converse online in real time. Through IM you can also play games, share files, listen to music, and send messages to cell phones. A 2004 study reported that approximately 42 percent of Internet users (more than 53 million Americans)

▼ | E-TALK

**Online and Offline Activities**
A report dated August 11, 2004, by the Pew Internet and American Life Project (The Internet and Daily Life, www.pewinternet.org/PPF/r/131/ report_display.asp, accessed February 10, 2005) noted that people are more likely to "get news, play games, pay bills, send cards, look up phone numbers and addresses, buy tickets, check sports scores, listen to music, schedule appointments, and communicate with friends" offline than online. Why do you think this is the case? Do you think the items on this list will change over the next 5 years? Over the next 20 years?

## TABLE 1.1 *Communication Tips*

**BETWEEN BLIND AND SIGHTED PEOPLE**

People vary greatly in their visual abilities; some are totally blind, some are partially sighted, and some have unimpaired vision. Ninety percent of individuals who are "legally blind" have some vision. All, however, have the same need for communication and information. Here are some tips for making communication between blind and sighted people more effective:

**If you're the sighted person and are talking with a blind person:**

1. *Identify yourself.* Don't assume the blind person will recognize your voice.
2. *Face your listener; you'll be easier to hear.* Don't shout. People who are visually impaired are not hearing impaired. Speak at your normal volume.
3. Because your gestures, eye movements, and facial expressions cannot be seen by the visually impaired listener, *encode into speech all the meanings you wish to communicate.*
4. *Use audible turn-taking cues.* When you pass the role of speaker to a person who is visually impaired, don't rely on nonverbal cues; instead, say something like "Do you agree with that, Joe?"
5. *Use normal vocabulary and discuss topics that you would discuss with sighted people.* Don't avoid terms like "see" or "look" or even "blind." Don't avoid discussing a television show or the way your new car looks; these are normal topics for all people.

**If you are a visually impaired person and are interacting with a sighted person:**

1. *Help the sighted person meet your special communication needs.* If you want your surroundings described, ask. If you want the person to read the road signs, ask.
2. *Be patient with the sighted person.* Many people are nervous talking with people who are visually impaired for fear of offending. Put them at ease in a way that also makes you more comfortable.

These suggestions were drawn from a variety of sources: www.cincyblind.org/, www.abwa.asn.au/, and www.dol.gov (all accessed October 9, 2006).

---

were using IM. Approximately 21 percent of IM users reported that they used it at work; of these, 40 percent used it to communicate with coworkers, 33 percent to communicate with friends and family, and 21 percent to reach both groups (Shiu & Lenhart, 2004). Among college students, as you probably know, the major purpose of IM seems to be to maintain "social connectedness" (Kindred & Roper, 2004).

But it is in business that IM is growing most impressively. Some 80 percent of U.S. corporations use IM. Within IBM, for example, some 2.5 million IMs are exchanged daily (Strom, 2006). Because IM tells you who else is now online, it enables members of a geographically separated workforce to contact others immediately—a decided advantage over e-mail, in which you have no idea when the person is going to read your message and get back to you. A nurse can instantly contact an online MD to ask a question, and a salesperson can consult with a supervisor to answer a customer's question immediately. In addition, IM builds a sense of community among users, even though they may physically be in different parts of the world.

Chat groups enable you to converse in real time. Unlike mailing lists, chat communication lets you see a member's message as it's being sent; there's virtually no delay, and recent innovations now enable you to communicate with voice as well as text. At any one time there are thousands of groups, so your chances of finding a topic you're interested in are high. As with e-mail and face-to-face conversation, the purposes of chat groups vary from communication that simply maintains connection with others (what many would call "idle chatter" or "phatic communication") to extremely significant discussions in science, education, health, politics, and just about any field you can name. Like mailing lists, chat groups have the great advantage that they enable you to communicate with people you would never meet and interact with face-to-face. Because chat groups are international, they provide excellent exposure to other cultures, other ideas, and other ways of communicating.

Blogs and interactive websites now enable you to communicate your opinions for others to read and react to and to communicate your reactions to what others say. Increasingly blogs are being used for more relational purposes, such as maintaining family or group ties and encouraging frequent communication among family or group members.

One of the major differences between face-to-face and computer-mediated communication is the contrast between the permanency of electronic communication and the evanescence of face-to-face communication. Here are a few of the consequences of this difference, all of which suggest added caution when you communicate electronically, whether via e-mail, chat room conversations, or blog posts:

- *Electronic messages are difficult to destroy.* Often e-mails that you think you deleted will remain on servers and workstations and may be retrieved by a clever hacker.
- *Electronic messages may easily be made public.* The ease of forwarding e-mails or newsgroup postings makes it especially important to remember that what you intend for one person may actually be received by many.
- *Electronic messages are not privileged communication.* They can easily be used against you, especially in the workplace. For example, criticism of others may one day come back to haunt you in accusations of discrimination.
- *Electronic messages provide permanent records.* This can make it impossible for you to say, for example, "That's not exactly what I said," because it will be exactly what you said; it will be there in black and white.
- *Electronic message files may be accessed.* And a file accessed by a nosy colleague at the next desk or by a visiting neighbor can then be sent to others.

Table 1.2 on page 12 presents some of the similarities and differences between face-to-face and computer-mediated communication. As you review the table, you may wish to add other similarities and differences or take issue with the ones identified here.

## Noise

**Noise** is anything that interferes with your receiving a message. At one extreme, noise may prevent a message from getting from source to receiver. A roaring noise or line static can easily prevent entire messages from getting through to your phone receiver. At the other extreme, with virtually no noise interference, the message of the source and the message received are almost identical. Most often, however, noise distorts some portion of the message a source sends as it travels to a receiver. Just as messages may be auditory or visual, noise comes in both auditory and visual forms. Four types of noise are especially relevant:

- *Physical noise* is interference that is external to both speaker and listener; it interferes with the physical transmission of the signal or message and would include the screeching of passing cars, the hum of a computer, sunglasses, extraneous messages, illegible handwriting, blurred type or fonts that are too small or difficult to read, misspellings and poor grammar, and popup ads.
- *Physiological noise* is created by barriers within the sender or receiver and would include visual impairments, hearing loss, articulation problems, and memory loss.

## TABLE 1.2 Face-to-Face and Computer-Mediated Communication

Throughout this text, face-to-face and computer-mediated communication are discussed, compared, and contrasted. Here is a brief summary of some communication concepts and some of the ways in which face-to-face and computer-mediated communication are similar and different. What other similarities and differences would you identify?

| HUMAN COMMUNICATION ELEMENT | FACE-TO-FACE COMMUNICATION | COMPUTER-MEDIATED COMMUNICATION |
|---|---|---|
| **Sender** | | |
| Presentation of self and impression management | • Visual appearance communicates who you are; personal characteristics (sex, approximate age, race, etc.) are overt and open to visual inspection; receiver controls the order of what is attended to; disguise is difficult. | • You present the self you want others to see; personal characteristics are covert and are revealed when you want to reveal them; speaker controls the order of revelation; disguise or anonymity is easy. |
| Speaking turn | • You compete for the speaker's turn and time with the other person(s); you can be interrupted. | • It's always your turn; speaker time is unlimited; you can't be interrupted. |
| **Receiver** | | |
| Number | • One or a few who are in your visual field. | • One, a few, or as many as you find in a chat room or have on your e-mail list, or who read your bulletin board posts. |
| Interests | • Limited to the interests of those you have the opportunity to meet; often difficult to find people who have the same interests you do, especially in isolated communities with little mobility. | • Virtually unlimited; you can more easily and quickly find people who match your interests. |
| Third parties | • Your messages can be overheard by or repeated to third parties, but not verbatim and not with complete accuracy. | • Your messages can be retrieved by others or forwarded verbatim to a third party or to hundreds of third parties (with or without your knowledge). |
| Impression formation | • Impressions are based on the verbal and nonverbal cues receiver perceives. | • Impressions are based on text messages (usually) receiver reads. |
| **Context** | | |
| Physical | • Where you both are; together in essentially the same physical space. | • Where you and receiver each want to be, separated in space. |
| Temporal | • As it happens; you have little control over the temporal context once you're in a communication situation. | • You can more easily choose the timing—when you want to respond. |
| | • Communication is *synchronous*—messages are exchanged at the same time. | • Communication may be synchronous, as in chat rooms and instant messaging, or may be *asynchronous*—messages are exchanged at different times, as in e-mail and bulletin board postings. |
| Channel | • Auditory + visual + tactile + proxemic. | • Visual for text (though both auditory and visual for graphics and video are available). |

| | | |
|---|---|---|
| | • Two-way channel enabling immediate interactivity. | • Two-way channels, some enabling immediate and some delayed interactivity. |
| **Messages** | | |
| Verbal and nonverbal | • Spoken words along with your gestures, eye contact, accent, paralinguistic cues, space, touch, clothing, hair, and all the other nonverbal cues. | • Written words in purely text-based CMC, though that's changing. |
| | | • Limited nonverbal cues; some can be created with emoticons or words and some (like smells and touch) cannot. |
| | • Rarely are abbreviations verbally expressed. | • Uses lots of abbreviations. |
| Permanence | • Temporary unless recorded; speech signals fade rapidly. | • Permanent unless erased. |
| Feedforward | • Conveyed nonverbally and verbally early in the interaction. | • In e-mail conveyed in the headings and subject line, as well as in the opening sentences. |
| Ethics and Deception | • Presentation of false physical self is more difficult, but not impossible; false psychological and social selves are easier. | • Presentation of false physical self as well as false psychological and social selves are relatively easy. |
| | • Nonverbal leakage cues often give you away when you're lying. | • Can probably lie more easily. |

- *Psychological noise* refers to mental interference in speaker or listener and includes preconceived ideas, wandering thoughts, biases and prejudices, closed-mindedness, and extreme emotionalism. You're likely to run into psychological noise when you talk with someone who is closed-minded or who refuses to listen to anything he or she doesn't already believe.

- *Semantic noise* is interference that occurs when the speaker and listener have different meaning systems; it would include language or dialectical differences, the use of jargon or overly complex terms, and ambiguous or overly abstract terms whose meanings can be easily misinterpreted. You see this type of noise regularly in the medical doctor who uses "medicalese" without explanation or in the insurance salesperson who speaks in the jargon of the insurance industry.

As you can see from these examples, noise is anything that distorts your receiving the messages of others or their receiving your messages.

A useful concept in understanding noise and its importance in communication is **signal-to-noise ratio.** In this term the word *signal* refers to information that you'd find useful, and *noise* refers to information that is useless (to you). So, for example, a mailing list or newsgroup that contains lots of useful information is high on signal and low on noise; one that contains lots of useless information is high on noise and low on signal.

All communications contain noise. Noise can't be totally eliminated, but its effects can be reduced. Making your language more precise, sharpening your skills for sending and receiving nonverbal messages, and improving your listening and feedback skills are some ways to combat the influence of noise.

## Effects

Communication always has some **effect** on those involved in the communication act. For every communication act, there is some consequence. For example, you

> **WHAT DO YOU SAY?**
> **Negative Communication Effects**
> An e-mail that you wrote to a close friend in anger (but never intended to send) was sent. You want to reduce the negative effects of such an e-mail. *What do you say?*

may gain knowledge or learn how to analyze, synthesize, or evaluate something. These are intellectual or cognitive effects. You may acquire new feelings, attitudes, or beliefs or change existing ones (affective effects). You may learn new bodily movements, such as how to throw a curve ball, paint a picture, give a compliment, or express surprise (psychomotor effects).

## Communication Competence

The term **communication competence** refers to your knowledge of how communication works and your ability to use communication effectively (Spitzberg & Cupach, 1989, 2002). Communication competence includes, for example, the knowledge that in certain contexts and with certain listeners, some messages and some ways of communicating are appropriate and effective and others are not.

The more you know about communication, the more choices you'll have available for your day-to-day interactions. It's like learning vocabulary. The more vocabulary you know, the more ways you have for expressing yourself. In a similar way, the aim of this book is to increase your communicative competence and thus to give you a broad range of options to use in your own communications.

This text both presents information about communication theory and research and explains the skills and techniques for more effective communication. In addition, the other themes of this book will help you sharpen and increase your competence in a variety of ways. These themes, in addition to communication skills, are culture, critical thinking, ethics, power, and listening (see Figure 1.5).

- *Competence and culture:* Communication competence is culture specific; that is, the principles of effective communication vary from one culture to another, and what proves effective in one culture may prove ineffective in another. For example, in American culture you would call a person you wished to date three or four days in advance. In certain Asian cultures, you might call the person's parents weeks or even months in advance. Thus, discussions of cultural implications accompany all of the major topics considered in this text.

- *Competence and critical thinking:* The ability to think critically about the communication situations you face and the options for communicating that you have available is crucial to your success and effectiveness. Consequently, opportunities for **critical thinking** and suggestions for thinking more critically in all communication situations are offered throughout this text.

- *Competence and ethics:* **Ethics** has been part of communication training for more than 2,000 years; *Essentials of Human Communication* follows in that tradition. There is a right-versus-wrong aspect to any and all communication acts, and this aspect is separate from that of effectiveness. For example, it might be effective to lie in selling a product, but most people would agree that it would not be ethical. Because of the central importance of ethics to all forms and functions of communication, *Communicating Ethically* boxes appear throughout this text.

- *Competence and power:* All communication transactions involve **power,** or the ability to control the behavior of others. In fact, you can look at the principles of communication covered in this text as principles of power—the power to speak your own mind, the power to influence a friend, the power to lead a group responsibly and efficiently, the power to get your point across to an audience. As motivational speaker Anthony Robbins put it, "Communication is power. Those who have mastered its effective use can change their own experience of the world and the world's experience of them." Because of the central importance of power in all forms of communication, concepts and principles relevant to power are discussed throughout the text.

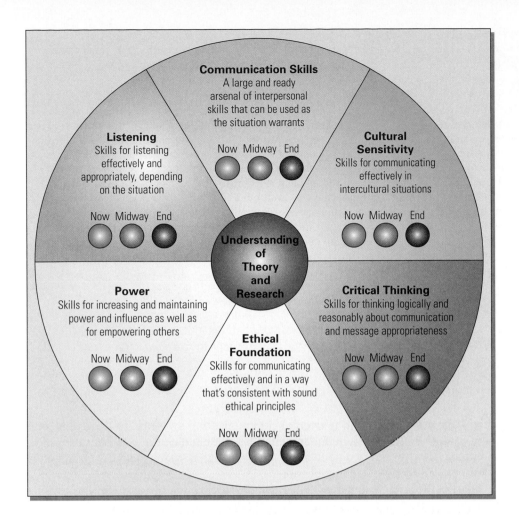

**Figure** *1.5*
**The Competent Communicator**
Indicate how competent you feel you are in each of these six areas right now: Give yourself scores from 1 (little competence) to 100 (a great deal of competence). Return to this midway through the course and at the end of the course and record your scores on the diagram. Your scores should improve significantly.

- *Competence and listening:* Communication is a two-way process; your ability to communicate effectively rests heavily on your ability to listen. An entire chapter, Chapter 3, is devoted to the principles and techniques of listening. In addition, each chapter contains a *Listen to This* box that connects listening with the content of the chapter and asks you to consider how you might apply listening skills to specific communication situations.

# Principles of Communication

Several principles are essential to an understanding of human communication in all its forms. These principles, as you'll see throughout the text, also have numerous practical implications for your own communication effectiveness.

## Communication Is a Process of Adjustment

The principle of **adjustment** states that communication can take place only to the extent that the communicators use the same system of signals (Pittenger, Hockett, & Danehy, 1960). You will be unable to communicate with another person to the extent that your language systems differ. Parents and children, for example, not only have largely different vocabularies, but also may assign different meanings to the terms they do share. Different cultures, even when they use a common language,

## Approaching Ethics

In making ethical decisions, you can take the position that ethics is objective or that it's subjective. An **objective view** of ethics claims that the morality of an act is absolute and exists apart from the values or beliefs of any individual, culture, or specific circumstance: Ethical standards apply to all people in all situations at all times. For example, if lying or false advertising is unethical, then, according to the objective view, that practice will be unethical regardless of the particular circumstances or of the values and beliefs of the culture.

A **subjective view** claims that the ethics of communication depends on the culture's values and beliefs as well as the particular circumstances. Thus, in a subjective view you might claim that lying is wrong to win votes or sell cigarettes, but that it is perfectly ethical if the end result is positive, as when someone tries to make people feel better by telling them they look great or tries to boost their confidence by saying that they're going to do well in a job interview.

*What Would You Do?* A colleague repeatedly takes home office supplies. He argues that because he is underpaid and was recently denied a well-deserved promotion, he's justified in taking additional compensation. You agree that he is underpaid and that he did deserve the promotion. He asks you if you think his behavior is unethical. What would you say if you took an objective view of ethics? What would you say if you took a subjective view? What would you say?

*When I do good, I feel good; when I do bad, I feel bad. That's my religion.*
—ABRAHAM LINCOLN

often have greatly different nonverbal communication systems. To the extent that these systems differ, meaningful and effective communication will not take place. In reality, however, no two people use identical signal systems, so this principle is relevant to all forms of communication.

Part of the art of communication is identifying the other person's signals, learning how they're used, and understanding what they mean. Those in close relationships will realize that learning the other person's signals takes a great deal of time and often a great deal of patience. If you want to understand what another person means (by smiling, by saying "I love you," by arguing about trivia, by making self-deprecating comments) rather than merely acknowledging what the other person says or does, you have to learn that person's system of signals.

This principle is especially important in intercultural communication. People from different cultures often use different signals—and sometimes use similar signals to mean quite different things. Focused eye contact means honesty and openness in much of the United States. But that same behavior may signify arrogance or disrespect in Japan and in many Hispanic cultures, particularly if engaged in by a youngster with someone significantly older.

**Communication Accommodation** An interesting theory revolving largely around adjustment is **communication accommodation theory.** This theory holds that speakers adjust to, or *accommodate* to, the speaking style of their listeners in order to gain, for example, social approval and greater communication efficiency (Giles, Mulac, Bradac, & Johnson, 1987). For example, when two people have a similar speech rate, they seem to be attracted more to each other than to those with dissimilar rates (Buller, LePoire, Aune, & Eloy, 1992).

Similarly, the speaker who uses language intensity similar to that of his or her listeners is judged to have greater credibility than the speaker who uses different intensity (Aune & Kikuchi, 1993). Still another study found that roommates who had similar communication attitudes (both roommates were high in communication competence and willingness to communicate, and low in verbal aggressiveness) were highest in roommate liking and satisfaction (Martin & Anderson, 1995). And in interethnic interactions, people who saw themselves as similar in communication styles were attracted to each other more than to those they perceived as having different communication styles (Lee & Gudykunst, 2001).

## Communication Is Ambiguous

**Ambiguity** is the condition in which a message can be interpreted in more than one way. Sometimes ambiguity is created by words that can be interpreted differently. Informal time terms offer good examples; *soon, right away, in a minute, early, late,* and similar terms can easily be understood very differently by different people. The terms are ambiguous. A more interesting type of ambiguity is grammatical ambiguity. You can get a feel for this type of ambiguity by trying to paraphrase—rephrase in your own words—the following sentences:

- What has the cat in its paws?
- Flying planes can be dangerous.
- They are frying chickens.

Each of these ambiguous sentences can be interpreted and paraphrased in at least two different ways:

- What monster has the cat in its paws? What does the cat have in its paws?
- To fly planes is dangerous. Planes that fly can be dangerous.
- Those people are frying chickens. Those chickens are for frying.

Although these examples are particularly striking—and are the work of linguists who analyze language—some degree of ambiguity exists in all communication: All messages are ambiguous to some degree. When you express an idea, you never communicate your meaning exactly and totally; rather, you communicate your meaning with some reasonable accuracy—enough to give the other person a reasonably clear idea of what you mean. Sometimes, of course, you're less accurate than you anticipated, and your listener gets offended when you only meant to be humorous or misunderstands your emotional meaning and trivializes something that is extremely important to you. Because of this inevitable uncertainty you may qualify what you're saying, give an example, or ask, "Do you know what I mean?"

▼ | **E-TALK**

**Translation**
If you want to understand a file written in a foreign language or translate a word or phrase, Google may be able to help. Go to Google's home page (www.google.com) and explore the relevant information under Language Tools.

## LISTEN TO THIS

*Wisdom is the reward you get for a lifetime of listening when you'd have preferred to talk.*

—Doug Larson

### Listening to Communicate

Listening is integral to all communication; it's coordinate with speaking. If you measured importance by the time you spend on an activity, then—according to the research studies available—listening would be your most important communication activity. Studies conducted from 1929 to 1980 show that listening was the most often used form of communication. In a study of college students conducted in 1980 (Barker, Edwards, Gaines, Gladney, & Holley), listening also occupied the most time: 53 percent compared to reading (17 percent), speaking (16 percent), and writing (14 percent). Because of the widespread use of the Internet, these studies now are dated and their findings of limited value. Your communication patterns are very different from those of someone raised and educated before widespread use of home computers. However, anecdotal evidence (certainly not conclusive in any way) suggests that listening still occupies a considerable portion of your communication time. And, if the popularity of cell phones is any indication, listening remains very important in your daily communications.

***Applying Listening Skills.*** *How much of your communication time do you spend in listening? In what situations do you listen most effectively? In what situations do you listen less effectively? How might you improve your listening in those situations where your listening is not as effective as it might be?*

**E-TALK**

**Online Uncertainty**
What kinds of uncertainty might you have with an online relationship partner that you wouldn't have in a face-to-face relationship? What kinds of uncertainty would occur more often offline than online?

These additional explanations help the other person understand your meaning and reduce uncertainty (to some degree).

Similarly, all relationships contain uncertainty. Consider your own close relationships and ask yourself the following questions. Answer using a six-point scale on which 1 = completely or almost completely uncertain and 6 = completely or almost completely certain. How certain are you about:

1. what you can or cannot say to each other in this relationship?

2. whether or not you and your partner feel the same way about each other?

3. how you and your partner would describe this relationship?

4. the future of the relationship?

It's very likely that you were not able to respond with 6s for all four questions, and equally likely that your relationship partner would not respond with all 6s. These questions—adapted from a relationship uncertainty scale (Knobloch & Solomon, 1999)—and similar others illustrate that you probably experience some degree of uncertainty about the norms that govern your relationship communication (question 1), the degree to which you each see the relationship in similar ways (question 2), the definition of the relationship (question 3), and the relationship's future (question 4).

You can look at the skills of human communication presented throughout this text as means for appropriately reducing ambiguity and making your meaning as unambiguous as possible.

## Communication Involves Content and Relationship Dimensions

Communication exists on at least two levels. A single message can refer to something external to both speaker and listener (for example, the weather) as well as to the relationship between speaker and listener (for example, who is in charge). These two aspects are referred to as **content and relationship dimensions** of communication (Watzlawick, Beavin, & Jackson, 1967). In the cartoon on the following page, the father is explicitly teaching his son the difference between content and relationship messages. In real life this distinction is rarely discussed (outside of textbooks and counseling sessions).

For example, let's say that a marketing manager at a Web design firm asks a worker to meet with her after the meeting. The content aspect of this request relates to what the manager wants the worker to do; namely, to meet with her after the meeting. The relationship aspect, however, has to do with the relationship between the manager and the worker; it states how the communication is to be dealt with. For example, the request indicates a status difference between the two parties: The manager can command the worker. If the worker commanded the manager, it would appear awkward and out of place—it would violate the normal relationship between manager and worker.

Some research shows that women send more **relationship messages** than men; they talk more about relationships in general and about the present relationship in particular. Men engage in more content talk; they talk more about things external to the relationship (Wood, 1994; Pearson, West, & Turner, 1995).

Problems often result from failure to distinguish between the content and the relationship levels of communication. Consider a couple, Pat and Chris. Pat made plans to attend a rally with friends during the weekend without first asking Chris, and an argument has ensued. Both would probably have agreed that attending the rally was the right choice to make. Thus, the argument is not centered on the content level. The argument, instead, centers on the relationship level. Chris expected to be consulted about plans for the weekend. Pat, in not doing this, rejected this definition of the relationship.

**WHAT DO YOU SAY?**
**Relationship Ambiguity**
You've dated someone three times and would like to invite your date to meet your parents, but you aren't sure how your date will perceive this invitation. *What do you say? In what context?*

## Communication Has a Power Dimension

Power, as mentioned earlier, has to do with your ability to influence or control the behaviors of another person. Power influences the way you communicate, and the way you communicate influences the power you wield. Research has identified six types of power: legitimate, referent, reward, coercive, expert, and information or persuasion power (French & Raven, 1968; Raven, Centers, & Rodrigues, 1975). Let's take a look at each.

You hold **legitimate power** when others believe you have a right—by virtue of your position—to influence or control their behaviors. For example, as an employer, judge, manager, or police officer you'd have legitimate power by virtue of these roles.

You have **referent power** when others wish to be like you. Referent power holders often are attractive, have considerable prestige, and are well liked and well respected. For example, you may have referent power over a younger brother because he wants to be like you.

You have **reward power** when you control the rewards that others want. Rewards may be material (money, promotion, jewelry) or social (love, friendship, respect). For example, teachers have reward power over students because they control grades, letters of recommendation, and social approval.

You have **coercive power** when you have the ability to administer punishments to or remove rewards from others if they do not do as you wish. Usually, people who have reward power also have coercive power. For example, teachers may give poor grades or withhold recommendations. But be careful: Coercive power may reduce your other power bases. It can have a negative impact when used, for example, by supervisors on subordinates in business (Richmond et al., 1984).

You have **expert power** when others see you as having expertise or special knowledge. Your expert power increases when you're seen as being unbiased and as

**"It's not about the story. It's about Daddy taking time out of his busy day to read you the story."**

## Skill Development Experience

### Distinguishing Content from Relationship Messages

*Content and relationship messages serve different communication functions. Being able to distinguish between these messages is a prerequisite for using and responding to them effectively.*

Deborah Tannen (2006), in her recent *You're Wearing That?*, gives lots of examples of content and relationship communication and the problems that can result from different interpretations. For example, the mother who says "Are you going to wear those earrings?" may think she's communicating solely a content message. To the daughter, however, the message is largely relational and is a criticism of the way she intends to dress. (Of course, the mother may have intended criticism.) Questions that appear to be objective and focused on content are often perceived as attacks, as in the title of Tannen's book. Identify the possible content and relational messages that a receiver might get in being asked the following questions:

- *You're* calling me?
- Did you say you're applying to *medical* school?
- You're in *love*?
- You paid *$100* for that?
- And that's *all* you did?

having nothing personally to gain from exerting this power. For example, judges have expert power in legal matters and doctors have expert power in medical matters.

You have **information power**—also called "persuasion power"—when others see you as having the ability to communicate logically and persuasively. For example, researchers and scientists may acquire information power because people perceive them as informed and critical thinkers.

The power you wield is not static; it can be increased or decreased depending on what you do and don't do. For example, you might increase your reward power by gaining wealth and using it to exert influence, or you might increase your persuasive power by mastering the principles of public speaking.

You can also decrease or lose power. Probably the most common way to lose power is by unsuccessfully trying to control another's behavior. For example, if you threaten someone with punishment and then fail to carry out your threat, you'll most likely lose power. Another way to lose power is to allow others to control you or to take unfair advantage of you. When you don't confront these power tactics of others, you lose power.

## Communication Is Punctuated

Communication events are continuous transactions that have no clear-cut beginning or ending. As a participant in or an observer of communication, you divide this continuous, circular process into causes and effects, or stimuli and responses. The **punctuation of communication** is the segmenting of the continuous stream of communication into smaller pieces (Watzlawick, Beavin, & Jackson, 1967). Some of these pieces you label causes (or stimuli) and others effects (or responses).

Consider this example: The manager of a local supermarket lacks interest in the employees, seldom offering any suggestions for improvement or any praise for jobs well done. The employees are apathetic and morale is low. Each action (the manager's lack of involvement and the employees' low morale) stimulates the other. Each serves as the stimulus for the other but there is no identifiable initial stimulus. Each event may be seen as a stimulus or as a response.

To understand what the other person in an interaction means from his or her point of view, see the sequence of events as punctuated by the other person. Further, recognize that punctuation does not reflect what exists in reality. Rather, it reflects the unique, subjective, and fallible perception of each individual (the other person as well as yourself).

## Communication Is Purposeful

You communicate for a purpose; some motivation leads you to communicate. When you speak or write, you're trying to send some message and trying to accomplish some goal. Although different cultures emphasize different purposes and motives (Rubin, Fernandez-Collado, & Hernandez-Sampieri, 1992), five general purposes seem relatively common to most if not all forms of communication:

- to learn: to acquire knowledge of others, the world, and yourself
- to relate: to form relationships with others, to interact with others as individuals
- to help: to assist others by listening, offering solutions
- to influence: to strengthen or change the attitudes or behaviors of others
- to play: to enjoy the experience of the moment

Some researchers argue that all communication is persuasive and that all our communications seek some persuasive goal. Some examples (Canary, Cody, & Manusov, 2000):

- Self-presentation goals: You communicate to give others the image you want them to have of you; for example, you get a special haircut for your date.

- Relationship goals: You communicate to form the relationships that will meet your needs; for example, you speak positively about people you want to like you.

- Instrumental goals: You communicate to get others to do something for you; for example, you flatter your boss before asking for a raise.

Popular belief and research findings both agree that men and women use communication for different purposes. Generally, as mentioned earlier, men seem to communicate more for information and women more for relationship purposes (Gamble & Gamble, 2003; Stewart, Cooper, Stewart, with Friedley, 2003). Gender differences also occur in computer communication. For example, women chat more for relationship reasons; men chat more to play and to relax (Leung, 2001).

## Communication Is Inevitable, Irreversible, and Unrepeatable

Communication is inevitable; that is, in interactional situations it is always taking place, even when a person may not intend or want to communicate. To understand the **inevitability** of communication, think about a student sitting in the back of a classroom with an expressionless face, perhaps staring out the window. Although the student might claim not to be communicating with the instructor, the instructor may derive a variety of messages from this behavior. Perhaps the instructor assumes that the student lacks interest, is bored, or is worried about something. In any event, the teacher is receiving messages even though the student may not intentionally be sending any (Watzlawick, Beavin, & Jackson, 1967; Motley, 1990a, 1990b; Bavelas, 1990). This does not mean that all behavior is communication. For instance, if the student looked out the window and the teacher didn't notice, no communication would have taken place. The two people must be in an interactional situation and the behavior must be perceived for the principle of inevitability to operate.

Notice, too, that when you're in an interactional situation, you cannot *not* respond to the messages of others. For example, if you notice someone winking at you, you must respond in some way. Even if you don't respond actively or openly, your lack of response is itself a response, and it communicates.

Another all-important attribute of communication is its **irreversibility**. Once you say something or click "send" on your e-mail, you cannot uncommunicate the message. You can, of course, try to reduce its effects. You can say, for example, "I really didn't mean what I said." But regardless of how hard you try to negate or reduce the effects of a message, the message itself, once it has been received, cannot be taken back. In a public speaking situation in which the speech is recorded or broadcast, inappropriate messages may have national or even international effects. Here, attempts to reverse what someone has said (for example, efforts to offer clarification) often have the effect of further publicizing the original statement.

In face-to-face communication, the actual signals (nonverbal messages and sound waves in the air) are evanescent; they fade almost as they are uttered. Some written messages, especially computer-mediated messages such as those sent through e-mail, are unerasable. E-mails among employees in large corporations or even at colleges are often stored on disk or tape and may not be considered private by managers and administrators (Sethna, Barnes, Brust, & Kaye, 1999). Much litigation has involved evidence of racist or sexist e-mails that senders thought had been erased but hadn't. E-mails and entire hard drives are finding their

▼ E-TALK

**Captology**
According to Wikipedia.com, captology is "the study of computers as persuasive technologies"; in other words, captology focuses on the ways in which computers and computer-mediated communication generally can influence beliefs, attitudes, and behaviors. How does computer-mediated communication influence you? Consider such areas as politics, personal finance, buying, personal relationships, and occupational effectiveness (http://captology.stanford.edu/notebook/archives/000087.html, accessed February 11, 2005; Fisher, 1998; Banerjee, 2005).

*"If your lips would keep from slips, five things observe with care; to whom you speak, of whom you speak, and how, and when, and where."*

—W. E. NORRIS

way into divorce proceedings. As a result of the permanency of computer-mediated communication, you may wish to be especially cautious in these messages.

In all forms of communication, because of irreversibility (and unerasability), be careful not to say things you may be sorry for later. Especially in conflict situations, when tempers run high, avoid saying things you may later wish to withdraw. Commitment messages—"I love you" messages and their variants—also need to be monitored. Messages that you considered private but that might be interpreted as sexist, racist, or homophobic may later be retrieved by others and create all sorts of problems for you and your organization. In group and public communication situations, when the messages are received by many people, it's especially crucial to recognize the irreversibility of communication.

Finally, communication is *unrepeatable*. A communication act can never be duplicated. The reason is simple: Everyone and everything is constantly changing. As a result, you can never recapture the exact same situation, frame of mind, or relationship dynamics that defined a previous communication act. For example, you can never repeat meeting someone for the first time, comforting a grieving friend, leading a small group for the first time, or giving a public speech. You can never replace an initial impression; you can only try to counteract this initial (and perhaps negative) impression by going through the motions again.

## Culture and Human Communication

**Culture** consists of the beliefs, ways of behaving, and artifacts of a group. By definition, culture is transmitted through communication and learning rather than through genes.

A walk through any large city, many small towns, or just about any college campus will convince you that the United States is largely a collection of lots of different cultures. These cultures coexist somewhat separately, but all influence one another. This coexistence has led some researchers to refer to these cultures as *cocultures* (Shuter, 1990; Samovar & Porter, 1991; Jandt, 2003).

*Gender* is considered a cultural variable largely because cultures teach boys and girls different attitudes, beliefs, values, and ways of communicating and relating to one another. This means that you act like a man or a woman in part because of what your culture has taught you about how men and women should act. This is not, of course, to deny that biological differences also play a role in the differences between male and female behavior. In fact, research continues to uncover biological roots of behavior we once thought was entirely learned—acting happy or shy, for example (McCroskey, 1997).

Yet we're living in a time of changing gender roles. Many men, for example, are doing a great deal more housekeeping chores and caring for their children. More obvious perhaps is that many women are becoming much more visible in fields once occupied exclusively by men—politics, law enforcement, the military, and the clergy are just some examples. And, of course, women are increasingly present in the corporate executive ranks; the glass ceiling may not have disappeared, but it has cracked.

Because your communication is heavily influenced by the culture in which you were raised, culture is highly relevant to communication, and a cultural perspective serves numerous important purposes.

### The Importance of Culture

Because of (1) demographic changes, (2) increased sensitivity to cultural differences, (3) economic interdependency, and (4) advances in communication technol-

**WHAT DO YOU SAY?**
**Irreversibility**
Without thinking you make some culturally insensitive remarks and immediately notice lots of nonverbal negative feedback. You want to explain that you're really not the kind of person who normally talks this way. *What do you say?*

ogy, it's impossible to communicate effectively without being aware of how culture influences human communication.

**Demographic Changes** Whereas at one time the United States was largely a country populated by Europeans, it's now a country greatly influenced by the enormous number of new citizens from Latin and South America, Africa, and Asia. This is especially true on college and university campuses. With these changes have come different customs and the need to understand and adapt to new ways of looking at communication. For example, consider health care workers and patients. Each group needs to understand how the other communicates about illness, sees ways to prevent health problems, and views taking medication. Police officers and civilians need to understand each other's views of "disorderly conduct," "the right of assembly," and "free speech."

**Sensitivity to Cultural Differences** As a people we've become increasingly sensitive to cultural differences. U.S. society has moved from an *assimilationist perspective* (the idea that people should leave their native culture behind and adapt to their new culture) to a view that values *cultural diversity* (people should retain their native cultural ways). And with some notable exceptions—hate speech, racism, sexism, homophobia, and classism come quickly to mind—we're more concerned with saying the right thing and ultimately with developing a society in which all cultures can coexist and enrich one another. At the same time, the ability to interact effectively with members of other cultures often translates into financial gain and increased employment opportunities and advancement prospects.

**Economic Interdependence** Today, most countries are economically dependent on one another. Our economic lives depend on our ability to communicate effectively across cultures. Similarly, our political well-being depends in great part on that of other cultures. Political unrest in any part of the world—Africa, Eastern Europe, or the Middle East, to take a few examples—affects our own security. Intercultural communication and understanding now seem more crucial than ever.

**Communication Technology** The rapid spread of communication technology has brought foreign and sometimes very different cultures right into our living rooms. News from foreign countries is commonplace. You see nightly—in vivid color—what is going on in remote countries. Technology has made intercultural communication easy, practical, and inevitable. Daily, the media bombard you with evidence of racial tensions, religious disagreements, sexual bias, and, in general, the problems caused when intercultural communication fails. And, of course, the Internet has made intercultural communication as easy as writing a note on your computer. You can now communicate by e-mail just as easily with someone in Europe or Asia, for example, as with someone in another city or state.

## Dimensions of Culture

Because of its importance in all forms of human communication, culture is given a prominent place in this text. Throughout this text I'll discuss theories and research findings that bear on culture and communication. Prominent among these discussions are the five major dimensions of culture. By way of a brief preview, these dimensions are:

■ *Uncertainty avoidance:* The degree to which a culture values predictability. In high-uncertainty-avoidance cultures, predictability and order are extremely important; in low-uncertainty-avoidance cultures, risk-taking and ambiguity are tolerated more easily. This dimension is considered in depth in the discussions of perception (Chapters 2 and 13).

- *Masculinity–femininity:* The extent to which cultures embrace traditionally masculine characteristics such as ambition and assertiveness or embrace traditionally feminine characteristics such as caring and nurturing others. This cultural distinction is explained in depth in the discussions of interpersonal relationships (Chapters 2, 6, and 13).

- *Power distance:* The way power is distributed throughout the society. In high-power-distance cultures, there is a great power difference between those in authority and others. In low-power-distance cultures, power is distributed more evenly. This dimension is discussed in detail in the discussion of small group communication (Chapters 8 and 13).

- *Individualism–collectivism:* A culture's emphasis on the importance of the individual or of the group. Individualist cultures value such qualities as self-reliance, independence, and individual achievement; collectivist cultures emphasize social bonds, the primacy of the group, and conformity to the larger social group. This dimension is examined in detail in the discussion of members and leaders in small group communication, in which this dimension takes on special importance (Chapters 9 and 13).

- *High and low context:* The extent to which information is seen as embedded in the context or tacitly known among members. In high-context cultures information is part of the context and does not have to be verbalized explicitly. In low-context cultures information is made explicit and little is taken for granted. This cultural dimension is discussed in connection with public speaking (Chapters 8, 10, and 13).

## The Aim of a Cultural Perspective

*"From the moment of his birth, the customs into which [a person] is born shape his experience and behavior. By the time he can talk, he is the little creature of his culture."*

—RUTH BENEDICT

Because culture permeates all forms of communication, it's necessary to understand its influences if you're to understand how communication works and master its skills. As illustrated throughout this text, culture influences communications of all types (Moon, 1996). It influences what you say to yourself and how you talk with friends, lovers, and family in everyday conversation. It influences how you interact in groups and how much importance you place on the group versus the individual. It influences the topics you talk about and the strategies you use in communicating information or in persuading. And it influences how you use the media and how much credibility you attribute to them.

A cultural emphasis helps you distinguish what is universal (true for all people) from what is relative (true for people in one culture but not for people in other cultures) (Matsumoto, 1991). The principles for communicating information and for changing listeners' attitudes, for example, will vary from one culture to another. If you're to understand communication, you need to know how its principles vary and how they must be qualified and adjusted on the basis of cultural differences. Success in communication—on your job and in your social life—will depend on your ability to communicate effectively with others who are culturally different from yourself.

Cultural differences exist across the communication spectrum—from the way you use eye contact to the way you develop or dissolve a relationship (Chang & Holt, 1996). But these differences should not blind you to the great number of similarities among even the most widely separated cultures. Close interpersonal relationships, for example, are common in all cultures, although they may be entered into for very different reasons by members of different cultures. Further, when reading about cultural differences, remember that they are usually matters of degree. For example, most

*Skill Development Experience*

### Making Cultural Beliefs Mindful

*Cultural beliefs exert powerful (often unconscious) influences on your communication. Bringing these beliefs to a mindfulness state will help you deal more effectively with their influences on your communication interactions, especially when you interact with people holding widely different beliefs.*

Here are five topics about which many people have strong cultural beliefs: *the nature of God, the importance of family, the rules of sexual appropriateness, the role of education,* and *the importance of money.* For any one, two, or three of these topics, try to answer these questions:

- Who taught you your beliefs about each topic? How did they teach you these beliefs?
- When and where were you taught your beliefs?
- Why do you suppose you were taught these beliefs? What motives led your "teachers" to pass on these beliefs to you?
- How productive do you feel these beliefs are in your current life situation?
- Would you try to pass these beliefs on to your children?
- What would your life be like if you held beliefs opposite to those you now hold?

cultures value honesty, but not all value it to the same extent. The advances in media and technology and the widespread use of the Internet, among other factors, are influencing cultures and cultural change and are perhaps homogenizing cultures, lessening intercultural differences and increasing similarities. They're also Americanizing various cultures—because the dominant values and customs evidenced in the media and on the Internet are in large part American, a product of the United States' current dominance in both media and technology.

This book's emphasis on cultural understanding does not imply that you should accept all cultural practices or that all cultural practices are equal (Hatfield & Rapson, 1996). For example, cockfighting, foxhunting, and bullfighting are parts of the cultures of some Latin American countries, England, and Spain, respectively; but you need not find these activities acceptable or equal to cultural practices in which animals are treated kindly. Further, a cultural emphasis does not imply that you have to accept or follow even the practices of your own culture. For example, even if the majority in your culture find cockfighting acceptable, you need not agree with or follow the practice. Similarly, you can reject your culture's values and beliefs; its religion or political system; or its attitudes toward the homeless, the disabled, or the culturally different. Of course, going against your culture's traditions and values is often very difficult. Still, it's important to realize that culture influences but does not determine your values or behavior. Often, for example, personality factors (your degree of assertiveness, extroversion, or optimism, for example) will prove more influential than culture (Hatfield & Rapson, 1996).

## Ethnic Identity and Ethnocentrism

As you learn your culture's ways, you develop an **ethnic identity,** a commitment to the beliefs and philosophy of your culture (Chung & Ting-Toomey, 1999). The degree to which you identify with your cultural group can be measured by your responses to measures such as the list below (from Ting-Toomey, 1981). Using a five-point scale from 1 = strongly disagree to 5 = strongly agree, indicate how true of you the following statements are:

- I am increasing my involvement in activities with my ethnic group.
- I involve myself in causes that will help members of my ethnic group.
- It feels natural being part of my ethnic group.
- I have spent time trying to find out more about my own ethnic group.
- I am happy to be a member of my ethnic group.
- I have a strong sense of belonging to my ethnic group.
- I often talk to other members of my group to learn more about my ethnic culture.

High scores (say, 5s and 4s) indicate a strong commitment to your culture's values and beliefs; low numbers (1s and 2s) indicate a relatively weak commitment.

A different type of cultural identification is ethnocentrism. Before reading about this important concept, examine your own cultural thinking by taking the self-test below.

## *Test* *Yourself*

## HOW ETHNOCENTRIC ARE YOU?

**INSTRUCTIONS:** Here are 18 statements representing your beliefs about your culture. For each statement indicate how much you agree or disagree, using the following scale: Strongly agree = **5**; agree = **4**; neither agree nor disagree = **3**; disagree = **2**; and strongly disagree = **1**.

_____ ❶ Most cultures are backward compared to my culture.

_____ ❷ My culture should be the role model for other cultures.

_____ ❸ Lifestyles in other cultures are just as valid as those in my culture.

_____ ❹ Other cultures should try to be like my culture.

_____ ❺ I'm not interested in the values and customs of other cultures.

_____ ❻ People in my culture could learn a lot from people in other cultures.

_____ ❼ Most people from other cultures just don't know what's good for them.

_____ ❽ I have little respect for the values and customs of other cultures.

_____ ❾ Most people would be happier if they lived like people in my culture.

_____ ❿ People in my culture have just about the best lifestyles of anywhere.

_____ ⓫ Lifestyles in other cultures are not as valid as those in my culture.

_____ ⓬ I'm very interested in the values and customs of other cultures.

_____ ⓭ I respect the values and customs of other cultures.

_____ ⓮ I do not cooperate with people who are different.

_____ ⓯ I do not trust people who are different.

_____ ⓰ I dislike interacting with people from different cultures.

_____ ⓱ Other cultures are smart to look up to my culture.

_____ ⓲ People from other cultures act strange and unusual when they come into my culture.

**HOW DID YOU DO?** This test gave you the opportunity to examine some of your own cultural beliefs—particularly those cultural beliefs that contribute to ethnocentrism. The person low in ethnocentrism would have high scores (4s and 5s) for items 3, 6, 12, and 13 and low scores (1s and 2s) for all the others. The person high in ethnocentrism would have low scores for items 3, 6, 12, and 13 and high scores for all the others.

**WHAT WILL YOU DO?** Use this test to bring your own cultural beliefs to consciousness so you can examine them logically and objectively. Ask yourself if your beliefs are productive and will help you achieve your professional and social goals, or if they're counterproductive and will actually hinder your achieving your goals.

*Source:* This test is taken from James W. Neuliep, Michelle Chaudoir, & James C. McCroskey (2001). A cross-cultural comparison of ethnocentrism among Japanese and United States college students. *Communication Research Reports, 18* (Spring), 137–146.

**WHAT DO YOU SAY?**
**Ethnocentrism**
Your friends are extremely ethnocentric, never acknowledging that other cultures have any value. You want to show them that their ethnocentrism is getting in the way of their learning and profiting from the contributions of other cultures. *What do you say?*

As you've probably gathered from taking this test, **ethnocentrism** is the tendency to see others and their behaviors through your own cultural filters, often as distortions of your own behaviors. It's the tendency to evaluate the values, beliefs, and behaviors of your own culture as superior and as more positive, logical, and natural than those of other cultures. Although ethnocentrism may give you pride in your own culture and its achievements and encourage you to sacrifice for the culture, it also may lead you to see other cultures as inferior and may make you unwilling to profit from the contributions of other cultures. For example, recent research shows a "substantial relationship" between ethnocentrism and homophobia (Wrench & McCroskey, 2003).

Ethnocentrism exists on a continuum (Table 1.3). People are not either ethnocentric or non-ethnocentric; rather, most are somewhere between these polar opposites. And, of course, your degree of ethnocentrism often varies depending on the group on which you focus. For example, if you're Greek American, you may have a

**TABLE 1.3** **The Ethnocentrism Continuum**

This table summarizes some of the interconnections between ethnocentrism and communication. In the table five degrees of ethnocentrism are identified; in reality, there are as many degrees as there are people. The "communication distances" are general terms that highlight the attitude that dominates that level of ethnocentrism. Under "communications" are some of the major ways people might interact given their particular degree of ethnocentrism. Can you identify your own ethnocentrism on this table? For example, are there groups to which you have low ethnocentrism? Middle? High? What accounts for these differences? This table draws on the work of several intercultural researchers (Lukens, 1978; Gudykunst & Kim, 1992; GudyKunst, 1991).

| DEGREE OF ETHNOCENTRISM | COMMUNICATION DISTANCE | COMMUNICATIONS |
|---|---|---|
| Low | Equality | You treat others as equals; you view different customs and ways of behaving as equal to your own. |
| | Sensitivity | You want to decrease distance between yourself and others. |
| | Indifference | You lack concern for others; you prefer to interact in a world of similar others. |
| | Avoidance | You avoid and limit interactions, especially intimate communication with interculturally different others. |
| High | Disparagement | You engage in hostile behavior and belittle others; you view different cultures and ways of behaving as inferior to your own. |

low degree of ethnocentrism when dealing with Italian Americans but a high degree when dealing with Turkish Americans or Japanese Americans. Your degree of ethnocentrism (and we're all ethnocentric to at least some degree) will influence your communication in all its forms, as we'll see throughout this text.

 ## Summary of Concepts and Skills

This chapter considered the nature of human communication, its major components, and some major communication principles.

1. Communication is transactional. Communication is a process of interrelated parts in which a change in one element produces changes in other elements.
2. Communication is the act, by one or more persons, of sending and receiving messages that are distorted by noise, occur within a context, have some effect (and some ethical dimension), and provide some opportunity for feedback.
3. The essentials of communication—the elements present in every communication act—are context (physical, cultural, social–psychological, and temporal); source–receiver; message; channel; noise (physical, psychological, and semantic); sending or encoding processes; receiving or decoding processes; feedback and feedforward; effect; and competence, including ethics.
4. Communication messages may vary in form and may be sent and received through any combination of sensory organs. Communication messages may also metacommunicate—communicate about other messages.
5. The communication channel is the medium through which the messages are sent.
6. Feedback consists of messages or information that is sent back to the source. It may come from the source itself or from the receiver. Feedforward messages are communications that preface other messages.
7. Noise is anything that distorts a message; it is present to some degree in every communication.
8. Communication ethics—the moral rightness or wrongness of a message—is an integral part of every effort to communicate.
9. Communication is a process of adjustment in which each person must adjust his or her signals to the understanding of the other if meaning is to be transmitted. In fact, communication accommodation theory holds that people imitate the speaking style of the other person as a way of gaining social approval.
10. Communication and relationships are always—in part—ambiguous.
11. Communication involves both content and relationship dimensions.

12. Communication and relationships invariably involve issues of power.
13. Communication sequences are punctuated for processing. Individuals divide the communication sequence into stimuli and responses in different ways.
14. Communication is purposeful. Through communication, you learn, relate, help, influence, and play.
15. In any interactional situation, communication is inevitable (you cannot not communicate, nor can you not respond to communication), irreversible (you cannot take back messages), and unrepeatable (you cannot exactly repeat messages).
16. Culture permeates all forms of communication, and intercultural communication is becoming more and more frequent as the United States becomes home to a variety of cultures and does business around the world.
17. Significant dimensions along which cultures may differ are uncertainty avoidance, masculinity–femininity, power distance, individualism–collectivism, and high and low context.
18. Ethnocentrism, existing on a continuum, is the tendency to evaluate the beliefs, attitudes, and values of our own culture positively and those of other cultures negatively.

Several important communication skills emphasized in this chapter are presented here in summary form (as they are in every chapter). These skill checklists don't include all the skills covered in the chapter but rather are representative of the most important skills. Place a check mark next to those skills that you feel you need to work on most.

_____ 1. I'm sensitive to contexts of communication. I recognize that changes in physical, cultural, social–psychological, and temporal contexts will alter meaning.

_____ 2. I assess my channel options and evaluate whether my message will be more effective if delivered face-to-face, through e-mail, or by some third party, for example.

_____ 3. I look for meaning not only in words, but also in nonverbal behaviors.

_____ 4. I am sensitive to the feedback and feedforward that I give to others and that others give to me.

_____ 5. I combat the effects of the various types of physical, psychological, and semantic noise that distort messages.

_____ 6. I listen not only to the more obvious content messages but also to the relational messages that I (and others) send, and I respond to the relational messages of others to increase meaningful interaction.

_____ 7. Instead of looking only at the punctuation patterns that I use, I also look at the patterns that others might be using in order to understand better the meanings communicated.

_____ 8. Because communication is transactional, I recognize that all elements influence all other elements in the communication process and that each person communicating is simultaneously a speaker/listener.

_____ 9. Because communication is purposeful, I look carefully at both the speaker's and the listener's purposes.

_____ 10. Because communication is inevitable, irreversible, and unrepeatable, I look carefully for hidden meanings, am cautious in communicating messages that I may later wish to withdraw, and am aware that any communication act occurs but once.

_____ 11. I am sensitive to cultural variation and differences, and I see my own culture's teachings and those of other cultures without undue bias.

# Key Word Quiz

## The Essentials of Human Communication

Match the terms about human communication with their definitions. Record the number of the definition next to the appropriate term.

a. _____ intrapersonal communication

b. _____ metamessages

c. _____ encoding

d. _____ communication competence

e. _____ computer-mediated communication

f. _____ feedback

g. _____ power

h. _____ transactional view of communication

i. _____ ethnocentrism

j. _____ ethnic identity

1. Communication between two or more people through some electronic means.

2. Knowledge of communication and the ability to apply that knowledge for effective communication.

3. The view of communication that sees each person as taking both speaker and listener roles simultaneously.

4. Communication with yourself.

5. Commitment to the beliefs and values of your culture.

6. The process of putting ideas into a code; for example, thinking of an idea and then describing it in words.

7. The tendency to see others and their behaviors through your own cultural filters.

8. The messages you get back from your own messages and from the responses of others to what you communicate.

9. Messages that refer to other messages.

10. The ability to influence the behaviors of others.

**Answers: a.** 4 **b.** 9 **c.** 6 **d.** 2 **e.** 1 **f.** 8 **g.** 10 **h.** 3 **i.** 7 **j.** 5

## Five for Discussion

1. What kinds of feedforward can you find in this book? What specific functions do these feedforwards serve?
2. Consider how cultural differences underlie some of the most hotly debated topics in the news today. The following, for example, is a brief list of some of these topics, here identified with specific questions. How would you answer these? How do your cultural attitudes, beliefs, and values influence your responses?
   a. Should Christian Science parents be prosecuted for preventing their children from receiving life-saving treatments such as blood transfusions?
   b. Should cockfighting be permitted? Or should it be declared illegal in all states as "cruelty to animals"?
   c. Should same-sex marriages be legalized?
   d. Should "safer sex" practices be taught in elementary schools, or is this a matter for parents to address with young children?
   e. Should doctor-assisted suicide be legalized?
3. In this age of multiculturalism, how do you feel about Article II, Section 1, of the U.S. Constitution? The relevant section reads: "No person except a natural-born citizen, or citizen of the United States at the time of the adoption of this Constitution, shall be eligible to the office of President."
4. With the growth of the Internet the question of a universal language—a language that everyone around the world would understand—has become a hot topic. In many ways—and largely because of the Internet—English is the world's universal language. What do you think of English as a universal language? Would you propose a different language? What arguments for and against English as a Universal language would you see as crucial in this debate (Kramarae, 1999)?
5. Do you agree with the assumption that everyone is ethnocentric to some degree? If so, where would you place yourself on the ethnocentric continuum when the "other" is a person of the opposite sex? A person of a different affectional orientation? A person of a different race? A person of a different religion?

## Log On! MyCommunicationLab

A variety of exercises will help you better understand the concepts and principles discussed in this chapter (www.mycommunicationlab.com): (1) Comparing Communication Channels, (2) Giving Effective Feedback, (3) How Can You Give Effective Feedforward? (4) Analyzing an Interaction, (5) How Do You Respond to Contradictory Messages? (6) Cultural Beliefs, (7) From Culture to Gender, and (8) Cultural Identities.

Also visit MyCommunicationLab for a wealth of study tools, activities, and video clips on the nature and varieties of human communication.

Explore our research resources at www.researchnavigator.com.

Research
Navigator.com

# The Self and Perception

Because you'll **learn about:**

- self-concept, self-awareness, and self-esteem.
- the process of self-disclosure.
- the nature and workings of perception.

Because you'll **learn to:**

- communicate with a better understanding of who you are.
- regulate your self-disclosures and respond appropriately to the disclosures of others.
- increase your own accuracy in perceiving other people and their messages.

*T*his chapter looks at the self—perhaps the most important element in any form of communication—and especially at the ways in which you and others perceive yourself. With this as a background, we will examine the ways in which we perceive others and the ways they perceive us.

# The Self in Human Communication

Who you are and how you see yourself influence not only the way you communicate but also how you respond to the communications of others. This first section explores the self: the self-concept and how it develops; self-awareness and ways to increase it; self-esteem and ways to enhance it; and self-disclosure, or communication that reveals who you are.

## Self-Concept

Your **self-concept** is your image of who you are. It's how you perceive yourself: your feelings and thoughts about your strengths and weaknesses, your abilities and limitations. Self-concept develops from the image that others have of you, comparisons between yourself and others, your cultural experiences, and your evaluation of your own thoughts and behaviors (Figure 2.1). Let's explore each of these components of the self-concept.

**Others' Images of You**   If you wished to see how your hair looked, you'd probably look in a mirror. But what would you do if you wanted to see how friendly or how assertive you are? According to the concept of the **looking-glass self** (Cooley, 1922), you'd look at the image of yourself that others reveal to you through the way they communicate with you.

### Figure *2.1*
**The Sources of Self-Concept**
This diagram depicts the four sources of self-concept, the four contributors to how you see yourself. As you read about self-concept, consider the influence of each factor throughout your life. Which factor influenced you most as a preteen? Which influences you most now? Which will influence you most 25 or 30 years from now?

Of course, you would not look to just anyone. Rather, you would look to those who are most significant in your life, such as your friends, family members, and romantic partners. If these significant persons think highly of you, you will see a positive self-image reflected in their behaviors; if they think little of you, you will see a more negative image.

**Comparisons with Others** Another way you develop self-concept is by comparing yourself with others, most often with your peers (Festinger, 1954). For example, after an exam, you probably want to know how you performed relative to the other students in your class. This gives you a clearer idea of how effectively you performed. If you play on a baseball team, it's important to know your batting average in comparison with the batting averages of others on the team. You gain a different perspective when you see yourself in comparison to your peers.

**Cultural Teachings** Your culture instills in you a variety of beliefs, values, and attitudes about such things as success (how you define it and how you should achieve it); the relevance of religion, race, or nationality; and the ethical principles you should follow in business and in your personal life. These teachings provide benchmarks against which you can measure yourself. Your ability to, for example, achieve what your culture defines as success contributes to a positive self-concept; your failure to achieve what your culture values contributes to a negative self-concept.

Especially important in self-concept are cultural teachings about gender roles—about how a man or woman should act. In fact, a popular classification of cultures is in terms of their masculinity and femininity (Hofstede, 1997). Masculine cultures socialize people to be assertive, ambitious, and competitive. For example, members of masculine cultures are more likely to confront conflicts directly and to competitively fight out any differences; they're more likely to emphasize win–lose conflict strategies. Feminine cultures socialize people to be modest and to emphasize close interpersonal relationships. Feminine cultures, for example, are more likely to emphasize compromise and negotiation in resolving conflicts; they're more likely to emphasize win–win solutions.

When you display the traits rewarded by your culture—whether they be masculine or feminine—you're likely to be rewarded and complimented, and this feedback is likely to contribute to a positive self-concept. Displaying contrary traits is likely to result in criticism which, in turn, will contribute to a more negative self-concept.

**Self-Interpretations and Self-Evaluations** Your self-interpretations (your reconstruction of your behavior in a given event and your understanding of it) and self-evaluations (the value—good or bad—that you place on that behavior) also contribute to your self-concept. For example, let's say you believe that lying is wrong. If you then lie and you view what you said as a lie (rather than as, say, a polite way of avoiding an issue), you will probably evaluate this behavior in terms of your internalized beliefs about lying and will react negatively to your own behavior. You may, for example, experience guilt about violating your own beliefs. On the other hand, let's say that you pull someone out of a burning building at great personal risk. You will probably evaluate this behavior positively; you'll feel good about your behavior and, as a result, about yourself.

## Self-Awareness

**Self-awareness** is basic to all communication and is achieved when you examine the several aspects of yourself as they might appear to others as well as to yourself. One tool that is commonly used for this examination is called the Johari window, a metaphoric division of the self into four areas (Figure 2.2).

**WHAT DO YOU SAY?**
**Blind Self**
You're going to enter a new job—one that you hope you'll keep for the major part of your professional career—and you really need honest feedback on your total performance at your present job. *What do you say? To whom? Through what channel?*

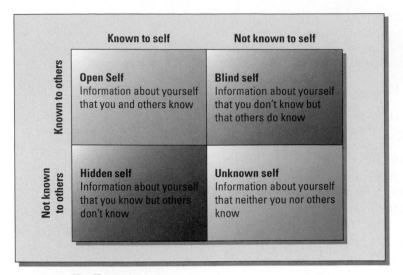

| | Known to self | Not known to self |
|---|---|---|
| **Known to others** | **Open Self**<br>Information about yourself that you and others know | **Blind self**<br>Information about yourself that you don't know but that others do know |
| **Not known to others** | **Hidden self**<br>Information about yourself that you know but others don't know | **Unknown self**<br>Information about yourself that neither you nor others know |

## Figure *2.2*
### The Johari Window

This diagram is a commonly used tool for examining what we know and don't know about ourselves. It can also help explain the nature of self-disclosure, covered later in this chapter. The window gets its name from its originators, *J*oseph Luft and *Harry* Ingham.

*Source:* from Joseph Luft *Group Process: An Introduction to Group Dynamics,* 3rd ed. Copyright © 1984. New York: McGraw-Hill. Reprinted by permission.

**Your Four Selves** Divided into four areas or "panes," the Johari window shows different aspects or versions of the self. The four versions are the open self, blind self, hidden self, and unknown self. These areas are not separate from one another but interdependent. As one dominates, the others recede to a greater or lesser degree; or, to stay with our metaphor, as one windowpane becomes larger, one or more others become smaller.

■ The *open self* represents all the information, behaviors, attitudes, and feelings about yourself that you know and that others also know. This could include your name, skin color, sex, age, religion, and political beliefs. The size of the open self varies according to your personality and the people to whom you're relating. You may be more open with some people than you are with others. For example, you may have a large open self about your romantic life with your friends (you tell them everything) but a very small open self about the same issues with, say, your parents.

■ The *blind self* represents knowledge about you that others have but you don't. This might include your habit of finishing other people's sentences or your way of rubbing your nose when you become anxious. A large blind self indicates low self-awareness and interferes with accurate communication. So it's important to reduce your blind self and learn what others know about you. You can do this by following the suggestions offered below, in "Growing in Self-Awareness."

■ The *unknown self* represents those parts of yourself that neither you nor others know. This is information that is buried in your subconscious. You may, for example, learn of your obsession with money, your fear of criticism, or the kind of lover you are through hypnosis, dreams, psychological tests, or psychotherapy.

■ The *hidden self* represents all the knowledge you have of yourself but keep secret from others. This windowpane includes all your successfully kept secrets, such as your fantasies, embarrassing experiences, and any attitudes or beliefs of which you may be ashamed. You probably keep secrets from some people and not from others; for example, you might not tell your parents you're dating someone of another race or religion, but you might tell a close friend.

**Growing in Self-Awareness** Because self-awareness is so important in communication, try to increase awareness of your own needs, desires, habits, beliefs, and attitudes. You can do this in various ways.

■ *Listen to others.* Conveniently, others are constantly giving you the very feedback you need to increase self-awareness. In every interaction, people comment on you in some way—on what you do, what you say, how you look. Sometimes these comments are explicit: "Loosen up" or "Don't take things so hard." Often they're "hidden" in the way others look at you or in what they talk about. Pay close attention to this kind of information.

■ *Increase your open self.* Revealing yourself to others will help increase your self-awareness. As you talk about yourself, you may see connections that you had previously missed. With feedback from others you may gain still more insight. Also, by increasing your open self, you increase the chances that others will reveal what they know about you.

- *Seek information about yourself.* Encourage people to reveal what they know about you. Use situations that arise every day to gain self-information: "Do you think I came down too hard on the kids today?" "Do you think I was assertive enough when asking for the raise?" But seek this self-awareness in moderation. If you do it too often, your friends will soon look for someone else with whom to talk.

- *Dialogue with yourself.* No one knows you better than you know yourself. Ask yourself self-awareness questions: What motivates me to act as I do? What are my short-term and long-term goals? How do I plan to achieve them? What are my strengths and weaknesses?

> "Let others confide in you. It may not help you, but it will surely help them."
>
> —ROGER G. IMHOFF

## Self-Esteem

**Self-esteem** is a measure of how valuable you think you are; people with high self-esteem think very highly of themselves, whereas people with low self-esteem view themselves negatively. Before reading further about this topic, consider your own self-esteem by taking the following self-test.

## Test ▶◀ Youself

### HOW'S YOUR SELF-ESTEEM?

**INSTRUCTIONS:** Respond to each of the following statements with True if the statement describes you at least some significant part of the time, or False if the statement describes you rarely or never.

_____ ❶ Generally, I feel I have to be successful in all things.

_____ ❷ A number of my acquaintances are often critical or negative of what I do and how I think.

_____ ❸ I often tackle projects that I know are impossible to complete to my satisfaction.

_____ ❹ When I focus on the past, I focus more often on my failures than on my successes and on my negative rather than my positive qualities.

_____ ❺ I make little effort to improve my personal and interpersonal skills.

**HOW DID YOU DO?** "True" responses to the questions would generally be seen as getting in the way of building positive self-esteem. "False" responses would indicate that you are thinking much the way a self-esteem coach would want you to think.

**WHAT WILL YOU DO?** The following discussion elaborates on the five tendencies suggested by the five questions in this test and illustrates why each tendency or mental habit creates problems for the development of healthy self-esteem. So this test is a good starting place. You might also want to log into the National Association for Self-Esteem's website (www.self-esteem-nase.org). There you'll find a variety of materials for examining and bolstering self-esteem.

The basic idea behind self-esteem is that when you feel good about yourself—about who you are and what you're capable of doing—you will perform better. When you think like a success, you're more likely to act like a success. When you think you're a failure, you're more likely to act like a failure. When you get up to give a speech and you visualize yourself as successful and effective, you're more likely to give a good speech. If, on the other hand, you think you're going to forget your speech or mispronounce words or mix up your presentation aids, you are less likely to be successful. Increasing self-esteem will, therefore, help you to function more effectively in school, in interpersonal relationships, and in careers. Here are five suggestions for increasing self-esteem that parallel the questions in the self-test.

**Attack Self-Destructive Beliefs** Challenge any beliefs you have about yourself that are unproductive or that make it more difficult for you to achieve your goals—for example, the belief that you have to succeed in everything you do, the belief that you have to be loved by everyone, the belief that you must be strong at all times, and/or the belief that you must please others (Butler, 1981; Einhorn, 2006). Replace these self-destructive beliefs with more productive ideas, such as "I succeed in many things, but I don't have to succeed in everything" and "It would be nice to be loved by everyone, but it isn't necessary to my happiness."

**Seek Out Nourishing People** Psychologist Carl Rogers (1970) drew a distinction between *noxious* and *nourishing* people. Noxious people criticize and find fault with just about everything. Nourishing people, on the other hand, are positive and optimistic. Most important, they reward us, they stroke us, they make us feel good about ourselves. To enhance your self-esteem, seek out these people—and avoid noxious people, who make you feel negatively about yourself. At the same time, seek to become more nourishing yourself so that you each build up the other's self-esteem.

**Work on Projects That Will Result in Success** Some people want to fail, or so it seems. Often, they select projects that will result in failure simply be-

---

cause they are impossible to complete. Avoid this trap and select projects that will result in success. Each success will help build self-esteem. Each success will make the next success a little easier. If a project does fail, recognize that this does not mean that you're a failure. Everyone fails somewhere along the line. Failure is something that happens to you; it's not something you've created, and it's not something inside you. Further, your failing once does not mean that you will fail the next time. So put failure in perspective.

**Remind Yourself of Your Successes** Some people have a tendency to focus, sometimes too much, on their failures, their missed opportunities, their social mistakes. If your objective is to correct what you did wrong or to identify the skills that you need to correct these failures, then focusing on failures can have some positive value. But if you merely focus on failure without any plans for correction, then you're likely to make life more difficult for yourself and to limit your self-esteem. To counteract the tendency to recall failures, remind yourself of your successes. Recall these successes both intellectually and emotionally. Realize why they were successes, and relive the emotional experience when you sank the winning basket or aced that test or helped your friend overcome personal problems. And while you're at it, recall too your positive qualities. For a start, read down the list of the essential interpersonal skills on the inside covers of this book and check off those you'd consider among your assets. To this list add any other qualities you number among your positive qualities.

**Secure Affirmation** It's frequently recommended that you remind yourself of your successes with affirmations—that you focus on your good deeds; on your positive qualities, strengths, and virtues; and on your productive and meaningful relationships with friends, loved ones, and relatives (Aronson, Cohen, & Nail, 1998; Aronson, Wilson, & Akert, 1999).

The idea behind this advice is that the way you talk to yourself will influence what you think of yourself. If you *affirm* yourself—if you tell yourself that you're a success, that others like you, that you will succeed on the next test, and that you will be welcomed when asking for a date—you will soon come to feel more positive about yourself. Self-affirmations include statements like: "I'm a worthy person," "I'm responsible and can be depended upon," "I'm capable of loving and being loved," "I'm a good team player," and "I can accept my past but also let it go."

However, not all researchers agree with this advice. Some argue that such affirmations—although extremely popular in self-help books—may not be very helpful. These critics contend that if you have low self-esteem, you're not going to believe your self-affirmations, because you don't have a high opinion of yourself to begin with (Paul, 2001). They propose that the alternative to self-affirmation is affirmation secured from others. You'd obtain this by, for example, becoming more competent in communication and interacting with more positive people. In this way you'd get more positive feedback from others—which, these researchers argue, is more helpful than self-talk in raising self-esteem.

Identification with people similar to yourself also seems to increase self-esteem. For example, deaf people who identified with the larger deaf community had greater self-esteem than those who didn't so identify (Jambor & Elliott, 2005). Similarly, identification with your cultural group also seems to encourage positive self-esteem (McDonald, McCabe, Yeh, Lau, Garland, & Hough, 2005).

# Self-Disclosure

**Self-disclosure** is a type of communication in which you reveal information about yourself (Jourard, 1968, 1971a, 1971b). You can look at self-disclosure as taking information from the hidden self and moving it to the open self. Overt statements

**WHAT DO YOU SAY?**
**Self-Esteem**
Your best friend has hit a new low in self-esteem—a long-term relationship failed, an expected promotion never materialized, a large investment went sour. You want to help your friend regain self-esteem. *What do you say? To whom? Through what channel?*

about the self (for example, "I'm getting fat") as well as slips of the tongue (for example, using the name of your ex instead of your present lover's name), unconscious nonverbal movements (for example, self-touching movements or eye avoidance), and public confessions (for example, "Well, Jerry, it's like this . . . ") all can be considered forms of self-disclosure. Usually, however, the term *self-disclosure* refers to the conscious revealing of information, as in the statements "I'm afraid to compete; I guess I'm afraid I'll lose" or "I love you."

Self-disclosure is "information"—something previously unknown by the receiver. This information may vary from the relatively commonplace ("I'm really afraid of that French exam") to the extremely significant ("I'm depressed; I feel like committing suicide"). For self-disclosure to occur, the communication must involve at least two people. You cannot self-disclose to yourself—the information must be received and understood by at least one individual.

## Factors Influencing Self-Disclosure

Many factors influence whether or not you disclose, what you disclose, and to whom you disclose. Among the most important factors are who you are, your culture, your gender, who your listeners are, and your topic and channel.

**Who You Are** Highly sociable and extroverted people self-disclose more than those who are less sociable and more introverted. People who are comfortable communicating also self-disclose more than those who are apprehensive about talking in general. Competent people engage in self-disclosure more than less competent people. Perhaps competent people have greater self-confidence and more positive things to reveal. Similarly, their self-confidence may make them more willing to risk possible negative reactions (McCroskey & Wheeless, 1976).

**Your Culture** Different cultures view self-disclosure differently. Some cultures (especially those high in masculinity) view disclosing inner feelings as weakness. Among some groups, for example, it would be considered "out of place" for a man to cry at a happy occasion such as a wedding, whereas in some Latin cultures that same display of emotion would go unnoticed. Similarly, it's considered undesirable in Japan for workplace colleagues to reveal personal information, whereas in much of the United States it's expected (Barnlund, 1989; Hall & Hall, 1987). Indians are reluctant to self-disclose for fear that what they say will reflect negatively on their reputation and family (Hastings, 2000). And in a study of Muslim, Druze, and Jewish adolescents in Israel, Muslim students disclosed most, Jewish students next, and Druze students least (Shechtman, Hiradin, & Zina, 2003).

There is some indication that the political climate at a given time will influence the cross-cultural self-disclosure patterns of all people. Significant self-disclosures between say, Christian Americans and Muslim Americans, for example, are likely to be more guarded than before September 11, 2001, and the Iraqi war, as are self-disclosures between recent immigrants and other Americans (Barry, 2003).

These differences aside, there also are important similarities across cultures. For example, people from Great Britain, Germany, the United States, and Puerto Rico are all more apt to disclose personal information—hobbies, interests, attitudes, and opinions on politics and religion—than information on finances, sex, personality, or interpersonal relationships (Jourard, 1971a). Similarly, one study showed self-disclosure patterns between American males to be virtually identical to those between Korean males (Won-Doornink, 1991).

**Your Gender** The popular stereotype of gender differences in self-disclosure emphasizes males' reluctance to speak about themselves. For the most part, research supports this view; women do disclose more than men. There are exceptions, however. For example, men and women make negative disclosures about

---

**WHAT DO YOU SAY?**
**Disclosure Pressure**
You're dating this wonderful person who self-discloses easily and fully and who, unfortunately, is putting pressure on you to reveal more about yourself. You just aren't ready to do so at this time. *What do you say? Through what channel?*

equally (Naifeh & Smith, 1984), and boys are more likely than girls to disclose family information on the Internet (www.CNN.com, accessed May 17, 2000). Another notable exception occurs in initial encounters. Here, men will disclose more intimately than women, perhaps "in order to control the relationship's development" (Derlega, Winstead, Wong, & Hunter, 1985). Still another exception is found in a study of American and Argentineans; here males indicated a significantly greater willingness to self-disclose than females (Horenstein & Downey, 2003).

Women disclose more than men about their previous romantic relationships, their feelings about their closest same-sex friends, their greatest fears, and what they don't like about their partners (Sprecher, 1987). Women also increase the depth of their disclosures as the relationship becomes more intimate, whereas men seem not to change their self-disclosure levels. Women have fewer taboo topics that they will not disclose to their friends than men do (Goodwin & Lee, 1994). Finally, women also self-disclose more to members of their extended families than men (Komarovsky, 1964; Argyle & Henderson, 1985; Moghaddam, Taylor, & Wright, 1993).

**Your Listeners** Self-disclosure occurs more readily in small groups than in large groups. **Dyads,** or groups of two people, are the most hospitable setting for self-disclosure. With one listener you can monitor your disclosures, continuing if there's support from your listener and stopping if there's not. With more than one listener, such monitoring becomes difficult, because the listeners' responses are sure to vary.

Research shows that you disclose most to people you like (Derlega, Winstead, Wong, & Greenspan, 1987) and to people you trust (Wheeless & Grotz, 1977). You also come to like those to whom you disclose (Berg & Archer, 1983). At times, self-disclosure occurs more in temporary than in permanent relationships—for example, between strangers on a train or plane, in a kind of "in-flight intimacy" (McGill, 1985). In this situation two people set up an intimate, self-disclosing relationship during a brief travel period, but they don't pursue the connection beyond that point. In a similar way, you might set up a relationship with one or several people on the Internet and engage in significant disclosure. Perhaps knowing that you'll never see these other people, and that they will never know where you live or work or what you look like, makes it easier to open up to them.

You are more likely to disclose when the person you are with discloses. This **dyadic effect** (what one person does, the other person also does) probably leads you to feel more secure and reinforces your own self-disclosing behavior. Disclosures are also more intimate when they're made in response to the disclosures of others (Berg & Archer, 1983). This dyadic effect, however, is not universal across all cultures. For example, while Americans are likely to follow the dyadic effect and reciprocate with explicit, verbal self-disclosure, Koreans aren't (Won-Doornink, 1985). As you can appreciate, this can easily cause intercultural differences; for example, an American may be insulted if his or her Korean counterpart doesn't reciprocate with self-disclosures that are similar in depth.

**Your Topic and Channel** You also are more likely to disclose about some topics than about others. For example, you're more likely to self-disclose information about your job or hobbies than about your sex life or financial situation (Jourard, 1968, 1971a). Further, you're more likely to disclose favorable information than unfavorable information. Generally, the more personal and negative the topic, the less likely you are to self-disclose.

In recent years research has addressed differences in self-disclosure depending on the channel—on whether communication is face-to-face or computer mediated. Some researchers have pointed to a *disinhibition effect* that occurs in online communication; people seem less inhibited in communicating by e-mail or in chat groups, for example, than in face-to-face situations. One reason may be that in online communication there is a certain degree of anonymity and invisibility (Suler,

▼ | E-TALK

**Self-Disclosure**
Some research indicates that self-disclosure occurs more quickly and at higher levels of intimacy online than in face-to-face situations (Joinson, 2001; Levine, 2000). Other research finds that people experience greater closeness and self-disclosure in face-to-face groups than in Internet chat groups (Mallen, Day, & Green, 2003). What has been your experience with self-disclosure in online and face-to-face situations?

2004). Research also finds that reciprocal self-disclosure occurs more quickly and at higher levels of intimacy online than it does in face-to-face interactions (Levine, 2000; Joinson, 2001).

The self-test "How willing to self-disclose are you?" focuses on the influences of four of the factors just discussed: you, your culture, your listeners, and your topic.

## Test ▶◀ Yourself

### HOW WILLING TO SELF-DISCLOSE ARE YOU?

**INSTRUCTIONS:** Respond to each of the following statements by indicating the likelihood that you would disclose such items of information to, say, other members of this class in a one-on-one *interpersonal* situation, in a five- or six-member *small group* situation, and in a *public communication* setting in which you would speak to all members of the class. Use the following scale to fill in all three columns:

**1** = would definitely self-disclose; **2** = would probably self-disclose; **3** = don't know; **4** = would probably not self-disclose; and **5** = would definitely not self-disclose.

| Information | Interpersonal Communication | Small Group Communication | Public Communication |
|---|---|---|---|
| ❶ My attitudes toward other religions, nationalities, and races | _____ | _____ | _____ |
| ❷ My financial status, how much money I earn, how much I owe, how much I have saved | _____ | _____ | _____ |
| ❸ My feelings about my parents | _____ | _____ | _____ |
| ❹ My sexual fantasies | _____ | _____ | _____ |
| ❺ My physical and mental health | _____ | _____ | _____ |
| ❻ My ideal romantic partner | _____ | _____ | _____ |
| ❼ My drinking and/or drug behavior | _____ | _____ | _____ |
| ❽ My most embarrassing moment | _____ | _____ | _____ |
| ❾ My unfulfilled desires | _____ | _____ | _____ |
| ❿ My self-concept | _____ | _____ | _____ |

**HOW DID YOU DO?** There are, of course, no right or wrong answers to this self-test. Generally, people will self-disclose most in the interpersonal communication situations, least in the public communication situations, and somewhere in between in small group settings.

**WHAT WILL YOU DO?** Taking this test, and ideally discussing it with others who also complete it, should get you started thinking about your own self-disclosing behavior and especially the factors that influence it. How does your personality influence your self-disclosure behavior? Are you more likely to disclose interpersonally than in small group or public situations? Are you more likely to disclose in small groups than in public situations? Are there certain people to whom you feel relatively free to disclose and others to whom you feel much less free? What distinguishes these two groups of people? Are there certain topics you are less willing to disclose than others? Are you more likely to disclose positive secrets than negative ones? Are there topics about which you wish you had the opportunity to self-disclose but somehow can't find the right situation? As a listener, are there topics you would rather not hear about from certain people?

## The Rewards and Dangers of Self-Disclosure

Self-disclosure often brings rewards, but it can also create problems. Whether or not you self-disclose will depend on your assessment of the possible rewards and dangers. Among the rewards of self-disclosure are:

- *Self-knowledge.* Self-disclosure helps you gain a new perspective on yourself and a deeper understanding of your own behavior.
- *Improved coping abilities.* Self-disclosure helps you deal with problems, especially guilt. Because you feel that past mistakes, for example, are a basis for rejection, you may develop guilt. By self-disclosing negative feelings and receiving support rather than rejection, you may be better able to deal with guilt, perhaps reducing or even eliminating it.
- *Communication enhancement.* Self-disclosure often improves communication. You understand the messages of others largely to the extent that you understand the individuals. You can tell what certain nuances mean, whether a person is serious or joking, and whether the person is being sarcastic out of fear or out of resentment.
- *More meaningful relationships.* By self-disclosing you tell others that you trust, respect, and care enough about them and your relationship to reveal yourself. This, in turn, leads the other individual to self-disclose and forms at least the start of a relationship that is honest and open and allows for more complete communication. Within a sexual relationship, self-disclosure increases sexual rewards and general relationship satisfaction. These two benefits in turn increase sexual satisfaction (Byers & Demmons, 1999).

Among the dangers of self-disclosure are:

- *Personal risks.* The more you reveal about yourself to others, the more areas of your life you expose to possible attack. Especially in the competitive context of work (or even romance), the more that others know about you, the more they'll be able to use against you.
- *Relationship risks.* Even in close and long-lasting relationships, self-disclosure can cause problems. Parents, normally the most supportive people in most individuals' lives, frequently reject children who self-disclose their homosexuality, their plans to marry someone of a different race, or their belief in another faith. Your best friends—your closest intimates—may reject you for similar self-disclosures.
- *Professional risks.* Sometimes self-disclosure may result in professional or material losses. Politicians who disclose that they have been in therapy may lose the support of their own political party and find that voters are unwilling to vote for them. Teachers who disclose disagreement with school administrators may find themselves being denied tenure, teaching undesirable schedules, and becoming victims of "budget cuts." In the business world self-disclosures of alcoholism or drug addiction often result in dismissal, demotion, or social exclusion.

Remember that self-disclosure, like any other communication, is irreversible (see Chapter 1). You cannot self-disclose and then take it back. Nor can you erase the conclusions and inferences listeners make on the basis of your disclosures. Remember, too, to examine the rewards and dangers of self-disclosure in terms of particular cultural rules. As with all cultural rules,

*"In order to have a conversation with someone, you must reveal yourself."*

—JAMES BALDWIN

**WHAT DO YOU SAY?**
**Corrective Self-Disclosure**
When you met your current partner—with whom you want to spend the rest of your life—you minimized the extent of your romantic history. You now want to come clean and disclose your "sordid" past. *What do you say? Through what channel?*

following rules about self-disclosure brings approval, and violating them brings disapproval.

## Guidelines for Self-Disclosure

Because self-disclosure is so important and so delicate a matter, here are some guidelines for (1) deciding whether and how to self-disclose, (2) responding to the disclosures of others, and (3) resisting the pressure to self-disclose.

### Guidelines for Making Self-Disclosures
In addition to weighing the potential rewards and dangers of self-disclosure, consider the following factors as well. These hints will help you raise the right questions before you make what must be your decision.

- *Consider the motivation for the self-disclosure.* Self-disclosure should be motivated by a concern for the relationship, for the others involved, and for yourself. Self-disclosure should serve a useful and productive function for all persons involved. Self-disclosing past indiscretions because you want to clear the air and be honest may be worthwhile; to disclose the same indiscretions to hurt your partner, however, is likely to damage the relationship.

- *Consider the appropriateness of the self-disclosure.* Self-disclosure should be appropriate to the context and to the relationship between you and your listener. Before making any significant self-disclosure, ask whether this is the right time (do you both have the time to discuss this at the length it requires?) and place (is the place free of distractions? is it private?). Ask, too, whether this self-disclosure is appropriate to the relationship. Generally, the more intimate the disclosure, the closer the relationship should be. It's probably best to resist mak-

*Skill Development Experience*

### Revealing Yourself

At what point in a relationship—if any—do you have an obligation to reveal the information listed below in the first column? Record your responses for romantic relationships in the second column and for friendships in the third. Use numbers from 1 to 10 to indicate at what point you would feel an obligation to reveal each type of information by visualizing a relationship existing on a continuum from 1 to 10, with 1 being initial contact and 10 being extreme intimacy. If you feel you would never have an obligation to reveal the information, use 0. After completing these items, try formulating in one sentence the obligation you have as a friend or romantic partner to reveal information about yourself.

*You don't have to reveal everything about yourself, but there may be obligations to reveal some information to certain relationship partners.*

| Information | Romantic Relationship | Friendship Relationship |
|---|---|---|
| HIV status | | |
| Past sexual experiences | | |
| Annual salary, net worth | | |
| Affectional orientation | | |
| Race, nationality, and religion | | |
| Social and political beliefs and attitudes | | |

ing intimate disclosures (especially negative ones) with nonintimates or with casual acquaintances, or in the early stages of a relationship.

- *Consider the disclosures of the other person.* During your disclosures, give the other person a chance to reciprocate with his or her own disclosures. If the other person does not reciprocate, reassess your own self-disclosures. It may be that for this person at this time and in this context, your disclosures are not welcome or appropriate. For example, if you reveal your romantic mistakes to a friend but your friend says nothing or reveals only the most minor details, it may be a cue to stop disclosing. Generally it's best to disclose gradually and in small increments so you can monitor your listener's responses and retreat if they're not positive enough.

- *Consider the possible burdens self-disclosure might entail.* Carefully weigh the potential problems that you may incur as a result of your disclosure. Can you afford to lose your job if you disclose your prison record? Are you willing to risk relational difficulties if you disclose your infidelities? Also, ask yourself whether you're making unreasonable demands on the listener. For example, consider the person who swears his or her mother-in-law to secrecy and then discloses having an affair with a neighbor. This disclosure places an unfair burden on the mother-in-law, who is now torn between breaking her promise of secrecy and allowing her child to believe a lie.

## Guidelines for Facilitating and Responding to Others' Self-Disclosures

When someone discloses to you, it's usually a sign of trust and affection. In carrying out this most important receiver function, keep the following guidelines in mind.

- *Practice the skills of effective and active listening.* The skills of effective listening (Chapter 3) are especially important when you're listening to self-disclosures: Listen actively, listen for different levels of meaning, listen with empathy, and listen with an open mind. Express an understanding of the speaker's feelings in order to give the speaker the opportunity to see his or her feelings more objectively and through the eyes of another. Ask questions to ensure your own understanding and to signal your interest and attention.

- *Support and reinforce the discloser.* Express support for the person during and after the disclosures. Try to refrain from evaluation. Concentrate on understanding and empathizing with the discloser. Make your supportiveness clear to the discloser through your verbal and nonverbal responses: Maintain eye contact, lean toward the speaker, ask relevant questions, and echo the speaker's thoughts and feelings. Men are generally more reluctant to show emotional support, at least to the degree that women do; the reason, according to recent research, is that men don't want their behavior to be seen as feminine (Burleson, Holmstrom, Gilstrap, 2005).

- *Be Willing to Reciprocate.* When you make relevant and appropriate disclosures of your own in response to the other person's disclosures, you're demonstrating your understanding of the other's meanings and at the same time your willingness to communicate on this meaningful level. If your colleague at work discloses an embarrassing dating situation and you reveal one of your own, you're indicating understanding on a deeper level than you would if you responded only with "That's funny" or "I know what you mean."

- *Keep the disclosures confidential.* When someone discloses to you, it's because the person wants you to know about his or her feelings and thoughts. If you reveal these disclosures to others, negative effects are inevitable. But most important, betraying a confidence is unfair; it debases what could be and should be a meaningful interpersonal experience. It's interesting to note that one of the netiquette rules of e-mail is that you shouldn't forward mail to third

▼ E-TALK

**Your Public Messages**
Will knowing that some undergraduate and graduate admissions offices and potential employers may examine your postings on social network sites influence what you write? If so, in what ways?

**WHAT DO YOU SAY?**
**Regulating Self-Disclosure**
You're currently engaged to Pat, but over the past few months you've been seeing someone else and have fallen in love. Now you want to break off your engagement and disclose this new relationship. *What do you say? Through what channel?*

**WHAT DO YOU SAY?**
**Disclosure Encouragement**
Your next-door neighbor is extremely secretive. You want to encourage greater disclosure but don't want to seem pushy or nosy. *What do you say? Through what channel?*

parties without the writer's permission. This rule is useful for self-disclosure generally: Maintain confidentiality; don't pass on disclosures made to you to others without the person's permission.

- *Don't use the disclosures against the person.* Many self-disclosures expose some kind of vulnerability or weakness. If you later turn around and use a disclosure against the person, you betray the confidence and trust invested in you. Regardless of how angry you may get, resist the temptation to use the disclosures of others as weapons. If your friend confides a fear of cats and you later use this to ridicule or tease the friend, you're likely to create relationship problems.

**Guidelines for Resisting Pressure to Self-Disclose** You may, on occasion, find yourself in a position in which a friend, colleague, or romantic partner pressures you to self-disclose. In such situations, you may wish to weigh the pros and cons of self-disclosure and make your own decision as to whether and what you'll disclose. If your decision is not to disclose and you're still being pressured, then you need to say something. Here are a few suggestions.

- *Don't be pushed.* Although there may be certain legal or ethical reasons for disclosing, generally you don't have to disclose if you don't want to. Realize that you're in control of what you reveal and of when and to whom you reveal it. Remember that self-disclosure has significant consequences. So if you're not sure you want to reveal something, at least not until you've had additional time to think about it, then don't.

- *Be indirect and move to another topic.* Avoid the question that asks you to disclose, and change the subject. If someone presses you to disclose your past financial problems, move the conversation to financial problems in general or nationally or change the topic to a movie you saw or to your new job. This is often a polite way of saying, "I'm not talking about it," and may be the preferred choice in certain situations and with certain people. Most often people will get the hint and will understand your refusal to disclose.

- *Be assertive in your refusal to disclose.* If necessary, say, very directly, "I'd rather not talk about that now" or "Now is not the time for this type of discussion."

With an understanding of the self in human communication, we can explore perception—the processes by which you come to understand yourself and others and, of course, the processes by which they come to understand you.

# Perception

**Perception** is your way of understanding the world; it helps you make sense out of what psychologist William James called the "booming buzzing confusion." More technically, perception is the process by which you become aware of objects, events, and especially people through your senses: sight, smell, taste, touch, and hearing. Perception is an active, not a passive, process. Your perceptions result both from what exists in the outside world and from your own experiences, desires, needs and wants, loves and hatreds. Among the reasons why perception is so important in communication is the fact that it influences your communication choices. The messages you send and listen to will depend on how you see the world, on how you size up specific situations, on what you think of the people with whom you interact.

## The Stages of Perception

Perception is a continuous series of processes that blend into one another. For convenience of discussion we can separate these processes into five stages: (1) You sense, you pick up some kind of stimulation; (2) you organize the stimuli in some way; (3) you interpret and evaluate what you perceive; (4) you store your perception in memory; and (5) you retrieve it when needed (Figure 2.3).

**Stage One: Stimulation**  At the first stage of perception, your sense organs are *stimulated*—you hear a new CD, you see a friend, you smell someone's perfume, you taste an orange, you feel another's sweaty palm. Naturally, you don't perceive everything; rather, you engage in *selective perception*, which includes selective attention and selective exposure.

In **selective attention,** you attend to those things that you anticipate will fulfill your needs or will prove enjoyable. For instance, when daydreaming in class, you don't hear what the instructor is saying until he or she calls your name. Your selective attention mechanism focuses your senses on the sound of your name.

The principle of **selective exposure** states that you tend to expose yourself to information that will confirm your existing beliefs, that will contribute to your objectives, or that will prove satisfying in some way. For example, after you buy a car, you're more apt to read and listen to advertisements for the car you just bought, because these messages tell you that you made the right decision. At the same time, you will tend to avoid advertisements for the cars that you considered but eventually rejected, because these messages would tell you that you made the wrong decision.

You're also more likely to perceive stimuli that are greater in intensity than surrounding stimuli and to perceive stimuli that have novelty value. For example, television commercials normally play at a greater intensity than regular programming to ensure that you take special notice. You're also more likely to notice the coworker who dresses in a novel way than you are to notice the one who dresses like everyone else.

**Stage Two: Organization**  At the second stage of perception, you organize the information your senses pick up. Three interesting ways in which you organize your perceptions are (1) by rules, (2) by schemata, and (3) by scripts.

*Organization by Rules.*   One frequently used rule is that of **proximity,** or physical closeness. The rule says that things that are physically close together constitute a unit. Thus, using this rule, you will tend to perceive people who are often together, or messages spoken one right after the other, as units, as belonging together. You also are likely to assume that the verbal and nonverbal signals sent at about the same time are related and constitute a unified whole.

Another rule is **similarity:** the idea that things that are physically similar or look alike belong together and form a unit. This principle leads you to see people who dress alike as belonging together. Similarly, you might assume that people who work at the same jobs, who are of the same religion, who live in the same building, or who talk with the same accent belong together.

"He didn't actually threaten me, but I perceived him as a threat."

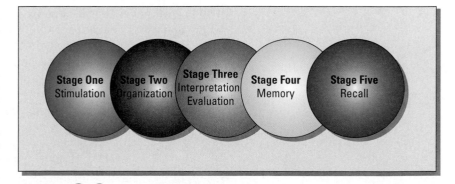

Figure *2.3*

**The Stages of Perception**

Perception occurs in five stages: stimulation, organization, interpretation–evaluation, memory, and recall. An understanding of how perception works will help make your own perceptions (of your self and of others) more accurate.

You use the principle of **contrast** when you conclude that some items (people or messages, for example) don't belong together because they're too different from each other to be part of the same unit. So, for example, in a conversation or a public speech, you'll focus your attention on changes in intensity or rate because these contrast with the rest of the message.

### Organization by Schemata.

Another way you organize material is by creating **schemata,** mental templates or structures that help you organize the millions of items of information you come into contact with every day as well as those you already have in memory. Schemata may thus be viewed as general ideas about people (Pat and Chris, Japanese, Baptists, New Yorkers); about yourself (your qualities, abilities, and even liabilities); or about social roles (the attributes of police officers, professors, or multimillionaires). The word *schemata*, by the way, is the plural of *schema* and is preferred to the alternative plural *schemas*.

You develop schemata from your own experience—actual experience as well as vicarious experience from television, reading, and hearsay. Thus, for example, you may have a schema that portrays college athletes as strong, ambitious, academically weak, and egocentric. And, of course, you've probably developed schemata for different religious, racial, and national groups; for men and women; and for people of different affectional orientations. Each group that you have some familiarity with will be represented in your mind in some kind of schema. Schemata help you organize your perceptions by allowing you to classify millions of people into a manageable number of categories or classes. As you'll soon see, however, schemata can also create problems—they can influence you to see what is not there or to miss seeing what is there.

### Organization by Scripts.

A **script** is a type of schema. Like a schema, a script is an organized body of information; but a script focuses on an action, event, or procedure. It's a general idea of how some event should unfold; it's the rules governing events and their sequence. For example, you probably have a script for eating in a restaurant with the actions organized into a pattern something like this: Enter, take a seat, review the menu, order from the menu, eat your food, ask for the bill, leave a tip, pay the bill, exit the restaurant. Similarly, you probably have scripts for how you do laundry, how you behave in an interview, the stages you go through in introducing someone to someone else, and the way you ask for a date.

Everyone relies on shortcuts—rules, schemata, and scripts, for example, are all useful shortcuts to simplify understanding, remembering, and recalling information about people and events. If you didn't have these shortcuts, you'd have to treat each person, role, or action differently from each other person, role, or action. This would make every experience totally new, totally unrelated to anything you already know. If you didn't use these shortcuts, you'd be unable to generalize, draw connections, or otherwise profit from previously acquired knowledge.

"No matter what else human beings may be communicating about, they are always communicating about themselves, about one another, and about the immediate context of the communication"
—R. Pittinger, Charles Hockett, and John Danehy

Shortcuts, however, may mislead you; they may contribute to your remembering things that are consistent with your schemata (even if they didn't occur) and distorting or forgetting information that is inconsistent.

Judgments about members of other cultures are often ethnocentric. Because you form schemata and scripts on the basis of your own cultural beliefs and experiences, you can easily (but inappropriately) apply these to members of other cultures. It's easy to infer that when members of other cultures do things that conform to your scripts, they're right, and when they do things that contradict your scripts, they're wrong—a classic example of ethnocentric thinking. As you can appreciate, this tendency can easily contribute to intercultural misunderstandings.

A similar problem arises when you base your schemata for different cultural groups on stereotypes that you may have derived from television or movies. So, for example, you may have schemata for religious Muslims that you derived from stereotypes presented in the media. If you then apply these schemata to all Muslims, you risk seeing only what conforms to your script and failing to see or distorting what does not conform to your script.

**Stage Three: Interpretation–Evaluation** The interpretation–evaluation step (a linked term because the two processes cannot be separated) is inevitably subjective and is greatly influenced by your experiences, needs, wants, values, expectations, physical and emotional state, gender, and beliefs about the way things are or should be—your rules, schemata, and scripts.

For example, when you meet a new person who is introduced to you as a college football player, you will tend to apply your schema to this person and view him as strong, ambitious, academically weak, and egocentric. You will, in other words, see this person through the filter of your schema for college athletes and evaluate him according to that schema. Similarly, when viewing someone asking for a date, you will apply your script to this event and view the event through the script. You will interpret the actions of the suitor as appropriate or inappropriate depending on your script for date-requesting behavior and on the ways in which the suitor performs the sequence of actions.

**Stage Four: Memory** You store in memory both your perceptions and their interpretations–evaluations. So, for example, you have in memory your schema for college athletes, and you know that Ben Williams is a football player. Ben Williams is then stored in memory with "cognitive tags" that tell you that he's strong, ambitious, academically weak, and egocentric. That is, despite the fact that you've not witnessed Ben's strength or ambitions and have no idea of his academic record or his psychological profile, you still may store your memory of Ben along with the qualities that make up your script for "college athletes."

Now, let's say that at different times you hear that Ben failed Spanish I (normally an A or B course at your school), that Ben got an A in chemistry (normally a tough course), and that Ben is transferring to Harvard as a theoretical physics major. Schemata act as filters or gatekeepers; they allow certain information to be stored in relatively objective form, much as you heard or read it, but may distort or prevent other information from being stored. As a result, these three items of information about Ben may get stored very differently in your memory along with your schema for college athletes.

For example, you may readily store the information that Ben failed Spanish, because it's consistent with your schema; it fits neatly into the template that you have of college athletes. Information that's consistent with your schema—as in this example—will strengthen your schema and make it more resistant to change (Aronson, Wilson, & Akert, 2002). Depending on the strength of your schema, you may also store in memory (even though you didn't hear it) the "information" that Ben did poorly in other courses as well. The information that Ben got an A in chemistry, because it contradicts your schema (it just doesn't seem right), may easily be distorted or lost. The information that Ben is transferring to Harvard, however, is a bit different. This information also is inconsistent with your schema; but it is so drastically inconsistent that you may begin to look at this mindfully. Perhaps you'll begin to question your schema for athletes, or perhaps you'll view Ben as an exception to the general rule. In either case, you're going to etch Ben's transferring to Harvard very clearly in your mind.

What you remember about a person or an event isn't an objective recollection but is more likely heavily influenced by your preconceptions or your schemata about what belongs and what doesn't belong. Your reconstruction of an event or

▼ **E-TALK**

**Impressions**
People will form judgments of you on the basis of your web page or blog. What types of Web design elements do you think would lead people to form a favorable impression of you, solely on the basis of your web page? Visit the web page of an instructor at your college whom you do not know. What impressions of this instructor do you get from the website? What specific website cues do you use to form these impressions?

person contains a lot of information that was not in your original experience and may omit a lot that was in this experience.

**Stage Five: Recall** At some later date, you may want to recall or access information you have stored in memory. Let's say you want to retrieve your information about Ben because he's the topic of discussion among you and a few friends. As you'll see in the discussion of listening in the next chapter, memory isn't reproductive; you don't simply reproduce what you've heard or seen. Rather, you reconstruct what you've heard or seen into a whole that is meaningful to you—depending in great part on your schemata and scripts—and it's this reconstruction that you store in memory. Now, when you want to retrieve this information from memory, you may recall it with a variety of inaccuracies. You're likely to:

- recall information that is consistent with your schema. In fact, you may not even recall the specific information you're looking for (say about Ben) but actually just your schema (which contains the information about college athletes and therefore about Ben).
- fail to recall information that is inconsistent with your schema. You have no place to put that information, so you easily lose it or forget it.
- recall information that drastically contradicts your schema, because it forces you to think (and perhaps rethink) about your schema and its accuracy; it may even force you to revise your schema.

## MEDIA LITERACY

### Who Are the Media?

- *Newspapers.* In 2003 there were 1,456 daily newspapers in the United States; most of these had circulations of under 50,000, though some numbered their readers in the millions (for example, in 2004 the two most widely read U.S. newspapers were *USA Today* with 2,192,098 readers and the *Wall Street Journal* with 2,101,017).
- *Television.* Since its development television (network and cable) has dominated the media. Ninety-eight percent of U.S. homes have television. According to Nielsen Media Research, men and women 55 and over watch the most television, logging around 40 hours a week.
- *Radio.* Although some 98 percent of U.S. households have radios, the radio is more background than foreground, except perhaps for talk radio, in which listeners become actively involved.
- *Film and video.* As of 2002, film and video constituted a $9.5 billion business. Viewed primarily as entertainment, films are persuasive messages; they teach cultural values in the country in which they were made and perhaps even more in countries to which they are exported.
- *Music.* CDs, music videos, concerts—as well as the presence of music in all the media—is still big business, though in 2002 the total value of music sold was $12.6 billion, a decline from $14.6 billion in 1999. Like film, music too expresses and teaches cultural values.
- *Internet, the Web, and blogs.* In 1993 approximately 3 million people were connected to the Internet. In early 2004 there were more than 800 million users world wide. These numbers will continue to grow in importance; online media are now essential tools for media literacy and for communication competence in general.

*Increasing Media Literacy.* *Continue the self-analysis of your own media behavior you began in the last chapter, but now look at the various different media and identify the ways you use each and the profits or rewards you get from using these media.*

*What the mass media offers is not popular art, but entertainment which is intended to be consumed like food, forgotten, and replaced by a new dish.*
—W. H. AUDEN

## Perceptual Processes

Before reading about common perceptual processes that can lessen your accuracy in perceiving other people, examine your own perception strategies by taking the following self-test, "How accurate are you at people perception?"

### HOW ACCURATE ARE YOU AT PEOPLE PERCEPTION?

**INSTRUCTIONS:** Respond to each of the following statements with T for true if the statement is usually or generally accurate in describing your behavior or with F for false if the statement is usually or generally inaccurate in describing your behavior.

_____ ❶ When I know some things about another person, I can pretty easily fill in what I don't know.

_____ ❷ I make predictions about people's behaviors that generally prove to be true.

_____ ❸ I base most of my impressions of people on the first few minutes of our meeting.

_____ ❹ I have clear ideas of what people of different national, racial, and religious groups are really like.

_____ ❺ I generally attribute people's attitudes and behaviors to their most obvious physical or psychological characteristic.

_____ ❻ I believe that the world is basically just, that good things happen to good people and bad things happen to bad people.

**HOW DID YOU DO?** This brief perception test was designed to raise questions about processes we'll shortly explore. All statements refer to perceptual processes that you may use but that may get you into trouble, leading you to form inaccurate impressions. These processes include implicit personality theory (statement 1), self-fulfilling prophecy (2), primacy–recency (3), and stereotyping (4). Statements 5 and 6 typify two kinds of mistakes we often make in attempting to attribute motives to other people's and even our own behaviors: overattribution (5) and the self-serving bias (6), which often involves a belief that the world is fundamentally just. Ideally, you would have responded to all of these statements with "false," indicating that you regularly avoid falling into these potential traps.

**WHAT WILL YOU DO?** As you read the rest of this chapter, think about these perceptual tendencies, and consider how you might avoid them so as to achieve more accurate and reasonable people perception. At the same time, recognize that situations vary widely and that this text's suggestions will prove useful in most but not all cases.

---

**Implicit Personality Theory** Consider the following brief statements. Note the word in parentheses that you think best completes each sentence:

- Carlo is energetic, eager, and (intelligent, stupid).
- Kim is bold, defiant, and (extroverted, introverted).
- Joe is bright, lively, and (thin, heavy).

▼ | E-TALK

**Online Dating**
According to a *New York Times* survey, online dating is losing its stigma as a place for losers (June 29, 2003, p. A1). Why do you think perceptions are changing in the direction of greater acceptance of online relationships? What is your current implicit personality theory of the "online dater"?

- Ava is attractive, intelligent, and (likable, unlikable).
- Susan is cheerful, positive, and (outgoing, shy).
- Angel is handsome, tall, and (friendly, unfriendly).

What makes some of these choices seem right and others seem wrong is your **implicit personality theory,** the system of rules that tells you which characteristics go with which other characteristics. Your theory may, for example, have told you that a person who is energetic and eager is also intelligent, although there's no logical reason why a stupid person could not be energetic and eager.

The widely documented **halo effect** is a function of the implicit personality theory (Dion, Berscheid, & Walster, 1972; Riggio, 1987). That is, if you believe a person has some positive qualities, you're likely to infer that she or he also possesses other positive qualities. There is also a reverse halo effect: If you know a person possesses several negative qualities, you're likely to infer that the person also has other negative qualities.

When using implicit personality theories, apply them carefully so as to avoid perceiving qualities that your theory tells you should be present in an individual when they actually are not. For example, you may see "goodwill" in a friend's "charitable" acts when a tax deduction may have been the real motive. Similarly, be careful of ignoring or distorting qualities that don't conform to your theory, but that are actually present in the individual. For example, you may ignore negative qualities in your friends that you would easily perceive in your enemies.

As you might expect, the implicit personality theories that people hold differ from culture to culture, from group to group, and even from person to person. For example, the Chinese have a concept called *shi gu*, which refers to a person who is skillful, devoted to family, worldly, and reserved (Aronson, Wilson, & Akert, 2002). This concept isn't easily encoded in English, as you can tell by trying to find a general concept that covers this type of person. In English, on the other hand, we have a concept of the "artistic type," a generalization that seems absent in the Chinese languages. Thus, although it is easy for speakers of English or Chinese to refer to specific concepts—such as socially skilled or creative—each language creates its own generalized categories. As a result, in Chinese languages, the qualities that make up *shi gu* are more easily seen as going together than they might be for an English speaker; they're part of the implicit personality theory of more Chinese speakers than, say, English speakers.

**The Self-Fulfilling Prophecy** A **self-fulfilling prophecy** occurs when you make a prediction that comes true because you act on it as if it were true (Merton, 1957). Put differently, a self-fulfilling prophecy occurs when you act on your schema as if it were true and in doing so you make it true (McNatt, 2001; Eden, 1992; Solomon et al., 1996; Einstein, 1995). For example, suppose you enter a group situation convinced that the other members will dislike you. Almost invariably you'll be proved right; the other members will appear to you to dislike you. What you may be doing is acting in a way that encourages the group to respond to you negatively. In this way, you fulfill your prophecies about yourself.

There are four basic steps in the self-fulfilling prophecy:

1. You make a prediction or formulate a belief about a person or a situation. For example, you expect Pat to be friendly in interpersonal encounters.

2. You act toward the person or situation as if that prediction or belief were true. For example, you act as if Pat were a friendly person.

3. Because you act as if the belief were true, it becomes true. For example, because of the way you act toward Pat, Pat becomes comfortable and friendly.

4. You observe your effect on the person or the resulting situation, and what you see strengthens your beliefs. For example, you observe Pat's friendliness, and this reinforces your belief that Pat is in fact friendly.

A widely known example of the self-fulfilling prophecy is the **Pygmalion effect.** In a classic study, teachers were told that certain pupils were late bloomers but were expected to do exceptionally well. The names of these students were actually selected at random by the experimenters. The results, however, were not random. The students whose names were given to the teachers actually performed at a higher level than their classmates. In fact, these students' IQ scores even improved more than did the other students'. The teachers' expectations probably prompted them to give extra attention to the selected students, thereby positively affecting their performance (Rosenthal & Jacobson, 1968; Insel & Jacobson, 1975).

**Primacy–Recency** Assume for a moment that you're enrolled in a course in which half the classes are extremely dull and half extremely exciting. At the end of the semester, you evaluate the course and the instructor. Will your evaluation be more favorable if the dull classes occur in the first half of the semester and the exciting classes in the second? Or will it be more favorable if the order is reversed? If what comes first exerts the most influence, you have a **primacy effect.** If what comes last (or most recently) exerts the most influence, you have a **recency effect.**

In the classic study on the effects of **primacy–recency** in interpersonal perception, college students perceived a person who was described as "intelligent, industrious, impulsive, critical, stubborn, and envious" more positively than a person described as "envious, stubborn, critical, impulsive, industrious, and intelligent" (Asch, 1946). Clearly, there's a tendency to use early information to get a general idea about a person and to use later information to make this impression more specific. The initial information helps you form a schema for the person. Once that schema is formed, you're likely to resist information that contradicts it.

One interesting practical implication of primacy–recency is that the first impression you make is likely to be the most important. The reason for this is that the schema that others form of you acts as a filter to admit or block additional information about you. If the initial impression or schema is positive, others are likely to remember additional positive information because it confirms their schema and to forget or distort negative information because it contradicts their schema. They are also more likely to interpret as positive information that is actually ambiguous. You win in all three ways—if the initial impression is positive.

**Stereotyping** One of the most common shortcuts in perception is stereotyping. A **stereotype** is a fixed impression of a group of people; it's a type of schema. We all have attitudinal stereotypes—of national, religious, sexual, or racial groups, or perhaps of criminals, prostitutes, teachers, or plumbers. If you have these fixed impressions, you will, on meeting a member of a particular group, often see that person primarily as a member of that group and apply to him or her all the characteristics you assign to that group. If you meet someone who is a prostitute, for example, there is a host of characteristics for prostitutes that you may apply to this one person. To complicate matters further, you will often "see" in this person's behavior the manifestation of characteristics that you would not "see" if you didn't know what the person did for a living. Stereotypes can easily distort accurate perception and prevent you from seeing an individual purely as an individual. Stereotypes can be especially prevalent in online communication; because there are few visual and auditory cues, it's not surprising that people often form impressions of online communication partners with a heavy reliance on stereotypes (Jacobson, 1999).

The tendency to group people and to respond to individuals primarily as members of groups can lead you to perceive an individual as possessing those qualities (usually negative) that you believe characterize his or her group (for example, "all Mexicans are . . . " or "all Baptists are . . ."). As a result, you may fail to appreciate the multifaceted nature of all individuals and groups. Stereotyping also can lead you to ignore each person's unique characteristics so that you fail to benefit from the special contributions each individual can bring to an encounter.

**WHAT DO YOU SAY?**
**Primacy–Recency**
Your partner forms initial impressions of people and never changes them. You want to show that this is illogical and prevents your partner from developing relationships with exciting people who may have given a negative first impression. *What do you say? Through what channel?*

### Taking Another's Perspective

*For effective communication to take place, each person needs to understand the perceptions of the other.*

Looking at the world through another's perspective, rather than only through your own, is pivotal in achieving mutual understanding. For each of the specific behaviors listed below, identify specific circumstances that would lead to a *positive perception* and specific circumstances that might lead to a *negative perception*. After you've completed these, state the principle of perception that you feel this exercise illustrated.

- A businessman ignores a homeless person who asks for money.
- A middle-aged man walks down the street with his arms around a teenage girl.
- A teenager gives a man $50 and walks away with a small envelope.

**Attribution** Attribution is the process by which you try to explain the reason or motivation for a person's behavior. One way to engage in attribution is to ask if the person was in control of the behavior. For example, suppose you invite your friend Desmond to dinner for 7 p.m. and he arrives at 9. Consider how you would respond to each of these reasons:

Reason 1: I just couldn't tear myself away from the beach. I really wanted to get a great tan.

Reason 2: I was driving here when I saw some young kids mugging an old couple. I broke it up and took the couple home. They were so frightened that I had to stay with them until their children arrived. Their phone was out of order, so I had no way of calling to tell you I'd be late.

Reason 3: I got in a car accident and was taken to the hospital.

Depending on the reason, you would probably attribute very different motives to Desmond's behavior. With reasons 1 and 2, you'd conclude that Desmond was in control of his behavior; with reason 3, that he was not. Further, you would probably respond negatively to reason 1 (Desmond was selfish and inconsiderate) and positively to reason 2 (Desmond was a Good Samaritan). Because Desmond was not in control of his behavior in reason 3, you would probably not attribute either positive or negative motivation to his behavior. Instead, you would probably feel sorry that he got into an accident.

You probably make similar judgments based on controllability in numerous situations. Consider, for example, how you would respond to the following situations:

- Doris fails her history midterm exam.
- Sidney's car is repossessed because he failed to keep up the payments.
- Margie is 150 pounds overweight and is complaining that she feels awful.
- Thomas's wife has just filed for divorce and he is feeling depressed.

You would most likely be sympathetic to each of these people if you felt that he or she was not in control of what happened; for example, if the examination was unfair, if Sidney lost his job because of employee discrimination, if Margie had a glandular problem, and if Thomas's wife wanted to leave him for a wealthy drug dealer. On the other hand, you probably would not be sympathetic if you felt that these people were in control of what happened; for example, if Doris partied instead of studying, if Sidney gambled his payments away, if Margie ate nothing but junk food and refused to exercise, and if Thomas had been repeatedly unfaithful and his wife finally gave up trying to reform him.

In perceiving and especially in evaluating other people's behavior, you frequently ask if they were in control of the behavior. Generally, research shows that if you feel a person was in control of negative behaviors, you'll come to dislike him or her. If you believe the person was not in control of negative behaviors, you'll come to feel sorry for and not blame the person. Attribution can lead to several potential errors: (1) the self-serving bias, (2) overattribution, and (3) the fundamental attribution error.

*The Self-Serving Bias.* The **self-serving bias** is an error usually made to preserve your self-esteem. You commit the self-serving bias when you take credit for the positive and deny responsibility for the negative. For example, you're more likely to attribute your positive outcomes (say, you get an A on an exam) to internal and controllable factors—to your personality, intelligence, or hard work (Bernstein, Stephan, & Davis, 1979; Duval & Silva, 2002). And you're more likely to attribute your negative outcomes (say, you get a D) to external and uncontrollable factors—to the exam's being exceptionally difficult or unfair.

*Overattribution.* **Overattribution** is the tendency to single out one or two obvious characteristics of a person and attribute everything that person does to this one or these two characteristics. For example, if a person is blind or was born into great wealth, there's often a tendency to attribute everything that person does to such factors. And so you might say, "Alex overeats because he's blind," or "Lillian is irresponsible because she never had to work for her money." To prevent overattribution, recognize that most behaviors and personality characteristics result from lots of factors. You almost always make a mistake when you select one factor and attribute everything to it. So when you make a judgment, ask yourself, for example, "Are there other factors that might be influencing Alex's eating habits or Lillian's irresponsible behavior?"

*The Fundamental Attribution Error.* The **fundamental attribution error** occurs when you overvalue the contribution of internal factors (for example, a person's personality) and undervalue the influence of external factors (for example, the context or situation the person is in). The fundamental attribution error is the tendency to conclude that people do what they do because that's the kind of

**WHAT DO YOU SAY?**
Overattribution
Your friends overattribute your behavior, attitudes, values, and just about everything you do to your racial origins. You want to explain the illogical nature of this overattribution. *What do you say? Through what channel?*

## LISTEN TO THIS

*I make progress by having people around me who are smarter than I am and listening to them. And I assume that everyone is smarter about something than I am.*
—HENRY J. KAISER

### Listening to Others' Perceptions

"Galileo and the Ghosts" is a technique for seeing how a particular group of people perceives a problem, person, or situation (DeVito, 2008). It involves two steps.

First, set up a mental "ghost-thinking team," much the way corporations and research institutes maintain think tanks. Select a team of four to eight "people" you admire, for example; historical figures like Aristotle or Galileo, fictional figures like Wonder Woman or Sherlock Holmes, public figures like Oprah Winfrey or Ralph Nader, or persons from other cultures or of a different gender or affectional orientation.

Next, pose a question or problem and then listen to how this team of ghosts perceives your problem. Of course, you're really listening to yourself—but to yourself acting in the roles of other people. The technique forces you to step outside your normal role and to consider the perceptions of someone totally different from you.

*Applying Listening Skills. Set up a ghost team to help you become a better friend, a more popular colleague at work, or a better student. Whom would you select? What specific questions would you ask? What might each team member say?*

**WHAT DO YOU SAY?**
**First Impression Correction**
You made a bad impression at work—you drank too much at an office party and played the clown. This is not the impression you want to give, and you need to change it fast. *What do you say? To whom? Through what channel?*

people they are, not because of the situation they're in. When Pat is late for an appointment, you're more likely to conclude that Pat is inconsiderate or irresponsible than to attribute the lateness to a bus breakdown or a traffic accident.

This fundamental attribution error is at least in part culturally influenced (Goode, 2000). Generally, for example, people in the United States are likely to explain behavior by saying that people did what they did because of who they are. When researchers asked Hindus in India to explain why their friends behaved as they did, the respondents gave greater weight to external factors than did respondents in the United States (Aronson, Wilson, & Akert, 2002). Generally, Americans have little hesitation in offering causal explanations of a person's behavior ("Pat did this because . . ."); Hindus, on the other hand, are generally reluctant to explain a person's behavior in causal terms (Matsumoto, 1994).

## Increasing Accuracy in Perception

Successful communication depends largely on the accuracy of your perception. You already know about barriers that can arise with perceptual processes—barriers such as the self-serving bias, overattribution, and the fundamental attribution error in attribution. There are, however, additional ways to think more critically about your perceptions and thereby to increase your perceptual accuracy. This section will offer some key strategies.

**Analyze Your Perceptions** Become aware of your perceptions and try to subject them to logical analysis and critical thinking. First, recognize your own role in perception. For example, your emotional and physiological state will influence the meaning you give to your perceptions. A movie may seem hysterically funny when you're in a good mood but just plain stupid when you're in a bad mood. Also, beware of your own biases; for example, do you tend to perceive only the positive in people you like and only the negative in people you don't like? Even your gender will influence your perceptions. Women consistently evaluate other people more positively than men on such factors as agreeableness, conscientiousness, and emotional stability (Winquist, Mohr, & Kenny, 1998).

Second, avoid early conclusions. On the basis of your observations of behaviors, formulate hypotheses to test against additional information and evidence rather than drawing conclusions you then look to confirm. At the same time, seek validation from others. Do others see things the same way you do? If not, ask yourself if your perceptions may be in some way distorted.

**Check Your Perceptions** Perception checking is another way to make your perceptions more accurate. The goal of perception checking is not to prove that your initial perception is correct but to explore further the thoughts and feelings of the other person. With this simple technique, you lessen your chances of misinterpreting another's feelings. In its most basic form, perception checking involves two components.

- Describe what you see or hear, recognizing that your perceptions are heavily influenced by who you are, your emotional state, and so on. At the same time, you may wish to describe what you *think* is happening. For example:
  - "You've called me from work a lot this week. You seem concerned about how things are at home."
  - "You've not wanted to talk with me all week. You say that my work is fine, but you don't seem to want to give me the same responsibilities that other editorial assistants have."
- Avoid mind reading; avoid trying to read the thoughts and feelings of another person just from observing their behaviors. A person's motives are not open to outside inspection; you can only make *assumptions* based on behaviors that

you observe. So seek confirmation. Ask the other person if your perception is accurate in as supportive a way as possible:

- "Are you worried about me or the kids?"
- "Are you displeased with my work? Is there anything I can do to improve my job performance?"

Try your hand at perception checking by asking yourself how you'd respond to the following statements:

- "Yeah, I finally married; it took me 43 years. And now comes the task of making do."
- "I can't imagine why I didn't get that job. I knew more about the company and the job than the interviewer did."
- "You'll never make it in this company; you're too bright, too dedicated."

**Reduce Your Uncertainty** Reducing uncertainty enables you to achieve greater accuracy in perception. Not surprisingly, you'll also find greater communication satisfaction when uncertainty is reduced (Neuliep & Grohskopf, 2000). In large part you learn about uncertainty and how to deal with it from your culture. In some cultures people do little to avoid uncertainty and have little anxiety about not knowing what will happen next. People in these cultures accept uncertainty as a normal part of life; they don't feel threatened by unknown situations. Examples of such low-anxiety cultures include those of Singapore, Jamaica, Denmark, Sweden, Hong Kong, Ireland, Great Britain, Malaysia, India, Philippines, and the United States. People in other cultures do much to avoid uncertainty and have a great deal of anxiety about not knowing what will happen next; they see uncertainty as a threatening issue that must be counteracted. Examples of such high-anxiety cultures include Greece, Portugal, Guatemala, Uruguay, Belgium, El Salvador, Japan, Yugoslavia, Peru, France, Chile, Spain, and Costa Rica (Hofstede, 1997).

Because weak-uncertainty-avoidance cultures have tolerance for ambiguity and uncertainty, members of these cultures minimize the importance of rules governing communication and relationships (Hofstede, 1997; Lustig & Koester, 2002). That is, they readily tolerate people who don't follow the same rules as the cultural majority; they may even encourage different approaches and perspectives. In contrast, strong-uncertainty-avoidance cultures create and enforce very clear-cut rules for communication.

Students from weak-uncertainty-avoidance cultures appreciate freedom in education and prefer vague assignments without specific timetables. These students want to be rewarded for creativity and will even accept an instructor's (occasional) lack of knowledge. Students from strong-uncertainty-avoidance cultures prefer highly structured experiences in which there is little ambiguity; they prefer specific objectives, detailed instructions, and definite timetables. These students expect to be judged on the basis of the right answers and expect the instructor to have all the answers all the time (Hofstede, 1997).

A variety of uncertainty reduction strategies can help reduce uncertainty in interpersonal communication (Berger & Bradac, 1982; Gudykunst, 1994).

- Observe the person while he or she is engaged in an active task, preferably interacting with others in relatively informal social situations. People are less apt to monitor their behaviors and more likely to reveal their true selves in informal situations.
- Set up situations so as to be able to observe a person in more specific and more revealing contexts. Employment interviews, theatrical auditions, and student teaching placements are examples of situations designed to reduce uncertainty by letting observers see how people act and react.
- Ask others for information. For example, you might ask a colleague if a third person finds you interesting and might like to have dinner with you.

▼ **E-TALK**

**Perceptual Accuracy**
How would you describe your own perceptual accuracy in face-to-face versus online relationships? What perceptual cues do you use in each situation?

> **WHAT DO YOU SAY?**
> **Relationship Uncertainty**
> You've been dating someone casually over the past six months. You want to move to a more exclusive relationship in which you date only each other. But first you want to discover whether your date feels as you do. *What do you say? To whom? Through what channel?*

- Interact with the individual. For example, you can ask questions: "Do you enjoy sports?" "What did you think of that computer science course?" "What would you do if you got fired?"

**Increase Your Cultural Sensitivity** Recognizing and being mindful of cultural differences will help increase your accuracy in perception. For example, Russian or Chinese performers such as ballet dancers will often applaud their audience by clapping. Americans seeing this may easily interpret this as egotistical. Similarly, a German man will enter a restaurant before the woman in order to see if the place is respectable enough for the woman to enter. This simple custom may appear rude to people from cultures in which it's considered courteous to allow the woman to enter first (Axtell, 1991).

Cultural awareness will help counteract the difficulty most people have in understanding the nonverbal messages of people from other cultures. For example, be aware that it's easier to decode emotions communicated facially by members of your own culture than to read emotions shown by members of other cultures (Weathers, Frank, & Spell, 2002). This "in-group advantage" will assist your perceptional accuracy for members of your own culture but will often hinder your accuracy for members of other cultures (Elfenbein & Ambady, 2002).

Within every cultural group, too, there are wide and important differences. Not all Americans are alike, and neither are all Indonesians, Greeks, Mexicans, and so on. When you make assumptions that all people of a certain culture are alike, you're thinking in stereotypes. In addition to recognizing differences between another culture and your own, recognizing differences among members of any given culture will help you perceive situations more accurately.

## Summary of Concepts and Skills

This chapter explored the self, the ways you perceive yourself, and perception, the way you perceive others and others perceive you.

1. Self-concept, the image that you have of yourself, is composed of feelings and thoughts about both your abilities and your limitations. Self-concept develops from the image that others have of you, the comparisons you make between yourself and others, the teachings of your culture, and your own interpretations and evaluations of your thoughts and behaviors.

2. The Johari window model of the self is one way to view self-awareness. In this model there are four major areas: the open self, the blind self, the hidden self, and the unknown self. To increase self-awareness, analyze yourself, listen to others to see yourself as they do, actively seek information from others about yourself, see yourself from different perspectives, and increase your open self.

3. Self-esteem is the value you place on yourself and may be enhanced by attacking self-destructive beliefs, seeking out nourishing others, working on projects that will result in success, and securing affirmation.

4. Self-disclosure is a form of communication in which information about the self that is normally kept hidden is communicated to one or more others.

5. Self-disclosure is more likely to occur when the potential discloser (1) feels competent, is sociable and extroverted, and is not apprehensive about communication; (2) comes from a culture that encourages self-disclosure; (3) is a woman; (4) is talking to supportive listeners who also disclose; and (5) talks about impersonal rather than personal topics and reveals positive rather than negative information.

6. The rewards of self-disclosure include increased self-knowledge, the ability to cope with difficult situations and guilt, communication efficiency, and chances for more meaningful relationships. The dangers of self-disclosure include personal and social rejection and material loss.

7. Before self-disclosing, consider the motivation for the self-disclosure, the possible burdens you might impose on your listener or yourself, the appropriateness of the self-disclosure, and the disclosures of the other person.

8. When listening to others' disclosures, try to understand what the discloser is feeling, support the discloser, be

willing to reciprocate, keep the disclosures confidential, and don't use the disclosures against the person.

9. When you don't want to disclose, try being firm, being indirect and changing the topic, or assertively stating your unwillingness to disclose.

10. Perception is the process by which you become aware of the many stimuli impinging on your senses. It occurs in five stages: Sensory stimulation occurs, sensory stimulation is organized, sensory stimulation is interpreted–evaluated, sensory stimulation is held in memory, and sensory stimulation is recalled.

11. The following processes can get in the way of accurate perception: (1) implicit personality theory, (2) self-fulfilling prophecy, (3) primacy–recency, (4) stereotyping, and (5) attribution.

12. Several strategies can increase the accuracy of interpersonal perceptions: (1) Analyze your perceptions; for example, recognize your role in perception, formulate hypotheses rather than conclusions, and be aware of your own biases. (2) Check perceptions; that is, describe what you see or hear and ask for confirmation. (3) Reduce uncertainty by, for example, collecting information about the person or situation and interacting and observing the interaction. And (4) be culturally aware, recognizing the differences between you and others as well as the differences among members of the culturally different group.

Throughout this discussion of the self and perception, a variety of skills were identified. Place a check mark next to those skills that you feel you need to work on most.

_____ 1. I seek to understand my self-concept and to be realistic about my strengths and my weaknesses.

_____ 2. I actively seek to increase self-awareness by talking with myself, listening to others, reducing my blind self, seeing myself from different perspectives, and increasing my open self.

_____ 3. I seek to enhance my self-esteem by attacking self-destructive beliefs, seeking out nourishing others, working on projects that will result in success, and securing affirmation.

_____ 4. I regulate my disclosures on the basis of the unique communication situation.

_____ 5. In deciding whether or not to self-disclose, I take into consideration my motivation, the possible burdens on my listener, the appropriateness to the other person and the context, the other person's disclosures, and the possible burdens the disclosures may impose on me.

_____ 6. I respond to the disclosures of others by trying to feel what the other person is feeling, using effective and active listening skills, expressing supportiveness, refraining from criticism and evaluation, and keeping the disclosures confidential.

_____ 7. I resist disclosing when I don't want to by being firm, by trying indirectness and changing the topic, and/or by stating assertively my refusal to disclose.

_____ 8. I think mindfully when I use perceptual shortcuts so that they don't mislead me and result in inaccurate perceptions.

_____ 9. I guard against ethnocentric thinking by viewing the behavior and customs of others from a multicultural view rather than from just my cultural view.

_____ 10. I bring to consciousness my implicit personality theories.

_____ 11. To guard against the self-fulfilling prophecy, I take a second look at my perceptions when they conform too closely to my expectations.

_____ 12. Recognizing how primacy–recency works, I actively guard against first impressions that might prevent accurate perceptions of future events; I formulate hypotheses rather than conclusions.

_____ 13. I recognize stereotyping in the messages of others and avoid it in my own.

_____ 14. I am aware of and am careful to avoid the self-serving bias, overattribution, and the fundamental attribution error when trying to account for another person's behavior.

_____ 15. I think critically about perception, analyzing my perceptions, checking my perceptions for accuracy, using uncertainty reduction strategies, and acting with cultural sensitivity.

## The Language of the Self and Perception

Match the terms about the self and perception with their definitions. Record the number of the definition next to the appropriate term.

a. _____ stereotype

b. _____ attribution

c. _____ self-fulfilling prophecy

d. _____ schemata

e. _____ social comparison

f. _____ implicit personality theory

g. _____ self-concept

h. _____ self-esteem

i. _____ self-disclosure

j. _____ self-serving bias

1. The mental templates or structures that help you organize new information as well as the information you already have in memory.

2. Concluding that a person has positive qualities because you know that he or she has other positive qualities.

3. The process by which you compare yourself with others, most often your peers.

4. Your image of who you are.

5. A measure of how valuable you think you are.

6. The process of talking to others about yourself, of revealing things that you normally keep hidden.

7. The tendency to take credit for positive outcomes and to deny responsibility for negative outcomes.

8. The process by which we try to explain the motivation for a person's behavior.

9. The process of making a prediction that comes true because you made the prediction and acted as if it were true.

10. A fixed impression of a group of people.

**Answers:** a. 10 b. 8 c. 9 d. 1 e. 3 f. 2 g. 4 h. 5 i. 6 j. 7

## Five for Discussion

1. How would you describe the current status of stereotyping—on your campus, in your family, or in your workplace—in relation to males and females, heterosexuals and homosexuals, believers and atheists, members of different races, or members of different religions? What effects do these stereotypes have on communication?

2. Popular wisdom and many television talk shows emphasize the importance of self-esteem. The self-esteem camp, however, has come under attack from critics (for example, Bushman & Baumeister, 1998; Baumeister, Bushman, & Campbell, 2000; Bower, 2001; Coover & Murphy, 2000; Hewitt, 1998). Much current thinking holds that high self-esteem is not necessarily desirable: It does nothing to improve academic performance, it does not predict success, and it may even lead to antisocial (especially aggressive) behavior. On the other hand, it's difficult to imagine how a person would function successfully without positive self-feelings. What do you think about the benefits or liabilities of self-esteem?

3. Racial profiling (the practice whereby the police focus on members of specific ethnic groups as possible crime suspects) has been widely reported and widely condemned as racist. In the aftermath of the attack on the World Trade Center and the Pentagon on September 11, 2001, racial profiling—of Muslims and those who looked "Arab"—became viewed by many as necessary in preventing further acts of terrorism. How do you view racial profiling?

4. As your relationship with another person becomes closer and more intimate, the two of you generally reduce your uncertainty about each other; you become more predictable to each other. Do you think this high predictability makes a relationship more stable or less stable? More enjoyable or less enjoyable?

5. An interesting variation on self-disclosure occurs when someone else takes information from your hidden self

and makes it public. Although third-party disclosure can concern any aspect of a person's hidden self—for example, an athlete's prison record or drug habit, a movie star's alcoholism, or a politician's financial dealings—the media have made a special case out of revealing a person's affectional orientation; the process is called "outing" (Gross, 1991; Signorile, 1993; Johansson & Percy, 1994). Those against outing argue that people have a right to privacy and no one else should take that right from them. Because outing can lead to severe consequences—for example, loss of a job, expulsion from the military, or social and physical harassment—opponents argue that no one but the individual himself or herself has the right to reveal such information. Those in favor of outing argue that it's an expedient political and social weapon to silence those gay men and lesbians who—perhaps in an effort to keep their own affectional orientation secret—support or refuse to protest homophobic policies. What do you think of outing?

## Log On! MyCommunicationLab

A variety of exercises and self-tests will help you work actively with the concepts discussed in this chapter (**www.mycommunicationlab.com**): (1) I'd Prefer to Be, (2) Time for Self-Disclosure, (3) Disclosing Your Hidden Self, (4) How Assertive Are Your Messages? (5) What Do You Have a Right to Know? (6) How Open Are You Interculturally? (7) How Shy Are You? (8) Applying Attribution Theory, (9) Perceiving My Selves, (10) Self-Perception, (11) Understanding the Process of Perception, (12) WHO? (13) Barriers to Accurate Perception, and (14) What Are Your Cultural Perceptions? (15) Perceptual Empathizing.

Take a look at MyCommunicationLab for a variety of study aids, exercises, and video clips on the nature and importance of the self and perception in all aspects of human communication.

Explore our research resources at **www.researchnavigator.com**.

Research
Navigator.com

# Listening in Human Communication

## *Why Read* This Chapter?

Because you'll **learn about:**

- listening and the ways in which you listen.
- how different cultures as well as men and women view listening.

Because you'll **learn to:**

- listen more effectively during each of the five listening stages.
- adjust your listening so that it's most effective for the specific situation.
- listen with an awareness of cultural and gender differences.

This chapter examines **listening,** which, according to the International Listening Association, is "the process of receiving, constructing meaning from, and responding to spoken and/or nonverbal messages" (Emmert, 1994, cited in Brownell, 2006). Here we look at the importance of listening, the nature of the listening process, the varied styles of listening you might use in different situations, and some cultural and gender differences in listening. The chapter also describes ways to avoid the major barriers to effective listening.

## The Importance of Listening: Task and Relationship Benefits

Regardless of what you do, listening will prove a crucial communication component and will serve both task and relationship functions. For example, one study concluded that in this era of technological transformation, employees' interpersonal skills are especially significant; workers' advancement will depend on their ability to speak and write effectively, to display proper etiquette, and *to listen attentively.* And in a survey of 40 CEOs of Asian and Western multinational companies, respondents cited a lack of listening skills as *the major shortcoming* of top executives (Witcher, 1999).

It's also interesting to note that the effective listener—to take just a few examples—is more likely to emerge as group leader, a more effective salesperson, a more attentive and effective health care worker, and a more effective manager (Johnson & Bechler, 1998; Kramer, 1997; Castleberry & Shepherd, 1993; Lauer, 2003; Stein & Bowen, 2003; Levine, 2004). In recent years medical educators, claiming that doctors are not trained to listen to their patients, have introduced what they call "narrative medicine" to teach doctors to listen to their patients and to recognize how their perceptions of their patients are influenced by their own emotions (Smith, 2003).

If you measured the importance of every activity by the time you spent on that activity, then—according to the research studies available—listening would be your most important communication activity. Studies conducted from 1929 to 1980 showed that listening was the most often used form of communication, followed by speaking, reading, and writing (Rankin, 1929; Werner, 1975; Barker, Edwards, Gaines, Gladney, & Holley, 1980; Steil, Barker, & Watson, 1983; Wolvin & Coakley, 1996). This was true of high school and college students as well as of adults from a wide variety of fields. Today, of course, these studies are dated; your communication patterns are very different from those of someone raised and educated before widespread use of computer-mediated communication. However, anecdotal evidence, although certainly not conclusive, suggests that listening probably is still the most used communication activity. Just think of how you spend your day; listening probably occupies a considerable amount of time.

Another way to look at the importance of listening is to consider the numerous benefits or payoffs that accrue to the effective listener. Listening serves the same purposes as those identified for human communication in general in Chapter 1: It enables you to learn, relate, influence, play, and help (Johnson & Bechler, 1998; Kramer, 1997; Castleberry & Shepherd, 1993; Levine, 2004; Brownell, 2006). Listening helps you *learn* by enabling you to acquire knowledge of others, the world, and yourself so as to avoid problems and make more reasonable decisions. Listening enables you to *relate;* to form and maintain relationships with others, to gain social acceptance and popularity, simply because people come to like those who are attentive and listen supportively. You also exert *influence* through listening; people are more likely to respect

*"Listening, not imitation, may be the sincerest form of flattery."*
—JOYCE BROTHERS

and follow those who they feel have listened to and understood them. Knowing when to suspend critical and evaluative listening and simply to listen to absurdities or incongruities enables you to fulfill the *play* function. And, of course, listening enables you to *help* others; to assist other people by hearing more, empathizing more, and coming to understand others more deeply.

## Stages of Listening

Listening is a collection of skills involving attention and concentration (receiving), learning (understanding), memory (remembering), critical thinking (evaluation), and feedback (responding). Listening can go wrong at any stage; by the same token, you can enhance your listening ability by strengthening the skills needed for each step of the process (Figure 3.1).

Note that the process of listening is circular: The responses of person A serve as the stimulation for person B, whose responses, in turn, serve as the stimulation for person A, and so on. All five stages overlap. When you listen, you're performing all five processes at essentially the same time. For example, when listening in conversation, you're not only paying attention to what other people are saying, but also critically evaluating what they just said and perhaps giving feedback. Let's take a look at each stage separately.

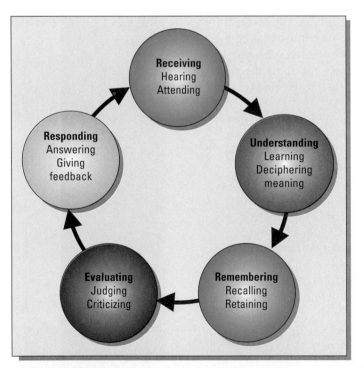

### Figure *3.1*

**A Five-Stage Model of the Listening Process**
This model depicts the various stages involved in listening. Note that receiving or hearing is not the same thing as listening, but is in fact only the first step in a five-step process. This model draws on a variety of previous models that listening researchers have developed (for example, Alessandra, 1986; Barker, 1990; Brownell, 1987; Steil, Barker, & Watson, 1983). In what other ways might you visualize the listening process?

## Receiving

*Hearing*, which is not the same as *listening*, begins and ends with the first stage of the listening process, receiving. Hearing simply happens when you open your ears or get within range of some auditory stimulus. Listening, on the other hand, is quite different. Listening begins but does not end with receiving (or hearing) messages the speaker sends.

At the *receiving* stage, you note not only what is said (verbally and nonverbally), but also what is omitted. For example, you receive not only the politician's summary of accomplishments in education, but also the omission of failures in health care or pollution control. This receiving stage of listening can be made more effective if you:

- focus attention on the speaker's verbal and nonverbal messages, on what is said and what is not said;
- avoid distractions in the environment;
- focus attention on the speaker's messages, not on what you will say next;
- maintain your role as listener by not interrupting the speaker; and
- confront **mixed messages**—messages that communicate different and contradictory meanings.

At times, speakers may ask hearers to cut them some slack and to receive their messages without prejudice, a process referred to as *disclaiming*. Some of the more popular *disclaimers* are these (Hewitt & Stokes, 1975):

- *Hedging* asks that you (the listener) separate the message from the speaker—that if you reject the message, you shouldn't also reject the speaker ("I didn't read the whole book, so I may not be entirely accurate, but . . .").

- *Credentialling* asks you not to disqualify the speaker for saying something that may be taken negatively ("You know, I'm not sexist, but it seems to me that . . . ").
- *Sin licenses* ask you for permission to deviate in some way from what is considered normal operating procedure ("This is probably not the place to say this, but . . . ").
- *Cognitive disclaimers* ask you to see the speaker as being in full possession of his or her faculties ("I know I drank a bit, but I'm as clear on this as ever . . . ").
- *Appeals for the suspension of judgment* ask you to hold off making a judgment until you hear the speaker out ("This may sound weird at first, but just listen to this . . . ").

In this brief discussion of receiving, and in fact throughout this chapter on listening, the unstated assumption is that both individuals can receive auditory signals without difficulty. But for many people who have hearing impairments, listening presents a variety of problems. Table 3.1 provides tips for communication between deaf and hearing people.

**E-TALK**

**Cell Phone Annoyances**
One researcher has argued that listening to the cell phone conversations of others is particularly annoying because you can only hear one side of the conversation; research participants rated cell phone conversations as more intrusive than two people talking face-to-face (Monk, Fellas, & Ley, 2004). Do you find the cell phone conversations of people near you on a bus or in a store annoying, perhaps for the reason given here?

## Understanding

Understanding occurs when you decode the speaker's signals, when you learn what the speaker means. *Understanding* means grasping both the thoughts that are expressed and the emotional tone that accompanies them—for example, the urgency, joy, or sorrow expressed in the message. The understanding phase of listening can be made more effective if you:

- relate the speaker's new information to what you already know (in what way will this new proposal change our present health care?);
- see the speaker's messages from the speaker's point of view, in part by not judging the message until it's fully understood as the speaker intended it;
- ask questions for clarification or request additional details or examples if needed; and/or
- rephrase (paraphrase) the speaker's ideas, a simple process that's especially important when listening to complicated instructions.

*Skill Development Experience*

### Paraphrasing for Understanding

Here are a few situations in which you might want to use paraphrasing to ensure that you understand the speaker's thoughts and feelings. For each situation (a) identify the thoughts and feelings you feel the speaker is expressing, and (b) put these thoughts and feelings into a paraphrase.

*Paraphrasing helps you check your understanding of the speaker and better remember what the speaker said while also helping to reinforce and support the speaker.*

1. A colleague says, "Did you hear I got engaged to Jerry? Our racial and religious differences are really going to cause difficulties for both of us. But, we'll work it through."
2. A classmate says, "I got a C on that paper. That's the worst grade I've ever received. I just can't believe that I got a C. This is my major. What am I going to do?"
3. A friend says, "That rotten, inconsiderate pig just up and left. He never even said good-bye. We were together for six months and after one small argument he leaves without a word. And he even took my bathrobe—that expensive one he bought for my last birthday."

**TABLE 3.1** *Communication Tips*

**BETWEEN DEAF AND HEARING PEOPLE**

People differ greatly in their hearing ability; some are totally deaf and can hear nothing, others have some hearing loss and can hear some sounds, and still others have impaired hearing but can hear most speech. Although many people with profound hearing loss can speak, their speech may seem labored and less clear than the speech of those with unimpaired hearing. Here are some suggestions to help deaf and hearing people communicate more effectively.

**If you have unimpaired hearing:**

1. Set up a comfortable context. Reduce the distance between yourself and the person with a hearing impairment. Reduce the background noise. Turn off the television and even the air conditioner.

2. Face the person and avoid any interference with the visual cues from your speech; for example, avoid smoking, chewing gum, or holding your hand over your mouth. Make sure the lighting is adequate.

3. Speak with an adequate volume, but avoid shouting, which can distort your speech and may insult the person. Be careful to avoid reducing volume at the ends of your sentences.

4. Because some words are easier to lip-read than others, it often helps if you can rephrase your ideas in different ways.

5. In group situations only one person should speak at a time.

6. Ask the person if there is anything you can do to make it easier for him or her to understand you.

7. Don't avoid terms like *hear, listen, music,* or *deaf* when they're relevant to the conversation. Trying to avoid these common terms will make your speech sound artificial.

8. Use nonverbal cues to help communicate your meaning; gestures indicating size or location and facial expressions indicating emotions and feelings are often helpful.

**If you have impaired hearing:**

1. Do your best to eliminate background noise.

2. Move closer to the speaker if this helps. Alert the other person that this closer distance will help you hear better.

3. If you feel the speaker can make adjustments that will make it easier for you to understand, ask. For example, ask the speaker to repeat a message, to speak more slowly or more distinctly, or to increase his or her volume.

4. If you hear better in one ear than in the other, position yourself accordingly and, if necessary, clue the other person in to this fact.

5. If necessary, ask the person to write down certain information, such as phone numbers or website addresses. Carrying a pad and pencil will prove helpful, both for this purpose and in the event that you wish to write something down for others.

*Sources:* These suggestions were drawn from a variety of sources: Tips for Communicating with Deaf People (Rochester Institute of Technology, National Technical Institute for the Deaf, Division of Public Affairs); www.his.com/~lola/deaf.html; www.zak.co.il/deaf-info/old/comm_strategies.html; and www.agbell.org. All websites accessed October 9, 2006.

## Remembering

Messages that you receive and understand need to be retained for some period of time. In some small group and public speaking situations, you can augment your memory by taking notes or by taping the messages. In most interpersonal communication situations, however, such note taking would be considered inappropriate, although you often do write down a phone number or an appointment or directions.

What you remember is not what was actually said, but what you think (or remember) was said. You don't simply *reproduce* in your memory what the speaker said; rather, you *reconstruct* the messages you hear into a system that makes sense to you—a concept noted in the discussion of perception in Chapter 2.

You can make this *remembering* phase of listening more effective if you:

- identify the central ideas and the major support advanced;

- summarize the message in an easier-to-retain form, not ignoring crucial details or qualifications;

- repeat names and key concepts to yourself or, if appropriate, aloud;

- take notes, if appropriate; and/or

- identify patterns and use them to organize what the speaker is saying (if this is a formal talk with a recognizable organizational structure).

## Evaluating

*Evaluating* consists of judging the messages you hear. At times you may try to evaluate the speaker's underlying intent, often without much conscious awareness. For example, Elaine tells you she is up for a promotion and is really excited about it. You may then try to judge her intention. Does she want you to use your influence with the company president? Is she preoccupied with the possible promotion and therefore telling everyone? Is she looking for a pat on the back? Generally, if you know the person well, you will be able to identify the intention and respond appropriately.

In other situations, your evaluation is more in the nature of critical analysis. For example, in a business meeting on upgrading office equipment, you'd evaluate the office manager's proposals while listening to them. As you're listening, you'd be asking yourself, "Are the proposals practical? Will they increase productivity? What is the evidence? Are there more practical alternatives?" This evaluation stage of listening can be made more effective if you:

- resist evaluating until you fully understand the speaker's point of view;

- assume that the speaker is a person of goodwill and give the speaker the benefit of any doubt by asking for clarification on issues you object to (are there any other reasons for accepting this new proposal?);

- distinguish facts from inferences (see Chapter 4), opinions, and personal interpretations by the speaker; and

- identify any biases, self-interests, or prejudices that might lead the speaker to slant information unfairly.

**WHAT DO YOU SAY?**
**Hate Speech**
Your work colleagues frequently use derogatory racial terms. You want to protest this kind of talk, but at the same time you don't want to alienate people you're going to have to work closely with for some time to come. *What do you say? To whom? Through what channel?*

## COMMUNICATING ETHICALLY

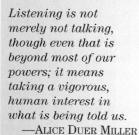

*Listening is not merely not talking, though even that is beyond most of our powers; it means taking a vigorous, human interest in what is being told us.*
—Alice Duer Miller

### Listening Ethically

Listening is a two-way process; both speaker and listener share in the success or failure of the interaction. And both participants share in the moral implications of the communication exchange. Two major principles govern the ethics of listening:

1. Give the speaker an honest hearing. Avoid prejudging the speaker. Put aside prejudices and preconceptions and evaluate the speaker's message fairly. At the same time, empathize with the speaker; try to understand emotionally as well as intellectually what the speaker means.
2. Give the speaker honest responses. Give open and honest feedback to the speaker. In a learning environment such as a communication class, this means giving honest and constructive criticism to help the speaker improve. It also means reflecting honestly on the questions that the speaker raises.

*What Would You Do?* *You're teaching a class in communication, and in the public speaking segment, one of your students wants to give a speech on "the benefits of steroids in sports." You know that this will cause all sorts of problems, and yet you wonder if you should place yourself in the position of censor. What would you do? What would you do if the student wanted to speak on ways to cheat on income taxes, how to create computer viruses, or the beauty of the anorexic body?*

## Essential Principles of Media Literacy Listening

Here are a few basic principles to illustrate the importance of listening in media literacy.

*In a day of virtual reality and computer simulations "seeing is NOT believing."*
—David Considine

1. Media messages are value-laden; the media contain the values of the producer and often of the primary audience. And these messages ethicize and socialize you—they give you an ethical standard and teach you the social rules you should be following. Electronic media—blogs, websites, and social networks such as MySpace or Friendster—are free or relatively inexpensive, and through these media people normally without influence voice their opinions and send out their persuasive messages. But mass media productions are (generally) expensive to create (feature films, television shows), so they are likely to reflect the values of the rich and powerful. Therefore, listen to television programs, for example, with a consciousness of the values that are embedded in the production—the sitcom as well as the news broadcast—and of how these might influence your thoughts and behaviors.

2. Media messages are informative and persuasive. They inform you of the news and at the same time persuade you that this is in fact the news; that is, that what the newspaper or TV covers represents the significant events of the day. And of course media persuade you on a more obvious level, with advertising. Almost all media messages have some persuasive aim. As a media-literate consumer, see these persuasive messages clearly so that you can analyze them and test their validity, rather than letting them influence you without awareness.

3. Media help construct your view of reality. What you know of the world and its people you probably learned largely from the media; some of it is accurate, and some of it isn't; some of it is slanted, and most of it is overly simplified. Listen to the ways in which the media influence how you see the world and to the ways in which they distort reality.

*Increasing Media Literacy.* *In what ways have the media influenced your beliefs about, for example, the war in Iraq, the U.S. economy, or the role of religion in government? How have the media influenced your peers' beliefs about these same issues? What specific media have the most influence on you? Why?*

## Responding

*Responding* occurs in two forms: (1) responses you make while the speaker is talking and (2) responses you make after the speaker has stopped talking. Responses made while the speaker is talking should be supportive and should acknowledge that you're listening. These responses are **backchanneling cues:** messages (words and gestures) that let the speaker know you're paying attention, as when you nod in agreement or say, "I see" or "Uh-huh."

Responses after the speaker has stopped talking are generally more elaborate and might include empathy ("I know how you must feel"); requests for clarification ("Do you mean this new health plan will replace the old one, or will it be just a supplement?"); challenges ("I think your evidence is weak"); and/or agreement ("You're absolutely right, and I'll support your proposal when it comes up for a vote"). You can improve this responding phase of listening if you:

■ express support for the speaker throughout the talk by using varied backchanneling cues (though using only one—for example, saying, "Uh-huh," throughout—will make it appear that you're not listening but are merely on automatic pilot);

■ express support for the speaker in your final responses; and

■ take ownership of your responses by stating your thoughts and feelings as your own and using "I-messages" (saying, "I think the new proposal will entail greater expense than you outlined" rather than "Everyone will object to the plan's cost").

**"I can't get off the phone, he won't stop listening!"**

Reprinted by permission of Jerry Marcus.

# Styles of Effective Listening

Before reading about the principles of effective listening, examine your own listening habits and tendencies by taking the following self-test, "How good a listener are you?" The "desirable" answers are obvious, of course, but try to give responses that are true for you in most of your listening experiences.

## HOW GOOD A LISTENER ARE YOU?

INSTRUCTIONS: Respond to each question using the following scale:

**1** = always; **2** = frequently; **3** = sometimes; **4** = seldom; and **5** = never.

_____ ❶ I listen to what the speaker is saying and feeling; I try to feel what the speaker feels.

_____ ❷ I listen objectively; I focus on the logic of the ideas rather than on the emotional meaning of the message.

_____ ❸ I listen without judging the speaker.

_____ ❹ I listen critically; I rarely suspend my critical, evaluative faculties.

_____ ❺ I listen to the literal meaning, to what the speaker says, rather than playing psychiatrist and focusing on the hidden or deeper meanings.

_____ ❻ I listen for the speaker's hidden meanings, to what the speaker means but isn't verbalizing.

**HOW DID YOU DO?** These statements focus on the ways of listening discussed in this chapter. All of these ways are appropriate at some times but not at others: It depends. So the only responses that are really inappropriate are "always" and "never." Effective listening is listening that is tailored to the specific communication situation.

**WHAT WILL YOU DO?** Consider how you might use your responses on this self-test to begin to improve your listening effectiveness. A good way to begin doing this is to review the statements and try to identify situations in which each statement would be appropriate and situations in which each would be inappropriate.

---

As stressed throughout this chapter, listening is situational: The type of listening that is appropriate will vary with the situation, each set of circumstances calling for a somewhat different combination of listening styles. The art of effective listening is largely a matter of making appropriate choices along the following four dimensions: (1) empathic and objective listening, (2) nonjudgmental and critical listening, (3) surface and depth listening, and (4) active and inactive listening. We'll take a look at each of these dimensions.

## Empathic and Objective Listening

If you're to understand what a person means and what a person is feeling, you need to listen with some degree of **empathy** (Rogers, 1970; Rogers & Farson, 1981). To empathize with others is to feel with them, to see the world as they see it, to feel

*"The opposite of talking isn't listening. The opposite of talking is waiting."*
—Fran Lebowitz

what they feel. Empathic listening will also help you enhance your relationships (Barrett & Godfrey, 1988; Snyder, 1992).

When you express empathy, it's often helpful to do it in two parts corresponding to the two parts in true empathy: thinking empathy and feeling empathy (Bellafiore, 2005). In *thinking empathy* you express an understanding of what the person means. For example, when you paraphrase someone's comment, showing that you understand the meaning the person is trying to communicate, you're communicating thinking empathy. The second part of empathy is *feeling empathy*; here you express your ability to feel what the other person is feeling. For example, if a friend told you of problems at home, you might respond by saying, "Your problems at home do seem to be getting worse. I can imagine how you feel so angry at times."

Although for most communication situations empathic listening is the preferred mode of responding, there are times when you need to go beyond it and to measure the speaker's meanings and feelings against some objective reality. It's important to listen as Peter tells you how the entire world hates him and to understand how Peter feels and why he feels this way. But then you need to look a bit more objectively at the situation and perhaps see Peter's paranoia or self-hatred. Sometimes you have to put your empathic responses aside and listen with objectivity and detachment. In adjusting your empathic and objective listening focus, keep the following recommendations in mind:

- Punctuate from the speaker's point of view (Chapter 1). That is, see the sequence of events as the speaker does and try to figure out how this perspective can influence what the speaker says and does.

- Engage in equal, two-way conversation. To encourage openness and empathy, try to eliminate any physical or psychological barriers to equality; for example, step from behind the large desk separating you from your employees. Avoid interrupting the speaker—a sign that what you have to say is more important.

- Seek to understand both thoughts and feelings. Don't consider your listening task finished until you've understood what the speaker is feeling as well as what he or she is thinking.

- Avoid "offensive listening"—the tendency to listen to bits and pieces of information that will enable you to attack the speaker or find fault with something the speaker has said.

- Strive especially to be objective when listening to friends or foes alike. Guard against "expectancy hearing," in which you fail to hear what the speaker is really saying and instead hear what you expect.

## Nonjudgmental and Critical Listening

Effective listening includes both nonjudgmental and critical responses. You need to listen nonjudgmentally—with an open mind and with a view toward understanding. But you also need to listen critically—with a view toward making some kind of evaluation or judgment. Clearly, it's important to listen first for understanding while suspending judgment. Only after you've fully understood the relevant messages should you evaluate or judge.

Supplement open-minded listening with critical listening. Listening with an open mind will help you understand the messages better; listening with a critical mind will help you analyze and evaluate the messages. In adjusting your nonjudgmental and critical listening, focus on the following guidelines:

- Keep an open mind. Avoid prejudging. Delay your judgments until you fully understand both the content and the intention the speaker is communicating.

### Listening to the Emotions of Others

Listening to the feelings of others is often difficult; it's often difficult to know how to react or what to say in response. Here are a few guidelines for making this often difficult process a little easier.

- *Don't equate "responding to another's feelings" with "solving the person's problems"* (Tannen, 1990). It's usually better to view your task as encouraging the person to express and perhaps to clarify his or her feelings in a supportive atmosphere.

- *Empathize.* Put yourself into the position of the other person. Be especially careful to avoid evaluating the other person's feelings. To say, for example, "Don't worry, you'll get promoted next year," can easily be interpreted as "your feelings are inappropriate."

- *Focus on the other person.* Avoid responding with your own problems. Although it's often useful to relate similar experiences that you've had, avoid refocusing the conversation on you and away from the other person.

- *Encourage the person to explore his or her feelings.* Use simple encouragers like "I see" or "I understand," or ask questions that let the speaker know that you're interested in hearing more.

***Applying Listening Skills.*** *Your best friend tells you that she suspects her boyfriend is seeing someone else. She's extremely upset and tells you that she wants to confront him with her suspicions but is afraid of what she'll hear. What listening guidelines would you suggest your friend use?*

*The first duty of love is to listen.*
—PAUL TILLICH

Avoid either positive or negative evaluation until you have a reasonably complete understanding.

- Avoid filtering out or oversimplifying difficult or complex messages. Similarly, avoid filtering out undesirable messages. Clearly, you don't want to hear that something you believe is untrue, that people you care for are unkind, or that ideals you hold are self-destructive. Yet it's important that you reexamine your beliefs by listening to these messages.

- Recognize your own biases. These may interfere with accurate listening and cause you to distort message reception through a process of **assimilation**—the tendency to integrate and interpret what you hear or think you hear in keeping with your own biases, prejudices, and expectations.

- Avoid uncritical listening when you need to make evaluations and judgments.

- Recognize and combat the normal tendency to *sharpen*—a process in which we tend to highlight, emphasize, and perhaps embellish one or two aspects of a message. Often the concepts that are sharpened are incidental remarks that somehow get emphasized and now stand out from the rest of the message.

## Surface and Depth Listening

In most messages there's an obvious meaning that you can derive from a literal reading of the words and sentences. But in reality, most messages have more than one level of meaning. Sometimes the other level is the opposite of the literal meaning; at other times it seems totally unrelated. Consider some frequently heard types of messages. Carol asks you how you like her new haircut. On one level, the meaning is clear: Do you like the haircut? But there's also another and perhaps more important level: Carol is asking you to say something positive about her appearance. In the same way, the parent who complains about working hard at the office or in the home may, on a deeper level, be asking for an expression of appreciation.

**"I was distracted for a moment. Go on."**

To appreciate these other meanings, you need to engage in depth listening. If you respond only to the surface-level communication (the literal meaning), you miss the opportunity to make meaningful contact with the other person's feelings and needs. If you say to the parent, "You're always complaining. I bet you really love working so hard," you fail to respond to this call for understanding and appreciation. In regulating your surface and depth listening, consider the following guidelines:

- **Focus on both verbal and nonverbal messages.** Recognize both consistent and inconsistent "packages" of messages and use these as guides for drawing inferences about the speaker's meaning. Ask questions when in doubt. Listen also to what is omitted. Remember that speakers communicate by what they leave out as well as by what they include.

- **Listen for both content and relational messages.** The student who constantly challenges the teacher is on one level communicating disagreement over content. However, on another level—the relationship level—the student may be voicing objections to the instructor's authority or authoritarianism. The instructor needs to listen and respond to both types of messages.

- **Make special note of statements that refer back to the speaker.** Remember that people inevitably talk about themselves. Whatever a person says is, in part, a function of who that person is. Attend carefully to those personal, self-referential messages.

- **Don't disregard the literal meaning of interpersonal messages.** Balance your listening between surface and underlying meanings. Respond to the different levels of meaning in the messages of others as you would like others to respond to yours—sensitively but not obsessively, readily but not overambitiously.

## Active and Inactive Listening

One of the most important communication skills you can learn is that of **active listening.** Consider the following interaction. You're disappointed that you have to redo your entire budget report, and you say, "I can't believe I have to redo this entire report. I really worked hard on this project and now I have to do it all over again." To this you get three different responses:

**Annette:** That's not so bad; most people find they have to redo their first reports. That's the norm here.
**Caroline:** You should be pleased that all you have to do is a simple rewrite. Peggy and Michael both had to completely redo their entire projects.
**Barbara:** You have to rewrite that report you've worked on for the last three weeks? You sound really angry and frustrated.

All three listeners are probably trying to make you feel better. But they go about it in very different ways and, it appears, with very different results. Annette tries to lessen the significance of the rewrite. This type of well-intended and extremely common response does little to promote meaningful communication and understanding. Caroline tries to give the situation a positive spin. In their responses, however, both Annette and Caroline are also suggesting that you should not be feeling the way you do; they're implying that your feelings are not legitimate and should be replaced with more logical feelings.

Barbara's response, however, is different from the others. Barbara uses active listening. Active listening owes its development to Thomas Gordon (1975), who made it a cornerstone of his P-E-T (Parent Effectiveness Training) technique; it is a process of sending back to the speaker what you as a listener think the speaker meant—both in content and in feelings. Active listening, then, is not merely repeat-

**WHAT DO YOU SAY?**
**Active Listening**
Your life partner comes home from work visibly upset and clearly has a need to talk about what happened—but simply says, "Work sucks!" You're determined to use active listening techniques. *What do you say? Through what channel?*

ing the speaker's exact words, but rather putting together into some meaningful whole your understanding of the speaker's total message.

Active listening helps you check your understanding of what the speaker said and, more important, what he or she meant. Reflecting back perceived meanings to the speaker gives the speaker an opportunity to offer clarification and correct any misunderstandings. Active listening also lets the speaker know that you acknowledge and accept his or her feelings. In the sample responses given above, Barbara listened actively and reflected back what she thought you meant while accepting what you were feeling. Note too that she also explicitly identified your emotions ("You sound angry and frustrated"), allowing you the opportunity to correct her interpretation. Still another function of active listening is that it stimulates the speaker to explore feelings and thoughts. Barbara's response encourages you to elaborate on your feelings and perhaps to better understand them as you talk them through. And finally, when combined with empathic listening, active listening proves the most effective approach for successful sales transactions (Comer & Drollinger, 1999).

Three simple techniques may help you succeed in active listening: Paraphrase the speaker's meaning, express understanding, and ask questions.

- *Paraphrase the speaker's meaning.* Stating in your own words what you think the speaker means and feels can help ensure understanding and demonstrates your interest. Paraphrasing gives the speaker a chance to extend what was originally said. But in paraphrasing, be objective; be especially careful not to lead the speaker in the direction you think he or she should go. Also, don't overdo paraphrasing. Paraphrase when you feel there's a chance for misunderstanding or when you want to express support for the other person and keep the conversation going.

- *Express understanding of the speaker's feelings.* In addition to paraphrasing the content, echo the feelings the speaker expressed or implied ("You must have felt horrible"). This expression of feelings will help you further check your perception of the speaker's feelings. It also will allow the speaker to see his or her feelings more objectively—especially helpful when they're feelings of anger, hurt, or depression—and to elaborate on these feelings.

- *Ask questions.* Asking questions strengthens your own understanding of the speaker's thoughts and feelings and elicits additional information ("How did you feel when you read your job appraisal report?"). Ask questions to provide just enough stimulation and support so the speaker will feel he or she can elaborate on these thoughts and feelings.

# Listening Differences: Culture and Gender

Listening is difficult in part because of the inevitable differences in the communication systems between speakers and listeners. Because each person has had a unique set of experiences, each person's communication and meaning system is going to be different from each other person's. When speaker and listener come from different cultures or are of different genders, the differences and their effects are naturally much greater.

## Listening and Culture

In today's multicultural world, where people from very different cultures live and work together, it's especially important to understand the ways in which cultural differences can influence listening. Three of these cultural influences on listening are (1) language and speech, (2) nonverbal behaviors, and (3) feedback.

**WHAT DO YOU SAY?**

**Listening Avoidance**

Your best friend's latest relationship has just broken up, and your friend comes to you in the hope that you'll listen to all the details. This seems to happen about once a week. You're fed up; you're determined not to spend the next three hours listening to this tale of woe. *What do you say?*

**Language and Speech** Even when a speaker and a listener speak the same language, they speak it with different meanings and different accents. Speakers of the same language will, at the very least, have different meanings for the same terms because they have had different experiences.

Speakers and listeners who have different native languages and who may have learned English as a second language will have even greater differences in meaning. If you learned your meaning for *house* in a culture in which everyone lived in their own house with lots of land around it, then communicating with someone whose meaning of house was learned in a neighborhood of high-rise tenements is going to be difficult. Although each of you will hear the word *house*, the meanings you'll develop will be drastically different. In adjusting your listening—especially in an intercultural setting—understand that the speaker's meanings may be very different from yours even though you're speaking the same language.

In many classrooms throughout the United States, there will be a wide range of accents. Those whose native language is a tonal one such as Chinese (in which differences in pitch signal important meaning differences) may speak English with variations in pitch that may be puzzling to others. Those whose native language is Japanese may have trouble distinguishing *l* from *r*, because Japanese does not include this distinction. The native language acts as a filter and influences the accent given to the second language.

**Nonverbal Behaviors** Speakers from different cultures have different *display rules*, cultural rules that govern which nonverbal behaviors are appropriate and which are inappropriate in a public setting. As you listen to other people, you also "listen" to their nonverbals. If nonverbal signals are drastically different from what you would expect on the basis of the verbal message, you may see them as a kind of noise or interference or even as contradictory messages. If a colleague at work, for example, consistently averts her eyes when talking with you, it may not be an indication of shyness or dishonesty (which are often associated with averted eyes), but merely a sign that your colleague's culture discourages direct eye contact. Different cultures often have very different meanings for the same nonverbal gesture. For example, the thumb and forefinger forming a circle means "OK" in most of the United States; but it means "money" in Japan, "zero" in some Mediterranean countries, and "I'll kill you" in Tunisia.

**Feedback** Members of some cultures give very direct and very honest feedback. Speakers from these cultures—the United States is a good example—expect feedback to be an honest reflection of what their listeners are feeling. In other cultures—Japan and Korea are good examples—it's more important to be positive than to be truthful. As a result, people may respond with positive feedback (say, in commenting on a business colleague's proposal) even though they don't really feel positive. Listen to feedback, as you would to all messages, with a full recognition that various cultures view feedback very differently.

## Listening and Gender

Deborah Tannen opens her chapter on listening in her best-selling *You Just Don't Understand: Women and Men in Conversation* (1990) with several anecdotes illustrating that when men and women talk, men lecture and women listen. The lecturer assumes the role of the superior or that of the teacher or expert. The listener is then made to assume the role of the inferior, the student, or the nonexpert.

Women, according to Tannen, seek to build rapport and establish relationships and so use listening to achieve these ends. For example, women use more listening cues that let the other person know they are paying attention and are interested. Men not only use fewer listening cues but also interrupt more. Additionally, men will often change the topic to an area they know more about or switch from a sub-

**WHAT DO YOU SAY?**

**Listening Cues**

Friends have told you that people don't address comments directly to you because you don't give listening cues to let the other person know that you're listening and that you're understanding what is being said. You're determined to change this. *What do you say?*

ject that is relational or people oriented to a topic that is more factual, such as sports statistics, economic developments, or political problems. Men, research shows, play up their expertise, emphasize it, and use it to dominate the conversation. Women play down their expertise.

Now, you might be tempted to conclude from this that women play fair in conversation and that men don't—for example, you might think that men consistently seek to put themselves in a position superior to women. But this may be too simple an explanation. Research shows that men communicate this way not only with women but with other men as well. Men are not showing disrespect for their female conversational partners; they are simply communicating as they normally do. Women, too, communicate as they do not only with men but also with other women.

Tannen argues that the goal of a man in conversation is to be accorded respect. Therefore, a man seeks to display his knowledge and expertise even if he has to change from a topic he knows little about to something he knows a great deal about. A woman, on the other hand, seeks to be liked; so she expresses agreement, rarely interrupts a man to take her turn as speaker, and gives a lot of verbal and nonverbal cues to show that she is listening.

Men and women also show that they are listening in different ways. A woman is more apt to give lots of listening cues, such as interjecting, "Yeah, uh-uh," nodding in agreement, and smiling. Women also make more eye contact when listening than men do; men are more apt to look around and away from the speaker (Brownell, 2006). A man is more likely to listen quietly, without giving lots of listening cues as feedback. Tannen also argues, however, that men do listen less to women than women listen to men. The reason, says Tannen, is that listening places the person in an inferior position whereas speaking places the person in a superior position.

There is no evidence to show that these differences represent any negative motives on the part of men to prove themselves superior or of women to ingratiate themselves. Rather, these differences in listening are largely the result of the way in which men and women have been socialized. Also, it should be mentioned that not all researchers would agree that there is sufficient evidence to support the claims that Tannen and others make about gender differences (Goldsmith & Fulfs, 1999). In any case, in U.S. society gender differences are undergoing many changes. So it's best to take all generalizations about gender as starting points for investigation and not as airtight conclusions.

 **E-TALK**

**Internet Noise**
Spam and pop-ups are visual noise and, like any kind of noise, interfere with your receiving the messages you want to receive. Check out the ways your ISP allows you to block unwanted messages. Blocking these intrusions will help you attend to the desired messages.

# *Skill Development Experience*

## Regulating Your Listening Perspective

In *situational listening* you regulate your listening style according to the specific circumstances. What listening styles would you most likely use in each of these situations? What listening styles would be obviously inappropriate in each situation?

1. Your steady dating partner for the last five years tells you that spells of depression are becoming more frequent and more long lasting.

2. Your five-year-old daughter says she wants to become a nurse.

3. Your brother tells you he's been accepted into Harvard's MBA program.

4. Your supervisor explains the new computerized mail system.

*Regulate your listening on the basis of the specific situation in which you find yourself.*

This chapter has discussed the way you listen and how you can listen more effectively.

1. Listening may be defined as "the process of receiving, constructing meaning from, and responding to spoken and/or nonverbal messages."
2. Listening serves a variety of purposes: You listen to learn; to relate to others; to influence the attitudes, beliefs, and behaviors of others; to play; and to help.
3. Listening is a five-step process consisting of receiving, understanding, remembering, evaluating, and responding. Receiving is essentially the hearing process; the messages from another person are received at this stage. Understanding is the stage of comprehension; you make sense out of the messages. In the remembering stage you store messages and your understanding of them in your memory for at least some time. In evaluating you judge the messages and apply your critical thinking skills to them. The final stage, responding, includes both the responses you make while the speaker is speaking and the responses you may make after the speaker has stopped talking.
4. Effective listening involves a process of making adjustments—depending on the situation—along dimensions such as empathic and objective listening, nonjudgmental and critical listening, surface and depth listening, and active and inactive listening.
5. Culture influences listening in a variety of ways. Contributing to listening difficulties are cultural differences in language and speech, nonverbal behaviors, and differences in giving feedback.
6. Men and women listen differently and perhaps for different reasons. For example, women give more messages that say, "I'm listening" than men. According to some theorists, women use listening to show empathy and to build rapport, whereas men minimize listening because it puts them in a subordinate position.

Throughout this discussion of listening, a variety of skills were identified. Place a check mark next to those skills that you feel you need to work on most.

_____ 1. I recognize that listening serves a variety of purposes, and I adjust my listening on the basis of my purposes; for example, to learn, relate, influence, play, or help.

_____ 2. I realize that listening is a multistage process, and I regulate my listening behavior as appropriate in receiving, understanding, remembering, evaluating, and responding.

_____ 3. In receiving messages I seek to increase my chances of effective listening by, for example, paying attention to the speaker's verbal and nonverbal messages; avoiding distractions; and focusing on what the speaker is saying, not on what I'm going to say next.

_____ 4. I facilitate understanding in listening by relating new information to what I already know and trying to see the messages from the speaker's point of view.

_____ 5. In remembering the speaker's messages, I try to identify the central ideas and the major supporting materials, summarize the main ideas, and repeat important concepts to etch them more firmly in my mind.

_____ 6. In evaluating messages, I first make sure I understand the speaker's point of view and seek to identify any sources of bias or self-interest.

_____ 7. In responding, I am supportive of the speaker and own my own thoughts and feelings.

_____ 8. I am especially careful to adjust my listening on the basis of the immediate situation between empathic and objective, nonjudgmental and critical, surface and depth, and active and inactive listening.

_____ 9. I practice active listening when appropriate by paraphrasing the speaker's meaning, expressing my understanding of the speaker's feelings, and asking questions.

_____ 10. I recognize the influence of culture on listening and the cultural differences in listening and take these into consideration when listening in intercultural situations.

_____ 11. I recognize gender differences in listening and take these into consideration when communicating with members of the opposite sex.

# Key Word Quiz

## The Language of Listening

Match the terms about listening with their definitions. Record the number of the definition next to the appropriate term.

a. _____ active listening

b. _____ paraphrasing

c. _____ situational listening

d. _____ disclaiming

e. _____ listening

f. _____ assimilation

g. _____ backchanneling cues

h. _____ memory

i. _____ I-messages

j. _____ empathic listening

1. The process of asking the listener to receive your message without prejudice, to give you a fair hearing.

2. A reconstructive rather than a reproductive process.

3. The tendency to integrate and interpret what you hear or think you hear in terms of your own expectations and biases.

4. A process of sending back to the speaker what you think the speaker meant.

5. Restating what another says but in your own words.

6. An approach to listening in which effective listening style depends on the specifics of the communication interaction.

7. A five-step process consisting of receiving, understanding, remembering, evaluating, and responding.

8. Listening responses that let the speaker know that you're paying attention.

9. Listening to what a person is feeling as well as to what the person is thinking.

10. Messages in which you take responsibility for your thoughts and actions rather than attributing these to others.

**Answers: a. 4; b. 5; c. 6; d. 1; e. 7; f. 3; g. 8; h. 2; i. 10; j. 9**

# Five for Discussion

1. Would you find it difficult to listen to friends who were complaining that the insurance premium on their Lexus SUV was going up? Would you find it difficult to listen to friends complain that their rent was going up and that they feared becoming homeless? If there is a difference, why?

2. Memory in listening (or in seeing or reading) is never perfect. You never store in your memory exactly what you hear (or see or read). A particularly interesting aspect of this, *false memory syndrome*, is the tendency to "remember" past experiences that never actually occurred. Most of the studies on false memory syndrome have centered on beliefs of abuse and other traumatic experiences. Often these false memories are implanted by therapists and interviewers whose persistent questioning over a period of time creates such a realistic scenario that the in-

dividual comes to believe these things actually occurred (Porter, Brit, Yuille, & Lehman, 2000). In what other, less dramatic ways can false memory syndrome occur?

3. Although empathy has an almost universally positive image, some evidence suggests that empathy also has a negative side. For example, people are most empathic with those who are similar—racially and ethnically as well as in appearance and social status. The more empathy you feel toward your own group, the less empathy—and possibly even the more hostility—you feel toward other groups. The same empathy that increases your understanding of your own group decreases your understanding of other groups. So although empathy may encourage group cohesiveness and identification, it can also create dividing lines between your group and

"them" (Angier, 1995). Have you ever experienced or witnessed these negative effects of empathy?

4. A popular belief, as this chapter has described, is that men listen the way they do to prove themselves superior and that women listen as they do to ingratiate themselves. Although there is no evidence to support this be-lief, it persists in the assumptions people make about the opposite sex. What do you believe accounts for the differences in the way men and women listen?

5. Consider this dialogue and note the active listening techniques used throughout:

**Pat:** That jerk demoted me. He told me I wasn't an effective manager. I can't believe he did that, after all I've done for this place.

**Chris:** I'm with you. You've been manager for like three or four months now, right?

**Pat:** A little over three months. It was probationary and all, but I thought I was doing a good job.

**Chris:** Can you get another chance?

**Pat:** Well, he said I could try again in a few months. But I don't know if I even want to try again.

**Chris:** I hear you. I hear you. Man, that sucks. What else did he say?

**Pat:** He said I had trouble getting the paperwork done on time.

**Chris:** What, were you late filing the reports?

**Pat:** A few times, I guess. There's just so much to get done. A lot of responsibility, you know?

**Chris:** I know. But, is there some way to delegate some of that paperwork?

**Pat:** Maybe. Something like that might work. I think if I could learn to manage my time better, I could make things right.

**Chris:** So, are you gonna give that manager's position another try?

**Pat:** You know, I think I might. I'm going to let him know tomorrow that I intend to apply again in the next few months.

## Log On! MyCommunicationLab

Useful exercises to further illustrate the concepts and principles of listening include (www.mycommunicationlab.com): (1) Sequential Communication, (2) Listening Actively, (3) Your Own Listening Barriers, and (4) Typical man. Typical woman.

Visit MyCommunicationLab for study guides, activities, and video clips on the nature of listening and its role in all forms of human communication.

Explore our research resources at www.researchnavigator.com.

Research
Navigator.com

# Verbal Messages

## Why Read This Chapter?

Because you'll **learn about:**

- the nature of verbal messages.
- the principles governing verbal messages.

Because you'll **learn to:**

- use verbal messages more effectively in all your communication experiences.
- avoid language that might be considered sexist, heterosexist, racist, or ageist, any of which would likely have negative consequences.
- avoid common pitfalls of language usage that can also distort your thinking.

*Y*our messages normally occur in "packages" consisting of both verbal and nonverbal signals (Pittenger, Hockett, & Danehy, 1960). Usually, verbal and nonverbal behaviors reinforce or support each other. For example, you don't usually express fear with words while the rest of your body relaxes. You don't normally express anger with your face while your words are warm and cheerful. Your entire being works as a whole—verbally and nonverbally—to express your thoughts and feelings. When you communicate, you use two major signal systems—verbal and nonverbal.

This chapter focuses on the verbal message system—the system's key principles, the concepts of confirmation and disconfirmation, and the ways you can use verbal messages most effectively. The next chapter will examine the nonverbal message system.

## Principles of Verbal Messages

As you grew up, you learned the language of the people around you. You learned its *phonological* or sound system; its *semantic* system, or system of word meanings; and its *syntactic* system, which enabled you to put words into meaningful sentence patterns. Our concern in this chapter is not with the grammatical structure of language (that's the linguist's job) but with the verbal messages you speak and hear and sometimes read. These verbal messages, of course, rely on the rules of grammar; you can't just make up sounds or words or string words together at random and expect to be understood. But following the rules of grammar, as we'll see, is not enough to achieve effective communication. Instead, you need to understand the principles of verbal messages. We'll look at five principles, beginning with the fact that verbal messages are both denotative and connotative.

### Messages Are Denotative and Connotative

You speak both denotatively and connotatively. **Denotation** has to do with the objective meaning of a term, the meaning you would find in a dictionary. It's the meaning that people who share a common language assign to a word. **Connotation** is the subjective or emotional meaning that specific speakers or listeners give to a word. Take as an example the word *death.* To a doctor, this word might mean (or denote) the time when the heart stops beating. This is an objective description of a particular event. On the other hand, to a mother who is informed of her son's death, the word means (or connotes) much more. It recalls her son's youth, ambition, family, illness, and so on. To her it is a highly emotional, subjective, and personal word. These emotional, subjective, or personal reactions are the word's connotative meaning.

Take another example: Compare the word *migrants* (used to designate Mexicans coming into the United States to better their economic condition) with the word *settlers* (meaning Europeans who came to the United States for the same reason) (Koppelman, with Goodhart, 2005). Though both terms describe essentially the same activity (and are essentially the same denotatively), they differ widely in their connotations, with one word often negatively evaluated and the other more often positively valued.

Semanticist S. I. Hayakawa (Hayakawa & Hayakawa, 1989) coined the terms **snarl words** and **purr words** to clarify further the distinction between denotation and connotation. Snarl words are highly negative: "She's an idiot," "He's a pig," "They're a bunch of losers." Purr words are highly positive: "She's a real sweetheart," "He's a dream," "They're the greatest." Snarl and purr words, although they may sometimes seem to have denotative meaning and to refer to the "real world," are actually connotative in meaning. These terms do not describe objective realities but rather express the speaker's feelings about people or events.

## Messages Vary in Abstraction

Consider the following list of terms:

entertainment

film

American film

Classic American film

*Casablanca*

At the top is an **abstraction** or general concept—the word *entertainment*. Note that *entertainment* includes all the other items on the list plus various other items—*television, novels, drama, comics,* and so on. *Film* is more specific and concrete. It includes all of the items below it as well as various other items such as *Indian film* or *Russian film.* It excludes, however, all entertainment that is not film. *American film* is again more specific than *film* and excludes all films that are not American. *Classic American film* further limits *American film* to those considered timeless. *Casablanca* specifies concretely the one item to which reference is made.

As this example illustrates, verbal messages vary from general and abstract to specific and concrete. Effective verbal messages include words from a wide range of abstractions. At times, a general term may suit your needs best; at other times, a more specific term may serve better. Generally, however, the specific term will prove the better choice. As you get more specific—less abstract—you more effectively guide the images that come to your listeners' minds.

## Messages Vary in Directness

Think about how you would respond to someone who said the following:

1A. "I'm so bored; I have nothing to do tonight."

2A. "I'd like to go to the movies. Would you like to come?"

1B. "Would you feel like hamburgers tonight?"

2B. "I'd like hamburgers tonight. How about you?"

Verbal messages may be direct or indirect. In these examples the messages numbered 1 represent **indirect speech:** They're attempts to get the listener to say or do something without committing the speaker, without the speaker's having to take responsibility. The messages numbered 2 represent more **direct speech**—they more clearly state the speaker's preferences and then ask if the listener agrees. (Note that many indirect messages are nonverbal, as when you glance at your watch to communicate that it is late and that you had better be going.)

Although the initial reaction is to favor direct statements as more honest and more open (which they are), indirect messages are not without merit. For example, indirect messages allow you to express a desire without insulting or offending anyone; they allow you to observe the rules of polite interaction. So instead of saying, "I'm bored with this conversation," you say, "It's getting late and I have to get up early tomorrow," or you look at your watch and pretend to be surprised by the time. In this way you can state your preference indirectly and so avoid offending someone.

Sometimes indirect messages allow you to ask for compliments in a socially acceptable manner. For example, if you say, "I was thinking of getting a nose job," you may be hoping to get a response such as "A nose job? You? Your nose is perfect."

**"I'd like you to head up the new team of the recently let go."**

Indirect messages, however, can also create problems. They're often ambiguous and can easily be misunderstood. A question such as "Do you enjoy French food?" may be a simple request for culinary information or an indirect way of asking if you'd like to go on a dinner date.

Indirect messages may also be seen as manipulative—as attempts to get something without openly asking for it, as in "All my friends have a really big party for their first anniversary." Although you're not explicitly asking for a big party, you are nevertheless asking for a big party.

## Message Meanings Are in People

To discover the meanings people try to communicate, it's necessary to look into the people in addition to the words. An example of the confusion that can result when this relatively simple fact is not taken into consideration was provided by Ronald D. Laing, H. Phillipson, and A. Russell Lee (1966) and analyzed with insight by Paul Watzlawick (1977). A couple on the second night of their honeymoon are sitting at a hotel bar. The woman strikes up a conversation with the couple next to her. The husband refuses to communicate with the couple and becomes antagonistic toward both them and his wife. The wife then grows angry because he has created such an awkward and unpleasant situation. Each becomes increasingly disturbed, and the evening ends in a bitter conflict, with each convinced of the other's lack of consideration. Eight years later, they analyze this argument. Apparently the concept *honeymoon* had meant different things to each. To the husband, their honeymoon would be a "golden opportunity to ignore the rest of the world and simply explore each other." He felt his wife's interaction with the other couple implied there was something lacking in him. To the wife, the honeymoon meant an opportunity to try out her new role as wife. "I had never had a conversation with another couple as a wife before," she said. "Previous to this I had always been a 'girlfriend' or 'fiancée' or 'daughter' or 'sister.'"

Also recognize that as you change, you also change the meanings you created out of past messages. Thus, although the message sent may not have changed, the meanings you created from it yesterday and the meanings you create today may be quite different. Yesterday, when a special someone said, "I love you," you created certain meanings. But today, when you learn that the same "I love you" was said to three other people or when you fall in love with someone else, you drastically change the meanings you perceive from those three words.

## Messages Are Influenced by Culture and Gender

Your verbal messages are influenced in large part by your culture and gender. Let's look first at some of the cultural influences.

**Cultural Influences**    Your culture teaches you that certain ways of using verbal messages are acceptable and certain ways are not. When you follow these **cultural rules** or principles in communicating, you're seen as a properly functioning member of the culture. When you violate the principles, you risk being seen as deviant or perhaps as insulting. Here are a variety of such principles:

- *The principle of cooperation.* The principle of **cooperation** holds that in any communication interaction, both parties will make an effort to help each other understand each other. That is, we assume cooperation. This general principle has four subprinciples or **conversational maxims.** As you read down the list, ask yourself how you follow these maxims in your everyday conversation:

  - The maxim of *quality:* Say what you know or assume to be true, and do not say what you know to be false.

**WHAT DO YOU SAY?**
**Cultural Maxims**
In introducing yourself to your class, you tell of your high grades, success in sports, and plans to transfer to Harvard. The students following you, however, all appear very modest. You quickly realize that you misunderstood the culture of this classroom. *What do you say?*

- The maxim of *relation*: Talk about what is relevant to the conversation.
- The maxim of *manner*: Be clear, avoid ambiguities (as much as possible), be relatively brief, and organize your thoughts into a meaningful pattern.
- The maxim of *quantity*: Be as informative as necessary to communicate the information.

■ *The principle of peaceful relations.* This principle holds that when you communicate, your primary goal is to maintain peaceful relationships. This means that you would never insult anyone; in fact, when communicating according to this principle, you may even express agreement with someone when you really disagree, which violates the principle of cooperation and the maxim of quality (Midooka, 1990).

■ *The principle of face-saving.* **Face-saving** messages are those that preserve the image of the other person and do nothing to make them appear in a negative light. The principle holds that you should never embarrass anyone, especially in public. Always allow people to save face, even if this means avoiding the truth—as when you tell someone he or she did good work although the job was actually poorly executed. Many Asian and Latin American cultures stress the value of indirectness because it helps people avoid overt criticism and the loss of face.

■ *The principle of self-denigration.* This principle advises you to avoid taking credit for accomplishments and to minimize your abilities or talents in conversation (Gu, 1997). At the same time, through self-denigration you would raise the image of the people with whom you're talking.

■ *The principle of directness.* As explained earlier, directness and indirectness communicate different impressions. Levels of directness also vary greatly from culture to culture. In most of the United States, directness is the preferred style. "Be up front" and "Tell it like it is" are commonly heard communication guidelines. Contrast these with the following two principles of indirectness found in the Japanese language (Tannen, 1994a):

**E-TALK**

**Chain E-mails**
In what ways do chain e-mails (with or without lengthy attachments) violate the conversational maxims listed here? What would be the face-to-face counterpart of chain e-mails?

## COMMUNICATING ETHICALLY

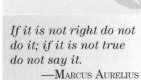

### Communicating in Cyberspace

The same principles that govern ethical face-to-face interaction should also prevail when you communicate on the Internet. Here, however, are a few ethical principles with special relevance to computer communication. It is unethical to:

1. *Invade the privacy of others.* Reading the files of another person or breaking into files that you're not authorized to read is unethical.
2. *Harm others or their property.* Creating computer viruses; publishing instructions for making bombs; or creating websites that promote racism, heterosexism, ageism, or sexism, for example, would be unethical.
3. *Spread falsehoods.* Lying on the Internet—about other people, about the powers of medical or herbal treatment, or about yourself—is unethical.
4. *Plagiarize.* Appropriating the work of another as your own, whether the original work appeared on the Internet or in a book or journal, is unethical.
5. *Steal the passwords, PIN numbers, or authorization codes that belong to others.*
6. *Copy software programs or download music that you haven't paid for.*

*If it is not right do not do it; if it is not true do not say it.*
—MARCUS AURELIUS

***What Would You Do?*** *As an experiment you develop a computer program that can destroy websites. Recently, you've come across a variety of websites that you feel promote child pornography. You wonder if you can ethically destroy these websites. What do you decide?*

- *Omoiyari*, close to empathy, says that listeners need to understand the speaker without the speaker's being specific or direct. This style places a much greater demand on the listener than would a direct speaking style.
- *Sassuru* advises listeners to anticipate a speaker's meanings and to use subtle cues from the speaker to infer his or her total meaning.

- *The principle of politeness.* Most cultures have a **politeness** principle, but cultures differ in the way they define politeness and in how much they emphasize politeness compared with, say openness or honesty (Mao, 1994; Strecker, 1993). It is often noted that Asians, especially the Chinese and Japanese, emphasize politeness more and mete out harsher social punishments for violations than would most people, in, say, the United States or Western Europe (Fraser, 1990).

Cultural differences often can create misunderstanding. For example, a person from a culture that values an indirect style of speech may be speaking indirectly to be polite. If, however, you're from a culture that values a more direct style of speech, you may assume that the person is using indirectness to be manipulative, because this may be how your culture regards indirectness.

**Gender Influences**     Verbal messages also reflect considerable gender influences. For example, take politeness (Holmes, 1995). Generally, studies from various different cultures show that women's speech is more polite than men's speech, even on the telephone (Brown, 1980; Wetzel, 1988; Holmes, 1995; Smoreda & Licoppe, 2000). Women seek areas of agreement in conversation and in conflict situations more often than men do. Similarly, young girls are more apt to try to modify expressions of disagreement, whereas young boys are more apt to express more "bald disagreements" (Holmes, 1995). Women also use more polite speech when seeking to gain another person's compliance than men do (Baxter, 1984).

The popular stereotype in much of the United States holds that women tend to be indirect in making requests and in giving orders—and that this indirectness communicates a powerlessness and discomfort with their own authority. Men, the stereotype continues, tend to be direct, sometimes to the point of being blunt or rude. This directness communicates power and comfort with their authority. Deborah Tannen (1994a) provides an interesting perspective on these stereotypes. Women are, it seems, more indirect in giving orders; they are more likely to say, for example, "It would be great if these letters could go out today" than "Have these letters out by three." But, Tannen (1994a, p. 84) argues, "issuing orders indirectly can be the prerogative of those in power" and does not show powerlessness. Power, to Tannen, is the ability to choose your own style of communication.

Men also can be indirect, but in different situations. For example, men are more likely to use indirectness when they express weakness, reveal a problem, or admit an error (Rundquist, 1992; Tannen, 1994a, 1994b). Men are more likely to speak indirectly when expressing emotions other than anger. They also tend to be more indirect when they refuse expressions of increased romantic intimacy. Men are thus indirect, the theory goes, when they are saying something that goes against the masculine stereotype.

There also are gender similarities. For example, in both the United States and New Zealand, men and women seem to pay compliments in similar ways (Manes & Wolfson, 1981; Holmes, 1995), and both men and women use politeness strategies when communicating bad news in an organization (Lee, 1993).

## Disconfirmation and Confirmation

The terms *confirmation* and *disconfirmation* refer to the extent to which you acknowledge another person. Consider this situation. You've been living with someone for the last six months and you arrive home late one night. Your partner, let's say Pat, is angry and complains about your being so late. Which of the following is most likely to be your response?

1. Stop screaming. I'm not interested in what you're babbling about. I'll do what I want, when I want. I'm going to bed.

2. What are you so angry about? Didn't you get in three hours late last Thursday when you went to that office party? So knock it off.

3. You have a right to be angry. I should have called to tell you I was going to be late, but I got involved in an argument at work, and I couldn't leave until it was resolved.

In response 1, you dismiss Pat's anger and even indicate dismissal of Pat as a person. In response 2, you reject the validity of Pat's reasons for being angry but do not dismiss either Pat's feelings of anger or Pat as a person. In response 3, you acknowledge Pat's anger and the reasons for it. In addition, you provide some kind of explanation and, in doing so, show that both Pat's feelings and Pat as a person are important and that Pat has the right to know what happened. The first response is an example of disconfirmation, the second of rejection, and the third of confirmation.

Psychologist William James once observed that "no more fiendish punishment could be devised, even were such a thing physically possible, than that one should be turned loose in society and remain absolutely unnoticed by all the members thereof." In this often-quoted observation, James identifies the essence of disconfirmation (Watzlawick, Beavin, & Jackson, 1967; Veenendall & Feinstein, 1995). **Disconfirmation** is a communication pattern in which we ignore someone's presence as well as that person's communications. We say, in effect, that this person and what this person has to say are not worth serious attention or effort—that this person and this person's contributions are so unimportant or insignificant that there is no reason to concern ourselves with her or him. The Amish community practices an extreme form of disconfirmation called "shunning," in which the community members totally ignore a person who has violated one or more of their rules. The specific aim of shunning is to get the person to repent and to reenter the community of the faithful. But it seems that all cultures practice some form of exclusion for those who violate important cultural rules.

Note that disconfirmation is not the same as **rejection.** In rejection, you disagree with the person; you indicate your unwillingness to accept something the other person says or does. In disconfirming someone, however, you deny that person's significance; you claim that what this person says or does simply does not count.

**Confirmation** is the opposite communication pattern. In confirmation you not only acknowledge the presence of the other person but also indicate your acceptance of this person, of this person's self-definition, and of your relationship as defined or viewed by this other person. Disconfirmation and confirmation may be communicated in a wide variety of ways. Table 4.1 shows just a few examples.

You can gain insight into a wide variety of offensive language practices by viewing them as types of disconfirmation—as language that alienates and separates. Four obvious disconfirming practices are racism, heterosexism, ageism, and sexism; and we'll look at these practices next.

Another -ism is **ableism**—discrimination against people with disabilities. This particular practice is handled throughout this text in a series of tables offering tips for communicating between people with and without a variety of disabilities:

- between blind and sighted people (Chapter 1)
- between people with and without disabilities (Chapter 2)
- between deaf and hearing people (Chapter 3)
- between people with and without speech and language disorders (Chapter 6)

▼ **E-TALK**

**Gender Differences in E-Mail**
Studies of gender differences find that women's e-mails are more relational and expressive and that they focus more on domestic and personal topics than do men's e-mails (Colley, Todd, Bland, Holmes, Khanom, & Pike, 2004). Do you find this difference in your own e-mail experience?

## TABLE 4.1 Confirmation and Disconfirmation

As you review this table, try to imagine a specific illustration for each of the ways of communicating disconfirmation and confirmation (Pearson, 1993; Galvin, Bylund, & Brommel, 2004).

**CONFIRMATION**

1. Acknowledge the presence and the contributions of the other by either supporting or taking issue with what the other says.

2. Make nonverbal contact by maintaining direct eye contact, touching, hugging, kissing, or otherwise demonstrating acknowledgment of the other; engage in *dialogue*—communication in which both persons are speakers and listeners, both are involved, and both are concerned with each other.

3. Demonstrate understanding of what the other says and means and reflect these feelings to demonstrate your understanding.

4. Ask questions of the other concerning both thoughts and feelings and acknowledge the questions of the other; return phone calls, and answer e-mails and letters.

5. Encourage the other to express thoughts and feelings, and respond directly and exclusively to what the other says.

**DISCONFIRMATION**

1. Ignore the presence and the messages of the other person; ignore or express (nonverbally and verbally) indifference to anything the other says.

2. Make no nonverbal contact; avoid direct eye contact; avoid touching the other person; engage in *monologue*—communication in which one person speaks and one person listens, there is no real interaction, and there is no real concern or respect for each other.

3. Jump to interpretation or evaluation rather than working at understanding what the other means; express your own feelings, ignore the feelings of the other, or give abstract, intellectualized responses.

4. Make statements about yourself; ignore any lack of clarity in the other's remarks; ignore the other's requests; and fail to answer questions, return phone calls, or answer e-mails and letters.

5. Interrupt or otherwise make it difficult for the other to express him- or herself; respond only tangentially or by shifting the focus in another direction.

## Racism

According to Andrea Rich (1974), "any language that, through a conscious or unconscious attempt by the user, places a particular racial or ethnic group in an inferior position is racist." **Racist language** expresses racist attitudes. It also, however, contributes to the development of racist attitudes in those who use or hear the language. Even when racism is subtle, unintentional, or even unconscious, its effects are systematically damaging (Dovidio, Gaertner, Kawakami, & Hodson, 2002).

Racism exists on both individual and institutional levels—a distinction made by educational researchers Kent Koppelman and R. Lee Goodhart (2005) and used throughout this discussion. *Individual racism* takes the form of negative attitudes and beliefs that people hold about specific races. Assumptions that certain races are intellectually inferior to others or that certain races are incapable of certain achievements are clear examples of individual racism. Prejudices against American Indians, African Americans, Hispanics, and Arabs have been with us throughout history and are still a part of many people's lives today. Such racism is seen in the negative terms some people use to refer to members of other races and to disparage their customs and accomplishments.

*Institutional racism* takes forms such as communities' de facto school segregation, companies' reluctance to hire members of minority groups, and banks' unwillingness to extend mortgages or business loans to members of some ethnic groups, or readiness to charge these groups higher interest rates.

Examine your own language racism. Do you:

- avoid using derogatory terms for members of a particular race?
- avoid basing your interactions with members of other races on stereotypes perpetuated by the media?

*"For me, words are a form of action, capable of influencing change."*

—INGRID BENGIS

*Skill Development Experience*

## Confirming, Rejecting, and Disconfirming

For each situation (a) write the three potential responses as indicated and (b) indicate what effects each type of response is likely to generate.

*Although each type of response serves a different purpose, confirming responses seem most likely to promote communication satisfaction.*

1. Enrique receives this semester's grades in the mail; they're a lot better than previous semesters' grades but are still not great. After opening the letter, Enrique says: "I really tried hard to get my grades up this semester." Enrique's parents respond:

   With disconfirmation: _____
   With rejection: _____
   With confirmation: _____

2. Carrie's boyfriend of seven years left her and married another woman. Carrie confides this to Samantha, who responds:

   With disconfirmation: _____
   With rejection: _____
   With confirmation: _____

- avoid mentioning race when it's irrelevant, as in references to "the African American surgeon" or "the Asian athlete?

- avoid attributing individuals' economic or social problems to the race of the individuals rather than to institutionalized racism or general economic problems that affect everyone?

## Heterosexism

Heterosexism also exists on both an individual and an institutional level. The term *individual heterosexism* refers to attitudes, behaviors, and language that disparage gay men and lesbians and to the belief that all sexual behavior that is not heterosexual is unnatural and deserving of criticism and condemnation. Such beliefs are at the heart of antigay violence and "gay bashing." Individual heterosexism also includes such beliefs as the idea that homosexuals are more likely than heterosexuals to commit crimes (actually, there's no difference) or to molest children (actually, child molesters are overwhelmingly heterosexual married men) (Abel & Harlow, 2001; Koppelman with Goodhart, 2005). It also includes the belief that homosexuals cannot maintain stable relationships or effectively raise children, a belief that contradicts research evidence (Fitzpatrick, Jandt, Myrick, & Edgar, 1994; Johnson & O'Connor, 2002).

*Institutional heterosexism* is easy to identify. For example, the ban on gay marriage in many states and the fact that at this time only one state (Massachusetts) allows gay marriage is a good example of institutional heterosexism. Other examples include the Catholic church's ban on homosexual priests, the U.S. military's prohibition against service by openly gay people, and the many laws prohibiting adoption of children by gay people. In some cultures (for example, in India, Malaysia, Pakistan, and Singapore) homosexual relations are illegal; penalties range from the punishment for a "misdemeanor" in Liberia to life in jail in Singapore and death in Pakistan.

**Heterosexist language** includes derogatory terms used for lesbians and gay men. For example, surveys in the military showed that 80 percent of those surveyed had heard "offensive speech, derogatory names, jokes or remarks about gays" and

### Hate Speech

Hate speech is speech that is hostile, offensive, degrading, or intimidating to a particular group of people. Women, African Americans, Muslims, Jews, Asians, Hispanics, and gay men and lesbians are among the major targets in the United States.

Hate speech occurs in all forms of human communication; it occurs when people utter insults to someone passing by, or when posters and fliers degrade specific groups; radio talk shows denigrate members of certain groups; computer games are reconfigured to make targets of members of minority groups; or websites insult, demean, and encourage hostility toward certain groups. Because the media are so powerful in influencing opinions and because they reach so many people, the issue of hate speech in the media takes on special importance (Ruscher, 2001).

One of the difficulties in attacking hate speech is that it's often difficult to draw a clear line between speech that is protected by the First Amendment right to freedom of expression but is simply at odds with the majority viewpoint and speech that is designed to denigrate members of certain groups and encourage hostility against them.

Some colleges are instituting hate speech codes—written statements of what constitutes hate speech as well as designation of penalties for hate speech. Proponents of such codes argue that they teach students that hate speech is unacceptable, is harmful to all people (but especially to minority group members who are the targets of such attacks), and may be curtailed in the same way as other undesirable acts (such as child pornography or rape). Opponents argue that such codes do not address the underlying prejudices and biases that give rise to hate speech, that codes stifle free expression, and that they may be used unfairly by the majority to silence minority opinion and dissent.

***Increasing Media Literacy.*** *Search for "hate speech" and "campus codes" or take a look at "The Price of Free Speech" at* **www.scu.edu/ethics/publications/iie/v5n2/codes.html** *(accessed June 3, 2006) for a review of the arguments for and against hate speech codes. After reading about hate speech and hate codes, formulate your own position on campus codes for hate speech. With this code in mind, examine a few media in terms of their own policies regarding hate speech.*

*It is not only true that the language we use puts words in our mouths; it also puts notions in our heads.*
—WENDELL JOHNSON

---

that 85 percent believed that such derogatory speech was "tolerated" (*New York Times*, March 25, 2000, p. A12). You also see heterosexism in more subtle forms of language usage; for example, a person who qualifies a professional—as in "gay athlete" or "lesbian doctor"—says in effect that athletes and doctors are not normally gay or lesbian.

Still another instance of heterosexism is the presumption of heterosexuality. Usually, people assume the person they're talking to or about is heterosexual. And usually they're correct, because most people are heterosexual. At the same time, however, this presumption denies the lesbian or gay identity a certain legitimacy. The practice is very similar to the social presumptions of whiteness and maleness that we have taken significant steps toward eliminating. Here are a few additional suggestions for avoiding heterosexist (or what some call homophobic) language. Do you:

- avoid offensive nonverbal mannerisms that parody stereotypes when talking about gay men and lesbians? Do you use the "startled eye blink" with which some people react to gay couples (Mahaffey, Bryan, & Hutchison, 2005)?

- avoid "complimenting" gay men and lesbians by saying that they "don't look it"? To gay men and lesbians, this is not a compliment. Similarly, expressing disappointment that a person is gay—often intended as a compliment, as in comments such as "What a waste!"—is not really a compliment.

- avoid making the assumption that every gay or lesbian knows what every other gay or lesbian is thinking? It's very similar to asking a Japanese person why

Sony is investing heavily in the United States or, as one comic put it, asking an African American, "What do you think Jesse Jackson meant by that last speech?"

■ avoid denying individual differences? Comments such as "Lesbians are so loyal" or "Gay men are so open with their feelings" ignore the reality of wide differences within any group and are potentially insulting to all groups.

■ avoid overattribution—the tendency to attribute just about everything a person does, says, and believes to the fact that the person is gay or lesbian? This tendency helps to activate and perpetuate stereotypes.

■ remember that relationship milestones are important to all people? Ignoring the anniversaries or birthdays of, say, a relative's partner is bound to cause resentment.

As you think about heterosexism, recognize that whereas heterosexist language will create barriers to communication, its absence will foster more meaningful communication: greater comfort, an increased willingness to disclose personal information, and a greater willingness to engage in future interactions (Dorland & Fisher, 2001).

**WHAT DO YOU SAY?**
**Homophobia**
You're bringing your college roommate home for the holidays. She's an outspoken lesbian, but your family is extremely homophobic. You want to prepare your family and your roommate for their holiday get-together. *What do you say? To whom? Through what channel?*

# Ageism

Although used mainly to refer to prejudice against older people, the term **ageism** also can refer to prejudice against other age groups. For example, if you describe all teenagers as selfish and undependable, you're discriminating against a group purely because of their age and thus are ageist in your statements. In some cultures—some Asian and African cultures, for example—the old are revered and respected. Younger people seek out elders for advice on economic, ethical, and relationship issues.

*Individual ageism* is seen in the general disrespect many have for older people and in their negative stereotypes. *Institutional ageism* is seen in mandatory retirement laws and age restrictions in certain occupations (rather than requirements based on demonstrated competence). In less obvious forms ageism emerges in the media's portrayal of old people as incompetent; complaining; and, as evidenced perhaps most clearly in both television and films, lacking romantic feelings. Rarely, for example, do television shows or films show older people working productively, being cooperative and pleasant, and engaging in romantic and sexual relationships.

Popular language is replete with examples of linguistic ageism; expressions such as "little old lady," "old hag," "old-timer," "over the hill," "old coot," and "old fogy" are just some examples. As with sexism, qualifying a description of someone in terms of his or her age demonstrates ageism. For example, if you refer to "a quick-witted 75-year-old" or "an agile 65-year-old" or "a responsible teenager," you're implying that these qualities are unusual in people of these ages and thus need special mention. You're saying that "quick-wittedness" and "being 75" do not normally go together. The problem with this kind of stereotyping is that it's simply wrong. There are many 75-year-olds who are extremely quick-witted (and many 30-year-olds who aren't).

You also communicate ageism when you speak to older people in overly simple words or explain things that don't need explaining. Nonverbally, you demonstrate ageist communication when, for example, you avoid touching an older person but touch others, or when you avoid making direct eye contact with the older person but readily do so with others, or when you speak at an overly high volume (suggesting that all older people have hearing difficulties).

One useful way to avoid ageism is to recognize and avoid the illogical stereotypes that ageist language is based on. Do you:

■ avoid talking down to a person because he or she is older? Most older people are not mentally slow but remain mentally alert.

- refrain from refreshing an older person's memory each time you see the person? Older people can and do remember things.

- avoid implying that relationships are no longer important? Older people continue to be interested in relationships.

- speak at a normal volume and maintain a normal physical distance? Being older does not necessarily mean being hard of hearing or being unable to see; most older people hear and see quite well, sometimes with hearing aids or glasses.

- engage older people in conversation as you would wish to be engaged? Older people are interested in the world around them.

Even though you want to avoid ageist communication, there are times when you may wish to make adjustments when talking with someone who does have language or communication difficulties. The American Speech and Hearing Association offers several useful suggestions (www.asha.org/public/speech/development/communicating-better-with-older-people.htm, accessed June 3, 2006):

- Reduce as much background noise as you can.

- Ease into the conversation by beginning with casual topics and then moving into more familiar topics. Stay with each topic for a while; avoid jumping too quickly from one topic to another.

- Speak in relatively short sentences and questions.

- Give the person added time to respond. Some older people react more slowly than others and need extra time.

- Listen actively. Practice the skills of active listening discussed in Chapter 3.

## Sexism

Sexism, like all the -isms discussed here, exists on both an individual and an institutional level. *Individual sexism* involves prejudicial attitudes and beliefs about men or women based on rigid beliefs about gender roles. These beliefs may include ideas such as the notion that all women should be caretakers, should be sensitive at all times, and should acquiesce to men's decisions concerning political or financial matters. Also sexist are the beliefs that all men are insensitive, interested only in sex, and incapable of communicating feelings.

*Institutional sexism*, on the other hand, results from customs and practices that discriminate against people because of their gender. Clear examples come from the world of business: the widespread practice of paying women less than men for the same job, and the frequent discrimination against women in the upper levels of management. Another clear example of institutionalized sexism is the divorce courts' practice of automatically, or almost automatically, granting child custody to the mother rather than the father.

Of particular interest here is **sexist language:** language that puts down someone because of his or her gender (but usually language derogatory toward women). The National Council of Teachers of English has proposed guidelines for nonsexist (gender-free, gender-neutral, or sex-fair) language. These guidelines concern the use of the generic word *man*, the use of generic *he* and *his*, and sex role stereotyping (Penfield, 1987). Consider your own communication behavior. Do you:

- avoid using *man* generically? Using the term to refer to both men and women emphasizes maleness at the expense of femaleness. Gender-neutral terms can easily be substituted. Instead of "mankind," say "humanity," "people," or "human beings." Similarly, the use of terms such as *policeman* or *fireman* and other terms that presume maleness as the norm—and femaleness as a deviation from this norm—are clear and common examples of sexist language.

- avoid using *he* and *his* as generic? Instead, you can alternate pronouns or restructure your sentences to eliminate any reference to gender. For example, the NCTE guidelines (Penfield, 1987) suggest that instead of saying, "The average student is worried about his grades," you say, "The average student is worried about grades."

- avoid sex role stereotyping? When you make the hypothetical elementary school teacher female and the college professor male or refer to doctors as male and nurses as female, you're sex role stereotyping, as you are when you mention the sex of a professional in terms such as "female doctor" or "male nurse."

## Sexual Harassment

This discussion of sexism leads naturally into a consideration of **sexual harassment,** a form of behavior that violates Title VII of the Civil Rights Act of 1964 as amended by the Civil Rights Act of 1991 (www.eeoc.gov/policy/, accessed June 3, 2006). There are two general categories of workplace sexual harassment: quid pro quo (a term borrowed from the Latin that literally means "something for something") and the creation of a hostile environment.

In **quid pro quo harassment,** employment opportunities (as in hiring and promotion) are made dependent on the granting of sexual favors. Conversely, quid pro quo harassment also includes situations in which reprisals and various negative consequences would result from the failure to grant such sexual favors. Put more generally, quid pro quo harassment occurs when employment consequences (positive or negative) hinge on a person's response to sexual advancements. If you don't get hired or promoted because you're unwilling to grant sexual favors to a superior, you're a victim of quid pro quo harassment.

**Hostile environment harassment** is broader and includes all sexual behaviors (verbal and nonverbal) that make a worker uncomfortable. Putting sexually explicit pictures on the bulletin board, using sexually explicit screen savers, telling sexual jokes and stories, and using sexual and demeaning language or gestures all constitute hostile environment harassment.

The Equal Employment Opportunity Commission (EEOC) definition of workplace sexual harassment sums up these two basic types. In the definition below items 1 and 2 refer to quid pro quo harassment and item 3 to hostile environment harassment:

> Unwelcome sexual advances, requests for sexual favors and other verbal or physical conduct of a sexual nature constitute sexual harassment when (1) submission to such conduct is made either explicitly or implicitly a term or condition of an individual's employment, (2) submission to or rejection of such conduct by an individual is used as the basis for employment decisions affecting such individual, or (3) such conduct has the purpose or effect of unreasonably interfering with an individual's work performance or creating an intimidating, hostile, or offensive working environment. (Friedman, Boumil, & Taylor, 1992)

If you are trying to determine whether someone's behavior constitutes sexual harassment, the following questions will help you assess your own situation objectively rather than emotionally (VanHyning, 1993):

1. Is this behavior real? Does it have the meaning it seems to have?
2. Is this behavior job related? Does it have something to do with or will it influence the way you do your job?

3. Have you rejected this behavior? Have you made your rejection of unwanted messages clear to the other person?

4. Have these unwanted messages persisted? Is there a pattern, a consistency to these messages?

If you answer yes to all four questions, then the behavior is likely to constitute sexual harassment (VanHyning, 1993).

Keep in mind three additional facts that are often misunderstood. First, people of either gender may sexually harass either gender. Although most cases brought to public attention are committed by men against women, women also may harass men. Further, harassment may be committed by men against men and by women against women. Second, anyone in an organization can be guilty of sexual harassment. Although most cases of harassment involve persons in authority who harass subordinates, this is not a necessary condition. Coworkers, vendors, and even customers may be charged with sexual harassment. Third, sexual harassment is not limited to business organizations but can and does occur in schools, in hospitals, and in social, religious, and political organizations.

What can you do about sexual harassment? If you encounter sexual harassment and wish to do something about it, consider these suggestions recommended by workers in the field (Petrocelli & Repa, 1992; Bravo & Cassedy, 1992; Rubenstein, 1993):

1. Talk to the harasser. Tell this person, assertively, that you do not welcome the behavior and that you find it offensive. Simply informing Fred that his sexual jokes aren't appreciated and are seen as offensive may be sufficient to make him stop.

2. Collect evidence—perhaps corroboration from others who have experienced similar harassment at the hands of the same individual, and/or perhaps a log of the offensive behaviors.

3. Utilize appropriate channels within the organization. Most organizations have established channels to deal with such grievances. In most cases this step will eliminate any further harassment.

4. If necessary, file a complaint with an organization or governmental agency or perhaps take legal action.

## Cultural Identifiers

Perhaps the best way to develop nonracist, nonheterosexist, nonageist, and nonsexist language is to examine the preferred cultural identifiers to use in talking to and about members of different groups. Remember, however, that preferred terms frequently change over time, so keep in touch with the most current preferences. The preferences and many of the specific examples identified here are drawn largely from the findings of the Task Force on Bias-Free Language of the Association of American University Presses (Schwartz, 1995).

Generally, the term *girl* should be used only to refer to very young females and is equivalent to *boy*. Neither term should be used for people older than say 13 or 14. *Girl* is never used to refer to a grown woman, nor is *boy* used to refer to people in blue-collar positions, as it once was. *Lady* is negatively evaluated by many because it connotes the stereotype of the prim and proper woman. *Woman* or *young woman* is preferred. *Older person* is preferred to *elder*, *elderly*, *senior*, or *senior citizen* (which technically refers to someone older than 65).

Generally, *gay* is the preferred term to refer to a man who has an affectional preference for other men, and *lesbian* is the preferred term for a woman who has an affectional preference for other women (Lever, 1995). (When used as a noun, *lesbian* means "homosexual woman"; the term *lesbian woman* is redundant.) *Homosexual* refers to both gays and lesbians, but more often to a sexual orienta-

**WHAT DO YOU SAY?**
**Misusing Cultural Identifiers**
During a conversation a group of classmates all use negative self-reference terms. Trying to be one of the group, you too use these terms—but almost immediately realize that the linguistic privilege allowing insiders to use self-derogatory names does not apply to outsiders. You don't want anyone to think that you normally talk this way. *What do you say?*

tion to members of a person's own sex. The terms *gay* and *lesbian* refer to a lifestyle and not just to sexual orientation. *Gay* as a noun, although widely used, may prove offensive in some contexts, as in "We have two gays on the team." Because most scientific thinking holds that sexuality is not a matter of choice, the term *sexual orientation*, rather than *sexual preference* or *sexual status* (which is also vague), is preferred.

Generally, most African Americans prefer *African American* to *black* (Hecht, Collier, & Ribeau, 1993), although *black* is often used with *white*, as well as in a variety of other contexts (for example, Department of Black and Puerto Rican Studies, the *Journal of Black History*, and Black History Month). The American Psychological Association recommends that both terms be capitalized, but the *Chicago Manual of Style* (the manual used by most newspapers and publishing houses) recommends using lowercase. The terms *Negro* and *colored*, although used in the names of some organizations (for example, the United Negro College Fund and the National Association for the Advancement of Colored People), are not used outside these contexts.

*White* is generally used to refer to those whose roots are in European cultures and usually does not include Hispanics. Analogous to *African American* (which itself is based on a long tradition of terms such as *Irish American* and *Italian American*) is the phrase *European American*. Few European Americans, however, call themselves that; most prefer their national origins emphasized, as in, for example, *German American* or *Greek American*. This preference may well change as Europe moves toward becoming a more cohesive and united entity. *People of color*—a more literary-sounding term, appropriate perhaps to public speaking but awkward in most conversations—is preferred to *nonwhite*, which implies that whiteness is the norm and nonwhiteness is a deviation from that norm. The same is true of the term *non-Christian:* It implies that people who have other beliefs deviate from the norm.

Generally, the term *Hispanic* refers to anyone who identifies himself or herself as belonging to a Spanish-speaking culture. *Latina* (female) and *Latino* (male) refer to persons whose roots are in one of the Latin American countries, such as the Dominican Republic, Nicaragua, or Guatemala. *Hispanic American* refers to United States residents whose ancestry is in a Spanish culture; the term includes Mexican, Caribbean, and Central and South Americans. In emphasizing a Spanish heritage, however, the term is really inaccurate, because it leaves out the large numbers of people in the Caribbean and in South America whose origins are African, Native American, French, or Portuguese. *Chicana* (female) and *Chicano* (male) refer to persons with roots in Mexico, although it often connotes a nationalist attitude (Jandt, 2003) and is considered offensive by many Mexican Americans. *Mexican American* is generally preferred.

*Inuk* (plural, *Inuit*), also spelled with two *n*'s (*Innuk* and *Innuit*), is preferred to *Eskimo* (a term the United States Census Bureau uses), which was applied to the indigenous peoples of Alaska and Canada by Europeans and literally means "raw meat eaters."

The word *Indian* technically refers only to someone from India, not to members of other Asian countries or to the indigenous peoples of North America. *American Indian* or *Native American* is preferred, even though many Native Americans do refer to themselves as *Indians* and *Indian people*. The word *squaw*, used to refer to a Native American woman and still used in some U.S. place names and in some textbooks, is to be avoided; its usage is almost always negative and insulting (Koppelman with Goodhart, 2005). In Canada, indigenous people are called *first people*. The term *native American* (with a lowercase *n*) is most often used to refer to persons born in the United States. Although technically the term could refer to anyone born in North or South America, people outside the United States generally prefer more specific designations such as *Argentinean, Cuban,* or *Canadian*. The term *native* means an indigenous inhabitant; it is not used to mean "someone having a less developed culture."

> **WHAT DO YOU SAY?**
> **Objecting to Disconfirmation**
> One of your instructors persists in calling the female students *girls*, refers to gay men and lesbians as *queers,* and uses racial terms that most people consider inappropriate. You want to object to this type of talk. *What do you say? To whom? Through what channel?*

*Words can destroy. What we call each other ultimately becomes what we think of each other, and it matters.*

—JEANNE J. KIRKPATRICK

### Listening without Prejudice

Just as racist, heterosexist, ageist, and sexist attitudes will influence your language, they can also influence your listening. In prejudiced listening, you hear what the speaker is saying through the stereotypes you hold. This type of listening occurs when you listen differently to a person because of his or her race, affectional orientation, age, or gender when these characteristics are irrelevant to the message.

Racist, heterosexist, ageist, and sexist listening can occur in a wide variety of situations. For example, when you dismiss a valid argument or attribute validity to an invalid argument because the speaker is of a particular race, affectional orientation, age, or gender, you're listening with prejudice.

However, there are many instances where these characteristics are relevant and pertinent to your evaluation of the message. For example, the sex of a speaker talking about pregnancy, fathering a child, birth control, or surrogate motherhood is, most would agree, probably relevant to the message. So, in these cases it is not sexist listening to take the gender of the speaker into consideration. It is, however, sexist listening to assume that only one gender can be an authority on a particular topic or that one gender's opinions are without value. The same is true when listening through a person's race, affectional orientation, or age.

***Applying Listening Skills.*** *Your friend Maria refuses to listen to men when they voice their opinions on any "women's issue"—whether it's abortion, women in religion, the glass ceiling, adoption rights, or divorce settlements. What would you say to Maria?*

*Muslim* (rather than the older *Moslem*) is the preferred form to refer to a person who adheres to the religious teachings of Islam. *Quran* (rather than *Koran*) is the preferred term for the scriptures of Islam. *Jewish people* is often preferred to *Jews*, and *Jewess* (a Jewish female) is considered derogatory.

When history was being written from a European perspective, Europe was taken as the focal point and the rest of the world was defined in terms of its location relative to that continent. Thus, Asia became the East or the Orient, and Asians became *Orientals*—a term that is today considered inappropriate or "Eurocentric." Thus, people from Asia are *Asians*, just as people from Africa are *Africans* and people from Europe are *Europeans*.

## Using Verbal Messages Effectively

Three general principles will help you use verbal messages more effectively and more critically. We'll look at each in turn. As you'll see, these principles all concern the connection between the way you think and the way you talk.

### Messages Symbolize Reality (Partially)

Language describes the objects, people, and events in the world with varying degrees of accuracy. But words and sentences are symbols; they're not actual objects, people, or events, even though we sometimes act as if they were. Two ways in which we sometimes act as if words and things were the same are communicating intensionally and communicating with an allness attitude.

**Intensional Orientation**   Have you ever reacted to the way something was labeled or described rather than to the actual item? Have you ever bought something because of its name rather than because of the actual object? If so, you were probably responding intensionally.

## Skill Development Experience

### Talking in E-Prime

**E-prime** (E′) refers to normal English without the verb *to be* (Bourland, 1965–1966; Bourland & Johnston, 1998; Einhorn, 2006). To appreciate further the difference between statements that use the verb *to be* and those that do not, (a) rewrite the following sentences without using the verb *to be* in any of its forms—*is, are, am, was,* and so on—in the second column; then (b) indicate the differences in meaning between the statement using *to be* and the e-prime rewrite in the third column.

*The verb* to be *suggests that qualities are in the person or thing rather than in the observer. The verb* to be *also implies a permanence that is not true of the world in which we live.*

| Normal English | E-Prime | Meaning Differences |
|---|---|---|
| 1. I'm not very good at making friends. | | |
| 2. They're just illiterate. | | |
| 3. I'm unpopular. | | |
| 4. I'm not a leader. | | |
| 5. I'm no public speaker. | | |

An **intensional orientation** (the *s* in *intensional* is intentional) is a tendency to view people, objects, and events in the way they are talked about—the way they are labeled. For example, if Sally were labeled "uninteresting," if you responded intensionally, you would evaluate her as uninteresting before listening to what she had to say. You would see Sally through a filter imposed by the label "uninteresting." The opposite tendency, **extensional orientation,** is the tendency to look first at the actual people, objects, and events and only afterward at their labels. In this case it would mean looking at Sally without any preconceived labels, guided by what she says and does, not by the words used to label her.

The way to avoid intensional orientation is to extensionalize. You can do this by focusing your attention on the people, things, and events in the world as you see them and not as they are presented in the words of others. For example, when you meet Jack and Jill, observe and interact with them. Then form your impressions. Don't respond to them as "greedy, money-grubbing landlords" because Harry labeled them this way. Don't respond to Carmen as "lazy and inconsiderate" because Elaine told you she was.

**Allness**   No one can know all or say all about anything. The parable of the six blind men and the elephant is an excellent example of an **allness** orientation and its problems. You may recall the John Saxe poem that tells of six blind men of Indostan who examined an elephant, an animal they had only heard about. The first blind man touched the elephant's side and concluded the elephant was like a wall. The second felt the tusk and said the elephant must be like a spear. The third held the trunk and concluded the elephant was like a snake. The fourth touched the knee and knew the elephant was like a tree. The fifth felt the ear and said the elephant was like a fan. And the sixth grabbed the tail and said the elephant was like a rope.

Each reached his own conclusion; each argued that he was correct and that the others were wrong. Each was correct and, at the same time, wrong. We are all in the position of the six blind men. We never see all of anything. We never experience anything fully. We see a part, then conclude what the whole is like. We have to draw conclusions on the basis of insufficient evidence (and we always have insufficient evidence). We must recognize that when we make judgments based only on a part, we are making inferences that can later prove wrong once we have more complete information.

A useful **extensional device** to encourage a **nonallness** orientation is to end each statement, explicitly or mentally, with **et cetera,** or **etc.**—a reminder that there is more to learn, more to know, and more to say: that every statement is inevitably incomplete. Instead of saying, for example, "I wouldn't like her; I saw the way she treated her father," you'd say, "I don't think I'd like her; I saw the way she treated her father, but I haven't seen her with other people, and I really don't know her father, et cetera." Be careful, however, that you do not use *etc.* as a substitute for being specific.

## Messages Express Both Facts and Inferences

A second key principle is the importance of avoiding **fact–inference confusion.** Often, when we listen or speak, we don't distinguish between statements of fact and those of inference. Yet there are great differences between the two. Barriers to clear thinking can develop if we treat inferences as facts.

For example, you can say, "She is wearing a blue jacket" as well as "He is harboring an illogical hatred." Although the sentences have similar structures, they are different. You can observe the jacket and the blue color, but how do you observe "illogical hatred"? Obviously, this is not a descriptive but an **inferential statement.** In contrast, a **factual statement** must be made by the observer after observation and must be limited to what is observed (Weinberg, 1959).

There is nothing wrong with making inferential statements. You must make them to talk about much that is meaningful to you. The problem arises when you act as if those inferential statements are factual. Consider the following anecdote (Maynard, 1963): A woman went for a walk one day and met a friend whom she had not seen, heard from, or heard of in 10 years. After an exchange of greetings, the woman said: "Is this your little boy?" and her friend replied, "Yes, I got married about six years ago." The woman then asked the child, "What is your name?" and the little boy replied, "Same as my father's." "Oh," said the woman, "then it must be Peter."

How did the woman know the boy's father's name when she had had no contact with her friend in the last 10 years? The answer is obvious, but only after we recognize that in reading this short passage we have made an unconscious inference. Specifically, we have inferred that the woman's friend is a woman. Actually, the friend is a man named Peter.

You may test your ability to distinguish facts from inferences by taking the following self-test, "Can you distinguish facts from inferences?" (based on tests constructed by William Haney [1973]).

## CAN YOU DISTINGUISH FACTS FROM INFERENCES?

**INSTRUCTIONS:** Carefully read the following report and the observations based on it. Indicate whether you think the observations are true, false, or doubtful on the basis of the information presented in the report. Write T if the observation is definitely true, F if the observation is definitely false, and ? if the observation may be either true or false. Judge each observation in order. Do not reread the observations after you have indicated your judgment, and do not change any of your answers.

A well-liked college teacher had just completed making up the final examinations and had turned off the lights in the office. Just then a tall, broad figure with dark glasses appeared and demanded the examination. The professor opened the drawer. Everything in the drawer was picked up and the individual ran down the corridor. The dean was notified immediately.

_____ ❶ The thief was tall, broad, and wore dark glasses.

_____ ❷ The professor turned off the lights.

_____ ❸ A tall figure demanded the examination.

_____ ❹ The examination was picked up by someone.

_____ ❺ The examination was picked up by the professor.

_____ ❻ A tall, broad figure appeared after the professor turned off the lights in the office.

_____ ❼ The man who opened the drawer was the professor.

_____ ❽ The professor ran down the corridor.

_____ ❾ The drawer was never actually opened.

_____ ❿ Three persons are referred to in this report.

**HOW DID YOU DO?** After you respond to all the statements, form small groups of five or six and discuss the answers. Look at each statement from each member's point of view. For each statement, ask yourself, "How can you be absolutely certain that the statement is true or false?" You should find that only one statement can be clearly identified as true and only one as false; eight should be marked ?.

**WHAT WILL YOU DO?** Think about this exercise and try to formulate specific guidelines that will help you distinguish facts from inferences.

---

To avoid fact–inference confusion, always make inferential statements tentatively and leave open the possibility of being wrong. If, for example, you treat the statement "Our biology teacher was fired for poor teaching" as factual, you eliminate alternative explanations. When making inferential statements, be psychologically prepared to be proved wrong. In this way, you'll be less hurt if you're shown to be wrong.

Be especially sensitive to this distinction when you're listening. Most talk is inferential. Beware of the speaker (whether in interpersonal, group, or public speaking) who presents everything as fact. Analyze closely and you'll uncover a world of inferences.

> "One great use of words is to hide our thoughts."
> —Voltaire

## Messages Can Obscure Distinctions

Language can obscure distinctions between people or events that are covered by the same label but are really quite different (indiscrimination). Language also can make it easy to focus on extremes rather than on the vast middle ground between opposites (polarization). And it can obscure the fact that change is constant and inevitable (static evaluation).

**Indiscrimination**   **Indiscrimination** is the failure to distinguish between similar but different people, objects, or events. It occurs when we focus on classes of things and fail to see that each thing is unique and needs to be looked at individually.

Although no two things are identical, our language provides us with common nouns, such as *teacher, student, friend, enemy, war, politician,* and *liberal.* These lead us to focus on similarities—to group together all teachers, all students, all politicians, and so on. At the same time, the terms divert attention away from the uniqueness of each person, each object, and each event.

This kind of misevaluation is at the heart of stereotyping on the basis of nationality, race, religion, sex, or affectional orientation. A stereotype, you'll remember from Chapter 2, is a fixed mental picture of a group that is applied to each individual in the group without regard to his or her unique qualities.

Whether stereotypes are positive or negative, they create the same problem. They provide us with shortcuts that are often inappropriate. For instance, when you meet a particular person, your first reaction may be to pigeonhole him or her into some category—perhaps religious, national, or academic. Then you assign to this person all the qualities that are part of your stereotype. Regardless of the category you use or the specific qualities you are ready to assign, you fail to give sufficient attention to the individual's unique characteristics. Two people may both be Christian, Asian, and lesbian, for example, but each will be different from the other. Indiscrimination is a denial of another's uniqueness.

A useful antidote to indiscrimination is an extensional device known as the **index.** This mental subscript identifies each individual as an individual, even though a group of these individuals may be covered by the same label. Thus, politician$_1$ is not politician$_2$; teacher$_1$ is not teacher$_2$. The index helps you to discriminate between without discriminating against. Use of the index would, for example, prevent you from grouping all Muslims or all Christians or all Jews in the same category. Each Muslim, each Christian, and each Jew is unique and needs a unique index number. So at the same time that you have to generalize and appreciate similarities, the index reminds you to also look at differences. For example, rather than saying, "I don't want you to hang around with Muslims," a parent might discriminate among Muslims and say something like "I don't want you to hang around with Abdul or Said."

**Polarization**    **Polarization** is the tendency to look at the world in terms of opposites and to describe it in extremes—good or bad, positive or negative, healthy or sick, intelligent or stupid. Polarization is often referred to as the fallacy of "either/or" or "black-and-white" thinking. In reality most people, objects, and events exist somewhere between the extremes. Yet we have a strong tendency to view only the extremes and to categorize things in terms of these polar opposites.

We create problems when we polarize in inappropriate situations. Consider this example: "The politician is either for us or against us." These options do not include all possibilities. The politician may be for us in some things and against us in other things or may be neutral.

To correct this tendency to polarize, beware of implying (and believing) that all individuals and events must fit into one extreme or the other, with no alternatives in between. And when others imply that there are only two sides or alternatives, look for the middle ground.

**Static Evaluation**    People and things change at a rapid rate, but our messages about them may not keep pace. The statements you make about an event or person need to change as quickly and as dramatically as people and events change. When you retain an evaluation (most often in the form of an internalized message) despite the changes in the person or thing, you're engaging in **static evaluation.**

"Say something. I forget what you sound like."

It's important to act in accordance with the notion of change, not merely to accept it intellectually. If you failed at something once, that does not necessarily mean that you'll fail again. If you were rejected once, that does not mean you'll be rejected again. You've changed since the first failure and the first rejection. You're a different person now, and you need to make new evaluations and initiate new efforts.

The mental **date** is a useful extensional device for keeping language (and thinking) up to date and for guarding against static evaluation. Date your statements and especially your evaluations; remember that Pat Smith$_{2001}$ is not Pat Smith $_{2007}$, that academic abilities$_{2002}$ are not academic abilities$_{2007}$. In talking and in listening, look carefully at messages that claim that what was true still is. It may or may not be. Look for change; be suspicious of the implication of nonchange.

# Summary of Concepts and Skills

Focusing on verbal messages, this chapter first looked at the nature of language and identified several major ways in which language works. The next section examined confirmation and disconfirmation and the related topics of racist, heterosexist, ageist, and sexist language. The final section presented ways to make verbal communication more effective.

1. Communication is a package of verbal and nonverbal signals.
2. Language is both denotative (objective and generally easily agreed upon) and connotative (subjective and generally highly individual in meaning).
3. Language varies in abstraction; it can range from extremely general to extremely specific.
4. Language varies in directness; it can state exactly what you mean, or it can hedge and state your meaning very indirectly.
5. Language meanings are in people, not simply in words.
6. Language is influenced by culture and gender.
7. Disconfirmation is the process of ignoring the presence and the communications of others. Confirmation means accepting, supporting, and acknowledging the importance of the other person.
8. Racist, heterosexist, ageist, and sexist language disconfirms, puts down, and negatively evaluates various groups.
9. To make verbal messages more effective, realize that language symbolizes reality and is not the reality itself; that language can express both facts and inferences but doesn't indicate this grammatically; that language can obscure distinctions, as when it provides lots of extreme terms but few terms to describe the middle ground; and that language tends to be static, whereas people and events are forever changing.

The study of verbal messages and of how meaning is communicated from one person to another has important implications for the skills of effective communication. Place a check mark next to those skills that you feel you need to work on most.

_____ 1. Because communication is a package of signals, I use my verbal and nonverbal messages to reinforce rather than to contradict each other.

_____ 2. I try to understand not only objective, denotative meanings, but also the speaker's subjective, connotative meanings.

_____ 3. I recognize that snarl and purr words describe the speaker's feelings and not objective reality.

_____ 4. I use terms varying in abstraction to best communicate my meanings.

_____ 5. I vary my directness depending on the situation and my communication goal.

_____ 6. I take special care to make spoken messages clear and unambiguous, especially when using terms for which people will have very different connotative meanings.

_____ 7. I recognize the cultural and gender differences in the use of verbal messages and avoid assuming that my principles are followed by members of other cultures.

_____ 8. I focus attention not only on words but also on the person communicating, recognizing that meanings are largely in the person.

_____ 9. I avoid disconfirmation and instead use responses that confirm the other person.

_____ 10. I avoid racist, heterosexist, ageist, and sexist language and, in general, language that puts down other groups.

_____ 11. I use the cultural identifiers that facilitate communication and avoid those that set up barriers to effective interaction.

_____ 12. I avoid responding intensionally to labels as if they are objects; instead, I respond extensionally and look first at the reality and secondarily at the words.

_____ 13. To avoid allness, I end my statements with an implicit "etc." in recognition that there is always more to be known or said.

_____ 14. I distinguish facts from inferences and respond to inferences with tentativeness.

_____ 15. I avoid indiscrimination by viewing the uniqueness in each person and situation.

_____ 16. I avoid polarization by using "middle ground" terms and qualifiers in describing the world, especially people.

_____ 17. I mentally date my statements and thus avoid static evaluation.

 ## Key Word Quiz

### The Language of Verbal Messages

Match the terms about verbal messages with their definitions. Record the number of the definition next to the appropriate term.

a. _____ quid pro quo harassment

b. _____ confirmation

c. _____ intensional orientation

d. _____ face-saving messages

e. _____ ableism

f. _____ denotation

g. _____ disconfirmation

h. _____ polarization

i. _____ connotation

j. _____ the maxim of quality

1. The objective meaning of a term; the meaning you'd find in a dictionary.

2. Messages that preserve the image of the other person.

3. The principle that speakers follow in saying what they know or assume to be true.

4. A communication pattern in which you ignore someone's presence as well as that person's communication.

5. A situation in which employment opportunities are made available in exchange for sexual favors.

6. The subjective or emotional meaning that specific speakers give a word.

7. A communication pattern in which you indicate your acceptance of the other person's self-definition.

8. The tendency to view people, objects, and events in the way they're talked about or labeled.

9. The tendency to talk and think in terms of extremes or opposites.

10. Discrimination against people with disabilities.

**Answers: a. 5 b. 7 c. 8 d. 2 e. 10 f. 1 g. 4 h. 9 i. 6 j. 3**

 ## Five for Discussion

1. In one study, when asked what they would like to change about the communication style of the opposite sex, men said they wanted women to be more direct, and women said they wanted men to stop interrupting and offering advice (Noble, 1994). What one change would you like to see in the communication style of the opposite sex? Of your own sex?

2. It's interesting to note that labels describing some of the major movements in art—for example, *impressionism* and *cubism*—were originally applied negatively. The terms were then adopted by the artists themselves and eventually became positive. A parallel can be seen in the use of the word *queer* by some lesbian and gay organizations. The purpose of these groups in using this iden-

tifier is to cause it to lose its negative connotation. One possible problem, though, is that certain identifiers may not lose their negative connotations but may simply reinforce negative social stereotypes. By using these terms, group members may come to accept the labels with their negative connotations and thus contribute to their own stereotyping. What's been your experience with people who refer to themselves with negative terms? How do you feel about this?

3. What cultural identifiers to describe yourself do you prefer? Have these preferences changed over time? How can you let other people know the designations that you prefer and those that you don't like? An interesting exercise—especially in a large and multicultural class—is for each student to write anonymously his or her preferred cultural identifiers on an index card and have them all read aloud.

4. A widely held assumption in anthropology, linguistics, and communication is that the importance of a concept to a culture can be measured by the number of words the language has for talking about the concept. For example, in English there are lots of words for money, transportation, and communication. With this principle

in mind, consider as an example the findings of Julia Stanley, who researched English-language terms indicating sexual promiscuity. Stanley found 220 terms referring to a sexually promiscuous woman but only 22 for a sexually promiscuous man (Thorne, Kramarae, & Henley, 1983). What does this suggest about attitudes and beliefs about promiscuity in men and women in English-speaking cultures? Do you think anything has changed since this study was conducted in the early 1980s?

5. In one research study, only 45 percent of the women actually confronted a man who made a sexist comment and of the women confronted only 15 percent responded directly to the person who made the comment. Among the reasons for such lack of confrontation are the social norms that teach us that it's best not to say anything, the pressure to be polite, and the concern about a prolonged confrontation (Swim & Hyers, 1999). Do you generally confront sexist remarks? Are you equally likely to confront racist and heterosexist remarks? Do you think things have changed since 1999, when this study was published?

## Log On! MyCommunicationLab

A variety of experiences related to verbal messages at www.mycommunicationlab.com will help you practice and extend some of the skills identified here: (1) Climbing the Abstraction Ladder, (2) Using the Abstraction Ladder as a Critical Thinking Tool, (3) "Must Lie" Situations, (4) Rephrasing Clichés, (5) Identifying the Barriers to Communication, (6) How Do You Talk about the Middle? (7) Recognizing Gender Differences, (8) How Direct Are You? (9) Is Lying Unethical? and (10) How Do You Feel about Communicating Feelings?

Also visit MyCommunicationLab for additional study aids, exercises, activities, and video clips on the nature and importance of verbal messages.

Explore our research resources at www.researchnavigator.com.

Research Navigator.com

# 5

# Nonverbal Messages

## Why Read This Chapter?

Because you'll **learn about:**

- what nonverbal communication is.
- the many forms of nonverbal communication.
- the many gender and cultural differences in nonverbal communication.

Because you'll **learn to:**

- use nonverbal messages to communicate a wide variety of meanings.
- use appropriate types of nonverbal communication to express your meanings.
- communicate appropriately on the basis of gender and cultural factors.

*N*onverbal communication is communication without words. You communicate nonverbally when you gesture, smile or frown, widen your eyes, move your chair closer to someone, wear jewelry, touch someone, raise your vocal volume, or even say nothing. The crucial aspect is that the message you send is in some way received by one or more other people. If you gesture while you are alone in your room and no one is there to see you, then, most theorists would argue, communication has not taken place. The same is true of verbal messages, of course; if you recite a speech and no one hears it, then communication has not taken place.

The ability to use nonverbal communication effectively can yield two major benefits (Burgoon & Hoobler, 2002). First, the greater your ability to send and receive nonverbal signals, the higher your popularity and psychosocial well-being are likely to be. Second, the greater your nonverbal skills, the more successful you're likely to be at influencing (as well as deceiving) others. Skilled nonverbal communicators are highly persuasive. This persuasive power can be used to help or support another, or it can be used to deceive and fool.

As you begin your study of nonverbal communication, keep the following suggestions in mind.

- *Analyze your own nonverbal communication patterns.* Self-analysis is essential if you're to use this material in any meaningful way; for example, to change some of your behaviors.

- *Observe. Observe. Observe.* Observe the behaviors of those around you as well as your own. See in everyday behavior what you read about here and discuss in class. This will help you bring to a mindful state what may now be automatic and mindless.

- *Resist the temptation to draw conclusions from nonverbal behaviors.* Instead, develop hypotheses (educated guesses) about what is going on, and test the validity of your hypotheses on the basis of other evidence.

- *Connect and relate.* Although textbooks (like this text) must present the areas of nonverbal communication separately, the various elements all work together in actual communication situations.

# The Functions of Nonverbal Communication

Let's consider the functions of nonverbal communication by looking at (1) the ways in which nonverbal communication messages are integrated with verbal messages and (2) the functions that researchers have focused on most extensively.

## Integrating Nonverbal and Verbal Messages

In face-to-face communication, you blend verbal and nonverbal messages to best convey your meanings. While speaking, you also smile, frown, or gesture, for example. And it's this combination of verbal and nonverbal signals that communicates your meanings. Here are six ways in which nonverbal messages interact with verbal messages (Knapp & Hall, 2002). Nonverbal messages:

- *Accent.* Nonverbal communication often serves to highlight or emphasize some part of the verbal message. You might, for example, raise your voice to underscore a particular word or phrase, bang your fist on the desk to stress your commitment, or look longingly into someone's eyes when saying "I love you."

- *Complement.* Nonverbal communication may add nuances of meaning not communicated by your verbal message. Thus, you might smile when telling a story (to suggest that you find it humorous) or frown and shake your head when recounting someone's deceit (to suggest your disapproval).

- *Contradict.* You may deliberately contradict your verbal messages with nonverbal movements—for example, by crossing your fingers or winking to indicate that you're lying.
- *Regulate.* Movements may serve to control, or indicate your desire to control, the flow of verbal messages, as when you purse your lips, lean forward, or make hand gestures to indicate that you want to speak. You might also put up your hand or vocalize your pauses (for example, with "um" or "ah") to indicate that you have not finished and are not ready to relinquish the floor to the next speaker.
- *Repeat.* You can nonverbally restate a verbal message. You can, for example, follow your verbal "Is that all right?" with raised eyebrows and a questioning look, or motion with your head or hand to repeat your verbal "Let's go."
- *Substitute.* You may also use nonverbal communication to take the place of verbal messages. For instance, you can signal "OK" with a hand gesture. You can nod your head to indicate yes or shake your head to indicate no.

## Researching Nonverbal Communication Functions

Although nonverbal communication serves the same functions as verbal communication, researchers have singled out several specific functions in which nonverbal messages are especially significant (Burgoon, Buller, & Woodall, 1996; Burgoon & Hoobler, 2002; Burgoon & Bacue, 2003).

**Forming and Managing Impressions**   It is largely through the nonverbal communications of others that you form impressions of them. Based on a person's body size, skin color, and dress, as well as on the way the person smiles or maintains eye contact, you form impressions—you judge who the person is and what the person is like. One nonverbal researcher groups these impressions into four categories: *credibility*, or how competent and believable you find the person; *likability*, or how much you like or dislike the person; *attractiveness*, or how attractive you find the person; and *dominance*, or how powerful the individual is (Leathers, 1997).

Of course, you reveal yourself largely through the same nonverbal signals you use to size up others. But not only do you communicate your true self nonverbally; you also manage the impression that you give to others. Impression management may, for example, mean appearing brave when you're really scared or happy when you're really sad.

**Forming and Defining Relationships**   Much of your relationship life is lived nonverbally. Largely through nonverbal signals, you communicate the nature of your relationship to another person; and you and that person communicate nonverbally with each other. Holding hands, looking longingly into each other's eyes, and even dressing alike are ways in which you communicate closeness in your interpersonal relationships. You also use nonverbal signals to communicate your relationship dominance and status (Knapp & Hall, 2002). The large corner office with the huge desk communicates high status, just as the basement cubicle communicates low status. A relaxed posture (rather than a tense bearing) and large gestures (rather than small gestures, which may make you appear uncertain) also contribute to the perception of higher status (Mehrabian, 1976).

**Structuring Conversation and Social Interaction**   When you're in conversation, you give and receive cues that you're ready to speak, to listen, to comment on what the speaker just said. These cues regulate and structure the interaction. These turn-taking cues may be verbal (as when you say, "What do you think?"), but most often they're nonverbal: A nod of the head in the direction of someone else, for example, signals that you're ready to give up your speaking turn

▼ E-TALK

**Communicating Closeness**
How would you establish a psychological closeness nonverbally in face-to-face communication? Lacking nonverbal signals, how would you do it in computer-mediated communication? After you've developed your responses, take a look at O'Sullivan, Hunt, and Lippert (2004).

and want this other person to say something. You also show that you're listening and that you want the conversation to continue (or that you're not listening and want the conversation to end) largely through nonverbal signals.

**Influence and Deception**   You can influence others not only through what you say, but you also exert influence through your nonverbal signals. A focused glance that says you're committed; gestures that further explain what you're saying; appropriate dress that says, "I'll easily fit in with this organization" are a few examples of ways in which you can exert nonverbal influence.

And with the ability to influence, of course, comes the ability to deceive—to lie, to mislead another person into thinking something is true when it's false or that something is false when it's true. One common example of nonverbal deception is using your eyes and facial expressions to communicate a liking for other people when you're really interested only in gaining their support in some endeavor. Not surprisingly, you also use nonverbal signals to try to detect deception in others. For example, you may well suspect a person of lying if he or she avoids eye contact, fidgets, and conveys inconsistent verbal and nonverbal messages. However research clearly shows that it is much more difficult to tell when someone is lying than you probably think it is. Using nonverbal cues in an attempt to detect lying is likely to get you into trouble by leading you to formulate incorrect conclusions (Burgoon & Hoobler, 2002; Burgoon & Bacue, 2003; Knapp & Hall, 2006; Park, Levine, McCornack, Morrison, & Ferrara, 2002).

**Emotional Expression**   Although people often explain and reveal emotions verbally, nonverbal expressions communicate a great part of your emotional experience. For example, you reveal your level of happiness or sadness or confusion largely through facial expressions. Of course, you also reveal your feelings by posture (for example, whether tense or relaxed), gestures, eye movements, and even the dilation of your pupils.

Nonverbal messages often help people communicate unpleasant messages, messages they might feel uncomfortable putting into words (Infante, Rancer, & Womack, 2003). For example, you might avoid eye contact and maintain large distances between yourself and someone with whom you didn't want to interact, or with whom you wanted to decrease the intensity of your relationship.

# The Channels of Nonverbal Communication

You communicate nonverbally through a wide range of channels: the body, the face and eyes, space, artifacts, touch, paralanguage and silence, and time.

## Body Messages

The body communicates with movements and gestures and just with its general appearance.

**Body Movements**   Nonverbal researchers identify five major types of body movements: emblems, illustrators, affect displays, regulators, and adaptors (Ekman & Friesen, 1969; Knapp & Hall, 2006).

**"I love your body—where did you get it?"**

© The New Yorker Collection 2006 Barbara Smaller from cartoonbank.com. All Rights Reserved.

**Emblems** are body gestures that directly translate into words or phrases—for example, the OK sign, the thumbs up for "good job," and the V for victory. You use these consciously and purposely to communicate the same meaning as the words. But emblems are culture specific, so be careful when using your culture's emblems in other cultures (see Figure 5.1 on page 121). For example, when President Richard Nixon visited Latin America and gestured with the OK sign, which he thought communicated something positive, he was quickly informed that this gesture was not universal. In Latin America the gesture has a far more negative meaning. Here are a few cultural differences in the emblems you may commonly use (Axtell, 1991):

- In the United States, you wave with your whole hand moving from side to side to say "hello"; but in a large part of Europe, that same signal means "no." In Greece such a signal would be considered insulting to the person to whom you were waving.

- The V for victory common throughout much of the world—if used with the palm toward your face—is as insulting in England as the raised middle finger is in the United States.

- In Texas the raised fist with raised little finger and index finger is a positive expression of support, because it represents the Texas longhorn steer. But in Italy it is an insult that means "cuckold." In parts of South America, it is a gesture used to ward off evil. In parts of Africa, it is a curse: "May you experience bad times."

- In the United States and much of Asia, hugs are rarely exchanged among acquaintances; but among Latin Americans and southern Europeans, hugging is a common greeting gesture, and failing to hug someone may communicate unfriendliness.

**Illustrators** enhance (literally "illustrate") the verbal messages they accompany. For example, when referring to something to the left, you might gesture toward the left. Most often, you illustrate with your hands, but you can also illustrate with head and general body movements. You might, for example, turn your head or your entire body toward the left. You might also use illustrators to communicate the shape or size of objects you're talking about. Recent research points to an interesting advantage of illustrators—namely, that they increase your ability to remember. In this research people who illustrated their verbal messages with gestures remembered 20 percent more than those who didn't gesture (Goldin-Meadow, Nusbaum, Kelly, & Wagner, 2001).

**Affect displays** are movements of the face (smiling or frowning, for example) but also of the hands and general body (body tenseness or relaxed posture, for example) that communicate emotional meaning. You use affect displays to accompany and reinforce your verbal messages, but also as substitutes for words. For example, you might smile while saying how happy you are to see your friend, or you might simply smile. (Affect displays, being primarily centered in the facial area, are covered in more detail in the next section.)

**Regulators** are behaviors that monitor, control, coordinate, or maintain the speech of another individual. When you nod your head, for example, you tell the speaker to keep on speaking; when you lean forward and open your mouth, you tell the speaker that you would like to say something.

**Adaptors** are gestures that satisfy some personal need, such as scratching to relieve an itch or moving your hair out of your eyes. **Self-adaptors** are self-touching movements (for example, rubbing your nose). **Alter-adaptors** are movements directed at the person with whom you're speaking—for example, removing lint from a person's jacket or straightening his or her tie or folding your arms in front of you to keep others a comfortable distance from you. **Object-adaptors** are gestures focused on objects—for example, doodling on or shredding a Styrofoam coffee cup. Table 5.1 summarizes these five types of body movements.

*"The body says what words cannot."*
—MARTHA GRAHAM

## TABLE 5.1 Five Body Movements

What other examples can you think of for these five movements?

| | NAME AND FUNCTION | EXAMPLES |
|---|---|---|
|  | EMBLEMS directly translate words or phrases; they are especially culture specific. | "OK" sign, "come here" wave, hitchhiker's sign |
|  | ILLUSTRATORS accompany and literally "illustrate" verbal messages. | Circular hand movements when talking of a circle; hands far apart when talking of something large |
|  | AFFECT DISPLAYS communicate emotional meaning. | Expressions of happiness, surprise, fear, anger, sadness, disgust/contempt |
|  | REGULATORS monitor, maintain, or control the speech of another. | Facial expressions and hand gestures indicating "keep going," "slow down," or "what else happened?" |
|  | ADAPTORS satisfy some need. | Scratching your head |

**Body Appearance**    Your general body appearance also communicates. Height, for example, has been shown to be significant in a wide variety of situations. Tall presidential candidates have a much better record of winning elections than do their shorter opponents. Tall people seem to be paid more and are favored by personnel interviewers over shorter job applicants (Keyes, 1980; DeVito & Hecht, 1990; Knapp & Hall, 2006). Taller people also have higher self-esteem and greater career success than do shorter people (Judge & Cable, 2004).

Your body also reveals your race, through skin color and tone, and may even give clues as to your nationality. Your weight in proportion to your height also will communicate messages to others, as will the length, color, and style of your hair.

Your general **attractiveness,** which includes both visual appeal and pleasantness of personality, is also a part of body communication. Attractive people have the advantage in just about every activity you can name. They get better grades in school, are more valued as friends and lovers, and are preferred as coworkers (Burgoon, Buller, & Woodall, 1996). Although we normally think that attractiveness is culturally determined—and to some degree it is—some research seems to show that definitions of attractiveness are becoming universal (*New York Times*, March 21, 1994, p. A14). A person rated as attractive in one culture is likely to be rated as attractive in other cultures—even in cultures in which people are generally quite different in appearance from people in the first culture.

## Facial and Eye Movements

The facial area, including the eyes, is probably the single most important source of nonverbal messages.

**Facial Communication**    Throughout your interpersonal interactions, your face communicates many things, especially your emotions. In fact, facial movements alone seem to communicate the degree of pleasantness, agreement, and sympathy felt; the rest of the body doesn't provide any additional information in those realms. But for other aspects—for example, the intensity with which an emotion is felt—both facial and bodily cues enter in (Graham, Bitti, & Argyle, 1975; Graham & Argyle, 1975). These cues are so important in communicating your full meaning that graphic representations are now commonly used in Internet communication. In some Internet Relay Chat groups (those that use GUI, Graphic User Interface), buttons are available to help you encode your emotions graphically. Table 5.2 identifies some of the more common "emoticons," icons that communicate emotions.

Some nonverbal research claims that facial movements may communicate at least the following eight emotions: happiness, surprise, fear, anger, sadness, disgust, contempt, and interest (Ekman, Friesen, & Ellsworth, 1972). Try to communicate surprise using only facial movements. Do this in front of a mirror and try to describe in as much detail as possible the specific movements of the face that make up a look of surprise. If you signal surprise like most people, you probably use raised and curved eyebrows, long horizontal forehead wrinkles, wide-open eyes, a dropped-open mouth, and lips parted with no tension. Even if there were differences from one person to another—and clearly there would be—you could probably recognize the movements listed here as indicative of surprise.

Of course, some emotions are easier to communicate and to decode than others. For example, in one study, participants judged happiness with accuracy ranging from 55 to 100 percent, surprise with 38 to 86 percent accuracy, and sadness with 19 to 88 percent accuracy (Ekman, Friesen, & Ellsworth, 1972). Research finds that women and girls are more accurate judges of facial emotional expression than men and boys (Hall, 1984; Argyle, 1988).

***Facial Management.*** As you grew up, you learned your culture's system of nonverbal communication. You also learned certain **facial management techniques** that enable you to express feelings so as to achieve certain desired effects—for example, to hide certain emotions and to emphasize others. Consider your own use of such facial management techniques. As you do so, think about the types of interpersonal situations in which you would use facial management techniques for each of the following purposes (Malandro, Barker, & Barker, 1989; Metts & Planalp, 2002). Would you

- *intensify?* For example, would you exaggerate your astonishment at a surprise party to make your friends feel better?
- *deintensify?* Would you cover up your own joy about good news in the presence of a friend who didn't receive any such news?
- *neutralize?* Would you cover up your sadness so as not to depress others?
- *mask?* Would you express happiness in order to cover up your disappointment at not receiving a gift you expected?
- *simulate?* Would you express an emotion you didn't feel?

## TABLE 5.2 Some Popular Emoticons

These are some of the emoticons used in computer communication. The first six are widely used in the United States; the last three are popular in Japan and illustrate how culture influences such symbols. Because Japanese culture considers it impolite for women to show their teeth when smiling, the emoticon for a woman's smile shows a dot signifying a closed mouth. Additional emoticons, acronyms, and abbreviations can be found at www.cafeshops.com/netlingo.

| EMOTICON | MEANING | EMOTICON | MEANING |
|----------|---------|----------|---------|
| :-) | Smile: I'm kidding | {*****} | Hugs and kisses |
| :-( | Frown; I'm feeling down | ^ . ^ | Woman's smile |
| ;-) | Wink | ^ _ ^ | Man's smile |
| * | Kiss | ^0^ | Happy |
| {} | Hug | | |

Facial management techniques help you display emotions in socially acceptable ways. For example, if someone gets bad news in which you secretly take pleasure, the social display rule dictates that you frown and otherwise nonverbally signal sorrow. If you place first in a race and your best friend barely finishes, the display rule requires that you minimize your expression of happiness—and certainly avoid any signs of gloating. If you violate these display rules, you'll appear insensitive. So, although facial management techniques may be deceptive, they're expected and even required by the rules for polite interaction.

### The Facial Feedback Hypothesis.

According to the **facial feedback hypothesis,** your facial expression influences your level of physiological arousal. People who exaggerate their facial expressions show higher physiological arousal than those who suppress these expressions. In research studies, those who neither exaggerated nor suppressed their expressions had arousal levels between these two extremes (Lanzetta, Cartwright-Smith, & Kleck, 1976; Zuckerman, Klorman, Larrance, & Spiegel, 1981). In one interesting study, subjects held a pen in their teeth in such a way as to simulate a sad expression. They were then asked to rate photographs. Results showed that mimicking sad expressions actually increased the degree of sadness the subjects reported feeling when viewing the photographs (Larsen, Kasimatis, & Frey, 1992). So not only does your facial expression influence the judgments and impressions others have of you; it also influences your own level of emotional arousal (Cappella, 1993).

## Eye Communication

The messages communicated by the eyes vary depending on the duration, direction, and quality of the eye behavior. For example, every culture has rather strict, though unstated, rules for the proper duration of eye contact. In one study conducted in England, the average length of gaze is 2.95 seconds. The average length of mutual gaze (two persons gazing at each other) is 1.18 seconds (Argyle & Ingham, 1972; Argyle, 1988). When eye contact falls short of this amount, members of some cultures may think the person is uninterested, shy, or preoccupied. When the appropriate amount of time is exceeded, they may perceive the person as showing unusually high interest or even hostility.

The direction of the gaze also communicates. In the United States it is considered appropriate to glance alternately at the other person's face, then away, then again at the face, and so on. The rule for public speakers is to scan the entire audience, not focusing for too long on or ignoring any one area of the audience. When you break these directional rules, you communicate different meanings—abnormally high or low interest, self-consciousness, nervousness over the interaction, and so on. How wide or narrow your eyes get during an interaction also communicates meaning, especially interest level and emotions such as surprise, fear, and disgust.

### The Functions of Eye Movements.

You communicate a variety of messages through eye movements. For example, you can seek feedback: In talking with someone, you might look at her or him intently, as if to say, "Well, what do you think?"

You can also inform the other person that the channel of communication is open and that he or she should now speak. You see this in college classrooms when the instructor asks a question and then locks eyes with a student. Without saying anything, the instructor conveys the expectation that the student will answer the question, and the student gets the message.

Eye movements also may signal the nature of a relationship, whether positive (an attentive glance) or negative (avoidance). You can also signal your power through "visual dominance behavior" (Exline, Ellyson, & Long, 1975). The average speaker, for example,

**"Look at me. Do I look worried?"**

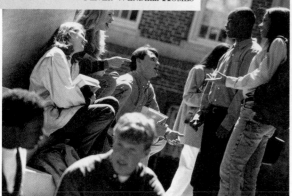

maintains a high level of eye contact while listening and a lower level while speaking. When people want to signal dominance, they may reverse this pattern—maintaining a high level of eye contact while talking but a lower level while listening. You'll see this pattern if you visualize a manager criticizing a subordinate. You'll probably picture the manager maintaining direct eye contact with the subordinate while criticizing, but using little eye contact when listening to excuses he or she considers inadequate.

Eye contact also can change the psychological distance between yourself and another person. When you catch someone's eye at a party, for example, you become psychologically close even though you are physically far apart. By avoiding eye contact—even when physically close, as in a crowded elevator—you increase the psychological distance between you and others.

Some researchers note that eye contact serves to enable gay men and lesbians to signal their homosexuality and perhaps their interest in another person—an ability referred to as "gaydar" (Nicholas, 2004).

When you avoid eye contact or avert your glance, you help others maintain their privacy. You may engage in this **civil inattention** when you see a couple arguing in public, for example (Goffman, 1967). You turn your eyes away (although your eyes may be wide open) as if to say, "I don't mean to intrude; I respect your privacy."

Eye avoidance also can signal lack of interest—in a person, a conversation, or some visual stimulus. At times you may hide your eyes to block off unpleasant stimuli; or you may close your eyes to block out visual stimuli and thus heighten other senses. For example, you may listen to music with your eyes closed. Lovers often close their eyes while kissing, and many prefer to make love in a dark or dimly lit room.

## Spatial Messages

Space is an especially important factor in nonverbal interpersonal communication, although we seldom think about it. Edward T. Hall (1959, 1963, 1966), who pioneered the study of spatial communication, called this study **proxemics**. We can sample this broad area by looking at proxemic distances and territoriality.

### Proxemic Distances
Hall (1959, 1966) distinguishes four distances that define types of relationships between people; each distance communicates specific kinds of messages.

At an **intimate distance,** ranging from actual touching to 18 inches, the presence of the other individual is unmistakable. Each person experiences the sound, smell, and feel of the other's breath. You use intimate distance for lovemaking and wrestling, for comforting and protecting. This distance is so short that most people do not consider it proper in public.

**Personal distance** constitutes the protective "bubble" that defines your personal space, which measures from 18 inches to 4 feet. This imaginary bubble keeps you protected and untouched by others. You can still hold or grasp another person at this distance—but only by extending your arms—allowing you to take certain individuals such as loved ones into your protective bubble. At the outer limit of personal distance, you can touch another person only if both of you extend your arms.

At **social distance,** ranging from 4 to 12 feet, you lose the visual detail you have at personal distance. You conduct impersonal business and interact at a social gathering at this social distance. The more distance you maintain in your interactions, the more formal they appear. Many people in executive and management positions place their desks so that they are assured of at least this distance from employees.

**Public distance,** measuring from 12 to 25 feet or more, protects you. At this distance you could take defensive action if threatened. On a public bus or train, for example, you might keep at least this distance from a drunk. Although you lose fine details of the face and eyes at this distance, you are still close enough to see what is happening. These four distances are summarized in Table 5.3.

## Territoriality

Another type of communication having to do with space is **territoriality,** a possessive reaction to an area or to particular objects. You interact basically in three types of territories (Altman, 1975):

- **Primary territories** are areas that you might call your own; these areas are your exclusive preserve. Primary territories might include your room, your desk, or your office.

- **Secondary territories** are areas that don't belong to you but which you have occupied and with which you're associated. They might include your usual table in the cafeteria, your regular seat in the classroom, or your neighborhood turf.

- **Public territories** are areas that are open to all people; they may be owned by some person or organization, but they are used by everyone. They are places such as movie theaters, restaurants, and shopping malls.

When you operate in your own primary territory, you have an interpersonal advantage, often called the **home field advantage.** In their own home or office, people take on a kind of leadership role: They initiate conversations, fill in silences, assume relaxed and comfortable postures, and maintain their positions with greater conviction. Because the territorial owner is dominant, you stand a better chance of getting your raise approved, your point accepted, or a contract resolved in your favor if you're in your own territory (your office, your home) rather than in someone else's (your supervisor's office, for example) (Marsh, 1988).

Like many animals, humans mark both their primary and secondary territories to signal ownership. Humans use three types of **markers:** central, boundary, and earmarkers (Goffman, 1971). **Central markers** are items you place in a territory to reserve it for you—for example, a drink at the bar, books on your desk, or a sweater over a library chair. Some teenagers, for example, perhaps because they can't yet own territories, often use markers to indicate a kind of pseudo-ownership or to appropriate someone else's turf or a public territory for their own

---

**TABLE 5.3**   Relationships and Proxemic Distances

Note that the four proxemic distances can be further divided into close and far phases and that the far phase of one level (say, personal) blends into the close phase of the next level (social). Do your relationships also blend into one another? Or are your personal relationships totally separate from your social relationships?

| RELATIONSHIP | DISTANCE | | RELATIONSHIP | DISTANCE | |
|---|---|---|---|---|---|
| Intimate Relationship | Intimate Distance<br>0 _____ 18 inches<br>Close phase    Far phase | | Social Relationship | Social Distance<br>4 _____ 12 feet<br>Close phase    Far phase | |
| Personal Relationship | Personal Distance<br>1½ _____ 4 feet<br>Close phase    Far phase | | Public Relationship | Public Distance<br>12 _____ 25+ feet<br>Close phase    Far phase | |

## Selecting Seats at the Company Meeting

The accompanying graphic represents a table with 12 chairs, one of which is occupied by the "boss." For each of the messages below, indicate (a) where you would sit to communicate each message and (b) any other possible messages that your choice of seat will likely communicate.

*Nonverbal choices (such as the seat you select or the clothes you wear) have an impact on communication and on your image as a communicator. Sometimes just an awareness of how things work will help you make effective communication choices.*

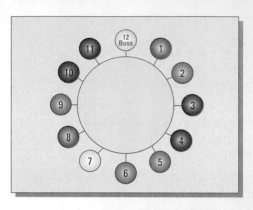

1. You want to ingratiate yourself with your boss.
2. You aren't prepared and want to be ignored.
3. You want to challenge the boss's proposal that is scheduled to come up for a vote.
4. You want to get to know better the person at seat number 7.

use (Childress, 2004). Examples of graffiti and the markings of gang boundaries come quickly to mind.

**Boundary markers** serve to divide your territory from that of others. In the supermarket checkout line, the bar placed between your groceries and those of the person behind you is a boundary marker, as are fences, armrests that separate your chair from those on either side, and the contours of the molded plastic seats on a bus.

**Ear markers**—a term taken from the practice of branding animals on their ears—are identifying marks that indicate your possession of a territory or object. Trademarks, nameplates, and initials on a shirt or attaché case are all examples of ear markers.

Markers are also important in giving you a feeling of belonging. For example, one study found that students who marked their college dorm rooms by displaying personal items stayed in school longer than did those who didn't personalize their spaces (Marsh, 1988).

Again, like animals, humans use territory to signal their status. For example, the size and location of your territory (your home or office, say) indicates something about your status. Status is also signaled by the unwritten law governing the right of invasion. Higher-status individuals have a "right" to invade the territory of lower-status persons, but the reverse is not true. The boss of a large company, for example, can barge into the office of a junior executive, but the reverse would be unthinkable. Similarly, a teacher may invade a student's personal space by looking over her or his shoulder as the student writes, but the student cannot do the same to the teacher.

## Artifactual Communication

**Artifactual messages** are messages conveyed through objects or arrangements made by human hands. Color, the clothing or jewelry you wear, the way you decorate space, and even bodily scents communicate a wide variety of meanings.

### WHAT DO YOU SAY?
**Proxemics**

Like the close-talker in an episode of *Seinfeld*, one of your team members at work maintains an extremely close distance when talking. In addition, this person is a heavy smoker and reeks of smoke. You need to say something. *What do you say? Through what channel?*

**Color Communication**   The colors with which we surround ourselves are important because there is some evidence that colors affect people physiologically. For example, respiration rates increase in the presence of red light and decrease in the presence of blue light. Similarly, eye blinks increase in frequency when eyes are exposed to red light and decrease when exposed to blue. These findings seem consistent with our intuitive feelings that blue is more soothing and red more provocative. At one school, in fact, after the administration changed the classroom walls from orange and white to blue, the students' blood pressure levels decreased and their academic performance improved (Ketcham, 1958; Malandro, Barker, & Barker, 1989).

"We're moving you to a cubicle, Harrison."

© Charles Barsotti

Colors surely influence our perceptions and behaviors (Kanner, 1989). People's acceptance of a product, for example, is strongly influenced by its package. For example, in one experiment consumers in the United States described the very same coffee taken from a yellow can as weak, from a dark brown can as too strong, from a red can as rich, and from a blue can as mild. Even our acceptance of a person may depend on the colors that person wears. Consider, for example, the comments of one color expert (Kanner, 1989, p. 23): "If you have to pick the wardrobe for your defense lawyer heading into court and choose anything but blue, you deserve to lose the case. . . ." Black is so powerful that it can work against the lawyer with the jury. Brown lacks sufficient authority. Green will probably elicit a negative response.

**Clothing and Body Adornment**   People make inferences about who you are partly on the basis of how you dress. Whether accurate or not, these inferences will affect what people think of you and how they react to you. Your social class, your seriousness, your attitudes (for example, whether you are conservative or liberal), your concern for convention, your sense of style, and perhaps even your creativity will all be judged—in part at least—by the way you dress. For instance, college students will perceive an instructor dressed informally as friendly, fair, enthusiastic, and flexible and the same instructor dressed formally as prepared, knowledgeable, and organized (Malandro, Barker, & Barker, 1989). In the business world, what you wear may communicate your position within the hierarchy and your willingness and desire to conform to the clothing norms of the organization. It also may communicate your level of professionalism, which seems to be the reason why some organizations favor dress codes (Smith, 2003).

Your jewelry also communicates messages about you. Wedding and engagement rings are obvious examples that communicate specific messages. College rings and political buttons likewise communicate messages. If you wear a Rolex watch or large precious stones, others are likely to infer that you are rich. Men who wear earrings will be judged differently from men who don't.

The way you wear your hair says something about who you are—from a concern about being up to date, to a desire to shock, to perhaps a lack of interest in appearances. Men with long hair, to take just one example, will generally be judged as less conservative than those with shorter hair. And in a study of male baldness, participants rated a man with a full head of hair as younger and more dominant, masculine, and dynamic than the same man without hair (Butler, Pryor, & Grieder, 1998).

Body piercing and tattoos communicate too. Nose and nipple rings and tongue and belly-button jewelry send a variety of messages. Although people wearing such jewelry may wish to communicate positive meanings, those interpreting the messages of body piercings seem to infer that wearers are communicating an unwillingness to conform to social norms and a willingness to take greater risks than those without such piercings (Forbes, 2001). It's worth noting that in a study of employers' perceptions, employers rated and ranked job applicants with eyebrow piercings significantly lower than those without such piercings (Acor, 2001). Nose-pierced job candidates received lower scores on measures of credibility such as

**WHAT DO YOU SAY?**
**Clothing Communication**
One of your friends has been passed over for promotion several times. You think you know the reason—your friend dresses inappropriately—and you want to help your friend. *What do you say? Through what channel? In what context?*

ratings of character and trustworthiness, as well as on sociability and hirability (Seiter & Sandry, 2003).

Tattoos—whether temporary or permanent—likewise communicate a variety of messages, often the name of a loved one or some symbol of allegiance or affiliation. Tattoos also communicate to the wearers themselves. For example, tattooed students see themselves (and perhaps others do as well) as more adventurous, creative, individualistic, and risk prone than those without tattoos (Drews, Allison, & Probst, 2000). In the context of health care, tattoos and piercings may communicate such undesirable traits as impulsiveness, unpredictability, and a tendency toward being reckless or violent (Rapsa & Cusack, 1990; Smith, 2003).

## Space Decoration

The decoration of your workplace tells a lot about you. The office with the mahogany desk and bookcase set and oriental rugs communicates your importance and status within the organization, just as a metal desk and bare floor indicate an entry-level employee much farther down in the company hierarchy.

Similarly, people will make inferences about you based on the way you decorate your home. The expensiveness of the furnishings may communicate your status and wealth; their coordination, your sense of style. The magazines on your coffee table may reflect your interests, and the arrangement of chairs around a television set may reveal how important watching television is to you. The contents of bookcases lining the walls reveal the importance of reading in your life. In fact, there is probably little in your home that does not send messages from which others will make inferences about you. Computers, wide-screen plasma televisions, well-equipped kitchens, and oil paintings of great grandparents, for example, all say something about the people who live in a home. At the same time, the lack of certain items will communicate something about you. Consider what messages you would get from a home where no television, phone, or books could be seen.

It's interesting to note that people also will make judgments about your personality on the basis of room decorations. For example, research finds that people will form opinions about your openness to new experiences (distinctive decorating usually communicates this, as would different types of books and magazines and travel souvenirs), conscientiousness, emotional stability, degree of extroversion, and agreeableness. And, not surprisingly, bedrooms prove more revealing than offices (Gosling, Ko, Mannarelli, & Morris, 2002).

## Smell Communication

Smell communication, or olfactory communication, is extremely important in a wide variety of situations; indeed, the study known as **olfactics** is now "big business" (Kleinfeld, 1992). Although we often think of women as the primary users of perfumes and scents, increasingly men are using them as well—not only the cologne and aftershave lotions they have long used but more recently body sprays, for which the market has been estimated at $180 million (Dell, 2005). Different scents have different effects. For example, there is some evidence (although clearly not very conclusive evidence) that the smell of lemon contributes to a perception of health. The smells of lavender and eucalyptus seem to increase alertness, and the smell of rose oil seems to reduce blood pressure. Research also finds that smells can influence your body's chemistry, which in turn influences your emotional state. For example, the smell of chocolate results in the reduction of theta brain waves, thus bringing a sense of relaxation and a reduced level of attention (Martin, 1998). Findings such as these have contributed to the growth of aromatherapy and to a new profession of aromatherapists (Furlow, 1996). Because humans possess "denser skin concentrations of scent glands than almost any other mammal," it has been argued that we need only to discover how we use scent to communicate a wide variety of messages (Furlow, 1996, p. 41). Two particularly important messages scent communicates are those of attraction and identification.

*Attraction Messages.*  In many animal species, the female gives off a scent that draws males, often from far distances, and thus ensures the continuation of the species. Humans (perhaps similarly) use perfumes, colognes, aftershave lotions, powders, and the like in an effort to enhance attractiveness. Women, research finds, prefer the scent of men who bear a close genetic similarity to themselves—a finding that may account in part for people's tendency to be attracted to others much like themselves (Ober, Weitkamp, Cox, Dytch, Kostyu, & Elias, 1997; Wade, 2002). You also use scents to make yourself feel better; after all, you also smell yourself. When the smells are pleasant, you feel better about yourself; when the smells are unpleasant, you feel less good about yourself and probably shower and perhaps put on some cologne.

*Identification Messages.*  Smell is often used to create an image or an identity for a product. Advertisers and manufacturers spend millions of dollars each year creating scents for cleaning products and toothpastes, for example. These fragrances have nothing to do with products' cleaning power; instead, they function solely to create an image for the products. There is also evidence that we can identify specific significant others by smell. For example, young children were able to identify the T-shirts of their brothers and sisters solely on the basis of smell (Porter & Moore, 1981). And one researcher goes so far as to advise, "If your man's odor reminds you of Dad or your brother, you may want genetic tests before trying to conceive a child" (Furlow, 1996, p. 41). Your man just may be a long-lost uncle or cousin.

> **WHAT DO YOU SAY?**
> **Artifactual Communication**
> One problem with a group of interns you're mentoring is that they've decorated their office spaces with items that communicate all the wrong messages. You need to address this seemingly minor but actually quite influential issue. *What do you say? In what context?*

# Touch Communication

**Touch communication**, or tactile communication, is perhaps the most primitive form of nonverbal communication (Montagu, 1971). Touch develops before the other senses; a child is stimulated by touch even in the womb. Soon after birth, the child is fondled, caressed, patted, and stroked. In turn, the child explores its world through touch and quickly learns to communicate a variety of meanings through touch.

Touching varies greatly from one culture to another. For example, African Americans touch each other more than European Americans, and touching declines from kindergarten to the sixth grade for European Americans but not for African American children (Burgoon, Buller, & Woodall, 1996). Japanese people touch each other much less than Anglo-Saxons, who in turn touch much less than southern Europeans (Morris, 1977; Burgoon, Buller, & Woodall, 1996).

Not surprisingly, touch also varies with your relationship stage. In the early stages of acquaintance, you touch little; in intermediate stages of relationship development (involvement and intimacy), you touch a great deal; and at stable or deteriorating stages of a relationship, you again touch little (Guerrero & Andersen, 1991).

**The Meanings of Touch**  Researchers in the field of **haptics,** or the study of touch communication, have identified the major meanings of touch (Jones & Yarbrough, 1985). Here are five of the most important.

- Touch may communicate *positive emotions* such as support, appreciation, inclusion, sexual interest or intent, and affection.
- Touch often communicates *playfulness*, either affectionately or aggressively.
- Touch may also *control* or direct the behaviors, attitudes, or feelings of another person. To get attention, for example, you may touch a person as if to say, "Look at me" or "Look over here."
- *Ritual* touching centers on greetings and departures, as in shaking hands to say hello or good-bye or hugging, kissing, or putting your arm around another's shoulder when greeting or saying farewell.

- *Task-related* touching occurs while you are performing some function—for example, removing a speck of dust from another person's face or helping someone out of a car.

**Touch Avoidance**     Much as we have a tendency to touch and be touched, we also have a tendency to avoid touch from certain people or in certain circumstances. Researchers in nonverbal communication have found some interesting relationships between **touch avoidance** and other significant communication variables (Andersen & Leibowitz, 1978).

Touch avoidance is positively related to communication apprehension: Those who fear oral communication also score high on touch avoidance. Touch avoidance is also high in those who self-disclose little. Both touch and self-disclosure are intimate forms of communication; people who are reluctant to get close to another person by self-disclosing also seem reluctant to get close by touching.

Touch avoidance is also affected by age and gender (Guerrero & Andersen, 1994; Crawford, 1994). Older people have higher touch-avoidance scores for opposite-sex persons than do younger people. As we get older, we are touched less by members of the opposite sex, and this decreased frequency may lead us to further avoid touching. Males score higher on same-sex touch avoidance than do females, which matches our stereotypes (Martin & Anderson, 1993). That is, men avoid touching other men, but women may and do touch other women. On the other hand, women have higher touch-avoidance scores for opposite-sex touching than do men (Andersen, Andersen, & Lustig, 1987).

## Paralanguage and Silence

**Paralanguage** is the vocal but nonverbal dimension of speech. It has to do with *how* you say something rather than what you say. As for silence: As we'll see, silence is the absence of sound but not of communication.

**Paralanguage**     An old exercise teachers used to increase students' ability to express different emotions, feelings, and attitudes was to have the students repeat a sentence while accenting or stressing different words each time. Placing the stress on different words easily communicates significant differences in meaning. Consider the following variations of the sentence "Is this the face that launched a thousand ships?"

1. *Is* this the face that launched a thousand ships?
2. Is *this* the face that launched a thousand ships?
3. Is this the *face* that launched a thousand ships?
4. Is this the face that *launched* a thousand ships?
5. Is this the face that launched *a thousand ships?*

Each sentence communicates something different—in fact, each asks a different question, even though the words are the same. All that varies the sentences is the stress on different words, one aspect of paralanguage.

In addition to stress, paralanguage includes such vocal characteristics as rate, volume, and rhythm. It also includes vocalizations you make in crying, whispering, moaning, belching, yawning, and yelling (Trager, 1958, 1961; Argyle, 1988). A variation in any of these vocal features communicates. When you speak quickly, for example, you communicate something different from when you speak slowly. Even though the words are the same, if the speed (or volume, rhythm, or pitch) differs, the meanings people receive will also differ.

***Judgments about People.***     Do you make judgments about people's personalities on the basis of their paralinguistic cues? For example, do you conclude that

## Expressing Praise and Criticism

*You cannot speak a sentence without using nonverbal signals, and these signals influence the meaning the receiver gets. Acquiring the skills of nonverbal communication will help you communicate your meanings more effectively, whether in interpersonal, small group, or public speaking.*

Consider how nonverbal messages can communicate praise and criticism by reading aloud each of the following statements, first to communicate praise, then to express criticism. In the second and third columns, record the nonverbal signals you used to help you communicate these differences in meaning between praise and criticism.

| Message | Nonverbal Cues to Communicate Praise | Nonverbal Cues to Communicate Criticism |
|---|---|---|
| You lost weight. You look happy. You're an expert. Your parents are something else. | | |

your colleague who speaks softly when presenting ideas at a meeting isn't sure of the ideas' usefulness and believes that no one really wants to listen to them? Do you assume that people who speak loudly have overinflated egos? Do those who speak with no variation, in a complete monotone, seem uninterested in what they are saying? Might you then assume that they have a lack of interest in life in general? All such judgments are based on little evidence, yet they persist in much popular talk.

Research has found that people can accurately judge the socioeconomic status (whether high, middle, or low) of speakers from 60-second voice samples (Davitz, 1964). Many listeners in this study made their judgments in less than 15 seconds. Participants also rated people whom they judged to be of high status as more credible than speakers judged to be of middle and low status.

Listeners also can accurately judge the emotional states of speakers from vocal expression alone. In these studies, speakers recite the alphabet or numbers while expressing emotions. Some emotions are easier to identify than others; it is easy to distinguish between hate and sympathy but more difficult to distinguish between fear and anxiety. And, of course, listeners vary in their ability to decode, and speakers in their ability to encode, emotions (Scherer, 1986).

***Judgments about Communication Effectiveness.***   Speech rate is an important component of paralanguage. In one-way communication (when one person is doing all or most of the speaking and the other person is doing all or most of the listening), those who talk fast (about 50 percent faster than normal) are more persuasive. That is, people agree more with a fast speaker than with a slow speaker and find the fast speaker more intelligent and objective (MacLachlan, 1979).

When we look at comprehension, rapid speech shows an interesting effect. When the speaking rate increases by 50 percent, the comprehension level drops by only 5 percent. When the rate doubles, the comprehension level drops only 10 percent. In terms of efficiency, then, these 5 and 10 percent comprehension losses are more than offset by the increased speed; faster speech rates are thus much more efficient in communicating information. If the speeds are more than twice that of normal speech, however, the comprehension level begins to fall dramatically.

Exercise caution in applying this research to all forms of communication (MacLachlan, 1979). While the speaker is speaking, the listener is generating, or

▼ | E-TALK

**Paralanguage**
When you have lots to communicate in a short time, the best you can do while speaking is to increase your rate. When you have a lot to communicate electronically, you can significantly compress your files to reduce the time they take to send and receive and to reduce the amount of storage space they take up. For more information on this see, for example, **www.eurekais.com/brock/aazip.htm** (accessed June 3, 2006).

### The Spiral of Silence

The *spiral of silence* theory argues that you're more likely to voice agreement than disagreement (Noelle-Neumann, 1973, 1980, 1991; Windahl, Signitzer, & Olson, 1992). The theory claims that when a controversial issue arises, you try to estimate public opinion on the issue and figure out which views are popular and which are not, largely by attending to the media (Gonzenbach, King, & Jablonski, 1999; Jeffres, Neuendorf, & Atkin, 1999). At the same time, you also judge the likelihood and the severity of punishment for expressing minority opinions. You then use these estimates to regulate your expression of opinions.

The theory continues: When you agree with the majority, you're more likely to voice your opinions than when you disagree. You may avoid expressing minority opinions because you don't want to be isolated from the majority or confront the unpleasant possibility of being proven wrong. Or, you may assume that the majority, because they're a majority, is right.

Not all people seem affected equally by this spiral (Noelle-Neumann, 1991). For example, younger people and men are more likely to express minority opinions than are older people and women. Educated people are more likely to express minority opinions than are those who are less educated. Similarly, the tendency to voice minority opinions will vary from one culture to another (Scheufele & Moy, 2000).

As people with minority views remain silent, the predominant media position gets stronger (because those who agree with it are the only ones speaking). As the media's position grows stronger, the voice of the opposition also gets weaker. Thus, the situation becomes an ever-widening spiral of silence.

*Increasing Media Literacy.*   *In what ways does the spiral of silence operate in your own media life? For example, do you contribute to this spiral of silence? Under what conditions are you most likely to conform to the predictions of this theory? What are its effects on your self-image and on your popularity with peers?*

> *I have noticed that nothing I have never said ever did me any harm.*
>
> —CALVIN COOLIDGE

---

framing, a reply. If the speaker talks too rapidly, the listener may not have enough time to compose a reply and may become resentful. Furthermore, the increased rate may seem so unnatural that the listener may focus on the speed rather than on the message being communicated.

**Silence**   "Speech," wrote Thomas Mann, "is civilization itself. The word, even the most contradictory word, preserves contact; it is silence which isolates." Philosopher Karl Jaspers, on the other hand, observed that "the ultimate in thinking as in communication is silence," and philosopher Max Picard noted that "silence is nothing merely negative; it is not the mere absence of speech. It is a positive, a complete world in itself." The one thing on which these contradictory observations agree is that **silence** communicates. Your silence communicates just as intensely as anything you verbalize (see Jaworski, 1993).

*Functions of Silence.*   Silence allows the speaker and the listener *time to think*, time to formulate and organize the meaning of the message. For example, a lawyer may have many sophisticated points to make during closing arguments to the jury. A skilled lawyer will use silence not only to give herself or himself time to present these issues in an organized way, but also to give the jury time to digest the information presented. Before messages indicative of intense conflict, as well as those confessing undying love, there is often silence. Again, silence seems to prepare the receiver for the importance of these messages.

Some people use silence as a *weapon* to hurt others. We often speak of giving someone "the silent treatment." After a conflict, for example, one or both individuals may remain silent as a kind of punishment. Silence used to hurt others may also take the form of refusal to acknowledge the presence of another person, as in disconfirmation (see Chapter 4); in this case, silence is a dramatic demonstration of the total indifference one person feels toward the other.

People sometimes use silence because of *personal anxiety* or shyness, or in response to threats. You may feel anxious or shy among new people and prefer to remain silent. By remaining silent you preclude the chance of rejection. Only when you break your silence and attempt to communicate with another person do you risk rejection.

People may also use silence *to prevent communication* of certain messages. In conflict situations silence is sometimes used to prevent certain topics from surfacing and to prevent one or both parties from saying things they may later regret. In such situations silence often allows people time to cool off before expressing hatred, severe criticism, or personal attack—which, as we've seen, are irreversible.

Like the eyes, face, or hands, silence can also be used to *communicate emotional responses* (Ehrenhaus, 1988). Sometimes silence communicates a determination to be uncooperative or defiant: By refusing to engage in verbal communication, you defy the authority or the legitimacy of the other person's position. Silence often communicates annoyance; in this case, it is usually accompanied by a pouting expression, arms crossed in front of the chest, and flared nostrils. Silence also may express affection or love, especially when coupled with long and longing gazes into another's eyes.

Of course, you also may use silence when you simply have *nothing to say,* when nothing occurs to you or when you do not want to say anything. James Russell Lowell expressed this well: "Blessed are they who have nothing to say and who cannot be persuaded to say it."

## Time Communication

The study of **temporal communication,** known technically as **chronemics,** concerns the use of time—how you organize it, react to it, and communicate messages through it (Bruneau, 1985, 1990).

An especially important aspect of temporal communication is **psychological time:** the relative importance we place on the past, present, or future. With a *past* orientation, we have a particular reverence for the past. We relive old times and

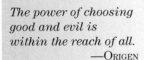

## COMMUNICATING ETHICALLY

### Communication Silence

In the U.S. legal system, although you have the right to remain silent so as not to incriminate yourself, you are obliged to reveal information about, for example, the criminal activities of others that you may have witnessed. But rightly or wrongly (and this in itself is an ethical issue), psychiatrists, lawyers, and some clergy are often exempt from this general rule. Similarly, a wife can't be forced to testify against her husband, nor a husband against his wife.

Unlike the legal system, however, most day-by-day communication situations lack written rules, so it's not always clear if or when silence is ethical. For example, most people (though not all) would agree that you have the right to withhold information that has no bearing on the matter at hand. Thus, your previous relationship history, affectional orientation, or religion is usually irrelevant to your ability to function as a doctor or police officer and may thus be kept private in most job-related situations.

*The power of choosing good and evil is within the reach of all.*
—ORIGEN

*What would you do?* *You witness a mother verbally abusing her three-year-old child. Your first impulse is to tell this woman that verbal abuse can have lasting effects on the child and often leads to physical abuse. At the same time, you don't want to interfere with a mother's rights. Nor do you want to aggravate a mother who may later take out her frustration on the child. What is your ethical obligation in this case? What would you do?*

regard the old methods as the best. We see events as circular and recurring and find that the wisdom of yesterday is applicable also to today and tomorrow. With a *present* orientation, we live in the present—for now—without planning for tomorrow. With a *future* orientation, we look toward and live for the future. We save today, work hard in college, and deny ourselves luxuries because we are preparing for the future. Before reading about some of the consequences of the way we view time, take the following self-test, "What time do you have?" to assess your own psychological time orientation.

## WHAT TIME DO YOU HAVE?

**INSTRUCTIONS:** For each statement, indicate whether the statement is true (T) or untrue (F) of your general attitude and behavior. A few statements are repeated; this is to facilitate interpreting your score.

_____ ❶ Meeting tomorrow's deadlines and doing other necessary work come before tonight's partying.

_____ ❷ I meet my obligations to friends and authorities on time.

_____ ❸ I complete projects on time by making steady progress.

_____ ❹ I am able to resist temptations when I know there is work to be done.

_____ ❺ I keep working at a difficult, uninteresting task if it will help me get ahead.

_____ ❻ If things don't get done on time, I don't worry about it.

_____ ❼ I think that it's useless to plan too far ahead because things hardly ever come out the way you planned anyway.

_____ ❽ I try to live one day at a time.

_____ ❾ I live to make better what is rather than to be concerned about what will be.

_____ ❿ It seems to me that it doesn't make sense to worry about the future, since fate determines that whatever will be, will be.

_____ ⓫ I believe that getting together with friends to party is one of life's important pleasures.

_____ ⓬ I do things impulsively, making decisions on the spur of the moment.

_____ ⓭ I take risks to put excitement in my life.

_____ ⓮ I get drunk at parties.

_____ ⓯ It's fun to gamble.

_____ ⓰ Thinking about the future is pleasant to me.

_____ ⓱ When I want to achieve something, I set subgoals and consider specific means for reaching those goals.

_____ ⓲ It seems to me that my career path is pretty well laid out.

_____ ⓳ It upsets me to be late for appointments.

_____ ⓴ I meet my obligations to friends and authorities on time.

_____ ㉑ I get irritated at people who keep me waiting when we've agreed to meet at a given time.

_____ ㉒ It makes sense to invest a substantial part of my income in insurance premiums.

_____ ㉓ I believe that "A stitch in time saves nine."

_____ ㉔ I believe that "A bird in the hand is worth two in the bush."

_____ ㉕ I believe it is important to save for a rainy day.

_____ ㉖ I believe a person's day should be planned each morning.

_____ ㉗ I make lists of things I must do.

_____ ㉘ When I want to achieve something, I set subgoals and consider specific means for reaching those goals.

_____ ㉙ I believe that "A stitch in time saves nine."

**HOW DID YOU DO?** This time test measures seven different factors. If you selected true (T) for all or most of the questions within any given factor, you are probably high on that factor. If you selected untrue (F) for all or most of the questions within any given factor, you are probably low on that factor.

The first factor, measured by questions 1 through 5, is a future, work motivation, perseverance orientation. People high in this factor have a strong work ethic and are committed to completing tasks despite difficulties and temptations. The second factor (6 through 10) is a present, fatalistic, worry-free orientation. High scorers on this factor live one day at a time, not necessarily to enjoy the day but to avoid planning for the next day or anxiety about the future. The third factor (11 through 15) is a present, pleasure-seeking, partying orientation. People high in this factor enjoy the present, take risks, and engage in a variety of impulsive actions. The fourth factor (16 through 18) is a future, goal-seeking, and planning orientation. High scorers on this factor derive special pleasure from planning and achieving a variety of goals.

The fifth factor (19 through 21) is a time-sensitivity orientation. People who score high are especially sensitive to time and its role in social obligations. The sixth factor (22 through 25) is a future, practical action orientation. People high in this factor do what they have to do—take practical actions—to achieve the future they want. The seventh factor (26 through 29) is a future, somewhat obsessive daily planning orientation. High scorers on this factor make daily "to do" lists and devote great attention to specific details.

**WHAT WILL YOU DO?** Now that you have some idea of how you treat the different types of time, consider how these attitudes and behaviors work for you. For example, will your time orientations help you achieve your social and professional goals? If not, what might you do about changing these attitudes and behaviors?

_Source:_ Adapted from "Time In Perspective" by Alexander Gonzalez and Philip G. Zimbardo. Reprinted with permission from _Psychology Today_ magazine. Copyright © 1985 (Sussex Publishers, Inc.).

Consider some of the findings on these time orientations (Gonzalez & Zimbardo, 1985). Future income is positively related to future orientation; the more future oriented you are, the greater your income is likely to be. Present orientation is strongest among lowest-income males and also among those with high emotional distress and hopelessness (Zaleski, Cycon, & Kurc, 2001).

The time orientation you develop depends largely on your socioeconomic class and your personal experiences (Gonzalez & Zimbardo, 1985). For example, parents in unskilled and semiskilled occupations are likely to teach their children a present-oriented fatalism and a belief that enjoying yourself is more important than planning for the future. Parents who are teachers or managers, or are in other profes-

▼ **E-TALK**

**Nonverbal Blog**
An interesting blog dealing with nonverbal communication is available at www.geocities.com/marvin_hecht/nonverbal.html (accessed June 3, 2006). Visit this site and examine the wide variety of information available. What do you find on this site that you would add to a chapter on nonverbal messages in interpersonal communication?

*You can't fake listening. It shows.*
—RAQUEL WELCH

### Listening with Nonverbals

Because much of ineffective listening is communicated nonverbally, it's useful to identify some general types of listeners who, largely through their nonverbal messages, make conversation difficult.

| Listen Type | Ineffective Listening Behavior | Effective Alternatives |
| --- | --- | --- |
| **The static listener** | Gives no feedback; remains relatively motionless and expressionless. | Get involved with the listener; react so the speaker knows that you're listening. |
| **The monotonous feedback giver** | Seems responsive, but the responses never vary; regardless of what you say, the response is the same. | Respond to the speaker with a broad repertoire of nonverbal feedback messages. |
| **The overly expressive listener** | Reacts to just about everything with extreme responses. | Consider moderation; keep the attention on the speaker and not on the listener reactions. |
| **The eye avoider** | Looks all around the room and at others but never at you. | Focus on the speaker visually and with a facing posture. |
| **The preoccupied listener** | Listens to other things at the same time, often with headphones or with the television on. | Really listen when you listen; give the speaker the same focused attention you'd like. |
| **The waiting listener** | Listens for a cue to take over the speaking turn. | Listen fully; it's not always easy, but it is considerate. |
| **The thought-completing listener** | Listens a little and then finishes your thought. | Listen to the speaker and not to yourself speaking for the speaker. |

***Applying Listening Skills.*** *What additional types of ineffective listening can you identify? What steps can you take to prevent yourself from falling into one of these ineffective listening patterns?*

sions teach their children the importance of planning and preparing for the future along with strategies for success.

Different time perspectives also account for much intercultural misunderstanding, because different cultures often teach their members drastically different time orientations. For example, members of some Latin cultures would rather be late for an appointment than end a conversation abruptly. The Latin person sees the lateness as politeness toward the person with whom he or she is conversing—but others may see it as impolite to the person with whom he or she had the appointment (Hall & Hall, 1987).

## Culture, Gender, and Nonverbal Communication

This chapter has already noted a few cultural and gender-related differences in nonverbal communication. The roles of culture and gender in certain areas of nonverbal communication, however, have become the focus of sustained research. Here we consider just a sampling of research on communication via gestures, the face and eyes, color, silence, touch, and time.

In general, research shows that women are better senders and receivers of non-verbal messages than are men (Hall, 1998; Burgoon & Hoobler, 2002). For example, in a review of 21 research studies, 71 percent found women to be superior senders of nonverbal signals. And in a review of 61 studies on decoding, 84 percent found women to be superior receivers (Hall, 1998).

## Gestures

As shown in Figure 5.1, there is much variation in gestures and their meanings among different cultures (Axtell, 1993). Consider a few additional common gestures that you might use even without thinking but that could easily get you into trouble if you used them in another culture:

- Folding your arms over your chest would be considered disrespectful in Fiji.
- Waving your hand would be insulting in Nigeria and Greece.
- Gesturing with the thumb up would be rude in Australia.
- Tapping your two index fingers together would be considered an invitation to sleep together in Egypt.
- Pointing with your index finger would be impolite in many Middle Eastern countries.
- Bowing to a lesser degree than your host would be considered a statement of your superiority in Japan.

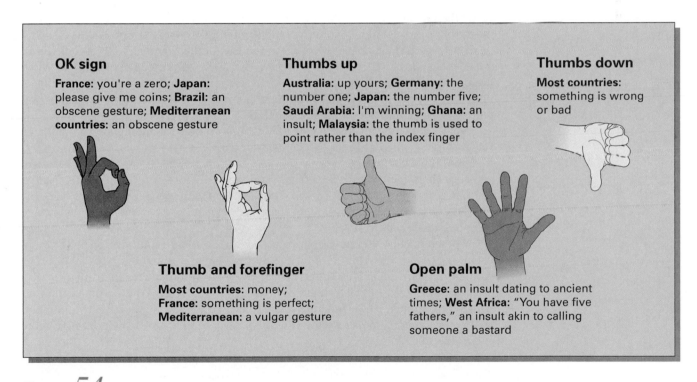

**OK sign**
**France:** you're a zero; **Japan:** please give me coins; **Brazil:** an obscene gesture; **Mediterranean countries:** an obscene gesture

**Thumbs up**
**Australia:** up yours; **Germany:** the number one; **Japan:** the number five; **Saudi Arabia:** I'm winning; **Ghana:** an insult; **Malaysia:** the thumb is used to point rather than the index finger

**Thumbs down**
**Most countries:** something is wrong or bad

**Thumb and forefinger**
**Most countries:** money; **France:** something is perfect; **Mediterranean:** a vulgar gesture

**Open palm**
**Greece:** an insult dating to ancient times; **West Africa:** "You have five fathers," an insult akin to calling someone a bastard

## Figure 5.1
**Some Cultural Meanings of Gestures**
Cultural differences in the meanings of nonverbal gestures are often significant. The over-the-head clasped hands that signify victory to an American may signify friendship to a Russian. To an American, holding up two fingers to make a V signifies victory or peace. To certain South Americans, however, it is an obscene gesture that corresponds to the American's extended middle finger. This figure highlights some additional nonverbal differences. Can you identify others?

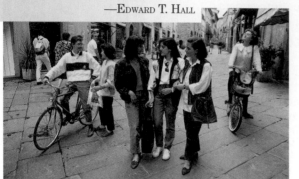
■ Inserting your thumb between your index and middle finger in a clenched fist would be viewed as a wish that evil fall on someone in certain African countries.

■ Resting your feet on a table or chair would be insulting in some Middle Eastern cultures.

## Facial Expression and Eye Movements

The wide variations in facial communication that we observe in different cultures seem to have to do more with which reactions are publicly permissible than with differences in the ways people show their emotions. For example, in one study Japanese and American students watched a film of an operation (Ekman, 1985). The experimenters videotaped the students both in an interview about the film and alone while watching the film. When alone, the students showed very similar reactions. In the interview, however, the American students displayed facial expressions indicating displeasure, whereas the Japanese students did not show any great emotion. Similarly, it's considered "forward" or inappropriate for Japanese women to reveal broad smiles, so women in Japan will hide their smiles, sometimes with their hands (Ma, 1996). Women in the United States, on the other hand, have no such restrictions and are more likely to smile openly. Thus, many differences may reflect not the way different cultures express emotions but rather the cultural rules for displaying emotions in public (Matsumoto, 1991).

Cultural differences also exist in the ways people decode the meanings of facial expressions. For example, researchers asked American and Japanese students to judge the meanings of smiling and neutral facial expressions. The Americans rated the smiling face as more attractive, more intelligent, and more sociable than the neutral face. The Japanese, however, rated the smiling face as more sociable but not as more attractive; and they rated the neutral face as more intelligent (Matsumoto & Kudoh, 1993). Another study found that participants rated people who smile as more likable and more approachable than people who don't smile or who only pretend to smile (Gladstone & Parker, 2002).

Not surprisingly, eye messages vary with both culture and gender. Americans, for example, consider direct eye contact an expression of honesty and forthrightness, but the Japanese often view this as a lack of respect. A Japanese person will glance at the other person's face rarely, and then only for very short periods (Axtell, 1990). Interpreting another's eye contact messages with your own cultural rules is a risky undertaking; eye movements that you may interpret as insulting may have been intended to show respect.

Women make eye contact more and maintain it longer (both in speaking and in listening) than men. This holds true whether women are interacting with other women or with men. This difference in eye behavior may result from women's greater tendency to display their emotions (Wood, 1994). When women interact with other women, they generally display affiliative and supportive eye contact, whereas when men interact with other men, they tend to avert their gaze (Gamble & Gamble, 2003).

## Colors

Colors vary greatly in their meanings from one culture to another. Table 5.4 presents some of these cultural differences—but before looking at the table, think about the meanings given to colors such as red, green, black, white, blue, yellow, and purple in your own culture(s).

## Touch

The functions and examples of touching discussed earlier were based on studies in North America; in other cultures these functions are not served in the same way. In

## TABLE 5.4 Some Cultural Meanings of Color

This table, constructed from research reported by a variety of researchers (Dreyfuss, 1971; Hoft, 1995; Dresser, 1996; Yunker, 2003; Singh & Pereira, 2005), summarizes some of the different meanings that colors may communicate and how colors are viewed in different cultures. As you read this table, consider the meanings you give to these colors and where your meanings came from.

| COLOR | CULTURAL MEANINGS AND COMMENTS |
|---|---|
| Red | Red signifies prosperity and rebirth in China and is used for festive and joyous occasions. It signifies masculinity in France and the United Kingdom, blasphemy or death in many African countries, and anger and danger in Japan. Red ink is used by Korean Buddhists only to write a person's name at the time of death or on the anniversary of the person's death; it therefore creates problems when American teachers use red ink to mark Korean students' homework. |
| Green | Green signifies capitalism, "go ahead," and envy in the United States; patriotism in Ireland; femininity among some Native Americans; fertility and strength in Egypt; youth and energy in Japan; and holiness in many Muslim cultures. |
| Black | Black signifies old age in Thailand, courage in parts of Malaysia, and death in much of Europe and North America. |
| White | White signifies purity in Thailand, purity and peace in many Muslim and Hindu cultures, death and mourning in Japan and other Asian countries, and victory and purity in much of Africa. |
| Blue | Blue signifies something negative in Iran, virtue and truth in Egypt, defeat among the Cherokee, national pride in Greece, and cleanliness in Scandinavia. |
| Yellow | Yellow signifies wealth and authority in China, caution and cowardice in the United States, happiness and prosperity in Egypt, envy and jealousy in Germany, and femininity in many countries throughout the world. |
| Purple | Purple signifies death in Latin America, royalty in Europe, virtue and faith in Egypt, grace and nobility in Japan, barbarism in China, and nobility and bravery in the United States. |

some cultures, for example, some task-related touching is viewed negatively and is to be avoided. Among Koreans it is considered disrespectful for a store owner to touch a customer in, say, handing back change; doing so is considered too intimate a gesture. Members of other cultures who are used to such touching may consider the Koreans' behavior cold and aloof. Muslim children in many countries are socialized to refrain from touching members of the opposite sex, a practice that can easily be interpreted as unfriendly by American children, who are used to touching one another (Dresser, 1996).

Students from the United States reported being touched twice as much as did the Japanese students. In Japan there is a strong taboo against strangers' touching, and the Japanese are therefore especially careful to maintain sufficient distance (Barnlund, 1975).

Some cultures, such as those of southern Europe and the Middle East, are contact cultures. Others, such as those of northern Europe and Japan, are noncontact cultures. Members of contact cultures maintain close distances, touch each other in conversation, face each other more directly, and maintain longer and more focused eye contact. Members of noncontact cultures maintain greater distance in their interactions, touch each other rarely if at all, avoid facing each other directly, and maintain much less direct eye contact. As a result, northern Europeans and Japanese may be perceived as cold, distant, and uninvolved by southern Europeans—who may in turn be perceived as pushy, aggressive, and inappropriately intimate.

## Paralanguage and Silence

Cultural differences also need to be taken into consideration in evaluating the results of studies on speech rate. In one study, for example, Korean male speakers

who spoke rapidly were given unfavorable credibility ratings, in contrast to the positive ratings received by Americans who spoke rapidly (Lee & Boster, 1992). Researchers have suggested that in individualistic societies a rapid-rate speaker is seen as more competent than a slow-rate speaker, whereas in collectivist cultures a speaker who uses a slower rate is judged more competent.

Similarly, not all cultures view silence as functioning in the same way (Vainiomaki, 2004). In the United States, for example, silence is often interpreted negatively. At a business meeting or even in informal social groups, the silent member may be seen as not listening or as having nothing interesting to add, not understanding the issues, being insensitive, or being too self-absorbed to focus on the messages of others. Other cultures, however, view silence more positively. In many situations in Japan, for example, silence is a response that is considered more appropriate than speech (Haga, 1988).

The traditional Apache, to take another example, regard silence very differently than European Americans (Basso, 1972). Among the Apache, mutual friends do not feel the need to introduce strangers who may be working in the same area or on the same project. The strangers may remain silent for several days. This period enables them to observe and evaluate each other. Once this assessment is made, the individuals talk. When courting, especially during the initial stages, the Apache remain silent for hours; if they do talk, they generally talk very little. Only after a couple has been dating for several months will they have lengthy conversations. These periods of silence are often erroneously attributed to shyness or self-consciousness. But the use of silence is explicitly taught to Apache women, who are especially discouraged from engaging in long discussions with their dates. Silence during courtship is a sign of modesty to many Apache.

## Time

Culture influences time communication in a variety of ways. Here we look at three: formal and informal time, monochronism and polychronism, and the social clock.

### Formal and Informal Time

Days are astronomically determined by the earth's rotation on its axis, months by the moon's movement around the earth, and years by the earth's rotation around the sun. But the rest of our time divisions are cultural (largely religious) in origin. In the United States and in most of the world, formal time divisions consist of units such as seconds, minutes, hours, days, weeks, months, and years. Some cultures, however, may use phases of the moon or changing seasons to delineate time periods. In the United States, if your college is on the semester system, your courses are divided into 50- or 75-minute periods that meet two or three times a week for 14-week periods. Eight semesters of 15 or 16 periods per week equal a college education. As these examples illustrate, formal time units are arbitrary. The culture establishes them for convenience.

**Informal time terms** denote approximate intervals—for example, "forever," "immediately," "soon," "right away," or "as soon as possible." Informal time expressions create the most communication problems, because the terms have different meanings for different people.

Attitudes toward time vary from one culture to another. For example, one study measured the accuracy of clocks in six cultures—Japan, Indonesia, Italy, England, Taiwan, and the United States. Japan had the most accurate and Indonesia the least accurate clocks. The researchers also measured the speed at which people in these six cultures walked; results showed that the Japanese walked the fastest, the Indonesians the slowest (LeVine & Bartlett, 1984).

TABLE 5.5 Monochronic and Polychronic Time

As you read down this table, based on Hall (1983) and Hall & Hall (1987), note the potential for miscommunication that might develop when M-time and P-time people interact. Have any of these differences ever created interpersonal misunderstandings for you?

| THE MONOCHRONIC-TIME PERSON | THE POLYCHRONIC-TIME PERSON |
|---|---|
| Does one thing at a time | Does several things at once |
| Treats time schedules and plans very seriously; feels they may be broken only for the most serious of reasons | Treats time schedules and plans as useful (not sacred); feels they may be broken for a variety of purposes |
| Considers the job the most important part of a person's life, ahead of even family | Considers the family and interpersonal relationships more important than the job |
| Considers privacy extremely important; seldom borrows or lends to others; works independently | Is actively involved with others; works in the presence of and with lots of people at the same time |

**Monochronism and Polychronism**   Another important cultural distinction exists between **monochronic** and **polychronic time orientations** (Hall, 1959, 1976; Hall & Hall, 1987). Monochronic peoples or cultures such as those of the United States, Germany, Scandinavia, and Switzerland schedule one thing at a time. These cultures compartmentalize time and set sequential times for different activities. Polychronic peoples or cultures such as those of Latin America, the Mediterranean, and the Arab world, on the other hand, schedule multiple things at the same time. Eating, conducting business with several different people, and taking care of family matters may all go on at once. No culture is entirely monochronic or polychronic; rather, these are general or preponderant tendencies. Some cultures combine both time orientations; in Japan and in parts of American culture, for example, both orientations can be found. Table 5.5 identifies some of the distinctions between these two time orientations.

**The Social Clock**   An especially interesting aspect of cultural time is the "social clock" (Neugarten, 1979). Your culture, and your more specific society within that culture, maintain a schedule that dictates the right times to do a variety of important things; for example, the right times to start dating, to finish college, to buy your own home, to have a child. You also may feel that you should be making a certain salary and working at a particular level of management by a certain age. Most people learn about and internalize this clock as they grow up. On the basis of your social clock, you evaluate your own social and professional development. If you're on time relative to the rest of your peers—for example, if you all started dating at around the same age or you're all finishing college at around the same age—then you will feel well adjusted, competent, and a part of the group. If you're late, you may experience feelings of dissatisfaction and inadequacy. It should be noted, however, that some research shows that this social clock has become more flexible in recent years; people in many societies are now more willing to tolerate deviations from the established, socially acceptable timetable for accomplishing many of life's transitional events (Peterson, 1996).

This chapter explored nonverbal communication—communication without words—and looked at the functions nonverbal messages serve, the channels of nonverbal communication, and some of the cultural and gender-related influences on and differences in nonverbal communication.

1. Nonverbal messages may be integrated with verbal messages to accent or emphasize a part of the verbal message; to complement or add nuances of meaning; to contradict verbal messages (as when people cross their fingers or wink to indicate that they're lying); to regulate, control, or indicate a desire to control the flow of verbal messages; to repeat or restate a verbal message; and/or to substitute or take the place of verbal messages.

2. Important relationship functions of nonverbal communication include forming and managing impressions, forming and defining relationships, structuring conversation and social interaction, influence and deception, and emotional expression.

3. The body communicates a variety of meanings with different types of nonverbal behaviors: emblems (which rather directly translate words or phrases); illustrators (which accompany and literally "illustrate" the verbal messages); affect displays (which communicate emotional meaning); regulators (which coordinate, monitor, maintain, or control the speech of another individual); and adaptors (which occur without conscious awareness and usually serve some kind of need, as in scratching an itch).

4. Facial movements may communicate a wide variety of emotions. The most frequently studied are happiness, surprise, fear, anger, sadness, and disgust/contempt. Through facial management techniques you can control your facial expression of emotions. The facial feedback hypothesis claims that facial display of an emotion can lead to physiological and psychological changes.

5. Eye movements may seek feedback, cue others to speak, signal the nature of a relationship, or compensate for increased physical distance.

6. Proxemics is the study of the communicative function of space and spatial relationships. Four major proxemic distances are: intimate distance, ranging from actual touching to 18 inches; personal distance, ranging from 18 inches to 4 feet; social distance, ranging from 4 to 12 feet; and public distance, ranging from 12 to 25 feet or more.

7. Your treatment of space is influenced by such factors as status, culture, context, subject matter, gender, age, and positive or negative evaluation of the other person.

8. Territoriality is a possessive reaction to an area of space or to particular objects. Markers are devices that identify a territory as ours; these include central, boundary, and ear markers.

9. Artifactual communication involves messages conveyed by human-made objects or arrangements; it includes communication through color, clothing and body adornment, space decoration, and smell.

10. Haptics is the study of touch communication. Touch may communicate a variety of meanings, the most important being positive affect, playfulness, control, ritual, and task-relatedness. Touch avoidance is the desire to avoid touching and being touched by others.

11. Paralanguage consists of the vocal but nonverbal dimension of speech. It includes stress, rate, pitch, volume, and rhythm as well as pauses and hesitations. On the basis of paralanguage we make judgments about people, conversational turns, and believability. Silence also serves important communication functions.

12. Chronemics, or the study of time communication, examines the messages communicated by our treatment of time. Psychological time has to do with people's orientations toward the past, present, or future.

13. Among important cultural and gender-related differences in nonverbal communication are variations in gestures, facial expressions and displays, the meanings of color, the appropriateness and uses of touch, the uses of paralanguage and silence, and the treatment of time.

This chapter has covered a wide variety of nonverbal communication skills. Place a check mark next to those skills that you feel you want to work on most.

_____ 1. I recognize the varied functions that nonverbal messages (my own and those of others) serve; for example, to form and manage impressions, to define relationships, and to structure conversations.

_____ 2. I use body and gesture messages to help communicate my desired meanings, and I recognize these messages in others.

_____ 3. I use my eyes to seek feedback, to inform others to speak, to signal the nature of my relationship with others, and to compensate for physical distance.

_____ 4. I give others the space they need; for example, I give extra space to those who are angry or disturbed.

_____ 5. I am sensitive to the markers (central, boundary, and ear markers) of others and use these markers to define my own territories.

_____ 6. I use artifacts thoughtfully to communicate desired messages.

_____ 7. I am sensitive to the touching behaviors of others and distinguish among touches that communicate positive emotion, playfulness, control, and ritual or task-related messages.

_____ 8. I recognize and respect each person's touch-avoidance tendency. I am especially sensitive to cultural and gender differences in touching preferences and in touch-avoidance tendencies.

_____ 9. I vary paralinguistic features (rate, emphasis, pauses, tempo, volume, etc.) to communicate my intended meanings.

_____ 10. I use silence to communicate varied meanings (for example, disappointment or the need for time to think) and I examine the silence of others for meanings just as I would eye movements or body gestures.

_____ 11. I interpret time cues with an awareness of the cultural perspective of the person with whom I am interacting.

_____ 12. I balance my time orientation and don't ignore the past, present, or future.

# Key Word Quiz

## The Language of Nonverbal Messages

Match the terms about nonverbal messages with their definitions. Record the number of the definition next to the appropriate term.

a. _____ facial feedback hypothesis

b. _____ artifactual communication

c. _____ civil inattention

d. _____ secondary territory

e. _____ adaptors

f. _____ paralanguage

g. _____ facial management techniques

h. _____ haptics

i. _____ central markers

j. _____ emblems

1. Body gestures that directly translate into words or phrases.

2. Gestures that satisfy some personal need, such as scratching.

3. Strategies that enable you to express feelings nonverbally so as to achieve your desired purpose.

4. Eye movements that respect another's privacy and avoid looking at something that might cause another embarrassment.

5. The assumption that your facial expressions influence the way you feel.

6. Items you place in a territory to reserve it for yourself or someone else.

7. The study of touch communication.

8. The vocal but nonverbal dimension of speech; includes, for example, vocal volume and stress.

9. Messages that are communicated through objects and their arrangements.

10. An area that doesn't belong to you but which you have occupied and with which you're associated.

**Answers: a.** 5 **b.** 9 **c.** 4 **d.** 10 **e.** 2 **f.** 8 **g.** 3 **h.** 7 **i.** 6 **j.** 1

## Five for Discussion

1. On a 10-point scale (with 1 indicating "not at all important" and 10 indicating "extremely important"), how important is body appearance to your own romantic interest in another person? Do the men and women you know conform to the stereotypes that say males are more concerned with the physical and females are more concerned with personality?

2. A tactic used by many defense lawyers (though some states currently prohibit this) in sex crimes against women, gay men, and lesbians is to blame the victim by referring to the way the victim was dressed and to imply that the victim, by virtue of the clothing worn, provoked the attack. What do you think of this tactic?

3. Here are a few findings from research on nonverbal sex differences (Hall, 1998; Stewart, Cooper, Stewart, with Friedley, 2003; Gamble & Gamble, 2003; Krolokke & Sorensen, 2006): (1) Women smile more than men; (2) women stand closer to each other than do men and are generally approached more closely than men; (3) both men and women, when speaking, look at men more than at women; (4) women both touch and are touched more than men; and (5) men extend their bodies, taking up greater areas of space, than women. What problems might these differences create when men and women communicate with each other?

4. Another type of time is biological time, the ways your body functions differently at different times. Your intellectual, physical, and emotional lives, according to theories of biorhythms, have cycles that influence your effectiveness. Detailed explanations and instructions for calculating your own intellectual, physical, and emotional cycles can be found in DeVito (1989); even better, you can visit a Web site that will compute your biorhythms, such as www.bio-chart.com or www.facade.com/biorhythm (both accessed June 3, 2006).

5. What nonverbal cues should you look for in judging whether someone likes you? List them in the order of their importance, beginning with 1 for the cue that is of most value in making your judgment. Do you really need two lists? One for judging a woman's liking and one for a man's?

## Log On! MyCommunicationLab

Several exercises and self-tests at www.mycommunicationlab.com will help you better understand how nonverbal communication works and will give you opportunities to practice the skills of nonverbal communication: (1) Facial Expressions, (2) Eye Contact, (3) Interpersonal Interactions and Space, (4) Artifacts and Culture: The Case of Gifts, (5) Communicating Vocally but Nonverbally, (6) Communicating Emotions Nonverbally, (7) Recognizing Verbal and Nonverbal Message Functions, (8) Integrating Verbal and Nonverbal Messages, (9) Coloring Meanings, (10) Deciphering Paralanguage Cues and (11) Do You Avoid Touch?

Also visit MyCommunicationLab for video clips, study aids, and activities that will further your understanding and mastery of the nonverbal message system.

Explore our research resources at www.researchnavigator.com.

Research Navigator.com

## PART TWO

Contexts of Human Communication

## Chapter

# 6

# Interpersonal Communication, Conversation, and Relationships

## *Why Read* This Chapter?

Because you'll **learn about:**

- interpersonal communication and relationships.
- the major types and theories of interpersonal relationships.
- the influence of culture and technology on your relationships.

Because you'll **learn to:**

- communicate in relationships (friendship, romance, family, and work) more effectively.
- assess and manage your own relationships in light of research and theory.
- communicate more effectively in different cultural and technological contexts.

*I*nterpersonal communication is communication that occurs between two people who have a relationship and who are thus influenced by each other's communication messages. It includes what takes place between a server and a customer, a son and his father, two people in an interview, and so on. This definition makes it almost impossible for communication between two people not to be considered interpersonal—inevitably, some relationship exists. Even a stranger asking directions from a local resident has established a clearly defined relationship as soon as the first message is sent. Sometimes this "relational" or "dyadic" definition of interpersonal communication is extended to include small groups of people, such as family members, groups of three or four friends, or work colleagues.

Another way to look at interpersonal communication is along a continuum ranging from relatively impersonal to highly personal (Miller, 1978, 1990). At the impersonal end of the spectrum, you have simple conversation between people who really don't know each other—the server and the customer, for example. At the highly personal end is the communication that takes place between people who are intimately interconnected—the father and son, for example (see Figure 6.1 on p. 132).

A few characteristics distinguish these two extremes. First, notice that in the impersonal example, the individuals are likely to respond to each other according to the roles they are currently playing: The server treats the customer not as a unique individual but as one of many customers, and the customer, in turn, acts towards the server not as a unique individual but as he or she would react to any server. The father and the son, however, react to each other as unique individuals.

Notice too that the server and the customer interact according to the rules of society governing the server–customer interaction. The father and the son, on the other hand, interact on the basis of personally established rules. The way they address each other, their touching behavior, and their degree of physical closeness, for example, are unique to them and are established by them rather than by society.

Still another difference is that the messages that the server and customer exchange are themselves impersonal; there is little self-disclosure and little emotional content, for example. In the father–son example, the messages may run the entire range and may at times be highly personal with lots of disclosure and emotion.

As you will realize, there are many gradations between these extremes. Some friendships, for example, are casual; others are highly intimate. Even romantic pairs vary in their levels of intimacy, and so do families.

This chapter introduces the forms of interpersonal communication. We'll begin with the nature of conversation and move on to friends, romances, and families, identifying the stages you go through, the types of relationships you form (and why you form them), and the influence of culture and technology on your interpersonal communication and relationships.

Before beginning your exploration of conversation, consider your apprehension by taking the following self-test.

## *Test* *Yourself*

## HOW APPREHENSIVE ARE YOU OFFLINE AND ONLINE?

**INSTRUCTIONS:** These two questionnaires consist of statements concerning your feelings about communication with other people face-to-face and online. For both questionnaires indicate the degree to which each statement applies to you by marking whether you (1) strongly agree, (2) agree, (3) are undecided, (4) disagree, or (5) strongly disagree with each statement. There are no right or wrong answers. Work quickly; record your first impression.

### How Apprehensive Are You in Face-to-Face Communication?

_____ ❶ While participating in a conversation with a new acquaintance, I feel very nervous.

_____ ❷ I have no fear of speaking up in conversations.

_____ ❸ Ordinarily I am very tense and nervous in conversations.

_____ ❹ Ordinarily I am very calm and relaxed in conversations.

_____ ❺ While conversing with a new acquaintance, I feel very relaxed.

_____ ❻ I'm afraid to speak up in conversations.

**HOW DID YOU DO?** Compute your score as follows: Begin with the number 18; it's used as a base so that you won't wind up with negative numbers.

1. To 18, add your scores for items 2, 4, and 5.

2. Subtract your scores for items 1, 3, and 6 from your step 1 total.

3. The result (which should be somewhere between 6 and 30) is your apprehension score for interpersonal conversations. A score above 18 indicates some degree of apprehension.

### How Apprehensive Are you in Computer-Mediated Communication?

_____ ❶ I look forward to the opportunity to interact with others on the computer.

_____ ❷ I feel that I am more skilled than most others when interacting with people online.

_____ ❸ I would enjoy giving a presentation to others online.

_____ ❹ I look forward to expressing myself during online meetings.

_____ ❺ I like to get involved in computer-based group discussion.

**HOW DID YOU DO?** Add up your responses; your score should range from 5 to 25. Low scores, say between 5 and 10, indicate little apprehension; high scores, say between 20 and 25, indicate significant apprehension.

**WHAT WILL YOU DO?** Are you more apprehensive in face-to-face than in online communication? Most people are (Rockwell & Singleton, 2002, Campbell & Neer, 2001). Can you pinpoint the reasons for your apprehension? If so, what possible remedies can you suggest? For example, if you're apprehensive because you fear mispronouncing certain terms, then consider looking these up in an audio dictionary.

_Source:_ The first scale is from James C. McCroskey, _An Introduction to Rhetorical Communication,_ 7/e. Published by Allyn & Bacon, Boston, MA. Copyright © 1997 by Pearson Education. Adapted by permission of the publisher. The second scale is from Scott and Timmerman (2005); the authors note that these test items are modified from McCroskey (1970).

## Conversation

**Conversation,** whether face-to-face or online, takes place in five steps: opening, feedforward, business, feedback, and closing, as shown in Figure 6.1. Of course, there are variations in the process, depending on whether your interaction is face-to-face or computer-mediated as well as on other factors. When reading about the

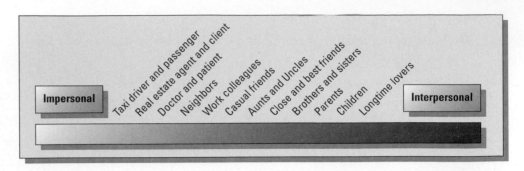

process of conversation, therefore, keep in mind the wide range of forms in which conversation can take place—face-to-face as well as via the Internet—and the similarities and differences between them.

Similarly, realize that not everyone speaks with the fluency and ease that many textbooks often assume. Speech and language disorders, for example, can seriously disrupt the conversation process if some elementary guidelines aren't followed. Table 6.1 offers suggestions for making such conversations run more smoothly.

## Opening

The first step in conversation is the opening, which usually involves some kind of greeting: "Hi." "How are you?" "Hello, this is Joe." In face-to-face conversation, greetings can be verbal or nonverbal but are usually both (Krivonos & Knapp, 1975; Knapp, 1984). In e-mail (and in most computer communication), the greetings are verbal with perhaps an emoticon or two thrown in. As video and sound are added to Internet connections, this difference from face-to-face conversation will diminish. Verbal greetings include, for example, verbal salutes ("Hi," "Hello"), initiation of the topic ("The reason I called . . ."), references to the other ("Hey, Joe, what's up?"), and personal inquiries ("What's new?" "How are you doing?"). Nonverbal greetings include waving, smiling, shaking hands, and winking (and their emoticon equivalents).

## Feedforward

In the second step of conversation, you usually give some kind of feedforward in which you may seek to accomplish a variety of functions. One function is to open the channels of communication, usually with some *phatic message* (see Chapter 1)—a message that signals that communication will take place rather than communicating any significant denotative information. An example would be "Haven't we met before?" or "Nice day, isn't it?" In e-mail you give feedforward simply by sending the message, which tells the other person that you want to communicate. Another function of feedforward is to preview future messages, as in, "I'm afraid I have bad news for you" or "Listen to this before you make a move" or "I'll tell you all the gory details." In office memos and e-mail, the feedforward function is served—in part—by headers that indicate the subject of your message, the recipients, and those who'll receive courtesy copies.

**"It's definitely true. Inane conversation is better with masks."**

## Business

The third step is the business, or the substance and focus, of the conversation. Business is a good term for this stage, because it emphasizes that most conversations are directed at achieving some goal. You converse to fulfill one or several of the general purposes of interpersonal

## TABLE 6.1 *Communication Tips*

### BETWEEN PEOPLE WITH AND WITHOUT SPEECH AND LANGUAGE DISORDERS

Speech and language disorders vary widely–from fluency problems such as stuttering, to indistinct articulation, to aphasia, or difficulty in finding the right word. A few simple guidelines greatly facilitate communication between people with and without speech and language disorders.

**If you're the person without a speech or language disorder:**

1. Avoid finishing sentences for someone who stutters or has difficulty finding words. It may communicate the idea that you're impatient and don't want to spend the extra time necessary to interact effectively.
2. Avoid giving directions to the person with a speech disorder. Saying "slow down" or "relax" will often prove insulting and can make further communication more difficult.
3. Maintain eye contact, and avoid showing signs of impatience or embarrassment.
4. If you don't understand what the person said, ask him or her to repeat it. Don't pretend that you understand when you don't.
5. Don't treat people who have language problems like children. A person with aphasia, say, may have difficulty with names or with nouns generally but is in no way childlike.

**If you're the person with a speech or language disorder:**

1. Let the other person know what your special needs are. For example, if you stutter, you might tell others that you have difficulty with certain sounds and so they need to be patient.
2. Demonstrate your comfort with and positive attitude toward the interpersonal situation. If you appear comfortable and positive, others will also.

*Sources:* These suggestions were drawn from a variety of sources: The National Stuttering Association, www.nsastutter.org; The National Aphasia Association, www.aphasia.org; and Constance Dugan, MA/CCC-SLP, www.conniedugan.com/, all accessed October 27, 2006.

communication: to learn, relate, influence, play, or help, as Chapter 1 described. In conversation you conduct this business through an exchange of speaker and listener roles—you talk about the new supervisor, what happened in class, or your vacation plans.

## Feedback

The fourth step of conversation, feedback, is the reverse of the second. In feedback you reflect back on the conversation. You normally do this immediately in face-to-face conversation and in your response to a previous e-mail. You say, for example, "So, you may want to send Jack a get-well card," or "Wasn't that the dullest meeting you ever went to?"

## Closing

The fifth and last step of the conversation process, the opposite of the first step, is the closing, the good-bye (Knapp, Hart, Friedrich, & Shulman, 1973; Knapp & Vangelisti, 2000). Like the opening, the closing may be verbal or nonverbal but usually is a combination of both. Just as the opening signals access, the closing signals the intention to end access. The closing usually also signals some degree of supportiveness—for example, you express your pleasure in interacting ("Well, it was good talking with you"). The closing may also summarize the interaction to offer more of a conclusion to the conversation.

Not all conversations divide neatly into these five steps, of course. Often the opening and the feedforward are combined, as when you see someone on campus and say, "Hey, listen to this," or when someone in a work situation says, "Well, folks, let's get the meeting going." In a similar way, the feedback and the closing may be combined: "Look, I've got to think more about this commitment, okay?"

As already noted, the business section is the longest part of the conversation. The opening and the closing are usually about the same length as the feedforward and feedback stages. When these relative lengths are severely distorted, you may feel that something is wrong. For example, when someone uses a long feedforward or too short an opening, you may suspect that what is to follow is extremely serious. If your supervisor calls you into the office to discuss your performance and spends the first five minutes talking about how important and difficult these performance appraisals are and how the company is putting pressure on appraisers to cover all aspects of a worker's performance, you can probably anticipate that you're in for some negative evaluation.

Different cultures have different rules and customs in conversation as in all aspects of communication. In some cultures, for example, the openings are especially short; in others they are elaborate, lengthy, and in some cases highly ritualized. And what is appropriate at a given step in one culture may not be appropriate in another culture. As you can see, it's easy to violate another culture's conversational rules in intercultural communication situations. Such violations may have significant consequences—because, if you are not aware of cultural differences, you may mistakenly interpret someone's "violations" as aggressiveness, stuffiness, or pushiness, take an immediate dislike to the person, and put a negative cast on future communications. Of course, knowing the other's cultural rules would clarify things for you. But in the absence of specific knowledge, it's probably wise to assume that when someone of another culture exhibits conversational behaviors that seem strange to you, the behaviors are cultural in origin and no offense is intended.

# Principles of Conversation

We can get a further perspective on conversation by looking at three principles: (1) turn-taking, (2) dialogue, and (3) immediacy.

*Skill Development Experience*

## Opening and Closing Conversations

*Opening and closing conversations can often be difficult. But these steps represent crucial communication skills: The way you open and close conversations will influence the impression that people form of you, and these impressions are likely to be long-lasting and highly resistant to change.*

How might you open a conversation with the persons described in each of these situations? What approaches would meet with favorable responses? What approaches would meet with unfavorable responses?

1. On the first day of class, you and another student are the first to come into the classroom and are seated in the room alone.
2. You've just started a new job in a large office where you're one of several computer operators. It seems as if most of the other people know each other.

How might you close each of the following conversations? What types of closings would be most effective? Which would be least effective?

1. You and a friend have been talking on the phone for the last hour, but at this point nothing new is being said. You have work to do and want to close the conversation.
2. After a long meeting, your colleague doesn't seem to know how to end the conversation and just continues to go over what has already been said. You have to get back to your desk.

# The Principle of Turn-Taking

Throughout the speaking–listening process, both speaker and listener exchange cues for what are called **conversational turns** (Burgoon, Buller, & Woodall, 1996; Duncan, 1972; Pearson & Spitzberg, 1990). These cues enable the speaker and listener to communicate about the communication in which they're currently engaged; that is, a form of **metacommunication** takes place through the exchange of these often subtle cues. The use of turn-taking cues—like just about every other aspect of human communication—will naturally vary from one culture to another. The description that follows here is largely valid for the United States and many Western cultures (Iizuka, 1993; Lee, 1984; Grossin, 1987; Ng, Loong, He, Liu, & Weatherall, 2000).

**Speaker Cues**    Speakers regulate the conversation through two major types of cues: turn-maintaining cues and turn-yielding cues. Using these cues effectively not only ensures communication efficiency but also increases likability (Place & Becker, 1991; Heap, 1992).

*Turn-Maintaining Cues.*    Through *turn-maintaining cues* a person can communicate the wish to maintain the role of speaker in a variety of ways:

- audibly inhaling breath to show that the speaker has more to say
- continuing a gesture or series of gestures to show that the thought is not yet complete
- avoiding eye contact with the listener so as not to indicate that the speaking turn is being passed along
- sustaining the intonation pattern to indicate that more will be said
- vocalizing pauses ("er," "umm") to prevent the listener from speaking and to show that the speaker is still talking

In most conversations we expect the speaker to maintain relatively brief speaking turns and to turn over the speaking role to the listener willingly (when so signaled by the listener). People who don't follow those unwritten rules are likely to be evaluated negatively.

*Turn-Yielding Cues.*    *Turn-yielding cues* tell the listener that the speaker is finished and wishes to exchange the role of speaker for the role of listener. They tell the listener (and sometimes they're addressed to a specific listener rather than to just any listener) to take over the role of speaker. For example, at the end of a statement you may add some cue such as "okay?" or "right?" to ask one of the listeners to assume the role of speaker. You also can indicate that you've finished speaking by dropping your intonation or by pausing at length (Wennerstrom & Siegel, 2003), by making direct eye contact with a listener, by asking some question, or by nodding in the direction of a particular listener.

In much the same way that you expect a speaker to yield the role of speaker, you also expect the listener to assume the speaking role willingly. Those who don't may be regarded as reticent or as unwilling to involve themselves and take equal responsibility for the conversation. Perhaps the most important violation is interrupting. Much research has addressed this issue, especially the question of whether men or women interrupt more. The research that has found a difference indicates that men interrupt more often than women, though much research finds no differences (Stratford, 1998; Crown & Cummins, 1998; Smith-Lovin & Brody, 1989; Donaldson, 1992).

**Listener Cues**    As a listener you can regulate the conversation by using three types of cues: turn-requesting cues, turn-denying cues, and backchanneling cues.

***Turn-Requesting Cues.***   *Turn-requesting cues* let the speaker know that you would like to say something and take a turn as speaker. Sometimes you can do this simply by saying, "I'd like to say something," but often it's done more subtly through some vocalized *er* or *um* that tells the speaker that you would now like to speak. The request to speak is also often made with facial and mouth gestures. Frequently a listener will indicate a desire to speak by opening his or her eyes and mouth wide as if to say something, by beginning to gesture with a hand, or by leaning forward.

***Turn-Denying Cues.***   You can use *turn-denying cues* to indicate your reluctance to assume the role of speaker; for example, by intoning a slurred "I don't know" or by giving some brief grunt that signals you have nothing to say. Often people accomplish turn denying by avoiding eye contact with the speaker (who wishes them now to take on the role of speaker) or by engaging in some behavior that is incompatible with speaking—for example, coughing or blowing their nose.

***Backchanneling Cues.***   People use *backchanneling cues* to communicate various types of information back to the speaker without assuming the role of the speaker. You can send a variety of messages with backchanneling cues (Burgoon, Buller, & Woodall, 1996; Pearson & Spitzberg, 1990). You can indicate your agreement or disagreement with the speaker through smiles or frowns, gestures of approval or disapproval, brief comments such as "right" or "never," or a vocalization such as *uh-huh*.

Backchanneling cues also indicate your degree of involvement or boredom with the speaker. Attentive posture, forward leaning, and focused eye contact will tell the speaker that you're involved in the conversation—and an inattentive posture, backward leaning, and avoidance of eye contact will communicate your lack of involvement.

You also can help regulate the speaker's rate of speech by giving the speaker pacing cues. You can, for example, ask the speaker to slow down by raising your hand near your ear and leaning forward and to speed up by continuously nodding your head. Or you can do this verbally by simply asking the speaker to slow down ("Slow down, I want to make sure I'm getting all this"). Similarly, you can tell the speaker to speed up by saying something like "and—?" or "go on, go on."

A request for clarification is still another function of backchanneling cues. A puzzled facial expression, perhaps coupled with a forward lean, will probably tell most speakers that you want some clarification. Similarly, you can ask for clarification by interjecting some interrogative: "Who?" "When?" "Where?" Some of these backchanneling cues are actually interruptions. These interruptions, however, are generally confirming rather than disconfirming. They tell the speaker that you are listening and are involved (Kennedy & Camden, 1988). Figure 6.2 diagrams the various turn-taking cues and shows how they correspond to the conversational wants of speaker and listener.

## The Principle of Dialogue

Often the term *dialogue* is used as a synonym for *conversation*. But dialogue is more than simple conversation; it's conversation in which there is genuine two-way interaction (Buber, 1958; Yau-fair Ho, Chan, Peng, & Ng, 2001; McNamee & Gergen, 1999). It's useful to distinguish the ideal dialogic communicator from his or her opposite, the totally monologic communicator.

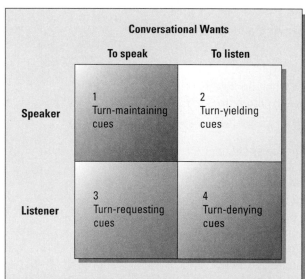

## Figure *6.2*
**Turn-Taking and Conversational Wants**
Quadrant 1 represents the speaker who wants to speak (continue to speak) and uses turn-maintaining cues; quadrant 2, the speaker who wants to listen and uses turn-yielding cues; quadrant 3, the listener who wants to speak and uses turn-requesting cues; and quadrant 4, the listener who wants to listen (continue listening) and uses turn-denying cues. Backchanneling cues would appear in quadrant 4, because they are cues that listeners use while they continue to listen.

Of course, no one totally and always engages in dialogue, and no one is totally monologic. These types are extremes and are intended to clarify the differences between these two types of communicators.

In **dialogue** each person is both speaker and listener, sender and receiver. It's conversation in which there is deep concern for the other person and for the relationship between the two. The objective of dialogue is mutual understanding and empathy. There is respect for the other person, not because of what this person can do or give but simply because this person is a human being and therefore deserves to be treated honestly and sincerely.

*"Two monologues do not make a dialogue."*

—JEFF DALY

In a dialogic interaction you respect the other person enough to allow that person the right to make his or her own choices without coercion, without the threat of punishment, without fear or social pressure. A dialogic communicator believes that other people can make decisions that are right for them and implicitly or explicitly lets them know that whatever choices they make, they will still be respected as people.

The dialogic communicator avoids negative criticism and negative personal judgments and instead practices using positive criticism ("I liked those first two explanations best; they were really well reasoned"). This person avoids dysfunctional communication patterns and keeps the channels of communication open by displaying a willingness to listen. While listening this person lets you know it by giving you cues (nonverbal nods, brief verbal expressions of agreement, paraphrasing) that tell you he or she is paying attention. When in doubt the dialogic communicator asks for clarification—asks for your point of view, your perspective—and thus signals a real interest in you and in what you have to say. This person does not manipulate the conversation so as to get positive comments.

Monologic communication is the opposite side: In **monologue** one person speaks and the other listens—there's no real interaction between participants. The monologic communicator is focused only on his or her own goals and has no real concern for the listener's feelings or attitudes; this speaker is interested in the other person only insofar as that person can serve his or her purposes.

The monologic communicator frequently uses negative criticism ("I didn't like that explanation") and negative judgments ("You're not a very good listener, are you?"). This communicator also often uses dysfunctional communication patterns such as expressing an unwillingness to talk or to listen to what the other person has to say. The monologic communicator rarely demonstrates that he or she understands you; this person gives no cues that he or she is listening (cues such as paraphrasing or expressing agreement with what you say). Nor would this person request clarification of your ideas, because he or she is less interested in you than in himself or herself. Still another characteristic of this person is a tendency to request that you say positive things about him or her ("How did you like the way I handled that?").

## The Principle of Immediacy

Of all the characteristics of effective communication, immediacy most clearly defines effective conversation. **Immediacy** has to do with the joining of speaker and listener; it's the creation of a sense of togetherness, of oneness. When you communicate immediacy, you convey a sense of interest and attention, a liking for and an attraction to the other person.

People respond more favorably to communication that is immediate than to communication that is not. For example, students of instructors who communicated immediacy felt that the instruction was better and the courses more valuable than students of instructors who did not communicate immediacy (Moore, Masterson, Christophel, & Shea, 1996; Witt & Wheeless, 2001; Daly & Vangelisti, 2003).

Students and teachers liked each other largely on the basis of immediacy (Wilson & Taylor, 2001; Baringer & McCroskey, 2000).

You can communicate immediacy in a variety of ways. Here are a few:

- Express psychological closeness and openness by, for example, maintaining physical closeness and arranging your body to exclude third parties. Maintain appropriate eye contact, limit looking around at others, smile, and express your interest in the other person.

- Use the other person's name; for example, say, "Joe, what do you think?" instead of "What do you think?"

- Orient your conversation to the other person. Focus on the other person's remarks. Make the speaker know that you heard and understood what was said, and give the speaker appropriate verbal and nonverbal feedback.

- Acknowledge the presence and importance of the other person. Ask for opinions and suggestions as appropriate.

- Communicate expressiveness by varying your vocal rate, volume, and rhythm to convey involvement and interest and use appropriate gestures, especially gestures that focus on the other person rather than yourself (for example, eye contact and leaning toward the other person instead of self-touching movements or directing your eyes to others in the room.

- Express immediacy with cultural sensitivity. In the United States, people generally see immediacy behaviors as friendly and appropriate. Members of other cultures, however, may view the same immediacy behaviors as overly familiar—as presuming closeness when only acquaintanceship exists (Axtell, 1993).

## The Stages of Interpersonal Relationships

You and another person don't become intimate friends immediately upon meeting. Rather, you build an intimate relationship gradually, through a series of steps or stages. The same is true of most relationships. To be sure, the "love at first sight" phenomenon creates a problem for this stage model of relationships. But rather than argue that such love cannot occur (my own feeling is that it can and frequently does), it seems wiser to claim simply that the stage model characterizes most relationships for most people most of the time.

The six-stage model in Figure 6.3 describes the main stages in most relationships: contact, involvement, intimacy, deterioration, repair, and dissolution. Each stage has an early and a late phase. These stages describe relationships as they are; they don't evaluate or prescribe how relationships should be. For a particular relationship, you might wish to modify the basic model. But as a general description of the course of relationships, the stages seem fairly standard. Do realize, of course, that both partners may not perceive their relationship in the same way; one person, for example, may see the relationship as having reached the intimate stage, but the other may not.

## Contact

At the initial phase of the **contact** stage, there is some kind of *perceptual contact*—you see, hear, and perhaps smell the person. From this you get a physical picture—gender, approximate age, height, and so on. After this perception there is usually *interactional contact*. Here the contact is superficial and relatively impersonal. This is the stage at which you exchange basic information that is preliminary to any more intense involvement ("Hello, my name is Joe"); you initiate interaction ("May I join you?") and engage in invitational communication ("May I buy you a drink?"). According to some researchers, it's at this stage—within the first four minutes of

### WHAT DO YOU SAY?
**Refusing a Date**
A fellow student in one of your classes has asked you for a date on each of the last three weekends. You don't want to go, so each time you made an excuse. But you realize that this can't go on, and you want to end these embarrassing requests and refusals. *What do you say? Through what channel? In what context?*

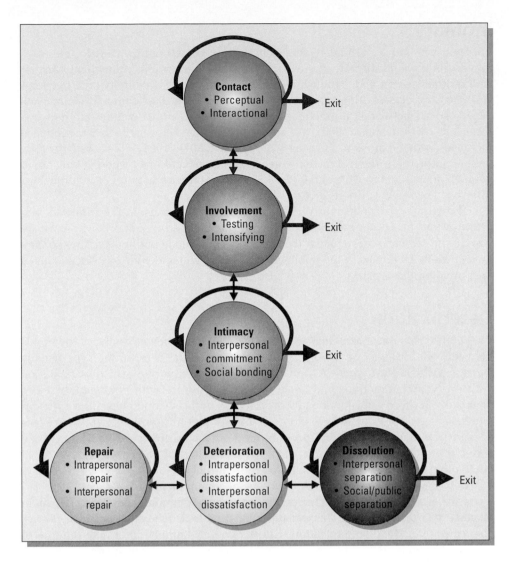

Figure *6.3*
**The Six Stages of Relationships**

Because relationships differ so widely, it's best to think of this or any relationship model as a tool for talking about relationships rather than as a specific map that indicates how you move from one relationship position to another. Can you identify other steps or stages that would further explain what goes on in relationship development? What happens when the two people in a relationship experience the stages differently? Can you provide an example from literature or from your own experience?

initial interaction—that you decide whether you want to pursue the relationship (Zunin & Zunin, 1972).

At the contact stage, physical appearance is especially important, because it's the characteristic most readily seen. Yet through verbal and nonverbal behaviors, personal qualities such as friendliness, warmth, openness, and dynamism are also revealed.

## Involvement

At the **involvement** stage a sense of mutuality, of being connected, develops. Here you experiment and try to learn more about the other person. At the initial phase of involvement, a kind of *testing* goes on. You want to see whether your initial judgment proves reasonable. So you may ask questions: "Where do you work?" "What are you majoring in?" If you want to get to know the person even better, you might continue your involvement by intensifying your interaction and by beginning to reveal yourself, though in a preliminary way. In a dating relationship, you might, for example, use a variety of strategies to help you move to the next stage and perhaps to intimacy. For example, you might increase contact with your partner; give your partner tokens of affection such as gifts, cards, or flowers; increase your own personal attractiveness; do things that suggest intensifying the relationship, such as flirting or making your partner jealous; and become more physically intimate (Tolhuizen, 1989).

**WHAT DO YOU SAY?**
**Relationship Résumé**
Although you've been mostly honest in your two-month Internet relationship, you have padded your relationship résumé—lopped off a few years and pounds and made your temporary job seem like the executive fast track. You now want to come clean. *What do you say?*

**E-TALK**

**Staying Together**
One study of people who met on the Internet found that those who met in places of common interest, who communicated over a period of time before they met in person, who managed barriers to greater closeness, and who managed conflict well were more likely to stay together than couples who did not follow this general pattern (Baker, 2002). Based on your own experiences, how would you predict which couples would stay together and which would break apart?

# Intimacy

The contact and involvement stages make up **relationship development**—a movement toward intimacy. At the **intimacy** stage you commit yourself still further to the other person and establish a relationship in which this individual becomes your best or closest friend, lover, or companion. You also come to share each other's social networks, a practice followed by members of widely different cultures (Gao & Gudykunst, 1995). Not surprisingly, your relationship satisfaction also increases with the move to this stage (Siavelis & Lamke, 1992). One research study defined intimacy as the feeling that you can be honest and open when talking about yourself and about thoughts and feelings that you don't reveal in other relationships (Mackey, Diemer, & O'Brien, 2000).

The intimacy stage usually divides itself into two phases. In the *interpersonal commitment* phase, the two people commit themselves to each other in a private way. In the *social bonding* phase, the commitment is made public—perhaps to family and friends, perhaps to the public at large. Here you and your partner become a unit, an identifiable pair.

# Deterioration

The relationship **deterioration** stage is characterized by a weakening of the bonds between the friends or lovers. The first phase of deterioration is usually *intrapersonal dissatisfaction:* You begin to experience personal dissatisfaction with everyday interactions and begin to view the future with your partner more negatively. If this dissatisfaction grows, you pass to the second phase, *interpersonal deterioration.* You withdraw and grow further and further apart. You share less of your free time. When you're together, there are awkward silences, fewer disclosures, less physical contact, and a lack of psychological closeness. Conflicts become more common and their resolution more difficult.

Relationship deterioration involves special communication patterns. These patterns are in part a response to the deterioration; you communicate the way you do because you feel that your relationship is in trouble. However, these patterns are also causative: The communication patterns you use largely determine the fate of your relationship. Here are a few communication patterns that characterize relationship deterioration.

- *Withdrawal.* Nonverbally, withdrawal is seen in the greater space the partners need and in the speed with which tempers and other signs of disturbance arise when that space is invaded. Other nonverbal signs of withdrawal include a decrease in eye contact and touching; less similarity in clothing; and fewer displays of items associated with the other person, such as bracelets, photographs, and rings (Miller & Parks, 1982; Knapp & Vangelisti, 2000). Verbally, withdrawal involves a decreased desire to talk and especially to listen. At times partners may use small talk not as a preliminary to serious conversation but as an alternative, perhaps to avoid confronting the serious issues.

- *Decline in self-disclosure.* Self-disclosing communications decline significantly. If the relationship is dying, you may think self-disclosure isn't worth the effort. Or you may limit your self-disclosures because you feel that the other person may not accept them or can no longer be trusted to be supportive and empathic.

- *Deception.* Deception increases as relationships break down. Sometimes this takes the form of clear-cut lies that people may use to avoid arguments over such things as staying out all night, not calling, or being seen in the wrong place with the wrong person. At other times, lies may be used because of a feeling of shame; you may not want the other person to think less of you. One of the problems with deception is that it has a way of escalating, eventually creating a climate of distrust and disbelief.

- *Negative versus positive messages.* During deterioration there's an increase in negative and a decrease in positive messages. Once you praised the other's behaviors, but now you criticize them. Often the behaviors have not changed significantly; what has changed is your way of looking at them. What was once a cute habit now becomes annoying; what was once "different" now becomes inconsiderate. When a relationship is deteriorating, there is a decline in requests for pleasurable behaviors ("Will you fix me my favorite dessert?") and a rise in requests to stop unpleasant or negative behaviors ("Will you stop monopolizing the phone?") (Lederer, 1984). Even the social niceties get lost as requests deteriorate from "Would you please make me a cup of coffee, honey?" to "Get me some coffee, will you?" to "Where's my coffee?"

## Repair

At the relationship **repair** stage, some relational partners may pause during deterioration and try to repair their relationship. Others, however, may progress—without stopping, without thinking—to dissolution.

At the first repair phase, *intrapersonal repair*, you analyze what went wrong and consider ways of solving your relational difficulties. You might at this stage consider changing your behaviors or perhaps changing your expectations of your partner. You might also evaluate the rewards of your relationship as it is now and the rewards to be gained if your relationship ended.

Should you decide that you want to repair your relationship, you might move to the *interpersonal repair* phase—you might discuss with your partner the problems in the relationship, the changes you want to see, and perhaps what you'd be willing to do and what you'd want your partner to do. This is the stage of negotiating new agreements and new behaviors. You and your partner might try to repair your relationship by yourselves, or you might seek the advice of friends or family, or perhaps go for professional counseling.

## Dissolution

The **dissolution** stage, the last stage in the relationship model, involves cutting the bonds that tie you together. In the beginning it usually takes the form of *interpersonal separation*: You might move into your own apartments and begin to lead

### Formulating Apologies

Formulate an appropriate **apology** for any one of the situations listed below, following these five steps (Slade, 1995, Coleman, 2002): (1) Demonstrate that you understand the problem and that the other person's feelings are justified. (2) Acknowledge responsibility. (3) Acknowledge your regret about what you did. (4) Request forgiveness; be specific. (5) Make it clear that this will never happen again.

*Well-formed apologies are often helpful in lessening the negative effects of your mishap; poorly formed apologies or attempts at making excuses may aggravate the situation.*

### Situations

1. Your boss (justifiably) accuses you of making lots of personal long-distance phone calls from work, a practice explicitly forbidden.
2. Your relationship partner catches you in a lie; you weren't at work but with a former lover.

"We swam. We made sand castles. I'm sorry, Michael—I thought you understood that this was just a summer thing."

© The New Yorker Collection 2002 Chris Weyant from cartoonbank.com. All Rights Reserved.

separate lives. If the separation works better than the original relationship, you enter the phase of *social* or *public separation.* Avoidance of each other and a return to a "single" status are among the primary characteristics of the dissolution of a relationship.

Given both the inevitability that some relationships will break up and the significant effects such breakups will have on you, here are some steps you can take to ease the pain during this difficult time. These suggestions apply to the termination of any type of relationship—whether a friendship or a love affair, and whether through death, separation, or breakup.

- *Break the Loneliness–Depression Cycle.* The two most common feelings following the end of a relationship are loneliness and depression. In most cases, fortunately, loneliness and depression are temporary. Depression, for example, rarely lasts forever. When depression does last, is especially deep, or disturbs your normal functioning, it's time to seek professional help.

- *Take Time Out.* Resist the temptation to jump into a new relationship while you still have strong feelings about the old one and before a new one can be assessed with some objectivity.

- *Bolster Self-Esteem.* If your relationship fails, you may experience a decline in self-esteem (Collins & Clark, 1989). Your task now is to regain the positive self-image you need in order to function effectively.

- *Seek Support.* Seeking the support of others is one of the best antidotes to the unhappiness caused when a relationship ends. Tell your friends and family of your situation—in only general terms, if you prefer—and make it clear that you want support. Seek out people who are positive and nurturing, and avoid those who will paint the world in even darker tones or blame you for what happened.

## LISTEN TO THIS

*Love is a fire. But whether it is going to warm your hearth or burn down your house, you can never tell.*

—JOAN CRAWFORD

### Listening to Stage Talk

Listen carefully to messages that express a desire to move the relationship in a particular way or to maintain it at a particular stage. This careful listening will help you better understand and manage your own interpersonal relationships. Over the next few days, listen carefully to all stage-talk messages. Listen to messages referring to your own relationships as well as messages that friends or coworkers disclose to you about their relationships. Collect these messages and classify them into the following categories.

- *Contact messages* express a desire for contact: "Hi, my name is Joe."

- *Closeness messages* express a desire to increased closeness, involvement, or intimacy: "I'd like to see you more often."

- *Maintenance messages* express a desire to stabilize the relationship at one stage: "Let's stay friends for now. I'm afraid to get more involved at this point in my life."

- *Distancing messages* express a desire for more space in a relationship. "*I think we should spend a few weeks apart.*"

- *Repair messages* express a desire to correct relationship problems: "Let's discuss this issue again, this time in a more constructive way? I didn't mean to hurt your feelings."

- *Dissolution messages* express a desire to break up the relationship: "Look, it's just not working out as we hoped; let's each go our own way."

***Applying Listening Skills.*** *What suggestions would you offer a friend whose work colleague—with whom your friend wants to have a working but not romantic relationship—has started giving closeness messages?*

# Interpersonal Relationship Types

Each relationship, whether friendship, love, a primary relationship, or a work relationship, is unique. Yet there are general types that research has identified—and these categories offer unusual insight into interpersonal relationships.

## Friendship

One theory of **friendship** identifies three major types: friendships of reciprocity, receptivity, and association (Reisman, 1979, 1981). The *friendship of reciprocity*, the ideal type, is characterized by loyalty, self-sacrifice: mutual affection, and generosity. A friendship of reciprocity is based on equality. Each individual shares equally in giving and receiving the benefits and rewards of the relationship.

In the *friendship of receptivity*, in contrast, there is an imbalance in giving and receiving; one person is the primary giver and the other the primary receiver. This is a positive imbalance, however, because each person gains something from the relationship. The different needs of both the person who receives affection and the person who gives it are satisfied. This is the friendship that may develop between a teacher and a student or between a doctor and a patient. In fact, a difference in status is essential for the friendship of receptivity to develop.

The *friendship of association* is transitory; it might be described as a friendly relationship rather than a true friendship. Associative friendships are the kind we often have with classmates, neighbors, or coworkers. There is no great loyalty, no great trust, no great giving or receiving. The association is cordial but not intense.

## Love

Like friends, lovers come in different styles as well. Before reading about these styles, take the following self-test to identify your own love style.

### WHAT KIND OF LOVER ARE YOU?

Respond to each of the following statements with T for "true" (if you believe the statement to be a generally accurate representation of your attitudes about love) or F for "false" (if you believe the statement does not adequately represent your attitudes about love).

_____ ❶ My lover and I have the right physical "chemistry" between us.

_____ ❷ I feel that my lover and I were meant for each other.

_____ ❸ My lover and I really understand each other.

_____ ❹ I believe that what my lover doesn't know about me won't hurt him/her.

_____ ❺ My lover would get upset if he/she knew of some of the things I've done with other people.

_____ ❻ When my lover gets too dependent on me, I want to back off a little.

_____ ❼ I expect to always be friends with my lover.

_____ ❽ Our love is really a deep friendship, not a mysterious, mystical emotion.

## Censoring Messages and Relationships

Throughout your life, the messages you receive are censored. When you were young, your parents may have censored certain television programs, magazines, and movies—perhaps even tapes and CDs—that they thought inappropriate, usually because they were too sexually explicit, showed too much violence, or used profanity. Moderators of computer mailing lists and chat groups also may censor messages; moderators may in fact ban certain members from participating in the group if their messages are considered inappropriate or destructive to the group.

Relationships, too, are often censored. When you were young, your parents may have encouraged you to play with certain children and not to play with others. Sometimes these decisions were based on the character of the other children. Sometimes they may have been based on the racial, religious, or national background or the affectional orientation of the would-be friends. Today, the most obvious situations in which interactions are prevented (or made more difficult than they should be) are those involving romantic relationships between interracial or homosexual couples, who frequently encounter difficulties in finding housing, employment, or acceptance in a community.

*What would you do?* *Your roommate has been concealing calls from someone who wants to date you because of a belief that this relationship would be bad for you. Is this ethical? If you were this roommate, what would you do?*

> *No person is your friend who demands your silence, or denies your right to grow.*
> —ALICE WALKER

_____ ⑨ Our love relationship is the most satisfying because it developed from a good friendship.

_____ ⑩ In choosing my lover, I believed it was best to love someone with a similar background.

_____ ⑪ An important factor in choosing a partner is whether or not he/she would be a good parent.

_____ ⑫ One consideration in choosing my lover was how he/she would reflect on my career.

_____ ⑬ Sometimes I get so excited about being in love with my lover that I can't sleep.

_____ ⑭ When my lover doesn't pay attention to me, I feel sick all over.

_____ ⑮ I cannot relax if I suspect that my lover is with someone else.

_____ ⑯ I would rather suffer myself than let my lover suffer.

_____ ⑰ When my lover gets angry with me, I still love him/her fully and unconditionally.

_____ ⑱ I would endure all things for the sake of my lover.

**HOW DID YOU DO?** This scale, from Hendrick and Hendrick (1990), is based on the work of Lee (1976), as is the discussion of the six types of love that follows. This scale is designed to enable you to identify your own beliefs about love. The statements refer to the six types of love described below: eros, ludus, storge, pragma, mania, and agape. Statements 1–3 are characteristic of the eros lover. If you answered "true" to these statements, you have a strong eros component to your love style. If you answered "false," you have a weak eros component. Statements 4–6 refer to ludus love; 7–9 to storge love; 10–12 to pragma love; 13–15 to manic love, and 16–18 to agapic love.

**WHAT WILL YOU DO?** Are there things you can do to become more aware of the different love styles and to become a more well-rounded lover? Incorporating the qualities of effective interpersonal communication—for example, being more flexible, more polite, and more other-oriented—will go a long way toward making you a more responsive love partner.

*Source:* From "A Relationship-Specific Version of the Love Attitudes Scale" by C. Hendrick and S. Hendrick. (1990), *Journal of Social Behavior and Personality 5,* 1990. Used by permission of Select Press.

**E-TALK**

**Privacy and Emotional Closeness**
In face-to-face relationships, emotional closeness compromises privacy; the closer you become, the less privacy you have. In online relationships, however, because you're more in control of what you reveal, you can develop close emotional relationships but also maintain your privacy (Ben-Ze'ev, 2003). Do you find this to be true? If not, how would you express the relationship between emotional closeness and privacy?

*Eros love* seeks beauty and sensuality and focuses on physical attractiveness, sometimes to the exclusion of qualities we might consider more important and more lasting. The erotic lover has an idealized image of beauty that is unattainable in reality. Consequently, the erotic lover often feels unfulfilled.

*Ludic love* seeks entertainment and excitement and sees love as fun, a game. To the ludic lover, love is not to be taken too seriously; emotions are to be held in check lest they get out of hand and make trouble. The ludic lover retains a partner only so long as the partner is interesting and amusing. When the partner is no longer interesting enough, it's time to change.

*Storge love* is a peaceful and tranquil love. Like ludus, storge lacks passion and intensity. Storgic lovers set out not to find a lover but to establish a companionable relationship with someone they know and with whom they can share interests and activities. Storgic love is a gradual process of unfolding thoughts and feelings and is sometimes difficult to separate from friendship.

*Pragma love* is practical and traditional and seeks compatibility and a relationship in which important needs and desires will be satisfied. The pragma lover is concerned with the social qualifications of a potential mate even more than with personal qualities; family and background are extremely important to the pragma lover, who relies not so much on feelings as on logic.

*Manic love* is an obsessive love that needs to give and receive constant attention and affection. When this is not given or received, or when an expression of increased commitment is not returned, reactions such as depression, jealousy, and self-doubt are often experienced and can lead to the extreme lows characteristic of the manic lover.

*Agapic love* is compassionate and selfless. The agapic lover loves both the stranger on the road and the annoying neighbor. Jesus, Buddha, and Gandhi practiced and preached this unqualified spiritual love—a love that is offered without concern for personal reward or gain and without any expectation that the love will be returned or reciprocated.

## Primary Relationships and Families

Primary relationships are central to family life. We should note, however, that the American **family** comes in many configurations and has undergone some profound changes in recent decades. Table 6.2 provides a few statistics on the U.S. family in 1970 and in 2000. One obvious example of change is the rise in one-parent families. There are now almost 12 million single-family households in the United States. In 1998 about 28 percent of children under 18 lived with just one parent (about 23 percent with their mother and about 4 percent with their father), according to the *World Almanac and Book of Facts, 2002.*

Another obvious example is the increasing number of people living together in an exclusive relationship who are not married. For the most part these cohabitants live as if they were married: There is an exclusive sexual commitment; there may be children; there are shared financial responsibilities, shared time, and shared space. These relationships mirror traditional marriages, except that in marriage the union is recognized by a religious body, the state, or both, whereas in a relationship of cohabitants it generally is not.

## TABLE 6.2  The Changing Face of Family

Here are a few statistics on the nature of the American family for 1970 and 2002, as reported by the *New York Times Almanac 2005* and *The World Almanac and Book of Facts 2005,* along with some possible trends these figures indicate. What other trends do you see occurring in the family?

| FAMILY CHARACTERISTIC | 1970 | 2002 | TRENDS |
|---|---|---|---|
| Number of members in average family | 3.58 | 3.21 | Reflects the tendency toward smaller families |
| Families without children | 44.1% | 52% | Reflects the growing number of families opting to not have children |
| Families headed by married couples | 86.8% | 76.3% | Reflects growing trends for heterosexual couples to live as a family without marriage, for singles to have children, and for gay men and lesbians to form families |
| Females as heads of households | 10.7% | 17.7% | Reflects the growing number of women having children without marriage and the increase in divorce and separation |
| Single-parent families | 13% | 27.8% | Reflects the growing trend for women (especially) to maintain families without a partner |
| Households headed by never-married women with children | 248,000 | 4.3 million | Reflects the growing trend for women to have children and maintain a family without marriage |
| Children living with only one parent | 12% | 23% | Reflects the growing divorce rate and the increased number of children born to unwed mothers |
| Children between 25 and 34 living at home with parents | 8% (11.9 million) | 9.3% (19.2 million) | Reflects the increased economic difficulties of establishing one's own home and perhaps the increased divorce rate and later dates for marriage (especially among men) |

Some families are headed by gay male or lesbian couples who live together as domestic partners or, in some cases spouses. Many of these couples have children from previous heterosexual unions, through artificial insemination, or by adoption. Although accurate statistics are difficult to secure, primary relationships among gays and lesbians seem more common than the popular media might lead us to believe. Research some decades ago (Blumstein & Schwartz, 1983) estimated the number of gay and lesbian couples to be 70 percent to more than 80 percent of the gay population (itself estimated variously at between 4 percent and 16 percent of the total population, depending on the definitions used and the studies cited).

The communication principles that apply to the traditional nuclear family (the mother-father-child family) also apply to these relationships. In the following discussion, the term *primary relationship* denotes the relationship between the two principal parties—the husband and wife, the lovers, or the domestic partners, for example—just as the term *family* now may denote a broader constellation that includes children, relatives, and assorted significant others.

A **primary relationship** is a relationship between two people that the partners see as their most important interpersonal relationship. An interesting typology of primary relationships (based on more than 1,000 couples' responses to questions concerning their degree of sharing, their space needs, their conflicts, and the time they spend together) identifies three basic types: traditionals, independents, and separates (Fitzpatrick, 1983, 1988, 1991; Noller & Fitzpatrick, 1993).

*Traditional couples* share a basic belief system and philosophy of life. They see themselves as a blending of two persons into a single couple rather than as two separate individuals. They're interdependent and believe that each individual's independence must be sacrificed for the good of the relationship. Traditionals believe in mutual sharing and do little separately. This couple holds to the traditional sex roles, and there are seldom any role conflicts. There are few power struggles and few conflicts, because each person knows and adheres to a specified role within the relationship. In their communications traditionals are highly responsive to each other. Traditionals lean toward each other, smile, talk a lot, interrupt each other, and finish each other's sentences.

*Independents* stress their individuality. The relationship is important, but never more important than each person's individual identity. Although independents spend a great deal of time together, they don't ritualize it, for example, with schedules. Each individual spends time with outside friends. Independents see themselves as relatively androgynous—as individuals who combine traditionally feminine and traditionally masculine roles and qualities. The communication between independents is responsive. They engage in conflict openly and without fear. Their disclosures are quite extensive and include high-risk and negative disclosures that are typically absent among traditionals.

*Separates* live together, but they view their relationship more as a matter of convenience than a result of their mutual love or closeness. They seem to have little desire to be together and, in fact, usually are together only at ritual occasions such as mealtime or holiday get-togethers. It's important to these separates that each has his or her own physical as well as psychological space. Separates share little; each seems to prefer to go his or her own way. Separates hold relatively traditional values and beliefs about sex roles, and each person tries to follow the behaviors normally assigned to each role. What best characterizes this type, however, is that each person sees himself or herself as a separate individual and not as a part of a "we."

▼ **E-TALK**

**Relationship Maintenance and E-Mail**
E-mail is one of the major ways in which meaningful relationships are maintained (Stafford, Kline, & Dimmick, 1999). In what specific ways can you envision e-mail being used to communicate relationship maintenance messages?

## MEDIA LITERACY

*True intimacy is a positive force only if it is a combining of strengths and energies with other mature persons for the continued growth of each.*

—LEO F. BUSCAGLIA

### Parasocial Relationships

**Parasocial relationships** are relationships that viewers perceive themselves to have with media personalities (Rubin & McHugh, 1987; Giles, 2001). At times viewers develop these relationships with real media personalities—Katie Couric, Regis Philbin, or Oprah Winfrey, for example. As a result they may watch these people faithfully and communicate with them in their own imaginations. At other times the relationship is with a fictional character—an investigator on *CSI*, a lawyer on *Law and Order*, or a doctor on a soap opera.

The chat sessions that celebrities hold on the Internet help further create the illusion of a real interpersonal relationship. And the screen savers of television performers make it difficult not to think of them in relationship terms when they face you every time you leave your computer idle for a few minutes.

Parasocial relationships develop in three stages (Rubin & McHugh, 1987):

1. The viewer develops an initial attraction to the character's social and task roles.
2. The viewer perceives there to be an interpersonal relationship between him or her and the character.
3. The viewer begins to believe that this is an important relationship.

As you might expect, these parasocial relationships are most important to those who spend a great deal of time with the media and who have few real-life interpersonal relationships (Rubin, Perse, & Powell, 1985; Cole & Leets, 1999).

***Increasing Media Literacy.*** *What role, if any, do parasocial relationships play in your life? What role do they play in the lives of your peers?*

# Theories of Interpersonal Communication and Relationships

Several theories offer insight into why and how we develop and dissolve our relationships. Here we'll examine five such theories: attraction, relationship rules, social penetration, social exchange, and equity.

## Attraction

**Attraction theory** holds that people form relationships on the basis of **attraction.** You are no doubt drawn, or attracted, to some people and not attracted to others. In a similar way, some people are attracted to you and some are not. If you're like most people, then you're attracted to others on the basis of four major factors:

- *Physical attractiveness and personality.* It's easily appreciated that people like physically attractive people more than they like physically unattractive people. What isn't so obvious is that we also feel a greater sense of familiarity with more attractive people than with less attractive people, that is, we're more likely to think we've met a person before if that person is attractive (Mohin, 2003). Also, although culture influences what people think is physical attractiveness and what isn't, some research indicates that there are certain facial features that seem to be thought attractive in all cultures—a kind of universal attractiveness (Brody, 1994). Additionally, you probably tend to like people who have a pleasant rather than an unpleasant personality (although people will differ on what is and what is not an attractive personality).

- *Similarity.* If you could construct your mate, according to the **similarity** principle, it's likely that your mate would look, act, and think very much like you (Burleson, Samter, & Luccetti, 1992; Burleson, Kunkel, & Birch, 1994). Generally, people like those who are similar to them in nationality, race, abilities, physical characteristics, intelligence, and attitudes. (Pornpitakpan, 2003). Sometimes people are attracted to their opposites in a pattern called **complementarity;** for example, a dominant person might be attracted to someone who is more submissive. Generally, however, people prefer those who are similar.

- *Proximity.* If you look around at people you find attractive, you will probably find that they are the people who live or work close to you. People who become friends are the people who have the greatest opportunity to interact with each other.

- *Reinforcement.* You're attracted to people who give rewards or reinforcements, which can range from a simple compliment to an expensive cruise. You're also attracted to people you reward (Jecker & Landy, 1969; Aronson, Wilson, & Akert, 2002). That is, you come to like people for whom you do favors.

> **WHAT DO YOU SAY?**
> **Compliance Resisting**
> Your friend asks you for a loan of $150 to pay off some bills. Unfortunately, you've never been paid back when you've lent money in the past, so you don't want to do it again. Yet you don't want to lose this otherwise wonderful friend. *What do you say?*

## Relationship Rules

You can gain an interesting perspective on interpersonal relationships by looking at them in terms of the rules that govern them (Shimanoff, 1980). The general assumption of **rules theory** is that relationships—friendship and love in particular—are held together by adherence to certain rules. When those rules are broken, the relationship may deteriorate and even dissolve.

Relationship rules theory helps us clarify several aspects of relationships. First, these rules help identify successful versus destructive relationship behavior. In addition, these rules help pinpoint more specifically why relationships break up and how they may be repaired. Further, if we know what the rules are, we will be better able to master the social skills involved in relationship development and maintenance. And because these rules vary from one culture to another, it is important to identify those unique to each culture so that intercultural relationships may be more effectively developed and maintained.

**Friendship Rules**    One approach to friendship argues that friendships are maintained by rules (Argyle & Henderson, 1984; Argyle, 1986). When these rules are followed, the friendship is strong and mutually satisfying. When these rules are broken, the friendship suffers and may die. For example, the rules for keeping a friendship include such behaviors as these: standing up for your friend in his or her absence, sharing information and feelings about successes, demonstrating emotional support for your friend, trusting and offering to help your friend when in need, and trying to make your friend happy when you're together. On the other hand, a friendship is likely to be in trouble when one or both friends are intolerant of the other's friends, discuss confidences with third parties, fail to demonstrate positive support, nag, and/or fail to trust or confide in the other. The strategy for maintaining a friendship then depends on your knowing the rules and having the ability to apply the appropriate interpersonal skills (Trower, 1981; Blieszner & Adams, 1992).

**Romantic Rules**    Other research has identified the rules that romantic relationships establish and follow. These rules, of course, will vary considerably from one culture to another. For example, the different attitudes toward permissiveness and sexual relations with which Chinese and American college students view dating influence the romantic rules each group will establish and live by (Tang & Zuo, 2000). Leslie Baxter (1986) has identified eight major romantic rules. Baxter argues that these rules keep the relationship together—or, when broken, lead to deterioration and eventually dissolution. The general form for each rule, as Baxter phrases it, is, "If parties are in a close relationship, they should . . .":

1. acknowledge each other's individual identities and lives beyond the relationship
2. express similar attitudes, beliefs, values, and interests
3. enhance each other's self-worth and self-esteem
4. be open, genuine, and authentic with each other
5. remain loyal and faithful to each other
6. have substantial shared time together
7. reap rewards commensurate with their investments relative to the other party
8. experience a mysterious and inexplicable "magic" in each other's presence

## Social Penetration

**Social penetration theory** is a theory not of why relationships develop but of what happens when they do develop; it describes relationships in terms of the number of topics that people talk about and their degree of "personalness" (Altman & Taylor, 1973). The **breadth** of a relationship has to do with the number of topics you and your partner talk about. The **depth** of a relationship involves the degree to which you penetrate the inner personality—the core—of the other individual. We can represent an individual as a circle and divide that circle into various parts. These parts represent the topics or areas of interpersonal communication, or breadth. Further, visualize the circle and its parts as consisting of concentric inner circles, rather like an onion. These represent the different levels of communication, or the depth.

When a relationship begins to deteriorate, the breadth and depth will, in many ways, reverse themselves, in a process called **depenetration.** For example, while ending a relationship, you might cut out certain topics from your interpersonal

▼ **E-TALK**

**Online Trust**
One research study finds that people who are trusting in their daily lives may experience greater difficulty in developing trust online (Feng, Lazar, & Preece, 2004; Henderson & Gilding, 2004). What do you find to be the relationship between face-to-face trusting and online trusting?

**WHAT DO YOU SAY?**
**Relationship Stage**
Your partner gives you a gift that contradicts your perception of your relationship stage. The gift is much too intimate and too expensive for the casual nature of what you believe your relationship is. *What do you say? Through what channel? In what context?*

communications. At the same time you might discuss the remaining topics in less depth. In some instances of relational deterioration, however, both the breadth and the depth of interaction increase. For example, when a couple breaks up and each is finally free from an oppressive relationship, they may—after some time—begin to discuss problems and feelings they would never have discussed when they were together. In fact, they may become extremely close friends and come to like each other more than when they were together. In these cases the breadth and depth of their relationship may increase rather than decrease (Baxter, 1983).

## Social Exchange and Equity

**Social exchange theory** claims that you develop relationships that will enable you to maximize your profits (Chadwick-Jones, 1976; Gergen, Greenberg, & Willis, 1980; Thibaut & Kelley, 1986)—a theory based on an economic model of profits and losses. The theory begins with the following equation: Profits = Rewards − Costs. Rewards are anything that you would incur costs to obtain. Research has identified six types of rewards in a love relationship: money, status, love, information, goods, and services (Baron & Byrne, 1984). For example, to get the reward of money, you might have to work rather than play. To earn the status of an A in an interpersonal communication course, you might have to write a term paper or study more than you want to.

Costs are things that you normally try to avoid, that you consider unpleasant or difficult. Examples might include working overtime; washing dishes and ironing clothes; watching your partner's favorite television show, which you find boring; or doing favors for those you dislike.

Using this basic economic model, social exchange theory claims that you seek to develop the friendships and romantic relationships that will give you the greatest profits; that is, relationships in which the rewards are greater than the costs. The most preferred relationships, according to this theory, are those that give you the greatest rewards with the least costs.

**Equity theory** uses the ideas of social exchange but goes a step farther and claims that you develop and maintain relationships in which the ratio of your rewards relative to your costs is approximately equal to your partner's (Walster, Walster, & Berscheid, 1978; Messick & Cook, 1983). For example, if you and a friend start a business and you put up two-thirds of the money and your friend puts up one-third, equity would demand that you get two-thirds of the profits and your friend get one-third. An equitable relationship, then, is simply one in which each party derives rewards that are proportional to their costs. If you contribute more toward the relationship than your partner, then equity requires that you should get greater rewards. If you both work equally hard, then equity demands that you should both get approximately equal rewards. Conversely, inequity will exist in a relationship if you pay more of the costs (for example, if you do more of the unpleasant tasks) but your partner enjoys more of the rewards. Inequity will also exist if you and your partner work equally hard but one of you gets more of the rewards.

Equity theory puts into clear focus the sources of relational dissatisfaction seen every day. For example, in a relationship both partners may have full-time jobs, but one partner may also be expected to do the major share of the household chores. Thus, although both may be deriving equal rewards—they have equally good cars, they live in the same three-bedroom house, and so on—one partner is paying more of the costs. According to equity theory, this partner will be dissatisfied because of this lack of equity.

Equity theory claims that you will develop, maintain, and be satisfied with relationships that are equitable. You will not develop, will terminate, and will be dissatisfied with relationships that are inequitable. The greater the inequity, the greater the dissatisfaction and the greater the likelihood that the relationship will end.

# Culture, Technology, Work, and Relationships

Interpersonal relationships vary widely depending on the culture, on the technological channels used, and on whether the relationships occur inside or outside the workplace. For a more complete understanding of interpersonal relationships today, we need to look at these three factors.

## Culture and Gender

Cultural contexts and gender distinctions vary greatly around the world. This text's discussion of relationships up to this point has assumed that you voluntarily choose your relationship partners—that you consciously choose to pursue certain relationships and not others. In some cultures, however, your parents choose your romantic partner for you. In some cases your husband or wife is chosen to unite two families or to bring some financial advantage to your family or village. An arrangement such as this may have been entered into by your parents when you were an infant or even before you were born. In most cultures, of course, even when arranged marriages are not the norm, there's pressure to marry "the right" person and to be friends with certain people and not others.

In the United States, researchers study and textbook authors write about dissolving relationships and how to survive relationship breakups. It's assumed that you have the right to exit an undesirable relationship. But in some cultures, you simply cannot dissolve a relationship once it's formed or once there are children. In the practice of Roman Catholicism, once people are validly married, they're always married and cannot dissolve that relationship. More important to such cultures may be issues such as "How do you maintain a relationship that has problems?" "What can you do to survive in this unpleasant relationship?" and "How can you repair a troubled relationship?" (Moghaddam, Taylor, & Wright, 1993).

Further, the culture will influence the difficulty that you go through when relationships break up. For example, married persons whose religion forbids divorce and remarriage will experience religious disapproval and condemnation as well as the same economic and social difficulties and emotional pain everyone else goes through. In the United States child custody almost invariably goes to the woman, and this presents an added emotional burden for the man. In Iran child custody goes to the man, which presents added emotional burdens for the woman. In India women experience greater difficulty than men in divorce because of their economic dependence on men, the cultural beliefs about women, and the patriarchal order of the family (Amato, 1994). And in Jordan it was only a few years ago that a wife was first granted a divorce. Previously only men had been granted divorces (*New York Times*, May 15, 2002, p. A6).

In most of the United States, interpersonal friendships are drawn from a relatively large pool. Out of all the people you come into regular contact with, you choose relatively few of these as friends. With computer chat groups, the number of friends you can have has increased enormously, as has the range from which these friends can be chosen. In rural areas and in small villages throughout the world, however, you would have very few choices. The two or three other children your age would become your friends, because these would be the only possible friends you could make.

Most cultures assume that relationships should be permanent or at least long-lasting. Consequently, it's assumed that people want to keep relationships together and will expend considerable energy to maintain relationships. Because of this bias, little research has studied how to move effortlessly from one intimate relationship to another or has suggested ways to do this more effectively and efficiently.

> **WHAT DO YOU SAY?**
> **Relationship Dissolution**
> You realize that your six-month relationship is going nowhere, and you want to break it off. It's just not exciting and not taking you where you want to go. *What do you say? Through what channel? In what context?*

Culture influences heterosexual relationships by assigning different roles to men and women. In the United States men and women are supposed to be equal—at least that is the stated ideal. As a result, both men and women can initiate relationships and both can dissolve them. Both men and women are expected to derive satisfaction from their interpersonal relationships; and when that satisfaction isn't present, either partner may seek to exit the relationship. In Iran, on the other hand, only the man has the right to dissolve a marriage, and he may initiate dissolution without giving reasons.

Gay and lesbian relationships are accepted in some cultures and condemned in others. In some areas of the United States, "domestic partnerships" may be registered; these partnerships grant gay men, lesbians, and (in some cases) unmarried heterosexuals rights that were formerly reserved only for married couples, such as health insurance benefits and the right to make decisions when one member is incapacitated. In Norway, Sweden, and Denmark, on the other hand, same-sex relationship partners have the same rights as married partners.

Not surprisingly, there are significant gender differences in interpersonal relationships. Perhaps the best-documented finding—already noted in the discussion of self-disclosure in Chapter 2—is that women self-disclose more than men. This difference holds throughout male and female friendships. Male friends self-disclose less often and with less intimate details than female friends do, and men generally do not view self-disclosure as a necessary aspect of their friendships (Hart, 1990). Women engage in significantly more affectional behaviors with their friends than do males, which may account for the greater difficulty men experience in initiating and maintaining close friendships (Hays, 1989). **Relational communication,** in all its forms and functions, seems a much more important dimension of women's friendships.

Men's friendships often are built around shared activities—attending a ball game, playing cards, working on a project at the office. Women's friendships, on the other hand, are built more around a sharing of feelings, support, and "personalism." In one study similarity (for example, in academic major, in status, in willingness to protect a friend in uncomfortable situations, and even in proficiency in playing Password) contributed greatly to relationship closeness between male–male friends but not between female–female or female–male friends (Griffin & Sparks, 1990). Perhaps, then, similarity is a criterion for male friendships but not for female or mixed-sex friendships.

There are also gender similarities and differences in love. Women and men seem to experience love to a similar degree (Rubin, 1973). However, women indicate greater love than men do for their same-sex friends. This may reflect a real difference between the sexes, or it may be a function of the greater social restrictions on men. A man is not supposed to admit his love for another man, but women are permitted to communicate their love for other women.

Men and women also differ in the types of love they prefer (Hendrick et al., 1984). For example, on a love self-test similar to the "What kind of lover are you?" test presented earlier, men scored higher on erotic and ludic love, whereas women scored higher on manic, pragmatic, and storgic love. No difference was found for agapic love.

Women report having their first romantic experiences earlier than men. The median age of first infatuation is 13 for women and 13.6 for men; the median age for first time in love is 17.1 for women and 17.6 for men (Kirkpatrick & Caplow, 1945; Hendrick et al., 1984).

Another gender difference frequently noted is that of romanticism. Research generally confirms that, contrary to popular depictions in the media, men are more romantic than women. For example, researchers have found that "men are more likely than women to believe in love at first sight, in love as the basis for marriage and for overcoming obstacles, and to believe that their partner and relationship will be perfect" (Sprecher & Metts, 1989). This difference seems to increase as the romantic relationship develops: Men become more romantic and women less romantic (Fengler, 1974).

One further gender difference concerns differences between men and women in breaking up relationships (Blumstein & Schwartz, 1983; cf. Janus & Janus, 1993). In a survey asking about their reasons for breaking up, only 15 percent of the men indicated that it was their own interest in another partner, whereas 32 percent of the women stated this as a cause of the breakup. These findings are consistent with their partners' perceptions as well; 30 percent of the men but only 15 percent of the women reported that their partner's interest in another person was the reason for the breakup.

In their reactions to broken romantic affairs, women and men exhibit both similarities and differences. For example, the tendency to recall only pleasant memories and to revisit places with past associations was about equal among women and men. However, men engage in more dreaming about the lost partner and in more daydreaming as a reaction to the breakup than women do.

## Technology

Perhaps even more obvious than culture or gender is the influence of technology on interpersonal relationships. Clearly, online interpersonal relationships are on the increase. The number of Internet users is rapidly increasing, and commercial websites devoted to introducing people are proliferating, making it especially easy to develop online relationships. The afternoon television talk shows frequently focus on computer relationships, especially on getting people together who have established a relationship online but who have never met. Clearly, many are turning to the Internet to find a friend or romantic partner. In MOOs (online role-playing games), 93.6 percent of the users formed ongoing friendship and romantic relationships (Parks & Roberts, 1998). Some are using the Internet as their only means of interaction; others are using it as a way of beginning a relationship and intend later to supplement computer talk with photographs, phone calls, and face-to-face meetings.

In one study, almost two-thirds of newsgroup users had formed new acquaintances, friendships, or other personal relationships with someone they met on the Internet. Almost one-third said that they communicated with their partner at least three or four times a week; more than half communicated on a weekly basis (Parks & Floyd, 1996).

Women, it seems, are more likely to form relationships on the Internet than men. About 72 percent of women and 55 percent of men had formed personal relationships online (Parks & Floyd, 1996). Not surprisingly, those who communicated more frequently formed more relationships.

As relationships develop on the Internet, network convergence occurs; that is, as a relationship between two people develops, they begin to share their network of other communicators with each other (Parks, 1995; Parks & Floyd, 1996). This, of course, is similar to what happens in relationships formed through face-to-face contact. Online work groups are also on the increase and have been found to be more task oriented and more efficient than face-to-face groups (Lantz, 2001). Online groups provide a sense of belonging that may once have been thought possible only through face-to-face interactions (Silverman, 2001).

There are lots of advantages to establishing relationships online. For example, online relationships let people avoid potential physical violence or sexually transmitted diseases. Unlike relationships established in face-to-face encounters, in which physical appearance tends to outweigh personality, Internet relationships allow your inner qualities to be communicated first. Rapport and mutual self-disclosure become more important than physical attractiveness in promoting intimacy (Cooper & Sportolari, 1997). And, contrary to some popular opinions, online

▼ | E-TALK

**Students Away at College**
When students go away to college, they often maintain close connections with their family and high school friends through cell phones, e-mail, and instant messaging. What advantages does this ease of connection provide? Can you identify any problems this might create?

**Cyberflirting**

One of the differences research finds between face-to-face and online flirting is that in the online situation reality and fantasy become somewhat blurred (Whitty, 2003a, 2003b). What other differences do you find between flirting in face-to-face and computer-mediated situations?

relationships rely just as heavily on the ideals of trust, honesty, and commitment as do face-to-face relationships (Whitty & Gavin, 2001). Friendship and romantic interaction on the Internet are a natural boon for shut-ins and for extremely shy people, for whom traditional ways of meeting someone are often difficult. Computer talk is empowering for those with "physical disabilities or disfigurements," for whom face-to-face interactions are often superficial and often end with withdrawal (Lea & Spears, 1995; Bull & Rumsey, 1988). By eliminating the physical cues, computer talk equalizes the interaction and doesn't put a person with a disfigurement, for example, at an immediate disadvantage in a society that emphasizes physical attractiveness. Online you're free to reveal as much or as little about your physical self as you wish, when you wish.

Another obvious advantage of online relationships is that the number of people you can reach is so vast that it's relatively easy to find someone who matches what you're looking for. The situation is comparable to your chances of finding a book that covers just what you need in a library of millions of volumes rather than in a collection of only a few thousand. Still another advantage for many is that the socioeconomic and educational status of people on the Net is significantly higher than you're likely to find in a bar or singles group.

Of course, there are also disadvantages. For one thing, you can't see the person. Unless you exchange photos or meet face-to-face, you won't know what the person looks like. Even if photos are exchanged, how certain can you be that the photos are of the person or that they were taken recently? In addition, you can't hear the person's voice, and this too hinders you in formulating a total picture. Of course, you can always add an occasional phone call to give you this information.

Online, people can present a false self with little chance of detection. For example, minors may present themselves as adults; and adults may present themselves as children for illicit and illegal sexual communications and, perhaps, meetings. Similarly, people can present themselves as poor when they're rich, as mature when they're immature, as serious and committed when they're just enjoying the experience. Although you can also misrepresent yourself in face-to-face relationships, the fact that it's easier to do online probably accounts for greater misrepresentation in computer relationships (Cornwell & Lundgren, 2001).

Another potential disadvantage—though some might argue it is actually an advantage—is that computer interactions may become all consuming and may substitute for face-to-face interpersonal relationships.

## Work

Workplace relationships, especially workplace romances, provide a unique perspective on the advantages and disadvantages of relationships. Real life is quite different from television depictions of workers, who are always best friends and who move in and out of interoffice romances with no difficulty—at least no difficulty that can't be resolved in 24 minutes.

Opinions vary widely concerning workplace romances. Some organizations, on the assumption that romantic relationships are basically detrimental to the success of the workplace, have explicit rules prohibiting dating among employees. In some organizations workers can even be fired for having such relationships.

On the positive side, the work environment seems a perfect place to meet a potential romantic partner. After all, by virtue of the fact that you're working in the same office, you're probably both interested in the same field, have similar training and ambitions, and spend considerable time together—all factors that foster the development of a successful interpersonal relationship.

Similarly, office romances can lead to greater work satisfaction. If you're romantically attracted to another worker, it can make going to work, working together, and even working added hours more enjoyable and more satisfying. If the relationship is good and mutually satisfying, the individuals are likely to develop empathy for each other and to act in ways that are supportive, cooperative, and friendly; in short, the workers are more likely to act with all the characteristics of effective communication noted throughout this book.

However, even when the relationship is good for the two individuals, it may not necessarily be good for other workers. Seeing the loving couple every day in every way may generate destructive office gossip. Others may see the lovers as a team that must be confronted as a pair; they may feel that they can't criticize one without incurring the wrath of the other.

Similarly, such relationships may cause problems for management when, for example, a promotion is to be made or relocation decisions are necessary. Can you legitimately ask one lover to move to Boston and the other to move to San Francisco? Will it be difficult for management to promote one lover to a position in which he or she will become the supervisor of the other?

The workplace also puts pressure on the individuals. Most organizations, at least in the United States, are highly competitive environments in which one person's success often means another's failure. A romantic couple may find, for example, that the self-disclosures that regularly accompany increased intimacy (which often reveal weaknesses, doubts, and misgivings) may actually prove a liability in this kind of competitive context.

There's a popular belief that women enter office romances to achieve some kind of personal gain. For example, a survey of 218 male and female business school graduates found that people perceived women as entering office romances for personal advancement, despite a lack of any evidence (Anderson & Fisher, 1991). So the woman who does participate in an office romance may have to deal with both male and female colleagues' suspicions that she is in this relationship just to advance her career.

Of course, when the romance goes bad or when it's one-sided, there are even more disadvantages. One obvious problem is that it can be stressful for the former partners to see each other regularly and perhaps to work together. And other workers may feel they have to take sides, being supportive of one partner and critical of the other. This can easily cause friction throughout the organization. Another and perhaps more serious issue is the potential for charges of sexual harassment, especially if the romance is between a supervisor and a worker. Whether the charges are legitimate or result merely from an unhappy love affair that had nothing to do with the organization, management will find itself in the middle, facing lawsuits and time and money lost from investigating and ultimately acting on the charges.

The generally negative attitude of management toward workplace relationships and the problems inherent in dealing with the normal stresses of both work and romance seem to outweigh the positive benefits that may be derived from such relationships. All in all, workers are generally advised not to romance their colleagues. Friendships seem the much safer course.

 ## Summary of Concepts and Skills

This chapter explored interpersonal communication, conversation, and relationships—their stages and types; the reasons why you form relationships; and the influence of culture, technology, and work on relationships.

1. Conversation consists of five general stages: opening, feedforward, business, feedback, and closing.
2. Three key principles of conversation are turn-taking, dialogue, and immediacy.

3. Relationships may be viewed in terms of six stages: contact, involvement, intimacy, deterioration, repair, and dissolution. Each of these stages can be further broken down into an early and a later phase.

4. Among the major causes of relationship deterioration are a lessening of the reasons for establishing the relationship, changes in the people involved, sexual difficulties, and work and financial problems.

5. Friendships may be classified as those of reciprocity, receptivity, and association.

6. Six primary love styles have been identified: eros, ludus, storge, mania, pragma, and agape.

7. Primary relationships and families may be classified into traditionals, independents, and separates.

8. Attraction depends on such factors as physical and personality attractiveness, similarity (especially attitudinal), reinforcement, and proximity.

9. The relationship rule approach views relationships as held together by adherence to an agreed-upon set of rules.

10. Social penetration theory describes relationships in terms of breadth (the number of topics you talk about) and depth (the degree of personalness with which you pursue the topics).

11. Social exchange theory holds that you develop relationships that yield the greatest profits. You seek relationships in which the rewards exceed the costs and are more likely to dissolve relationships when the costs exceed the rewards.

12. Equity theory claims that you develop and maintain relationships in which the rewards are distributed in proportion to costs. When your share of the rewards is less than would be demanded by equity, you are likely to experience dissatisfaction and exit the relationships.

13. Relationships of all kinds and in all their aspects are heavily influenced by culture, as are the theories that explain relationships and the topics research focuses on.

14. Gender differences in both friendship and love are often considerable and influence the ways in which these relationships are viewed and the communication that takes place within them.

15. All aspects of relationships—from development through maintenance, and sometimes to dissolution—are greatly influenced by the Internet and the opportunities it affords for communication.

16. Romantic relationships in the workplace present both opportunities and dangers.

Check your competence in using the skills of effective relationship communication by placing a check mark next to the skills you want to work on most.

_____ 1. I understand that conversation occurs in stages and that each stage serves a different function.

_____ 2. I follow the principles of turn-taking in conversation, giving appropriate speaker and listener cues and responding to the cues of others.

_____ 3. I engage in dialogic rather than monologic conversation.

_____ 4. I adjust my immediacy cues as appropriate to the conversation and the relationship.

_____ 5. I understand that relationships occur in stages and that each stage communicates a different relationship.

_____ 6. I adjust my communication patterns on the basis of the relationship's intimacy.

_____ 7. I can identify changes in communication patterns that may signal deterioration.

_____ 8. I can use the accepted repair strategies to heal an ailing relationship—for example, reversing negative communication patterns, using cherishing behaviors, and adopting a positive action program.

_____ 9. I can deal with relationship dissolution and apply such skills as breaking the loneliness-depression cycle, bolstering self-esteem, and seeking support.

_____10. I understand the different types of friendships and can identify the goals that each type serves.

_____11. I understand the different types of love and can appreciate the varied ways in which people can love.

_____12. I understand the varied types of primary relationships and families and can see the similarities and differences among them.

_____13. I can effectively manage physical proximity, reinforcement, and emphasizing similarities as ways to increase interpersonal attractiveness.

_____14. I can apply the rules of friendship and romantic relationships as appropriate.

_____15. I can identify, and to some extent control, the rewards and costs of my relationships.

_____16. I can appreciate the other person's perception of relationship equity and can modify my own behavior to make the relationship more productive and satisfying.

_____17. I understand relationships as influenced by both culture and gender and I take these differences into consideration when understanding interpersonal relationships.

_____18. I understand the differences between face-to-face and online relationships and can modify my behavior accordingly.

_____19. I take into consideration the advantages and the disadvantages of workplace romantic relationships.

# Key Word Quiz

## The Language of Interpersonal Communication, Conversation, and Relationships

Match the terms about interpersonal communication with their definitions. Record the number of the definition next to the appropriate term.

a. _____ phatic communication

b. _____ turn-maintaining cues

c. _____ dialogue

d. _____ immediacy

e. _____ agapic love

f. _____ turn-denying cues

g. _____ monologue

h. _____ depenetration

i. _____ storge love

j. _____ social exchange

1. Genuine two-way interaction.

2. A theory claiming that you develop relationships in which the profits are greater than the costs.

3. Signals indicating your reluctance to assume the role of speaker.

4. The process by which a deteriorating relationship decreases in breadth and depth.

5. A love that is peaceful and tranquil.

6. Communication in which one person speaks and the other listens.

7. A love that is compassionate and selfless.

8. Signals that indicate that the speaker wishes to continue speaking.

9. The quality of togetherness, of oneness, that joins speaker and listener.

10. Communication that opens the channels of communication.

**Answers: a. 10 b. 8 c. 1 d. 9 e. 7 f. 3 g. 6 h. 4 i. 5 j. 2**

# Five for Discussion

1. In an analysis of 43 published studies on gender differences in interrupting, men interrupted significantly more than women (Anderson et al., 1998). Among the explanations offered is the idea that men interrupt out of a desire to shift the focus to areas of their competence and away from possible areas of incompetence and to maintain power and control. Do you find that your own experience with gender differences in interrupting supports these findings? Based on your own experiences, how would you explain the reasons for interrupting?

2. Another way of looking at conversational rule violations is as breaches of etiquette. When you fail to follow the rules of etiquette, you're often breaking a conversational rule. Numerous websites focus on etiquette in different communication situations. For the etiquette of online conversation, for example, see www.internetiquette.org/; for web etiquette see www.w3.org/Provider/Style/Etiquette.html; and for cell phone etiquette see www.cell-phone-etiquette.com/index.htm. Visit one or more of these websites and record any rules you find particularly applicable to interpersonal communication and conversation.

3. Not surprisingly, each culture has its own conversational taboos—topics that should be avoided, especially by visitors from other cultures. A few examples: In Norway avoid talk of salaries and social status; in Spain avoid the topics of family, religion, jobs, and negative

comments on bullfighting; in Egypt avoid talk of Middle Eastern politics; in Japan avoid talking about World War II; in the Philippines avoid talk of politics, religion, corruption, and foreign aid; in Mexico avoid talking about the Mexican-American war and illegal aliens; in the Caribbean avoid discussing race, local politics, and religion (Axtell, 1993). Are there certain topics that you do not want members of other cultures to talk about? Why? Can you identify taboo topics in family communication? In workplace communication? In classroom communication?

4. The "matching hypothesis" claims that people date and mate with people who are very similar to themselves in physical attractiveness (Walster & Walster, 1978). When this does not happen—for example, when a very attractive person dates someone of average attractiveness—the observer may begin to look for "compensating factors" in the less attractive partner that may make up for the person's lower level of physically attractive-

ness. What evidence can you find to support or contradict this theory? How would you go about testing this theory?

5. Some cultures consider sexual relationships to be undesirable outside of marriage; others see sex as a normal part of intimacy and chastity as undesirable. Intercultural researchers (Hatfield & Rapson, 1996) cite a meeting where colleagues from Sweden and the United States were discussing ways of preventing AIDS. When members of the U.S. delegation suggested teaching abstinence, their Swedish colleagues asked, "How will teenagers ever learn to become loving, considerate sexual partners if they don't practice?" "The silence that greeted the question," note the researchers, "was the sound of two cultures clashing" (Hatfield & Rapson, 1996, p. 36). How have your cultural beliefs and values influenced what you consider appropriate relationship behavior?

# Log On! MyCommunicationLab

A variety of exercises are available to help you work actively with the concepts discussed in this chapter (www.mycommunicationlab.com): (1) Mate Preferences: I Prefer Someone Who . . . , (2) The Television Relationship, (3) Explaining Relationship Problems, (4) Relational Repair from Advice Columnists, (5) Male and Female, and (6) Interpersonal Relationships in Songs and Greeting Cards. In addition, several self-tests will help you further explore some of the concepts alluded to in this chapter: (7) How Confirming Are You? (8) How Committed Are You? (9) How Romantic Are You? (10) What Type of Relationship Do You Prefer? (11) Talking Cherishing, and (12) What Do You Believe about Relationships?

Also visit MyCommunicationLab for additional study tools, activities, and video clips on conversation and interpersonal relationships.

Explore our research resources at www.researchnavigator.com.

Research
Navigator.com

# Chapter

# 7

# Managing Interpersonal Conflict

## Why Read This Chapter?

Because you'll **learn about:**

- the nature and principles of interpersonal conflict.
- the strategies that people use in conflict situations.

Because you'll **learn to:**

- engage in interpersonal conflicts so that they result in strengthening, not weakening your relationship.
- manage conflicts so that both parties emerge from the conflict reasonably satisfied.

*O*f all your interpersonal interactions, those involving conflict are among your most important. Interpersonal conflict often creates ill will, anxiety, and problems for relationships. But, as you'll soon see, conflict also can create opportunities for improving and strengthening relationships.

# What Is Interpersonal Conflict?

Interpersonal conflict is a special type of conflict, so we need here to define this type of conflict and to see how it may focus on both content and relationship issues.

## A Definition of Interpersonal Conflict

**Interpersonal conflict** is disagreement between or among connected individuals—coworkers, close friends, lovers, or family members. The word *connected* emphasizes the transactional nature of interpersonal conflict—the fact that each person's position affects the other person. Thus, the positions in interpersonal conflicts are to some degree both interrelated and incompatible.

Interpersonal conflict is a part of every interpersonal relationship, whether between parents and children, brothers and sisters, friends, lovers, or coworkers. If conflict doesn't exist, then the relationship is probably dull, irrelevant, or insignificant.

To appreciate the inevitability of conflict, consider the broad range of topics on which relationship partners disagree to the point of conflict (Canary, 2003). For example, one study on the issues argued about by gay, lesbian, and heterosexual couples identified six major sources of conflict that were virtually identical for all couples (Kurdek, 1994). The issues are listed here in order, with the first being the most often mentioned. How many of these do you argue about?

- intimacy issues such as affection and sex
- power issues such as excessive demands or possessiveness, lack of equality in the relationship, friends, or leisure time
- personal flaws issues such as drinking or smoking, personal grooming, or driving style
- personal distance issues such as frequent absences or school or job commitments
- social issues such as politics, social problems, parents, or personal values
- distrust issues such as previous lovers or lying

Another study found that among couples, four conditions typically led up to the partners' "first big fight": uncertainty over commitment, jealousy, violation of expectations, and personality differences (Siegert & Stamp, 1994). In work situations, conflict among top managers most often revolved around issues of executive responsibility and coordination. Other conflicts involved differences on organizational objectives, allocation of resources, and appropriate management style (Morrill, 1992). In a study of same-sex and opposite-sex friends, the four issues most often argued about involved problems with sharing living space or possessions, violations of friendship rules, difficulties in sharing activities, and incompatible ideas or opinions (Samter & Cupach, 1998).

Just as you experience conflicts in face-to-face communication, you can experience the same kinds of conflicts online. Some conflict situations, however, are unique to online communication. A few examples:

- Sending commercial messages to those who didn't request them often creates conflict. Junk mail is junk mail; but on the Internet, the receiver often has to pay for the time it takes to read and delete these unwanted messages. Even if there is no financial cost, there is still a loss of time.

▼ **E-TALK**

**E-mail and Interpersonal Conflict**
In what ways do you find that e-mail can escalate interpersonal conflict? In what ways might it help resolve conflict?

- Sending messages to an entire listserv when they're relevant to only one member may annoy members who expect to receive only messages relevant to the entire group and not personal exchanges between two people. This often occurs when someone sends a message seeking specific information, and then individual members reply not just to the person seeking the information but to the entire listserv. Sometimes the reply is simply, "I can't help you with that question," a message relevant only to the person asking the question and not to the entire listserv.

- Spamming—sending someone unsolicited mail, repeatedly sending the same mail, or posting the same message in lots of newsgroups, even when the message is irrelevant to the focus of the group—often causes conflict. As with commercial messages, dealing with spam absorbs valuable time and energy. Also, of course, spamming clogs the system, slowing it down for everyone.

- Flaming, or sending messages that personally attack another user, often occurs in newsgroups. Frequently, flaming leads to flame wars, in which everyone in the group gets into the act and attacks each other. Generally, flaming and flame wars prevent you from achieving your goals and are counterproductive.

- Trolling, or putting out purposely incorrect information or outrageous viewpoints to watch other people correct you or get emotionally upset by your messages, obviously can lead to conflict, though some see it as fun.

- Ill-timed cell phone calls and text messaging often interfere with more important matters and may easily be resented. And, of course, if the recipient doesn't respond as the message sender wishes, conflict of a different sort can be generated.

▼ E-TALK

**Flaming**
What specific kinds of messages do you consider flaming? What messages would you consider the face-to-face counterpart of flaming (O'Sullivan & Flanagin, 2003)?

## Content and Relationship Conflict

Using concepts developed in Chapter 1, you can distinguish between content conflict and relationship conflict. *Content conflict* centers on objects, events, and persons that are usually, though not always, external to the parties involved in the conflict. Content conflicts have to do with the millions of issues that we argue and fight about every day—the merit of a particular movie, what to watch on television, the fairness of the last examination or job promotion, the way to spend our savings.

*Relationship conflicts* are equally numerous. Examples include clashes that arise when a younger brother refuses to obey his older brother, two partners each want an equal say in making vacation plans, or a mother and daughter each want to have the final word concerning the daughter's lifestyle. Here the conflicts are concerned not so much with external objects as with the relationships between the individuals—with issues like who is in charge, how equal are the members in a primary relationship, or who has the right to set down rules of behavior.

Of course, content and relationship dimensions are always easier to separate in a textbook than they are in real life, in which many conflicts contain elements of both. For example, you can probably imagine both content and relationship dimensions in each of the "content" issues mentioned earlier. And yet certain issues seem more one way than the other. For example, intimacy and power issues are largely relational, whereas differences on political and social issues are largely content focused.

*"The ultimate test of a relationship is to disagree, but to hold hands.*

—Alexandria Penney

## Principles of Conflict

Interpersonal conflict is a complex and often difficult-to-understand process. The following principles will help clarify how interpersonal conflict

"I can't remember what we're arguing about, either. Let's keep yelling, and maybe it will come back to us."

works: (1) conflict can be negative or positive, (2) conflict is influenced by culture and gender, and (3) conflict styles have consequences.

## Conflict Can Be Negative or Positive

Although interpersonal conflict is always stressful, it's important to recognize that it has both negative and positive aspects.

**Negative Aspects**     Conflict often leads to increased negative regard for the opponent. One reason for this is that many conflicts involve unfair fighting methods (which we'll examine shortly) and are focused largely on hurting the other person. When one person hurts the other, increased negative feelings are inevitable; even the strongest relationship has limits.

At times, conflict may lead you to close yourself off from the other person. When you hide your true self from an intimate, you prevent meaningful communication from taking place. Because the need for intimacy is so strong, one or both parties may then seek intimacy elsewhere. This often leads to further conflict, mutual hurt, and resentment—qualities that add heavily to the costs carried by the relationship. Meanwhile, rewards may become difficult to exchange. In this situation, the costs increase and the rewards decrease, which often results in relationship deterioration and eventual dissolution.

**Positive Aspects**     The major value of interpersonal conflict is that it forces you to examine a problem and work toward a potential solution. If both you and your opponent use productive conflict strategies (as will be described below), the relationship may well emerge from the encounter stronger, healthier, and more satisfying than before. And you may emerge stronger, more confident, and better able to stand up for yourself (Bedford, 1996).

Through conflict and its resolution, you also can stop resentment from increasing and let your needs be known. For example, suppose I need lots of attention when I come home from work, but you need to review and get closure on the day's work. If we both can appreciate the legitimacy of these needs, then we can find solutions. Perhaps you can make your important phone call after my attention needs are met, or perhaps I can delay my need for attention until you get closure about work. Or perhaps I can learn to provide for your closure needs and in doing so get my attention needs met. We have a win–win solution; each of us gets our needs met.

Consider, too, that when you try to resolve conflict within an interpersonal relationship, you're saying in effect that the relationship is worth the effort; otherwise you would walk away from such a conflict. Usually, confronting a conflict indicates commitment and a desire to preserve the relationship.

## Conflict Is Influenced by Culture and Gender

As in other areas of interpersonal communication, it helps to consider conflict in light of the influences of culture and gender. Both exert powerful influences on how people view and resolve conflicts.

**Conflict and Culture**     Culture influences both the issues that people fight about and the ways of dealing with conflict that people consider appropriate and inappropriate. Researchers have found, for example, that cohabiting 18-year-olds are more likely to experience conflict with their parents about their living style if they live in the United States than if they live in Sweden, where cohabitation is much more accepted. Similarly, male infidelity is more likely to cause conflict between

American spouses than in southern European couples. Students from the United States are more likely to engage in conflict with another U.S. student than with someone from another culture; Chinese students, on the other hand, are more likely to engage in a conflict with a non-Chinese student than with another Chinese (Leung, 1988).

The types of conflicts that arise depend on the cultural orientation of the individuals involved. For example, in **collectivist cultures,** such as those of Ecuador, Indonesia, and Korea, conflicts are more likely to center on violations of collective or group norms and values. Conversely, in **individualist cultures,** such as those of the United States, Canada, and western Europe, conflicts are more likely to occur when people violate individual norms (Ting-Toomey, 1985).

Americans and Japanese differ in their view of the aim or purpose of conflict. The Japanese (a collectivist culture) see conflicts and conflict resolution in terms of compromise; Americans (an individualist culture), on the other hand, see conflict in terms of winning (Gelfand, Nishii, Holcombe, Dyer, Ohbuchi, & Fukuno, 2001). Also, different cultures seem to teach their members different views of conflict strategies (Tardiff, 2001). For example, in Japan it's especially important that you not embarrass the person with whom you are in conflict, especially if the disagreement occurs in public. This face-saving principle prohibits the use of such strategies as personal rejection or verbal aggressiveness. In another example, many Middle Eastern and Pacific Rim cultures discourage women from direct and forceful expressions; rather, these societies expect more agreeable and submissive postures. Also, in general, members of collectivist cultures tend to avoid conflict more than members of individualist cultures (Dsilva & Whyte, 1998; Haar & Krabe, 1999; Cai & Fink, 2002).

Even within a given general culture, more specific subgroups differ from one another in their methods of conflict management. African American men and women and European American men and women, for example, engage in conflict in very different ways (Kochman, 1981). The issues that cause and aggravate conflict, the conflict strategies that are expected and accepted, and the entire attitude toward conflict vary from one group to the other (Collier, 1991; Hecht, Jackson, & Ribeau, 2003).

The cultural norms of organizations also influence the types of conflicts that occur and the ways people may deal with them. Some work environments, for example, would not tolerate employees' expressing disagreement with high-level management; others might welcome it. In individualist cultures there is greater tolerance for conflict, even when it involves different levels of an organizational hierarchy. In collectivist cultures there's less tolerance. And, not surprisingly, the culture influences how the conflict will be resolved. For example, managers in the United States (an individualist culture) deal with workplace conflict by seeking to integrate the demands of the different sides; managers in China (a collectivist culture) are more likely to call on higher management to make decisions—or not to resolve the conflict at all (Tinsley & Brett, 2001).

**Conflict and Gender**  Do men and women engage in interpersonal conflict differently? One of the few stereotypes that is supported by research is that of the withdrawing and sometimes aggressive male. Men are more apt to withdraw from a conflict situation than are women. It has been argued that this may happen because men become more psychologically and physiologically aroused during conflict (and retain this heightened level of arousal much longer than do women) and so may try to distance themselves and withdraw from the conflict to prevent further arousal (Gottman & Carrere, 1994; Canary, Cupach, & Messman, 1995; Goleman, 1995a).

"I was thinking about what we should do this weekend, and I have a few ideas for you to reject."

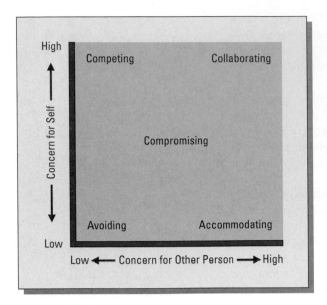

**Figure** *7.1*

**Five Conflict Styles**

This figure is adapted from Blake and Mouton's (1984) approach to managerial leadership and conflict. Try to locate your usual conflict style on this grid. How well does this style work for you?

Women, on the other hand, want to get closer to the conflict; they want to talk about it and resolve it. Even adolescents reveal these differences; in a study of boys and girls aged 11 to 17, boys withdrew more than girls, but were more aggressive when they didn't withdraw (Lindeman, Harakka, & Keltikangas-Jarvinen, 1997). Similarly, a study of offensive language found that girls were more easily offended by language than boys; but boys were more apt to fight when they were offended by the words used (Heasley, Babbitt, & Burbach, 1995a, 1995b). Another study showed that young girls used more prosocial strategies than boys (Rose & Asher, 1999).

Other research has found that women tend to be more emotional and men more logical when they argue (Schaap, Buunk, & Kerkstra, 1988; Canary, Cupach, & Messman, 1995). Women have been defined as conflict "feelers" and men as conflict "thinkers" (Sorenson, Hawkins, & Sorenson, 1995). Another difference is that women are more apt to reveal their negative feelings than are men (Schaap, Buunk, & Kerkstra, 1988; Canary, Cupach, & Messman, 1995).

Among Mexican Americans, studies found that men preferred to achieve mutual understanding by discussing the reasons for the conflict, whereas women focused on being supportive of the relationship. Among Anglo Americans, men preferred direct and rational argument; women preferred flexibility (Collier, 1991). These, of course, are merely examples—but the underlying principle is that techniques for dealing with interpersonal conflict will be viewed differently by men and women.

Nevertheless, from a close examination of the research, it would have to be concluded that the differences between men and women in interpersonal conflict are a lot less clear in reality than they are in popular stereotypes. Much research fails to find the differences that cartoons, situation comedies, novels, and films portray so readily. For example, several studies dealing with both college students and men and women in business found no significant differences in the way men and women engage in conflict (Wilkins & Andersen, 1991; Canary & Hause, 1993; Canary, Cupach, & Messman, 1995).

## Conflict Styles Have Consequences

The way in which you engage in conflict has consequences for the resolution of the conflict and for the relationship between the conflicting parties. Figure 7.1 identifies five basic styles or ways of engaging in conflict and is especially relevant to understanding interpersonal conflicts (Blake & Mouton, 1984). Descriptions of the five styles, plotted among the dimensions of concern for self and concern for the other person, provide insight into the ways people engage in conflict and highlight some of the advantages and disadvantages of each style. As you read through these styles, try to identify your own conflict style as well as the styles of those with whom you have close relationships.

**Competing: I Win, You Lose**    The competitive style involves great concern for your own needs and desires and little for those of others. As long as your needs are met, the conflict has been dealt with successfully (for you). In conflict motivated by competitiveness, you'd be likely to be verbally aggressive and to blame the other person.

This style represents an "I win, you lose" philosophy. This is the conflict style of a person who simply imposes his or her will on the other: "I make the money, and we'll vacation at the beach or not at all." But this philosophy can easily lead to resentment on the part of the person who loses, which can easily cause additional conflicts. Further, the fact that you win and the other person loses probably means that the conflict hasn't really been resolved but only concluded (for now).

**Avoiding: I Lose, You Lose**   Conflict avoiders are relatively unconcerned with their own or with their opponents' needs or desires. They avoid any real communication about the problem, change topics when the problem is brought up, and generally withdraw from the scene both psychologically and physically.

As you can appreciate, the avoiding style does little to resolve any conflicts and may be viewed as an "I lose, you lose" philosophy. If a couple can't agree about where to spend their vacation, but each person refuses to negotiate a resolution to the disagreement, the pair may not take any vacation at all, and both sides lose. Interpersonal problems rarely go away of their own accord; rather, if they exist, they need to be faced and dealt with effectively. Avoidance merely allows the conflict to fester and probably grow, only to resurface in another guise.

"She asked for a divorce, but I outsmarted her and ran into the next room."

**Accommodating: I Lose, You Win**   In accommodating you sacrifice your own needs for the needs of the other person(s). Your major purpose is to maintain harmony and peace in the relationship or group. This style may help maintain peace and may satisfy the opposition; but it does little to meet your own needs, which are unlikely to go away.

Accommodation represents an "I lose, you win" philosophy. If your partner wants to vacation in the mountains and you want to vacation at the beach, and you, instead of negotiating an agreement acceptable to both, give in and accommodate, then you lose and your partner wins. And although this style may make your partner happy (at least on this occasion), it's not likely to prove a lasting resolution to an interpersonal conflict. You'll eventually sense unfairness and inequality and may easily come to resent your partner and perhaps even yourself.

**Collaborating: I Win, You Win**   In collaborating you address both your own and the other person's needs. This style, often considered the ideal, takes time and a willingness to communicate—and especially to listen to the perspectives and needs of the other person.

Ideally, collaboration enables each person's needs to be met, an "I win, you win" situation. For example, you might both agree to split the vacation—one week in the mountains and one week at the beach. Or you might agree to spend this year's vacation at one resort and next year's at the other. This is obviously the style that, in an ideal world, most people would choose for interpersonal conflict.

**Compromising: I Win and Lose, You Win and Lose**   The compromising style is in the middle: There's some concern for your own needs and some concern for the other's needs. Compromise is the kind of strategy you might refer to as "meeting each other halfway," "horse trading," or "give and take." This strategy is likely to result in maintaining peace, but there will be a residue of dissatisfaction over the inevitable losses that each side has to endure.

Compromise represents an "I win and lose, you win and lose" philosophy. So, if you and your partner can't vacation at both the beach and the mountains, then you might settle for weekend trips or using the money to have a hot tub installed instead. These may not be your first choices, but they're not bad and may satisfy (to some degree at least) each of your vacation wants.

**WHAT DO YOU SAY?**
**Resolving Differences**
You've just moved into a new apartment. Unfortunately, your next-door neighbors play their stereo loud and long into the night. You need to say something but just aren't sure how to go about it. *What do you say? To whom? Through what channel?*

## Generating Win–Win Solutions

*Win–win solutions exist for most interpersonal conflict situations (though not necessarily all), if the people involved are willing to put in a little effort to find them.*

For any one of the situations below, (a) generate as many win–lose solutions as you can—solutions in which one person wins and the other loses; (b) generate as many possible win–win solutions as you feel the individuals involved in the conflict could reasonably accept; and (c) explain in one sentence the difference between win–lose and win–win solutions

1. Pat and Chris have decided to get a pet. Pat wants a cat; Chris wants a dog.
2. Pat, who has been in a 12-year relationship with Chris, recently received a $10,000 bonus and has already used the whole amount for a down payment on a new car. Chris is expecting to receive a $5,000 share of the bonus.
3. Pat smokes and smells up the apartment. Chris hates this, and they argue about it almost daily.

# Conflict Management Strategies

In managing conflict you can choose from a variety of productive or unproductive strategies, which we'll investigate here. Realize, however, that the strategies you choose will be influenced by numerous factors, among them (1) the goals to be achieved, (2) your emotional state, (3) your cognitive assessment of the situation, (4) your personality and communication competence, and (5) your family history (Koerner & Fitzpatrick, 2002). Understanding these factors may help you select more appropriate and more effective strategies. And recent research finds that using productive conflict strategies can have lots of beneficial effects, whereas using inappropriate strategies may be linked to poorer psychological health (Weitzman & Weitzman, 2000; Weitzman, 2001; Neff & Harter, 2002).

The *goals* (short-term and long-term) you wish to achieve will influence what conflict strategies seem appropriate to you. If you just want to salvage today's date, you may want to simply "give in" and basically ignore the difficulty. If you want to build a long-term relationship, on the other hand, you may want to fully analyze the cause of the problem and look for strategies that will enable both parties to win.

Your *emotional state* will influence your strategies. You're unlikely to select the same strategies when you're sad as when you're angry. You will tend to use different strategies if you're seeking to apologize than if you're looking for revenge.

Your *cognitive assessment* of the situation will exert powerful influence. For example, your attitudes and beliefs about what is fair and equitable will influence your readiness to acknowledge the fairness in the other person's position. Your own assessment of who (if anyone) is the cause of the problem will also influence your conflict style. You may also assess the likely effects of various possible strategies. For example, what do you risk if you fight with your boss by using blame or personal rejection? Do you risk alienating your teenager if you use force?

Your *personality and communication competence* will influence the way you engage in conflict. For example, if you're shy and unassertive, you may tend to avoid conflict rather than fighting actively. If you're extroverted and have a strong desire to state your position, then you may be more likely to fight actively and to argue forcefully.

Your *family history* will influence the strategies you use, the topics you choose to fight about, and perhaps your tendencies to obsess or forget about interpersonal conflicts. If, for example, your parents argued aggressively about religious differences, you might tend to be aggressive when your partner expresses different religious beliefs; it's what you learned growing up. If you haven't unlearned family conflict patterns, you are likely to repeat them.

Discussions elsewhere in this book have already covered a wide variety of conflict resolution skills. For example, active listening is a skill that has wide application in conflict situations (see Chapter 3). Similarly, using confirming rather than disconfirming language will contribute to effective interpersonal conflict resolution. The following discussion identifies additional strategies—including the unproductive strategies that should be avoided as well as their recommended productive counterparts. As you'll see and as research confirms, using productive conflict strategies can have lots of beneficial effects (Weitzman & Weitzman, 2000; Weitzman, 2001).

## Avoidance and Fighting Actively

Conflict **avoidance** may involve actual physical flight. You may leave the scene of the conflict (walk out of the apartment or go to another part of the office or shop), fall asleep, or blast the stereo to drown out all conversation. It also may take the form of emotional or intellectual avoidance, in which you may leave the conflict psychologically by not dealing with any of the arguments or problems raised.

## MEDIA LITERACY

### Cultivation Theory

According to cultivation theory, the media, especially television, are the primary means by which you form your perceptions of your society and your culture (Gerbner, Gross, Morgan, & Signorielli, 1980). What you watch and how often you watch TV will influence your perception of the world and of people (Signorielli & Lears, 1992; Shanahan & Morgan, 1999; Vergeer, Lubers, & Scheepers, 2000).

Cultivation theory argues that heavy television viewers form an image of reality that is inconsistent with the facts (Potter, 1986, Potter & Chang, 1990). For example:

- Heavy television viewers see their chances of being a victim of a crime to be 1 in 10. In reality it's 1 in 50.
- Heavy viewers think that 20 percent of the world's population lives in the United States. In reality it's 6 percent.
- Heavy viewers believe that the percentage of workers in managerial or professional jobs is 25 percent. It's actually 5 percent.
- Heavy viewers in the United States are more likely to believe that "hard work yields rewards" and that "good wins over evil" than are light viewers.
- Heavy sports program viewers were more likely to believe in the values of hard work and good conduct.
- Heavy soap opera viewers are more likely to believe that "luck is important" and that "the strong survive" than are light viewers.
- Heavy viewers may be more materialistic than light viewers (Harmon, 2001).

In reality, media portrayals of violence, infidelity, and racial and gender stereotypes do *not* represent reality; these portrayals are often extreme so that they can more easily capture your attention. Most media depictions are not (and aren't supposed to be) reality. Media literacy will help you realize that.

***Increasing Media Literacy.*** *In what ways do you think cultivation theory might apply to you? What might you do to lessen such influence?*

*People in the United States still have a "Tarzan" movie view of Africa. That's because in the movies all you see are jungles and animals. . . . We [too] watch television and listen to the radio and go to dances and fall in love.*

—Miriam Makeba

**Nonnegotiation** is a special type of avoidance. Here you refuse to discuss the conflict or to listen to the other person's argument. At times nonnegotiation takes the form of hammering away at your own point of view until the other person gives in—a technique called "steamrolling."

Instead of avoiding the issues, take an active role in your interpersonal conflicts. Involve yourself on both sides of the communication exchange. Be an active participant as a speaker and as a listener; voice your own feelings and listen carefully to the voicing of your opponent's feelings. This is not to say that periodic moratoriums are not helpful; sometimes they are. But in general, be willing to communicate.

Another part of active fighting involves owning your thoughts and feelings. For example, when you disagree with your partner or find fault with her or his behavior, take responsibility for these feelings. Say, for example, "I disagree with . . ." or "I don't like it when you. . . ." Avoid statements that deny your responsibility; for example, "Everybody thinks you're wrong about . . ." or "Chris thinks you shouldn't. . . ."

Focus on the present, on the here and now, rather than on issues that occurred two months ago. Similarly, focus your conflict on the person with whom you're fighting, not on the person's parents, child, or friends.

## Force and Talk

When confronted with conflict, many people prefer not to deal with the issues but rather to force their position on the other person. **Force** may be emotional or physical. In either case, however, the issues are avoided and the "winner" is the combatant who exerts the most force. This is the technique of warring nations, quarreling children, and even some normally sensible and mature adults.

In one study, more than 50 percent of both single people and married couples reported that they had experienced physical violence in their relationships. If symbolic violence was included (for example, threatening to hit the other person or throwing something), the percentages rose above 60 percent for singles and above 70 percent for marrieds (Marshall & Rose, 1987). In another study, 47 percent of a sample of 410 college students reported some experience with violence in a dating relationship. In most cases the violence was reciprocal—each person in the relationship used violence. In cases in which only one person was violent, the research results are conflicting. For example, some surveys (e.g., Deal & Wampler, 1986; Cate et al., 1982) have found that in such cases the aggressor was significantly more often the female partner. Other research, however, has tended to confirm the widespread view that men are more likely to use force than women (DeTurck, 1987).

Men are more apt than women to use violent methods to achieve compliance.

The only real alternative to force is talk. Instead of resorting to force, talk and listen.

## Defensiveness and Supportiveness

Although talk is preferred to force, not all talk is equally productive in conflict resolution. One of the best ways to look at destructive versus productive talk is to look at how the style of your communications can create unproductive **defensiveness** or a productive sense of **supportiveness,** a system developed by Jack Gibb (1961). The type of talk that generally proves destructive and sets up defensive reactions in the listener is talk that is evaluative, controlling, strategic, indifferent or neutral, superior, and certain.

"What's amazing to me is that this late in the game we *still* have to settle our differences with rocks."

**Evaluation**    When you evaluate or judge another person or what that person has done, that person is likely to become resentful and defensive and is likely to respond with attempts to defend himself or herself and perhaps at the same time to become equally evaluative and judgmental. In contrast, when you describe what happened or what you want, it creates no such defensiveness and is generally seen as supportive. The distinction between evaluation and description can be seen in the differences between **you-messages** and **I-messages**.

| Evaluative You-Messages | Descriptive I-Messages |
| --- | --- |
| You never reveal your feelings. | I sure would like hearing how you feel about this. |
| You just don't plan ahead. | I need to know what our schedule for the next few days will be. |
| You never call me. | I'd enjoy hearing from you more often. |

If you put yourself in the role of the listener hearing these statements, you probably can feel the resentment or defensiveness that the evaluative messages (you-messages) would create and the supportiveness from the descriptive messages (I-messages).

**Control**    When you try to control the behavior of the other person, when you order the other person to do this or that, or when you make decisions without mutual discussion and agreement, defensiveness is a likely response. Control messages deny the legitimacy of the person's contributions and in fact deny his or her importance. They say, in effect, "You don't count; your contributions are meaningless." When, on the other hand, you focus on the problem at hand—not on controlling the situation or getting your own way—defensiveness is much less likely. This problem orientation invites mutual participation and recognizes the significance of each person's contributions.

**Strategy**    When you use strategy and try to get around other people or situations through **manipulation**—especially when you conceal your true purposes—others are likely to resent it and to respond defensively. But when you act openly and with **spontaneity,** you're more likely to create an atmosphere that is equal and honest.

**Neutrality**    When you demonstrate **neutrality**—in the sense of indifference or a lack of caring for the other person—it's likely to create defensiveness. Neutrality seems to show a lack of empathy or interest in the thoughts and feelings of the other person; it is especially damaging when intimates are in conflict. This kind of talk says, in effect, "You're not important or deserving of attention and caring." When, on the other hand, you demonstrate empathy, defensiveness is unlikely to occur. Although it can be especially difficult in conflict situations, try to show that you can understand what the other person is going through and that you accept these feelings.

**Superiority**    When you present yourself as superior to the other person, you're in effect putting the other person in an inferior position, and this is likely to be resented. Such superiority messages say in effect that the other person is inadequate or somehow second class. A superior attitude is a violation of the implicit equality contract that people in a close relationship have—namely, the assumption that each person is equal. The other person may then begin to attack your superiority; the conflict can easily degenerate into a conflict over who's the boss, with personal attack being the mode of interaction.

▼ **E-TALK**

**Positiveness**
One study found that, generally at least, people are more positive in dealing with conflict in face-to-face situations than in computer-mediated communication (Zornoza, Ripoll, & Peiró, 2002). Do you notice this to be true? If so, why do you think it's true?

### Early Conflict Resolution

This exercise helps you look at your own pattern for dealing with conflict starters—comments that signal the start of interpersonal conflicts. For each conflict starter below, (a) write an unproductive response—that is, a response that is likely to cause the conflict to escalate; (b) write a productive response—that is, a response that will likely lessen the potential conflict; and (c) in one sentence explain the major difference that you see between the productive and the unproductive responses.

*Impending conflicts are often signaled at a stage when they can be confronted and resolved before they escalate and prove more difficult to resolve.*

1. You're late again. You're always late. Your lateness is so inconsiderate!
2. I just can't bear another weekend of sitting home watching cartoon shows with the kids.
3. Well, there goes another anniversary that you forgot.
4. You think I'm fat, don't you?
5. You never want to do what I want. We always have to do what you want.

**Certainty**   The person who appears to know it all is likely to be resented, so **certainty** often sets up a defensive climate. After all, there is little room for negotiation or mutual problem solving when one person already has the answer. An attitude of **provisionalism**—"Let's explore this issue together and try to find a solution"—is likely to be much more productive than **closed-mindedness**.

## Face-Detracting and Face-Enhancing Strategies

Another dimension of conflict strategies is that of face orientation. Face-detracting or face-attacking strategies involve attacks on the person's self-image; these are strategies designed to embarrass or insult the other person, often in a public setting, and often involve treating the other person as incompetent or untrustworthy, as unable or bad (Donohue & Kolt, 1992). The effects of such attacks can range from mildly embarrassing the other person to severely damaging his or her ego or reputation. When such attacks become extreme, they may be similar to verbal aggressiveness—a tactic explained below. So be especially careful to avoid "fighting words"—words that are sure to escalate the conflict rather than helping to resolve it. Words like *stupid, liar,* and *bitch* as well as words like *always* and *never* (as in "you always . . ." or "you never . . .") invariably create additional problems.

One popular but destructive face-detracting strategy is **beltlining** (Bach & Wyden, 1968). Much like fighters in a ring, each person has a "beltline" in interpersonal conflict. When you hit above the "belt," the person is able to absorb the emotional blow. When you hit below it, however, you can inflict serious injury. With most interpersonal relationships, especially those of long standing, you know where the beltline is. You know, for example, that to talk about Pat's infertility or Chris's failure to get a permanent job is to hit below the belt. This type of face-detracting strategy causes added problems for all persons involved in a conflict. Keep blows to areas your opponent can absorb and handle.

Face-enhancing techniques, on the other hand, enhance the other person's self-image and self-esteem and involve helping the other person maintain a positive image—the image of a person who is competent and trustworthy, able and good. There is some evidence to show that even when you get what you want, say in a bargaining situation, it's wise to help the other person retain positive face. This makes it less likely that future conflicts will arise (Donohue & Kolt, 1992). Not surprisingly, people are more likely to make an effort to support someone's "face" if they like the person than if they don't (Meyer, 1994).

Generally, collectivist cultures like those of Korea and Japan place greater emphasis on face, especially on maintaining a positive image in public. Face is generally less crucial in individualist cultures such as that of the United States. And yet there are, of course, many shadings to any such broad generalization. For example, in parts of China, whose highly collectivist culture puts great stress on face-saving, criminals are paraded publicly at rallies and humiliated before being put to death (Tyler, 1996). Perhaps the importance of face-saving in China gives this particular punishment a meaning that it could not have in more individualistic cultures. But be careful not to think of all individualist or collectivist cultures as similar. For example, one study indicated that Germans had more face concerns than Americans, although both are individualist cultures; and Chinese had more face concerns than Japanese, although both are collectivist cultures (Oetzel, Ting-Toomey, Masumoto, Yokochi, Pan, Takai, & Wilcox, 2001).

Confirming the other person's definition of self (Chapter 2), avoiding attack and blame, and using excuses and apologies as appropriate are some generally useful face-enhancing strategies.

**WHAT DO YOU SAY?**
**Empathy**
Your roommate just made the dean's list (as did you) and as a reward received a new Mercedes from a rich uncle. Your roommate is ecstatic and runs to you to share the news. You want to demonstrate empathy, but in all honesty you're annoyed that some people just seem to get everything. *What do you say?*

## Blame and Empathy

Sometimes conflict is caused by the actions of one of the individuals. Sometimes it's caused by clearly identifiable outside forces. Most of the time, however, it's caused by a wide variety of factors. Any attempt to single out one or two factors for **blame** is sure to fail. Yet a frequently used fight strategy is to blame someone for the situation. Consider, for example, a couple who are fighting over their child's getting into trouble with the police. Instead of dealing with the problem itself, the parents may blame each other for the child's troubles. Such blaming, of course, does nothing to resolve the problem or to help the child.

Perhaps the best alternative to blame is **empathy.** Do your best to empathically understand your opponent's feelings, and validate those feelings as appropriate. Once again, in expressing **affirmation** and validation you are not necessarily expressing agreement on the issue in conflict; you're merely respecting your partner's feelings. This simple strategy has also been found to reduce verbal aggressiveness (Infante, Rancer, & Jordan, 1996).

## Silencers and Facilitating Open Expression

Silencers are a wide variety of unproductive fighting techniques that literally silence the other individual. One frequently used silencer is crying. When a person is unable to deal with a conflict or when winning seems unlikely, he or she may cry, and thus silence the other person.

Another silencer is to feign extreme emotionalism—to yell and scream and pretend to be losing control. Still another is to develop some "physical" reaction—headaches and shortness of breath are probably the most popular. One of the major problems with such silencers is that we as opponents can never be certain that they are mere tactics; they may be real physical reactions that we should pay attention to. Regardless of what we do, the conflict remains unexamined and unresolved.

In addition to avoiding silencers, avoid power tactics (raising your voice or threatening physical force) that suppress or inhibit freedom of expression. Such tactics are designed to put the other person down and to subvert real interpersonal equality. Grant other people permission to express themselves freely and openly, to be themselves.

"Walking down here and asking if I can get you some more detergent from the store is just the beginning of my fence-mending agenda."

## Gunnysacking and Present Focus

The word **gunnysacking** refers to the unproductive process of storing up grievances—as if in a gunnysack—and then unloading them when an argument arises (Bach & Wyden, 1968). The immediate occasion for unloading stored-up grievances may be relatively simple (or so it may seem at first); for example, you come home late one night without calling. Instead of arguing about this, the gunnysacker pours out a mass of unrelated past grievances. As you probably know from experience, gunnysacking does nothing to help resolve conflict and often begets further gunnysacking. Frequently the trigger problem never gets addressed. Instead, resentment and hostility escalate. Therefore, focus on the present, on the here and now, rather than on issues that occurred two months ago. Similarly, focus your conflict on the person with whom you're fighting, not on the person's mother, child, or friends.

"A slip of the foot may soon be recovered; but that of tongue perhaps never."
—THOMAS FULLER

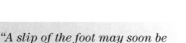

## Verbal Aggressiveness and Argumentativeness

An especially interesting perspective on conflict has emerged from work on verbal aggressiveness and argumentativeness, concepts that were developed by communication researchers but that have quickly spread to other disciplines such as psychology, education, and management, among others (Infante, 1988; Rancer, 1998; Wigley, 1998; Rancer & Avtgis, 2006). Understanding these two concepts will help you understand some of the reasons why things go wrong and some of the ways in which you can use conflict to improve rather than damage your relationships.

**Verbal Aggressiveness** **Verbal aggressiveness** is a method of winning an argument by inflicting psychological pain, by attacking the other person's self-concept. The technique is a type of disconfirmation, in

### Ethical Fighting

Throughout this chapter, a distinction has been made between effective and ineffective conflict strategies. But all communication strategies also have an ethical dimension, so we need to look at the ethical implications of conflict resolution strategies. For example:

- Does conflict avoidance have an ethical dimension? For example, is it unethical for one relationship partner to refuse to discuss disagreements?
- Can the use of physical force to influence another person ever be ethical? Can you identify a situation in which it would be appropriate for someone with greater physical strength to overpower another to enforce his or her point of view?
- Are face-detracting strategies inherently unethical, or might it be appropriate to use them in certain situations? Can you identify such situations?
- What are the ethical implications of verbal aggressiveness?

*What would you do?* At your highly stressful job you sometimes use cocaine with your colleagues. This happens several times a month, but you don't use drugs of any kind at any other times. Your partner asks you if you take drugs. Because your coke use is so limited, but mainly because you know that admitting it will cause a huge conflict in your already shaky relationship, you wonder if you can ethically lie. What would you do?

*Honest disagreement is often a good sign of progress.*
—GANDHI

that it seeks to discredit the individual's view of self. To explore this tendency further, take the following self-test of verbal aggressiveness.

*Test* ▶ *Yourself*

## HOW VERBALLY AGGRESSIVE ARE YOU?

**INSTRUCTIONS:** This scale measures how people try to obtain compliance from others. For each statement, indicate the extent to which you feel it's true for you in your attempts to influence others. Use the following scale:

**5** = strongly agree, **4** = agree, **3** = undecided, **2** = disagree, and **1** = strongly disagree.

_____ ❶ If individuals I am trying to influence really deserve it, I attack their character.

_____ ❷ When individuals are very stubborn, I use insults to soften their stubborness.

_____ ❸ When people behave in ways that are in very poor taste, I insult them in order to shock them into proper behavior.

_____ ❹ When people simply will not budge on a matter of importance, I lose my temper and say rather strong things to them.

_____ ❺ When individuals insult me, I get a lot of pleasure out of really telling them off.

_____ ❻ I like poking fun at people who do things that are stupid in order to stimulate their intelligence.

▼ E-TALK

**Aggressiveness in Internet Communication**
How does verbal aggressiveness differ in face-to-face and in computer-mediated communication?

_____ ❼ When people do things that are mean or cruel, I attack their character in order to help correct their behavior.

_____ ❽ When nothing seems to work in trying to influence others, I yell and scream in order to get some movement from them.

_____ ❾ When I am unable to refute others' positions, I try to make them feel defensive in order to weaken their positions.

_____ ❿ When people refuse to do a task I know is important without good reason, I tell them they are unreasonable.

**HOW DID YOU DO?** In order to compute your verbal aggressiveness score, simply add up your responses. A total score of 30 would indicate the neutral point, not especially aggressive but not especially confirming of the other either. If you scored about 35, you would be considered moderately aggressive; and if you scored 40 or more, you'd be considered very aggressive. If you scored below the neutral point, you'd be considered less verbally aggressive and more confirming when interacting with others. In looking over your responses, make special note of the characteristics identified in the 10 statements that refer to the tendency to act verbally aggressive. Note those inappropriate behaviors that you're especially prone to commit.

**WHAT WILL YOU DO?** Because verbal aggressiveness is likely to seriously reduce communication effectiveness, you probably want to reduce your tendencies to respond aggressively. Review the times when you acted verbally aggressive. What effect did such actions have on your subsequent interactions? What effect did they have on your relationship with the other person? What alternative ways of getting your point across might you have used? Might these have proved more effective? Perhaps the most general suggestion for reducing verbal aggressiveness is to increase your argumentativeness.

_Source:_ From a 20-item scale developed by Infante and Wigley (1986) and factor analyzed by Beatty, Rudd, and Valencic (1999). See "Verbal Aggressiveness" by Dominic Infante and C. J. Wigley, _Communication Monographs_ 53, 1986, and Michael J. Beatty, Jill E. Rudd, & Kristin Marie Valencic, "A Re-evaluation of the Verbal Aggressiveness Scale: One Factor or Two?" _Communication Research Reports_, 1999, Vol. 16, 10–17. Copyright © 1986 by the National Communication Association. Reprinted by permission of the publisher and authors.

**Argumentativeness**    Contrary to popular belief, argumentativeness is a quality to be cultivated rather than avoided. The term **argumentativeness** refers to your willingness to argue for a point of view, your tendency to speak your mind on significant issues. It's the mode of dealing with disagreements that is the preferred alternative to verbal aggressiveness (Infante & Rancer, 1995).

## HOW ARGUMENTATIVE ARE YOU?

**INSTRUCTIONS:** This questionnaire contains statements about your approach to controversial issues. Indicate how often each statement is true for you personally according to the following scale:

**1** = almost never true, **2** = rarely true, **3** = occasionally true, **4** = often true, and **5** = almost always true.

_____ ❶ While in an argument, I worry that the person I am arguing with will form a negative impression of me.

_____ ❷ Arguing over controversial issues improves my intelligence.

_____ ❸ I enjoy avoiding arguments.

_____ ❹ I am energetic and enthusiastic when I argue.

_____ ❺ Once I finish an argument, I promise myself that I will not get into another.

_____ ❻ Arguing with a person creates more problems for me than it solves.

_____ ❼ I have a pleasant, good feeling when I win a point in an argument.

_____ ❽ When I finish arguing with someone, I feel nervous and upset.

_____ ❾ I enjoy a good argument over a controversial issue.

_____ ❿ I get an unpleasant feeling when I realize I am about to get into an argument.

_____ ⓫ I enjoy defending my point of view on an issue.

_____ ⓬ I am happy when I keep an argument from happening.

_____ ⓭ I do not like to miss the opportunity to argue a controversial issue.

_____ ⓮ I prefer being with people who rarely disagree with me.

_____ ⓯ I consider an argument an exciting intellectual challenge.

_____ ⓰ I find myself unable to think of effective points during an argument.

_____ ⓱ I feel refreshed and satisfied after an argument on a controversial issue.

_____ ⓲ I have the ability to do well in an argument.

_____ ⓳ I try to avoid getting into arguments.

_____ ⓴ I feel excitement when I expect that a conversation I am in is leading to an argument.

> "The aim of an argument or discussion should not be victory, but progress."

**HOW DID YOU DO?** To compute your argumentativeness score follow these steps:

1. Add your scores on items 2, 4, 7, 9, 11, 13, 15, 17, 18, and 20.

2. Add 60 to the sum obtained in step 1.

3. Add your scores on items 1, 3, 5, 6, 8, 10, 12, 14, 16, and 19.

To compute your argumentativeness score, subtract the total obtained in step 3 from the total obtained in step 2. The following guidelines will help you interpret your score: Scores between 73 and 100 indicate high argumentativeness; scores between 56 and 72 indicate moderate argumentativeness; and scores between 20 and 55 indicate low argumentativeness.

**WHAT WILL YOU DO?** The researchers who developed this test note that both high and low argumentatives may experience communication difficulties. The high argumentative, for example, may argue needlessly, too often, and too forcefully. The low argumentative, on the other hand, may avoid taking a stand even when it is appropriate to do so. Persons scoring somewhere in the middle are probably the more interpersonally skilled and adaptable, arguing when it is necessary but avoiding arguments that are needless and repetitive. Does your experience

## WHAT DO YOU SAY?
**Verbal Aggressiveness**
Your partner persists in being verbally aggressive whenever you have an argument. Regardless of what the conflict is about, your self-concept is attacked, and you've had enough. You want to stop this kind of attack. *What do you say? Through what channel? In what context?*

support this observation? What specific actions might you take to improve your argumentativeness?

*Source:* From Dominic Infante and Andrew Rancer, "A Conceptualization and Measure of Argumentativeness" *Journal of Personality Assessment* 46 (1982): 72–80. Copyright 1982 Lawrence Erlbaum Associates, Inc. Reprinted by permission of Lawrence Erlbaum Associates, Inc., and the authors.

***Some Differences between Argumentative and Verbally Aggressive Messages.*** As you can appreciate, there are numerous differences between argumentative and verbally aggressive messages. Here are just a few (Infante & Rancer, 1996, Rancer & Atvgis, 2006).

| Argumentativeness | Verbal Aggressiveness |
|---|---|
| Is *constructive;* the outcomes are positive in a variety of communication situations (interpersonal, group, organizational, family, and intercultural). | Is destructive; the outcomes are negative in a variety of communication situations (interpersonal, group, organizational, family, and intercultural). |
| Leads to relationship *satisfaction.* | Leads to relationship dissatisfaction, not surprising for a strategy that aims to attack another's self-concept. |
| May prevent *relationship violence,* especially in domestic relationships. | May lead to relationship violence. |
| Enhances *organizational life;* for example, subordinates prefer supervisors who encourage argumentativeness. | Damages organizational life and demoralizes workers on varied levels. |
| Enhances *parent–child communication* and enables parents to gain greater compliance. | Prevents meaningful parent–child communication and makes corporal punishment more likely. |
| Increases the user's *credibility;* argumentatives are seen as trustworthy, committed, and dynamic. | Decreases the user's credibility, in part because it's seen as a tactic to discredit the opponent rather than addressing the argument. |
| Increases the user's *power of persuasion* in varied communication contexts; argumentatives are more likely to be seen as leaders. | Decreases the user's power of persuasion. |

***Some Differences between Argumentative and Verbally Aggressive People.*** People scoring high in argumentativeness see themselves as having more competence than low argumentatives in speaking in varied contexts. They're more self-assured and more self-confident in communication situations generally. They are also less defensive and more willing to admit mistakes (Rancer, Kosberg, & Silvestri, 1992).

Not surprisingly, high argumentatives score lower in communication apprehension than do low argumentatives. Also, it's been found that training in argumentativeness seems to lower communication apprehension (Wigley, 1987).

Generally, those who score high in argumentativeness have a strong tendency to state their position on controversial issues and to argue against the positions of others. A high scorer sees arguing as an exciting, intellectually challenging exercise and as an opportunity to win a kind of contest. The person who scores low in argumentativeness tries to prevent arguments. This person experiences satisfaction not from arguing but from avoiding arguments. The low-argumentativeness person sees arguing as unpleasant and unsatisfying. Not surprisingly, this person has little confidence in his or her ability to argue effectively. The moderately argumentative person possesses some of the qualities of the high argumentative and some of the qualities of the low argumentative.

Men generally score higher in argumentativeness (and in verbal aggressiveness) than women. Men also are more apt to be perceived (by both men and women) as more argumentative and verbally aggressive than women (Nicotera & Rancer, 1994). Some cultural and regional differences in argumentativeness and verbal aggressiveness have been found, though there are also great similarities. For example, in studies of Japanese and Americans, Americans scored higher on the general tendency to argue; no differences were found, however, between Japanese men and American men or between Japanese women and American women on verbal aggressiveness (Infante & Rancer, 1996).

High and low argumentatives also differ in the ways in which they view argument (Rancer, Kosberg, & Baukus, 1992). High argumentatives see arguing as enjoyable and its outcomes as pragmatic. In their view arguing has a positive impact on their self-concept, has functional outcomes, and is highly ego-involving. Low argumentatives, on the other hand, believe that arguing has a negative impact on their self-concept, that it has dysfunctional outcomes, and that it's not very ego-involving. They see arguing as offering little enjoyment and few pragmatic outcomes.

***Some Suggestions for Cultivating Argumentativeness.*** Here are some suggestions for developing argumentativeness and for preventing it from degenerating into aggressiveness (Infante, 1988):

- Treat disagreements as objectively as possible; avoid assuming that because someone takes issue with your position or your interpretation, they're attacking you as a person.
- Center your arguments on issues rather than personalities. Avoid attacking a person (rather than a person's arguments), even if this would give you a tactical advantage—it will probably backfire at some later time and make your relationship or group participation more difficult.
- Reaffirm the other person's sense of competence; compliment the other person as appropriate.
- Allow the other person to state her or his position fully before you respond; avoid interrupting.
- Stress equality, and stress the similarities that you have with the other person or persons; stress your areas of agreement before attacking the disagreements.
- Express interest in the other person's position, attitude, and point of view.
- Avoid getting overemotional; using an overly loud voice or interjecting vulgar expressions will prove offensive and eventually ineffective.
- Allow people to save face; never humiliate another person.

 ## Summary of Concepts and Skills

This chapter looked at the nature of interpersonal conflict and at how best to manage conflict.

1. Interpersonal conflict (in face-to-face situations and in cyberspace) is a disagreement between or among connected individuals whose positions are to some degree both interrelated and incompatible.

2. Conflict can be content or relationship oriented but is usually a combination of both.
3. Conflict can have both negative and positive effects.
4. Conflict is heavily influenced by both culture and gender, and any effective management of conflict needs to consider these influences.

5. Conflict management strategies are influenced by the goals you seek, your emotional state, your cognitive assessment of the situation, your personality and communication competence, and your family history.
6. Conflict management strategies include making decisions between win–win and win–lose strategies; active fighting and avoidance; talk and force; supportiveness and defensiveness; face-enhancing and face-detracting strategies; empathy and blame; open expression and silence; present orientation and gunnysacking; and argumentativeness and verbal aggressiveness.

The skills covered in this chapter are vital to managing interpersonal conflict. Place a check mark next to those skills you want to work on most.

_____ 1. I seek to derive positive benefits from interpersonal conflict and to avoid conflict's possible negative outcomes.

_____ 2. I engage in conflict with an understanding of the cultural and gender influences.

_____ 3. I understand the consequences of different conflict styles and adjust my style of conflict depending on the specific circumstances.

_____ 4. I look for win–win strategies rather than win–lose strategies.

_____ 5. I engage in conflict actively rather than avoid the problem.

_____ 6. I talk conflict differences through rather than try to force my way of thinking on the other person.

_____ 7. I express support rather than encourage defensiveness.

_____ 8. I use I-messages (rather than you messages) and assume responsibility for my thoughts and feelings.

_____ 9. I use face-enhancing rather than face-detracting tactics.

_____ 10. I express empathy rather than try to blame the other person.

_____ 11. I facilitate open expression rather than try to silence the other.

_____ 12. I focus on the present rather than gunnysack.

_____ 13. I use the skills of argumentativeness rather than verbal aggressiveness.

# Key Word Quiz

## The Language of Conflict Management

Match the terms about interpersonal conflict management with their definitions. Record the number of the definition next to the appropriate term.

a. _____ interpersonal conflict

b. _____ accommodating style

c. _____ face-detracting strategies

d. _____ gunnysacking

e. _____ beltlining

f. _____ collaborating style

g. _____ verbal aggressiveness

h. _____ neutrality

i. _____ content conflict

j. _____ argumentativeness

1. An "I win, you win" approach to conflict management.
2. The willingness to argue for a point of view and to speak your mind without attacking the other person.
3. A kind of indifference that is likely to create defensiveness.
4. Disagreement between connected individuals.
5. Conflict strategies that attack the other person's self-image.
6. A conflict strategy in which stored-up prior grievances are introduced into the present conflict.
7. A conflict strategy in which one person attacks the other with criticisms that are difficult to absorb.
8. Disagreement that addresses issues external to the relationship and that does not challenge the agreed-upon interpersonal relationship between the conflicting parties.
9. A method of trying to win an argument by inflicting psychological pain or distress.
10. An approach to conflict in which you sacrifice your own needs for the needs of the other person.

**Answers: a. 4 b. 10 c. 5 d. 6 e. 7 f. 1 g. 9 h. 3 i. 8 j. 2**

## Five for Discussion

1. Using the concepts of the productive and unproductive conflict strategies discussed here, how would you describe the conflicts that take place in your family? Among your friends? In what ways might these conflicts be managed more effectively?
2. Several reasons have been advanced to account for the observation that men are more likely to withdraw from interpersonal conflict than are women: (1) Men have difficulty dealing with conflict, (2) the culture has taught men to avoid conflict, and/or (3) withdrawal is an expression of power (Noller, 1993). What arguments can you advance for or against any of these hypotheses?
3. On the basis of your own experiences and observations, how would you describe the issues that men and women argue about and the strategies they use? For example, are there certain types of issues that men are more likely to argue about and others that women are more likely to argue about? And do men and women argue in the same way?
4. What does your own culture teach about conflict and its management? What strategies does your culture prohibit? Are some strategies prohibited in conflicts with certain people (say, your parents) but not in conflicts with others (say, your friends)? Does your culture prescribe certain ways of dealing with conflict? Does it have different expectations for men and for women? To what degree have you internalized these teachings? What effect do these teachings have on your actual conflict behaviors?
5. One of the most puzzling findings on domestic violence is that many victims interpret it as a sign of love. For some reason, they see being beaten or verbally abused as a sign that their partner is fully in love with them. Also, and equally puzzling, is that many victims blame themselves for the physical or psychological violence instead of blaming their partners (Gelles & Cornell, 1985). Why do you think this is so? What part does force or violence play in your own interpersonal relationship conflicts?

## Log On! MyCommunicationLab

Two useful exercises on interpersonal conflict are available at this book's website, www.mycommunicationlab.com: (1) Analyzing a Conflict Episode and (2) How Do You Fight? Like a Man? Like a Woman? and (3) Responding to Confrontations.

Also visit MyCommunicationLab for more activities, video clips, and study tools for interpersonal relationships.

Explore our research resources at www.researchnavigator.com.

# Small Group Communication

## Why Read This Chapter?

Because you'll **learn about:**

- the nature of small group communication, whether face-to-face or online.
- the types of small groups and the influence of culture.
- the formats that different types of groups follow.

Because you'll **learn to:**

- communicate in groups with an understanding of the unique nature of the small group.
- communicate in brainstorming groups more creatively and more effectively.
- share information (learn and teach) in groups more effectively.
- solve or manage problems in groups more efficiently and more effectively.

*C*onsider the number of **groups** to which you belong. Your family is the most obvious example, but you're probably also a member of a team, a class, a club, an organization, a sorority or fraternity, a collection of friends, or perhaps a band or theater group. Some of your most important and satisfying communications probably take place in small groups like these. In this chapter we look at the nature and characteristics of small groups and examine three types of small groups.

# The Small Group

A **small group** is a relatively small number of individuals who share a common purpose and follow similar organizing rules. It's a collection of individuals, few enough in number that all may communicate with relative ease as both senders and receivers. Generally, a small group consists of approximately 5 to 12 people; if the group is much larger than 12 people, communication becomes difficult. To constitute a group, members must share a common purpose. This does not mean that all members must have exactly the same purpose. But there must be some similarity in their reasons for interacting.

Groups operate by following certain organizing rules. Sometimes these rules are extremely rigid—as in groups operating under parliamentary procedure, in which comments must follow prescribed rules. At other times, the rules are more loosely defined, as in a social gathering. Even here, however, there are rules—for example, two people do not speak at the same time; a member's comments or questions are responded to, not ignored; and so on.

# Small Group Types

You can get a clearer idea of the nature of small groups by considering some different types of small groups. You're already familiar with these various types, though their names may be new.

**Relationship and Task Groups**   One way to look at the types of small groups is in terms of their general purposes. Groups serve two broad and overlapping categories of purposes: There are social or relationship groups, on the one hand, and work or task groups, on the other.

**Social or relationship groups** are what sociologists call *primary groups*. These are the groups in which you participate early in life; they include, for example, your immediate family, your group of friends at school, and perhaps your neighbors. Usually these groups serve your relationship needs for affiliation, affirmation, and affection. Some of these groups, like family, are extremely long-lasting; some, like a group of friends at college, may last only a year or two. It is largely through participating in primary groups and through your strong identification with fellow members that you develop your self-concept.

**Task groups** (sociologists call these *secondary groups*) are groups formed to accomplish something. Some task groups are put together to solve a specific problem; for example, a committee of college professors might be established to hire a new faculty member, select a textbook, or serve on a graduate student's dissertation committee. Once the specific task is accomplished, the group is dissolved. Other task groups have more long-range concerns—a committee to oversee diversity in the workplace, to monitor fairness in advertising, or to rate feature films may be an ongoing, permanent group.

*"Never doubt that a small group of thoughtful, committed citizens can change the world. Indeed, it is the only thing that ever has."*
—MARGARET MEAD

## WHAT DO YOU SAY?
### Group Norms
The first 20 minutes of just about every meeting at work invariably revolves around personal talk. You really don't enjoy this interaction; you want to participate in the work part of the meeting but not in the interpersonal part. *What do you say? To whom? Through what channel?*

Unlike the relationship group, which is informal and in which the reward of participation comes simply from being together, the task group is more formal, and the reward of participation here comes from accomplishing the specific task.

Another interesting difference between task and relationship groups is that in relationship groups each member is irreplaceable and unique. In task groups, by contrast, each member plays a role but can be replaced by a similarly competent individual. For example, in a group formed to develop a core curriculum for undergraduates, the professor representing the sciences could easily be replaced by another science professor, and the group would remain essentially the same.

Task and relationship functions often overlap, however. In fact, it would be difficult to find a group in which these two functions were not combined in some way at some times. The coworkers who bowl together or the two chemistry professors who begin dating are clear examples of how the functions often overlap. Not surprisingly, when groups normally devoted to one function start serving another function, they often encounter difficulties. For example, the much-in-love couple who are effective at home may find their relationship under stress when they open a business together.

**Reference and Membership Groups**    Another way of looking at small groups is in terms of their values and of the influence of these values on group members. Two such value-related categories are reference and membership groups.

A *reference group* is a group from which you derive your values and norms of behavior. It serves as a standard against which you compare yourself; you judge your successes and your failures in comparison with those of members of the reference group. Reference groups may be primary (relationship) or secondary (task). At different times you may, for example, compare yourself with and measure your successes against those of your siblings or cousins (primary groups) and/or your classmates or coworkers (generally, secondary groups).

A *membership group* is a group that you participate in but do not use to guide or measure yourself. Membership and reference groups are often the same. For the most part, you participate in the groups whose values you share; at the same time, you are likely to acquire the values of the groups in which you participate. At times membership and reference groups may differ, however. For example, while you are studying to be a doctor, you are not yet a member of the doctor group. You may nevertheless have learned the norms and values of this group, so you may take this as your reference group and, in the process, come to emulate its norms and values as you journey toward your MD.

## Small Group Stages

With knowledge of the various kinds of groups, we can now look at how groups interact in the real world. Small group interaction develops in much the same way as a conversation. As in conversation (see Chapter 6), there are five stages: opening, feedforward, business, feedback, and closing. The *opening* period is usually a getting-acquainted time during which members introduce themselves and engage in small talk ("How was your weekend?" "Does anyone want coffee?"). After this preliminary get-together, there is usually some *feedforward*—some attempt to identify what needs to be done, who will do it, and so on. In a more formal group, the agenda (which is a perfect example of feedforward) may be reviewed and the tasks of the group identified. The *business* portion is the actual discussion of the tasks—the problem solving, the sharing of information, or whatever else the group needs to achieve. At the *feedback* stage, the group may reflect on what it has done and perhaps on what remains to be done. Some groups may even evaluate their performance at this stage. At the *closing* stage, the group members again return to their focus on individuals and will perhaps exchange closing comments ("Good seeing you again," "See you next time").

## ▼ E-TALK

### Uses and Gratifications
One study identified seven gratifications people can derive from online communication: being in a virtual community, seeking information, aesthetic experience, financial compensation, diversion, personal status, and maintaining relationships (Song, LaRose, Eastin, & Lin, 2004). How would you describe the gratifications you yourself receive from online communication?

### The Third-Person Effect

How powerful is the effect of the media on your attitudes and behavior as compared to, say, media's influence on a group of your peers? Are you influenced less than your peers? About the same as your peers? More than your peers? In a variety of studies conducted on college students, researchers have found that students believe that they are influenced less by the media than their peers are. For example, only 25 percent of teens think the media's portrayal of sex on television influences their own behavior, but nearly 75 percent of teens believe these portrayals influence their peers (Davison, 1983; Media Education Foundation, 2006a). Whether the topic is political advertising, rap music, or pornography, students feel they are less susceptible to media influence than their peers (Hoffner et al., 2001). This belief, called the third-person effect, is especially strong when media messages are negative or socially unacceptable; for example, people think that messages of violence, racism, or sexism influence them much less than they influence their peers. The third-person effect is weakened (though still present) when the message is more acceptable (for example, public service announcements).

Very likely you're influenced by the media about as much as the person next to you. With increased media literacy, however, you'll be in a stronger position to regulate and control media influence.

*The worst of all deceptions is self-deception.*

—PLATO

***Increasing Media Literacy.*** *What implications does this theory have for your own media behavior? For example, is it possible that you are influenced more by the media than you think you are? If so, what might you do to become more aware of the media's influence and ultimately to lessen it?*

---

Note that the group focus shifts from people to task and then back again to people. A typical pattern would look like Figure 8.1. Different groups will naturally follow different patterns. For example, a work group that has gathered to solve a problem is likely to spend a great deal more time focused on the task—whereas an informal social group, say two or three couples who get together for dinner, will spend more time focused on people concerns. Similarly, the amount of time spent on the opening or business or closing, for example, will vary with the type and purposes of the group.

## Small Group Formats

Small groups serve their functions in a variety of formats. Among the most popular are the roundtable, panel, symposium, and symposium–forum formats.

In the **roundtable,** group members arrange themselves in a circular or semicircular pattern. They share information or solve a problem without any set pattern of who speaks when. Group interaction is informal, and members contribute to the discussion as they see fit. A leader or moderator may be present and may, for example, try to keep the discussion focused on the topic or encourage more reticent members to contribute.

The **panel** format is similar to the roundtable; however, panel participants are "experts." As in the roundtable format, members' remarks are informal and there is no set pattern for who speaks when. Another difference is that the panel is observed by an audience, whose members may interject comments

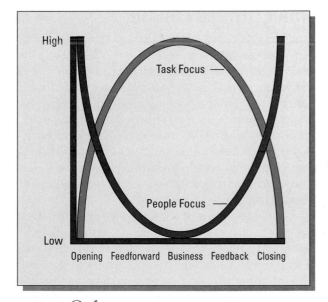

### Figure *8.1*
**Small Group Stages and the Focus on Task and People**

Do the groups to which you belong follow these five stages when interacting? How do these groups divide their focus between people and task?

or ask questions. Many television talk shows, such as *The Oprah Winfrey Show*, use this format. A variation is the two-panel format, which includes an expert panel and a lay panel. The lay panel discusses the topic but turns to the expert panel when in need of technical information, additional data, or direction.

The **symposium** consists of a series of prepared presentations much like public speeches. All speeches address different aspects of a single topic. The leader of a symposium introduces the speakers, provides transitions from one speaker to another, and may provide periodic summaries.

The *symposium–forum* consists of two parts: a symposium of prepared speeches and a **forum** consisting largely of questions and comments from the audience and responses from the symposium speakers. The symposium leader introduces the speakers and moderates the question-and-answer session.

These four formats, illustrated in Figure 8.2 are general patterns that describe a wide variety of groups. Within each type, there will naturally be considerable variation. For example, in the symposium–forum, there is no set pattern for how much time will be spent on the symposium part and how much on the forum part. Combinations may also be used. Thus, for example, group members may each present a position paper (basically a symposium) and then participate in a roundtable discussion.

## Figure *8.2*
**Small Group Formats**
With how many of these group formats have you had experience?

## Small Groups Online

Small groups use a wide variety of channels. Often, of course, group interactions take place face-to-face; this is the channel that probably comes to mind when you think of groups. But today much small group interaction also takes place online—and online groups serve both relationship or social purposes on the one hand and business and professional purposes on the other. As noted in Chapter 6, some research, in fact, shows that online social groups provide a sense of belongingness that may once have been thought possible only through face-to-face interactions (Silverman, 2001). At the same time, additional research on online work groups shows that online groups are more task oriented and more efficient than face-to-face groups (Lantz, 2001).

Two major types of online groups may be noted here: the mailing-list group and the chat group. In conjunction with the following discussions, take a look at the "Credo for Free and Responsible Use of Electronic Communication Networks" at **www.natcom.org**. The "Credo" is one attempt by a national communication association to articulate some of the ethical issues in electronic group communication.

**Mailing-List Groups**   As described in Chapter 1, mailing-list groups are groups of people interested in particular topics who communicate with one another through e-mail. Generally, you subscribe to a list and communicate with all other members by addressing your mail to the group e-mail address. Any message you send to this address

**"Honey, please don't talk to Daddy when he's in a chat room."**

will be sent to all members who subscribe to the list at the same time; there are no asides to the person sitting next to you (as in face-to-face groups). A huge number of mailing lists are available at **www.liszt.com**. A list of frequently asked questions and mailing-list addresses can be found at **www.intuitive.com/social-faq.html**. Of course you could also go to one of the search engines and search for mailing lists.

Communication through mailing lists does not take place in real time. It's like regular e-mail; you may send your message today, but it may not be read until next week, and you may not get an answer for another week. Much of the spontaneity created by real-time communication is lost. For example, you may be very enthusiastic about a topic when you send your e-mail but may practically forget about it by the time someone responds.

**Chat Groups**   Unlike mailing lists, chat group communication takes place in real time; you see and in many cases hear a member's message as it's being sent, with virtually no delay. As in mailing lists and face-to-face conversation, the purposes of chat groups vary from communication that simply maintains connection with others (what many would call "idle chatter" or phatic communication) to extremely significant interchanges of ideas.

Communication in a chat group resembles the conversation you would observe at a large party. The whole group of "guests" divides up into small groups varying from 2 on up, and members of each subgroup discuss their own topic or their own aspect of a general topic. For example, in a group about food, 10 people may be discussing food calories, 8 people may be discussing restaurant food preparation, and 2 people may be discussing the basic food groups, all on this one channel. So although you may be communicating primarily in one group (say, dealing with restaurant food), you also have your eye trained to pick up something particularly interesting in another group, much as you do at a party. Chat groups also notify you when someone new comes into the group and when someone leaves the group. Like mailing lists, chat groups have the great advantage that they enable you to communicate with people you would never meet or interact with otherwise. Because such groups are international, they provide excellent exposure to other cultures, other ideas, and other ways of communicating.

In face-to-face group communication, you're expected to contribute to the ongoing discussion. In chat groups, however, you can simply observe; in fact, you're encouraged to lurk—to observe the group's interaction before you say anything yourself. In this way you'll be able to learn the customs of the group and not violate any of its rules or norms.

## Small Group Culture

Many groups—especially those of long standing—develop cultural norms and are greatly influenced by their own high- or low-context orientation. Each of these cultural dimensions influences the group and its members.

**Group Norms**   **Group norms** are rules or standards identifying which behaviors are considered appropriate (such as being willing to take on added tasks or directing conflict toward issues rather than toward people) and which are considered inappropriate (such as arriving late or failing to contribute actively). These rules for appropriate behavior are sometimes explicitly stated in a company contract or policy: "All members must attend department meetings." Sometimes they are unstated: "Group members should be well groomed." Regardless of whether or not norms are spelled out, they are powerful regulators of members' behaviors.

Norms may apply to individual members as well as to the group as a whole and, of course, will differ from one group to another (Axtell, 1990, 1993). For example, although Americans prefer to get right down to business, the Japanese prefer rather

▼ **E-TALK**

**Blogging**
If you want an easy way to create a presence for yourself on the Web, consider a personal blog—"a web application which contains periodic, reverse chronologically ordered posts on a common webpage" and coined as a combination of "web" and "log" (http://en.wikipedia.org/wiki/Blog). Blog hosts such as Blogger (www.blogger.com) enable you to do this very easily. While you're online, visit my blog at http://tcbdevito.blogspot.com.

▼ **E-TALK**

**Blogging Frequency**
At the end of 2004, approximately 8 million Americans said they had created blogs, and 27 percent of Internet users said they read blogs (The State of Blogging, www.pewinternet.org/PPF/r/144/report_display.asp, dated January 2, 2005, accessed February 10, 2005). If you have not done so already surf a few blogs. What personal or professional values might blogs have for you?

### Telling Secrets

Close friends, family members, or workplace colleagues often exchange secrets with the implied stipulation that they not be revealed to outsiders. For example, if you promised to keep a group member's financial status secret, then it would be considered unethical if you revealed this information to people outside the group who had no right to know anything about it. But there are other kinds of instances in which it's not so easy to tell whether revealing a secret would be considered unethical.

Ethicist Sissela Bok (1983) argues that it's unethical to reveal secrets when the revelation would invade the privacy that everyone has a right to; for example, when a secret concerns matters that are no one else's business. It also would be unethical to reveal a secret that could hurt the individuals involved. Conversely, there are likely to be situations when you may have an obligation to reveal the secret. For example, Bok (1983) argues that you have an obligation to reveal a secret when keeping the information hidden will do more harm than good.

*What would you do?* *An instructor who supervises your study group confides in you that she is a confirmed racist and proud of it. What do you do? A 16-year-old member of your wilderness group confides that she's having unprotected sex with her married history teacher. What do you do? A community religious leader confides in you that he is skimming a portion of the members' contributions to fund his retirement. What do you do?*

> *Good people do not need laws to tell them to act responsibly, while bad people will find a way around the laws.*
>
> —Plato

elaborate socializing before addressing the business at hand. In the United States, men and women in business are expected to interact when making business decisions as well as when socializing. In Muslim and Buddhist societies, however, religious restrictions prevent mixing the sexes. In some cultures (for example, those of the United States, Bangladesh, Australia, Germany, Finland, and Hong Kong), punctuality for business meetings is very important. But in others (for example, those of Morocco, Italy, Brazil, Zambia, Ireland, and Panama), punctuality is less important; being late is no great insult and in some situations is even expected. In the United States and in much of Asia and Europe, meetings are held between two parties. In many Persian Gulf states, however, a business executive is likely to conduct meetings with several different groups—sometimes dealing with totally different issues—at the same time. In this situation you have to share what in the United States would be "your time" with these other groups. In the United States very little interpersonal touching goes on during business meetings; in Arab countries touching (for example, hand holding) is common and is a gesture of friendship.

You're more likely to accept the norms of your group's culture when you feel your group membership is important and you want to continue your membership in the group. You're also more likely to accept these norms when your group is cohesive: when you and the other members are closely connected, are attracted to one another, and depend on one another. Lastly, you're more apt to accept these norms if you'd be punished by negative reactions or exclusion from the group for violating them (Napier & Gershenfeld, 1989).

> *"A group is best defined as a dynamic whole based on interdependence, rather than on similarity."*
>
> —Kurt Lewin

### High- and Low-Context Cultures

A cultural distinction that has special relevance to small group communication (and to public speaking, as we'll see in Chapter 10) is that between high- and low-context cultures. A **high-context culture** is a culture in which much of the information conveyed in communication is in the context or in the person rather than explicitly coded in verbal messages. In a high-context culture, people have lots of information in common, and this shared knowledge does not have to be made explicit. A **low-context culture,** on the other hand, is a culture in which most of the information in communication is explicitly stated in verbal messages. In a low-context culture, people do not assume that they share certain information and so make all crucial details explicit.

According to Edward T. Hall (1976), who first identified this dimension, and Singh and Pereira (2004), who applied this dimension to electronic communication, high-context cultures include those of countries in Asia, Africa, and South America (such as Japan, China, Korea, Malaysia, and Indonesia), whereas low-context cultures are those of many countries in Northern Europe (Denmark, Germany, Switzerland), North America (the United States, Canada), and Australia and New Zealand.

To appreciate the distinction between high and low context, consider giving directions:

"I don't know how it started, either. All I know is that it's part of our corporate culture."

| **High-Context Situation** | **Low-Context Situation** |
|---|---|
| **A person who knows the neighborhood asks you:** *"Where's the voter registration center?"* | **A newcomer to your city asks you:** *"Where's the voter registration center?"* |
| **You answer:** *"Next to the laundromat on Main Street"* or *"The corner of Albany and Elm."* | **You answer:** *"Make a left at the stop sign. Then go two blocks and turn right. The office is next to a wash-and-dry service called Green's Laundromat."* |

With someone who knows the neighborhood (a high-context situation), you can assume the person knows local landmarks (like Green's Laundromat). With a newcomer (a low-context situation), you cannot assume the person shares any information with you. So you have to use directions that a stranger will understand; you have to be more explicit and include more information than you would in a high-context situation, where you can assume that you have neighborhood information in common.

As you can expect, members of high-context cultures spend a lot of time getting to know each other before engaging in any important transactions. Because of this prior personal knowledge, a great deal of information is shared and therefore does not have to be explicitly stated. High-context societies, for example, rely more on nonverbal cues in reducing uncertainty (Sanders, Wiseman, & Matz, 1991). Members of low-context cultures spend less time getting to know each other and therefore do not have that shared knowledge. As a result everything has to be stated explicitly. When this simple difference is not taken into account, misunderstandings can easily result. For example, the directness and explicitness characteristic of the low-context culture may prove insulting, insensitive, or unnecessary to members of a high-context culture. Conversely, to members of a low-context culture, someone from a high-context culture may appear vague, underhanded, even dishonest in his or her reluctance to be explicit or to engage in communication that a low-context culture would consider open and direct.

Members of high-context cultures also tend to be reluctant to question the judgments of their superiors. So, for example, if a product were being manufactured with a defect, workers might hesitate to communicate this back to management (Gross, Turner, & Cederholm, 1987). Similarly, workers might detect problems in procedures proposed by management but never communicate their concerns back to management. In an intercultural organization knowledge of this tendency would alert a low-context management to look more deeply into the absence of communication.

**WHAT DO YOU SAY?**
**Group Pressure**
All of your colleagues at your new job pad their expense accounts. You don't want to go along with this, but if you don't, everyone else will be found out. You don't want to make waves, yet you don't want to do something unethical. *What do you say? To whom? Through what channel?*

# Small Group Apprehension

Just as you may have some apprehension in interpersonal conversations (Chapter 6), you probably experience apprehension to some degree in group discussions. Because small groups vary so widely, you're likely to experience different degrees of apprehension depending on the nature of the specific group. Work groups, for example, may cause greater apprehension than groups of friends. And interacting with superiors is likely to generate greater apprehension than meeting with peers or subordinates. Similarly, the degree of familiarity you have with the group members and the extent to which you see yourself as a part of the group (as opposed to an outsider) also will influence your apprehension. You may wish at this point to take the following self-test, "How apprehensive are you in group discussions?"

## *Test* ▷ *Yourself*

### HOW APPREHENSIVE ARE YOU IN GROUP DISCUSSIONS?

**INSTRUCTIONS:** This brief test is designed to measure your apprehension in small group communication situations. The questionnaire consists of six statements concerning your feelings about communication in group discussions. Indicate the degree to which each statement applies to you by marking whether you (1) strongly agree, (2) agree, (3) are undecided, (4) disagree, or (5) strongly disagree. (Each of these answers then becomes the "score" for each item.) There are no right or wrong answers. Do not be concerned that some of the statements are similar. Work quickly; just record your first impression.

_____ ❶ I dislike participating in group discussions.

_____ ❷ Generally, I am comfortable while participating in group discussions.

_____ ❸ I am tense and nervous while participating in group discussions.

_____ ❹ I like to get involved in group discussions.

_____ ❺ Engaging in a group discussion with new people makes me tense and nervous.

_____ ❻ I am calm and relaxed while participating in group discussions.

**HOW DID YOU DO?** To obtain your apprehension for group discussions score, use the following formula:

> Start with 18; add the scores for items 2, 4, and 6; then subtract the scores for items 1, 3, and 5.
> A total above 18 shows some degree of apprehension.

**WHAT WILL YOU DO?** Think about the kinds of groups that generate the most apprehension for you. Can you identify the major characteristics of these high-apprehension groups? How do these differ from groups generating little apprehension? What other factors might influence your small group apprehension? When you read the suggestions for reducing apprehension given in Chapter 10, consider how you might use them in the various types of groups in which you participate.

*Source:* From James C. McCroskey, *An Introduction to Rhetorical Communication,* 7th ed. Copyright © 1997 by Allyn and Bacon. Reprinted by permission.

# Brainstorming Groups

Many small groups exist solely to generate ideas. **Brainstorming** is a process often used in such groups; it's a technique for analyzing a problem through a process of generating as many ideas as possible (Osborn, 1957; Beebe & Masterson, 2006). Although brainstorming also can be useful when you're trying to come up with ideas by yourself—ideas for speeches or term papers, ideas for a fun vacation, or ways to make money—it is more typically seen in small group settings. Organizations have come to embrace brainstorming, because it lessens group members' inhibitions and encourages all participants to exercise their creativity. It also fosters cooperative teamwork; members soon learn that their own ideas and creativity are sparked by the contributions of others. The technique builds member pride and ownership in the final solution or product or service, because all members contribute to it.

*"The best way to have a good idea is to have a lot of ideas."*
—Linus Pauling

Brainstorming occurs in two phases. The first is the brainstorming period itself; the second is the evaluation period. The procedures are simple. First, a problem is selected. The "problem" may be almost anything that is amenable to many possible solutions or ideas—for example, how to devise an effective advertising campaign, how to recruit new members to the organization, or how to market a new product. Before the actual session, group members are informed of the problem so they can think about the topic. When the group meets, each person contributes as many ideas as he or she can think of. Companies often use chalkboards, whiteboards, or easels to record all the ideas. A brainstorming group may appoint one person to be the scribe; that person keys the group's notes into a laptop for instant circulation via e-mail to other group members after the group has concluded its business. During the initial idea-generating session, members follow four rules:

1. No evaluation is permitted at this stage. All ideas are recorded for the group to see (or hear later). Any evaluation—whether verbal or nonverbal—is criticized by the leader or members. Prohibiting evaluation encourages group members to participate freely.

   This first rule is perhaps the most difficult for members to follow, so you might want to practice responding to what are called "idea killers." For example, what might you say if someone were to criticize an idea with the following comments?

   - We tried it before and it didn't work.
   - No one would vote for it.
   - It's too complex.
   - It's too simple.
   - It would take too long.
   - It'll cost too much.
   - We don't have the facilities.
   - What we have is good enough.
   - It just doesn't fit us.
   - It's not possible.

2. Quantity of ideas is the goal. The more ideas generated, the more likely it is that a useful solution will be found.

3. Combinations and extensions of ideas are encouraged. Although members may not criticize a particular idea, they may extend or combine it. The value of a particular idea may well lie in the way it stimulates another member.

4. Freewheeling (developing as wild an idea as possible) is desirable. A wild idea can be tempered easily, but it's not so easy to elaborate on a simple or conservative idea.

After all the ideas are generated—a period that lasts about 15 or 20 minutes—the group evaluates the entire list. Unworkable ideas are crossed off the list; those showing promise are retained and evaluated. During this phase, criticism is allowed.

## Skill Development Experience

# Information-Sharing Groups

The purpose of information-sharing groups is to acquire new information or skills by sharing knowledge. In most information-sharing groups, all members have something to teach and something to learn; a good example is a group of students sharing information to prepare for an exam. In others, the group interaction takes place because some members have information and some do not. An example is a discussion between patients and health care professionals.

## Educational or Learning Groups

Members of educational or learning groups may follow a variety of discussion patterns. For example, a historical topic such as the development of free speech or equal rights might be developed chronologically, with the discussion progressing from the past into the present and perhaps predicting the future. Issues in developmental psychology, such as a child's language development or physical maturity, might also be discussed chronologically. Other topics lend themselves to spatial development. For example, the development of the United States might take a spatial pattern—from east to west—or a chronological pattern—from 1776 to the present. Other suitable patterns, depending on the topic and the group's needs, might be cause and effect, problem and solution, or structure and function.

Perhaps the most popular discussion pattern is the topical pattern. A group might discuss the legal profession by itemizing and discussing each of the profession's major functions. Another might consider a corporation's structure in terms of its major divisions. Groups could further systematize each of these topics by, say, listing the legal profession's functions in order of importance or complexity, or ordering the corporation's major structures in terms of decision-making power.

## Focus Groups

A different type of learning group is the **focus group,** a kind of in-depth interview of a small group. The aim here is to discover what people think about an issue or product; for example, what do men between 18 and 25 think of the new aftershave lotion and its packaging? What do young executives earning more than $70,000 think of buying foreign luxury cars?

In the focus group, the leader tries to discover the members' beliefs, attitudes, thoughts, and feelings so as to guide decisions on, for example, changing the scent or redesigning the packaging or constructing advertisements for luxury cars. It is the leader's task to prod members to analyze their thoughts and feelings on a deeper level and to use the thoughts of one member to stimulate the thoughts of others.

Generally, a focus group leader assembles approximately 12 people. The leader explains the process, the time limits, and the general goal of the group—let's say, for example, to discover why these 12 individuals requested information on the XYZ health plan but purchased a plan from another company. Here, of course, the 12 group members are standing in for or representing the general population. The leader, who is usually a professional facilitator rather than a member of the organization itself, asks a variety of questions. In our example these might be questions such as How did you hear about the XYZ health plan? What other health plans did you consider before making your actual purchase? What influenced you to buy the plan you eventually bought? Were any other people influential in helping you make your decision? Through the exploration of these and similar questions, the facilitator and the relevant organizational members (who may be seated behind a one-way mirror, watching the discussion) may put together a more effective health plan or more effective advertising strategies.

# Problem-Solving Groups

A **problem-solving group** meets to solve a particular problem or to reach a decision on some issue. In a sense, this is the most demanding kind of group. It requires not only a knowledge of small group communication techniques but also a thorough knowledge of the particular problem on the part of all group members. Also, for the most successful outcome, it usually demands faithful adherence to a set of procedural rules.

In companies or other organizations, problem-solving group members may all come from the same area or department; all may be sales representatives or all may be teachers, for example. At other times the group members make up what has come to be called an integrated work team, which consists of members from different areas of the organization who have related goals and who must work together to accomplish them (Hill, 1997). For example, a publishing company work team might consist of people from the editorial, design, advertising, production, and marketing departments.

## LISTEN TO THIS

*The wisest mind has something yet to learn.*
—George Santayana

### Listening in Small Groups

Listening in small groups is much the same as listening in conversation. Yet there are some listening suggestions that seem especially appropriate in small groups, whether social or business.

- Respond visibly but in moderation; an occasional nod of agreement or a facial expression that says "that's interesting" usually is sufficient. Too little response says you aren't listening, but too much response says you aren't listening critically.

- Avoid playing with your hair or a pencil or drawing pictures on a Styrofoam cup; these adaptors signal discomfort.

- Maintain an open posture. When seated around a table, resist covering your face, chest, or stomach with your hands; these nonverbals may make you appear defensive.

- Avoid interrupting the speaker or completing the speaker's thoughts; these are generally perceived as indicating a lack of communication savvy and business etiquette.

***Applying Listening Skills.*** *Jennifer is a bright and diligent worker, but at company meetings she seems so uninvolved that other members ignore her; they don't ask her advice and don't even make eye contact with her. What listening advice would you give Jennifer to make her appear more involved and more a part of the group interactions?*

## The Problem-Solving Sequence

The **problem-solving sequence** identifies six steps and owes its formulation to philosopher John Dewey's insights into how people think (see Figure 8.3). These steps are designed to make problem solving more efficient and effective.

**Define and Analyze the Problem**    In many instances the nature of the problem is clearly specified. For example, a work team might discuss how to package the new CD-ROMs for Valentine's Day. In other instances, however, the problem may be vague, and it may be up to the group to define it. For example, the general problem may be poor campus communications, but such a vague and general topic is difficult to tackle in a problem-solving discussion. So, for purposes of discussion, a group might be more specific and focus on improving the college website.

Define the problem as an open-ended question ("How can we improve the college website?") rather than as a statement ("The website needs to be improved") or as a yes/no question ("Does the website need improvement?"). The open-ended question allows greater freedom of exploration.

Limit the problem to a manageable area for discussion. A question like "How can we improve communication at the college?" is too broad and general. Focus on one subdivision of the issue—such as, in this example, the student newspaper, student–faculty relationships, registration, examination scheduling, student advisory services, or the college website.

**Establish Criteria for Evaluating Solutions**    Decide how you'll evaluate the solutions before proposing any of them. Identify the standards or criteria you'll use in evaluating solutions or in preferring one solution over another. Generally, problem-solving groups consider two types of criteria: practical and value criteria. As an example of practical criteria, you might decide that the solutions must not increase the budget or that a solution must lead to a 10 percent increase in website visits.

## Figure *8.3*

**The Problem-Solving Sequence**

Although most small group theorists would advise you to follow the problem-solving pattern as presented here, others would alter it somewhat. For example, some would advise you to reverse steps 2 and 3: to identify possible solutions first and then consider the criteria for evaluating them (Brilhart & Galanes, 1992). The advantage of this approach is that you're likely to generate more creative solutions, because you will not be restricted by standards of evaluation. The disadvantage is that you may spend a great deal of time generating impractical solutions that will never meet the standards you will eventually propose.

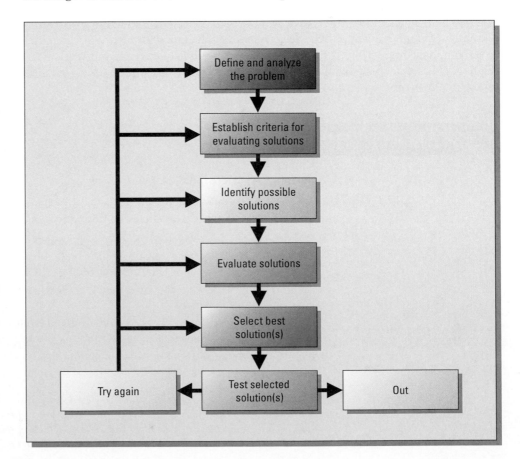

The value criteria are more difficult to identify. For example, value criteria might state that the website information must not violate anyone's right to privacy or must provide a forum for all members of the college community.

**Identify Possible Solutions**   Identify as many solutions as possible. Focus on quantity rather than quality. Brainstorming may be particularly useful at this point. Solutions to the website improvement problem might include incorporating reviews of faculty publications, student evaluations of specific courses, reviews of restaurants in the campus area, outlines for new courses, and employment information.

**Evaluate Solutions**   After all solutions have been proposed, evaluate each. For example, does incorporating reviews of area restaurants meet the criteria? Would it increase the budget, for example? Would posting grades violate students' rights to privacy? Each potential solution should be matched against the evaluating criteria.

Critical thinking pioneer Edward deBono (1987) suggests we use six "thinking hats" to evaluate solutions. In the **critical-thinking-hats technique** you wear each hat to look at the problem and the proposed solutions from a different perspective.

- The *fact hat* focuses on the data—the facts and figures that bear on the problem. For example, what are the relevant data on the website? How can I get more information on the website's history? How much does it cost to construct and maintain? Can we include advertising?

- The *feeling hat* focuses on your feelings, emotions, and intuitions concerning the problem. How do you feel about the website and about making major changes?

- The *negative argument hat* asks you to become the devil's advocate. Why might this proposal fail? What are the problems with publishing outlines and reviews of courses? What is the worst-case scenario?

- The *positive benefits hat* asks you to look at the upside. What opportunities will this new format open up? What benefits will publishing outlines and reviews of courses provide for the students? What is the best-case scenario?

- The *creative new idea hat* focuses on new ways of looking at the problem and can easily be combined with brainstorming techniques discussed earlier in this chapter. What other ways can you look at this problem? What other functions can a website serve? Can the website serve the nonacademic community as well?

- The *control of thinking hat* helps you analyze what you've done and are doing. It asks that you reflect on your own thinking processes and synthesize the results. Have you adequately defined the problem? Are you focusing too much on insignificant issues? Have you given enough attention to the possible negative effects?

**Select the Best Solution(s)**   Select the best solution and put it into operation. Let's assume that reviews of faculty publications and outlines for new courses best meet the evaluating criteria for solutions. The group might then incorporate these two new items into the website.

Groups use different decision-making methods when deciding, for example, which solution to accept. The method to be used should, naturally, be stated at the outset of the group discussion. The three main decision-making methods are:

- *Decision by authority:* Group members voice their feelings and opinions, but the leader, boss, or chief executive makes the final decision. This method has the advantages of being efficient and of giving greater importance to the suggestions of more experienced members. The big disadvantage is that members may feel that their contributions have too little influence and therefore may not participate with real enthusiasm.

- *Majority rule:* The group agrees to abide by the majority decision and may vote on various issues as the group searches to solve its problem. Like decision by

**WHAT DO YOU SAY?**
**Responding to a Group**
While surfing the Net you come upon a social network where members have been trashing one of your favorite instructors. *What do you say? To whom? Through what channel?*

**WHAT DO YOU SAY?**
**Critical Thinking**
You're on a team charged with designing the packaging for a new shampoo, and you want to use the six critical thinking hats technique to evaluate the proposed solutions. *What do you say (for each hat)?*

*"A problem well stated is a problem half solved."*
—Charles F. Kettering

authority, this method is efficient. A disadvantage is that it may lead the group to limit discussion by calling for a vote once a majority has agreed. Also, members not voting with the majority may feel disenfranchised and left out.

■ *Consensus:* In some situations, consensus means unanimous agreement; for example, a criminal jury must reach a unanimous decision to convict or acquit a defendant. In most business groups, consensus means that members agree that they can live with the solution; they agree that they can do whatever the solution requires (Kelly, 1994). Consensus is especially helpful when the group wants each member to be satisfied and committed to the decision and to the decision-making process as a whole (DeStephen & Hirokawa 1988; Beebe & Masterson, 2006). Consensus obviously takes the most time of any of the decision-making methods and can lead to a great deal of inefficiency, especially if members wish to prolong the discussion process needlessly or selfishly.

Note that these decision-making methods may be used at any point in the problem-solving sequence. For example, the vice-president may decide what problem to study (decision by authority) or the members may vote on what criteria the solution should meet (decision by majority vote).

**Test Selected Solution(s)**     After putting the solution(s) into operation, test their effectiveness. The group might, for example, poll the students or college employees about the new website. Or the group might analyze the number of visits to the website to see if the number of visits increased by the desired 10 percent. If the selected solutions prove ineffective, the group will need to return to a previous stage and repeat that part of the process. This often involves selecting other solutions to test. But it also may mean going even farther back in the process—to a reanalysis of the problem, an identification of other solutions, or a restatement of criteria, for example.

## Problem Solving at Work

The problem-solving sequence discussed here is used widely in work settings in a variety of different types of groups. Three group interaction types that rely largely on the problem-solving sequence are popular in business: the nominal group technique, the Delphi method, and quality circles.

**The Nominal Group Technique**     The **nominal group** technique is a method of problem solving that uses limited discussion and confidential voting to obtain a group decision. It is extremely useful for increasing the number of ideas generated by group members (Roth, Schleifer, & Switzer, 1995). A nominal group is especially helpful when some members are reluctant to voice their opinions in a regular problem-solving group or when the issue is controversial or sensitive—for example, "what can be done about sexism, racism, or homophobia in the workplace," "office romantic relationships," or "ways to downsize." With this technique each member contributes equally and each contribution is treated equally. Another advantage of this technique is that it can be accomplished in a relatively short period of time. The nominal group procedure can be divided into seven steps (Kelly, 1994):

1. The problem is defined and clarified for all members.

2. Each member writes down (without discussion or consultation with others) his or her ideas on or possible solutions to the problem.

3. Each member—in sequence—states one idea from his or her list, which is recorded on a board or flip chart so everyone can see it. This process is repeated until all suggestions are stated and recorded. Duplicates are then eliminated. Group agreement is secured before ideas are combined.

## Solving Problems in Groups

*Patterns like this problem-solving sequence, although they may seem artificial at first, will actually help you move a discussion along without unnecessary detours and will give you the assurance that you'll cover all essential steps.*

Together with four, five, or six others, problem-solve one of the following questions: (a) *What should we do about the homeless?* (b) *What should we do to improve student morale?* (c) *What should we do to better prepare ourselves for the job market?* (d) *How can we improve student–faculty communication?* or (e) *What should be the college's responsibility concerning students and faculty with HIV or AIDS?* Before beginning discussion of the topic, prepare a discussion outline, answering the following questions:

1. What is the problem? What causes it? What are its effects?
2. What criteria should a solution have to satisfy?
3. What are some possible solutions?
4. What are the advantages and disadvantages of each of these solutions?
5. What solution seems best (in light of the advantages and disadvantages)?
6. How might we test this solution?

4. Each suggestion is clarified (without debate). Ideally, each suggestion should be given equal time.

5. Each member rank-orders the suggestions.

6. The rankings of the members are combined to get a group ranking, which is then written on the board.

7. Clarification, discussion, and possible reordering may follow.

The highest-ranking solution might then be selected to be tested, or several high-ranking solutions may be put into operation.

**The Delphi Method**    The **Delphi method** utilizes a group of experts, but there is no interaction among them; instead, they communicate by repeatedly responding to questionnaires (Tersine & Riggs, 1980; Kelly, 1994). The method is especially useful when you want to involve people who are geographically distant from one another, when you want all members to act as part of the solution and to uphold it, and when you want to minimize the effects of dominant members or even of peer pressure. For example, the Delphi method might be used by a group of communication professors to write a statement of ethical guidelines for technological communication or by a group of health care professionals to identify the requirements for nurse practitioners. The method is best explained as a series of steps (Kelly, 1994):

1. The problem is defined (for example, "We need to improve intradepartmental communication"). What each member is expected to do is specified (for example, "Each member should contribute five ideas on this specific question").

2. Each member then anonymously contributes five ideas in writing. This stage used to be completed through questionnaires sent through traditional mail but now is more frequently done through e-mail, which greatly increases the speed with which this entire process can be accomplished.

3. The ideas of all members are combined, written up, and distributed to all members, who may be asked to, say, select the three or four best ideas from this composite list.

4. Members then select the three or four best ideas and submit them.

5. From these responses another list is produced and distributed to all members, who may be asked to select the one or two best ideas.

6. Members then select the one or two best ideas and submit them.

7. From these responses another list is produced and distributed to all members. The process may be repeated any number of times, but usually three rounds are sufficient for achieving a fair degree of agreement.

8. The "final" solutions are identified and are communicated to all members.

**Quality Circles**   **Quality circles** are groups of workers (usually 6 to 12) whose task it is to investigate and make recommendations for improving the quality of some organizational function. The members are drawn from the workers whose area is being studied. Thus, for example, if the problem is to improve advertising on the Internet, the quality circle membership would consist of people from the advertising and information technology departments. Generally, the motivation for establishing quality circles is economic; the company's aim is to improve quality and profitability. Another related goal is to improve worker morale; because quality circles involve workers in decision making, workers may feel empowered and more essential to the organization (Gorden & Nevins, 1993).

The basic idea is that people who work on similar tasks will be better able to improve their departments or jobs by pooling their insights and working through problems they share. The quality circle style of problem solving is often considered one of the major reasons for the success of many businesses in Japan, where it's widely used. In the United States, hundreds of organizations use quality circles, but generally with less success than in Japan (Gorden & Nevins, 1993; Tang & Butler, 1997).

Quality circle members investigate problems using any method they feel might be helpful—for example, face-to-face problem-solving groups, nominal groups, or the Delphi method. The group then reports its findings and its suggestions to those who can do something about it. In some cases the quality circle members may implement their solutions without approval from upper management levels.

## Summary of Concepts and Skills

This chapter provided an overview of the small group's nature, the ways in which some major types of small groups (brainstorming, information-sharing, and problem-solving) work, and the popular small group formats.

1. A small group is a collection of individuals, few enough for all members to communicate with relative ease as both senders and receivers. The members are related by some common purpose and have some organization or structure.

2. Small groups may be looked at in terms of relationship and task. Relationship groups generally serve relationship needs for affiliation, affirmation, and affection and include family and friendship networks. Task groups are formed to accomplish something, often a work-related goal, and may then be disbanded.

3. Small groups also may be categorized as reference groups (groups from which you derive your values and norms of behavior) or as membership groups (groups in which you participate but whose values you don't necessarily adopt).

4. Small group interactions generally follow the five stages of conversation: opening, feedforward, business, feedback, closing.

5. Four popular small group formats are the roundtable, the panel, the symposium, and the symposium–forum.

6. Two popular Internet groups are the mailing-list group and the chat group. Both are changing the way we think about small group communication.

7. Small groups develop norms (rules or standards of behavior) and are heavily influenced by the larger culture of which the groups are a part.

8. The brainstorming group attempts to generate as many ideas as possible by avoiding critical evaluation and encouraging quantity, combinations and extensions, and freewheeling.

9. Information-sharing groups (for example, educational or learning groups or focus groups) attempt to acquire new information or skill through a mutual sharing of knowledge or insight.

10. The problem-solving group attempts to solve a particular problem, or at least to reach a decision that may be a preface to solving the problem, and may do so through decision by authority, majority rule, or consensus.

11. The six steps in the problem-solving approach are: Define and analyze the problem, establish criteria for evaluating solutions, identify possible solutions, evaluate solutions, select best solution(s), and test solution(s).

12. A useful technique for analyzing problems is the six critical thinking hats technique, in which you approach a problem in terms of facts, feelings, negative arguments, positive benefits, creative ideas, and overall analysis.

13. Three problem-solving techniques popular in business today are the nominal group, the Delphi method, and quality circles.

The skills covered in this chapter focus on your ability to function effectively in a variety of small groups. Place a check mark next to those skills you want to work on most.

_____ 1. I actively seek to discover the norms of the groups in which I function and take these norms into consideration when interacting in the group.

_____ 2. I can communicate in online groups such as mailing-list and chat groups.

_____ 3. I can adjust my messages and listening in light of differences between high- and low-context cultures.

_____ 4. I follow the general rules when brainstorming: I avoid negative criticism, strive for quantity, combine and extend the contributions of others, and contribute as wild an idea as I can.

_____ 5. I appropriately restimulate a brainstorming group that has lost its steam.

_____ 6. I employ organizational structure in educational or learning groups.

_____ 7. I follow the six steps when in group problem-solving situations: Define and analyze the problem, establish the criteria for evaluating solutions, identify possible solutions, evaluate solutions, select the best solution(s), and test selected solution(s).

_____ 8. I use the six critical thinking hats technique and think about problems and solutions in terms of facts, feelings, negative arguments, positive benefits, creative ideas, and overall analysis.

_____ 9. I can make use of techniques such as the nominal group, the Delphi method, and quality circles.

# Key Word Quiz

## The Language of Small Group Communication

Match the terms about small group communication with their definitions. Record the number of the definition next to the appropriate term.

a. _____ primary groups

b. _____ norms

c. _____ task groups

d. _____ brainstorming

e. _____ reference group

f. _____ high-context culture

g. _____ symposium

h. _____ consensus

i. _____ Delphi method

j. _____ focus group

1. Groups that are formed to accomplish specific goals.

2. A series of prepared presentations introduced and co-ordinated by a leader.

3. A kind of in-depth interview of a small group.

4. Rules or standards identifying which behaviors are considered appropriate and which are considered inappropriate in a group.

5. A type of agreement in which group members all agree that a solution is acceptable.

6. Groups in which you participate early in life and which serve needs such as those for affiliation, affirmation, and affection.

7. A culture in which much of the information in communication is not explicitly coded in verbal messages but is considered common knowledge to all participants.

8. Problem-solving technique in which a small group of experts communicate by responding to questionnaires rather than interacting with one another.

9. A group from which you derive your values and norms of behavior.

10. A small group process for generating ideas.

Answers: a. 6 b. 4 c. 1 d. 10 e. 9 f. 7 g. 2 h. 5 i. 8 j. 3

## Five for Discussion

1. Studies find that persons high in communication apprehension are less effective in idea-generation groups than those low in apprehension (Jablin, 1981; Comadena, 1984; Cragan & Wright, 1990). Why might this be so?

2. What norms govern your class in human communication? Your family? Your place of work? What one rule, norm, or principle of small group interaction do you find is violated most often? How would the groups you participate in be different if this rule were followed instead of violated?

3. What type of criteria would an advertising agency use in evaluating a proposed new campaign to sell soap? A university in evaluating a new multicultural curriculum? Parents in evaluating a preschool for their children?

4. Visit the Creativity Web at http://members/optusnet .com.au/~charles57/creative/index2.html for a wealth of links to all aspects of creativity—quotations, affirmations, humor, discussions of the brain and the creative process, and more. What can you find here that might be of value to brainstorming and to idea generation generally?

5. Groups frequently make more extreme decisions than do individuals—a tendency known as group polarization (Brauer, Judd, & Gliner, 1995; Friedkin, 1999; Bullock, McCluskey, Stamm, Tanaka, Torres, & Scott, 2002). For example, groups tend to take greater risks if the members are already willing to take some risks, or to become even more cautious if the members are already cautious. Have you ever observed this group polarization tendency? What happened? What implications does this theory have for, say, teenagers who join a gang? For athletes who join a new team?

## Log On! MyCommunicationLab

Networking, a group process somewhat different from those discussed here, is presented briefly at www.mycommunicationlab.com. Also visit MyCommunicationLab for video clips on small group communication as well as additional exercises and study tools. These will give you additional perspectives on the different types of small groups.

Explore our research resources at www.researchnavigator.com.

Research
Navigator.com

# 9

# Members and Leaders in Small Group Communication

## Why Read This Chapter?

Because you'll **learn about:**

- small group members, their roles, and ways of participating.
- approaches to and functions of leadership.
- the role of culture in members' and leaders' behaviors.

Because you'll **learn to:**

- participate more effectively as a member of a small group.
- lead a variety of small groups more effectively.
- participate in and lead groups in light of significant cultural differences.

s you saw in Chapter 8, you're a part of many different groups, and you serve a wide variety of roles and functions in these groups. This chapter focuses on both membership and leadership in small groups. By gaining insight into these roles and functions, you'll increase your own effectiveness as a group member and leader.

## Members in Small Group Communication

Each of us serves many **roles,** patterns of behaviors that we customarily perform and that we're expected by others to perform. Javier, for example, is a part-time college student, father, bookkeeper, bowling team captain, and sometime poet. That is, he acts as a student—attends class, reads textbooks, takes exams, and does the things we expect of college students. He also performs those behaviors associated with fathers, bookkeepers, and so on. In a similar way, you develop ways of behaving when participating in small groups.

## Member Roles

Kenneth Benne and Paul Sheats (1948) proposed a classification of members' roles in small group communication that still provides the best overview of this important topic (Lumsden & Lumsden, 1993; Beebe & Masterson, 2006). They divide members' roles into three general classes: group task roles, group building and maintenance roles, and individual roles. Leaders, of course, often perform these roles as well.

### Group Task Roles

*Group task roles* help the group focus on achieving its goals. Effective group members serve several roles. Some people do lock into a few specific roles, but this single focus is usually counterproductive—it's better for the roles to be spread more evenly among the members and for the roles to be alternated frequently. Here are some examples of group task roles.

- *The information seeker or giver* or *the opinion seeker or giver* asks for or gives facts or opinions, seeks clarification of issues being discussed, and presents facts or opinions to group members: "Sales for May were up 10 percent. Do we have the sales figures for June?"

- *The evaluator–critic* evaluates the group's decisions, questions the logic or practicality of the suggestions, and provides the group with both positive and negative feedback: "That's a great idea, but it sounds expensive."

- *The procedural technician* or *recorder* takes care of various mechanical duties, such as distributing group materials and arranging the seating; writes down the group's activities, suggestions, and decisions; and/or serves as the group's memory: "We have another meeting scheduled to discuss just this issue, so perhaps we can skip it for today."

### Group Building and Maintenance Roles

No group can be task oriented at all times. Group members have varied interpersonal relationships, and these need to be nourished if the group is to function effectively. Group members need to be satisfied if they are to be productive. Group building and maintenance roles serve these relationship needs. Here are some examples of these roles.

- *The encourager* or *harmonizer* provides members with positive reinforcement through social approval or praise for their ideas

**"Remember, in this negotiation you're the 'Paula Abdul.'"**

and mediates the various differences between group members: "Pat, another great idea."

- *The compromiser* tries to resolve conflict between his or her ideas and those of others and offers compromises: "This looks like it could work if each department cut back at least 10 percent."
- *The follower* goes along with members, passively accepts the ideas of others, and functions more as an audience than as an active member: "If you all agree, that's fine with me."

**Individual Roles**   Group task roles and group building and maintenance roles are productive. They help the group achieve its goal and are group oriented. Individual roles, on the other hand, are counterproductive. They hinder the group from achieving its goal and are individual rather than group oriented. Such roles, often termed dysfunctional, hinder the group's effectiveness in terms of both productivity and personal satisfaction. Here are some examples of individual roles.

- *The aggressor* or *blocker* expresses negative evaluation of members and attacks the group, is generally disagreeable, and opposes other members or their suggestions regardless of their merit: "That's a terrible idea. It doesn't make any sense."
- *The recognition seeker* and *the self-confessor* try to focus attention on themselves, boast about their accomplishments rather than the task at hand, and express their own feelings rather than focus on the group: "The system I devised at B&B was a great success; everyone loved it. We can do the same thing here."
- *The dominator* tries to run the group or members by pulling rank, flattering members, or acting the role of boss: "I've been here the longest; I know what works and what doesn't work."

A popular individual role born on the Internet is *trolling*, the practice of posting messages that you know are false or outrageous just so you can watch the group members correct you or get emotionally upset by your message. As in any group, behavior such as trolling or flaming wastes time and energy and diverts the group from its primary objective.

## Member Participation

Here are several guidelines to help make your participation in small group communication more effective and enjoyable. These guidelines may look familiar, as they are in fact an elaboration and extension of the basic characteristics of effective interpersonal communication described in Chapter 6.

**Be Group Oriented**   When participating in a small group, you serve as a member of a team. You share common goals with the other group members, and your participation is valuable to the extent that it advances this shared goal. So in a team situation, you need to pool your talents, knowledge, and insights to promote the best possible solution for the group. Although a group orientation calls for the participation and cooperation of all group members, this guideline does not suggest that you abandon your individuality, personal values, or beliefs for the group's sake. Individuality *with* a group orientation is most effective. And because the most effective and the most creative solutions often emerge from a combination of ideas, approach small group situations with flexibility; come to the group with ideas and information but without firmly formulated conclusions. The importance of a group orientation is also seen in one of the rules of netiquette, which holds that you should not protest the subject of, say, a mailing list or a chat group. If you don't wish to be group oriented and discuss what the group is discussing, you're expected to unsubscribe from the mailing list or withdraw from the group.

**▼ E-TALK**

**Loneliness and the Computer**
One study finds that lonely people are more likely to use the Internet to obtain emotional support than are those who are not lonely. Further, lonely people are more satisfied with their online relationships than are those who are not lonely (Morahan-Martin & Schumacher, 2003). How would you explain the reasons for these findings?

**WHAT DO YOU SAY?**
**Asserting Yourself in a Group**
In your meetings at work, the supervisor consistently ignores your cues that you want to say something—and when you do manage to say something, no one reacts. You're determined to change this situation. *What do you say? To whom? Through what channel?*

## Responding to Individual Roles

For each of the three individual roles described on page 201 and identified in the left column, write a response or two that you as a leader might make in order to deal with this dysfunctional role playing. Be careful that your responses don't alienate the individual or the group.

*One major value of small group interaction is that everyone profits from the insights of everyone else; individual roles can get in the way of that important function.*

| Individual, Dysfunctional Roles | Responding to Individual Roles |
|---|---|
| *The aggressor:* Expresses negative evaluation of the group and its members | |
| *The blocker:* Is disagreeable, opposing other members and their ideas regardless of their merit | |
| *The self-confessor:* Personalizes everything instead of focusing on the group | |

**Center Conflict on Issues**  Conflict in small group situations is inevitable; it's a natural part of the give and take of ideas. Recognize that conflict is a natural part of the small group process that often promotes a better outcome. To manage conflict effectively, however, center it on issues rather than on personalities. When you disagree, make it clear that your disagreement is with the ideas expressed, not with the person who expressed them. For example, if you think that a colleague's ideas to raise funds for your social service agency are impractical and shortsighted, concentrate your criticisms on your colleague's proposed plan and suggest ways that the plan could be improved rather than attacking your colleague personally. Similarly, when you find someone disagreeing with you, try not to take it personally or to react emotionally. Rather, view the disagreement as an opportunity to discuss issues from an alternative point of view. In the language of the Internet, don't flame—don't attack the person. And don't contribute to flame wars by flame baiting, or saying things that will further incite the personal attacks.

**Be Critically Open-Minded**  When members join a group with their minds already made up, the small group process degenerates into a series of debates in which each person argues for his or her position—a clear example of members' taking on individual and dysfunctional roles. Group goals are neglected and the group process breaks down.

*"Do not wait for leaders; do it alone, person to person."*
—MOTHER TERESA

Let's say you have spent several hours developing what you think is the best, most effective advertising campaign to combat your company's low sales numbers. At the group meeting, however, members' reactions are extremely critical. Instead of becoming defensive, listen to their criticisms and try to think of ways that your plan could be modified to be as effective as possible for the company. To avoid this situation in the future, try to come to the group with ideas rather than conclusions; with suggestions rather than final decisions; and, of course, with information that will contribute to the discussion and the group goal. Try not to decide on solutions or draw conclusions before discussing them with the group. Be willing to accept other people's suggestions as

## Justifying the Ends

Do the ends justify the means? Is it ethical for a group to do things that would normally be considered unethical? For example, would it be ethical for an advertising team to write deliberately misleading advertising, if the end it hoped to achieve were worthy, such as keeping children from using drugs? Those taking an objective position (see the Communicating Ethically box in Chapter 1) would argue that the ends do not justify the means—that a lie, for example, is always wrong regardless of the specific situation. Those taking a subjective position would argue that at times the end would justify the means and at times it wouldn't; it would depend on the specific means and ends in question.

*What would you do?* *Would you lie about your past to your romantic partner to preserve peace and stability in the relationship? Would you misrepresent yourself on an Internet group to spice things up? Would you make up statistics to support your point of view in a forum because you know that what you are advocating will benefit the audience?*

> *You cannot make yourself feel something you do not feel, but you can make yourself do right in spite of your feelings.*
> —Pearl S. Buck

well as to revise your own in light of the discussion. Listen openly but critically to comments of all members (including your own).

**Ensure Understanding**   Make sure all participants understand your ideas and information. If something is worth saying, it's worth making clear. When in doubt, ask: "Is that clear?" "Did I explain that clearly?" Make sure, too, that you fully understand other members' contributions, especially before you disagree with them. In fact, it's often wise to preface any expression of disagreement with some kind of paraphrase to ensure you really are in disagreement. For example, you might say, "If I understand you correctly, you feel that marketing should bear sole responsibility for updating the product database." After waiting for the response, you would state your thoughts.

**Beware of Groupthink**   The concept of **groupthink** provides an especially useful perspective on thinking critically in the small group situation. In groupthink agreement among members becomes extremely important—so important that it tends to shut out realistic and logical analysis of a problem or of possible alternatives (Janis, 1983; Mullen, Tara, Salas, & Driskell, 1994). The term *groupthink* itself is meant to signal a "deterioration of mental efficiency, reality testing, and moral judgment that results from in-group pressures" (Janis, 1983, p. 9).

Many specific behaviors of group members can lead to groupthink—the unwillingness to invite disagreement and reexamination of the issue. One of the most significant behaviors occurs when the group limits its discussion to only a few alternative solutions. Another occurs when the group does not reexamine its decisions despite indications of possible dangers. Yet another happens when the group spends little time discussing why certain initial alternatives were rejected. For example, if the group rejects a certain alternative because it is too costly, members will devote little time, if any, to ways of reducing the cost.

In groupthink, members are extremely selective concerning the information they consider seriously. Members tend to ignore facts and opinions contrary to the group's position, and they readily and uncritically accept those that support the group's position. The following symptoms should help you recognize groupthink in groups you observe or participate in (Janis, 1983; Schafer & Crichlow, 1996).

> **WHAT DO YOU SAY?**
> **Groupthink**
> Your work group is displaying all the symptoms of groupthink you've read about. You want to get the group's members to reevaluate their decision-making processes. *What do you say? To whom? Through what channel?*

### Gatekeepers

The concept of "gatekeeping" in communication, introduced by Kurt Lewin in his *Human Relations* (1947), involves both *the process* by which a message passes through various gates and *the people or groups* that allow the message to pass (gatekeepers).

As you were growing up, your parents—your first gatekeepers—gave you certain information and withheld other information. For example, depending on the culture in which you were raised, you may have been told about Santa Claus and the tooth fairy but not about cancer or mutual funds. When you went to school, your teachers served a similar gatekeeping function. They taught you about certain historical events, for example, but not others. Textbook authors also serve a gatekeeping function (Robinson, 1993), as do editors of newspapers and magazines; television producers, writers, and advertisers; and those who regulate and monitor Internet messages. All these gatekeepers allow certain information to come through and cause other information to be filtered out (Lewis, 1995; Bodon, Powell, & Hickson, 1999).

Often the purpose of gatekeeping by the media is to increase profits, as when different media emphasize (open the gates for) stories about celebrities, violence, and sex—because these sell—and deemphasize (close the gates on) minority issues, classical drama, or antireligious viewpoints. At times the media may gatekeep because of legal restrictions.

So, when you hear a news broadcast, read an article, or listen to a commentator, ask yourself if you're seeing or hearing an incomplete or unrealistic picture. What might not have passed through the gate?

*Increasing Media Literacy.* How do one, two, or three of the following people function as gatekeepers in your ability to acquire information: The editor of your local or college newspaper, Oprah Winfrey, your romantic partner (past or present), the president of the United States, network news shows, or the advertising department of a large corporation?

*"All the news that's fit to print."*
—New York Times
SLOGAN

*"All the news that fits we print."*
—POPULAR ALTERNATIVE
RESPONSE

---

- Group members believe all are in unanimous agreement, whether this is stated or not.
- Members censor their own doubts.
- Group pressure is applied to any member who expresses doubts or questions the group's arguments or proposals.
- Group members think the group and its members are invulnerable.
- Members create rationalizations to avoid dealing with warnings or threats.
- Members believe their group is moral.
- Members perceive those opposed to the group in simplistic, stereotyped ways.
- Group members emerge whose function it is to guard the information that gets to other members, especially when it might create diversity of opinion.

## Leaders in Small Group Communication

In many small groups, one person serves as leader. In others, several people share leadership. In some groups a person may be appointed or serve as leader because she or he holds a high position within the company or hierarchy. In other groups, the leader emerges as the group proceeds in fulfilling its functions or may be voted as leader by the group members. In any case, the role of the leader or leaders is vital to the well-being and effectiveness of the group. In fact even in leaderless groups, in which all members are equal, leadership functions must still be served.

# Approaches to Leadership

Not surprisingly, **leadership** has been the focus of considerable research attention. Researchers have identified several views of leadership, which are termed *approaches*. Looking at a few of these approaches will give you a better idea of the varied ways in which leadership may be viewed and a better grasp of what leadership is and how it may be achieved.

**The Traits Approach**     The *traits approach* views the leader as the one who possesses those characteristics or skills (or traits) that contribute to leadership. This approach is valuable for stressing the characteristics that often (though not always) distinguish leaders from nonleaders. For example, some of the world's leading corporations seek technology project managers and leaders by looking for people who have "the right mix of technological savvy, teambuilding skills, communication know-how, and interpersonal management skills" (Crowley, 1999, p. 76). Research has found that traits more frequently associated with leadership than others include intelligence, self-confidence, determination, integrity, and sociability (Northouse, 1997). And Attila the Hun, who had much to say about leadership and particularly about the traits of effective leaders, noted that effective leaders demonstrate empathy, courage, accountability, dependability, credibility, stewardship, loyalty, desire, emotional stamina, physical stamina, decisiveness, anticipation, timing, competitiveness, self-confidence, responsibility, and tenacity (Roberts, 1987). If you demonstrate these qualities, the traits approach argues, you'll find yourself in leadership positions.

   The problem with the traits approach is that these qualities often vary with the group situation, with the members, and with the culture in which the leader functions. Thus, for some groups (for example, a new computer game company), a youthful, energetic, humorous leader might be effective; for other groups (for example, a medical diagnosis team), an older, more experienced and serious leader might be effective.

**The Functional Approach**     The *functional approach* to leadership focuses on what the leader should do in a given situation. We've already encountered some of these functions in the discussion of group roles. Other functions associated with leadership are setting group goals, giving the group members direction, and summarizing the group's progress (Schultz, 1996). Additional functions are identified in the section entitled "Functions of Leadership" later in this chapter.

**The Transformational Approach**     The *transformational approach* describes a "transformational" (also called visionary or charismatic) leader who elevates the group's members, enabling them not only to accomplish the group task but also to emerge as more empowered individuals (Hersey, Blanchard, & Johnson, 2001). At the center of the transformational approach is the concept of charisma, that quality of an individual that makes us believe or want to follow him or her. Gandhi, Martin Luther King Jr., and John F. Kennedy are often cited as examples of transformational leaders. These leaders were role models, were seen as extremely competent and able, and articulated moral goals (Northouse, 1997). We'll return to this concept of charisma and to these qualities when we examine credibility in Chapter 13.

**The Situational Approach**     The *situational approach* holds that the effective leader adjusts his or her emphasis between task accomplishment (identifying and focusing on the specific problem that the group must solve) and member satisfaction (providing for the psychological and interpersonal needs of the group members) on the basis of the specific group situation. This twofold function, you'll

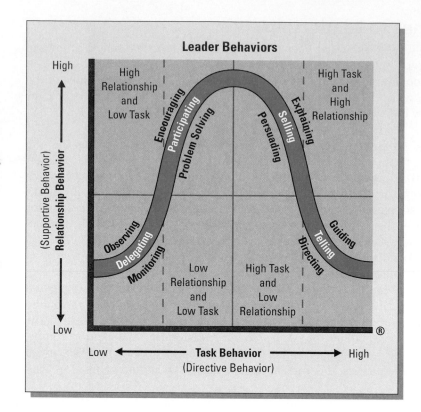

notice, rests on essentially the same distinction between relationship and task groups that we considered in Chapter 8. Some groups call for a high focus on task issues and need little people encouragement; this might be the case, for example, with a group of experienced scientists researching a cure for AIDS. In contrast, a group of recovering alcoholics might require leadership that stressed the members' emotional needs. The general idea of situational leadership is that there is no one style of leadership that fits all situations; each situation will call for a different combination of emphasis on task and member satisfaction (Fielder, 1967).

An interesting extension of this basic approach views leadership as consisting of four basic styles, illustrated in Figure 9.1 (Hersey, Blanchard, & Johnson, 2001). This theory claims that groups differ in their task and relationship maturity. In a group with task maturity, the members are knowledgeable about and experienced with the topic, task, and group process. Because of this maturity, the members are able to set realistic and attainable goals and are willing to take on responsibility for their decisions. In a group with relationship maturity, the members are motivated to accomplish the task and are confident in their abilities to accomplish it.

Effective leadership, then, depends on the leader's assessment of the group's task and relationship maturity. And, to complicate matters just a bit, the maturity of a group will change as the group develops—so the particular style of leadership will have to change in response. This theory identifies four leadership styles:

- The *telling style*, most appropriate for the group lacking both task and relationship maturity, is highly directive; the leader, who is significantly more knowledgeable or more powerful than the members, tells the group what has to be done and what they have to do to accomplish it. The experienced surgeon might use this style in leading a group of young interns through the required surgical procedures.

- The *selling style* is both directive and supportive. The leader using this style, sometimes called *coaching*, tries to sell the members on the task to be accomplished, much as a coach would energize and motivate a team before a big game.

- The *participating style* is nondirective and highly supportive; the leader's focus is almost entirely on member satisfaction and member relationships. A leader supervising a group of volunteers working for a political candidate might use this style; the group would already be committed to the task but might need to be supported to continue their volunteering.

- The *delegating style*, often used with mature and knowledgeable groups, is low in both direction and support. This leader allows the group members to set their own goals, to define the problem as they see fit, and to progress through the problem-solving process with little leader interference.

As you can tell from these descriptions, the leader exerts more control with immature groups (telling and selling) and less control with mature groups (participating and delegating). As groups become more mature, members assume greater responsibility and control and leaders' control diminishes.

At this point you should find it interesting to analyze your own leadership qualities by taking the following self-test, "Are you leader material?" It will help personalize the preceding discussion on the four approaches to leadership.

**WHAT DO YOU SAY?**
**Situational Leadership**
You're in an introductory Internet Design team whose leader uses a delegating style which isn't working. Group members are all new to this business and need more direction and guidance. You've been elected to clue the leader into appropriate and inappropriate styles. *What do you say? Through what channel?*

# Test ► ◄ Yourself

## ARE YOU LEADER MATERIAL?

**INSTRUCTIONS:** This self-test will help you think about yourself in the role of leader. Respond to the following statements in terms of how you perceive yourself and how you think others perceive you, using a 10-point scale on which 10 = extremely true and 1 = extremely false.

| Others See Me As | I See Myself As | Perceptions |
|---|---|---|
| ___ ❶ | ___ ❶ | Popular with group members |
| ___ ❷ | ___ ❷ | Knowledgeable about the topics discussed |
| ___ ❸ | ___ ❸ | Dependable |
| ___ ❹ | ___ ❹ | Effective in establishing group goals |
| ___ ❺ | ___ ❺ | Competent in giving directions |
| ___ ❻ | ___ ❻ | Capable of energizing group members |
| ___ ❼ | ___ ❼ | Charismatic (dynamic, engaging, powerful) |
| ___ ❽ | ___ ❽ | Empowering of group members |
| ___ ❾ | ___ ❾ | Moral and honest |
| ___ ❿ | ___ ❿ | Skilled in satisfying both task and relationship needs |
| ___ ⓫ | ___ ⓫ | Flexible in adjusting leadership style on the basis of the situation |
| ___ ⓬ | ___ ⓬ | Able to delegate responsibility |

**HOW DID YOU DO?** This test was designed to encourage you to look at yourself in terms of the four approaches to leadership discussed in the text. Perceptions 1–3 refer to the traits approach to leadership, which defines a leader as someone who possesses certain qualities. Perceptions 4–6 refer to the functional approach, which defines a leader as someone who performs certain functions. Perceptions 7–9 refer to the transformational approach, which defines a leader as someone who enables the group members to become the best they can be. Perceptions 10–12 refer to the situational approach, which defines a leader as someone who can adjust his or her style to balance the needs of the specific situation.

To compute your scores:

- Add your scores for items 1–3: _____. This will give you an idea of how you and others see you in terms of the leadership qualities identified by the trait approach.

- Add your scores for items 4–6: _____. This will give you an idea of how you and others see you in relation to the varied leadership functions considered in the functional approach.

- Add your scores for items 7–9: _____. This will give you an idea of how you and others see you as a transformational leader.

- Add your scores for items 10–12: _____. This will give you an idea of how you and others see you as a situational leader.

**WHAT WILL YOU DO?** As you read the remainder of this chapter and this book, try to identify specific skills and competencies you might learn that would enable you to increase your scores on all four approaches to leadership. Also, try searching the Web for information on "leadership" as well as, say, topics such as "business leadership" and "political leaders."

## General Styles of Leadership

In addition to the styles identified in the situational approach to leadership (see Figure 9.1 on p. 206), small group theorists also distinguish among laissez-faire, democratic, and authoritarian leaders (Bennis & Nanus, 1985; Hackman & Johnson, 1991). As you'll see, these three styles represent a different way of looking at leadership style.

The **laissez-faire leader** takes no initiative in directing or suggesting alternative courses of action. Rather, this leader allows the group to develop and progress on its own, even allowing it to make its own mistakes. The laissez-faire leader answers questions and provides information only when specifically asked. During the interaction, this leader neither compliments nor criticizes group members or the group's progress. Generally, this type of leadership results in a satisfied but inefficient group.

The **democratic leader** provides direction but allows the group to develop and progress the way its members wish; this form of leadership is similar to the "participating style" in the situational approach. The democratic leader encourages group members to determine their own goals and procedures and aims to stimulate self-direction and self-actualization of the group members. Unlike the laissez-faire leader, the democratic leader does contribute suggestions and does comment on member and group performance. Generally, this form of leadership results in both satisfaction and efficiency.

The **authoritarian leader** is the opposite of the laissez-faire leader. As in the "telling style" of leadership in the situational approach, this leader determines group policies and makes decisions without consulting or securing agreement from the members. The authoritarian leader discourages member-to-member communication and encourages communication from member to leader. This person is concerned with getting the group to accept his or her

*"Be willing to make decisions. That's the most important quality in a good leader. Don't fall victim to what I call the 'ready-aim-aim-aim-aim syndrome.' You must be willing to fire.""*

—T. BOONE PICKENS

decisions rather than making its own. If the authoritarian leader is a competent individual, the group may be highly efficient, but its members are likely to be less personally satisfied.

## Functions of Leadership

Keeping the various views of leadership in mind, especially the situational theory with its concern for both task and people, we can look at some of the major functions leaders serve. These functions are not exclusively the leader's; they are often shared or served wholly by group members. But when there's a specific leader, she or he is expected to perform these functions.

**Leaders Prepare Members and Start Interaction**   Groups form gradually and often need to be eased into meaningful discussion. As the leader, you need to prepare members for the small group interaction as well as for the discussion of a specific issue or problem. Don't expect diverse members to work together cohesively to solve a problem without first becoming familiar with one another. Similarly, if members are to discuss a specific problem, a proper briefing may be necessary. If materials need to be distributed before the actual discussion, consider e-mailing them to members. Or perhaps members need to view a particular film or television show. Whatever the preparations, you need to organize and coordinate them. Once the group is assembled, you may need to stimulate the members to interact.

**Leaders Maintain Effective Interaction**   Even after the group has begun to interact, you'll need to monitor the members' effective interaction. When the discussion begins to drag, you may need to step in and motivate the group: "Do we have any additional comments on the proposal to eliminate required courses?" "What do you, as members of the college curriculum committee, think about the proposal?" You'll also want to ensure that all members have an opportunity to express themselves.

**Leaders Guide Members through the Agreed-on Agenda**   As the leader, you need to keep the discussion on track by asking relevant questions, summarizing the group discussions periodically, or by offering a transition from one issue to the next. This involves following the tasks to be accomplished by the group as outlined in the meeting agenda and efficiently managing the amount of time allotted for each event.

**Leaders Ensure Member Satisfaction**   Members have different psychological needs and wants, and many people enter groups because of them. Even though a group may, for example, deal with political issues, members may have come together for psychological as well as for political reasons. If a group is to be effective, it must achieve the group goal (in this case, political) without denying the psychological purposes or goals that motivate many of the members to come together. One way to meet these needs is for you as leader to allow digressions and personal comments, assuming they are not too frequent or overly long. Another way is to be supportive and reinforcing.

**Leaders Empower Group Members**   An important function of a leader (though not limited to leadership) is to empower others—to help group members (as well as your relational partner, coworkers, employees, other students, or siblings) to gain increased power over themselves and their environment. For example, both as a leader and in your daily life, try to:

**WHAT DO YOU SAY?**
**Leadership Styles**
The appointed leader of your work group is extremely authoritarian, and the entire group has asked you to confront the leader to change to a more democratic style. *What do you say? Through what channel?*

*"Leadership appears to be the art of getting others to want to do smething you are convinced should be done."*

—Vance Packard

## Farcus
by David Waisglass
Gordon Coulthart

**"The kids want to know what's next on the agenda."**

■ Raise other's self-esteem. Compliment, reinforce. Resist fault-finding; it doesn't benefit anyone and in fact disempowers.

■ Share skills and decision-making power and authority.

■ Be constructively critical. Be willing to offer your perspective—to lend an ear to a first-try singing effort or to listen to a new poem. Be willing to react honestly to suggestions from all group members and not just those in high positions.

■ Encourage growth in all forms (academic, relational, and professional). The empowerment of others enhances your own growth and power.

### Leaders Encourage Ongoing Evaluation and Improvement
All groups encounter obstacles as they try to solve a problem, reach a decision, or generate ideas. No group is totally effective. All groups have room for improvement. To improve, the group must focus on itself. Along with trying to solve some external problem, it must try to solve its own internal problems—for example, personal conflicts, failure of members to meet on time, or members who come unprepared. When you notice some serious group failing, address it, perhaps posing this very issue (say, member lateness) as a problem to be solved.

### Leaders Manage Conflict
As in interpersonal relationships, conflict is a part of small group interaction. And it's a leader's responsibility to deal with it effectively. The conflict management techniques that are useful in small groups are the same techniques that we considered in the context of interpersonal communication

## *Skill Development Experience*

### Empowering Group Members

For each situation, indicate what you might say to help empower the other person, using such strategies as (a) raising the other person's self-esteem; (b) listening actively and supportively; (c) being open, positive, and empathic; and (d) avoiding verbal aggressiveness or any unfair conflict strategies.

1. Your partner is having lots of difficulties—he recently lost his job, he received poor grades in a night class, and he is gaining a lot of weight. At the same time, you're doing extremely well. You want to give your partner back his confidence.

2. You're managing four college interns who are working on redesigning your company's website, three men and one woman. The men are extremely supportive of one another and regularly contribute ideas. Although equally competent, the woman doesn't contribute; she seems to lack confidence. Because the objective of this redesign is to increase the number of female visitors, you really need the woman intern's input and want to empower her.

3. You're a third-grade teacher. Most of the students are from the same ethnic–religious group; three, however, are from a very different group. The problem is that these three have not been included in the social groupings of the students; they're treated as outsiders. As a result, these children stumble when they have to read in front of the class and make a lot of mistakes at the chalkboard (though they consistently do well in private). You want to empower these students.

*Power is not a zero-sum game; contrary to some popular opinion, empowering others adds to rather than subtracts from your own power.*

### Listening to Complaints

Complaints—whether in an interpersonal, small group, or organizational situation—are essential sources of feedback; they tell you that at least one person, if not many, is dissatisfied with the way things are going and that something may need changing. If you wish to keep this channel of vital information open, listen to complaints positively.

- Welcome complaints; let the person know that you view complaints as helpful sources of information and that you're listening.
- Express concern for both thoughts and feelings. For example, respond both to the complaint about the inadequate copying facilities and to the frustration the worker feels in turning in work that looks sloppy.
- Respect confidentiality. Let the person know that you'll treat the complaint in confidence or that you'll reveal it only to those he or she wishes.
- Ask the person what he or she would like you to do about the complaint. Sometimes, all a person wants is for someone to hear the complaint and to appreciate its legitimacy.
- Express thanks to the person for voicing the complaint and verbalize your intention to follow-up on the complaint.

*Applying Listening Skills. Suppose you are working as a manager at McDonald's and a regular customer complains about the server: "I don't like the way she treated me, and I'm not coming back here." What would you say to the customer? What would you say to the server?*

*Listen long enough and the person will generally come up with an adequate solution.*
—Mary Kay Ash

(Chapter 7). You may wish to review these now and look at them as small group conflict management strategies.

## Mentoring

Another function of leadership that extends well beyond the small group situation is that of mentoring. A **mentoring** relationship occurs when an experienced individual helps to train a less experienced person. An accomplished teacher, for example, might mentor a younger teacher who is newly arrived or who has never taught before. The mentor guides the new person through the ropes, teaches the strategies and techniques for success, and otherwise communicates his or her accumulated knowledge and experience to the "mentee."

The mentoring relationship provides an ideal learning environment. It's usually a one-on-one relationship between expert and novice, a relationship that is supportive and trusting. There's a mutual and open sharing of information and thoughts about the job. The relationship enables the novice to try out new skills under the guidance of an expert, to ask questions, and to obtain the feedback so necessary to learning complex skills. Mentoring is perhaps best characterized as a relationship in which the experienced and powerful mentor empowers the novice, giving the novice the tools and techniques needed for gaining the same power the mentor now holds.

One study found the mentoring relationship to be one of the three primary paths for career achievement among African American men and women (Bridges, 1996). And another study (of middle-level managers) demonstrated that those who had mentors and participated in mentoring relationships got more promotions and higher salaries than those who didn't have mentors (Scandura, 1992).

At the same time, the mentor benefits from clarifying his or her thoughts, from seeing the job from the perspective of a newcomer, and from considering and formulating answers to a variety of questions. Just as a teacher learns from teaching, a mentor learns from mentoring.

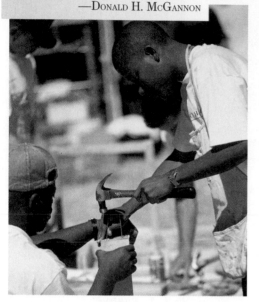
# Membership, Leadership, and Culture

Most of the research (and also the resulting theory) concerning small group communication, membership, and leadership has been conducted in universities in the United States and reflects American culture. So it's important that we look at both membership and leadership from the point of view of different cultures.

For example, each culture maintains its own belief system, which influences group members' behavior. Members of many Asian cultures, influenced by Confucian principles, believe that "the protruding nail gets pounded down" and are therefore not likely to voice disagreement with the majority of the group. Americans, on the other hand, influenced by the belief that "the squeaky wheel gets the grease," are more likely to voice disagreement or to act in ways different from other group members in order to get what they want (Hofstede, 1997).

Also, each culture has its own rules of preferred and expected leadership style. In the United States, the general and expected style for a group leader is democratic. Our political leaders are elected by a democratic process; similarly, company directors are elected by the shareholders of their corporations. In other situations, of course, leaders are chosen by those in authority. The president of a company will normally decide who will supervise and who will be supervised. Even in this situation, however, the supervisor is expected to behave democratically—to listen to the ideas of the employees; to take their views into consideration when decisions are to be made; to keep them informed of corporate developments; and not to discriminate on the basis of sex, race, or affectional orientation. Also, we expect that organizational and other group leaders will be changed fairly regularly, much as we change political leaders on a regular basis. In some other cultures, leaders get their positions by right of birth. They are not elected, nor are they expected to behave democratically. Similarly, their tenure as leaders is usually extremely long and may in fact last their entire lives. Their leadership roles are then passed on to their children. In other cases leaders may be chosen by a military dictator.

## Individual and Collective Orientations

Small group cultures and cultures in general differ in the extent to which they promote individualistic values (for example, power, achievement, hedonism, and stimulation) versus collectivist values (for example, benevolence, tradition, and conformity).

One of the major differences between an **individual orientation** and a **collective orientation** is in the extent to which an individual's goals or the group's goals are given precedence. Individual and collective tendencies are, of course, not mutually exclusive; this is not an all-or-none orientation, but rather one of emphasis. You probably have both tendencies. Thus, you may, for example, compete with other members of your basketball team to make the most baskets or win the most valuable player award (and thus emphasize individual goals). At the same time, however, you will—in a game—act in a way that will benefit the entire team (and thus emphasize group goals). In actual practice, both individual and collective tendencies will help both you and your team achieve your goals. Still, most people and most cultures have a dominant orientation: They're more individually oriented (they see themselves as independent) or more collectively oriented (they see themselves as interdependent) in most situations, most of the time (Singelis, 1994).

In an *individualist culture*, as discussed in Chapter 7, you're responsible to your own conscience; responsibility is largely an individual matter. Examples of individualist cultures include those of the United States, Australia, United Kingdom, Netherlands, Canada, New Zealand, Italy, Belgium, Denmark, and Sweden

(Hofstede, 1997; Singh & Pereira, 2004). In a *collectivist culture* you're responsible to the rules of the social group; all members share responsibility for accomplishments as well as for failures. Examples include the cultures of Guatemala, Ecuador, Panama, Venezuela, Colombia, Indonesia, Pakistan, China, Costa Rica, and Peru (Hofstede, 1997; Singh & Pereira, 2004). Individualistic cultures foster competition, whereas collectivist cultures promote cooperation.

In a small group situation in an individualist culture, you might compete for leadership, and there would likely be a very clear distinction between leaders and members. In a collectivist culture, in contrast, group leadership would be shared and rotated; there would likely be little distinction between leader and members. These orientations will also influence the kinds of communication members consider appropriate in an organizational context. For example, individualistic members will favor clarity and directness, but collectivists will favor face-saving and the avoidance of hurting others or arousing negative evaluations (Kim & Sharkey, 1995).

One obvious consequence of this difference in orientation can be seen in how individualistic and collectivist groups treat members who commit serious errors. A group governed by individualistic norms is likely to single out, reprimand, and perhaps fire an errant member. Further, the leader or supervisor is likely to distance himself or herself from this member for fear that the error will reflect negatively on his or her leadership. In a more collectivist culture, the error is more likely to be seen as a group mistake. The group is unlikely to single out the member—especially not in public—and the leader is likely to bear part of the blame. The same is true when one member comes up with a great idea. In individualist cultures that person is likely to be singled out for praise and rewards, even though the effort was to benefit the group. In collectivist cultures the group is recognized and rewarded for the idea.

Another example of cultural differences is the phenomenon of suicide bombers, people who will give up their own life in support of a cause in which they believe. In individualistic cultures the mentality of the suicide bomber is difficult to understand, because it is so foreign to everything such cultures teach and value. But for those from collectivist cultures, the larger social group is more important than the individual; the sacrifice of an individual life for the life of the group is entirely consistent with the collectivist cultural orientation.

## High and Low Power Distances

In some cultures power is concentrated in the hands of a few, and there is a great difference between the power held by these people and that held by the ordinary citizen. These are called high-power-distance cultures. Examples are the cultures of Malaysia, Panama, Guatemala, Philippines, Venezuela, Mexico, China, the Arab world, Indonesia, and Ecuador (Hofstede, 1997; Singh & Pereira, 2004). In low-power-distance cultures, power is more evenly distributed throughout the citizenry; examples include Austria, Israel, Denmark, New Zealand, Ireland, Norway, Sweden, Finland, Switzerland, and Costa Rica (Hofstede, 1997; Singh & Pereira, 2004). To understand the importance of cultural differences on the dimension of power distance, consider Iraq. Ever since the war in Iraq started, the United States and some allies have been trying to change the political culture of that country. Put in terms of power distance, the United States is trying to change Iraq from a high-power-distance culture, in which the few in authority made the decisions for the many, to a low-power-distance culture in which people will be relatively equal (that is, a democracy). Yet it is important to note that even in democracies where everyone is equal under the law (or should be), there are still great power distances between those in authority—the employers, the police, the politicians—and the ordinary citizen, as there are between those who are rich and those who are poor. These distances affect interpersonal and group communication in many ways.

The power distance between groups will influence both friendship and dating relationships (Andersen, 1991). For example, in India (high power distance) friendships and romantic relationships are expected to take place within your cultural

**WHAT DO YOU SAY?**
**Leader Guidance**
Members of your group are not participating equally. Of the eight members, three monopolize the discussion; the other five say as little as possible. *What do you say? To whom?*

▼ **E-TALK**

**Cultural Tours**
Virtual tours offer an interesting way of viewing a wide variety of areas. The most popular tours, which millions of Americans have taken, include museums, vacation spots, schools, real estate, historical exhibits, parks, places such as the Taj Mahal and the White House, and hotels (Virtual Tours, Pew/Internet, Data Memo 202-419-4500, http://www.pewinternet.org, dated December, 2004, accessed February 10, 2005). What are some of the virtual tours currently available that you might use to learn about different cultures?

**Organizational Hierarchies**
Some theorists believe that computer-mediated communication will eventually eliminate the hierarchical structure of organizations, largely because CMC "encourages wider participation, greater candor, and an emphasis on merit over status" (Kollock & Smith, 1996, p. 109). If this prediction came true, it would mean that high-power-distance organizational cultures would move in the direction of lower power distance and would gradually become more democratic. What evidence can you find bearing on this issue?

class; in Sweden (low power distance) a person is expected to select friends and romantic partners on the basis not of class or culture but of individual factors such as personality, appearance, and the like.

In low-power-distance cultures, there is a general feeling of equality, which is consistent with acting assertively; so you're expected to confront a friend, partner, or supervisor assertively (Borden, 1991). In high-power-distance cultures, direct confrontation and assertiveness may be viewed negatively, especially if directed at a superior.

In high-power-distance cultures, you're taught to have great respect for authority; people in these cultures see authority as desirable and beneficial and generally do not welcome challenges to authority (Westwood, Tang, & Kirkbride, 1992; Bochner & Hesketh, 1994). In low-power-distance cultures, there's a certain distrust for authority; it's seen as a kind of necessary evil that should be limited as much as possible. This difference in attitudes toward authority can be seen right in the classroom. In high-power-distance cultures, there's a great power distance between students and teachers; students are expected to be modest, polite, and totally respectful. In low-power-distance cultures, students are expected to demonstrate their knowledge and command of the subject matter, participate in discussions with the teacher, and even challenge the teacher—something many high-power-distance culture members wouldn't even think of doing.

High-power-distance cultures rely more on symbols of power. For example, titles (Dr., Professor, Chef, Inspector) are more important in high-power-distance cultures. Failure to include these honorifics in forms of address is a serious breach of etiquette. Low-power-distance cultures rely less on symbols of power, so there is less of a problem if you fail to use a respectful title (Victor, 1992)—although you may create problems if, for example, you call a medical doctor, police captain, military officer, or professor Ms. or Mr.

The groups in which you'll participate as a member or a leader will vary in power distance; some will be high-power-distance groups and others will be low. You need to recognize which is which, to follow the cultural rules generally, and to break the rules only after you've thought through the consequences.

# Summary of Concepts and Skills

This chapter looked at membership and leadership in the small group. We examined the roles of members—some productive and some counterproductive—and considered leadership theories, leadership styles, leadership functions, and cultural factors in small groups.

1. A popular classification of small group member roles divides them into three types: group task roles, group building and maintenance roles, and individual roles.

2. Among the group task roles are those of information seeker or giver, opinion seeker or giver, evaluator–critic, and procedural technician or recorder. Among the group building and maintenance roles are encourager/harmonizer, compromiser, and follower. Among the individual (dysfunctional) roles are aggressor/blocker, recognition seeker/self-confessor, and dominator.

3. Group members should be group oriented, center conflict on issues, be critically open-minded, and ensure understanding.

4. Groupthink is an excessive concern with securing agreement that discourages critical thinking and the exploration of alternative ways of doing things.

5. Three theories of leadership help to clarify aspects of leadership. The traits approach identifies characteristics, such as intelligence and self-confidence, that contribute to leadership. The transformational approach focuses on leaders as people who raise the performance of group members and empower them. The situational approach views leadership as varying its focus between accomplishing the task and serving the members' social and emotional needs, depending on the specific group and the unique situation.

6. An extension of the situational approach to leadership identifies four leadership styles: the telling, selling, participating, and delegating styles. The appropriate style to use depends on the group's level of task and relationship maturity.

7. Three general leadership styles are laissez-faire, democratic, and authoritarian.

8. Among the leader's task functions are to prepare members and start the group interaction, maintain effective interaction, guide members through the agreed-on agenda, ensure member satisfaction, empower members, encourage ongoing evaluation and improvement, prepare members for the discussion, and manage conflict.

9. Mentoring refers to the relationship where an experienced and knowledgeable individual helps guide and train a less-experienced person.

10. Group membership and leadership attitudes and behaviors are likely to be heavily influenced by culture, especially by the individual–collective and power-distance orientations.

The skills identified in this discussion center on increasing your ability to function more effectively as a small group member and leader. Place a check mark next to those skills you feel you should work on most.

_____ 1. I avoid playing the popular but dysfunctional individual roles in a small group—those of aggressor, blocker, recognition seeker, self-confessor, or dominator.

_____ 2. When participating in a small group, I am group rather than individual oriented, center the conflict on issues rather than on personalities, am critically open-minded, and make sure that my meanings and the meanings of others are clearly understood.

_____ 3. I recognize the symptoms of groupthink and actively counter my own groupthink tendencies as well as those evidenced in the group.

_____ 4. I adjust my leadership style according to the task at hand and the needs of group members.

_____ 5. As a small group leader, I start group interaction, maintain effective interaction throughout the discussion, keep members on track, ensure member satisfaction, encourage ongoing evaluation and improvement, and prepare members for the discussion as necessary.

_____ 6. I recognize and appreciate the cultural differences that people have toward group membership and leadership.

 Key Word Quiz

## The Language of Small Group Membership and Leadership

Match the terms about group membership and leadership with their definitions.
Record the number of the definition next to the appropriate term.

a. _____ groupthink

b. _____ collective orientation

c. _____ individual roles

d. _____ laissez-faire leader

e. _____ transformational leader

f. _____ group task roles

g. _____ mentoring

h. _____ group building and maintenance roles

i. _____ low-power-distance culture

j. _____ gatekeeper

1. The process or relationship in which a more experienced member helps train a less experienced member.

2. Member roles that help the group focus on achieving its goals.

3. A person or organization that monitors and censors the messages that get through to people.

4. A cultural view that holds that the group is more important than the individual.

5. Group roles of which encouraging, compromising, and following are examples.

6. A leader who takes no initiative in directing or suggesting alternative courses of action.

7. A dysfunctional process in which group agreement becomes more important than critical analysis.

8. A leader who elevates and empowers group members.

9. Group roles of which expressing aggressiveness, dominating, and seeking self-recognition are examples.

10. A culture in which there is a feeling of equality and in which there is little difference in power among members.

Answers: a. 7; b. 4; c. 9; d. 6; e. 8; f. 2; g. 1; h. 5; i. 10; j. 3

## Five for Discussion

1. Can you identify roles that you habitually play in certain groups? Do you tend to take these roles in your friendship, love, and family relationships as well? Being as honest with yourself as you can, how might you change the roles you serve?

2. Have you ever been in a group when groupthink was operating? If so, what were the groupthink symptoms you observed? What effect did groupthink have on the process and conclusions of the group?

3. It's been found that the person with the highest rate of participation in a group is the member most likely to be chosen leader (Mullen, Salas, & Driskell, 1989). Do you find this to be true of the groups in which you have participated? Why do you suppose this relationship exists?

4. In a social group at a friend's house, any leadership other than laissez-faire would be difficult to tolerate. When all members of a working committee are about equal in their knowledge of the topic or when the members are very concerned with their individual rights, the democratic leader seems the most appropriate. When time and efficiency are critical or when group members continue to lack motivation despite repeated democratic efforts, authoritarian leadership may be the most effective. In what other situations would laissez-faire, democratic, or authoritarian leadership style be appropriate? Does serving individual roles in a group make a member unpopular with other group members?

5. How would you describe the groups of which you're a member in terms of task and relationship maturity? What implications does the level of maturity have for the leadership of these groups?

## Log On! MyCommunicationLab

Three useful self-tests to help you further explore the concepts of leadership and leader influence are available at **www.mycommunicationlab.com**: (1) How Machiavellian Are You? (2) "What kind of Leader Are You?" and (3) How Individualistic Are You?

Also visit MyCommunicationLab for other activities, study aids, and video clips on members and leaders in small group communication situations.

Explore our research resources at **www.researchnavigator.com**.

Research
Navigator.com

# 10

# Public Speaking Preparation (Steps 1–6)

## Why Read This Chapter?

Because you'll **learn about:**

- the nature and importance of public speaking.
- audience analysis, research, and organization.

Because you'll **learn to:**

- manage your apprehension.
- select and narrow your topic and purpose.
- analyze your audience and adapt your speech to them.
- research your topic.
- organize your speech.

*B*efore getting to the steps for preparing and presenting a public speech, let's define public speaking and consider the benefits that will reward your public speaking efforts. In addition, we'll address what is probably your number one problem; namely, the fear that so often accompanies giving speeches. As a preface to this chapter and the remaining discussions of public speaking in Chapters 11 through 13, become familiar with Allyn and Bacon's public speaking website (see www.abacon.com/pubspeak).

# The Nature of Public Speaking

**Public speaking** is a form of communication in which a speaker addresses a relatively large audience with a relatively continuous discourse, usually in a face-to-face situation. A student delivering a report to a political science class, a teacher lecturing on the structure of DNA, a minister preaching a sermon, and a politician delivering a campaign speech are all examples of public speaking. Also, delivering a speech to a television camera to be broadcast to an entire nation or over the radio to be heard by a few thousand or a few million people is similar in many ways to what we traditionally think of as public speaking. It differs in that these mediated messages are not face-to-face, so the audience cannot respond immediately to the message, and the speaker cannot make adjustments on the basis of this feedback.

The closest electronic counterpart to public speaking is probably the newsgroup, a public forum for the exchange of ideas. One difference between newsgroups and face-to-face public speaking is that the messages in newsgroups are written. Another difference is that in electronic communication, as in television or radio, feedback from listeners is delayed rather than immediate, so the speaker cannot make on-the-spot adjustments. Voice and video enhancements are eliminating (or at least blurring) these differences. Even given these differences, the principles of public speaking discussed in this and the remaining chapters apply to these mediated and electronic communications as well as to face-to-face communication.

In addition to the speeches that you will give in this class and during your college career, you will also be called on to make formal and informal speeches throughout your life. For example, you may make a presentation about a new product at a sales meeting; present your company's rules and regulations to a group of new employees; explain the benefits of a new playground to members of your local PTA; or give a speech about your family genealogy at a family reunion. Regardless of the circumstances under which you give a speech, you will find the 10 steps to public speaking preparation discussed in this chapter and the next extremely practical.

## Benefits and Skills of Public Speaking

Public speaking draws together a wide variety of social, academic, and career skills. Although these skills are central to public speaking, they also enrich other competencies. Among these are your ability to present yourself to others with confidence and self-assurance, and your ability to conduct research efficiently and effectively. Public speaking skills will further help you to understand human motivation, to analyze and evaluate the validity of persuasive appeals, and to use persuasion effectively.

Public speaking will also develop and refine your general communication abilities by helping you

- explain complex concepts clearly
- organize a variety of messages for clarity and persuasiveness
- develop logical, emotional, and ethical appeals to support an argument
- communicate credibility
- improve your listening and delivery skills

It's important to remember, however, that effective public speakers aren't born; they're made. Through instruction, exposure to different speeches, feedback, and individual learning experiences, you can become an effective speaker. Regardless of your present level of competence, you can improve your public speaking skills through proper training.

## Managing Your Communication Apprehension

Now that you have a good idea of what public speaking is and what benefits you'll derive from studying it, consider what is probably your major concern: **communication apprehension,** or stage fright. People experience apprehension in all types of communication (as illustrated throughout this text), but it is in the public speaking situation that apprehension is most common and most severe (McCroskey, 1997; Richmond & McCroskey, 1998). To measure your own fear of speaking in public, take the apprehension self-test that follows.

### HOW APPREHENSIVE ARE YOU ABOUT PUBLIC SPEAKING?

**INSTRUCTIONS:** This questionnaire consists of six statements concerning your feelings about public speaking. Indicate the degree to which each statement applies to you by marking whether you (1) strongly agree, (2) agree, (3) are undecided, (4) disagree, or (5) strongly disagree with each statement. There are no right or wrong answers. Don't be concerned that some of the statements are similar to others. Work quickly; just record your first impression.

_____ ❶ I have no fear of giving a speech.

_____ ❷ Certain parts of my body feel very tense and rigid when I am giving a speech.

_____ ❸ I feel relaxed while giving a speech.

_____ ❹ My thoughts become confused and jumbled when I am giving a speech.

_____ ❺ I face the prospect of giving a speech with confidence.

_____ ❻ While giving a speech, I get so nervous that I forget facts I really know.

**HOW DID YOU DO?** To obtain your public speaking apprehension score, use the following formula: Start with 18 points; add the scores for items 1, 3, and 5; then subtract the scores for items 2, 4, and 6.

A score above 18 shows some degree of apprehension. Most people score above 18, so if you scored relatively high, you're among the vast majority of people. You may find it interesting to compare your apprehension scores from this test and the test in Chapter 8. Most people would score higher on public speaking apprehension than on apprehension in group discussions.

**WHAT WILL YOU DO?** As you read the suggestions for reducing apprehension in the text, consider what you can do to incorporate these ideas into your own public speaking experiences. Consider too how these suggestions might be useful in reducing apprehension more generally—for example, in social situations and in small groups and meetings.

The following suggestions will help you reduce your public speaking apprehension, as well as any communication apprehension in small group and interpersonal communication situations (Beatty, 1988; Richmond & McCroskey, 1998).

***Gain Experience.*** New and different situations such as public speaking are likely to make you anxious, so try to reduce their newness and differentness. The best way to do this is to get as much public speaking experience as you can. With experience, your initial fears and anxieties will give way to feelings of control, comfort, and pleasure. Experience will show you that the feelings of accomplishment in public speaking are rewarding and will outweigh any initial anxiety. Also, try to familiarize yourself with the public speaking context. For example, try to rehearse in the room in which you will give your speech.

***Think Positively.*** When you see yourself as inferior—when, for example, you feel that others are better speakers or that they know more than you do—anxiety increases. To gain greater confidence, think positive thoughts and be especially thorough in your preparation. At the same time, maintain realistic expectations for yourself. Fear increases when you feel that you can't meet your own or your audience's expectations (Ayres, 1986). Keep in mind that your second speech does not have to be better than that of the previous speaker, but that it should be better than your first speech.

***See Public Speaking as Conversation.*** When you're the center of attention, as you are in public speaking, you feel especially conspicuous; this often increases anxiety. It may help, therefore, to think of public speaking as another type of conversation (some theorists call it "enlarged conversation"). Or, if you're comfortable talking in small groups, visualizing your audience as an enlarged small group may dispel some anxiety.

***Stress Similarity.*** When you feel similar to (rather than different from) your audience, your anxiety should lessen. Therefore, try to emphasize the similarity between yourself and your audience, especially when your audience consists of people from cultures different from your own (Stephan & Stephan, 1992). With a culturally different audience, you're likely to feel less similarity with your listeners and thus to experience greater anxiety (Gudykunst & Nishida, 1984; Gudykunst, Yang, & Nishida, 1985). With all audiences, but especially with multicultural gatherings, stress similarities in experiences, attitudes, and values; it will make you feel more at one with your listeners.

***Prepare and Practice Thoroughly.*** Much of the fear you experience is a fear of failure. Adequate and even extra preparation will lessen the possibility of failure and the accompanying apprehension. Because apprehension is greatest during the beginning of the speech, try memorizing the first few sentences of your talk. If there are complicated facts or figures, be sure to write these out and plan to read them; this will remove from your mind any worry about forgetting them.

***Move About and Breathe Deeply.*** Physical activity—gross bodily movements as well as the small movements of the hands, face, and head—lessens apprehension. Using a visual aid, for example, will temporarily divert attention from you and will allow you to get rid of your excess energy. If you breathe deeply a few times before getting up to speak, you'll sense your body relax. This will help you overcome your initial fear of walking to the front of the room.

***Avoid Chemicals as Tension Relievers.*** Unless prescribed by a physician, avoid any chemical means for reducing apprehension. Tranquilizers, marijuana, and artificial stimulants are likely to create problems rather than to reduce

*The human brain starts working the moment you're born and never stops until you stand up to speak in public.*

—GEORGE JESSEL

### Listening to Help Reduce Apprehension

As a listener, you can help speakers with their apprehension.

■ *Positively reinforce the speaker.* A nod, a smile, an attentive appearance throughout the speech will help put the speaker at ease. Resist the temptation to check your IMs or talk with a friend.

■ *Ask questions in a supportive manner.* If there's a question period, ask information-seeking questions rather than firing off critical challenges. And ask questions in a way that won't encourage defensiveness. Instead of saying, "Your criticism of heavy metal music is absurd," say, "Why do you find the lyrics of heavy metal harmful?"

■ *Don't focus on errors.* If the speaker fumbles, don't put your head down, cover your eyes, or otherwise communicate your awareness of the fumble. Instead, continue listening to the content of the speech; let the speaker know that you're focused on what is being said.

**Applying Listening Skills.** *You notice that the speaker approaching the front of the room to give a speech is visibly nervous. What specifically can you do as a listener to help the speaker manager this apprehension and get through the speech?*

---

them. They're likely to impair your ability to remember the parts of your speech, to accurately read audience feedback, and to regulate the timing of your speech. And, of course, alcohol does nothing to reduce public speaking apprehension (Himle, Abelson, & Haghightgou, 1999).

## Culture and Public Speaking

As with all forms of communication, public speaking needs also to be seen within a cultural context. Your audiences are likely to be multicultural, and understanding the sometimes vastly different cultural perspectives of your listeners will help you construct a more culturally sensitive and thus more effective speech.

Of particular relevance to public speaking is the distinction between low and high context, which you learned about in Chapter 8 (pp. 186–187). You'll recall that people in low-context cultures want explicit information, whereas members of high-context cultures are more apt to rely on the context and what is known from previous interactions. In a *low-context culture*, most information is explicitly stated in a speech or, in more formal transactions, in written (contract) form. In a *high-context culture*, much of the information in communication is in the context or in the person—for example, information shared through previous communications, through assumptions about each other, and through shared experiences. Much key information is not explicitly stated in an actual speech.

Because members of low-context cultures generally expect information to be communicated explicitly, audiences from such cultures will probably wish to hear a direct statement of your position and an explicit statement of what you want the audience to learn or do. In contrast, people in high-context cultures prefer a less explicit statement and prefer to be led indirectly to your conclusion. An explicit statement ("Vote for Smith" or "Buy Viterall") may be interpreted as too direct and even insulting.

Another frequent difference and source of misunderstanding between high- and low-context cultures has to do with *face-saving* (Hall & Hall, 1987), as discussed in Chapter 4. People in high-context cultures such as that of Japan place great emphasis on face-saving. For example, they may tend to avoid argument for fear of causing others to lose face, whereas people in low-context cultures (with

> **WHAT DO YOU SAY?**
> **Apprehension Management**
> This is your first experience with public speaking, and you're very nervous; you're afraid you'll forget your speech or stumble somehow. So you're wondering if it would be a good idea to alert your audience to your nervousness. *What do you say?*

### Using Cultural Beliefs as Assumptions

How effective would it be to use each of the following cultural beliefs as a basic assumption in a speech to your public speaking class? Use the following scale: A = the audience would favorably accept this assumption and would welcome a speaker with this point of view; B = some members would listen open-mindedly, but others wouldn't; or C = the audience would reject this assumption and would not welcome a speaker with this point of view. On the basis of this analysis, what might you do and what should you not do in your next speech?

*Knowing your audience's cultural beliefs will help you identify with your listeners, avoid offending them, and adapt your speech in light of their beliefs.*

_____ 1. Religious differences are the main causes of war.
_____ 2. The group is more important than the individual.
_____ 3. The rich (countries, individuals) are morally obligated to give to the poor.
_____ 4. Men and women should each enter occupations for which they are biologically suited.
_____ 5. Pleasure is the only real goal in life.

their individualistic orientation) are more likely to use argument to win a point. Similarly, in high-context cultures criticism should take place only in private, to enable the person being criticized to save face; low-context cultures may not make this public/private distinction. Again, in high-context cultures speakers who attack the character of others may be accused of using unethical face-detracting strategies and may be disbelieved.

Members of high-context cultures are reluctant to say no for fear of offending and causing a person to lose face. So, for example, it's necessary to understand when a Japanese executive's yes means yes and when it means no. The difference is not in the words, but in the way they're used. As you can imagine, problems arise when people from a low-context culture interpret this reluctance to be direct—to say no when you mean no—as a weakness or as an unwillingness to confront reality. Be aware that audiences of high-context cultures are likely to give you positive feedback even if they dislike or don't understand your speech; it is up to you to look deeper for signs of disagreement or comprehension problems.

With the nature of public speaking and its benefits in mind, with an understanding of communication apprehension and some techniques for managing it, and with a sense of the importance of culture in public speaking, we can look at the first 6 of the 10 essential steps for preparing an effective public speech, as summarized in Figure 10.1. The final 4 steps will be covered in Chapter 11.

## Step 1: Select Your Topic and Purpose

The first step in preparing an effective public speech is to select the topic on which you'll speak and the general and specific purposes you hope to achieve.

### Your Topic

Select a worthwhile topic that will prove interesting to the audience. If your first speech is to be informative, select a topic that your audience probably knows little about but that will make them curious to learn more. If your first speech is persua-

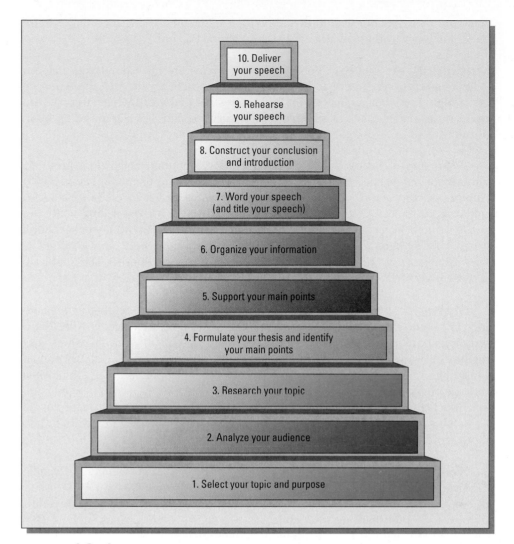

## Figure *10.1*

**The Steps in Public Speaking Preparation and Delivery**

Speakers differ in the order in which they follow these steps. Some speakers, for example, prefer to begin with audience analysis, asking themselves what the audience is interested in and then selecting the topic and purpose. Some speakers prefer to identify their main points before conducting extensive research; others prefer to allow the propositions to emerge from the research. The order presented here will prove useful to most speakers for most situations, but vary the order when it serves your purposes. As long as you cover all steps, you should be in good shape.

sive, you might select a topic about which you and the audience agree, and aim to strengthen their attitudes. Or you might select a topic on which you and the audience disagree; your aim then would be to persuade them to change their attitudes in your direction.

Not surprisingly, the appropriateness of a speech topic will vary with the culture of the audience. For example, each culture has its own topics that will often cause conflict. Generally these subjects should be avoided, especially by visitors from other cultures. Although the topics that are **taboo** vary from one culture to another and from one time to another, generally it is best to avoid criticizing any deeply held belief whether about religion or politics or education or child rearing practices. If you're going to address an audience with members from cultures other than your own, find out what these taboo topics are and avoid them or at least present them in a way that will not cause them to tune you out.

**Finding Your Topic**   Public speaking topics are all around you. Select a topic area that you're interested in and know something about. And, of course, select a topic that your audience will find interesting and worthwhile. You can find topics by examining lists of suitable topics, surveys, and news items or by brainstorming.

*Topic Lists.*   Most public speaking textbooks contain suggestions for topics suitable for public speeches as do books for writers (e.g., Lamm, & Lamm, 1999). This text's companion website (www.ablongman.com/devito) contains a list of hundreds of topics. Another source of topics is the list of best-selling nonfiction books printed in most newspaper book reviews or found in well-stocked bookstores. Or visit one of the online bookstores (www.amazon.com, www.bn.com, or www.borders.com) and search the lists of their most popular books. The popularity of these books tells you that people are interested in these topics.

*Surveys.*   An excellent way to determine what is worthwhile to your audience is to look at some of the national and regional polls concerning what issues people feel are most significant. Search for polling sites with your favorite search engine or start with one of the most widely used, the Gallup poll at www.gallup.com. Surveys of major concerns of people appear regularly in newspapers and magazines and are perhaps the most timely. Some search engines and websites list the topics that users ask for or visit most often; these, too, are useful for helping you discover what people are interested in and what they want to hear about more.

*News Items.*   Still another useful starting point is a good daily newspaper. Here you'll find the important international, domestic, financial, and social issues all conveniently covered in one place. The editorial page and letters to the editor are also useful for learning what concerns people. News magazines such as *Time* and *Newsweek* and business-oriented magazines such as *Forbes, Money, Business Week,* and *Fortune* will provide a wealth of suggestions. News shows such as *20/20* and *60 Minutes* and the numerous talk shows often discuss the very issues that concern us all. And, of course, you can surf the Net and discover a host of topics that command people's interest and attention in health, education, politics, religion, science, technology, or just about any other area in which you're interested.

**Limiting Your Topic**   Plan to cover a limited topic in depth, rather than a broad topic superficially. The limiting process is simple: Repeatedly divide the topic into its significant parts. For example, divide your general topic into its component parts, then divide one of these parts into its component parts. Continue until you arrive at a topic that seems manageable—a topic that you can reasonably cover in some depth in the allotted time.

For example, take television programs as a general topic area. Television programs, without some limitation, would take a lifetime to cover adequately. But you could divide this general subject into subtopics such as comedy, children's programs, educational programs, news, movies, soap operas, game shows, and sports. You might then take one of these topics, say comedy, and divide it into subtopics. You might consider comedy on a time basis and divide television comedy into its significant time periods: pre-1960, 1961–1989, 1990 to the present. Or you might focus on situation

"My summer vacation: How I made money in a bear market."

comedies. Here you might examine a topic such as "Women in Television Comedy," "Race Relations in Situation Comedy," or "Families in Television Comedies." At this stage the topic is beginning to look manageable. Figure 10.2 presents a tree diagram to further illustrate this process. The diagram begins with a topic even broader than television programs—mass communication. Notice how from the general "Mass Communication" you can get to the relatively specific "Same-Sex or Opposite-Sex Business Relationships in Television Soaps."

## Your Purpose

In some cases you'll select your topic and purpose almost simultaneously. At other times you'll select your topic and later formulate your purpose. In preparing public speeches, you'll need to formulate both a general and a specific purpose.

### Your General Purpose

The two major kinds of public speeches are informative and persuasive. The informative speech creates understanding; it clarifies, enlightens, corrects misunderstandings, demonstrates how something works, or explains how something is structured (see Chapter 12). The persuasive speech, on the other hand, influences attitudes or behaviors. It may strengthen existing attitudes or change the audience's beliefs. Or it may move the audience to act in a particular way (see Chapter 13).

### Your Specific Purpose

Your specific purpose identifies the information you want to communicate (in an informative speech) or the attitude or behavior you want to change (in a persuasive speech). For example, your specific purpose in an informative speech might be

- to inform my audience of three ways to save time using the Internet for research
- to inform my audience about how the new interoffice e-mail system works
- to inform my audience of the benefits of integrated work teams

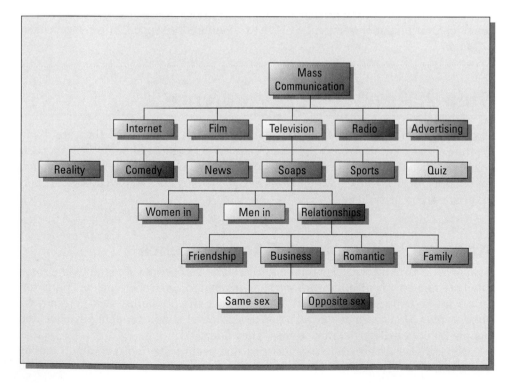

**Figure 10.2**
**Tree Diagram for Limiting Speech Topics**
Here is a tree diagram illustrating how a topic may be divided until it becomes manageable for a short speech. If you draw your tree diagram freehand, it's likely to look a lot messier than this, with cross-outs and false starts indicated. If you do the diagram on the computer—even with the Table function—then it's likely to look more like the example in this figure. Construct a different tree diagram by selecting Internet, film, radio, or advertising as a topic and subdividing it until you reach a level that would be appropriate for a 5- to 10-minute informative or persuasive speech.

# *Skill Development Experience*

## Limiting Topics

Here are a few overly general topics. Using one of the methods discussed in this chapter (or any other method you're familiar with), limit one of these topics to a subject that would be reasonable for a 5- to 10-minute speech: (1) sports, (2) male–female relationships, (3) parole, (4) surveillance on the Internet, (5) children, (6) student problems, (7) morality, (8) fitness, (9) religion, and (10) violence.

Your specific purpose in a persuasive speech might be

- to persuade my audience that all cigarette advertising should be abolished
- to persuade my audience that the college should establish courses on the prevention of AIDS and other STDs
- to persuade my audience to contribute time to working with students with disabilities

Whether you intend to inform or to persuade, limit your specific purpose so you'll be able to go into it in some depth. Your audience will benefit more from a speech that covers a small area in depth than from one that covers a broad topic superficially.

Avoid the common pitfall of trying to accomplish too much in too short a time. For example, "to inform my audience about the development of AIDS and the recent testing procedures for HIV infection" is actually two specific purposes. Select one of them and build your speech around it. Follow the same principle in developing your specific purpose for your persuasive speeches. Thus, for example, "to persuade my audience of the prevalence of AIDS in our community and to influence them to contribute money for AIDS services" contains two specific purposes. Select either one.

# Step 2: Analyze Your Audience

If you are to inform or persuade an audience, you must know who they are. What do they already know? What would they want to know more about? What are their opinions, attitudes, and beliefs? Where do they stand on the issues you wish to address? Specifically, you will want to look at the sociological and psychological characteristics of your audience.

## Analyze the Sociology of the Audience

In analyzing an audience, be careful not to assume that people covered by the same label are necessarily all alike. As soon as you begin to use a sociological characteristic with an expressed or implied "all," consider the possibility that you may be stereotyping. Don't assume that all women or all older people or all highly educated people think or believe the same things. They don't.

Nevertheless, there are characteristics that seem to be more common among one group than another, and it is these characteristics that you want to explore in analyzing your audience. Four of the most important factors are (1) cultural factors, (2) age, (3) gender, and (4) religion and religiousness.

**Cultural Factors**    Cultural factors such as nationality, ethnicity, and cultural identity are crucial in audience analysis. Largely because of different training and experiences, the interests, values, and goals of various cultural groups also will differ. Further, cultural factors will influence each of the remaining factors; for example, attitudes toward age and gender will differ greatly from one culture to another.

Perhaps the primary question to ask is "Are the cultural beliefs and values of the audience relevant to your topic and purpose?" In other words, might the cultural membership(s) of your audience members influence the way they see the topic? If so, find out what these beliefs and values are and take these into consideration as you build your speech.

**Age**    Different age groups have different attitudes and beliefs, largely because they have had different experiences in different contexts. Take these differences into consideration in preparing your speeches. For example, let's say that you're an investment counselor and you want to persuade your listeners to invest their money to increase their income. Your speech would have to be very different if you were addressing an audience of retired people (say, people in their 60s) than if the audience consisted of young executives (say, people in their 30s).

In considering the age of your audience, ask yourself if age groups differ in the goals, interests, and day-to-day concerns that may be related to your topic and purpose. Graduating from college, achieving corporate success, raising a family, and saving for retirement are concerns that differ greatly from one age group to another. Ask too if groups differ in their ability to absorb and process information. Will they differ in their responses to visual cues? With a young audience it may be best to keep up a steady, even swift pace. With older persons you may wish to maintain a more moderate pace.

**Gender**    Gender is one of the most difficult audience variables to analyze. The rapid social changes taking place today make it difficult to pin down the effects of gender. As you analyze your audience in terms of gender, ask yourself if men and women differ in the values that they consider important and that are related to your topic and purpose. Traditionally, men have been found to place greater importance on theoretical, economic, and political values. Traditionally, women have been found to place greater importance on aesthetic, social, and religious values. In framing appeals and in selecting examples, use the values your audience members consider most important.

Ask too if your topic will be seen as more interesting by one gender or the other. Will men and women have different attitudes toward the topic? Men and women do not, for example, respond in the same way to such topics as abortion, rape, and equal pay for equal work. Select your topics and supporting materials in light of the genders of your audience members. When your audience is mixed, make a special effort to give men ways to connect to "women's" topics and women ways to connect to "men's" topics.

**Religion and Religiousness**    The religion and religiousness of your listeners will often influence the audience's responses to your speech. Religion permeates all topics and all issues. On a most obvious level, we know that attitudes on such issues as birth control, abortion, and divorce are closely connected to religion. Similarly, views about premarital sex, marriage, child-rearing, money, cohabitation, responsibilities toward parents, and thousands of other issues are clearly influenced by religion. Religion is also important, however, in areas where its connection is not so obvious. For example, religion influences people's ideas concerning such topics

**▼ E-TALK**

**Attraction and Gender Differences**
It is commonly thought that in Internet personal ads, men often describe themselves as "financially secure" and women describe themselves as "physically attractive." But some research finds that the ads describing women as ambitious, financially independent, and successful got more responses than those describing them as attractive, lovely, and slim (Strassberg & Holty, 2003). How might you use this finding in selecting materials for your speech?

as obedience to authority; responsibility to government; and the usefulness of qualities such as honesty, or of feelings such as guilt or happiness.

Ask yourself if your topic or purpose might be seen as an attack on the religious beliefs of any segment of your audience. If so, then you might want to make adjustments—not necessarily to abandon your purpose, but to rephrase your arguments or incorporate different evidence. When dealing with any religious beliefs, and particularly when disagreeing with them, recognize that you're going to meet stiff opposition. Proceed slowly and inductively. That is, present your evidence and argument before expressing your disagreement.

## Analyze the Psychology of the Audience

Focus your psychological analysis of the audience on three questions: How willing is your audience? How knowledgeable is your audience? And how favorable is your audience?

**How Willing Is Your Audience?**    If you face an audience that is willing (even anxious) to hear your speech, you'll have an easy time relating your speech to them. If, however, your audience is listening unwillingly, consider the following suggestions:

- Secure their attention as early in your speech as possible—and maintain their interest throughout—with supporting materials that will speak to their motives, interests, and concerns.
- Reward the audience for their attendance and attention; compliment them for being there, and show respect for what they know and think.
- Relate your topic and supporting materials directly to your audience's needs and wants; show them how what you are saying will help them achieve what they want.
- Show the audience why they should listen to your speech by connecting your purpose to their purposes, their motives.
- Involve the audience directly in your speech by showing them that you understand their perspective, by asking rhetorical questions, and by referring to their experiences and interests.
- Focus on a few very strong issues or even on a single strong issue.

**How Knowledgeable Is Your Audience?**    Listeners differ greatly in the knowledge they have of your topic. If your audience knows little about your topic, consider these suggestions:

- Don't talk down to audience members.
- Don't confuse a lack of knowledge with a lack of intelligence.

If your audience knows a great deal about your topic, consider these suggestions:

- Let the audience know that you are aware of their knowledge and expertise and that your speech will not simply repeat what they already know but will go beyond that.
- Emphasize your credibility, especially your competence in this general subject area (see Chapter 13).

**How Favorable Is Your Audience?**    If you face an audience that has unfavorable attitudes toward your topic or your purpose, or even toward you, consider these suggestions:

- Build on commonalities; emphasize not the differences but the similarities between you and the audience.

### The Media and Disconfirmation

In analyzing your audience, be especially careful not to rely on media stereotypes. The media are responsible for propagating discriminatory stereotypes of all types; a media-literate individual needs to be able to recognize these and to see that these are not reality but extreme examples, often created for comic effect or to maintain a viewer's attention. For example, men and women on television comedy shows are often depicted in an unpleasant light. Most men on TV are portrayed as incompetent, relationally inept, insensitive clods who are absorbed with sports, are ignorant of the important things in life, and will never learn how to relate to women. And women are portrayed as complaining, never satisfied, and abnormally thin. Old folks are portrayed as inept, complaining, loud, and offensive. And of course old people shown on TV have lost and will never again find romance; for older people the kisses, for example, have to be nonsexual.

Racism is rampant in the media's portrayal of Muslims; almost all the Muslims on television are negatively constructed and are much more likely to be terrorists than they are to be teachers or lawyers or store owners or carpenters. Also, consider the negative stereotypes of gay men and lesbians; they're extremes that you rarely see in real life.

*Increasing Media Literacy.* *No specific examples were given here to support the accusation of media stereotypes. Examine the current lineup of television situation comedies and dramas, and try to identify examples that support or contradict the idea that media engage in stereotyping.*

*Whoever controls the media—the images—controls the cultures.*
—ALLEN GINSBERG

- Build your speech from areas of agreement, through areas of slight disagreement, up to the major differences.
- Strive for small gains.
- Ask for a fair hearing.

Here, for example, in a speech about research on the biological differences between men and women, a topic that many listeners might have preconceived ideas about, Stephanie Cagniart, a student at the University of Texas at Austin, simply explained that despite much opposition this topic was too important to ignore:

> But because the May 2005 *Scientific American* notes that this research may hold the key to gender equality, as well as lead to far more effective treatments for mental disorders and transform our educational system, we can't ignore this debate.

## Analysis and Adaptation during the Speech

In your classroom speeches, you'll face a known audience, an audience you've already analyzed and for which you've made appropriate adaptations. At other times, however, you may face an audience that you've not been able to analyze beforehand or that differs greatly from what you expected. In these cases you'll have to analyze and adapt as you speak. Here are a few suggestions.

**Focus on Listeners as Message Senders**   As you're speaking, look at your listeners. Remember that just as you're sending messages to your audience, they're also sending messages to you. Pay attention to these messages, and make necessary adjustments on the basis of what they tell you.

You can make a wide variety of adjustments to each type of audience response. For example, if your audience shows signs of boredom, increase your volume, move closer to them, or tell them that what you're going to say will be of value to them. If your audience shows signs of disagreement or hostility, stress a similarity you have with them. If your audience looks puzzled or confused, pause a moment and rephrase your ideas, provide necessary definitions, or insert an internal summary. If your audience seems impatient, say, for example, "my last argument" instead of your originally planned "my third argument."

**Ask "What If" Questions**   The more preparation you put into your speech, the better prepared you'll be to make on-the-spot adjustments and adaptations. For example, let's say you have been told that you're to explain the opportunities available to the nontraditional student at your college. You've been told that your audience will consist mainly of working women in their 30s and 40s who are just beginning college. As you prepare your speech with this audience in mind, ask yourself "what if" questions. Some examples:

- What if the audience has a large number of men?
- What if the audience consists of women much older than 40?
- What if the audience members come with their spouses or their children?

Keeping such questions in mind will force you to consider alternatives as you prepare your speech. This way, you'll have adaptations readily available if you face a new or different audience.

**Address Audience Responses Directly**   Another way of dealing with audience responses is to confront them directly. To those who are giving disagreement feedback, for example, you might say:

> You may disagree with this position, but all I ask is that you hear me out and see if this new way of doing things will not simplify your accounting procedures.

Or, to those who seem puzzled, you might say:

> I know this plan may seem confusing, but bear with me; it will become clear in a moment.

Or, to those who seem impatient, you might respond:

> I know this has been a long day, but give me just a few more minutes and you'll be able to save hours recording your accounts.

> By responding to your listeners' reactions and feedback, you acknowledge your audience's needs. You let them know that you hear them, that you're with them, and that you're responding to their very real needs.

# Step 3: Research Your Topic

*"The ultimate goal of all research is not objectivity, but truth."*
—HELENE DEUTSCH

Throughout the process of preparing your public speeches, you'll conduct research to find examples, illustrations, and definitions to help you inform your listeners; testimony, statistics, and arguments to support your major ideas; personal anecdotes, quotations, and stories to help you bring your topics to life.

## General Research Principles

Here are a few principles to help you research your speeches more effectively and more efficiently.

■   Begin your search by examining what you already know. Write down what you know, for example, about books, articles, or websites that you're familiar with on the topic or people who might know something about the topic.

- Continue your search by getting an authoritative but general overview of the topic. An encyclopedia article, book chapter, or magazine article will serve this purpose well. This general overview will help you see the topic as a whole and how its various parts fit together.

- Follow up the general overview with increasingly more detailed and specialized sources. Fortunately, many of the general articles contain references or links to direct this next stage of your search for more specific information.

## Libraries

Libraries are the major storehouses of information and have added to their concentration on print sources a major focus on computerized databases. Often you'll go to a library to access other libraries or databases maintained by local and national governments, cultural institutions, and various corporations and organizations. Of course, you'll also go to a brick-and-mortar library to access materials that are not on the Net or that you want in print. Because each library functions somewhat differently, your best bet in learning about a specific library, such as your own college's, is to talk with your librarian about what the library has available and how materials are most easily accessed. Here are a few online libraries that you'll find especially helpful.

- Quick Study, the University of Minnesota's Library Research Guide (http://tutorial.lib.umn.edu), will help you learn how to find the materials you need and will answer lots of questions you probably have about research.

- To locate a list of library catalogs to help you find the location of the material you need, try www.lights.com/webcats. By clicking on "library-type index," you'll get a list of categories of libraries; for example, government or medical or religious.

- The largest library in the United States is the Library of Congress, which houses millions of books, maps, multimedia resources, and manuscripts. Time spent at this library (begin with www.loc.gov) will be well invested. The home page will guide you to a wealth of information.

- Maintained by the National Archives and Records Administration, the presidential libraries may be accessed at www.nara.gov/nara/present/address.html.

- The Virtual Library is a collection of links to 14 subject areas; for example, agriculture, business and economics, computing, communication and media, and education. Visit this at www.vlib.org.

- If you're not satisfied with your own college library, visit the online catalogs of the libraries of some of the large universities, such as the University of Pennsylvania (www.library.upenn.edu/resources/reference/reference.html) or the University of Illinois (http://gateway.library.uiuc.edu).

- The Internet Public Library (www.ipl.org) is actually not a library; it's a collection of links to a wide variety of materials. But it will function much like the reference desk at any of the world's best libraries.

## News Sources

Often you'll want to read reports on natural disasters, political speeches, congressional actions, obituaries, financial news, international developments, United Nations actions, or any of a host of other topics. Or you may wish to locate the time of a particular event and learn something about what else was going on in the world at that particular time. For this type of information, you may want to consult a reliable newspaper. Especially relevant are newspaper indexes, newspaper databases, newspaper and magazine websites, news wire services, and news networks on line.

- *Newspaper indexes.* One way to start a newspaper search is to consult one of the newspaper indexes. For example, the *National Newspaper Index* covers 27 newspapers, including the *Christian Science Monitor*, the *Wall Street Journal*, the *Los Angeles Times*, and the *Washington Post*. Each of these newspapers also has its own index. The *New York Times* is available through Research Navigator (www.ablongman.com/researchnavigator).

- *Electronic newspaper databases.* Many newspapers can be accessed online or through CD-ROM databases to which your college library probably subscribes. The *New York Times* database, for example, contains complete editorial content of the paper, one of the world's most comprehensive newspapers. All aspects of news, sports, editorials, columns, obituaries, New York and regional news, and the *New York Times Book Review* and *Magazine* are included. The *New York Times* and the *Financial Times* are both available through Research Navigator.

- *Newspaper and newsmagazine websites.* Most newspapers now maintain their own websites, from which you can access current and past issues. Here are a few to get you started: www.latimes.com/ (*Los Angeles Times*), www.usatoday.com/ (*USA Today*), http://journal.link.wsj.com/ (*Wall Street Journal*), and www.nytimes.com (the *New York Times*). The *Washington Post* (www.washingtonpost.com) maintains an especially extensive website; two particularly useful websites are www.newslink.org/menu.html, which provides access to a variety of online newspapers and magazines, and Hotlinks to Newspapers Online, which provides links to more than 1,000 daily, 400 weekly, and 100 international newspapers (www.newspaperlinks.com).

- *News wire services.* Three wire services should prove helpful. The Associated Press can be accessed at www1.trib.com/NEWS/Apwire.html, Reuters at www.reuters.com/, and PR Newswire at www.prnewswire.com/. The advantage of getting your information from a news wire service is that it's more complete than you'd find in a newspaper, which has to cut copy to fit space requirements—and which, in some cases, may put a politically or socially motivated spin on the news.

- *News networks online.* All of the television news stations maintain extremely useful websites. Here are some of the most useful: Access CNN at www.cnn.com/, ESPN at espn.sportszone.com/, ABC News at www.abcnews.com/newsflash, CBS News at www.cbs.com/news/, and MSNBC News at www.msnbc.com/news.

## Biographical Material

*"There is no such thing as an uninteresting subject; there are only uninteresting people."*
—G. K. Chesterton

As a speaker you'll often need information about particular individuals. For example, you may want to look up authors of books or articles to find out something about their education, their training, or their other writings. Or you may want to find out if there have been critical evaluations of their work in, say, book reviews or articles about them or their writings. Knowing something about your sources helps you to evaluate their competence, present their credibility to the audience, and answer audience questions about them.

The *Biography and Genealogy Master Index*—in print, on CD-ROM, or online—indexes several hundred biographical indexes. This index will send you to numerous specialized works, such as *The Dictionary of American Biography* (DAB), which contains articles on famous deceased Americans from all areas of accomplishment; *Current Biography*, which is the best single source for living individuals and includes both favorable and unfavorable comments on its subjects; and *Who's Who in America*, which also covers living individuals.

In addition, there are a host of other, more specialized works whose titles indicate their scope: *The Dictionary of Canadian Biography, Directory of American Scholars, International Who's Who, Who Was Who in America, American Men and Women of Science, Notable American Women, Who's Who in the Arab World, Who's Who in Finance and Industry, Who's Who in American Politics, Who's Who Among Black Americans, Who's Who of American Women, Who's Who Among Hispanic Americans*, and the *Biographical Directory of the American Congress*.

Not surprisingly, there are lots of Internet sources for biographical information. For example, http://mgm.mit.edu:8080/pevzner/Nobel.html provides links to biographical information on all Nobel Prize winners. If you want information on members of the House of Representatives, try www.house.gov. And www.biography.com/ will provide you with brief biographies of some 25,000 famous people, living and dead. Other excellent sources include Lives, the Biography Resource at http://amillionlives.com, and the Biographical Dictionary at http://s9.com/biography, which covers more than 28,000 men and women.

**WHAT DO YOU SAY?**
**Asking A Favor**
You're preparing a speech on the architectural ideas for rebuilding Ground Zero, and you want to ask some of the famous architects a few questions so you can integrate their most recent thoughts (and interject a more personalized note) into your speech. *What do you say? Through what channel?*

## Academic Research Articles

Academic research forms the core of what we know about people and the world; it is the most valid and the most reliable you're likely to find. Research articles report on studies conducted by academicians around the world. For the most part, these articles are conducted by unbiased researchers using the best research methods available. Further, before publication this research is subjected to careful critical review by experts in the specific field of the research.

Each college library subscribes to a somewhat different package of CD-ROM and online research databases. These databases contain information on the nature and scope of the database and user-friendly directions for searching, displaying, printing, and saving the retrieved information to disk.

## Book Sources

Each library catalogs its books, journals, and government documents in a slightly different way, depending on its size and the needs of its users. All, however, make use of some form of computerized catalog. These are uniformly easy and efficient to use. The catalog is the best place to find out what books are in your college library or in libraries whose books you can secure on interlibrary loan, for example.

Browsing through any large brick-and-mortar bookstore is almost sure to give you insights into your topic. If you're talking about something that people are interested in today, there's likely to be a book dealing with it on the bookshelf of most bookstores. Visit too some of the online bookstores, such as Amazon (www.amazon.com), Barnes & Noble (www.bn.com), or Borders (www.borders.com). In addition, other useful sites include http://aaup.pupress.princeton.edu/ (Association of American University Presses), www.cs.cmu.edu/~spok/most-banned.html (contains links to texts of books that have been banned in the United States and elsewhere), and www.booksite.com/ (contains search tools for locating more than 2 million books). Some online bookstores now enable you to search some of the books for specific topics and to read a paragraph or so on each topic.

## Using and Evaluating Web Materials

Although you'll no doubt use a variety of research sources—both print and electronic—it's a lot easier to do your research by computer. Perhaps the greatest advantage is that in computer research you browse through a larger number of sources in less time and with greater accuracy and thoroughness than you could do manually. And you can usually do this research at your own convenience and from your own home.

In using computerized sources—on CD-ROMs and, most often, on the Web—you've already noticed that the amount of information available often makes finding specific information difficult. Two general guides will help you at the start. First, learn the databases that contain the information you want to find. A *database* is simply organized information contained in one place that can be accessed with relative ease. A dictionary, an encyclopedia, an index to magazines, and a collection of abstracts from hundreds of journals are all examples of databases. Databases may be in print (for example, *Psychological Abstracts*) or computerized (for example, the communication database in Research Navigator). Because each library subscribes to a different set of databases, find out which databases are available at your college library as well as at other libraries to which you have access. Review the available databases, single out those that will be especially helpful to you, and learn as much as you can about them. For example, if you're researching a medical topic, then the *Medline* database will prove especially useful. *Medline* can be searched for free at the National Library of Medicine's website, www.nlm.nih.gov. If you're looking for sociological statistics, then the U.S. census figures will be essential; you'll want to become familiar with the Census Bureau's website, www.census.gov).

Second, learn about the search engines and directories that will help you find the information you need and learn how to use them efficiently. A *search engine* is a program that searches a database or index of Internet sites for the specific words you submit. These search engines are easily accessed through your Internet browser. Both Netscape and Internet Explorer have search functions as a part of their own home pages; they also provide convenient links to the most popular search engines and directories.

A *directory* is a list of subjects or categories of Web links. You select the category you're most interested in, and then a subcategory of that, and then a subcategory of that until you reach your specific topic. A directory doesn't cover everything; rather, the documents that it groups under its various categories are selected by the directory's staff members from those they feel especially worthwhile. Many search engines also provide directories, so you can use the method you prefer.

Some search engines are *metasearch engines*; these search the databases of a variety of search engines at the same time. These programs are especially useful if you want a broad search and you have the time to sift through lots of websites. Some of the more popular include Ask Jeeves at www.ask.com, Google at www.google.com, Dog Pile at www.dogpile.com, and Vivisimo at www.vivisimo.com. Other useful search engines (some of which also contain directories) include Yahoo! (www.yahoo.com), Alta Vista (http://altavista.digital.com), and go (www.go.com).

In using search engines (and in searching many CD-ROM databases), it's often helpful to limit your search with "operators"—words and symbols that define relationships among the terms for which you're searching. Perhaps the most common are AND, OR, and NOT. Searching for *drugs AND violence* will limit your search to only those documents that contain both words—in any order. Searching for *drugs OR violence* will expand your search to all documents containing either word, and searching for *drugs and violence* will yield only documents containing that exact phrase. Searching for *violence AND schools NOT elementary* will yield documents containing both *violence* and *schools* except those that contain the word *elementary*. Each search engine uses a somewhat different system for limiting searches, so you'll have to learn the specific system used by your favorite search engines.

You may want to try your hand using search engines and these "Boolean operators" (for example, AND, OR, +, −) and see how efficiently you can locate such information as the following:

- the literacy rate for Cuba
- the major religions of Nigeria
- the principles and beliefs of Islam
- the speeches of the presidents of the United States

- the rules for playing golf
- the author of the quotation, "All the great speakers were bad speakers at first."
- what is the prime rate and who sets it
- the use and origin of the word *spam*
- the members of the European Union
- the academic vita of a professor at your school

One caution on online research: Keep in mind that anyone can "publish" on the Internet. An article on the Internet can be written by world-renowned scientists or by elementary school students; by fair and objective reporters or by those who would spin the issues to serve their own political, religious, or social purposes. And it's not always easy to tell which is which. Find out what the author's qualifications are. One useful technique is to pursue the Internet links, often included in the document, to the sources from which the author of an article derived, say, his or her statistics or predictions or arguments. Recognize also, however, that much information on the Internet is identical to the information you regularly read in print. Encyclopedias, newspapers and newsmagazines, and professional journals that appear on the Internet are identical to the print copies, so there's no need to draw distinctions between print and Internet information when dealing with sites such as these. Additional suggestions for using Web sources may be found at www.slu.edu/departments/english/research and http://nuevaschool.org/~debbie/library/research.

## Integrating Research into Your Speech

By integrating and acknowledging your sources of information in your speech, you'll give fair credit to those whose ideas and statements you're using; at the same time you'll help establish your own reputation as a responsible researcher.

Be certain to mention the sources in your speech by citing at least the author and, if helpful, the publication and the date. Check out some of the speeches reprinted in this book and note especially how the speakers integrated their sources in the speech. In your written outline, you would then give the complete bibliographical reference.

Here is an example of how you might cite your source:

My discussion of the causes of anorexic nervosa is based on the work of Dr. Peter Rowan of the Priory Hospital in London. In an article titled "Introducing Anorexia Nervosa," which I last accessed on October 5, 2006, Rowan notes that "this is a disorder of many causes that come together." It's these causes that I want to cover in this talk.

The speaker would then, in the reference list following the speech, identify the author, title of the article, URL address, and the speaker's date of visit. It would look like this:

Rowan, P. Introducing Anorexia nervosa. www.priory-hospital.co.uk.htm/anorexia.htm (Accessed October 5, 2006).

Although it's possible to overdo the oral citation—giving more information than the listeners really need—it is more risky to leave out potentially useful information. Because your speeches in this course are learning experiences, it will be better to err on the side of being more rather than less complete.

Avoid useless expressions such as "I have a quote here" or "I want to quote an example." Let the audience know that you're quoting by pausing before the quote, taking a step forward, or referring to your notes to read the extended quotation. If you want to state more directly that this is a quotation, you might do it this way:

Tony Alessandra, in his book *Charisma*, defines this essential quality most clearly. "Charisma," says Alessandra, "is the ability to influence others positively by connecting with them physically, emotionally, and intellectually."

> **WHAT DO YOU SAY?**
> **Correcting Errors**
> In your speech you say that more than 70 percent of the students at your school favor banning alcohol on campus. Toward the end of the speech, you realize that you mixed up the figures; only 30 percent actually favor banning alcohol. During the question-and-answer period no one asks about the figures. *What do you say?*

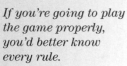

### Plagiarism

Because plagiarism is such an important issue in public speaking, this ethics box is a bit longer than others. It will cover the nature of plagiarism, the reasons plagiarism is unacceptable, and what you can do to avoid plagiarism.

#### What Is Plagiarism?

**Plagiarism** is the process of passing off the work (ideas, words, illustrations) of others as your own. Understand that plagiarism is not the act of using another's ideas—we all do that. Rather, it is using another's ideas without acknowledging that they are the ideas of this other person; it is presenting the ideas as if they were yours. Plagiarism exists on a continuum, ranging from appropriating an entire term paper or speech written by someone else to using a quotation or research finding without citing the author.

Plagiarism also includes situations in which you get help from a friend without acknowledging this assistance. In some cultures—especially collectivist cultures (cultures that emphasize the group and mutual cooperation) such as those of Korea, Japan, and China—teamwork is strongly encouraged. Students are encouraged to help other students with their work. But in the United States and in many individualist cultures (cultures that emphasize individuality and competitiveness), teamwork without acknowledgment is considered plagiarism.

In U.S. institutions of higher education, plagiarism is a serious violation of the rules of academic honesty and is subject to serious penalties, sometimes even expulsion. Further, as with all crimes, ignorance of the law is not an acceptable defense against charges of plagiarism. This last point is especially important, because people often commit plagiarism through a lack of information as to what does and what does not constitute plagiarism.

#### Why Plagiarism Is Unacceptable

Here are just a few reasons why plagiarism is wrong.

- Plagiarism is a violation of another's intellectual property rights. Much as it would be wrong to take another person's watch without permission, it is wrong to take another person's ideas without giving due credit.
- You're in college to develop your own ideas and ways of expressing them; plagiarism defeats this fundamental purpose.
- Evaluations (everything from grades in school to promotions in the workplace) assume that what you present as your work is in fact your work.

#### Avoiding Plagiarism

Let's start with the easy part. In a speech or essay, you do not have to—and should not—cite sources for common knowledge, which is information that is readily available in numerous sources and not likely to be disputed. For example, the population of Thailand, the amendments to the U.S. Constitution, the actions of the United Nations, or the way the heart pumps blood are all common knowledge, and you should not cite the almanac or the political science text from which you got such information. On the other hand, if you were talking about the attitudes of people from Thailand or the reasons the Constitutional amendments were adopted, then you would need to cite your sources, because this information is not common knowledge and may well be disputed.

For information that is not common knowledge, you need to acknowledge your source. Here are a few simple rules that will help you avoid even the suggestion of plagiarism (for more extended discussion see Stern, 2007):

1. *Acknowledge the source of any ideas you present that are not your own.* If you learned of an idea in your history course, then cite the history instructor or history textbook. If you read an idea in an article, then cite the article.
2. *Acknowledge the words of another.* It's obvious when you're quoting another person exactly; then of course, you need to cite the person you're quoting. You should also cite the person even when you paraphrase their words, because you are still using the other person's ideas. When paraphrases need to be credited may not always be clear, so some of the plagiarism

websites established by different universities include exercises and extended examples; see, for example, Indiana University's at www.indiana.edu/~uts/wts/plagiarism.html or Purdue University's at http://owl.english.purdue.edu/handouts/print/reseach/r-plagiar.html. The same is true when using the organizational structure of another person; just say, for example: "I'm following the line of reasoning proposed by James McCroskey in his discussion of apprehension."

3. *Acknowledge help from others.* If your roommate gave you examples or ideas, or helped you style your speech, acknowledge the help. Notice that in some of the award-winning speeches that are reprinted as models in this book, the speech coaches are mentioned.

*What would you do?* *You're really pressed to come up with a persuasive speech on a contemporary social issue, and you just don't have the time to research it. Fortunately, a friend at another school wrote a term paper for her sociology course and got an A on it. You could easily adapt it to your required public speaking assignment. You figure that it's similar to using research you'd find in newspapers and magazines; and besides, you're writing the outline and delivering the speech. Would you use your friend's paper? If so, how would you acknowledge your sources?*

## Citing Research Sources

In citing references, first find out what style manual is used in your class or at your school. Generally, it will be one or another of the style manuals developed by the American Psychological Association (APA), the Modern Language Association (MLA), or the University of Chicago (in their *Chicago Manual of Style*). Different colleges and different departments within a given college often rely on different formats for citing research, which, quite frankly, makes a tedious process even worse. Fortunately, there are a variety of websites that provide exactly the information you'll need to cite any reference you might have. For example, Purdue University offers an excellent site that covers APA and MLA style formats and provides examples for citing books, articles, newspaper articles, websites, e-mail, online posting, electronic databases, and more (http://owl.english.purdue.edu/handouts/research). This site also provides extremely useful advice for searching the Web and evaluating website information. Another excellent website is Capital Community College's Guide for Writing Research Papers (http://webster.commnet.edu). Like the Purdue website, this one also provides useful guides to research and to writing research papers. Guidelines for using the *Chicago Manual of Style* may be found at Ohio State's website (www.lib.ohio-state.edu/). This site provides guidance for citing all types of print and electronic sources. Another valuable source is the Columbia Guide to Online Style (www.columbia.edu/cu/cup/cgos/idx_basic.html). This site provides detailed instructions and examples for citing MOOs, MUDs, and IRCs, Telnte sites, e-mail, listservs, and newsgroup communications, and even software programs and video games. Still another helpful guide is the International Federation of Library Associations and Institutions website (www.ifla.org/I/training/citation/citing.html), which provides guidelines for citing electronic sources and links to various other websites concerned with citing research. After reviewing these websites, print out the one or two that you find most useful so that you can have them in easy reach.

## Step 4: Formulate Your Thesis and Identify Your Main Points

In this step, you choose your thesis and then use it to generate your major points or ideas.

# Choose Your Thesis

The **thesis** is the main idea that you want to convey to the audience. The thesis of Lincoln's Second Inaugural Address was that northerners and southerners should work together for the good of the entire country. The thesis of many science fiction movies is that working together, people, often from very different cultures and different areas of life, can repel any force and achieve just about anything.

Let's say, for example, you're planning to deliver a persuasive speech in favor of the election of Senator Winters. Your thesis statement might be "Winters is the best candidate." This is what you want your audience to believe, what you want your audience to remember even if they forget everything else. In an informative speech, on the other hand, the thesis statement focuses on what you want your audience to learn. For example, for a speech on jealousy, a suitable thesis might be "Two main theories of jealousy exist."

The thesis and the purpose of a speech are similar in that they both guide you in selecting and organizing your materials. In some ways, however, they are different:

- Thesis and purpose differ in their form of expression. The thesis is phrased as a complete declarative sentence. The purpose is phrased as an infinitive phrase ("to inform . . . ," "to persuade . . .").
- The thesis focuses on the message; the purpose focuses on the audience. The thesis succinctly identifies the central idea of your speech. The purpose identifies the change you hope to bring about in your audience—for example, to impart information, to change attitudes, to influence people to act in a certain way.

Especially in the early stages of mastering public speaking, formulate both your thesis statement and your purpose. From there, you will be able to construct a more coherent and more understandable speech. Limit your thesis statement to one central idea. A statement such as "We should support Winters and the entire Democratic party" contains not one but two basic ideas.

As we have discussed, in low-context cultures (the United States, Germany, and Sweden, for example) most audiences wish to hear a direct statement of the speaker's position and an explicit statement of what he or she wants the audience to do. In contrast, high-context cultures of purpose (Japan, China, and Arab countries, for example) prefer a less explicit statement and prefer to be led indirectly to the speaker's conclusion.

# Generate Your Main Points

Use your thesis statement to generate your main points. Once you phrase the thesis statement, the main divisions of your speech will suggest themselves. Here, for example, is how student speaker Stephanie Cagniart expressed her thesis along with a clear orientation of the main points she would cover in her speech:

> The commerce clause is being used by the federal government to dictate social issues—from gun control to same-sex marriage—in a way that threatens our individual liberties and undermines states' rights. So let's first, examine why the commerce clause has broadened; second, explore this abuse's dangers; and finally, investigate how we can scale back what the October 20, 2005, *Wanderer Magazine* calls "the clause that ate the Constitution."

To take another example, let's say you are giving a speech on the values of a college education to a group of people in their 30s and 40s who are considering returning to college. Your thesis is *"A college education is valuable."* You then ask yourself, "Why is it valuable?" From these answers you generate your major propositions. You might first brainstorm the question and identify as many answers as you can. Your list might look something like this:

## WHAT DO YOU SAY?
**Unpopular Thesis**
You've decided to tackle the hypocrisy you see in classmates who publicly support the values of racial equality but privately express racist attitudes. You're afraid, however, that your audience will walk out on you as soon as you state your thesis. *What do you say?*

A college education is valuable because:

1. It helps you get a job.
2. It increases your potential to earn a good salary.
3. It gives you greater job mobility.
4. It helps you secure more creative work.
5. It helps you appreciate the arts more fully.
6. It helps you understand an increasingly complex world.
7. It helps you understand different cultures.
8. It helps you avoid taking a regular job for a few years.
9. It helps you meet lots of people and make friends.
10. It helps you increase personal effectiveness.

For purposes of illustration, let's stop at this point. You have 10 possible main points—too many to cover in a short speech. Further, not all are equally valuable or relevant to your audience. Look over the list to make it shorter and more relevant. Here are some suggestions:

## Eliminate Points That Seem Least Important

You might want to eliminate, say, number 8—because it's inconsistent with the positive values of college, the thesis of your speech. Further, your audience is unlikely to be able to stop working to go to college full time.

## Combine Points That Have a Common Focus

Notice, for example, that the first four points center on jobs. You might, therefore, consider grouping them under a general heading:

A college education will help you secure a better job.

This might be one of your major propositions, which you can develop by defining what you mean by "a better job." You might also use some of the ideas you generated in your brainstorming session. This main point and its elaboration might look like this:

    I. A college education will help you secure a better job.

        A. College graduates earn higher salaries.

        B. College graduates enter more creative jobs.

        C. College graduates have greater job mobility.

Note that A, B, and C are all aspects or subdivisions of "a better job."

## Select Points That Are Most Relevant

Ask yourself what will interest your audience most. On this basis, you might drop number 5 on the assumption that your audience will be more interested in more practical outcomes. You might eliminate number 9 on the assumption that your audience is not looking to college to help them make friends; they probably have lots of friends and families that occupy most of their time. Further, you might conclude that this audience cares a lot about personal effectiveness, so you might make this your second major proposition:

    II. A college education will help you increase your personal effectiveness.

Much as you developed the subordinate points in your first proposition by defining what you meant by "a good job," you would define what you mean by "personal effectiveness":

"Sorry, Pop, but your message is no longer relevant to the younger audience."

II. A college education will help you increase your personal effectiveness.

    A. A college education will help you increase your ability to communicate.

    B. A college education will help you acquire learning skills.

    C. A college education will help you acquire coping skills.

You then follow the same procedure used to generate these subordinate points (A, B, and C) to develop the subheadings. For example, you might divide A into two major subheads:

    A. A college education will improve your ability to communicate.

        1. A college education teaches writing skills.

        2. A college education teaches speech skills.

**Use Two, Three, or Four Main Points**    Remember, your aim is not to cover every aspect of a topic but to emphasize selected parts. Further, you want to have enough time to amplify and support the points you present. With too many propositions, this becomes impossible. Also, you don't want to present too much information, because your audience will simply not be able to remember it.

**Phrase Propositions in Parallel Style**    To make it easier for listeners to follow and remember your speech, use similar structures in wording your major propositions.

NOT THIS:

Mass Media Functions

   I. The media entertain.

  II. The media function to inform their audiences.

 III. Creating ties of union is a major media function.

 IV. The conferral of status is a function of all media.

THIS:

Mass Media Functions

   I. The media entertain.

  II. The media inform.

 III. The media create ties of union.

 IV. The media confer status.

**Develop Main Points Separately and Distinctly**    Don't overlap your main points.

NOT THIS:

   I. Color and style are important in clothing selection.

THIS:

   I. Color is important in clothing selection.

  II. Style is important in clothing selection.

## Step 5: Support Your Main Points

Now that you've researched your topic and identified your thesis and your main points, you need to support each point. In the informative speech, your support primarily amplifies the concepts you discuss. Specifically, you might use:

1. *Examples*, *illustrations*, and the *testimony* of various authorities to breathe life into abstract or vague concepts
2. *Definitions* to clarify complex terms and to provide different ways of looking at some process or event
3. *Statistics* (summary figures) to explain trends in a wide variety of topics
4. *Presentation aids*—charts, maps, objects, slides, films, tapes, CDs, and so on—to help clarify vague concepts

These forms of amplification are covered in detail in Chapter 12.

In a persuasive speech, your support is proof—material that offers evidence, argument, and motivational appeal and that establishes your credibility and reputation. To persuade your audience to adopt the new production guidelines, for example, you might claim that the guidelines will save time. You must then substantiate your claim by giving proof. You might, for example, show that the new system saves an average of 30 minutes per job, that new employees take less time to learn the new system, and that the new system results in fewer errors and thereby less lost time.

You can persuade your audience with several types of support:

1. *Logical support* includes reasoning from specific instances and from general principles, from causes and effects, and from signs.
2. *Motivational support* includes appeals to the audience's emotions and to their desires for status, financial gain, or increased self-esteem: "No one wants to be at the low end of the hierarchy. Our new Management Seminar will help you climb that corporate ladder faster and easier than you ever thought possible."
3. *Credibility appeals* involve establishing your own personal reputation or credibility, especially your competence, high moral character, and charisma.

These forms of support are covered in depth in Chapter 13.

# Step 6: Organize Your Information

Organize your materials to help the audience understand and remember what you say. We'll look at six patterns you might use to organize the body of a speech: time, spatial, topical, problem–solution, cause–effect, and the motivated sequence. Additional help on organization may be found on the website for this text (www.mycommunicationlab.com).

## Time Pattern

Organizing major issues on the basis of some time, or temporal, relationship is popular for informative speeches. Generally, when you use a time-related pattern, you organize the speech into two, three, or four major parts. You might begin with the past and work up to the present or future, or begin with the present or future and work back to the past. For example, you might organize a speech on children's development of speech and language according to a temporal pattern.

*General Purpose: To inform*

*Specific Purpose: To inform my audience of the four stages in the child's acquisition of language.*

*Thesis: The child goes through four stages in learning language.*

    I. Babbling occurs first.

    II. Lallation occurs second.

▼ E-TALK

**Web Page Organization**
How would you describe the organization of a typical web page? In what ways does its organization differ from that of a public speech? Why do you suppose there are such differences?

III. Echolalia occurs third.

IV. Communication occurs fourth.

Most historical topics lend themselves to organization by a time pattern. Topics such as events leading to the Civil War, how to plant a vegetable garden, and the history of the Internet are all candidates for temporal patterning.

## Spatial Pattern

Similar to temporal patterning is patterning the main points of a speech on the basis of space. Both temporal and spatial patterns are especially appropriate for informative speeches. Discussions of most physical objects fit well into spatial patterns. For example, a presentation on the structure of a hospital, a school, a skyscraper, or even a dinosaur might lend itself to this pattern. Here, a speech on places to visit in Central America uses a spatial pattern.

*General Purpose: To inform*

*Specific Purpose: To inform my audience of a great way to visit Central America.*

*Thesis: You can have a great visit to Central America by visiting four countries.*

    I. First, visit Guatemala.

    II. Second, visit Honduras.

    III. Third, visit Nicaragua.

    IV. Fourth, visit Costa Rica.

## Topical Pattern

The topical pattern divides the speech topic into subtopics or component parts. This pattern is an obvious choice for organizing a speech on a topic such as, say, the branches of government.

*General Purpose: To inform*

*Specific Purpose: To inform my audience of the ways the three branches of government work.*

*Thesis: Three branches govern the United States.*

    I. The legislative branch is controlled by Congress.

    II. The executive branch is controlled by the President.

    III. The judicial branch is controlled by the courts.

Problems facing the college graduate, great works of literature, and the world's major religions are other examples of speech topics that lend themselves to a topical organizational pattern.

## Problem–Solution Pattern

As its name indicates, the problem–solution pattern divides the main ideas into two main parts: problems and solutions. Let's say you're trying to persuade an audience that home health aides should be given higher salaries and increased benefits. In the first part of the speech, you might discuss some of the problems confronting home health aides: Industry lures away the most qualified graduates of the leading universities, many health aides leave the field after two or three years, and the occupation suffers from a low status in many undergraduates' minds. In the second part, you would consider the possible solutions to these problems: making health aides' salaries competitive with those in private industry, making benefits as attractive as those offered by industry, and raising the status of the health aide profession.

The speech, in outline form, would look like this:

*General Purpose: To persuade*

*Specific Purpose: To persuade my audience of the solutions to the three main problems of the home health care industry.*

*Thesis: The home health care industry can be improved with three changes.*

I. Three major problems confront home health care.
   A. Industry lures away the most qualified graduates.
   B. Numerous excellent health aides leave the field after a few years.
   C. Home health care is currently a low-status occupation.
II. Three major solutions to these problems exist.
   A. Increase salaries for home health aides.
   B. Make benefits for health aides more attractive.
   C. Raise the status of the home health care profession.

## Cause–Effect/Effect–Cause Pattern

Especially appropriate for persuasive speeches and similar to the problem–solution pattern of organization is the cause–effect or effect–cause pattern. Using this pattern, you divide the speech into two major sections—causes and effects. For example, a speech on the reasons for highway accidents might fit into a cause–effect pattern. In such a speech you might first consider the causes of highway accidents—unlicensed drivers, alcohol and drugs, the roles of anger and ill temper—and then some of the effects, such as accidents, deaths, and property damage. Similarly, illnesses or low self-esteem can be explained with a cause–effect pattern. An outline of the causes and effects of low self-esteem might look something like this:

*General Purpose: To persuade*

*Specific Purpose: To persuade my audience of the causes and effects of low self-esteem.*

*Thesis: Low self-esteem is caused by a history of criticism and unrealistic goals, which lead to depression and an unwillingness to socialize.*

I. Low self-esteem often has two main causes.
   A. A history of criticism can contribute to low self-esteem.
   B. Unrealistic goals can contribute to low self-esteem.
II. Low self-esteem often has two main effects.
   A. Depression is one frequent effect.
   B. An unwillingness to socialize with others is another frequent effect.

## The Motivated Sequence

The **motivated sequence** is a pattern in which you arrange information to motivate your audience to respond positively to your purpose (McKerrow, Gronbeck, Ehninger, & Monroe, 2000). This pattern is useful for organizing both informative and persuasive speeches. It consists of five steps: (1) attention, (2) need, (3) satisfaction, (4) visualization, and (5) action. An extended discussion of the motivated sequence may be found at www.ablongman.com/devito.

**1. Attention**    Make the audience give you their undivided attention. If you execute this step effectively, your audience should be anxious to hear what you have to say. You can gain audience attention by, for example, asking a rhetorical question, referring to specific audience members, or using a dramatic or humorous story. These and other ways of gaining attention are discussed more fully in Chapter 13.

**2. Need**    Now you prove that a need exists. The audience should feel that they need to learn or do something. You can establish need by:

- stating the need or problem as it exists or will exist
- illustrating the need with specific examples, illustrations, statistics, testimony, and other forms of support
- pointing to how this need affects your specific listeners—for example, their financial status, career goals, or individual happiness

For example, in a speech to convince people in their 60s and 70s to purchase home computers, you might say in this step, "A survey of persons in their 60s and 70s reported that one of their greatest needs was easy and rapid access to medical information. If you are like those in this survey, then the home computer may be your answer."

**3. Satisfaction**    In the satisfaction step, you present the "solution" that satisfies the need you demonstrated in step 2. This step should convince the audience that what you are informing them about or persuading them to do will satisfy the need. You answer the question "How will the need be satisfied by what I am asking the audience to learn, believe, or do?" This step usually contains two types of information:

- a clear statement (with examples and illustrations if necessary) of what you want the audience to learn, believe, or do
- a statement of how or why what you are asking them to learn, believe, or do will lead to satisfying the need identified in step 2

For example, you might say, "With a home computer, you'll be able to get information on thousands of potential drug interactions in seconds." You might then show your listeners how this would be done with, perhaps, an actual demonstration.

**4. Visualization**    Visualization intensifies the audience's feelings or beliefs. It takes the audience beyond the present place and time and helps them imagine the situation as it would be if the need were satisfied as suggested in step 3. You can accomplish this by (1) demonstrating the positive benefits to be derived if this advocated proposal is put into operation or (2) demonstrating the negative consequences that will occur if your plan is not followed.

Of course, you could combine the two methods and demonstrate both the positive benefits of your plan and the negative effects of the existing situation or of a competing proposal. For example, you might say, "With this simple CD-ROM and these few Web addresses, you'll be able to stay at home and get valuable medical information." You might then demonstrate with a specific example how they would find this information.

**5. Action**    In the action step, you tell the audience what they should *do* to satisfy the need you have identified. Your goal is to move the audience in a particular direction. For example, you might want them to speak for Farrington or against Williamson, to attend the next student government meeting, or to work for a specific political candidate. Here are a few ways to accomplish this step.

- State exactly what audience members should do.
- Appeal to your listeners' emotions.
- Give the audience guidelines for future action.

*"Speech is power; speech is to persuade, to convert, to compel."*
—RALPH WALDO EMERSON

For example, you might say, "Read this pamphlet, 'Life on the Computer after 60,' and take a walk to your neighborhood computer store and talk with the salespeople." Or you might suggest that they consider taking an appropriate adult education course at the local community college.

Notice that an informative speech could have stopped after the satisfaction step. You accomplish the goal of informing the audience about some advantages of home computers for older people with the satisfaction step. In some cases, though, you may believe it helpful to progress through the action step to emphasize your point.

In a persuasive speech, on the other hand, you must go at least as far as visualization if you limit your purpose to strengthening or changing attitudes or beliefs. If you aim to get your listeners to behave in a certain way, you'll need to go all the way through the action step.

## Additional Patterns

The six organizational patterns just considered are the most common and are useful for many public speeches. But there are other patterns that also may prove appropriate for some presentations.

**Structure–Function**    The structure–function pattern is useful in informative speeches in which you want to discuss how something is constructed—its structure—and what it does—its function. This pattern might be useful, for example, in a speech about what an organization is and what it does, about the parts of a university and how they operate, or about the sensory systems of the body and their functions. This pattern might also be useful in a discussion about the nature of a living organism: its anatomy (or structure) and its physiology (or function).

**Comparison and Contrast**    A comparison-and-contrast pattern can work well in informative speeches in which you want to analyze two different theories, proposals, departments, or products in terms of their similarities and differences.

# THE PUBLIC SPEAKING SAMPLE ASSISTANT

### A POORLY CONSTRUCTED INFORMATIVE SPEECH

This speech was written to illustrate some broad as well as some rather subtle errors that a beginning speaker might make in constructing a persuasive speech. First, read the entire speech without reading any of the comments or questions in the right-hand column. After you've read the entire speech, reread each paragraph and respond to the critical thinking questions. What other questions might prove productive to ask?

### THREE JOBS

Well, I mean, hello. Er . . . I'm new at public speaking, so I'm a little nervous. I've always been shy. So don't watch my knees shake.

This nervous reaction is understandable but is probably best not shared with the listeners. After all, you don't want the audience to be uncomfortable for you.

*continued*

Ehm, let me see my notes here. [Mumbles to self while shuffling notes: "One, two, three, four, five—oh, they're all here."] Okay, here goes.

Three jobs. That's my title, and I'm going to talk about three jobs.

The Health Care Field. This is the fastest-growing job in the country; one of the fastest, I guess I mean. I know that you're not interested in this topic and that you're all studying accounting. But there are a lot of new jobs in the health care field. The *Star* had an article on health care and said that health care will be needed more in the future than it is now. And now, you know, like they need a lot of health care people. In the hospital where I work—on the west side, uptown—they never have enough health aides and they always tell me to become a health aide, like, you know, to enter the health care field. To become a nurse. Or maybe a dental technician. But I hate going to the dentist. Maybe I will.

I don't know what's going to happen with the president's health plan, but whatever happens, it won't change the need for health aides. I mean, people will still get sick so it really doesn't matter what happens with health care.

The Robotics Field. This includes things like artificial intelligence. I don't really know what that is, but it's like growing real fast. They use this in making automobiles and planes and I think in computers. Japan is a leading country in this field. A lot of people in India go into this field, but I'm not sure why.

The Computer Graphics Field. This field has a lot to do with designing and making lots of different products, like CAD and CAM. This field also includes computer-aided imagery—CAI. And in movies, I think. Like *Star Wars* and *Terminator 2*. I saw *Terminator 2* four times. I didn't see *Star Wars* but I'm gonna rent the video. I don't know if you have to know a lot about computers or if you can just like be a designer and someone else will tell the computer what to do.

I got my information from a book that Carol Kleiman wrote, *The 100 Best Jobs for the 1990s and Beyond*. It was summarized in last Sunday's *News*.

Going through your notes makes the audience feel that you didn't prepare adequately and may just be wasting their time.

This is the speaker's orientation. Is this sufficient? What else might the speaker have done in the introduction? The title seems adequate but is not terribly exciting. After reading the speech, try to give it a more appealing title. In general, don't use your title as your opening words.

Here the speaker shows such uncertainty that we question his or her competence.

And we begin to wonder, why is the speaker talking about this to us?
A report in the *Star* may be entertaining, but it doesn't constitute evidence. What does this reference do to the credibility you ascribe to the speaker?

Everything in the speech must have a definite purpose. Asides such as this comment about not liking to go to the dentist are probably best omitted.

Here the speaker had an opportunity to connect the topic with important current political events but failed to say anything that was not obvious.

Introducing these topics like this is clear but is probably not very interesting. How might each of the three main topics have been introduced more effectively?
Notice how vague the speaker is—"includes things like," "and I think in computers," "I'm not sure why." Language like this communicates very little information to listeners and leaves them with little confidence that the speaker knows what he or she is talking about.

Again, there is little that is specific. CAD and CAM are not defined, and CAI is explained as "computer-aided imagery," but unless we already knew what these were, we would still not know even after hearing the speaker. Again, the speaker inserts personal notes (for example, seeing *Terminator 2* four times) that have no meaningful connection to the topic.

The speaker uses only one source and, to make matters worse, doesn't even go to the original source but relies on a summary in the local newspaper. Especially with a topic like this, listeners are likely to want a variety of viewpoints and additional reliable sources.

Note too that the speech lacked any statistics. This is a subject that demands facts and figures. Listeners will want to know how many jobs will be available in these fields, what these fields will look like in 5 or 10 years, how much these fields pay, and so on.

My conclusion. These are three of the fastest-growing fields in the U.S. and in the world I think—but not in Third World countries, I don't think. China and India and Africa. More like Europe and Germany. And the U.S.—the U.S. is the big one. I hope you enjoyed my speech. Thank you.

I wasn't as nervous as I thought I'd be. Are there any questions?

Using the word *conclusion* to signal that you're concluding is not a bad idea, but work it into the text instead of using it like a heading in a book chapter.

Again, the speaker makes us question his or her competence and preparation by the lack of uncertainty. Again, personal comments are best left out.

In this type of speech, you not only explain each theory or proposal, but also explain primarily how they are similar and how they are different.

**Pro and Con, Advantages and Disadvantages**    The pro-and-con pattern, sometimes called the advantages–disadvantages pattern, is useful in informative speeches in which you want to explain objectively the advantages (the pros) and the disadvantages (the cons) of a plan, method, or product.

**Claim and Proof**    The claim-and-proof pattern is especially appropriate for a persuasive speech in which you want to prove the truth or usefulness of a particular proposition. It's the pattern that you see frequently in trials: The prosecution makes a claim that the defendant is guilty and presents proof in the form of varied evidence—for example, evidence that the defendant had a motive, had the opportunity, and had no alibi. This pattern divides your speech into two major parts. In the first part you explain your claim (for example, "Tuition must not be raised," "Library hours must be expanded," or "Courses in AIDS education must be instituted"). In the second part you offer your evidence or proof as to why, for example, tuition must not be raised.

**Multiple Definition**    The multiple-definition pattern serves well in informative speeches in which you want to explain the nature of a concept (What is a born-again Christian? What is a scholar? What is multiculturalism?). In this pattern each major heading consists of a different type of definition or way of looking at the concept. A variety of definition types are discussed in Chapter 12.

**Who, What, Why, Where, When**    The "who, what, why, where, when" pattern is the primary pattern in journalism and is useful in informative speeches in which you want to report or explain an event—for example, a robbery, political coup, war, or trial. You divide your speech into five major parts, each answering one of the five "W" questions.

**Fiction–Fact**    This pattern may be useful when you wish to clarify certain misconceptions that people have about various things. For example, if you were giving a speech on fiction and fact about the flu, you might use this pattern. You could first give the fiction (for example, you can get the flu from a flu shot, or antibiotics can help the flu, or older people spread the flu most often) and then follow it by the fact—you can't get the flu from the flu shot; antibiotics are useful only against bacteria, not against viruses; and children, rather than older people, spread the flu most often and most easily.

Because your chosen organizational pattern will serve primarily to help your listeners follow your speech, you may want to tell your listeners (in your introduction or as a transition between the introduction and the body of your speech) what pattern you'll be following. Here are just a few examples:

- "In our discussion of language development, we'll follow the baby from the earliest sign of language through true communication."
- "In touring Central America, we'll travel from north to south."
- "I'll first explain the problems with raising tuition and then propose a workable solution."
- "First we'll examine the causes of hypertension and then we'll look at its effects."

This chapter focused on the first six steps in preparing a public speech. The next chapter explains the remaining four steps.

## Summary of Concepts and Skills

This chapter explained the nature of public speaking and described the first six steps involved in preparing an effective public speech.

1. In public speaking a speaker addresses a relatively large audience with a relatively continuous discourse, usually in a face-to-face situation.
2. Public speaking effectiveness will yield a variety of personal, social, academic, and professional benefits.
3. Apprehension can be managed by gaining experience, thinking positively, seeing public speaking as conversation, stressing similarity, preparing and practicing thoroughly, moving about and breathing deeply, and avoiding chemicals as tension relievers (unless prescribed by a physician).
4. Public speaking takes place within a cultural context and that context must be taken into consideration in preparing and delivering speeches.
5. The preparation of a public speech involves 10 steps: (1) Select your topic and purpose; (2) analyze your audience; (3) research your topic; (4) formulate your thesis and identify your major propositions; (5) support your propositions; (6) organize your speech materials; (7) word your speech; (8) construct your conclusion and introduction; (9) rehearse your speech; and (10) deliver your speech. The first 6 of these were discussed in this chapter; the remaining 4 are discussed in Chapter 11.
6. Speech topics should deal with significant issues that interest the audience. Subjects and purposes should be limited in scope.
7. When analyzing the audience, consider audience members' age; sex; cultural factors; occupation, income, and status; and religion and religiousness. Also consider the psychology of the audience: the degree to which the audience is willing to hear your speech, their attitudes toward the topic and thesis, and the knowledge they possess of the topic.
8. Research your topic, beginning with general sources and gradually exploring more specific and specialized sources.
9. Formulate the thesis of your speech. Develop your main points by asking relevant questions about this thesis.
10. Support your main points with a variety of materials that amplify and provide evidence.
11. Organize your speech materials into a clear, easily identifiable pattern. Useful patterns include time, spatial, topical, problem–solution, cause–effect/effect–cause, and the motivated sequence. Other available patterns include structure–function, comparison and contrast, pro and con, claim and proof, multiple definition, the five W's (who, what, why, where, when), and fiction–fact.

These first six steps in preparing a public speech entail a variety of specific skills. Place a check mark next to those skills you most want to work on.

_____ 1. When preparing a public speech, I follow a logical progression of steps, such as the sequence outlined here.

_____ 2. I select appropriate topics and purposes and narrow them to manageable proportions.

_____ 3. I analyze my audience in terms of members' sociological and psychological characteristics, and I adapt the speech on the basis of these findings.

_____ 4. I research topics effectively and efficiently and critically evaluate the reliability of the research material.

5. After selecting my thesis (the main assertion), I expand it by asking strategic questions to develop my main ideas or propositions.

6. After generating my possible main points, I eliminate those points that seem least important to my thesis, combine those that have a common focus, and select those most relevant to my audience.

7. I support my propositions with amplifying materials such as examples, statistics, and visual aids and with logical, emotional, and ethical proofs.

8. When organizing the speech's main points, I select a pattern appropriate to the subject matter, purpose, and audience.

# Key Word Quiz

## The Language of Public Speaking

Match the terms about public speaking with their definitions. Record the number of the definition next to the appropriate term.

a. _____ topical pattern

b. _____ database

c. _____ high context

d. _____ thesis

e. _____ motivated sequence

f. _____ public speaking

g. _____ logical proof

h. _____ visualization

i. _____ plagiarism

j. _____ specific purpose

1. A speech pattern consisting of attention, need, satisfaction, visualization, and action.

2. The act of presenting another's material as your own.

3. A form of communication in which a speaker addresses a relatively large audience with a relatively continuous discourse.

4. One of the steps in the motivated sequence, in which the audience is shown what will happen if the speaker's plan is adopted.

5. A situation in which much of the information in communication is in the person and is not made explicit.

6. Statement identifying the information you want to communicate or the attitude you want to change.

7. An organized body of information contained in one place that can be easily accessed.

8. Reasoning from specific instances, causes and effects, and signs.

9. A pattern of speech organization in which a topic is divided into its subtopics.

10. The main idea of your speech.

Answer: a. 9 b. 7 c. 5 d. 10 e. 1 f. 3 g. 8 h. 4 i. 2 j. 6

# Five for Discussion

1. George and Iris want to give their speeches on opposite sides of Megan's law—the law requiring that community residents be notified if a convicted sex offender is living in close proximity. George is against the law and Iris is for it. If George and Iris were giving their speeches to your class, what would you advise each of them to do concerning the statement of their theses?

2. You're to give a speech to your class on the need to establish a day care center at your college for parents who attend school but have no means to hire people to take care of their children. You want to use the motivated sequence. How would you gain attention? Establish the need? Satisfy the need? Visualize the problem solved? Ask for action?

3. Log on to one of the libraries mentioned in this chapter and identify two or three ways in which this library can be of value to you for the courses you're taking this semester or for your future speeches.

4. Log on to Freeality.com (www.freeality.com/encyclop .htm), which provides links to a variety of reference works. Explore one of these references and, in a two-minute speech, explain its value to the class.

5. Conduct a biographical search for some famous person you're interested in by using one of the biographical dictionaries mentioned in this chapter or by simply typing the person's name in the search box of your favorite search engine.

# Log On! MyCommunicationLab

Several exercises that extend and elaborate on the concepts discussed in this chapter are available at www.mycommunicationlab.com: (1) Metaphors, Similes, and Public Speaking, (2) Using Performance Visualization to Reduce Apprehension, (3) Reducing Apprehension through Systematic Desensitization, (4) Predicting Listeners' Attitudes, (5) Analyzing an Unknown Audience, (6) Predicting Audience Attitudes, (7) Generating Main Ideas from Thesis Statements, (8) Electronic Research, and (9) Dictionary of Topics. In addition, several self-tests relevant to this chapter are available: What Do You Know about Research? How Are Cultural Beliefs and Theses Related? and How Well Do You Know Your Audience?

Also visit MyCommunicationLab for other activities, study aids, and video clips on public speaking preparation.

Explore our research resources at www.researchnavigator.com.

Research
Navigator.com

# 11

# Public Speaking Preparation and Delivery (Steps 7–10)

## *Why Read* This Chapter?

**Because you'll learn about:**

- language in public speaking.
- rehearsal and delivery.
- speech criticism.

**Because you'll learn to:**

- use language to best achieve your purposes.
- construct effective introductions and conclusions.
- rehearse your speech efficiently and effectively.
- deliver your speech with effective voice and body action.
- critically analyze a speech and express that criticism constructively.

At this point, you're probably deep into your speech preparation. You've selected and limited your topic. You've analyzed your audience, and you have begun thinking of adaptations you can make on the basis of the nature of your specific audience. You've researched the topic. You've selected your thesis and identified the main points you want to focus on. You've organized the points and selected appropriate supporting materials. This chapter continues explaining the process of preparing a speech and offers suggestions on wording the speech, crafting the conclusion and introduction, rehearsing the speech, and finally delivering the completed public speech.

# Step 7: Word Your Speech

When you're reading, you can look up an unfamiliar word or reread difficult portions or sections you didn't catch because of momentary lapses in attention. When you're listening, you don't have this luxury. Because of differences between reading and listening, and because your listeners will hear your speech only once, your talk must be instantly intelligible.

Researchers who have examined a great number of speeches and writings have found several important differences between them (DeVito, 1965, 1981; Akinnaso, 1982). Generally, spoken language consists of shorter, simpler, and more familiar words than does written language. There is more qualification in speech than in writing; for example, when you speak, you generally make greater use of such qualifying expressions as *although*, *however*, and *perhaps*. When you write, you usually edit these out. Spoken language also contains a greater number of self-reference terms—*I*, *me*, *my*. And it contains more expressions that incorporate the speaker as part of the observation (for example, "It seems to me that . . ." or "As I see it . . .").

For most speeches, this "oral style" is appropriate. The specific suggestions offered throughout this section will help you style a speech that will retain the best of the oral style while maximizing comprehension and persuasion.

## Clarity

Clarity in speaking style should be your primary goal. Here are some guidelines to help you make your speech clear.

***Be Economical.*** Don't waste words. Notice the wasted words in expressions such as "at 9 a.m. *in the morning*," "we *first* began the discussion," "I *myself personally*," and "blue *in color*." By withholding the italicized terms, you eliminate unnecessary words and move closer to a more economical and clearer style.

***Use Specific Terms and Numbers.*** As we get more and more specific, we get a clearer and more detailed picture. Be specific. Don't say "dog" when you want your listeners to picture a St. Bernard. Don't say "car" when you want them to picture a limousine. The same is true of numbers. Don't say "earned a good salary" if you mean "earned $90,000 a year." Don't say "taxes will go up" when you mean "taxes will increase 7 percent."

***Use Guide Phrases.*** Use guide phrases to help listeners see that you're moving from one idea to another. Use phrases such as "now that we have seen how . . . , let us consider how . . . ," and "my next argument. . . ." Terms such as *first, second, and also, although*, and *however* will help your audience follow your line of thinking.

***Use Short, Familiar Terms.*** Generally, favor the short word over the long word. Favor the familiar over the unfamiliar word. Favor the more commonly used over the rarely used term. Use *harmless* instead of *innocuous*, *clarify* instead of *elucidate*, *use* instead of *utilize*, *find out* instead of *ascertain*, *cost* or *expense* instead of *expenditure*.

**Carefully Assess Idioms.** Idioms are expressions that are unique to a specific language and whose meaning cannot be deduced from the individual words used. Expressions such as "to kick the bucket," and "doesn't have a leg to stand on" are idioms. Either you know the meaning of the expression or you don't; you can't figure it out from only a knowledge of the individual words. The positive side of idioms is that they give your speech a casual and informal style; they make your speech sound like a speech and not like a written essay. The negative side is that idioms create problems for audience members who are not native speakers of your language. Many such listeners will simply not understand the meaning of your idioms.

**Vary the Levels of Abstraction.** Combining high abstraction (the very general) and low abstraction (the very concrete) seems to work best. Too many generalizations without specifics will prove vague and difficult for your audience to comprehend. Too many specifics without any generalizations will leave them wondering what the big picture is. Here, for example, is an excerpt from a speech on the homeless. Note that in the first paragraph we have a relatively abstract description of homelessness. In the second paragraph we get into specifics. In the last paragraph the abstract and the concrete are connected.

> *[Here the speaker begins with relatively general or abstract statements.]* Homelessness is a serious problem for all metropolitan areas throughout the country. It's currently estimated that there are now more than 200,000 homeless in New York City alone. But what is this really about? Let me tell you what it's about.
>
> *[Here the speaker gets to specifics.]* It's about a young man. He must be about 25 or 30, although he looks a lot older. He lives in a cardboard box on the side of my apartment house. We call him Tom, although we really don't know his name. All his possessions are stored in this huge box. I think it was a box from a refrigerator. Actually, he doesn't have very much, and what he has easily fits in this box. There's a blanket my neighbor threw out, some plastic bottles Tom puts water in, and some Styrofoam containers he picked up from the garbage from Burger King. He uses these to store whatever food he finds.
>
> *[The conclusion combines the general and the specific.]* What is homelessness about? It's about Tom and 200,000 other "Toms" in New York and thousands of others throughout the rest of the country. And not all of them even have boxes to live in.

# Vividness

Select words that make your ideas vivid, that make them come alive in the listeners' minds.

**Use Active Verbs.** Favor verbs that communicate activity. The verb *to be*, in all its forms—*is, are, was, were,* and *will be*—is relatively inactive. Try replacing such forms with action verbs. Instead of saying "Management will be here tomorrow," consider "Management descends on us [or jets in] tomorrow."

**Use Figures of Speech.** A figure of speech is a stylistic device in which words are used beyond their literal meaning. One of the best ways to achieve vividness is to use figures of speech. Table 11.1 presents a few that you may find helpful.

**Use Imagery.** Another way to inject vividness into your speech is to appeal to the audience's senses, especially their visual, auditory, and tactile senses. Using imagery can make your listeners see, hear, and feel what you're talking about.

## TABLE 11.1  Figures of Speech

These are just a few of the many figures of speech you can use in your speeches. Too many similes or too much hyperbole is likely to make your speech sound unnatural and overly formal, so use these sparingly. On the other hand, a good figure goes a long way toward making your speech memorable. Can you think of additional examples for each of the figures identified here?

| FIGURE | DEFINITION | EXAMPLES |
|---|---|---|
| Alliteration | Repetition of the same initial consonant sound in two or more words close to one another | Fifty Famous Flavors March Madness |
| Hyperbole | Use of extreme exaggeration | I'm so hungry I could eat a horse. |
| Metaphor | Comparison of two unlike things | She's a lion when she wakes up. He's a real bulldozer. |
| Personification | Attribution of human characteristics to inanimate objects | This room cries out for activity. My car is tired and wants water. |
| Simile | Comparison of two unlike objects using the words *like* or *as* | This chairperson takes charge like a bull. The teacher is as gentle as a lamb. |
| Rhetorical Question | A question used to make a statement or produce some desired effect rather than to secure an answer, which is obvious | Do you want to be popular? Do you want to get promoted? Do you want to get an "A" on the exam? |

*Visual imagery* enables you to describe people or objects in images the audience can see. When appropriate, describe visual qualities such as height, weight, color, size, shape, length, and contour. Let your audience see the sweat pouring down the faces of coal miners and the short, overweight executive in a pin-striped suit smoking an enormous cigar. *Auditory imagery* helps you appeal to the audience's sense of hearing. Let listeners hear the car screeching, the wind whistling, the bells chiming, and the roar of the angry tenants. *Tactile imagery* enables you to make the audience feel the temperature or texture you're talking about. Let listeners feel the cool water running over their bodies, the fighter's punch, the sand beneath their feet, and a lover's soft caress.

## Appropriateness

Appropriate language is consistent in tone with your topic, your audience, and your own self-image. It's language that does not offend anyone or make anyone feel uncomfortable. It's language that seems natural given the situation. Here are some guidelines to help you choose appropriate language.

***Speak at the Appropriate Level of Formality.*** Although public speaking usually takes place in a relatively formal situation, relatively informal language seems to work best in most situations. One way to achieve a more informal style is to use contractions: *don't* instead of *do not*, *I'll* instead of *I shall*, and *wouldn't* instead of *would not*. Contractions give a public speech the sound and rhythm of conversation—a quality listeners generally like.

***Avoid Written-Style Expressions.*** Avoid expressions that are more familiar in writing, such as "the former" or "the latter" as well as expressions such as "the argument presented above." These make listeners feel you're reading to them rather than talking with them.

***Avoid Slang, Vulgar, and Offensive Expressions.*** Be careful not to offend your audience with language that embarrasses them or makes them think you have little respect for them. Although your listeners may use such expressions, they generally resent their use by public speakers. Above all, avoid terms that might be interpreted as sexist, heterosexist, ageist, or racist (see Chapter 4).

## Personal Style

Audiences favor speakers who use a personal rather than an impersonal style—who speak *with* them rather than *at* them. A personal style makes the audience feel more involved with the speaker and with the speech topic.

***Use Personal Pronouns.*** Say "I," "me," "he," "she," and "you." Avoid expressions such as the impersonal *one* (as in, "One is led to believe that . . ."), *this speaker*, or *you, the listeners*. These expressions are overly formal and distance the audience, creating barriers rather than bridges.

***Direct Questions to the Audience.*** Involve the audience by asking them questions. With a small audience, you might even briefly take responses. With larger audiences, you might ask the question, pause to allow the audience time to consider their responses, and then move on. When you direct questions to your listeners, you make them feel a part of the experience. For example, in a speech on abortion, you might ask, "Do you know anyone who had an abortion?" and then pause to consider a few responses from your audience. With a larger audience you might simply say, "I'd like you to think about the people you know who have had abortions. What were their reasons for undergoing abortion?"

***Create Immediacy.*** Immediacy is a connectedness, a relatedness, a oneness with your listeners. Create immediacy by referring directly to your listeners, using *you;* say, "*You'll* enjoy reading . . ." instead of "Everyone will enjoy reading. . . ." Refer to commonalities between you and the audience. Say, for example, "We're all children of immigrants," or, "We all want to see this agency run smoother and receive fewer complaints from clients." Refer also to shared experiences and goals. Say, for example, "We all need a more responsive PTA." Finally, recognize and refer to audience feedback. Say, for example, "I can see from your expressions that we're all here for the same reason."

## Power

Public speaking, perhaps even more than interpersonal or small group communication, often requires a powerful style—a style that is certain, definite, and persuasive. Perhaps the first step to achieving a powerful style of speech is to eliminate the powerless forms that you may use now. Listed below are the major characteristics of powerless speech (Molloy, 1981; Kleinke, 1986; Johnson, 1987; Dillard & Marshall, 2003; Lakoff, 1975; Timmerman, 2002). As you consider this list, think of your own speech. Do you avoid the following speech behaviors?

*"If you have an important point to make, don't try to be subtle or clever. Use a pile-driver. Hit the point once. Then come back and hit it agin. Then hit it a third time—a tredmendous whack."*
—WINSTON CHURCHHILL

- *Hesitations* make you sound unprepared and uncertain. Example: "I, er, want to say that, ah, this one is, er, the best, you know?"

- *Too many intensifiers* make your speech monotonous and don't allow you to stress what you do want to emphasize. Example: "Really, this was the greatest; it was truly phenomenal."

- *Disqualifiers* signal a lack of competence and a feeling of uncertainty. Examples: "I didn't read the entire article, but . . . ." "I didn't actually see the accident, but . . . ."

- *Tag questions* ask for another's agreement and therefore may signal your need for agreement—and your own uncertainty. Examples: "That was a great movie, wasn't it?" "She's brilliant, don't you think?"
- *Self-critical statements* signal a lack of confidence and may make public your own inadequacies. Examples: "I'm not very good at this." "This is my first public speech."
- *Slang and vulgar language* signal low social class and hence little power. Examples: "No problem!" "@*+#?$!!"

## Sentence Construction

Effective public speaking style also requires careful attention to the construction of sentences. Here are some guidelines that will help you achieve a clear, vivid, appropriate, and personal speaking style.

***Favor Short over Long Sentences.***   Short sentences are more forceful and economical. They are easier to understand and to remember. Listeners don't have the time or inclination to unravel long and complex sentences. Help them to listen more efficiently: Use short rather than long sentences.

***Favor Direct over Indirect Sentences.***   Direct sentences are easier to understand. They are also more forceful. Instead of saying, "I want to tell you the three main reasons why we should not adopt the Bennett Proposal," say, "We should not adopt the Bennett Proposal. Let me give you three good reasons."

***Favor Active over Passive Sentences.***   Active sentences are easier to understand. They also make your speech livelier and more vivid. Instead of saying, "The lower court's original decision was reversed by the Supreme Court," say, "The Supreme Court reversed the lower court's decision." Instead of saying, "The change was favored by management," say, "Management favored the change."

***Favor Positive over Negative Sentences.***   Positive sentences are easier to comprehend and to remember (DeVito, 1976; Clark, 1974). Notice how sentences A and C are easier to understand than B and D.

   A.  The committee rejected the proposal.

   B.  The committee did not accept the proposal.

   C.  This committee works outside the normal company hierarchy.

   D.  This committee does not work within the normal company hierarchy.

***Vary the Type and Length of Sentences.***   The advice to use short, direct, active, and positive sentences is valid most of the time. But too many sentences of the same type or length will make your speech boring. Use variety while generally following the guidelines given above.

## Step 8: Construct Your Conclusion and Introduction

Your conclusion and introduction need special care, because they will determine, in large part, the effectiveness of your speech. Construct your conclusion first and your introduction next.

# The Conclusion

Devote special care to this brief but crucial part of your speech. In your conclusion, summarize your main points and close.

**Summarize**   You may summarize your speech in a variety of ways.

***Restate Your Thesis.***   Restate the essential thrust of your speech—your thesis or perhaps the purpose you hoped to achieve.

***Restate the Importance of Your Thesis.***   Tell the audience again why your topic or thesis is so important. Here is how Carrie Willis (Schnoor, 2000, p. 15), a student from Tallahassee Community College, in a speech on "drowsy driving," restated the importance of her thesis and summarized the main points of her speech:

> While this problem is as old as cars, it's not disappearing. And it won't disappear until you choose to do something about it. Today, we have gained a better understanding of the problem of falling asleep at the wheel, and why it continues to exist, while finally suggesting several initiatives to help end this epidemic. Six innocent college students were killed, all because someone didn't take the precautionary steps to avoid the tragedy. So next time you're on the road and you find yourself dozing off, pull over and take a nap, because those 30 minutes could save your life.

***Restate Your Main Points.***   Simply reiterate your two, three, or four main points. For example, in a speech on problems with volunteer fire departments, one student speaker restated his propositions like this: "By examining how volunteer firefighters are jeopardizing our safety, why our communities remain so dependent, and finally prescribing some solutions, we have set the stage for reform" (Schnoor, 1999, p. 46).

In a speech on hate crimes, the speaker restates the thesis and its importance and summarizes the major points all in one simple statement: "Today we've seen the reality of hate crimes against homosexuals, some of the reasons these crimes are committed, the limitations of our current legislation, and the need for the Hate Crimes Prevention Act of 1998" (Schnoor, 1999, p. 61).

**Close**   The conclusion's second function is to provide closure—to give the speech a crisp and definite end. Don't leave your audience wondering whether you've finished.

***Use a Quotation.***   A quotation that summarizes your thesis or provides an interesting perspective on your point of view often provides effective closure. Make sure that it's clearly and directly related to your speech purpose; otherwise, the audience will spend their time trying to figure out the connection.

***Pose a Challenge or Question.***   You may wish to end your speech with a provocative question or challenge:

- "What do you intend to do about the company's refusal to increase wages?"
- "Go home and clean high-cholesterol foods out of your refrigerator."
- "Sign this petition; it will help put an experienced person in office."
- "What are you going to do to help end the AIDS crisis?"

Here's how one student, in a speech on the problems with our diet culture, challenged her audience: "There's a whole generation of kids out there who need our action. This is our wakeup call as a society. Don't diet—eat smart. For your sake, and for the sake of the children in your life" (Schnoor, 1999, p. 127).

***Motivate Your Audience to Do Something.*** Remind your audience of what they should now do. For example:

- "The next time you go online, visit one of the websites I mentioned . . . ."
- "You can sign up to volunteer at the desk in the Student Union . . . ."
- "So, read the article in this handout; it could change your life. . . ."

***Thank the Audience.*** Speakers frequently thank their audience. If you do this, do it a bit more elaborately than by simply saying "Thank you." You might relate the thanks to your thesis: "I really appreciate your attention and hope you'll join us in Sunday's protest." Or you might say, "Thank you for your attention and your active concern about this crisis," or "I want to thank you for listening and for your willingness to sign Williams's petition."

## The Introduction

In your introduction, try to accomplish two goals: First, gain your audience's attention, and second, orient the audience—tell them a little bit about what you'll talk about.

**Gain Attention**   In your introduction, focus the audience's attention on your topic. Then work to maintain that attention throughout your speech.

***Ask a Question.*** Questions are effective because they are a change from normal statements and involve the audience. They tell the audience that you're talking directly to them and care about their responses.

Questions are also useful in setting the stage for what will follow. Here, for example, is how Ashley Hatcher, a student from the University of Texas at Austin, gained attention and also identified what she was going to cover:

> Dennis Rader was your typical family man, described by neighbors as "affable and pleasant." But to their surprise, as CNN of March 1, 2005, explains, this church council president and father of two was uncovered as the BTK serial killer—named for his method, bind, torture, kill—who terrorized the Midwest for three decades. After his 2005 conviction one question remained: How did a seemingly normal man with no psychological abnormalities become a serial killer?

***Refer to Specific Audience Members.*** Involving members directly makes them perk up and pay attention. Depending on the nature of the audience and your knowledge of specific members, you might say something like "Pat, you defended the NRA, whereas Chris, you argued against it. And Pablo, you argued for a pro-life position on abortion, but Sarah, you argued for a pro-choice position. Even in a small class such as this, there are wide differences in beliefs, values, and attitudes. And that's what I want to talk about today: differences in beliefs and how these can cause conflict in our relationships."

***Refer to Recent Happenings.*** Being familiar with recent news events, the audience will pay attention to your approach. For example, in a speech on the war in Iraq, you might cite recent car bombings, the most recent statistics on the number of Americans and Iraqis who died, or the results of recent elections. In fact, speeches on some topics (such as the war in Iraq) would require that you demonstrate familiarity with recent events.

***Use Illustrations or Dramatic or Humorous Stories.*** We are all drawn to illustrations and stories about people—they make a speech vivid and con-

> **WHAT DO YOU SAY?**
> **Unexpected Feedback**
> You have just introduced your speech with a story you found extremely humorous; you laughed out loud after you finished it. Unfortunately, the audience just didn't get it—not one smile in the entire audience. *What do you say?*

crete. Use them to secure audience attention in the introduction and to maintain it throughout.

***Use Visual Aids.*** These will engage attention because they are new and different. Chapter 12 provides lots of specific examples.

## Orient the Audience
Previewing what you're going to say will help your listeners follow your thoughts more closely. You can orient the audience in several ways.

***Give the Audience a General Idea of Your Subject.*** One student, for example, in a speech on the problems of Internet education, oriented her audience not only to the topic but also to her problem–solution organizational pattern: "I am going to describe the problem of phony academic institutions on the Internet, focusing primarily on the misleading nature of their names as an advertising strategy. I will then provide some simple solutions to aid the general public in avoiding and exposing these disreputable organizations" (Schnoor, 1999, p. 10).

***Give a Detailed Preview of Your Main Points.*** Identify the propositions you will discuss—for example, "In this brief talk, I will cover four major attractions of New York City: the night life, the theater, restaurants, and museums."

***Identify the Goal You Hope to Achieve.*** A librarian addressing my public speaking class oriented the audience by stating goals in this way: "Pay attention for the next few minutes and you'll be able to locate anything we have in the library by using the new touch-screen computer access system."

"I'll tell you what this election is about. It's about homework, and pitiful allowances, and having to clean your room. It's also about candy, and ice cream, and staying up late."

## Avoiding Some Common Faults
Here are a few tips for avoiding the mistakes that beginning speakers often make.

***Don't Start Your Speech Immediately.*** Instead, survey your audience; make eye contact and engage their attention. Stand in front of the audience with a sense of control. Pause briefly, then begin speaking.

***Don't Display Discomfort or Displeasure.*** When you walk to the speaker's stand, display enthusiasm and a desire to speak. People much prefer listening to a speaker who shows that she or he enjoys speaking to them.

***Don't Apologize.*** A common fault is to apologize for something in your speech. Don't. Your inadequacies, whatever they may be, will be clear enough to any discerning listener. Don't point them out. In the United States, avoid expressions such as "I am not an expert on this topic," "I wanted to illustrate these ideas with a DVD but I couldn't get my hands on a player," or "I didn't do as much reading on this topic as I should have." And never start a speech with "I'm not very good at giving public speeches."

Be aware, however, that this rule does not hold in all cultures. For example, in Iran, a speaker would be expected to use self-deprecating terms to indicate humility and modesty (Keshavarz, 1988). A similar modesty claim would be expected in many Asian cultures.

> **WHAT DO YOU SAY?**
> **Introductions**
> You're scheduled to give a speech on careers in computer technology to high school students who have been forced to attend this career day on Saturday. If you don't win over this unwilling audience in your introduction, you figure you're finished. *What do you say?*

**WHAT DO YOU SAY?**
**Audience Adaptation**
You're one of four running for president of your building's tenant association. Each candidate must give a brief talk stating what he or she would do for the building. All the tenants except you belong to the same race. You wonder if you should mention race in your talk? *What do you say?*

***Don't Preface Your Introduction.*** Don't begin with such common but ineffective statements as "I'm really nervous, but here goes," "Before I begin my talk, I want to say . . . ," or "I hope I can remember everything I want to say." Statements such as these may call your credibility into question; after all, who wants to believe someone who isn't sure they can remember their speech? Such statements also make it difficult for you to open your speech with a strong attention grabber. You don't want your audience's first impression of you to be of someone who is nervous or may forget his or her speech.

***Don't Introduce New Material in Your Conclusion.*** Once you reach your conclusion, it's too late to introduce new material. Instead, reinforce what you have already said, summarize your essential points, or give new expression to ideas already covered.

***Don't Race Away from the Speaker's Stand.*** After your last statement, pause, maintain audience eye contact, and then walk (don't run) to your seat. Show no signs of relief; focus your attention on whatever activity is taking place. Glance over the audience and sit down. If a question period follows your speech and you're in charge of this, pause after completing your conclusion. Ask audience members in a direct manner if they have any questions. If there's a chairperson who will ask for questions, pause after your conclusion, then nonverbally signal to the chairperson that you're ready.

## Transitions and Internal Summaries

**Transitions** (sometimes called "connectives") are words, phrases, or sentences that connect the various parts of your speech. Because your audience will hear your speech just once, they may not see the connections you want them to see. By using transitions, you can help your listeners see how one point leads to another or where one argument ends and another begins. Use transitions in at least the following places:

- between the introduction and the body of the speech
- between the body and the conclusion
- between the main points in the body of the speech

*Skill Development Experience*

### Constructing Conclusions and Introductions

*Because the conclusion and the introduction are often the parts that listeners remember most, give special attention to these brief but crucial parts of your speech.*

Prepare a conclusion and an introduction to a hypothetical speech on one of the topics listed here, making sure that in your conclusion you (1) review the speech's main points and (2) provide closure, and that in your introduction you (1) gain attention and (2) orient the audience.

1. Foreign language requirements should be abolished.
2. All wild-animal killing should be declared illegal.
3. Properties owned by religious institutions should be taxed.
4. Assisted suicide should be legalized.
5. Gambling should be declared illegal by all states.

Here are the major transitional functions and some stylistic devices that you might use to serve these functions.

1. *To announce the start of a main point or piece of evidence:* "First . . . ," "A second argument . . . ," "A closely related problem . . . ," "If you want further evidence, look at . . . ," "My next point . . . ," or "An even more compelling argument. . . ."

2. *To signal that you're drawing a conclusion from previously given evidence and argument:* "Thus . . . ," "Therefore . . . ," "So, as you can see . . . ," or, "It follows, then, that. . . ."

3. *To alert the audience that you're introducing a qualification or exception:* "But . . . ," "However, also consider . . . ," or, "On the other hand. . . ."

4. *To remind listeners of what you've just said and to stress that it's connected with another issue you now want to consider:* "In contrast to . . . ," "Consider also . . . ," "Not only . . . , but also . . . ," or "In addition to . . . , we also need to look at. . . ." One student speaker, Andrew Farmer, did this simply and effectively by saying: "But while the project is astounding *[a point just explained]*, there are also some challenges *[the next point to be made]*. For example, . . ."

5. *To signal the part of your speech that you're approaching:* "By way of introduction . . . ," "In conclusion . . . ," "Now, let's discuss why we are here today . . . ," or, "So, what's the solution? What should we do?"

You can enhance a transition nonverbally by pausing between the transition and the next part of your speech. This will help the audience see that you're beginning a new part of your speech. You might also take a step forward or to the side after saying your transition to echo the movement from one part of your speech to another.

Closely related to the transition is the **internal summary**, a statement that summarizes what you have already discussed. Usually it summarizes some major subdivision of your speech. Incorporate several internal summaries into your speech—perhaps working them into the transitions connecting, say, the major arguments or issues. An internal summary that is also a transition might look something like this:

> The three arguments advanced here were (1) . . . , (2) . . . , (3) . . . . Now, what can we do about them? I think we can do two things. First, . . .

Another example:

> Inadequate recreational facilities, poor schooling, and a lack of adequate role models seem to be the major problems facing our youngsters. Each of these, however, can be remedied and even eliminated. Here's what we can do.

Now that you have completed your speech, you need to put it all together in the form of an outline, something you have already been doing as you identified your main points and amplified them with illustrations and definitions, for example. Here we look at three kinds of outline: the preparation outline, the template outline, and the delivery outline.

## The Preparation Outline

This preparation outline in the Public Speaking Sample Assistant Box on page 262 (as well as the template and delivery outlines that are discussed next) will help you not only to organize your thoughts more coherently, but also to deliver your speech more effectively.

# THE PUBLIC SPEAKING SAMPLE ASSISTANT

**THE PREPARATION OUTLINE**

Here is a relatively detailed preparation outline similar to the outline you might prepare when constructing your speech. The sidenotes should clarify both the content and the format of a preparation outline.

TITLE: HAVE YOU EVER BEEN CULTURE SHOCKED?

Thesis: Culture shock can be described in four stages.

Purpose: To inform my audience of the four phases of culture shock.

Generally, the title, thesis, and purpose of the speech are prefaced to the outline. When the outline is an assignment that is to be handed in, additional information may be required.

INTRODUCTION

I. How many of you have experienced culture shock?

   A. Many people experience culture shock, a reaction to being in a culture very different from what they were used to.

   B. By understanding culture shock, you'll be in a better position to deal with it if and when it comes.

II. Culture shock occurs in four stages (Oberg, 1960).

   A. The Honeymoon occurs first.

   B. The Crisis occurs second.

   C. The Recovery occurs third.

   D. The Adjustment occurs fourth.

[Let's follow the order in which these four stages occur beginning with the first stage, the honeymoon.]

BODY

I. The Honeymoon occurs first.

   A. The honeymoon is the period of fascination with the new people and culture.

   B. You enjoy the people and the culture.

      1. You love the people.

         a. For example, the people in Zaire spend their time very differently from the way New Yorkers do.

         b. For example, my first 18 years living on a farm was very different from life in a college dorm.

      2. You love the culture.

         a. The great number of different religions in India fascinated me.

         b. Eating was an especially great experience.

Note the general format for the outline; the headings are clearly labeled, and the indenting helps you clearly see the relationship between the items. For example, in introduction II, the outline format helps you to see that A, B, C, and D are explanations for II.

Note that the introduction, body, and conclusion are clearly labeled and separated visually.

Although the speaker assumes that the audience is familiar with culture shock, he or she still includes a brief definition in case some audience members don't know what it is and to refresh the memory of others.

Note that references are integrated throughout the outline, just as they would be in a term paper. In the actual speech, the speaker might say: "Anthropologist Kalervo Oberg, who coined the term *culture shock*, said it occurs in four stages."

The introduction serves two functions: it gains attention by involving the audience and by stressing the importance of the topic to the audience's desire to gain self-understanding, and it orients the audience to what is to follow. This particular orientation identifies both the number and the names of the stages. If this speech were much longer and more complex, this orientation might also have included brief definitions of each stage.

Another function often served by the introduction is to establish a relationship between yourself as the speaker, the topic, and the audience. In this particular speech, this function might have been served by your telling the audience how you experienced culture shock and how knowing the stages helped you cope with the difficulties. You might then tell the audience that the same would be true for them and thus connect all three major elements of the speech.

The transition at the end of the introduction tells the audience to expect a four-part presentation. Also, the numbers repeated throughout the outline will further aid the audience in keeping track of where you are in the speech. Most important, the transition tells the audience that the speech will follow a temporal thought pattern.

Notice the parallel structure throughout the outline. For example, note that I, II, III, and IV in the body are all phrased in exactly the same way. Although this may seem unnecessarily repetitive, it will help your audience follow your speech more closely and will also help you structure your thoughts logically.

[But, like many relationships, contact with a new culture is not all honeymoon; soon there comes a crisis.]

    II.   The Crisis occurs second.

        A.  The crisis is the period when you begin to experience problems.

           1.  One-third of American workers abroad fail because of culture shock (Samovar & Porter, 1991, p. 232).

           2.  The personal difficulties are also great.

        B.  Life becomes difficult in the new culture.

           1.  Communication is difficult.

           2.  It's easy to offend people without realizing it.

[As you gain control over the various crises, you begin to recover.]

    III.  The Recovery occurs third.

        A.  The recovery is the period when you learn how to cope.

        B.  You begin to learn intercultural competence (Lustig & Koester, 2003).

           1.  You learn how to communicate.

              a.  Being able to go to the market and make my wants known was a great day for me.

              b.  I was able to ask for a date.

           2.  You learn the rules of the culture.

              a.  The different religious ceremonies each have their own rules.

              b.  Eating is a ritual experience in lots of places throughout Africa.

[Your recovery leads naturally into the next and final stage, the adjustment.]

    IV.  The Adjustment occurs fourth.

        A.  The adjustment is the period when you come to enjoy the new culture.

        B.  You come to appreciate the people and the culture.

[Let me summarize, then, the stages you go through in experiencing culture shock.]

CONCLUSION

    I.  Culture shock can be described in four stages.

        A.  The honeymoon is first.

        B.  The crisis is second.

        C.  The recovery is third.

        D.  The adjustment is fourth.

    II.  By knowing the four stages, you can better understand the culture shock you may now be experiencing on the job, at school, or in your private life.

---

Notice that there are lots of examples in this speech. These examples are identified only briefly in the outline and would naturally be elaborated on in the speech.

Notice, too, the internal organization of each major point. Each main assertion in the body contains a definition of the stage (IA, IIA, IIIA, and IVA) and examples (IB, IIB, IIIB, and IVB) to illustrate the stage.

When you cite a specific fact, some style manuals require that you include the page number in the source reference.

Note that each statement in the outline is a complete sentence. You can easily convert this outline into a phrase or key word outline for use in delivery. The full sentences, however, will help you see relationships among items more clearly.

The transitions are inserted between all major parts of the speech. Although they may seem too numerous in this abbreviated outline, they will be appreciated by your audience because the transitions will help them follow your speech.

Notice that these four points correspond to IIA, B, C, and D of the introduction and to I, II, III, and IV of the body. Notice how the similar wording adds clarity.

This step provides closure; it makes it clear that the speech is finished. It also serves to encourage reflection on the part of the audiences as to their own experiences of culture shock.

**REFERENCES**

Lustig, Myron W., & Koester, Jolene. (2006). *Intercultural competence: Interpersonal communication across cultures* (5th ed.). Boston: Allyn and Bacon.

Oberg, Kalervo. (1960). Culture shock: Adjustment to new cultural environments. *Practical Anthropology*, 7, 177–182.

Samovar, Larry A., & Porter, Richard E. (1991). *Communication between cultures*. Belmont, CA: Wadsworth.

This reference list includes only those sources that appear in the completed speech.

## The Template Outline

Another useful type of outline is the **template.** Much as a template in PowerPoint guides you to fill in certain information in particular places, the template outline serves a similar function; it ensures that you include all the relevant material in reasonable order. At the same time, it also helps you see your speech as a whole—and may reveal gaps that need to be filled or items that are discussed at too great a length. In a sense the template outline is mechanical (some might say too mechanical), but it's an extremely useful device for organizing a speech. As you become more familiar with the public speaking process, as with PowerPoint, you'll soon be able to develop your speech, and your slides, without any template or wizard.

The sample template outline in the Public Speaking Sample Assistant box presented below would be appropriate for a speech using a time, spatial, or topical organization pattern. Note that in this outline there are three main points (I, II, and III in the body). These correspond to items IIA, B, C, and D in the introduction (where you would orient the audience) and to IA, B, C, and D in the conclusion (where you would summarize your major propositions). The transitions are signaled by square brackets. As you review this outline—the watermarks will remind you of the functions of each outline item—you will see how it can be adapted for use with other organization patterns, such as problem–solution, cause–effect, or the motivated sequence. Additional template outlines for a variety of organizational patterns may be found at **www.ablongman.com/devito.**

# THE PUBLIC SPEAKING SAMPLE ASSISTANT

**THE TEMPLATE OUTLINE**

Thesis: _____ *your main assertion; the core of your speech*

Specific Purpose: _____ *what you hope to achieve from this speech*

*Introduction*

    I. _____ *gain attention*

    II. _____ *orient audience*

        A. _____ *first main point; same as I in body*

        B. _____ *second main point; same as II in body*

C. _____ third main point; same as III in body _____

[Transition: _____ connect the introduction to the body _____]

*Body*

    I. _____ first main point _____

       A. _____ support for I (the first main point) _____

       B. _____ further support for I _____

[Transition: _____ connect the first main point to the second _____]

    II. _____ second main point _____

       A. _____ support for II (the second main point) _____

       B. _____ further support for II _____

[Transition: _____ connect the second main point to the third _____]

    III. _____ third main point _____

       A. _____ support for III _____

       B. _____ further support for III _____

[Transition: _____ connect the third main point (or all main points) to the conclusion _____]

*Conclusion*

    I. _____ summary _____

       A. _____ first main point; same as I in body _____

       B. _____ second main point; same as II in body _____

       C. _____ third main point: same as III in body _____

    II. _____ Closure _____

## The Delivery Outline

The **delivery outline** assists you in presenting the speech. Don't use your preparation outline: you may feel inclined to read from it, which is not an effective way to give a speech. So write a brief delivery outline such as that presented in the next Public Speaking Sample Assistant Box, which was constructed from the preparation outline on culture shock. If you're using PowerPoint—discussed in detail in the next chapter—then your delivery outline is going to be either the PowerPoint slides themselves or the speaker's notes that you generate along with your PowerPoint presentation (see pages 300–301 and 303–304). Here are some guidelines for delivery outlines.

- *Be brief.* Don't allow the outline to stand in the way of speaker–audience contact. Use key words to trigger in your mind the ideas you wish to discuss. Notice how brief the sample delivery outline is compared to the preparation outline. You'll be able to use this brief outline effectively without losing eye contact with the audience. It uses abbreviations (for example, CS for culture shock) and phrases rather than complete sentences. And yet it's detailed enough to include all essential parts of your speech, even transitions.

- *Be delivery-minded.* Include any delivery guides you might wish to remember while you're speaking—for example, notes to pause or to show the visual aid.

- *Rehearse your speech with this delivery outline.* Make your rehearsal as close to the real thing as possible.

**THE DELIVERY OUTLINE**

PAUSE!

LOOK OVER THE AUDIENCE!

I. Many experience CS

    A. CS: the reaction to being in a culture very different from your own

    B. By understanding CS, you'll be better able to deal with it

PAUSE—SCAN AUDIENCE

II. CS occurs in 4 stages (WRITE ON BOARD)

    A. Honeymoon

    B. Crisis

    C. Recovery

    D. Adjustment

[Let's examine these stages of CS]

PAUSE/STEP FORWARD

I. Honeymoon

    A. fascination w/ people and culture

    B. enjoyment of people and culture

        1. Zaire example

        2. farm to college dorm

[But, life is not all honeymoon—the crisis]

II. Crisis

    A. problems arise

        1. 1/3 Am workers fail abroad

        2. personal difficulties

    B. life becomes difficult

        1. communication

        2. offend others

[As you gain control over the crises, you learn how to cope]

PAUSE

III. Recovery

    A. period of learning to cope

    B. you learn intercultural competence

        1. communication becomes easier

        2. you learn the culture's rules

[As you recover, you adjust]

IV. Adjustment

    A. learn to enjoy (again) the new culture

    B. appreciate people and culture

[These then are the 4 stages; let me summarize]

PAUSE

CONCLUSION

    I.   CS occurs in 4 stages: honeymoon, crisis, recovery, & adjustment

    II.  By knowing the 4 stages, you can better understand the culture shock you may now be experiencing on the job, at school, or in your private life.

PAUSE

ASK FOR QUESTIONS

# Step 9: Rehearse Your Speech

Let's start the discussion of rehearsal by identifying the general methods of delivery. Then we can look at some general suggestions for making your rehearsals efficient and effective.

## Methods of Delivery

Speakers vary widely in delivery methods. Some speak off-the-cuff with no apparent preparation. Others read their speeches from manuscript. Others construct a detailed outline and compose the speech at the moment of delivery. These represent the three general methods of delivery: impromptu, manuscript, and extemporaneous.

**The Impromptu Method**   An **impromptu speech** involves speaking without preparation. On some occasions, you can't avoid impromptu speaking. In a classroom, you may be asked to comment on the speaker and speech you just heard: In effect, you give an impromptu speech of evaluation. At meetings, people are often asked for impromptu comments on various issues. Or you may have to fill in for someone who has not shown up. You can greatly improve impromptu speaking by cultivating public speaking ability in general. The more proficient you are as a speaker, the better you will be impromptu.

**The Manuscript Method**   If you give a **manuscript speech,** you write out the speech and read it. This is the safest method when exact timing and wording are required. For example, it could be disastrous if a political leader did not speak from manuscript on sensitive issues. An ambiguous word, phrase, or sentence that proved insulting, belligerent, or conciliatory might cause serious problems. With a manuscript speech, you can control style, content, organization, and all other elements. A variation of the manuscript method is to write out the speech and then memorize it. You then recite the entire speech from memory, much as an actor recites a part in a play. The great disadvantages of the manuscript method are that the speech doesn't sound natural and there is no opportunity to adjust the speech on the basis of audience feedback.

**The Extemporaneous Method**   The **extemporaneous speech** is useful when exact timing and wording are not required. Good lecturing by college teachers is extemporaneous. They have prepared thoroughly, know what they want to say, and have the lecture's organization clearly in mind. But they are not committed to exact wording. This method allows greater flexibility for feedback. Should a

**WHAT DO YOU SAY?**
**Time Problem**
Your speech has run overtime, and you've been given the 30-second stop signal. You wonder if it would be best to ignore the signal and simply continue your speech or if you should you wrap up in 30 seconds. In either case, *What do you say?*

point need clarification, you can elaborate when it will be most effective. It's also easy to be natural, because you're being yourself. And you may move about and interact with the audience.

The major disadvantage of this method is that you may stumble and grope for words. You can address this disadvantage by rehearsing the speech several times. Although you can't give the precise attention to style that you can in the manuscript and memorized methods, you can memorize certain key phrases.

I recommend the extemporaneous method for most situations. Overall, it offers the greatest advantages with the fewest disadvantages. However, consider the advantages of memorizing certain parts of your speech:

- Even in extemporaneous speaking, memorize your opening and closing lines—perhaps the first and last two or three sentences. This will help you focus your attention on the audience at the two most important moments of your speech.

- Memorize the main points and the order in which you will present them. After all, if you expect your audience to remember these points, they will expect you to remember them as well.

## Rehearsing the Speech

Rehearsal should enable you to see how the speech will flow as a whole and to make any necessary changes and improvements. It will also allow you to time your

## MEDIA LITERACY

*Small groups of people can, and do, make the rest of us think what they please about a given subject.*
—EDWARD BERNAYS

### Advertising and Public Relations

The word *advertising* refers to the paid promotion of a product or service in print, on television, on the Web, or anywhere a picture or an apt phrase may be placed. The term *public relations* refers to those activities that promote a positive relationship between an organization and the public. (Rodman, 2001). Like public speeches, advertising and public relations serve two major functions: to inform and to persuade.

- Advertising makes you aware of a particular product or service, a function that's especially important with new products. Advertising also informs you about the product, perhaps describing its ingredients or its uses or telling you where to buy it or how much it costs. Public relations also informs you—about, for example, a political candidate or what an organization is doing to control a crisis, combat crime, or promote better race relations or cancer awareness.

- Beyond information, however, the main purpose of both advertising and public relations is to create a favorable image—whether of a product, so you'll buy it, or of a person or organization. For example, beer and soft drink advertisers often associate friendship and fun with their products so that when you see their products you'll have a positive feeling and ultimately buy the product. And just about every political candidate has a public relations firm helping to form an image that voters will trust and ultimately vote for.

What you see and hear—whether in a television advertisement or in a political candidate's speech—has been carefully constructed by experts in persuasion and represents only a very small part of the entire product, person, or organization. A breakfast cereal's fiber content may be included in a TV commercial, but rarely is the sugar or salt content. And while an organization's charitable donations and a candidate's popular positions may be made public, activities and qualities that might turn people off are kept hidden.

*Increasing Media Literacy.* *Perhaps the best defense against being duped by the media is to recognize how advertising and public relations have influenced you in the past. How would you describe their influence on your own behavior?*

speech so that you stay within the allotted time. The following procedures should help you use your rehearsal time most effectively.

- Rehearse the speech from beginning to end, rather than in parts. Be sure to include all the examples and illustrations (and audiovisual aids if any) in your rehearsal.

- Time the speech during each rehearsal. Adjust your speech—both what you say and your delivery rate—on the basis of this timing.

- Rehearse the speech under conditions as close as possible to those under which you'll deliver it. If possible, rehearse in the room in which you'll present the speech and in front of a few supportive listeners. Get together with two or three other students or colleagues so you can each serve both as speaker and as listener/critic.

- Rehearse the speech in front of a full-length mirror to help you see how you'll appear to the audience. Practice your eye contact, your movements, and your gestures in front of the mirror.

- Don't interrupt your rehearsal to make notes or changes; do these between rehearsals. If possible, record your speech (ideally, on videotape) so you can hear and see exactly what your listeners will hear and see. This will also enable you to see whether you exhibit habits or tics that you may want to alter before you give the "real" speech.

- Rehearse at least three or four times, or as long as your rehearsals continue to result in improvements.

▼ | E-TALK

**Rehearsal**
How would you describe the "rehearsal" you go through in online messages and in public speeches?

## Step 10: Deliver Your Speech

Use your voice and body to complement and reinforce your verbal message.

## Voice

Your voice is your major tool in delivering your message. Use your vocal volume and rate, articulation and pronunciation, and pauses to complement and reinforce your message.

**Volume**  The **volume** of your voice is its relative loudness or softness. In an adequately controlled voice, volume varies according to factors such as the distance between you and your listeners, the competing noise, and the emphasis you want to give an idea. A voice that is too soft will require listeners to strain to hear, and they will soon tire of listening. A voice that is too loud will intrude on the listeners' psychological space. Vary your volume to best reflect your ideas—perhaps increasing volume for key words or phrases, lowering volume when talking about something extremely serious. Be especially careful not to fade away at the ends of sentences.

**Rate**  Your speech **rate** is the speed at which you speak. About 140 words per minute is average for speaking as well as for reading aloud. If you talk too fast, you deprive your listeners of the time they need to digest what you're saying. If your rate is too slow, your listeners' thoughts will wander. So speak at a pace that engages but doesn't bore and that allows listeners time for reflection. Vary your rate during the speech to call attention to certain points and to add variety.

**Articulation and Pronunciation**  **Articulation** results from movements of the speech organs as they modify and interrupt the air stream from the lungs. Different movements of the tongue, lips, teeth, palate, and vocal cords produce different sounds. **Pronunciation** consists of the production of syllables or words according to some accepted standard, such as that of a dictionary. Let's consider some of the most common problems associated with faulty articulation and pronunciation.

***Errors of Omission (Articulation).*** Omitting sounds or even syllables is a common articulation problem that you can easily overcome with concentration and practice. Here are some examples:

| Incorrect | Correct |
|---|---|
| gov-a-ment | gov-ern-ment |
| hi-stry | hi-sto-ry |
| wanna | want to |
| studyin | studying |
| a-lum-num | a-lum-i-num |
| comp-ny | comp-a-ny |
| vul-ner-bil-ity | vul-ner-a-bil-ity |

***Errors of Substitution (Articulation).*** Substituting an incorrect sound for the correct one is also easy to fix. Among the most common substitutions are [d] for [t] and [d] for [th]; for example, *wader* for the correct *waiter*, *dese* for the correct *these*, *bedder* for the correct *better*, and *ax* for the correct *ask*. Other prevalent substitution errors include *ekcetera* for the correct *etcetera*, *congradulations* for the correct *congratulations*, and *lenth* for the correct *length*.

***Errors of Addition (Articulation).*** These errors involve adding sounds where they don't belong. Some examples include:

| Incorrect | Correct |
|---|---|
| acrost | across |
| athalete | athlete |
| Americar | America |
| idear | idea |
| filim | film |
| lore | law |

If you make any of these errors, you can correct them by following these steps:

1. Become conscious of your own articulation patterns and the specific errors you're making. Recording yourself on tape will help you become more aware of your own speech patterns and possible errors.
2. Listen carefully to the articulation of accomplished speakers—for example, broadcasters.
3. Practice the correct patterns until they become part of your normal speech behavior.

***Errors of Accent (Pronunciation).*** Each word has its own accepted **accent** or stress pattern. Examples of words that are often accented incorrectly include *New Orleáns*, *ínsurance*, *compárable*, and *orátor* for the correct *New Órleans*, *insúrance*, *cómparable*, and *órator*.

***Errors of Adding Sounds (Pronunciation).*** For some words, many people add sounds that are not part of the standard pronunciation. In the first three examples, the error involves pronouncing letters that are a part of the written word but should remain silent. In the last four examples, sounds are inserted where they don't belong.

| Incorrect | Correct |
|-----------|---------|
| homage | omage |
| Illinois | Illinoi |
| evening | evning |
| athalete | athlete |
| airaplane | airplane |
| burgalar | burglar |
| mischievious | mischievous |

One way to correct pronunciation problems is to check a word's pronunciation in a dictionary. Learn to read your dictionary's pronunciation key. Another way is to listen to a dictionary on CD-ROM so you can hear the standard pronunciation.

**Pauses**   Pauses are interruptions in the flow of speech. *Filled pauses* are gaps that you fill with vocalizations such as *er*, *um*, and *ah*. Even expressions such as *well* and *you know*, when used merely to fill up silence, are filled pauses. These pauses are ineffective and detract from the strength of your message. They will make you appear hesitant, unprepared, and unsure.

*Unfilled pauses*, silences interjected into the stream of speech, can be especially effective if used correctly. Here are a few examples of places where unfilled pauses—silences of a few seconds—can enhance your speech.

**WHAT DO YOU SAY?**
**Audience Inactivity**
You're giving a speech on the problems of teenage drug abuse, and you notice that the back rows of your audience have totally tuned you out; they're reading, chatting, working on their laptops. *What do you say?*

 *Skill Development Experience*

## Checking Your Pronunciation

Here are additional words that are often mispronounced. Consult a print or online dictionary (ideally, one with audio capabilities) and record the correct pronunciations here.

| Words Often Mispronounced | Correct Pronunciation | Words Often Mispronounced | Correct Pronunciation |
|---------------------------|----------------------|---------------------------|----------------------|
| Abdomen | | Herb | |
| Accessory | | Hierarchy | |
| Arctic | | Library | |
| Buffet | | Nausea | |
| Calvary | | Nuclear | |
| Clothes | | Probably | |
| Costume | | Prostate | |
| Diagnosis | | Relevant | |
| Especially | | Repeat | |
| Espresso | | Salmon | |
| Et cetera | | Sandwich | |
| February | | Similar | |
| Foliage | | Substantive | |
| Forte | | Xenophobia | |

*Mispronouncing words in public speaking may significantly detract from your credibility. Feeling unsure about how to pronounce any word in your speech also is likely to contribute to your own communication apprehension.*

- Pause at transitional points. This will signal that you're moving from one part of the speech or from one idea to another. It will help listeners separate the main issues you're discussing.

- Pause at the end of an important assertion. This allows the audience to think about its significance.

- Pause after asking a rhetorical question. This will give the audience time to think about how they would answer.

- Pause before an important idea. This will help signal that what comes next is especially significant.

- Pause before you begin your speech (to scan and assess the audience and gather your thoughts) and after you finish it (to allow your ideas to sink in and to dispel any idea that you're anxious to escape).

## Body Action

You speak with your body as well as with your mouth. The total effect of the speech depends not only on what you say but also on how you present it. As shown in Table 11.2, body action can communicate your power, your self-assurance, your comfort and control of the public speaking situation. The four aspects of body action that are especially important in public speaking are eye contact, facial expression, gestures and posture, and movement.

**Eye Contact** The most important single aspect of bodily communication is eye contact. Keep in mind, however, that cultures differ widely on the amount and intensity of eye contact they consider appropriate. In some cultures, eye contact that is too intense may be considered offensive. In most of the United States, audiences want and expect to be looked at rather directly. Not surprisingly, then, the two major problems with eye contact are not enough eye contact and eye contact that does not cover the audience fairly. Speakers who do not maintain enough eye contact appear distant, unconcerned, and less trustworthy than speakers who look directly at their audience. And, of course, without eye contact, you will not be able to secure that all-important audience feedback. Maintain eye contact with the entire audience. Involve all listeners in the public speaking transaction. Communicate equally with the audience members on the left and on the right, in both the back and the front of the room.

*"Within many cultures around the world, it is believed that the eyes are the windows to the soul. In public speaking, since we usually want to arouse both spirit and soul, the eyes become the most important physical equipment of all."*

—ROGER E. AXTELL

**Facial Expression** If you believe in your thesis, you'll probably display your meanings appropriately and effectively. Nervousness and anxiety, however, can prevent you from relaxing enough for your positive emotions to come through. But time and practice will allow you to relax, and your feelings will reveal themselves appropriately and automatically.

**Gestures and Posture** Spontaneous and natural gestures will help illustrate your verbal messages. If you feel relaxed and comfortable with yourself and your audience, you'll generate natural body action without conscious or studied attention. When delivering your speech, stand straight but not stiff. Try to communicate a command of the situation rather than any nervousness you may feel. Avoid putting your hands in your pockets or leaning on the desk or chalkboard. With practice, you'll feel more at ease and will communicate this in the way you stand before the audience.

**Movement** If you move too little, you may appear fearful or distant. If you move too much, you may lead the audience to concentrate on the movement itself, wondering where you'll wind up

**TABLE 11.2** Powerful Body Action

Here are examples of body actions that are likely to enhance your power as a public speaker (Lewis, 1989; Burgoon & Bacue, 2003; Burgoon & Hoobler, 2002; Guerrero, DeVito, & Hecht, 1999):

| SUGGESTIONS FOR COMMUNICATING POWER WITH BODILY ACTION | ANTICIPATED EFFECT |
|---|---|
| Avoid self-manipulations (playing with your hair or touching your face, for example) and backward leaning. | These signals communicate an ill-at-ease feeling; avoiding them will show your comfort and will enhance your persuasiveness. |
| Walk slowly and deliberately to and from the podium. | To appear hurried is to seem as if you were rushing to meet the expectations of others; taking your time conveys an air of control. |
| Use facial expressions and gestures as appropriate. | Appropriate facial expressions and gestures help you express your concern for the other person and for the interaction and help you communicate your comfort and control of the situation. |
| Use consistent packaging; be careful that your verbal and nonverbal messages do not contradict each other. | Consistency between verbal and nonverbal messages communicates assurance, confidence, and conviction. |

next. Use movement to emphasize transitions and to introduce important assertions. For example, when making a transition, you might step forward to signal that something new is coming. Similarly, use movement to signal an important assumption, bit of evidence, or closely reasoned argument.

## Using Notes

Speakers who prepare their speeches around a series of slides such as you'd produce with one of the presentation software packages (such as PowerPoint or Corel Presentations) may use their slides as their notes. In most public speaking classes, your notes will consist of a delivery outline and your audiovisual aids. Effective delivery depends on the smooth use of notes—whether a series of slides or transparencies or an $8\frac{1}{2}$-by-11-inch piece of paper—during the speech. A few simple guidelines may help you avoid common errors (McCroskey, 1997; Kesselman-Turkel & Peterson, 1982).

- Use only your delivery outline when presenting your speech; never use the preparation outline. One $8\frac{1}{2}$-by-11-inch page should be sufficient for most speeches. This aid will relieve anxiety over forgetting your speech but not be extensive enough to prevent meaningful speaker–audience interaction.

- Know your notes intimately. Rehearse at least twice with the same notes you will take to the speaker's stand.

- Use your notes with "open subtlety." Don't make your notes more obvious than necessary, but don't try to hide them. Don't gesture with them, but don't turn away from the audience to steal a glance at them, either. Watch the way television talk show personalities use notes; many of these media hosts provide useful models you might want to imitate.

## Critically Evaluating Speeches

Part of your function in learning public speaking is learning to evaluate finished, delivered speeches and to express your evaluations in a clear and constructive way.

**Willingness to Criticize**
How would you compare your
willingness to criticize, say, an
acquaintance in e-mail versus
face-to-face interaction?
Would the substance of the
criticism change? Would the
way you expressed it change?

# Speech Evaluation

The following questions, which come from topics covered in this chapter and Chapter 11, can serve as a beginning guide to speech evaluation. Use them to check your own speeches as well as to evaluate the speeches of others. In addition, see Table 11.3 for tips on identifying common language fallacies you'll want to watch out for.

### The subject and purpose

1. Is the subject worthwhile? Relevant? Interesting to the audience and speaker?
2. What is the speech's general purpose (to inform, to persuade)?
3. Is the topic narrow enough to be covered in some depth?
4. Is the specific purpose clear to the audience?

### The audience

5. Has the speaker considered the culture, age, gender, occupation, income, status, and religion of the audience? How does the speaker take these factors into consideration?
6. Has the speaker considered and adapted to the willingness, favorableness, and knowledge of the audience?

### The thesis and major propositions

7. Is the speech's thesis clear and limited to one main idea?
8. Are the speech's main points clearly related to the thesis?
9. Are there an appropriate number of main points in the speech (not too many, not too few)?

### Research

10. Is the speech adequately researched? Are the sources reliable and up to date?
11. Does the speaker seem to understand the subject thoroughly?

### Supporting materials

12. Is each major proposition adequately and appropriately supported?
13. Do the supporting materials amplify what they purport to amplify? Do they prove what they purport to prove?

### Organization

14. How is the body of the speech organized? What is the organization pattern?
15. Is the organization pattern appropriate to the speech and to the audience?

### Wording

16. Is the language clear, vivid, and appropriate?
17. Are the sentences short, direct, active, positive, and varied?

### The conclusion, introduction, and transitions

18. Does the conclusion effectively summarize and close the speech?
19. Does the introduction gain the audience's attention and provide a clear orientation?
20. Are there adequate transitions?

### Delivery

21. Does the speaker maintain eye contact with the audience?

22. Are the volume and rate appropriate to the audience, occasion, and topic?

23. Are the voice and body actions appropriate to the speaker, subject, and audience?

## Expressing Your Evaluation

The major purpose of classroom evaluation is to improve class members' public speaking technique. Through constructive criticism, you, as a speaker and as a listener–critic, will more effectively learn the principles of public speaking. You will be shown what you do well and what you can improve.

For all the benefits of evaluation, however, many people resist this process. The main source of resistance seems to be that evaluations and suggestions for improvement are often perceived as personal attacks. Before reading the specific suggestions for expressing criticism, take the self-test, "What's wrong with these comments?" Then consider the suggestions for offering criticism more effectively that follow the self-test.

---

**TABLE 11.3** Fallacies of Language

In listening to and critically evaluating speeches, look carefully for language fallacies—ways in which speakers often use language to subvert instead of clarify truth and accuracy. In the discussion of verbal messages (Chapter 4), five such barriers to language accuracy were identified: polarization, fact–inference confusion, allness, static evaluation, and indiscrimination. Here we focus on words that mislead and give listeners the wrong impression. After you read these verbal fallacies, review some of the commercial websites for vitamins, clothing, books, music, or any such topic you're interested in and try to find examples of misleading language. It won't be difficult.

| FALLACY | EXAMPLES | CRITICAL RESPONSE |
|---|---|---|
| *Weasel words* are those whose meanings are slippery and difficult to pin down (Hayakawa & Hayakawa, 1989). | For example, the medicine that claims to "work better than Brand X" doesn't specify how much better or in what respect it performs better. *Better* is a weasel word, as are *help*, *virtually*, *as much as*, *like* (as in *it will make you feel like new*), and *more economical*. | Ask yourself: Exactly what is being claimed? For example, "What does 'may reduce cholesterol' mean? What exactly is being asserted?" |
| *Euphemisms* make the offensive or taboo appear positive and appealing, or at least neutral. | Euphemisms are all around. Calling the firing of 200 workers *downsizing* or *reallocation of resources* is euphemistic. | Don't let polite words get in the way of accurate firsthand perception. The word is not the thing; words just symbolize the thing (sometimes inaccurately). |
| *Jargon* is the specialized language of a professional class; it becomes a problem when used with those who are not professionals in the field. | The specialized languages of communication, computer, and psychology professionals are examples, as in *content and relationship messages*, *blogosphere*, and *attribution*. | Don't be intimidated by jargon; ask questions when you don't understand. |
| *Doublespeak* is language used to deceive or confuse rather than to inform. | The use of words to obscure meaning or to confuse people. | As with jargon, don't allow words to intimidate you; when in doubt, find out. |
| *Gobbledygook* is overly complex language that overwhelms the listener instead of communicating meaning. | Big and relatively uncommon words and foreign terms (especially Latin or French) are examples. | Don't confuse complex language with truth or accuracy; ask for simplification when appropriate. |

*I love criticism just as long as it's unqualified praise.*

—NOEL COWARD

## Listening to Criticism

Although it's a valuable part of public speaking and of life in general, listening to criticism is difficult. Here are some suggestions for making listening to criticism easier and more effective.

- *Listen with an open mind.* Encourage the critics to share their insights, demonstrate your willingness to listen, and listen with an open mind. At the same time, recognize that when someone criticizes your speech, he or she is not criticizing your worth as an individual. So be open to criticism, but don't take it too personally; view critical messages as objectively as you can.

- *Accept the critic's viewpoint.* If the critic says the evidence wasn't convincing, it doesn't help to identify the 12 references that you used in your speech; this critic simply was not convinced. Instead, think about why your evidence was not convincing to this critic. Perhaps you didn't emphasize the credibility of the sources or didn't clarify their relevance to your proposition.

- *Seek clarification.* If you don't understand the criticism, ask for clarification. If you're told that your specific purpose was too broad, but it's unclear to you how you might improve it, ask the critic how you might narrow the specific purpose.

***Applying Listening Skills.*** *You've just given a speech you thought was pretty good. Yet your audience looked bored, and during the criticism period one person says, "Your speech didn't hold my attention. I was bored. You really should have prepared more." In truth you put a great deal of time into this speech, and you know you incorporated just about every attention-gaining device imaginable. How do you respond?*

## *Test* ▶◀ *Yourself*

### WHAT'S WRONG WITH THESE COMMENTS?

**INSTRUCTIONS:** Examine each of the following critical comments. For the purposes of this exercise, assume that each comment represents the critic's complete criticism. What's wrong with each?

_____ ❶  I loved the speech. It was great. Really great.

_____ ❷  The introduction didn't gain my attention.

_____ ❸  You weren't interested in your own topic. How do you expect us to be interested?

_____ ❹  Nobody was able to understand you.

_____ ❺  The speech was weak.

_____ ❻  The speech didn't do anything for me.

_____ ❼  Your position was unfair to those of us on athletic scholarships; we earned those scholarships.

_____ ❽  I found four things wrong with your speech. First, . . .

_____ ❾  You needed better research.

_____ ❿  I liked the speech; we need more police on campus.

**HOW DID YOU DO?**  Before reading the following discussion, try to explain why each of these statements is ineffective.

**Say Something Positive**   Because most people suffer from apprehension and anxiety in public speaking, criticism is difficult to take. So emphasize the positive. First, positively comment on effective speech elements: "Your visual aids made the cost comparison so easy for me to see and really convinced me to change brands." Second, use positive comments as a preface to any negative ones. There are always positive characteristics, and it's more productive to mention these first. Thus, instead of saying—as in the self-test—"The speech didn't do anything for me," tell the speaker what you liked first and then bring up a weakness and suggest how it might be corrected: "Your introduction really made me realize that many colleges have problems with campus violence, but I wasn't convinced early on that we have one here at Andrews. I would have preferred to hear the examples that you gave near the end of the speech—which were excellent, by the way—in the introduction. Then I would have been convinced we had a problem and would have been more anxious to hear your solutions."

**Be Specific**   Criticism is most effective when it's specific. Statements such as "I thought your delivery was bad" or "I thought your examples were good" or, as in the self-test, "I loved the speech. . . . Really great" and "The speech was weak" are poorly expressed evaluations. These statements don't specify what the speaker might do to improve delivery or to capitalize on the examples used. When commenting on delivery, refer to specifics such as the evidence used, the language, the delivery, or whatever else is of consequence, as in "I thought that more recent examples of arson would have made the need for new legislation more convincing" or "Your opening story really got me involved and totally on your side."

**Be Objective**   When evaluating a speech, transcend your own biases as best you can. Avoid statements like the self-test example "Your position was unfair. . . . We earned those scholarships." Examine the speech from the point of view of the (detached) critic. Evaluate, for example, the validity of the arguments and their suitability to the audience, the language, the supporting materials. Analyze, in fact, all the ingredients that went into the preparation and presentation of the speech.

**Limit Criticism**   Cataloging a speaker's weak points, as in "I found four things wrong with your speech," will overwhelm, not help, the speaker. If you're one of many critics, chances are that others will bring up the same criticisms you noted and you can feel comfortable limiting your criticism to one or perhaps two points. You might say, for example, "The one thing I would change is your opening quotation; it was interesting but a bit long and somewhat difficult to follow. I think if you had paraphrased the idea, it would have had a greater impact." If you're the sole critic, then you'll want to evaluate the entire speech.

**Be Constructive**   Give the speaker the insight that you feel will help him or her in future public speaking situations. For example, "The introduction didn't gain my attention" doesn't tell the speaker how he or she might have gained your attention. Instead, you might say, "The example about the computer crash would have more effectively gained my attention in the introduction."

**Focus on Behavior**   Focus criticism on what the speaker said and did during the actual speech. Try to avoid the very natural tendency to

*Anyone can be accurate and even profound, but it is damned hard work to make criticism charming."*

—H. L. MENCKEN

## Criticizing Ethically

Just as the speaker and the listener have ethical obligations, so does the critic.

- First, the ethical critic separates personal feelings about the speaker from the evaluation of the speech. A liking for the speaker should not lead you to give positive evaluations to the speech, nor should disliking the speaker lead you to give negative evaluations.
- Second, the ethical critic separates personal feelings about the issues from an evaluation of the validity of the arguments. Recognize the validity of an argument even if it contradicts a deeply held belief; at the same time, recognize the fallaciousness of an argument even if it supports a deeply held belief.
- Third, the ethical critic is culturally sensitive and aware of his or her own ethnocentrism; the ethical critic doesn't negatively evaluate customs and beliefs simply because they differ from her or his own. Conversely, the ethical critic does not positively evaluate a speech just because it supports her or his own cultural beliefs and values. The ethical critic does not discriminate against or favor speakers simply because they're of a particular gender, race, affectional orientation, nationality, religion, or age group.

*What Would You Do?* *You and your best friend are taking this course together. Your friend just gave a pretty terrible speech, and unfortunately, the instructor has asked you to offer a critique. The wrinkle here is that the grade the instructor gives will be heavily influenced by what the student critic says. So, in effect, your critique will largely determine your friend's grade. You'd like to give your friend a positive critique so he can earn a good grade—which he badly needs. Besides, you figure, you can always tell him the truth later and even help him to improve. What would you do?*

*We are here on earth to do good for others. What the others are here for, I don't know.*
—W. H. AUDEN

mind-read the speaker, to assume that you know why the speaker did one thing rather than another. Instead of saying, "You weren't interested in your topic" (a comment that attacks the speaker), say, "I would have liked to see greater variety in your delivery. It would have made me feel you were more interested." Instead of saying, "You didn't care about your audience," say, "I would have liked it if you looked more directly at us while speaking."

**Own Your Own Criticism** Take responsibility for your criticism. The best way to express this ownership is to use I-messages rather than you-messages. Instead of saying, "You needed better research," say, "I would have been more persuaded if you had used more recent research."

I-messages also will prevent you from using "should messages," a type of expression that almost invariably creates defensiveness and resentment. When you say, "You should have done this," or, "You shouldn't have done that," you assume a superior position and imply that what you're saying is correct and that what the speaker did was incorrect. When you own your evaluations and use I-messages, on the other hand, you're offering your perceptions. It's then up to the speaker to deal with them.

**Be Culturally Sensitive** There are vast cultural differences in what is considered proper when it comes to criticism. In some cultures public criticism, even if it's designed to help teach important skills, is considered inappropriate. As noted in Chapters 4, 7, and 9, some cultures place a heavy emphasis on face-saving, on allowing the other person always to remain in a positive light (James, 1995). In cultures in which face-saving is important, members may prefer not to say anything negative in public—and may even be reluctant to say anything positive, for fear that the omissions may be construed as negatives. In cultures emphasizing face-saving (generally high-context cultures), criticism should take place only in private to enable the person to save face. Communication rules such as the following prevail in these cultures.

- Don't express negative evaluation in public; instead, compliment the person.
- Don't prove someone wrong, especially in public; express agreement even if you know the person is wrong.
- Don't correct someone's errors; don't even acknowledge them.
- Don't ask difficult questions lest the person not know the answer and lose face or be embarrassed; generally, avoid asking questions.

# THE PUBLIC SPEAKING SAMPLE ASSISTANT

## A POORLY CONSTRUCTED PERSUASIVE SPEECH

This speech was written to illustrate some really broad as well as some rather subtle errors that a beginning speaker might make in constructing a persuasive speech. First, read the entire speech without reading any of the questions in the right-hand column. Then, after you've read the entire speech, reread each paragraph and respond to the critical thinking questions. What other questions might prove productive to ask?

## XXX HAS GOT TO GO

*Speech*

You probably didn't read the papers this weekend, but there's a XXX movie, I mean video, store that moved in on Broad and Fifth Streets. My parents, who are retired teachers, are protesting it, and so am I. My parents are organizing a protest for the next weekend.

There must be hundreds of XXX video stores in the country, and they all need to be closed down. I have a lot of reasons.

First, my parents think it should be closed down. My parents are retired teachers and have organized protests over the proposed new homeless shelter and to prevent the city from making that park on Elm Street. So they know what they're doing.

The XXX video place is un-Godly. No people would ever go there. Our religious leader is against it and is joining in the protest.

These stores bring crime into the neighborhood. I have proof of that. Morristown's crime increased after the XXX video store opened. And in Martinsville, where they got rid of the video store, crime did not increase. If we allow the video store in our own town, then we're going to be like Morristown and our crime is going to increase.

*Critical Thinking Questions*

What do you think of the title of the speech?

Visualizing yourself as a listener, how would the opening comment make you feel?

Does the speaker gain your attention?

What thesis do you think the speaker will support?

Does mentioning "my parents" help or hurt the speaker's credibility?

What is the speaker's thesis?

What impression are you beginning to get of the speaker?

How do the speaker's parents sound to you? Do they sound like credible leaders with a consistent cause? Or chronic protesters (with perhaps a negative agenda)?

What evidence is offered to support the assertion that you should believe the speaker's parents? Is this adequate?

What would you need to know about these people before believing them?

What does this statement assume about the audience?

How would your public speaking class respond to this statement? What are some reasons why the speaker might not have explained how XXX video stores are un-Godly? How will those in the audience who are not religious react to this statement?

What do you think of the reasoning used here? Are there other factors that could have influenced Morristown's crime increase? Is there any evidence that getting rid of the video store resulted in the stable crime rate in Martinsville? What assumption about the audience does the speaker make in using Martinsville and Morristown as analogies?

These stores make lots of garbage. The plastic wrappings from the videos will add to our already overextended and overutilized landfill. And a lot of them are going to wind up as litter on the streets.

The XXX Video House stays open seven days a week, 24 hours a day. People will be forced to work at all hours and on Sunday, and that's not fair. And the store will increase the noise level at night with the cars pulling up and all.

The XXX Video House—that's its name, by the way—doesn't carry regular videos that most people want. So why do we want them?

The XXX Video House got a lease from an owner who doesn't even live in the community, someone by the name of, well, it's an organization called XYZ Management. And their address is Carlson Place in Jeffersonville. So they don't even live here.

A neighboring store owner says he thinks the store is in violation of several fire laws. He says they have no sprinkler system and no metal doors to prevent the spread of a fire. So he thinks they should be closed down, too.

Last week on *Oprah*, three women were on and they were in the XXX movie business and they were all on drugs and had been in jail and they said it all started when they went into the porno business. One woman wanted to be a teacher, another wanted to be a nurse, and the other wanted to be a beautician. If there weren't any XXX video stores, then there wouldn't be a porn business and, you know, pornography is part of organized crime and so if you stop pornography you take a bite out of crime.

One of the reasons I think it should be closed is that the legitimate video stores—the ones that have only a small selection of XXX movies somewhere in the back—will lose business. And if they continue to lose business, they'll leave the neighborhood and we'll have no video stores.

That's a lot of reasons against XXX movie houses. I have a quote here: Reason is "a portion of the divine spirit set in a human body." Seneca.

In conclusion and to wrap it up and close my speech, I want to repeat and say again that XXX video stores should all be closed down. They corrupt minors. And they're offensive to men and women and especially women. I hope you'll all protest with the Marshalls—my mother and father—and there will be lots of others there, too.

Do you agree with this argument about the garbage? Is this argument in any way unique to the video store? Is it likely that people will open the wrappers and drop them on the street?

What validity do you give to each of these arguments? Given the 24-hour policy, how might you construct an argument against the video store? Are there advantages of a neighborhood store's 24-hour policy that the audience may be thinking of and thus countering the speaker's argument? If there are, how should the speaker deal with them?

Upon hearing this, would you be likely to extend this argument and start asking yourself, "Do we now close up all stores that most people don't want?"

Is there a connection between who the owner is and whether the video store should or should not be closed? Could the speaker have effectively used this information in support of the thesis to close the video store?

What credibility do you ascribe to the "neighboring store owner"? Do you begin to wonder whether the speaker would simply agree to have the store brought up to the fire code laws?

What is the cause and what is the effect that the speaker is asserting? How likely is it that the proposed cause actually produced the effect? Might there have been causes other than pornography that might have led these women into drugs?

What credibility do you give to people you see on talk shows? Does credibility vary with the specific talk show?

Do you accept the argument that there would be no pornography business without video stores? What would have to be proved to you before you accepted this connection?

How do you respond to the expression "take a bite out of crime"?

Is the speaker implying that this is the real reason against XXX video stores?

Do you start wondering whether the speaker is against XXX video—as seemed in the last argument—or just against stores that sell these exclusively? What effect does this impression have on your evaluation of the speaker's credibility and thesis?

How do you feel about the number of "reasons"? Would you have preferred fewer reasons more fully developed or more reasons?

What purpose does this quotation serve?

Might the speaker have introduced the conclusion differently?

Now what is the speaker's thesis?

What do you think of the argument that XXX video stores are offensive? What effect does this argument have coming here in the conclusion?

Do you think you'd go to the protest? Why?

In some cultures, being kind to the person is more important than telling the truth, so members may say things that are complimentary but untrue in a logical sense.

In contrast, people in cultures that are highly individualistic and competitive (the United States, Germany, and Sweden are examples) may find public criticism a normal part of the learning process. Thus, people in these cultures may readily criticize others and are likely to expect the same "courtesy" from other listeners. After all, these people may reason, "If I'm going to criticize your skills to help you improve, I expect you to help me in the same way." People from cultures that are more collectivist and that emphasize the group rather than the individual (Japan, Mexico, and Korea are examples) are likely to find giving and receiving public criticism uncomfortable, however. They may feel that it's more important to be polite and courteous than to help someone learn a skill. Cultural rules aimed at maintaining peaceful relations among the Japanese (Midooka, 1990) and politeness among many Asian cultures (Fraser, 1990) may conflict with the Western classroom cultural norm that supports voicing criticism.

The difficulties are compounded when you interpret unexpected behavior through your own cultural filters. For example, if a speaker who expects comments and criticism gets none, he or she may interpret the silence to mean that the audience didn't care or wasn't listening. But they may have been listening very intently. They may simply be operating according to a different cultural rule, a rule that says it's impolite to criticize or evaluate another person's work, especially in public.

**WHAT DO YOU SAY?**
**Criticizing A Speech**
A student has just given a speech on the glory of bullfighting, something you define as animal cruelty. To the speaker, however, bullfighting is an important part of the culture. As you bristle inside, the instructor asks you to critique the speech. *What do you say?*

## Summary of Concepts and Skills

This chapter looked at the last four steps in the public speaking process: wording the speech, constructing the conclusion and the introduction, rehearsing, and delivering the speech.

1. Compared with written style, oral style contains shorter, simpler, and more familiar words; greater qualification; and more self-referential terms.
2. Effective public speaking style is clear (be economical and specific; use guide phrases and short, familiar, and commonly used terms); vivid (use active verbs, strong verbs, figures of speech, and imagery); appropriate to your audience (speak on a suitable level of formality; avoid written-style expressions; avoid slang, vulgar, and offensive terms); personal (use personal pronouns, ask questions, and create immediacy); and powerful (avoid behaviors that convey powerlessness).
3. When constructing sentences for public speeches, favor short, direct, active, and positively phrased sentences. Vary the type and length.
4. Conclusions should summarize and close the speech. Introductions should gain attention and orient the audience as to what is to follow.
5. Transitions and internal summaries help connect the parts of the speech and help the listeners better remember the speech.
6. Preparation, template, and delivery outlines all serve different functions and will help any speaker, but especially the beginning speaker, in preparing and presenting effective public speeches.
7. There are three basic methods of delivering a public speech. The impromptu method involves speaking without any specific preparation. The manuscript method involves writing out the entire speech and reading it to the audience. The extemporaneous method involves thorough preparation and memorizing the main ideas and their order of appearance, but not a commitment to exact wording.
8. Use rehearsal to time and perfect your speech from beginning to end; rehearse under realistic conditions, and with listeners if possible.
9. When you deliver your speech, regulate your voice for greatest effectiveness. Adjust your volume on the basis of the distance between you and your audience and the emphasis you wish to give certain ideas, for example. Adjust your rate on the basis of time constraints, the speech's content, and the listening conditions.
10. Avoid the major problems of articulation and pronunciation; errors of omission, substitution, addition, and accent.
11. Use unfilled pauses to signal a transition between the major parts of the speech, to allow the audience time to think, to allow the audience to ponder a rhetorical question, and to signal the approach of a particularly important idea. Avoid filled pauses; they weaken your message.

12. Effective body action involves maintaining eye contact with your entire audience, allowing your facial expressions to convey your feelings, using your posture to communicate command of the public speaking interaction, gesturing naturally, and moving around a bit.

13. When expressing critical evaluations, try to say something positive, be specific, be objective, limit your criticism, be constructive, focus on behavior, own your own criticism, and be culturally sensitive.

This chapter stressed several significant skills for style and delivery. Place a check mark next to those skills you want most to work on.

_____ 1. I word my speech so it's clear, vivid, appropriate, and personal.

_____ 2. I construct sentences that are short, direct, active, and positive, and I vary the type and length of sentences.

_____ 3. I construct conclusions that summarize the major ideas of the speech and bring the speech to a crisp close.

_____ 4. I construct introductions that gain attention and preview what is to follow.

_____ 5. I use transitions and internal summaries to connect the parts of the speech and to help listeners remember what I say.

_____ 6. In general, I use the extemporaneous method of delivery.

_____ 7. I rehearse my speech often, perfect my delivery, rehearse the speech as a whole, time the speech at each rehearsal, approximate the specific speech situation as much as possible, see and think of myself as a public speaker, and incorporate any delivery notes that may be of value during the actual speech presentation.

_____ 8. I vary my vocal volume and rate to best reflect and reinforce my verbal messages and avoid the common problems with volume and rate.

_____ 9. I avoid the articulation and pronunciation errors of omission, substitution, addition, accent, and pronouncing sounds that should be silent.

_____ 10. I use pauses to signal transitions, to allow listeners time to think, and to signal the approach of a significant idea.

_____ 11. During the speech delivery I maintain eye contact with the entire audience, allow my facial expressions to convey my feelings, gesture naturally, and incorporate purposeful body movements.

_____ 12. When expressing critical evaluations of the speeches of others, I try to say something positive, be specific, be objective, be constructive, be culturally sensitive, and own my own responses.

 Key Word Quiz

## The Language of Public Speaking Preparation

Match the terms about public speaking preparation with their definitions. Record the number of the definition next to the appropriate term.

a. _____ impromptu speech

b. _____ powerless forms of language

c. _____ internal summary

d. _____ extemporaneous speech

e. _____ written style expressions

f. _____ transitions

g. _____ tag questions

h. _____ idiom

i. _____ articulation

j. _____ simile

1. An expression that is unique to specific language and whose meaning cannot be deduced from the individual words.

2. Words, phrases, or sentences that connect the various parts of the speech and guide the listeners to focus on your next argument or idea.

3. Messages that ask for agreement.

4. Speech made off-the-cuff, without preparation.

5. The production of words resulting from movements of the speech organs.

6. Faults such as hesitations, disqualifiers, and self-critical statements.

7. A statement that recaps what you've discussed so far.

8. A speech that is thoroughly prepared and organized in detail but in which only certain aspects of style are predetermined.

9. A figure of speech that compares two unlike objects, using words such as *like* or *as*.

10. Expressions such as "the former" and "the above."

Answers: a. 4 b. 6 c. 7 d. 8 e. 10 f. 2 g. 3 h. 1 i. 5 j. 9

## Five for Discussion

1. When images are too vivid, they may divert an audience from following a logically presented series of thoughts or arguments (Frey & Eagly, 1993). The listener's brain focuses on these extremely vivid images and loses the speaker's train of thought. So if you suspect that your listeners may concentrate on the imagery rather than the idea, drop the imagery. In the same way that a speech can be too vivid, can a speech be too clear? Too appropriate? Too personal?

2. What do you think is the single most important principle for preparing and delivering an effective public speech? What mistake is most frequently made in public speaking?

3. What would you say to students in a public speaking class who may be reluctant to voice public criticism?

4. As a public speaker, do you think you'd get greater power and be more influential by using task cues (cues that stress your ability to do the job, such as maintaining eye contact, using a relatively rapid speech rate, speaking fluently, and gesturing appropriately) or by using dominance cues (cues that threaten, such as speaking in a loud and angry voice, pointing fingers, maintaining rigid posture, using forceful gestures, and lowering the eyebrows)? Results from one study show that you'd be more influential if you used task cues (Driskell, Olmstead, & Salas, 1993). Listeners also would see you as more competent and more likable. If you used dominance cues, on the other hand, you'd be more likely to be perceived as less competent, less influential, less likable, and more self-oriented. The implication of these findings is that if you wish to gain influence and be liked, you should use task cues and avoid dominance cues. How might you use the results of this study to enhance your influence in public speaking? What kinds of cues would you seek to avoid?

5. Visit one of the websites for quotations; for example, try www.bartleby.com or http://us.imdb.com/ (a database of quotations from films). Select a quotation suitable for use with the speech on culture shock in the Public Speaking Sample Assistant on pages 262–264, and explain how you would use this in this speech.

## Log On! MyCommunicationLab

Several exercises and two self-tests at www.mycommunicationlab.com will help personalize the material presented here: (1) Making Concepts Specific, (2) Rephrasing Clichés, (3) Organizing a Scrambled Outline, (4) Can You Distinguish Commonly Used Words? and (5) How Flexible Are You as a Public Speaker? In addition, there is an extended discussion of the (6) Motivated Sequence and a variety of (7) template outlines to help you organize your speeches.

Also visit MycommunicationLab for other activities, study aids, and video clips on public speaking preparation.

Explore our research resources at www.researchnavigator.com.

# The Informative Speech

## Why Read This Chapter?

Because you'll **learn about:**

- the ways in which information is communicated from speaker to audience most effectively.
- the varied types of informative speeches.

Because you'll **learn to:**

- apply the principles of communicating information to a variety of informative speeches.
- develop a variety of informative speeches.
- use presentation software with maximum effectiveness.

$\mathcal{T}$his chapter covers speeches of information, through which you tell your listeners something they didn't already know; the next chapter covers speeches of persuasion, through which you change your listeners' attitudes or beliefs or get them to do something. (A thorough discussion of a third kind of speech, the "special occasion speech," may be found on the CD-ROM and at www.ablongman.com/devito.) Before beginning your journey into these types of speeches—or after giving your next speech—you may want to examine your own satisfaction as a public speaker by taking the self-test "How satisfying is your public speaking?"

# Guidelines for Informative Speaking

To communicate information is to tell your listeners something they don't know, something new. You can inform your audience about a new way of looking at old things or an old way of looking at new things. You may discuss a theory not previously heard of or a familiar concept not fully understood. You may talk about events that the audience may be unaware of or explain happenings they may have misconceptions about. Regardless of what type of informative speech you intend to give, the following guidelines should help.

## Limit the Amount of Information

There's a limit to the amount of information that a listener can take in at one time. Resist the temptation to overload your listeners. Instead of enlarging the breadth of information you communicate, expand its depth. It's better to present two new items of information and explain these in depth with examples, illustrations, and descriptions than to present five items without this needed amplification. The speaker who attempts to discuss the physiological, psychological, social, and linguistic differences between men and women, for example, is clearly trying to cover too much and is going to be forced to cover these areas only superficially, with the

$\mathcal{T}est$ ▶ ◀ $\mathcal{Y}ourself$

### HOW SATISFYING IS YOUR PUBLIC SPEAKING?

Respond to each of the following statements by recording the number best representing your feelings after a recent speech, using this scale:

**1** = strongly agree; **2** = moderately agree; **3** = slightly agree; **4** = neutral; **5** = slightly disagree; **6** = moderately disagree; and **7** = strongly disagree.

_____ ❶ The audience let me know that I was speaking effectively.

_____ ❷ My speech accomplished nothing.

_____ ❸ I would like to give another speech like this one.

_____ ❹ The audience genuinely wanted to get to know me.

_____ ❺ I was very dissatisfied with my speech.

_____ ❻ I was very satisfied with the speech.

_____ ❼ The audience seemed very interested in what I had to say.

_____ ❽ I did not enjoy the public speaking experience.

_____ ❾ The audience did not seem supportive of what I was saying.

_____ ❿ The speech flowed smoothly.

**HOW DID YOU DO?** To compute your score, follow these steps:

1. Add the scores for items 1, 3, 4, 6, 7, and 10.

2. Reverse the scores for items 2, 5, 8, and 9 so that 7 becomes 1, 8 becomes 2, 5 becomes 3, 4 remains 4, 3 becomes 5, 2 becomes 6, and 1 becomes 7.

3. Add the reversed scores for items 2, 5, 8, and 9.

4. Add the totals from steps 1 and 3 to yield your communication satisfaction score.

You may interpret your score along the following scale:

| 10 | 20 | 30 | 40 | 50 | 60 | 70 |
|---|---|---|---|---|---|---|
| Extremely Satisfying | Quite Satisfying | Fairly Satisfying | Average | Fairly Unsatisfying | Quite Unsatisfying | Extremely Unsatisfying |

How accurately do you think this scale captures your public speaking satisfaction?

**WHAT WILL YOU DO?** As you become a more successful and effective public speaker, your satisfaction is likely to increase. What else can you do to increase your satisfaction?

*Source:* This test was adapted for public speaking on the basis of the conversational satisfaction test developed by Michael Hecht (1978), "The Conceptualization and Measurement of Interpersonal Communication Satisfaction," *Human Communication Research, 4*, 253–264, and is used by permission of the author and International Communication Association.

---

result that little or no new information will be communicated. Even covering one of these areas completely is likely to prove difficult. Instead, select one subdivision of one area—say, language development or differences in language problems—and develop that in depth.

## Adjust the Level of Complexity

As you know from attending college classes, information can be presented in very simple or very complex form. The level of complexity on which you communicate your information should depend on the wide variety of factors considered throughout this book: the level of knowledge your audience has, the time you have available, the purpose you hope to achieve, the topic on which you're speaking, and so on. If you simplify a topic too much, you risk boring or, even worse, insulting your audience. On the other hand, if your talk is too complex, you risk confusing your audience and failing to communicate your message.

Generally, beginning speakers err by being too complex and not realizing that a 5- or 10-minute speech isn't long enough to make an audience understand sophisticated concepts or complicated processes. At least in your beginning speeches, try to keep it simple rather than complex. Make sure the words you use are familiar to your audience; alternatively, explain and define any unfamiliar terms as you use them. For example, remember that jargon and technical vocabulary familiar to the computer hacker may not be familiar to everyone.

## Stress Relevance and Usefulness

Listeners remember information best when they see it as relevant and useful to their own needs or goals. Notice that as a listener you yourself regularly demonstrate this principle. You may, for example, attend to and remember certain information because it will help you make a better impression in your job interview, make you a better parent, or enable you to deal with relationship problems. Like you, listeners attend to information that will prove useful to them.

If you want the audience to listen to your speech, relate your information to their needs, wants, or goals. Throughout your speech, but especially in the beginning, make sure your audience knows that the information you're presenting will be relevant and useful to them. For example, you might say something like:

> We all want financial security. We all want to be able to buy those luxuries we read so much about in magazines and see every evening on television. Wouldn't it be nice to be able to buy a car without worrying about where you're going to get the down payment or how you'll be able to make the monthly payments? Actually, that's not an unrealistic goal, as I'll demonstrate in this speech. In fact, I'll show you several investment strategies that have enabled many people to increase their income by as much as 40 percent.

## Relate New Information to Old

Listeners will learn information more easily and retain it longer when you relate it to what they already know. So, relate the new to the old, the unfamiliar to the familiar, the unseen to the seen, the untasted to the tasted. Here, for example, Teresa Jacob, a student from Ohio State University (Schnoor, 1997, p. 97), relates the problems of drug interactions (the new) to mixing chemicals in the school lab (the old or familiar).

> During our high school years, most of us learned in a chemistry class the danger of mixing harmless chemicals in lab. Add one drop of the wrong compound, and suddenly you've created a stink bomb, or worse, an explosion. Millions of Americans run the same risk inside their bodies each day by combining drugs that are supposed to help restore or maintain good health.

## Make Your Speech Easy to Remember

The principles of public speaking (principles governing use of language, delivery, and supporting materials, for example) will all help your listeners remember your speech. If, for example, you stress interest and relevance—as already noted—the audience is more likely to remember what you say because they'll see it as important and relevant to their own lives. But here are a few extra suggestions.

- *Repeat the points you want the audience to remember.* Help your audience to remember what you want them to remember by repeating your most important points.
- *Use guide phrases.* Guide your audience's attention to your most memorable points by saying, for example, "The first point to remember is that . . ." or "the argument I want you to remember when you enter that voting booth is. . . ."
- *Use internal summary transitions.* Internal summary transitions will remind the audience of what you have said and how it relates to what is to follow. This kind of repetition will reinforce your message and help your listeners remember your main points.
- *Pattern your messages.* If the audience can see the logic of your speech, they'll be better able to organize what you say in their own minds. If they can see that you're following a temporal pattern or a spatial pattern, for example, it will be easier for them to retain more of what you say, because they'll have a framework into which they can fit what you say.
- *Focus audience attention.* The best way to focus the listeners' attention is to tell them to focus their attention. Simply say, "I want you to focus on three points that I'll make in this speech. First, . . . " or "What I want you to remember is simply this . . ."

**WHAT DO YOU SAY?**
**Unexpected Events**
You're going to speak on the new version of Microsoft Windows, which you've used the last few weeks. Unfortunately, the speaker before you turns out to be a Microsoft program designer and gives a speech on exactly your topic. *What do you say?*

### Listening to New Ideas

A useful technique in listening to new ideas—whether these are presented in informative speeches, in small group situations, or in conversation—is PIP'N, a technique that derives from the insights of Carl Rogers (1970) on paraphrase and from Edward deBono's (1976) PMI (plus, minus, interesting) technique. PIP'N involves four steps that follow each letter in the acronym (DeVito, 1996):

P = *Paraphrase*. Put into your own words what you think the speaker is saying. In what other words can you express the speaker's meaning?

I = *Interesting*. Identify something interesting that you find in the idea. Why might this idea be interesting to you or to others?

P = *Positive*. Identify something positive about the idea. What's good about it?

N = *Negative*. Identify any negatives that you think the idea might entail. What are potential problems with this idea?

***Applying Listening Skills.*** *How might you use PIP'N? For practice, you may want to try PIP'N on the PIP'N technique itself: (1) Paraphrase the PIP'N technique, (2) say why the technique is interesting, (3) say something positive about it, and (4) say something negative about it.*

*We can, if we are able to listen as well as to speak, become better informed and wiser as we grow older, instead of being stuck like some people with the same little bundle of prejudices at 65 that we had at 25.*
　　—S. I. HAYAKAWA

# Supporting Materials

In explaining your main points, you'll use a variety of supporting materials—materials that amplify and clarify what you want your audience to understand. Principal among these are (1) examples, illustrations, and narration, (2) testimony, (3) statistics, and (4) definitions. Additional types of supporting material are identified in Table 12.1.

## Examples, Illustrations, and Narratives

Examples, illustrations, and narratives are specific instances in varying degrees of detail that help you explain your ideas. An *example* is a relatively brief specific instance ("Pat's on the varsity and has a 4.0"). An *illustration* is a longer and more detailed example ("Pat has always been an athlete but at the same time has always maintained an outstanding academic record, and there are many others on the varsity that have been both athletes and scholars, effectively destroying the stereotype of the dumb jock"). A *narrative* is longer still and is presented in the form of an anecdote or short story. The parables in many religious works are good examples of narratives used to illustrate a general principle.

Examples, illustrations, and narratives help make an idea vivid and memorable in the listeners' minds. To talk in general terms about starvation throughout the world is likely to have little effect on most listeners. But an example, illustration, or narrative of a nine-year-old girl roaming the streets eating garbage and prostituting herself for food would make the idea vivid and real.

Examples, illustrations, and narratives may be factual or imaginary. Thus, in explaining friendship, you might tell about an actual friend's behavior. Or you might formulate a composite ideal friend and describe how this person would act in a particular situ-

*"He or she is greatest who contributes the greatest original practical example."*
　　—WALT WHITMAN

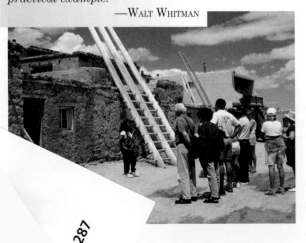

## TABLE 12.1 Additional Forms of Support

Along with examples, illustrations, narratives, testimony, statistics, and definitions, you'll also find the following forms of support useful and relevant.

| FORMS OF SUPPORT | SUGGESTIONS FOR USING |
|---|---|
| *Quotations,* verbatim reproductions of what someone else has said, often add spice and wit as well as authority to your speeches. Quotations from either historical or contemporary figures can allow you to explain an idea in a particularly clever or humorous way. | Quotations work best when they're short, easily comprehended, and easily remembered. If quotes are long, it may be best to paraphrase them. Most important, connect the quotations directly to the point you're making, and do so as smoothly as possible (avoid the too-often-used "I have a quote"). And always give credit to the source, whether you quote directly or paraphrase. |
| *Comparisons and contrasts* clarify the similarities and differences between two ideas, events, or concepts. | Focus on major similarities and differences; avoid itemizing all possible ones. If necessary, supplement your speech with a presentation aid that visualizes the most crucial information. |
| *Simple statements of fact or a series of facts* often help to illustrate and support a statement for position. | Make sure you clearly link the facts or series of facts to your main points. State the connections when introducing the facts and perhaps again after you've finished identifying the list of facts. |
| *Repetition* (repeating ideas in the same words at strategic places during the speech) and *restatement* (repeating ideas in different words) add clarity and emphasis and will help compensate for listeners' inevitable lapses in attention. | Steer a clear course between too little repetition and restatement and too much. If your ideas are relatively complex or your audience is unfamiliar with the topic, then you can use repetition and restatement more liberally. |

ation. Both approaches are useful and effective. In using these forms of support, be sure to include only those details that are needed to help your audience understand the point you're making. Don't clutter up an otherwise pointed example with unnecessary details. Also, because it is the example, illustration, or narrative that listeners will remember most clearly, be sure to connect this very explicitly to the proposition in your speech.

For example, former New York mayor Rudolph Giuliani, in his address to the United Nations after the World Trade Center attack of September 11, 2001, gave relevant examples to support his proposition that we are a land of immigrants and must continue to be so (www.ci.nyc.ny.us/html/om/html/96/united.html):

> New York City was built by immigrants, and it will remain the greatest city in the world as long as we continue to renew ourselves with and benefit from the energizing spirit from new people coming here to create a better future for themselves and their families. Come to Flushing, Queens, where immigrants from many lands have created a vibrant, vital commercial and residential community. Their children challenge and astonish us in our public school classrooms every day. Similarly, you can see growing and dynamic immigrant communities in every borough of our city: Russians in Brighton Beach, West Indians in Crown Heights, Dominicans in Washington Heights, the new wave of Irish in the Bronx, and Koreans in Willow Brook on Staten Island.

As another example, in a speech on unfair sentencing practices, student Jillian Collum provided a particularly dramatic illustration. After stating that a man was sentenced to 55 years in prison (under the federal mandatory minimum sentencing laws) for selling marijuana, she said:

> The sentencing brief noted that if Angelos had provided weapons to a terrorist organization, hijacked an aircraft, committed second-degree murder, and raped a 10-year-old child he would have received a lower combined sentence than he got for selling about $1,000 worth of marijuana.

## Testimony

*Testimony* may consist of experts' opinions or of witnesses' accounts. Testimony supports your ideas by adding a note of authority. You might, for example, cite an economist's predictions concerning the size of the deficit or the growth rate of the economy. Or you might discuss an art critic's evaluation of a painting or an art movement.

You might also consider using an eyewitness's testimony. You might, for example, cite the testimony of an eyewitness to an accident, an inmate who spent two years in a maximum-security prison, or a patient who underwent an operation.

In your use of testimony, be sure to use sources that the audience values highly. For example, if you were addressing an audience of devout Catholics who were active participants in their church, the testimony of the pope or a cardinal would likely be influential. But if your audience were composed of Muslims, Jews, Buddhists, or atheists, then it's unlikely that these sources would be as influential. To some listeners, these sources might even have a negative effect. So do a thorough audience analysis before you select your testimonials.

In presenting the testimony, stress the person's credibility. For example, when you cite an authority, make sure the person is in fact an authority. Tell the audience who the authority is and state the basis for the individual's expertise. The testimony will be much more effective when your audience is convinced that this person is worth listening to. For example, let's say you wanted to use the testimony of Jeff Bezos in a speech on the future of Internet selling. To establish the credibility and expertise of Bezos, you might note that Bezos is the founder of Amazon.com, one of the top Internet retail sites, and was *Time's* man of the year.

Here, for example, is how student Ashley Hatcher established the credibility of her testimony:

> As the 2005 book *The Structure of the Innate Mind* states, the answer may lie in Homicide Adaptation Theory, the conclusion of an unprecedented six-year study conducted by leading evolutionary psychologists David Buss and Joshua Duntley from the University of Texas.

## Statistics

Let's say you want to show that suspects' poverty influences their likelihood of criminal conviction, or that significant numbers of people now get their news from the Internet. To support these types of main points, you might use *statistics*—

**WHAT DO YOU SAY?**

**Testimony**

You want to present the testimony of a retired judge to explain the problems that probation causes. For your purposes, what would be the ideal qualifications of this judge? How might you weave these qualifications into your speech? *What do you say?*

*Skill Development Experience*

### Critically Evaluating Testimony

*Not all testimony is worth believing or using in your speech; distinguish reliable and credible testimony from that which is unreliable and lacking in credibility.*

If you were presenting someone's testimony on one of these issues, how would you establish the person's qualifications so that your audience would accept what he or she said?

- Nutritionist on the importance of a proper diet
- Real estate agent explaining the difference between a condo and a coop
- Nurse on the nature of bipolar disorder
- An MD on how to feed your pet
- Drama teacher on how to write a play

summary figures that help you communicate the important characteristics of complex sets of numbers. For most speeches and most audiences, simple statistics work best: (1) measures of central tendency, (2) measures of correlation, and (3) percentages.

*Measures of central tendency* (the mean and the median in particular) describe the general pattern in a group of numbers. The mean is the arithmetic average of a set of numbers, whereas the median is the middle score; 50 percent of cases fall above the median and 50 percent fall below it. When using such measures, make it clear why each figure is important. For example, if you wanted to show that significant numbers of people now get their news from the Internet, you might give the average number or mean of online users and newspaper readers and television viewers each year for the last 10 years. These statistics would then allow you to show that people who get their news from the Internet are increasing but that those getting the news from papers and television are declining.

*Measures of correlation* describe how closely two or more things are related. For example, there's a high positive correlation between smoking and lung cancer; smokers have a much greater incidence of lung cancer than nonsmokers. Correlations can also be negative. For example, there's a negative correlation between the amount of money you have and the likelihood that you'll be convicted of a crime; as your income level increases, your likelihood of criminal conviction decreases. When using correlations, make clear to your audience why the relationship between, say money and criminal conviction is important and how it relates to the proposition you want to support.

*Percentages* allow you to express a score as a number per 100. That is, if 78 percent of people favored coffee over tea, it would mean that 78 out of every 100 people favored coffee over tea. Percentages might be useful if you wanted to show, say, the relative amount of a proposed tuition increase, the growth of cable television over a 10-year period, or divorce rates in different parts of the world. In some cases you might want to compare percentages. For example, you might compare the percentage tuition increase at your school to the national average increase or to the rate of inflation or cost of living. To illustrate the growth of instant messaging, you might note the percentage by which its usage has grown in each of the last 5 years.

In using statistics, consider these suggestions:

- Make sure the statistics are clear, remembering that your audience will hear the figures only once. Round off figures so they're easy to comprehend and retain. For example, instead of saying that the median income of workers in your city is "$49,347," consider saying "about $50,000."

- Make explicit the meaning of the statistics. For example, if you state that the average home health aide makes less than $30,000 a year, you need to compare this figure to the salaries of other workers and to your proposition that home health aide salaries need to be increased. Don't just rattle off statistics; use them to support a specific proposition.

- Reinforce your oral presentation of statistics with some type of presentation aid—perhaps a graph or a chart. Numbers presented without some kind of visual reinforcement are difficult to grasp and remember. When possible, let your audience both see and hear the numbers.

- Use statistics in moderation. Most listeners' capacity for numerical data presented in a speech is limited, so use figures sparingly.

## Definitions

*Definitions*, essentially explanations of terms and concepts that may not be familiar to your listeners, may be useful as a form of support in many types of speeches. The speech of definition also is a major type of information speech, and later in this chapter we'll examine speeches of definition. Here we focus on definitions as a form of support. Below are several ways in which definitions might be used.

**Define by Etymology** One way to define a term is to trace its historical or linguistic development, or *etymology*. In defining the word *communication*, for example, you might note that it comes from the Latin *communis*, meaning "common"; in "communicating" you seek to establish a commonness, a sameness, a similarity with another individual. And *woman* comes from the Anglo-Saxon *wifman*, which meant literally a "wife man," where the word man was applied to both sexes. Through phonetic change *wifman* became *woman*. Most larger dictionaries and, of course, etymological dictionaries will help you find useful etymological definitions.

Or you might define a term by noting not its linguistic etymology, but how it came to mean what it now means. For example, you might note that the word *spam* on the Net comes from a *Monty Python* television skit in which every item on the menu contained the product Spam. Much as the diner in the skit was forced to get Spam, so the Net surfer gets spam—even when he or she wants something else.

**Define by Authority** You often can clarify a term by explaining how a particular *authority* views it. You might, for example, define *lateral thinking* by authority and say that Edward deBono, who developed the concept of lateral thinking in 1966, noted that "lateral thinking involves moving sideways to look at things in a different way. Instead of fixing on one particular approach and then working forward from that, the lateral thinker tries to find other approaches." Or you might use the authority of cynic and satirist Ambrose Bierce and define *love* as nothing but "a temporary insanity curable by marriage" and *friendship* as "a ship big enough to carry two in fair weather, but only one in foul."

*"The beginning of wisdom is the definition of terms."*
—SOCRATES

**Define by Negation** You also might define a term by noting what the term is not; that is, define it by *negation*. "A wife," you might say, "isn't a cook, a cleaning person, a babysitter, a seamstress, a sex partner. A wife is. . . ." Or, "A teacher isn't someone who tells you what you should know but rather one who. . . ."

Here Michael Marien (1992) defines *futurists* first negatively and then positively:

> Futurists do not use crystal balls. Indeed, they're generally loath to make firm predictions of what will happen. Rather, they make fore-

## Speaking Ethically

One interesting approach to ethics that has particular relevance to public speaking is Karl Wallace's (1955; see also Johannesen, 1990) "Ethical Basis of Communication." Wallace suggested four principles or guidelines.

- The speaker must have a thorough knowledge of the topic, an ability to answer relevant questions, and an awareness of the significant facts and opinions bearing on the topic.
- The speaker must present both facts and opinions fairly, without bending or spinning them to personal advantage. The speaker must allow the listener to make the final judgment.
- The speaker must reveal the sources of these facts and opinions and must help the listeners evaluate any biases and prejudices in the sources.
- The speaker must acknowledge and respect opposing arguments and evidence. Any attempt to hide valid opposing arguments from the audience is unethical.

*Never let your sense of morals get in the way of doing what's right.*
—ISAAC ASIMOV

*What Would You Do?* *You're giving a persuasive speech arguing for condom machines in rest rooms on campus. You know, however, that the money to install these machines will have to come from an increase in student fees. You wonder if you can ethically give the speech without mentioning that student fees will have to be increased. After all, you don't have time to include all arguments and evidence, even those that support your position. You also figure that it's the listeners' responsibility to ask where the money is coming from and not your job to tell them. What would you do?*

casts of what is probable, sketch scenarios of what is possible, and/or point to desirable futures—what is preferable and what strategies we should pursue to get there.

**Define by Direct Symbolization** You also might define a term by direct *symbolization*—by showing the actual thing or a picture or model of it. For example, a sales representative explaining a new computer keyboard would obviously use an actual keyboard in the speech. Similarly, a speech on magazine layout or types of fabrics would include actual layout pages or fabric samples.

**Define by Operations** Definition by *operations* involves describing how you would construct the object. For example, in defining a chocolate cake, you could tell how to bake a cake.

# Presentation Aids

*Presentation aids*—visual or auditory means for clarifying ideas—are really a form of supporting material. But because they're so important in public speaking today, because they're so numerous and varied, and because technology has provided a wealth of alternatives and some pretty sophisticated techniques, we'll look at presentation aids separately here and will consider them in considerable detail.

As you plan any type of speech, consider using some kind of presentation aid. Ask yourself how you can visually present what you want your audience to remember. For example, if you want your audience to see the growing impact of the sales tax, consider showing them a chart of rising

"Can you help me with my ethics homework, or would that be missing the point?"

Reprinted courtesy of Bunny Hoest and Parade Magazine.

sales tax over the last 10 years. Of course, you can deliver your entire speech supplemented by overhead slides—as created in, say, PowerPoint.

Presentation aids are not added frills; they are integral parts of your speech. Aids will help you:

- *gain attention and maintain interest.* Listeners perk up when the speaker says, "I want you to look at this chart showing the employment picture for the next five years" or "Listen to the vocal range in this voice."

- *add clarity.* Adding pictures to your words will provide added clarification. Some concepts, such as comparison figures, architectural designs, or anatomical features, are best communicated through a combination of oral and visual messages.

- *reinforce your main ideas.* Help ensure that your listeners understand and remember what you've said through a combination of the verbal and the nonverbal.

- *establish your credibility and confidence.* Especially when your aids appear highly professional, they'll show that you care enough about both your listeners and your topic to do this "extra" work.

- *reduce your apprehension.* When you concentrate on coordinating your speech with your presentation aids, you're less likely to focus on yourself. This focus away from the self will often decrease apprehension.

## Types of Presentation Aids

Among the presentation aids you have available are the object itself, models of the object, graphs, word charts, maps, people, and photographs and illustrations.

**The Object Itself**   As a general rule (to which there are many exceptions), the best presentation aid is the object itself. Bring it to your speech if you can. Notice that infomercials sell their products not only by talking about them but by showing them to potential buyers. You see the jewelry, the clothing, the new mop from a wide variety of angles and in varied settings.

**The 5th Wave**   By Rich Tennant

"WELL, SHOOT! THIS EGGPLANT CHART IS JUST AS CONFUSING AS THE BUTTERNUT SQUASH CHART AND THE GOURD CHART. CAN'T YOU JUST MAKE A PIE CHART LIKE EVERYONE ELSE?"

©The 5th Wave, www.the5thwave.com

**Models**   Models—replicas of the actual object—are useful for a variety of purposes. For example, if you wanted to explain complex structures such as the human hearing or vocal mechanism, the brain, or the structure of DNA, a model would prove useful. Models help to clarify relative size, position, and how each part interacts with each other part.

**Graphs**   Graphs are useful for showing differences over time, clarifying how a whole is divided into parts, and comparing different amounts or sizes. Figure 12.1 shows various types of graphs that can be drawn freehand or generated with the graphics capabilities of any word-processing or presentation software. Keep your graphs as simple as possible. In a pie chart, for example, don't have more than five segments. Similarly, in a bar graph limit the number of items to five or fewer. As in the graphs shown in Figure 12.1, be sure you add the legend, the labels, and the numerical values you wish to emphasize.

**Word Chart**   Word charts (which also can contain numbers and even graphics) are useful for identifying the key points in one of your propositions or in your entire speech—in the order in which you cover them, of course. Figure 12.2 on page 297 is a good example of a simple word chart that identi-

### Product Placement

James Bond's Aston Martin and E.T.'s Reese's Pieces were early examples of product placement: the insertion of brand-name products in movies and TV shows. Today, paid product placement is becoming increasingly popular throughout all media—even print media. The reason is that it means big money to the media producers and effective advertising for products. For example, the makers of *Tomorrow Never Dies*, one of the Bond movies, earned $34 million for placing in the movie such products as BMW, Omega watches, Heineken beer, Avis rental cars, and Bollinger champagne (Rodman, 2001).

In 2004 the total number of product placements on television was 81,739; in 2005 it rose to 107,839 (*New York Times*, March 20, 2006, p. C3). In 2005, *The Contender*—a reality boxing show on NBC—had 7,502 product placements (including both the presence of the product or its mention), more than any other show; for example, characters were shown drinking Gatorade and driving a Toyota truck. In televised sports, products are advertised not only during commercial breaks but on billboards, in the names of the stadiums, or on the players' sneakers.

It's estimated that in 2004 magazines earned some $160.9 million and newspapers earned approximately $65 million for product placements—for advertising products without telling readers that these were in fact advertisements designed to sell the products (Lamb, 2005).

The use of product placement in news shows has created the most debate. For example, *Good Morning America* broadcast one of its shows from a Norwegian Cruise Line ship. Although no fees were paid for the product placement, the Cruise Line reportedly did pay for the airfare, room, and board for 300 contest winners on a cruise to the West Indies (Schiller, 2006). And the *New York Times* has already agreed to allow "watermark" ads to appear behind news and editorial articles (Mandese, 2006).

***Increasing Media Literacy.*** *Product placements will surely increase over the coming years and will invade all media forms. When you see a product in a movie or television show, keep in mind that its manufacturer paid heavily for its being there.*

*Let advertisers spend the same amount of money improving their product that they do on advertising, and they wouldn't have to advertise it.*
—WILL ROGERS

---

fies the major topics discussed in the speech. Or you could use a word chart to clarify relationships among roles in an organization or to identify the steps in a process—for example, the stages of language acquisition or setting up TIVO, dealing with sexual harassment, or downloading the latest version of Netscape (Figures 12.3 and 12.4). Another use of charts is to show information you want your audience to write down. Emergency phone numbers, addresses, titles of recommended books, and website URLs are examples of types of information that listeners will welcome in written form.

**Maps**   If you want to illustrate the locations of geographic features such as cities, lakes, rivers, or mountain ranges, maps will obviously prove useful as presentation aids. But maps also can be used for illustrating population densities, immigration patterns, world literacy rates, varied economic conditions, the spread of diseases, and hundreds of other issues you may wish to examine in your speeches. A wide variety of maps may be downloaded from the Internet and then shown as slides or transparencies. Chances are you'll find a map on the Internet for exactly the purpose you need.

**People**   If you want to demonstrate the muscles of the body or different voice patterns, skin complexions, or hairstyles, consider using people as your aids. Aside from the obvious assistance they provide in demonstrating their muscles or voice qualities, people help to secure and maintain the attention and interest of the audience.

**Photographs and Illustrations**   Types of trees, styles of art, kinds of exercise machines, or the horrors of war—all can be made more meaningful with

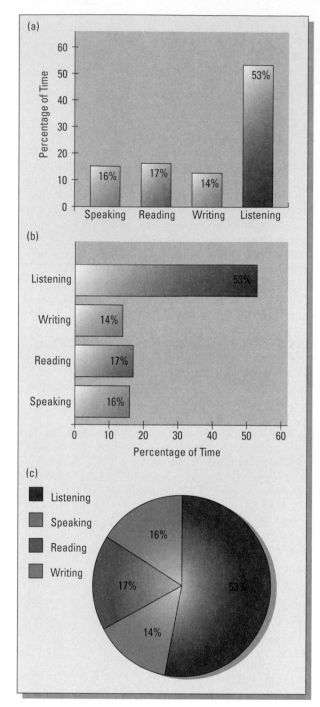

**Figure** *12.1*
**Three Graphs**
These three graphs illustrate data from a study on the amounts of time people spend on the four communication activities (Barker, Edwards, Gaines, Gladney, & Holley, 1980). All three of these graphs are useful for illustrating comparisons. These are just three types of graphs that are easily constructed using the graphics software integrated with most word-processing packages or, of course, with the more sophisticated graphics programs.

photographs and illustrations. The best way to use these images is to convert them to slides. If you're using a computer presentation program (explained below) and you have a scanner, you can import your photos into your presentation with relative ease. Or you can have them converted to slides. Once they're converted to slides, you'll be able to project them in a format large enough for everyone to see clearly. You'll also be able to point to specific parts of the photo as you explain the devastation of war or the fine art of combining colors and textures. You also can convert the images to transparencies to use with a transparency projector, although you'll lose some of the detail that you would have in slides.

Another way to use photographs and illustrations is to have them enlarged and printed in a size large enough for the entire audience to see. Try to mount these on cardboard so they'll be easier to handle. Most copy shops provide this service—though the cost may be considerable, especially if you have several photos to convert and you need them in color. Nevertheless, this is an option that may prove useful in some situations. Passing pictures around the room is generally a bad idea, however. Listeners will wait for the pictures to circulate to them, will wonder what the pictures contain, and will miss a great deal of your speech in the interim.

## The Media of Presentation Aids

Once you've decided on the type of presentation aid you'll use, you need to decide on the medium you'll use to present it. Acquire skill in using both low-tech (the chalkboard or flip chart) and high-tech (the computerized slide show) resources. In this way you'll be able to select your presentation aids from the wide array available, choosing on the basis of the message you want to communicate and the audience to whom you'll be speaking.

**Chalkboards**   The easiest aid to use, though not necessarily the most effective, is the chalkboard. The chalkboard may be used effectively to record key terms or important definitions or even to outline the general structure of your speech. Don't use it when you can present the same information with a preplanned chart or model. It takes too long to write out anything substantial. If you do write on the board, be careful not to turn your back to the audience, even briefly. In just a few moments, you can easily lose the attention of your audience.

**Chartboards**   Chartboards are useful when you have one or two relatively simple graphs or charts that you want to display during your speech. If you want to display them for several minutes, be sure you have a way of holding them up. For example, bring masking tape if you intend to secure them to the chalkboard, or enlist the aid of an audience member to hold them up. Black lettering on a white board generally works best; it provides the best contrast and is the easiest for people to read.

**Flip Charts**   Flip charts—large pads of paper (usually about 24 × 24 inches) mounted on a stand or easel—can be used to record a variety of information that you reveal by flipping the pages as you deliver your speech. For example, if you were to discuss the various departments in an organization, you might have the key points relating to each department on a separate page of your flip chart. As you discussed the advertising department, you'd show the chart relevant to the advertising department. When you moved on to discuss the personnel department, you'd flip to the chart dealing with personnel.

**Slides and Transparencies**   Slides and transparencies are helpful in showing a series of visuals that may be of very different types; for example, photographs, illustrations, charts, or tables. The slides can easily be created with many of the popular computer programs (discussed later in "Computer-Assisted Presentations," p. 299). To produce actual 35mm slides, you'll need considerable lead time, so be sure to build this into your preparation time. If you don't have access to a slide projector or if you don't have the lead time needed to construct 35mm slides, consider the somewhat less sophisticated transparencies. You can create your visual in any of the word-processing or spreadsheet programs you normally use, then use a laser printer or copier to produce the transparencies.

**Audio and Videotapes, CDs, and DVDs**   Consider the value of using music or recorded speech to support your ideas—and also to add a note of variety that will set your speeches apart from most other speakers' presentations. A speech on advertising jingles, music styles, or dialects would be greatly helped, for example, by having actual samples for the audience to hear on CDs or tapes. Similarly, videotapes can serve a variety of purposes in public speaking. Basically, you have two options with videotapes. First, you can tape a scene from a film or television show with your DVD or VCR recorder and show it at the appropriate time in your speech. Thus, for example, you might record examples of sexism in television sitcoms, violence on television talk shows, or types of families depicted in feature films and show these excerpts during your speech. Second, you can create your own video with a simple

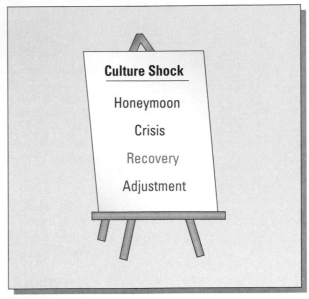

**Figure** *12.2*
**Word Chart**
The relative value of this chart and, in fact, of any visual aid depends on the effect it has on the audience.

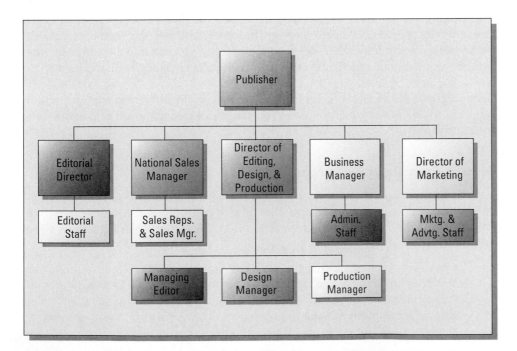

**Figure** *12.3*
**An Organizational Chart**
This figure was constructed in Illustrator. But organizational charts can easily be constructed using the table function on most word processors and then enlarged for an entire audience to see.

Figure *12.4*
**A Flowchart**
This chart identifies the stages a child goes through in learning language. Flowcharts are often useful to guide the audience through the entire speech—each section of the chart might represent a main point of your speech.

camcorder. Videos are best used in small doses; in many instances just 20- or 30-second excerpts will prove sufficient to illustrate your point. Avoid using long excerpts that will divert attention from your message; just use enough video to help your listeners understand the point you're making, not to rehash an entire plot line.

**Handouts**   Handouts, printed materials that you distribute to the audience, are especially helpful when you wish to explain complex material and/or to provide listeners with a permanent record of some aspect of your speech. Handouts also are useful for presenting complex information that you want your audience to refer to throughout the speech. Handouts encourage listeners to take notes, especially if you leave enough white space or even provide a specific place for notes, which keeps them actively involved in your presentation. A variety of handouts can be easily prepared with many of the computer presentation packages that we'll consider in the last section of this chapter.

Of course, if you distribute your handouts during your speech, you run the risk of your listeners' reading the handout and not concentrating on your speech. On the other hand, if the listeners are getting the information you want to communicate—even if it's primarily from the handout—that isn't too bad. You can encourage listeners to listen to you when you want them to and to look at the handout when you want them to by simply telling them, "Look at the graph on the top of page two of the handout; it summarizes recent census figures on immigration" or "We'll get back to the handout in a minute; now, however, I want to direct your attention to this next slide" (or "to the second argument"). If you distribute your handouts at the end of the speech, they won't interfere with your presentation but may never get read. After all, listeners may reason, they heard the speech, so why bother going through the handout as well? To counteract this very natural tendency, you can include additional material in your handout and mention this to your audience when you distribute it.

Once you have the idea that you want to present in an aid and you know the medium you want to use, direct your attention to preparing and using the aid so it best serves your purpose.

## Preparing Presentation Aids

In preparing presentation aids, make sure that they add clarity to your speech, that they're appealing to the listeners, and that they're culturally sensitive.

Clarity is the most important consideration. To achieve clarity, follow a few simple suggestions:

- *Use easily seen colors.* Use colors that will make your message instantly clear; light colors on dark backgrounds or dark colors on light backgrounds provide the best contrast and seem to work best for most purposes. Be careful of using yellow, which is often difficult to see, especially if there's glare from the sun.
- *Use direct phrases.* Avoid complete sentences. Use bullets to highlight your points or your support (as in the slides in Figure 12.5 on p. 300). Just as you

phrase your main points in parallel style, phrase your bullets in parallel style; in many cases this involves using the same part of speech (for example, all nouns or all infinitive phrases). And make sure that any connection between a graphic and its meaning is immediately clear. If it isn't, explain it.

- *Use the aid to highlight a few essential points.* Don't clutter it with too much information. Usually four bullets on a slide or chart, for example, are as much information as you should include.

- *Use easily read typefaces.* Typefaces vary widely in readability; select a typeface that can easily be read from all parts of the room.

- *Give the aid a title.* A general heading for the slide, chart, or transparency will help to further guide your listeners' attention and focus.

Presentation aids should be appealing to your audience. At the same time, although presentation aids should be attractive enough to engage the attention of the audience, they should not be so attractive that they're distracting. The almost nude body draped across a car may be effective in selling underwear, but would probably detract if your objective is to explain the profit-and-loss statement of General Motors.

Presentation aids should be culturally sensitive. Be sure that they can easily be interpreted by people from other cultures. Also, be careful that icons don't reveal an ethnocentric bias. For example, using the American dollar sign to symbolize "wealth" might be quite logical in your public speaking class but might be interpreted as ethnocentric if used with an audience of international visitors.

## Using Presentation Aids

Your presentation aids will be more effective if you follow a few simple guidelines.

- *Know your aids intimately.* Be sure you know in what order your aids are to be presented and how you plan to introduce them. Know exactly what goes where and when.

- *Pretest the presentation aids.* Be certain that aids can be seen easily from all parts of the room. Don't underestimate, for example, how large lettering must be to be seen by those in the back of the room.

- *Rehearse your speech with the presentation aids.* Do all your rehearsal with your presentation aids so that you'll be able to introduce and use them smoothly and effectively. Practice your actual movements with the aids you'll use. If you're going to use a chart, how will you use it? Will it stand by itself? Will you ask another student to hold it for you?

- *Integrate presentation aids into your speech seamlessly.* Just as a verbal example should flow naturally into the text and seem an integral part of the speech, so should a presentation aid. The aid should appear not as an afterthought but as an essential part of the speech.

- *Avoid talking to your aids.* Talk to your audience at all times. Know your aids so well that you can point to what you want without breaking eye contact with your audience.

- *Use your aids only when they're relevant.* Show each aid when you want the audience to concentrate on it; then remove it. If you don't remove it, the audience's attention may remain focused on the visual when you want them to focus on your next assertion.

## Computer-Assisted Presentations

Computer-assisted presentations possess all of the advantages of aids already noted (for example, maintaining interest and attention, adding clarity, and reinforcing your message). In addition, however, they have advantages all their own—so many, in fact, that you'll want to seriously consider using this technology in your

**E-TALK**

**Access for Persons with Disabilities**
For persons with impaired vision, accessing information through print can be difficult; today, however, computer technology is making it a lot easier (Williamson, Wright, Schauder, & Bow, 2001). In what specific ways might you adjust your presentation aids or your explanation of them to help the visually impaired?

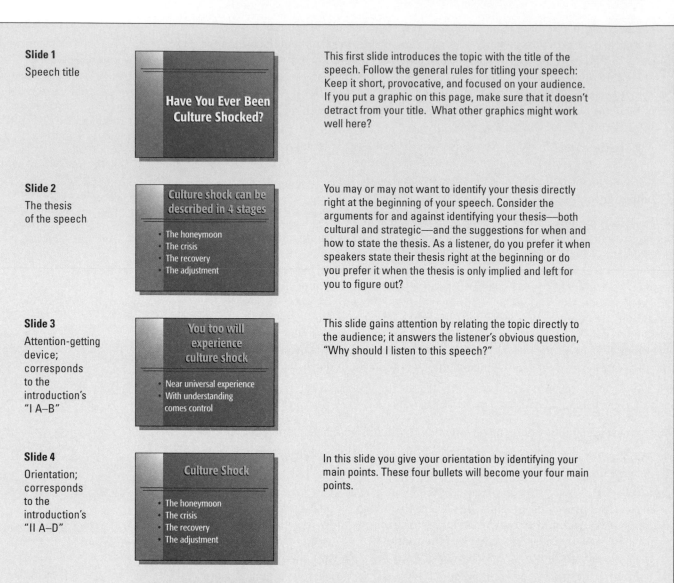

**Slide 1**

Speech title

This first slide introduces the topic with the title of the speech. Follow the general rules for titling your speech: Keep it short, provocative, and focused on your audience. If you put a graphic on this page, make sure that it doesn't detract from your title. What other graphics might work well here?

**Slide 2**

The thesis of the speech

You may or may not want to identify your thesis directly right at the beginning of your speech. Consider the arguments for and against identifying your thesis—both cultural and strategic—and the suggestions for when and how to state the thesis. As a listener, do you prefer it when speakers state their thesis right at the beginning or do you prefer it when the thesis is only implied and left for you to figure out?

**Slide 3**

Attention-getting device; corresponds to the introduction's "I A–B"

This slide gains attention by relating the topic directly to the audience; it answers the listener's obvious question, "Why should I listen to this speech?"

**Slide 4**

Orientation; corresponds to the introduction's "II A–D"

In this slide you give your orientation by identifying your main points. These four bullets will become your four main points.

**Slide 5**

First main point; corresponds to the body's "I A–B"

This is your first main point. You'd introduce it, perhaps, by saying, "The honeymoon occurs first." If you wanted your audience to keep track of the stage numbers, you could use numbers in your slides; for example, "1. The Honeymoon" or "Stage 1, The Honeymoon." The graphic of the heart is meant to associate culture shock with good times and a romancelike experience. As a listener, would you prefer that the speaker explain this graphic or say nothing about it?

**Figure *12.5***
**A Slide Show Speech**

speeches. They give your speech a professional, up-to-date look, and in the process add to your credibility. They show that you're prepared and that you care about your topic and audience.

Various presentation software packages are available. Figure 12.5 illustrates what a set of slides might look like; the slides are built around the "culture shock" speech outline discussed in Chapter 11 and were constructed in PowerPoint. As you review this figure, try to visualize how you'd use a slide show to present your next speech.

**Slide 6**

Second main point; corresponds to the body's "II A–B"

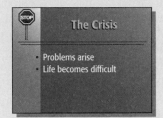

This is your second point and follows in format the previous slide. Again, a graphic is used. Can you think of a better graphic?

**Slide 7**

Third main point; corresponds to the body's "III A–B"

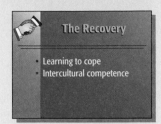

This is your third main point and again follows the format of the previous two slides.

**Slide 8**

Fourth main point; corresponds to the body's "IV A–B"

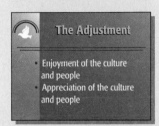

This is your fourth main point; the sound of applause is programmed to come on with this slide, reinforcing the idea that we do adjust to culture shock. Examine the sound effects you have available; what other sound effects would you use in this speech?

**Slide 9**

Summary; corresponds to the conclusion's "I A–D"

This is your summary of your four points; notice that it's the same as your orientation (Slide 4). This slide violates the general rule to use graphics in moderation. What do you think of the repetition of graphics? Do you think they add reinforcement? Do they detract from the verbal message?

**Slide 10**

Closure; corresponds to the conclusion's "II"

This slide is intended to wrap up the speech—it contains the title and two graphics that will support the speaker's concluding statement: "By knowing about culture shock you'll be in a better position to deal with it at school and on the job." Notice that the conclusion is tied to the introduction by a similarity in font and text color; it helps signal that this is the last slide and the end of the speech.

**Figure *12.5***
**A Slide Show Speech** *(continued)*

**Ways of Using Presentation Software**   Presentation software enables you to produce a variety of aids. For example, you can construct your slides on your computer, and then have 35mm slides developed from disk. To do this you'd have to have a slide printer or send the files out (you can do this via modem) to a lab specializing in converting electronic files into 35mm slides. You may have access to a slide printer at your school, so do check first. Similarly, your local office supply store or photocopy shop may have exactly the services you need.

Or you can create your slides and then show them on your computer screen. If you're speaking to a very small group, it may be possible to have your listeners gather around your computer as you speak. With larger audiences, however, you'll need a computer projector or LCD projection panel. Assuming you have a properly equipped computer in the classroom, you can copy your entire presentation to a floppy, Zip, Flash, or CD-ROM disk and bring it with you the day of the speech.

Computer presentation software also enables you to print out a variety of materials to use as handouts: slides, slides with speaker's notes, slides with room for listener notes, and outlines of your speech. You can print out your complete set of slides to distribute to your listeners. Or you can print out a select portion of the slides, or even slides that you didn't have time to cover in your speech but which you'd like your audience to look at later. The most popular options are to print out two, three, or up to six slides per page. The two-slide option provides for easy readability and is especially useful for slides of tables or graphs that you want to present to your listeners in an easy-to-read size. The three-slide option is probably the most widely used; it prints the three slides down the left side of the page with space for listeners to write notes on the right. This option is useful if you want to interact with your audience and you want them to take notes as you're speaking. Naturally, you'd distribute this handout before you began your speech, during your introduction, or perhaps at the point when you wanted your listeners to begin taking notes. A sample three-slide printout with space for notes is shown in Figure 12.6. If you want to provide listeners with a complete set of slides, then the six-slide option may be the most appropriate. You can, of course, also print out any selection of slides you wish—perhaps only those slides that contain graphs, or perhaps only those slides that summarize your talk.

Another useful option is to print out your slides with your speaker's notes for your own use. That way you'll have your slides and any notes you may find useful—examples you want to use, statistics that would be difficult to memorize, quotations that you want to read to your audience, delivery notes, or anything that you care to record. The audience will see the slides but not your notes; of course. As discussed in Chapter 11, it's generally best to record these notes in outline form, with key words rather than complete sentences. This will prevent you from falling into the trap of reading your speech. A sample printout showing a slide plus speaker's notes is provided in Figure 12.7 on page 304.

The speech outline is another useful handout. Two outline options are generally available: the collapsed outline and the full outline. The collapsed outline contains only the slide titles and will give your audience a general outline of your talk. If you want your listeners to fill in the outline with the information you'll talk about, then you can distribute this collapsed outline at the beginning of your speech. The full outline option (slide titles plus bullets) gives listeners a relatively complete record of your speech and also can be helpful if you cover a lot of technical information that listeners will have to refer to later. You might hand out a full outline, for example, if you were giving a speech on company health care or pension plans and you wanted to provide your listeners with detailed information on each option, or if you wanted to provide listeners with addresses and phone numbers. As mentioned earlier, you would normally distribute a full outline not at the beginning but after your speech, because such a complete outline could lead your audience to read and not to listen.

You also can create overhead transparencies from your computer slides. You can make these on many printers and most copiers simply by just substituting transparency paper for regular paper.

**Suggestions for Designing Slides**   Your slides will be more effective and easier to produce if you follow these simple suggestions.

- *Use the templates provided by your software.* Allow the design wizards to help you choose colors and typefaces. These are created by professional designers

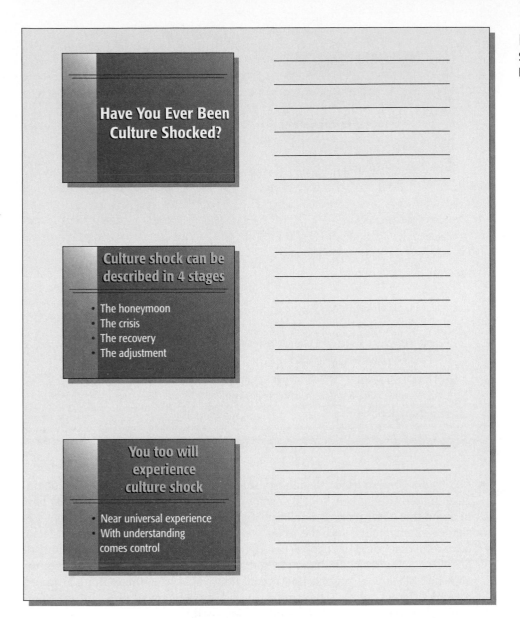

Figure *12.6*
**Slides with Space for Listeners' Notes**

who are experts at using colors, fonts, and layouts to create clear and appealing renderings.

- *Use consistent typeface, size, and color.* Give each item in your outline that has the same level head (for example, all your main points) the same typeface, size, and color throughout your presentation. This will help your listeners follow the organization of your speech. If you're using one of the predesigned templates, this will be done for you. Notice that this principle was followed (for the most part) in the slides in Figure 12.5—but that it was broken in one case, to connect the introduction and the conclusion, which are in a color and typesize different from the rest of the slides. Another way you might break this rule would be to design your internal summaries a bit differently from the regular slides to signal their unique function. This would prove especially effective in a long speech with frequent internal summaries.

- *Be brief.* Your objective in designing these slides is to provide the audience with key words and ideas that will reinforce what you're saying; you don't want your audience to spend their time reading rather than listening. Generally, put one complete thought on a slide, and don't try to put too many words on one slide.

Figure *12.7*
**Slide and Speaker's Notes**

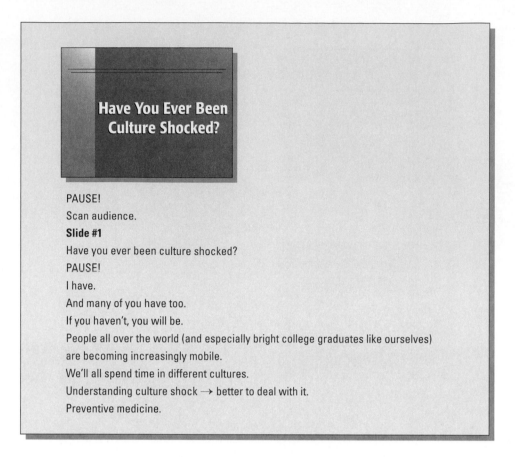

PAUSE!
Scan audience.
**Slide #1**
Have you ever been culture shocked?
PAUSE!
I have.
And many of you have too.
If you haven't, you will be.
People all over the world (and especially bright college graduates like ourselves)
are becoming increasingly mobile.
We'll all spend time in different cultures.
Understanding culture shock → better to deal with it.
Preventive medicine.

- *Use colors for contrast.* Remember that many people have difficulty distinguishing red from green; so if you want to distinguish ideas, it is probably best to avoid this color pairing. Similarly, if you're going to print out your slides in shades of gray, make sure the tones you choose provide clear contrasts. Also, be careful that you don't choose colors that recall holidays that have nothing to do with your speech—for example, red and green may evoke Christmas, or orange and black may suggest Halloween. Remember, too, the cultural attitudes toward different colors; for example, among some Asian cultures, writing a person's name in red means that the person has died.

- *Use only the visuals that you really need.* Presentation software packages make inserting visuals so easy that they may encourage you to include too many. Use visuals when you have room on the slide and when the visual is directly related to your speech thesis and purpose. The visual should advance your speech purpose. If it does, use it; if it doesn't, lose it.

- *Use transitions.* As verbal transitions help you move from one part of your speech to another, presentational transitions help you move from one slide to the next with the desired effect—blinds folding from left or right or top or bottom or a quick fade. Generally, it's best to use the same transition for all slides in a single presentation. You might vary this a bit by, say, having the last slide introduced by a somewhat different transition, but any more variation is likely to weaken the listeners' focus on your message. In choosing transitions, select a pattern that is consistent with your speech purpose; don't use a perky black-and-yellow checkerboard transition in a speech on child abuse, for example.

- *Use sound effects.* A wide variety of sound effects come with most presentation packages, ranging from individual sounds—foghorn, drumroll, or doorbell—to excerpts from musical compositions. Consider using sound effects in your speech, perhaps especially with your transitions. But, as with graphics, go easy; overdoing it is sure to make your speech seem carelessly put together. In the slides in Figure 12.5, I programmed "applause" (one of the readily available sound effects) to come on as Slide 8—the adjustment—comes on. As you read through the slides in Figure 12.5, you may find additional places where sound could be used effectively.

- *Use build effects.* Help focus your listeners' attention with "build effects," the ways in which your bulleted items come onto the screen. For example, you can have each bulleted phrase fly from the top of the screen into its position; with the next mouse click, the second bullet flies into position. Or you can have your bullets slide in from right to left or from left to right. And so on.

- *Use graphs and tables when appropriate.* Graphs and tables are useful, as noted earlier, when you want to communicate complex information that would take too much text for one slide to explain. Consider the advantages of graph animation. Just as you can display individual bullets as you discuss them, you can display the graph in parts so as to focus the audience's attention on exactly the part of the graph you want. Incidentally, you can achieve somewhat the same effect with transparencies, by covering up the graph and gradually revealing the parts you want the audience to focus on.

- *Anticipate questions.* If there's a question-and-answer period following your speech, consider preparing a few extra slides for your responses to questions you anticipate being asked. Then, when someone asks you an expected question, you can say: "I anticipated that someone might ask that question; it raises an important issue. The data are presented in this chart." You can then show the slide and explain it more fully. This is surely going the extra mile, but it can help make your speech a real standout.

- *Use the spell-check.* You don't want your professional-looking slides to contain misspellings; spelling errors can ruin your credibility and seriously damage the impact of your speech.

- *Anticipate technical problems.* If you're planning a slide show, consider what you'll do if the equipment doesn't work. A useful backup procedure is to have lower-tech alternatives (for example, transparencies and/or handouts) ready just in case something goes wrong.

**Rehearsing with Presentation Programs**   Presentation packages are especially helpful in enabling you to rehearse your speech and time it precisely. As you rehearse, the computer program records the time you spend on each slide and will display that time under each slide; it will also record the presentation's total time. You can see these times at the bottom of each slide in a variety of views, but they won't appear in the slides the audience sees or in a printed handout, such as appears in Figure 12.5. You can use these times to program each slide to run automatically, or you can use the times to see if you're devoting the amount of time to each of your ideas that you want to. If you find in your rehearsal that your speech is too long, these times can help you see which parts may be taking up too much time and perhaps could be shortened.

Presentation software allows you to rehearse individually selected slides as many times as you want. But make sure that you go through the speech from beginning to end toward the end of your rehearsal period. Rehearse with this system as long as improvements result; when you find that rehearsal no longer serves any useful purpose, then stop.

Another aspect of rehearsal is checking out the equipment available in the room you'll speak in and its compatibility with the presentation software you're using. If possible, rehearse with the very equipment you'll have available on the day you're speaking. In this way you can adjust to or remedy any incompatibilities or idiosyncrasies that you come across. You'll discover how long it takes to warm up

**WHAT DO YOU SAY?**
**Technical Problems**
You've prepared a great slide show for your informative speech. Unfortunately, the projector that you need to show the slides never arrives. But you have to give your speech and you have to (or do you?) explain something of what happened. *What do you say?*

the slide projector or to load PowerPoint, so you won't have to use up your speaking time for these preparations.

**The Actual Presentation**    During your actual presentation you can control your slides with your mouse, advancing to the next one or going back to a previously shown slide. If you set the package to run automatically, programming each slide to be shown for its own particular amount of time, you won't be tied to the mouse—assuming you don't have a remote mouse. You can, of course, override the automatic programming by simply clicking your mouse either to advance or to go back to a slide that perhaps went by too quickly.

As with any presentation aid, make sure that you focus on the audience; don't allow the computer or the slides to get in the way of your immediate contact with the audience.

You may wish to use the pen—actually your mouse—to write on or to highlight certain words or figures in the slides. But it's not very easy to write with a mouse, so don't plan on writing very much. Underlining or circling key terms or figures is probably the best use for the pen.

Now that we have considered the principles of informative speaking, types of supporting materials, and presentation aids, let's turn to three types of informative speeches: speeches of description, definition, and demonstration.

# Speeches of Description

In a speech of *description*, you're concerned with explaining an object, person, event, or process. Examples of speeches in which you describe an object or person might include the structure of the brain, the contributions of Thomas Edison, the parts of a telephone, the layout of Philadelphia, the hierarchy of a corporation, or the components of a computer system.

Examples of speeches in which you describe an event or process might include the attacks of September 11, 2001; the process of organizing a bodybuilding contest; how a newspaper is printed; how a child acquires language; how people purchase stocks online; or the events leading to the Iraq War.

## Thesis and Main Points

The thesis of a speech, as explained in Chapter 10, is your single most important concept; it is what you most want your audience to remember. The thesis of a speech of description simply states what you'll describe in your speech; for example, "The child acquires language in four stages," or "There are three steps to purchasing stock online," or "Four major events led to the Iraq war."

The main points of a speech of description are the major subdivisions of the thesis. You derive your main points from your thesis by asking strategic questions. For example, what are the four stages in child language acquisition? What are the three steps to purchasing stock online. What events led to the Iraq war?

## Support

Obviously you don't want to simply list your main points; instead, you want to flesh them out and to make them memorable, interesting, and most of all clear. In a speech of description you do this by using a variety of materials that amplify and support your main ideas, including examples, illustrations, testimony, statistics, and presentation aids.

Because this is a speech of description, give extra consideration to the types of description you might use in your supporting materials. Try to describe the object or event with lots of different descriptive categories, from physical to social, psychological, and economic categories.

## Organization

Consider using a spatial or a topical organization when describing objects and people. Consider using a temporal pattern when describing events and processes. For example, if you were to describe the layout of Philadelphia, you might start from the north and work down to the south (using a spatial pattern). If you were to describe the contributions of Thomas Edison, you might select the three or four major contributions and discuss each of these equally (using a topical pattern).

If you were describing the events leading up to the Iraq war, you might use a temporal pattern, starting with the earliest and working up to the latest. A temporal pattern would also be appropriate for describing how a hurricane develops or how a parade is put together.

Consider the "Who? What? Where? When? and Why?" pattern of organization. These journalistic categories are especially useful when you want to describe an event or a process. For example, if you're going to describe how to purchase a house, you might want to consider the people involved (who?), the steps you have to go through (what?), the places you'll have to go (where?), the timing or sequence of the steps (when?), and the advantages and disadvantages of buying the house (why?).

Here is an example of how the bare bones of a descriptive speech might look. Notice that the speaker derives the main points from asking a question of the thesis.

General purpose: _____ *To inform.* _____

Specific purpose: _____ *To describe the way fear works in intercultural* _____
_____ *communication* _____

Thesis: _____ *Fear influences intercultural communication. (How does fear* _____
_____ *influence intercultural communication?)* _____

I. _____ *We fear disapproval.* _____

II. _____ *We fear embarrassing ourselves.* _____

III. _____ *We fear being harmed.* _____

In delivering such a speech, the speaker might begin by saying:

> Three major fears interfere with intercultural communication. First, we fear disapproval—from members of our own group as well as from members of the other person's group. Second, we fear embarrassing ourselves, even making fools of ourselves, by saying the wrong thing or appearing insensitive. And third, we may fear being harmed—our stereotypes of the other group may lead us to see its members as dangerous or potentially harmful to us.
>
> Let's look at each of these fears in more detail. We'll be able to see clearly how they influence our own intercultural communication behavior.
>
> Consider, first, the fear of disapproval. [The speaker would then amplify and support this fear of disapproval, giving examples of disapproval seen in his or her own experience, the testimony of communication theorists on the importance of such fear, research findings on the effects that such fear might have on intercultural communication, and so on.]

## Speeches of Definition

What is leadership? What is a born-again Christian? What is the difference between sociology and psychology? What is a cultural anthropologist? What is safe sex? These are all topics for informative speeches of definition.

A *definition* is a statement of the meaning or significance of a concept or term. Use definitions when you wish to explain difficult or unfamiliar concepts or when you wish to make a concept more vivid or forceful.

In giving a speech of definition, you may focus on defining a term, defining a system or theory, or pinpointing the similarities and/or differences among terms or systems. A speech of definition may be on a subject new to the audience or may present a familiar topic in a new and different way.

Examples of speeches in which you define a term might include What is a smart card? What is machismo? What is creativity? What is affirmative action? What is multiculturalism? What is political correctness?

Examples of speeches in which you'd define a system or theory might include What is the classical theory of public speaking? What are the parts of a generative grammar? What are the major beliefs in Confucianism? What is expressionism? What is futurism? What is the "play theory" of mass communication?

Examples of speeches in which you'd define similar and dissimilar terms or systems might include football and soccer: What's the difference? What do Christians and Muslims have in common? Oedipus and Electra: How do they differ? Other examples: Genetics and heredity, Animal and human rights, and Keyword and directory searches.

## Thesis and Main Points

The thesis in a speech of definition is a statement identifying the term or system and your intention to define it or to contrast it with other terms; for example, "Christianity and Islam have much in common" or "You can search for information through keywords or a through directory."

In a speech of definition, once again, you derive the main points from asking questions of your thesis; for example, what do Christianity and Islam have in common? How do online and text dictionaries differ? Your main points will then consist of, say, the factors that Christianity and Islam have in common or the several ways in which online and text dictionaries differ.

## Support

Once you have each of the main points for your speech of definition, support them with examples, testimony, and the like. For example, one of your main points in the Christianity–Islam example might be that both religions believe in the value of good works. You might then quote from the New Testament and from the Quran to illustrate this belief, or you might give examples of noted Christians and Muslims who exemplified this characteristic, or you might cite the testimony of religious leaders who talked about the importance of good works.

Because this is a speech of definition, you'd want to give special attention to all your definitions, as discussed earlier (pp. 291–293).

## Organization

For a speech of definition, an obvious organizational pattern is the pattern of multiple definitions (see Chapter 10). Alternatively, you might consider using a topical order, in which each main idea is treated equally. In either case, however, proceed from the known to the unknown. Start with what your audience knows and work up to what is new or unfamiliar. Let's say you want to explain the concept of phonemics, with which your particular audience happens to be totally unfamiliar. The specific idea you wish to get across is that each phoneme stands for a unique sound. You might proceed from the known to the unknown and begin your definition with something like this:

## Preparing an Informative Speech

Consult the Dictionary of Topics at **www.mycommunicationlab.com** for suggestions for informative speech topics. Select a topic; then:

*Working repeatedly with the process of preparing a speech will ultimately make the process easier, more efficient, and more effective.*

1. Formulate a thesis and a specific purpose suitable for an informative speech of approximately 10 minutes.
2. Analyze this class as your potential audience and identify ways in which you can relate this topic to their interests and needs.
3. Generate at least two main points from your thesis.
4. Support these main points with examples, illustrations, definitions, testimony, and so on.
5. Construct a conclusion that summarizes your main ideas and brings the speech to a definite close.
6. And finally, construct an introduction that gains attention and orients your audience.

Discuss these outlines in small groups or with the class as a whole. Try to secure feedback from other members on how you can improve your outline.

We all know that in the written language each letter of the alphabet stands for a unit of the written language. Each letter is different from every other letter. A *t* is different from a *g* and a *g* is different from a *b* and so on. Each letter is called a "grapheme." In English we know we have twenty-six such letters.

We can look at the spoken language in much the same way. Each sound is different from every other sound. A *t* sound is different from a *d* and a *d* is different from a *k* and so on. Each individual sound is called a "phoneme."

Now, let me explain in a little more detail what I mean by a "phoneme."

Here is an example of how you might go about constructing a speech of definition.

In this example, the speaker selects three major types of lying for discussion and arranges these in a topical pattern.

General purpose: ———————————— *To inform.* ————————————

Specific purpose: ————— *To define lying by explaining the major types of lying.* —————

Thesis: ————— *There are three major kinds of lying. (What are the three major kinds of lying?)* —————

   I. ————— *Concealment is the process of hiding the truth.* —————

   II. ————— *Falsification is the process of presenting false information as if it were true.* —————

   III. ————— *Misdirection is the process of acknowledging a feeling but misidentifying its cause.* —————

In delivering such a speech, the speaker might begin by saying:

A lie is a lie is a lie. True? Well, not exactly. Actually, there are a number of different ways we can lie. We can lie by concealing the truth. We can lie by falsification, by presenting false information as if it were true. And we can lie by misdirection, by acknowledging a feeling but misidentifying its cause.

Let's look at the first type of lie—the lie of concealment. Most lies are lies of concealment. Most of the time when we lie we simply conceal the truth. We don't actually make any false statements. Rather we simply don't reveal the truth. Let me give you some examples I overheard recently.

# Speeches of Demonstration

In using *demonstration*, or in a speech devoted entirely to demonstration, you show the audience how to do something or how something operates. Examples of speeches in which you demonstrate how to do something might include how to give mouth-to-mouth resuscitation, how to drive defensively, how to mix colors, how to ask for a raise, how to burglarproof your house, or how to use PowerPoint in business meetings.

Examples of speeches in which you demonstrate how something operates might include how the body maintains homeostasis, how perception works, how divorce laws work, how e-mail works, how a hurricane develops, or how a heart bypass operation is performed.

## Thesis and Main Points

The thesis for a speech of demonstration identifies what you will show the audience how to do or how something operates; for example, "E-mail works through a series of electronic connections from one computer to a server to another computer," or "You can burglarproof your house in three different ways," or "Three guidelines will help you get that raise."

You derive the main points for your speech of demonstration by asking a simple How or What question of your thesis: How do these electronic connections work? What are the things you can do to burglarproof your house? What are the guidelines for asking for a raise?

## Support

To support each of the main ideas in a speech of demonstration, you can use a variety of materials. For example, you might show diagrams of houses with different burglarproofing arrangements, demonstrate how various locks work, or show how different security systems work.

Presentation aids are especially helpful in speeches of demonstration. A good example of this is the signs in restaurants demonstrating the Heimlich maneuver. These signs demonstrate the sequence of steps with both words and pictures. The combination of verbal and graphic information makes it easy to understand this important process. In a speech on this topic, however, it would be best to use only the pictures as aids so that written words would not distract your audience from your oral explanation.

## Organization

In most cases, a temporal pattern will work best in speeches of demonstration. Demonstrate each step in the sequence in which it's to be performed. In this way, you'll avoid one of the major difficulties in demonstrating a process—backtracking. Don't skip steps even if you think they're familiar to the audience. They may not be. Connect each step to the next with appropriate transitions. For example, in explaining the Heimlich maneuver, you might say,

> Now that you have your arms around the choking victim's chest, your next step is to. . . .

Assist your listeners by labeling the steps clearly; for example, say, "The first step," "The second step," and so on.

Begin with an overview. It's often helpful, when demonstrating, to give a broad general picture and then present each step in turn. For example, suppose you were talking about how to prepare a wall for painting. You might begin with a general overview to give your listeners a general idea of the process, saying something like this:

> In preparing the wall for painting, you want to make sure that the wall is smoothly sanded, free of dust, and dry. Sanding a wall isn't like sanding a block of wood. So let's look first at the proper way to sand a wall.

Here is an example of the speech of demonstration. In this example, the speaker identifies and demonstrates how to listen actively.

General purpose: _____ *To inform.* _____

Specific purpose: _____ *To demonstrate three techniques of active listening.* _____

Thesis: _____ *We can engage in active listening. (How can we engage in active* _____
*listening?)*

   I. _____ *Paraphrase the speaker's meaning.* _____

   II. _____ *Express understanding of the speaker's feelings.* _____

   III. _____ *Ask questions.* _____

In delivering the speech, the speaker might begin by saying:

> Active listening is a special kind of listening. It's listening with total involvement, with a concern for the speaker. It's probably the most important type of listening you can engage in. Active listening consists of three steps: paraphrasing the speaker's meaning, expressing understanding of the speaker's feelings, and asking questions.
>
>   Your first step in active listening is to paraphrase the speaker's meaning. What is a paraphrase? A paraphrase is a restatement in your own words of the speaker's meaning. That is, you express in your own words what you think the speaker meant. For example, let's say that the speaker said. . . .

This three-part classification of information speeches into speeches of demonstration, definition, and description is only one way of looking at informative speeches. You may be interested in some alternative classifications of information speeches that other writers in public speaking have devised.

George Grice and John Skinner (2004), for example, offer an eight-part system:

- Speeches about people (Cesar Chavez, Margaret Mead)
- Speeches about objects (electric cars, the Great Wall of China)
- Speeches about places (Ellis Island, the Nile)
- Speeches about events (sinking of the *Titanic*, Woodstock festivals)
- Speeches about processes (cartooning, waterproofing)
- Speeches about concepts (liberty, nihilism)
- Speeches about conditions (McCarthyism, the civil rights movement)
- Speeches about issues (the use of polygraph tests, fetal tissue research)

Stephen Lucas (2004) uses a four-part classification:

- Speeches about objects, persons, places, or things; for example, the contributions of a noted scientist or philosopher
- Speeches about processes or series of actions; for example, an explanation of how to do something
- Speeches about events or happenings; for example, the story of your first date
- Speeches about concepts, beliefs, or ideas; for example, a review of theories of economics

**WHAT DO YOU SAY?**
**Demonstrating**
You want to demonstrate to your audience how to paste a photo or document into the text of an e-mail. Your audience is probably mixed in terms of their knowledge of technology generally—some know a great deal and others know very little. You want to gain the attention of your entire audience early in your speech. *What do you say?*

# THE PUBLIC SPEAKING SAMPLE ASSISTANT

AN EXCELLENT INFORMATIVE SPEECH

## CONTROLLING THE WEATHER: MOSHE ALAMARO'S PLAN FOR HURRICANE MITIGATION

### *Jillian Collum\**

Unbeknownst to most Americans, in 1984 the United States came under attack from a terrorist group bent on overthrowing our government. Their leader had constructed a machine to create devastating storms. Their goal was clear, and the entire group was committed, well funded and animated. Fortunately, the Cobra Commander's plan failed thanks to some real American heroes—the GI Joes, who used giant mirrors to absorb the machine's solar power. Though the ability to harness natural phenomena has traditionally been restricted to masked cartoon terrorists, one real-life scientist now believes that he too has discovered how to control the weather. But instead of attacking the United States, he wants to protect it. The *Houston Chronicle* of July 12, 2005, reports that Moshe Alamaro, a visiting researcher in MIT's Department of Earth, Atmospheric and Planetary Sciences, has drafted a plan to fight back against hurricanes. Alamaro's "hurricane mitigation" system calls for creating tropical storms to consume all of the warm ocean water that would normally fuel an approaching hurricane. A January 27, 2006, article from the National Oceanic and Atmospheric Administration's website explains that, in 2005, Hurricanes Katrina, Wilma, Rita and Dennis caused over $120 billion in damage, and took the lives of over 1,400 people. Even more alarming, *The New Scientist* of December 24, 2005, notes that the number of strong hurricanes has almost doubled in the last 35 years. And as global warming further increases water temperatures, we could see even more devastating hurricane seasons in the future. So, in order to understand how Moshe Alamaro plans to protect us from the increasing danger of these storms, we must first, explore how Alamaro's plan works; next, examine how it will be enacted; and finally, discuss the drawbacks and future implications of this new effort to keep deadly storms at bay.

Cobra Commander's evil plans generally took about thirty minutes to carry out. Moshe Alamaro, however, took a little bit longer when he first presented his ideas at an April 2005 Weather Modification Association conference. To explore his plan, we'll discuss how hurricanes work, and how Alamaro plans to mitigate them.

Did this introduction gain your attention and make you want to continue reading/listening?

Here you start wondering—is this fact or fiction? And in this way the speaker gains your attention. After you complete reading the speech, return to this introduction and try to identify other ways the speaker might have introduced the topic and gained the audience's attention.

When this speech was given (in March 2006), the weather was much in the news, and Hurricane Katrina was referred to almost daily in newspapers' coverage of the rebuilding of New Orleans. The speaker's topic is certainly most timely. Moreover, it addresses something many people have wondered about, "Why can't science tell us how to prevent these weather problems from causing so much destruction?"

How might you have illustrated how great a sum $120 billion is? How might you have illustrated what the doubling of the yearly number of strong hurricanes over the last 35 years means in terms of their frequency?

Here the speaker explains the importance of the topic briefly. Most people listening to this speech are likely to appreciate the importance of the topic and the need for methods to combat these natural catastrophes.

Here the speaker orients the audience and explains that she'll cover three topics: how the plan works, how it will be enacted, and the future of this effort.

Here the speaker wisely repeats her first point rather than merely assuming that the audience will remember, from the orientation, that the first point concerns how the plan works. And, to further guide the listeners, she explains that she'll explain the plan by first explaining how hurricanes work.

Hurricanes are obviously huge, deadly storms, but the *Washington Post* of October 3, 2005, explains that they start out as clusters of regular thunderstorms. These clusters pick up heat and moisture from surface water, which then cools and condenses into clouds and rain, causing the storm to grow larger. This means: The more warm water available to feed the storm, the bigger it will get. According to Canada's *National Post* of August 30, 2005, warm waters have turned recent storms into giants—Katrina was a weak category one hurricane when it passed over southern Florida, but after traveling over the warm waters of the gulf, it grew into a catastrophic category four hurricane almost 400 miles wide.

Here is a very simple explanation of how hurricanes grow, which is a necessary step to understanding how Alamaro's plan works.

But Moshe Alamaro plans to neutralize the threat by depriving it of its energy source. His plan is simple: Create man-made tropical storms in the paths of approaching hurricanes. Because tropical storms consume the same fuel as hurricanes—warm water—Alamaro believes that placing tropical storms in front of approaching hurricanes would leave the bigger storms with far less fuel. Without this energy, hurricanes won't be able to grow as large. The *Economist Technology Quarterly* of June 11, 2005, likens this to firefighters' practice of lighting small fires in front of approaching wildfires. The small controlled fires consume fuel, leaving the bigger fire with no energy source when it passes over the area. If this principle is applied to hurricanes, residents in hurricane-prone areas will one day experience more tropical storms, but not so many devastating hurricanes.

Here the speaker explains the plan and also helps the audience understand it by relating it to something they're already familiar with—namely, the practice of using small fires to fight large fires.

While Cobra Commander had a clear plan for defeating the U.S., Moshe Alamaro has a clear plan for taking on hurricanes. We'll explore his ideas further by examining how and where he plans to create tropical storms.

If you're familiar with Cobra Commander, then these frequent references work well. Would they work in your class?

The *Scripps Howard News Service* reported on June 30, 2005 that Alamaro plans to tow a barge equipped with about twenty jet engines into the path of an oncoming hurricane, then ignite the engines with the jets facing upward. The resulting updrafts would siphon heat from the ocean. This heat and moisture would cool and condense into clouds and rain as it rose, creating the man-made tropical storm that would weaken the hurricane. In a February 24, 2006, personal interview, Moshe Alamaro explained that the 20 jet engines would create approximately 100 tons of thrust. Since a barge can carry 1,000 tons, there is no danger of it sinking. Additionally, the previously cited *Economist* reveals that the costs for this project would be relatively low, since jet engines could be retrieved from retired U.S. and Soviet bombers. This would mean that protecting Central America and the southern U.S. would cost less than $1 billion a year, a small price to pay compared to the $120 billion in hurricane damage in 2005 alone.

In his presentation to the Weather Modification Association, Alamaro suggested two ways to carry out his plan. First, barges carrying the jet engines could be dispatched to intercept advancing hurricanes. However, this plan could be logistically difficult, since hurricanes can quickly switch course. So Alamaro also suggested a second plan, which would call for barges to continuously patrol the shoreline during hurricane season. These barges would then create tropical storms to preemptively lower the ocean's temperature in any areas where it may be high. This would mean that when hurricanes did come through an area, they would have less warm water with which to grow. *Popular Science* of October 2005 reveals that we may begin to see this plan take shape within the next five years.

Because Cobra Commander was so diabolical, the Joes always had to be wary of the next obstacle he was planning for them. Moshe Alamaro knows he too will face challenges, in the form of drawbacks and implications.

Like most events in nature, hurricanes serve a purpose. According to the Central Florida Hurricane Center website on November 7, 2005, hurricanes serve to redistribute excess heat from the tropics to the mid-latitudes in order to keep the global climate system balanced. The *Boston Globe* of September 6, 2004, reports that hurricanes have other beneficial purposes—they refresh waterways, revive dry areas, and bulk up barrier islands with redistributed sand. Also, in his report to the Weather Modification Association, Alamaro cautioned that if the man-made tropical storm gets too close to the target hurricane, there is a small possibility the two could merge, forming an even larger hurricane. So, while Alamaro's plan has the potential to prevent hurricane damage, it could disrupt our environment by eliminating the beneficial aspects of these storms, or it could make a dangerous storm even stronger.

Finally, Alamaro's plan may result in the weaponization of hurricanes. According to the April 2005 Weather Modification Association report, it may be possible to design the man-made tropical storms to steer the target hurricane in a particular direction. The *Boston Globe* of July 3, 2005, notes that militaries— both cartoon and real—have long dreamed of controlling the weather to gain an edge over their enemies. In fact, during the Vietnam War, the U.S. military sprayed silver iodide on clouds to create rain over the Ho Chi Minh Trail in order to make it muddy and impassable to foes. So, it isn't hard to imagine how militaries, or even terrorist organizations, may be interested in steering hurricanes toward well-populated areas to wreak havoc on their enemies. But while Alamaro's plan does have the potential for harm, it could also be used to save millions of dollars and thousands of lives.

Here the speaker goes into her second point—how the plan will work. This is relatively straightforward and follows clearly from the first point. If you chose to use a transition here, how might you phrase it?

Here the speaker offers a transition from the second point to the third and links this to Cobra Commander. In what other ways might you have phrased a transition?

How would you describe the research presented in this speech?

Here the speaker explains the drawbacks and implications fairly and objectively. We don't feel the speaker is minimizing the dangers of the plan, and perhaps because of this we believe the speaker. In other words, the fairness of these explanations heightens the speaker's credibility.

Though Cobra Commander's efforts to create dangerous storms were thwarted, Mother Nature continues to throw deadly disasters our way, meaning that anyone who figures out how to stop them will be a real American hero. After examining how Moshe Alamaro's "hurricane mitigation" plan works, how it will be carried out, and its drawbacks and future implications, we finally know all about this promising new technology. And as the GI Joes taught us, "knowing is half the battle."

*Jillian Collum is a student at the University of Texas at Austin. This speech was delivered at the 2006 American Forensic Association National Individual Events Tournament in Gainsville, Florida, and is reprinted by permission of the speaker.

The speaker's conclusion serves two major purposes. The speaker summarizes the speech's main points and closes with a quotation relating back to the theme of Cobra Commander.

## Summary of Concepts and Skills

This chapter covered the nature of the informative speech and ways you can most effectively communicate information.

1. When preparing informative speeches, observe the guidelines for informative speaking: Limit the amount of information, adjust the level of complexity, stress the information's relevance and usefulness, relate new information to information the audience already knows, and make your speech easy to remember.
2. To make your ideas clear to your audience, use amplifying materials such as examples, illustrations, and narratives; testimony; statistics; definitions; and visual aids.
3. Three general types of informative speeches are speeches of description, in which you explain an object, person, event, or process; speeches of definition, in which you define a term, system, theory, or set of principles; and speeches of demonstration, in which you explain how something works or how to do something.

Effective public speakers need to master a variety of informing skills. Place a check mark next to those skills you want most to work on.

_____ 1. In my informative speeches I follow the principles of informative speaking: I stress the information's usefulness, relate new information to information the audience already knows, present information through several senses, adjust the level of complexity, limit the amount of information I present, and recognize cultural variations.

_____ 2. For my informative speeches I select a variety of amplifying materials; examples, illustrations, and narratives; testimony; definitions; statistics; and visual aids.

_____ 3. When developing a speech of information, I follow the suggestions for constructing speeches of description, definition, and demonstration.

## Key Word Quiz

### The Language of Informative Speaking

Match the terms about informative speaking with their definitions. Record the number of the definition next to the appropriate term.

a. _____ speech of description
b. _____ correlation
c. _____ statistics

1. An expert's opinion or a witness's account.
2. A relatively brief specific instance.
3. A means of defining a term by tracing its historical or linguistic development.

**d.** _____ speech of demonstration

**e.** _____ example

**f.** _____ etymology

**g.** _____ testimony

**h.** _____ measures of central tendency

**i.** _____ narrative

**j.** _____ illustration

4. A speech in which you explain an object, person, event, or process.

5. Statistical figures of which the mean and the median are examples.

6. A relatively long illustration presented as an anecdote or story.

7. Summary figures that help you communicate important aspects of complex sets of numbers.

8. A speech in which you show listeners how to do something or how something works.

9. A longer and more detailed example.

10. A measure of how closely two or more things are related.

**Answers.** a. 4 b. 10 c. 7 d. 8 e. 2 f. 3 g. 1 h. 5 i. 6 j. 9

## Five for Discussion

1. To keep usefulness in the forefront, assume—as you're preparing and refining your speech—that each person in the audience is going to be asking, "What's in this for me?" "How will this benefit me?" "Why should I be here listening to this speech?" How would you answer these audience questions in relation to your next speech topic?

2. What is the single most important principle of informative speaking? What one principle do you see violated most often?

3. How would you use statistics to illustrate "the increase in school violence," "the federal deficit," "the cost of war," or "the rise in drug use in corporations"?

4. Compare the news available on the website of one of the major newspapers (for example, the _Washington Post_ or _New York Times_ site) with the news presented by a wire service such as the Associated press (www.ap.org) or Reuters (www.reuters.com). Which do you prefer? Why?

5. The Onelook Dictionary Search website at www. onelook.com will enable you to search a wide variety of dictionaries at the same time. Visit this site and search for two or three words whose definitions may be important in one of your future speeches.

## Log On! MyCommunicationLab

Two exercises and a self-test will help you work actively with presentation aids (www.ablongman.com/devito): (1) Analyzing Presentation Aids, (2) Preparing a Two-minute Speech, and (3) Can You Distinguish Universal from Culture-Specific Icons?

Explore our research resources at www.researchnavigator.com.

Research Navigator.com

# The Persuasive Speech

*Y*ou'll no doubt find yourself in a wide variety of situations in which you'll have to persuade others—to urge others to accept or reject a union proposal, redesign a company's website, negotiate a business deal, or donate blood or money or time, to give just a few examples. As with having to provide information, the higher up you go in your organization's hierarchy, the more you'll find yourself having to persuade others.

## Goals of Persuasion

**Persuasion** is the process of influencing another person's *attitudes, beliefs, values,* and/or *behaviors.* Here is a brief glossary of the terms in this definition:

- **Attitude:** The tendency to respond to something in a certain way. For example, if your audience has a positive attitude toward the current administration, then they're likely to favor the policies, proposals, and values of the administration. If they have a negative attitude, they're likely to oppose administration policies and the like.

- **Belief:** The conviction in the existence or reality of something or in the truth of some assertion. For example, if your audience believes that soft drugs lead to hard drugs, then they're likely to oppose legalizing marijuana and perhaps to favor harsher penalties for soft drug use.

- **Value:** An indicator of what people feel is good or bad, ethical or unethical, just or unjust. For example, if your audience positively values "free speech," then they'll likely oppose increased restrictions on what can and cannot be said publicly and will likely oppose increased surveillance of their e-mail or phone calls.

- **Behavior:** Overt, observable actions, such as voting for increased funding for education, voting for a particular person, contributing money to the Red Cross, or buying a Ford.

Your persuasive speeches may focus on influencing listeners' attitudes, beliefs, values, and/or behaviors. You may want to accomplish any one of the following three general goals of persuasive speaking:

- *To strengthen or weaken attitudes, beliefs, or values.* Persuasion often aims to strengthen audience views. For example, religious sermons usually seek to strengthen the existing beliefs of the congregation. Similarly, many public service announcements try to strengthen existing beliefs about, say, recycling, smoking, or safe sex. At times, however, you may want to weaken the existing beliefs of the audience—to suggest that what they currently believe may not be entirely true. For example, you might want to weaken the favorable attitudes people might have toward a particular political party or policy.

- *To change attitudes, beliefs, or values.* Sometimes you'll want to change how your audience feels. You might want to change their attitudes to the college's no-smoking rules, to change their beliefs about television's influence on viewer violence, or to change their values about the efficacy of war.

- *To motivate to action.* Ultimately, your goal is to get people to do something— for example, to vote for one person rather than another, to donate money to a fund for the homeless, or to take a course in personal finance.

It's useful to view the effects of persuasion as a continuum ranging from one extreme to another. Let's say, to take one issue currently in the news, that you want to give a persuasive speech on same-sex marriage. You might visualize your audience as existing on a continuum ranging from strongly in favor to strongly opposed, as shown in Figure 13.1. Your task is to move your audience in the direction of your persuasive purpose, which you can do in any of three ways (corresponding to the goals of per-

**Figure *13.1***

**The Persuasion Continuum**

Any movement along the continuum would be considered persuasion.

suasion identified above). You can design your persuasive speech to attempt to:

- Strengthen or weaken your listeners' attitudes, beliefs, or values about same-sex marriage.
- Change your listeners' attitudes, beliefs, or values about same-sex marriage.
- Move your listeners to act—to protest, write letters, or sign a petition.

If your purpose is to persuade the audience to *oppose* same-sex marriage, then in Figure 13.1 any movement toward the right will be successful persuasion; if your purpose is to persuade listeners to *support* same-sex marriage, then any movement toward the left will be successful persuasion. Notice, however, that it's quite possible to give a speech in which you attempt to move your listeners in one direction but actually succeed in moving them in the other direction. This "negative persuasion" effect could occur, for example, if the audience perceived you as dishonest or self-promoting or felt that you presented biased evidence or faulty reasoning.

# Guidelines for Persuasive Speaking

You can become more successful in strengthening or changing attitudes or beliefs and in moving your listeners to action by following these guidelines for persuasive speaking.

## Anticipate Selective Exposure

Listeners expose themselves to information selectively; as discussed in Chapter 2, they listen in accordance with the principle of *selective exposure*. According to this principle, (1) listeners will actively seek out information that supports their opinions, beliefs, values, decisions, and behaviors; and (2) listeners will actively avoid information that contradicts their existing opinions, beliefs, attitudes, values, decisions, and behaviors.

Let's say you're giving a speech on the need to reduce spending on college athletic programs. If your audience consists largely of people who agree with you, you can lead with your thesis and show them that you're on the same side. Your introduction might go something like this:

> Our college athletic program is absorbing money that we can more profitably use for the library and computer labs. Let me explain how the excessive money now going to athletic programs could be better spent in these other areas.

But if you want to persuade an audience that holds attitudes different from those you're advocating, you'll need to anticipate selective exposure and proceed inductively; that is, hold back on your thesis until you've given your evidence and argument, then relate this evidence and argument to your thesis. If you present your listeners with your thesis first, they may tune you out without giving your position a fair hearing.

## Ask for Reasonable Amounts of Change

Persuasion is most effective when it strives for small changes and works over a period of time. Put in terms of the continuum of persuasion shown in Figure 13.1, the

**WHAT DO YOU SAY?**

**Changing Behavior**

You're supervising a workforce of 20 people. Your problem is that computer parts are being stolen by one or more of the workers, and you've been assigned the task of stopping the thefts. You decide to tackle this in your weekly meeting with the workers. *What do you say?*

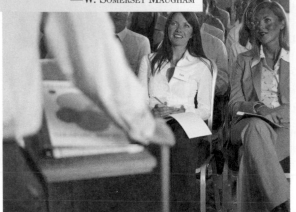

**amounts of change principle** suggests that you'll be more successful if you ask for small (rather than large) movements. Conversely, the greater and more important the change you want your audience to make, the more difficult your task will be.

The reason is simple: Listeners demand a greater number of reasons and a lot more evidence before making big changes—such as, say, changing careers, moving to another state, or investing in stocks.

On the other hand, listeners are more easily persuaded (and demand less evidence) for making small changes—such as, say, attending a particular lecture or donating a small amount of money to a charity. Also, people change gradually, in small degrees, over time. For example, a persuasive speech stands a better chance when it tries to get a drinker to attend just one Alcoholics Anonymous meeting than when it advocates giving up alcohol for life.

So in your classroom speeches, set reasonable goals for what you want the audience to do. Remember you have only perhaps 10 to 15 minutes, and in that time you cannot move the proverbial mountain. Instead, ask for small changes in attitudes, beliefs, values, or behavior; for example, ask your listeners to visit a particular website (perhaps even a site dedicated to beliefs or values that they do not currently share), to vote in the next election, or to buy the new virus protection software.

When you're addressing an audience that is opposed to your position and your goal is to change their attitudes, beliefs, or values, it is even more important that you focus on small changes. Let's say, for example, that your ultimate goal is to get a pro-life group to favor abortion on demand. Obviously, this goal is too great to achieve in one speech. Therefore, you need to strive for small changes. Here, for example, is an excerpt in which the speaker tries to get a pro-life audience to agree that at least some abortions should be legal. The speaker begins as follows:

> One of the great lessons I learned in college was that most extreme positions are wrong. Most of the important truths lie somewhere between the extreme opposites. And today I want to talk with you about one of these truths. I want to talk with you about rape and the problems faced by the mother carrying a child conceived in this most violent of all violent crimes.

Notice that the speaker does not state a pro-choice position but instead focuses on one situation involving abortion and attempts to get the audience to agree that in some cases abortion should be legal.

## Identify with Your Audience

If you can show your audience that you and they share important attitudes, beliefs, and values, you'll clearly advance your persuasive goal. For example, if you know your listeners are concerned with helping the homeless, you might share your own experiences in working at a homeless shelter. Other similarities are also important. For example, in some cases similarity of cultural, educational, or social background may help you identify yourself with your audience. Be aware, however, that insincere or dishonest attempts at identification are likely to backfire and create problems. So avoid even implying similarities between yourself and your audience that don't exist.

As a general rule, never ask the audience to do what you have not done yourself; always demonstrate that you have done what you want the audience to do. If you don't, the audience will rightfully ask, "Why haven't you done it?" In addition, show your listeners that you're glad to have done what you're asking them to do. For example, tell them of the satisfaction you derived from working in the homeless shelter or from donating blood or from reading to blind students.

# Supporting Materials

In addition to the supporting materials described in Chapter 12—for example, materials such as examples or testimony or statistics—three forms of support are of special importance in persuasive speeches: logical, emotional, and credibility appeals.

## Logical Appeals

When you use logical appeals—when you argue on the basis of **logic** supported by reliable facts and evidence—your listeners are more likely to remain persuaded over time and are more likely to resist counterarguments that may come up in the future (Petty & Wegener, 1998). In using logical appeals be sure to avoid the common fallacies of logic, as outlined in Table 13.1. Instead, follow the several principles of the main categories of logical appeals: (1) specific instances, (2) causes and effects, and (3) sign.

| TABLE 13.1 | Fallacies: Pseudo-Argument |
| --- | --- |

Certain persusasive tactics have the feel of real arguments but in fact are fallacies; that is, they appear to address the issues but really don't. Here are a few such pseudo-arguments (Lee & Lee 1972, 1995; Pratkanis & Aronson, 1991; Herrick, 2004). As you read the table, try to recall a recent speech in which any of these fallacies were used. Were you influenced by the pseudo-arguments? Were you persuaded?

| FALLACY | EXAMPLES | CRITICAL RESPONSES |
| --- | --- | --- |
| **Name calling** gives an idea, a group of people, or an ideology a name that the audience evaluates negatively. | "They're antilabor; what do you expect?" "It's just another example of tax-and-spend." | Avoid condemning an idea or person without evidence; as a listener, don't let negative labels prevent critical analysis. |
| **Transfer** associates an idea with something people respect (to gain audience approval) or with something people dislike (to gain rejection). | "The proposal is in the best tradition of equality and democracy." "This is just another form of apartheid." | Not all language aims to describe or present facts objectively; much language is emotive and appeals to listeners' emotions, not to their reason. |
| **Testimonial** involves using the authority of some positively evaluated person to gain audience approval (or of some negatively evaluated person to gain rejection.) | Soap opera stars for automobiles, athletes for underwear, and attractive models for everything from cereal to shampoo. | The spokesperson is usually no more an authority on the product than the audience is; he or she is simply getting paid to endorse the product. |
| **Plain folks** identifies the speaker and the proposal with the audience. | "We're all middle class and we need a break." "As parents—and I'm a parent just like you—we know. . . . " | The speaker's membership in the same groups as the audience has nothing to do with the validity of what's said. |
| **Card stacking** involves selecting only the evidence that supports the speaker's case and ignores contrary evidence. | Almost any political campaign speech. | Most issues have many sides; if an issue is presented with only one side, it may mean that the other side is being hidden. |
| **Bandwagon** involves persuading you to accept or reject an idea so as to go along with "everybody" or "the right people." | "Economists agree that. . . ." "The entire faculty agrees that. . . ." | Agreement is not proof; most of the world once thought the earth was flat or that women were too emotional to vote. |
| **Attack** involves accusing another person of some wrongdoing so that the issue under discussion never gets examined. | "How can we support a candidate who has been unfaithful and has lied?" | A person's personal reputation and past behavior may have nothing to do with the real issues. |

**"In the interest of streamlining the judicial process, we'll skip the evidence and go directly to sentencing."**

## Reasoning from Specific Instances and Generalizations

In reasoning from **specific instances** (or examples), you examine several specific instances and then conclude something about the whole. This form of reasoning, known as induction, is useful when you want to develop a general principle or conclusion but cannot examine the whole. For example, you sample a few communication courses and conclude something about communication courses in general; you visit several Scandinavian cities and conclude something about the whole of Scandinavia.

In reasoning from specific instances, be sure to examine a sufficient number of instances. Two general guidelines will help you determine how much is enough.

- First, the larger the group you wish covered by your conclusion, the greater the number of specific instances you should examine. If you wish to draw conclusions about members of an entire country or culture, you'll have to examine a considerable number of people before drawing even tentative conclusions. On the other hand, if you're attempting to draw a conclusion about a bushel of 130 apples, sampling a few is probably sufficient.

- Second, the greater the diversity of items in the class, the more specific instances you will have to examine. Pieces of pasta in boiling water are all about the same; thus, sampling one usually tells you something about all the others. On the other hand, college courses are probably very different from one another, so valid conclusions about the entire range of college courses will require a much larger sample.

## Reasoning from Causes and Effects

In reasoning from **causes and effects,** you may go in either of two directions: (1) You may reason from cause to effect; for example, smoking (the cause) contributes to lung cancer (the effect). Or (2) you may reason from effect to cause; for example, low reading scores among elementary school children (the effect) are due to poverty (the cause).

In order to establish a cause–effect connection, you'd need to prove that possible causes other than the one you're postulating are not producing the effect. And so you'd need to ask if causes other than smoking may contribute to lung cancer, or if factors other than poverty contribute to low reading scores. Usually, you'd not be able to rule out *all* other factors, but it's important to demonstrate that the factors you are identifying are the main contributors. For example, you'd need to show that although other factors also may contribute to lung cancer, smoking is a major (if not the major) culprit. Similarly, you'd need to demonstrate that poverty more than any other factor accounts for low reading scores. Scientific studies on the effects of smoking on cancer rates and the effects of poverty on reading scores would enable you to establish these cause–effect relationships.

You'd also want to demonstrate that the causation is in the direction you say it is. If two things occur together, it's often difficult to determine which is the cause and which is the effect. For example, a lack of interpersonal intimacy and a lack of self-confidence often occur in the same person. A person who lacks self-confidence seldom has successful intimate relationships with others. But which is the cause and which is the effect? Does the lack of intimacy "cause" low self-confidence, or does low self-confidence "cause" a lack of intimacy? Of course, it might also be that some other previously unexamined cause (a history of negative criticism, for example) might be contributing to both the lack of intimacy and the low self-confidence.

## Reasoning from Sign

Reasoning from **sign** involves drawing a conclusion on the basis of the presence of clues or symptoms that frequently occur together.

## Reversing Media's Influence

Although you generally think of the media as exerting influence on you, you can also exert influence on the media—on radio, television, newspapers and magazines, film, and the Internet (Jamieson & Campbell, 1997; Postman & Powers, 1992; Media Education Foundation, 2006b):

■ Register your complaints. Write letters, send e-mail, call a television station or advertiser, or fill out the feedback forms provided on many websites expressing your views. Write to a public forum such as a newspaper or newsgroup, or contact the Federal Communication Commission (FCC) or other regulatory agencies. Use any of the variety of websites (www.vote.com is perhaps the most popular) that encourage users to voice their opinions and then forward these to the appropriate agencies.

■ Exert group pressure. Join with others who think the same way you do. Bring group pressure to bear on television networks, newspapers, advertisers, Internet sites, and manufacturers.

■ Protest through an established organization. There's probably an organization already established for the issue with which you're concerned. Search the Internet for relevant newsgroups, professional organizations, and chat rooms that focus on your topic.

■ Protest by taking part in a social movement, a technique used throughout history to gain civil rights. Such movements have the potential advantage of securing media coverage that might enable you to communicate your message to a large audience.

■ Create legislative pressure. Exert influence on the state or federal level by influencing your local political representatives (through voting, calls, letters, and e-mails), who will in turn influence representatives at higher levels of the political hierarchy.

*Increasing Media Literacy. Let's say that you're unhappy about the way in which the national and local media (television and newspapers) have treated the abortion controversy. How would you go about exerting pressure on the media to better reflect your own position in their coverage?*

Medical diagnosis is a good example of reasoning by sign. The general procedure is simple. If a sign and an object, event, or condition are frequently paired, the presence of the sign is taken as proof of the presence of the object, event, or condition. For example, fatigue, extreme thirst, and overeating serve as signs of hyperthyroidism, because they frequently accompany the condition.

In reasoning from sign, you need to demonstrate that the signs necessitate the conclusion. If a person has frequent fatigue, extreme thirst, and overeats but doesn't gain weight, how certain may you be of the "hyperthyroid" conclusion? With most medical and legal matters, we can never be absolutely certain, but we can be certain beyond a reasonable doubt.

You'd also want to show that other signs cannot logically point to the same conclusion. In the thyroid example, extreme thirst could be brought on by any number of factors. Similarly, the fatigue and the overeating could be attributed to other causes. Yet taken together, the three signs seem to point to thyroid problems as a reasonable diagnosis. Generally, the more signs that point toward the conclusion, the more confidence you can have that it's valid.

## Emotional Appeals

*Emotional appeals*, often called motivational appeals, are appeals to your listeners' feelings, needs, desires, and wants, and are extremely powerful in persuasion. When you use emotional appeals, you appeal to those forces that energize, move, or motivate people to develop, change, or strengthen their attitudes or ways of

## Listening to Anecdotal Evidence

Often you'll hear people use anecdotes to "prove" a point: "Women are like that; I have three sisters." "That's the way Japanese managers are; I've seen plenty of them." One reason this type of "evidence" is inadequate is that it relies on too few observations; it's usually a clear case of overgeneralizing on the basis of too little evidence. A second reason is that one person's observations may be unduly clouded by his or her own attitudes and beliefs. People's attitudes toward women or the Japanese, for example, are likely to influence their perception and can lead them to see what they want to or expect to see.

***Applying Listening Skills.*** *How would you respond as a critic if a speaker "reasoned" from nothing more than anecdotal "evidence"?*

*How dangerous it always is to reason from insufficient data.*
—Sherlock Holmes

behaving. Not surprisingly, the motivated sequence pattern discussed in Chapter 10 is directly relevant to the use of emotional appeals. Table 13.2 summarizes the motivated sequence as a persuasive strategy and illustrates the numerous ways in which emotional appeals can be employed in persuasive speeches. Let's now look more closely at how motivational appeals work.

Developed more than 30 years ago, one of the most useful analyses of human motives remains Abraham Maslow's fivefold hierarchy of needs, reproduced in Figure 13.2 on page 326 (Maslow, 1970; Benson & Dundis, 2003; Hanley & Abell, 2002; Kiel, 1999). One of the assumptions of Maslow's hierarchy is that people seek to fulfill the needs at the lowest level first, and that only when those needs are satisfied do the needs at the next level begin to influence behavior. For example, people would not concern themselves with the need for security or freedom from fear if they were starving (if their need for food had not been met). Similarly, they would not be concerned with friendship if their need for protection and security was not fulfilled. The implication for you as a speaker is that you have to know what needs of your audience are unsatisfied. These are the needs you can appeal to in motivating your listeners.

Here are several useful motivational appeals organized around Maslow's hierarchy. As you review these, try to visualize how you might use each appeal in your next speech.

### Physiological Needs
In many parts of the world, and even in parts of the United States, the basic physiological needs of people are not fully met, and thus are powerful motivating forces. In such circumstances the speaker who promises to meet fundamental physiological needs is the one the people will follow.

### Safety Needs
Those who do not have their basic safety and freedom-from-fear needs met will be motivated by appeals to security, protection, and freedom from physical and psychological harm. You see such **fear appeals** in advertisements for burglar protection devices for home and car, in political speeches promising greater police protection in schools, and in the speeches of motivational gurus who promise freedom from anxiety.

Sometimes the safety motive is seen in individuals' desire for order, structure, and organization—motives clearly appealed to in advertisements for personal data assistants like the BlackBerry, cell phones, and information management software.

### Belonging and Love Needs
Belonging and love needs comprise a variety of specific motives. For example, most people are motivated to love and be loved.

## TABLE 13.2  The Motivated Sequence as a Persuasive Strategy

This table summarizes persuasive strategies in terms of the motivated sequence.

| STEP | PURPOSE | AUDIENCE QUESTION SPEAKER SHOULD ANSWER | AUDIENCE RESPONSE YOU WANT TO AVOID | IDEAL AUDIENCE RESPONSE | SPEECH MATERIALS TO USE | CAUTIONS TO OBSERVE |
|---|---|---|---|---|---|---|
| Attention | Focus listeners' attention on you and your message. | Why should I listen? Why should I use my time listening? | This is boring. This is irrelevant. This is of no interest to me. | This sounds interesting. Tell me more. | Attention-gaining materials. | Make attention relevant to speech topic. |
| Need | Demonstrate that there is a problem that affects them. | Why do I need to know or do anything? | I don't need to hear this. Things are fine now. This won't benefit me. | Ok, I understand; there's a problem. | Supporting materials (examples, statistics, testimony). | Don't overdramatize the need. |
| Satisfaction | Show listeners how they can satisfy the need. | How can I do anything about this? | I really can't do anything. It's beyond my control. | I can change things. | Supporting materials, logical, motivational, and credibility appeals. | Answer any objections listeners might have to your plan. |
| Visualization | Show listeners what their lives will be like with the need satisfied. | How would anything be different or improved? | I can't see how anything would be different. Nothing's going to change. | *Wow!* Things look a lot better this way. | Motivational appeals, illustrations and language high in imagery. | Be realistic; don't visualize the world as perfect once your listeners do as you suggest. |
| Action | Urge listeners to do something to solve the problem. | What can I do to effect this change? | I can't do anything. I'll be wasting my time and energy. | Let me sign up. Here's my contribution. I'll participate in the campaign. | Motivational appeals, specific language. | Be specific. Ask for small attitude changes and easily performed behaviors. |

For most persons, love and its pursuit occupy a considerable amount of time and energy. If you can teach your audience how to be loved and how to love, your audience will be not only attentive but also grateful.

As humans, we also want affiliation—friendship and companionship. We want to be a part of a group, despite our equally strong desire for independence and individuality. Notice how advertisements for dating services, singles clubs, apartments with lounges and club rooms, and cruises appeal to this need for affiliation.

**Self-Esteem Needs**  We all want to see ourselves as self-confident, worthy, and contributing human beings. Inspirational speeches, speeches of the "you're the greatest" type, never seem to lack receptive and suggestible audiences.

Self-esteem derives, at least in part, from the approval of others (something that is important in all cultures, but especially in collectivist cultures). Most people are concerned with approval from peers, family, teachers, elders, and even children. And beyond contributing to positive self-esteem, approval from others helps

## Figure *13.2*

**Maslow's Hierarchy of Needs**

Which of these motives would be most effective in moving your class members to, say, believe that campus violence is a real problem? Which might move them to donate their used books to students who can't afford them?

*Source:* From Abraham Maslow, *Motivation and Personality.* Copyright © 1970. Reprinted by permission of Prentice-Hall, Inc, Upper Saddle River, NJ.

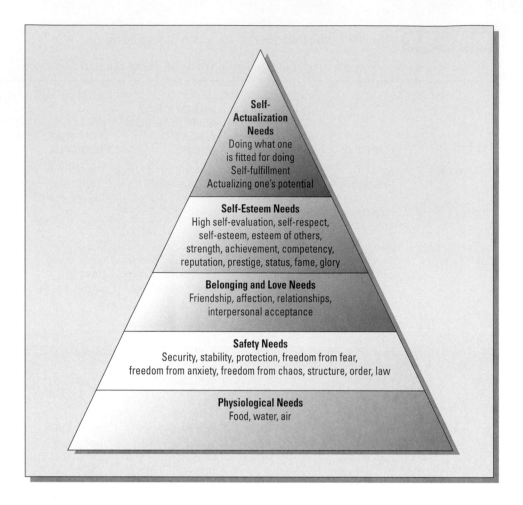

**Self-Actualization Needs**
Doing what one is fitted for doing
Self-fulfillment
Actualizing one's potential

**Self-Esteem Needs**
High self-evaluation, self-respect, self-esteem, esteem of others, strength, achievement, competency, reputation, prestige, status, fame, glory

**Belonging and Love Needs**
Friendship, affection, relationships, interpersonal acceptance

**Safety Needs**
Security, stability, protection, freedom from fear, freedom from anxiety, freedom from chaos, structure, order, law

**Physiological Needs**
Food, water, air

▼ **E-TALK**

**Self-Esteem**
An investigation of self-esteem found that when engaged in communication situations involving interpersonal risk, low-self-esteem persons preferred e-mail, whereas high-self-esteem persons preferred face-to-face interaction (Joinson, 2004). How would you explain this finding?

us achieve other important goals. For example, if we have peer approval, we probably also have influence. If we have approval, we're likely to have status. Show your audience how they can increase their own likeability and you'll have a most attentive group of listeners.

Self-esteem is raised by success. People want to succeed in what they set out to do. If your speech can help them be successful, they'll listen. At the same time, recognize that different cultures will define success very differently. In some cultures success may mean money; in others it may mean group popularity; in still others it may mean security. Show your listeners how what you have to say will help them achieve the goals they seek, and you'll likely have an active and receptive audience.

Financial gain, in our culture and in many others, makes people feel good and raises their self-esteem. Concern for lower taxes, for higher salaries, and for fringe benefits are clearly related to the financial gain motive. Show the audience that what you're saying or advocating will make them money, and they'll listen with considerable interest—much as they read the get-rich-quick books that constantly flood the bookstores and your e-mail mailbox.

**Self-Actualization Needs** At the top of Maslow's hierarchy is the self-actualization motive. This motive influences attitudes and behaviors only after all other needs are satisfied. Because those other needs are very rarely all satisfied, it might seem that the time spent appealing to self-actualization needs would be better spent on other motives. And yet regardless of how satisfied or unsatisfied our other desires may be, each of us has a desire to self-actualize, to become what we

### Emotional Appeals

Emotional appeals are all around. Persons who want to censor the Internet may appeal to parents' fears about their children's accessing pornographic materials; those who want to restrict media portrayals of violence may appeal to people's fear of increased violence in their own communities. The real estate broker who appeals to your desire for status, the friend who wants a favor and appeals to your desire for social approval, and the car salesperson who appeals to your desire for sexual rewards are familiar examples.

*What Would You Do?* *You're a parent of two young teenagers, and you want to dissuade them from engaging in sex. Would it be ethical for you to use fear appeals to get them to avoid sexual relationships? Similarly, would it be ethical to use fear appeals in a public campaign to help prevent sexually transmitted diseases? Would it be ethical to use fear appeals if your motive was to sell SUVs?*

*Whoever is happy will make others happy too.*
—ANNE FRANK

feel we're fit for. If we see ourself as a poet, we must write poetry. If we see ourself as a teacher, we must teach. Even if we don't pursue these as occupations, we nevertheless have a desire to write poetry or to teach. Appeals to self-actualization needs—to people's yearning "to be the best they can be"—encourage listeners to strive for their highest ideals and often will be welcomed by your listeners.

## Credibility Appeals

Your **credibility** is the degree to which your audience regards you as a believable spokesperson. It is not something you have or don't have in any objective sense; rather, your credibility is in the minds of your audience. If your listeners see you as competent and knowledgeable, of good character, and charismatic or dynamic, they'll find you credible (that is, believable). As a result, you'll be more effective in changing their attitudes or in moving them to do something.

This section focuses on how to communicate competence, character, and charisma to your audience. At the same time, however, realize that many speakers will attack your competence, character, and charisma as a persuasive strategy to weaken your own believability. Table 13.3 provides a few examples of unfair personal attacks.

What makes a speaker credible will vary from one culture to another. In some cultures people see competence as the most important factor in, say, their choice of a teacher for their preschool children. In other cultures the most important factor might be the goodness or moral tone of the teacher or perhaps the reputation of the teacher's family. At the same time, each culture may define each of the factors in credibility differently. For example, "character" may mean following the rules of a specific religion in some cultures and following your individual conscience in others. The Quran, the Torah, and the New Testament will be ascribed very different levels of credibility depending on the religious beliefs of the audience. And this will be true even when all three books say essentially the same thing.

Before reading any farther about the ways to establish your credibility, you may wish to take the self-test "How credible are you?"

"I've never actually stormed a castle, but I've taken a bunch of siege-management courses."

## TABLE 13.3  Fallacies: Personal Attacks

Fallacies of argument are all around us; these are arguments that seem logical on the surface but when inspected more closely can be recognized as illogical, irrelevant, and often unethical (Lee & Lee, 1972, 1995; Pratkanis & Aronson, 1991; Herrick, 2004). Here are a few such fallacies that focus on attacking the person. Identify fallacies like these in the speeches of others and eliminate them from your own reasoning. As you read this table, try to recall examples of such personal attacks from your own communication experiences. What effects did these fallacies have on your feelings about the speaker or about the speaker's position?

| FALLACY | EXAMPLES | CRITICAL RESPONSE |
|---|---|---|
| *Personal interest:* In one form of personal interest the speaker disqualifies someone because he or she isn't directly affected by the proposal or doesn't have firsthand knowledge. In another form the speaker disqualifies someone because he or she will benefit in some way from the proposal. | Arguing that because someone is rich, middle class, or poor, he or she will (or will not) benefit greatly from a proposed tax cut, and thus that the person's position on the tax cut is invalid. | The legitimacy of an argument can be judged only on the basis of the evidence and reasoning presented. That someone doesn't have firsthand knowledge or will benefit from what is advocated does not reflect on their argument's validity—though listeners may always question credibility. |
| *Character attacks:* Often referred to as *ad hominem arguments*, character attacks involve accusing another person of wrongdoing or of some character flaw. | Arguments such as "How can we support a candidate who has smoked pot (or avoided the military)?" or "Do you want to believe someone who has been unfaithful on more than one occasion?"—often heard in political discussions. | The purpose of character attack is to discredit the person (which may have nothing to do with the validity of the argument) or to divert attention from the issue under discussion. |
| *Name calling:* Referred to frequently as "poisoning the well," name-calling gives an idea, a group of people, or a philosophy a bad name to try to get listeners to condemn the idea without analyzing the argument and evidence. | Any term that an audience evaluates negatively, such as "terrorist," "racist," or "sexist." | The name someone gives a speaker or an idea may have nothing to do with the speaker or idea; it may be (and often is) a diversionary tactic to get listeners not to look at the logical argument and evidence. |
| *Virtue words:* This fallacy is the opposite of name-calling. With virtue words—often referred to as **glittering generalities**—the speaker tries to make you accept some person or idea by evoking things you value highly. | Associating persons or ideas with "the war against terrorism," "free speech," or "academic freedom." | The use of "virtue words" aims to get listeners to ignore the evidence and simply give their approval. Examine the person or the idea, not the language a speaker uses. |

## HOW CREDIBLE ARE YOU?

**INSTRUCTIONS:** Respond to each of the following phrases to indicate how you think members of your class see you when you deliver a public speech. Use the following scale:

Definitely true = **5**; probably true = **4**; neither true nor untrue = **3**; probably untrue = **2**; and definitely untrue = **1**.

_____ ❶ Knowledgeable about the subject matter

_____ ❷ Experienced

_____ ❸ Informed about the subject matter

_____ ❹ Fair in the presentation of material (evidence and argument)

_____ ⑤ Concerned with the audience's needs

_____ ⑥ Consistent over time on the issues addressed in the speech

_____ ⑦ Assertive in personal style

_____ ⑧ Enthusiastic about the topic and in general

_____ ⑨ Active rather than passive

**HOW DID YOU DO?** This test focuses on the three qualities of credibility—competence, character, and charisma—and is based on a large body of research (for example, McCroskey, 1997; Riggio, 1987). Items 1 to 3 refer to perceived competence: How capable do you seem to the audience? Items 4 to 6 refer to character: Does the audience see you as a good and moral person? Items 7 to 9 refer to charisma: Does the audience see you as dynamic and active? Total scores will range from a high of 45 to a low of 9. If you scored relatively high (say around 32 or higher), then you feel your audience sees you as credible. If you scored relatively low (say below 27), then you feel your audience sees you as lacking in credibility.

**WHAT WILL YOU DO?** Think about how you might go about increasing your credibility. What specific steps can you take to change any audience perception with which you may be unhappy? As you read the following discussion, consider how you might strengthen your competence, character, and/or charisma.

**Competence**   To demonstrate your **competence,** show your listeners that you are knowledgeable and thoroughly familiar with your topic. The more knowledge and expertise the audience sees you as having, the more likely the audience will believe you, just as you are more likely to believe a teacher or doctor if you think he or she is knowledgeable on the subject at hand.

One way to demonstrate your competence is simply to tell listeners about it. Let the audience know of any special experience or training that qualifies you to speak on your topic. If you're speaking on communal living and you've lived on a commune yourself, then say so in your speech.

Another way to demonstrate competence is to cite a variety of research sources. Make it clear to your audience that you've thoroughly researched your topic. Do this by mentioning some of the books you've read, the persons you've interviewed, the articles you've consulted. Weave these references throughout your speech; don't bunch them together. At the same time, stress the competencies of your sources. Say something like "Senator Cardova, who headed the finance committee for three years and was formerly a professor of economics at MIT, thinks. . . ."

**Character**   An audience will see you as credible and will believe you if they perceive you as someone of high moral **character,** someone whom is honest and whom they can trust.

One way to establish your moral character is to stress fairness. Stress, for example, that you've examined both sides of the issue (if indeed you have). If you're presenting both sides of an issue (arguing for Plan A and against Plan B, for example), then make it clear that your presentation is accurate and fair. Be particularly careful not to omit any argument the audience may already have thought of—this is a sure sign that your presentation isn't fair or balanced.

Also, make it clear to the audience that you're interested in their welfare rather than seeking self-gain. If the audience feels that you're "out for yourself," they'll justifiably question your credibility. Tell

"This is what happens when ethical standards are set artificially high."

your audience how the new legislation will reduce *their* taxes, how recycling will improve *their* community, how a knowledge of sexual harassment will make *their* workplace more comfortable and stress free.

**Charisma**    **Charisma** is a combination of your personality and dynamism as seen by the audience. An audience will perceive you as credible (and believable) if they like you and if they see you as friendly and pleasant rather than aloof and reserved. Similarly, audiences favor the dynamic speaker over the hesitant, nonassertive speaker. They'll perceive you as less credible if they see you as shy, introverted, and soft-spoken rather than as extroverted and forceful.

One way to stress charisma is to demonstrate a positive outlook. Show the audience that you have a positive orientation to the public speaking situation and to the entire speaker–audience encounter. Positive and forward-looking people are seen as more credible than negative and backward-looking people. Stress your pleasure at addressing the audience. Stress hope rather than despair, happiness rather than sadness.

Demonstrate enthusiasm. The lethargic speaker, the speaker who somehow plods through the speech, is the very opposite of the charismatic speaker. Let the audience see your energy.

Be emphatic. Use language that's vivid and concrete rather than colorless and vague. Use gestures that are clear and decisive rather than random and hesitant. Demonstrate a firm commitment to the position you're advocating.

## Supporting Materials in Cultural Perspective

The cultural distinctions introduced in earlier chapters (see, for example, Chapter 1, pp. 22–28) become especially important in persuasion; the appeals you'd use to influence one cultural group would not be the same you'd use for a different group. You can appreciate the importance of this by reviewing five key dimensions of culture with persuasive strategies in mind, noting, for example, the types of appeals that will work and those that won't work in different cultures (Singh & Pereira, 2005).

- *Individualist and collectivist cultures.* In addressing members of a collectivist culture, you'd need to emphasize the importance of family, of loyalty (to brand names or local organizations), and of national identity and pride. On the other hand, if you were trying to appeal to members of individualistic cultures, you'd emphasize such themes as independence, nonconformity, and uniqueness. In collectivist cultures, to stress your own competence or that of your corporation may be taken as a suggestion that your audience members are inferior or that their corporations are not as good as yours. In individualist cultures, if you don't stress your competence, your listeners may assume it's because you don't have any.

- *High- and low-power-distance cultures.* With members of a high-power-distance culture, references to important and prominent people and to what they believe and advocate will prove effective. In contrast, in a low-power-distance culture these appeals will prove less effective than would, say, references to or testimonials from people much like the people you wanted to influence.

- *High- and low-uncertainty-avoidance cultures.* Audiences high in uncertainty avoidance want information from experts (or supported by experts)—they want to know very clearly where they can go for information and guidance. These audiences also value tradition, so appeals to the past will prove effective with such groups. Audiences low in uncertainty avoidance can tolerate more ambiguity, and appeals to the new and different will be more effective.

"Excellent sermon."

## Developing Persuasive Strategies

The objective of this exercise is to stimulate the discussion of persuasive strategies on a variety of contemporary cultural issues. The exercise may be completed individually, in small groups, or with the entire class.

What persuasive strategies would you use to convince your class of the validity of either side in any of the following points of view? For example, what persuasive strategies would you use to persuade your class members that interracial adoption should be encouraged or discouraged? The points of view are simplified for purposes of this exercise and are by no means intended to represent complete descriptions of these complex issues.

- *Points of view: Interracial adoption.* Those in favor of interracial adoption argue that the welfare of the child—who might not get adopted if made to wait for someone of the same race—must be considered first. Regardless of race, adoption is good for the child and therefore is a positive social process. Those opposed to interracial adoption argue that children need to be raised by those of the same race if they are to develop self-esteem and become functioning members of their own ethnic group. Interracial adoption is therefore a negative social process.

- *Points of view: Gay men and lesbians in the military.* Those in favor argue that gay men and lesbians should be accorded exactly the same rights and responsibilities as heterosexuals—no more, no less; equality means equality for all. Those opposed argue that gay men and lesbians will undermine the image of the military and will make heterosexuals uncomfortable.

- *Points of view: Affirmative action.* Those in favor of affirmative action argue that because of the injustices in the way certain groups (racial, national, gender) have been treated, members of such groups should now be given preferential treatment to correct the imbalance caused by social injustices. Those opposed to affirmative action argue that merit must be the sole criterion for promotions, jobs, entrance to colleges and graduate schools, and so on, and that affirmative action is just reverse racism; one form of injustice cannot correct another form of injustice.

*Working with a variety of persuasive strategies will increase your competence as both speaker and listener.*

- *Masculine and feminine cultures.* Audiences from cultures high in masculinity will be motivated by appeals to achievement, adventure, and enjoyment and will welcome the "hard sell"; listeners high in femininity will be motivated by "soft sell" appeals to harmony and aesthetic qualities.

- *High- and low-context Cultures.* Listeners from high-context cultures will favor appeals that are indirect and implied; listeners from low-context cultures will want detail, directness, and explicitness.

## Persuasive Speeches on Questions of Fact

*Questions of fact* concern what is or is not true, what does or does not exist, what did or did not happen. Some questions of fact are easily answered. These include many academic questions you're familiar with: Who was Aristotle? How many people use the Internet to get news? When was the first satellite launched? Questions of fact also include more mundane questions: What's on television? When is the meeting? What's Jenny's e-mail address? You can easily find answers to these

> **WHAT DO YOU SAY?**
> **Persuasive Appeals**
> You want to give a speech urging your listeners to vote in favor of establishing a hate speech code at the college. You want to use both logical and emotional appeals. *What do you say?*

**Preparing a Persuasive Speech**

Consult the online Dictionary of Topics available with Chapter 13 materials at www.mycommunicationlab.com for suggestions for persuasive speech topics. Select a topic; then:

1. Formulate a thesis and a specific purpose suitable for a persuasive speech of approximately 13 to 15 minutes.
2. Analyze this class as your potential audience and identify ways in which you can relate this topic to their interests and needs.
3. Generate at least two main points from your thesis.
4. Support these main points with logical, motivational, and credibility appeal.
5. Construct a conclusion that summarizes your main ideas and brings the speech to a definite close.
6. Construct an introduction that gains attention and orients your audience.

Discuss these outlines in small groups or with the class as a whole. Try to secure feedback from other class members on how you can improve your outline.

*Practicing persuasion with a variety of topics will help you learn the principles and strategies of this crucial art.*

questions by looking at some reference book, finding the relevant website, or asking someone who knows the answer.

The questions of fact that we deal with in persuasive speeches are a bit different. Although these questions also have answers, the answers are not that easy to find and in fact may never be found. The questions concern controversial issues for which different people have different answers. Daily newspapers abound in questions of fact. To take a random example, the June 4, 2006, edition of the *New York Times* dealt with questions of fact that included such issues as these: Were the 17 Canadian residents arrested guilty of plotting to attack targets in southern Ontario? Did the Alabama Boy Scouts inflate their numbers by some 13,000 members in order to get increased funding and benefit the careers of scouting officials? Will a needle exchange program in New Jersey reduce the spread of AIDS? Did the American military kill 24 Iraqi civilians in cold blood in Haditha? Has technology improved business productivity in recent years?

## Thesis and Main Points

For a persuasive speech on a question of fact, you'll formulate a thesis on the basis of a factual statement such as: "This company has . . . ," "The plaintiff was . . . ," "The death was a case of . . . ."

If you were preparing a persuasive speech, you might phrase your thesis as "This company discriminates against women." Whether or not the company does discriminate is a question of fact; clearly the company either does or does not discriminate. Whether you can prove it does or it doesn't, however, is another issue.

Once you've formulated your thesis, you can generate your main points by asking the simple question "How do you know this?" or "Why would you believe this is true (factual)?" The answers to one of these questions will enable you to develop your main points. The bare bones of your speech might then look something like this:

General purpose: _____ *To persuade.*

Specific purpose: _____ *To persuade my listeners that this company discriminates against women.*

Thesis: _____ *This company discriminates against women. (How can we tell that this company discriminates against women?)*

I. _____ *Women earn less than men.*

II. _____ *Women are hired less often than men.*

III. _____ *Women occupy fewer managerial positions than men.*

Make sure that you clearly connect your main points to your thesis in your introduction, when introducing each of the points, and again in your summary. Don't allow the audience to forget that the lower salaries that women earn directly supports the thesis that this company discriminates against women.

## Support

Having identified your main points, you would then begin searching for information to support them. Taking the first point, you might develop it something like this:

I. Women earn less than men.
   A. Over the past five years, the average salary for editorial assistants was $6,000 less for women than it was for men.
   B. Over the past five years, the entry-level salaries for women averaged $4,500 less than the entry-level salaries for men.
   C. Over the past five years, the bonuses earned by women were 20 percent below the bonuses earned by men.

The above speech focuses entirely on a question of fact; the thesis itself is a question of fact. In other speeches, however, you may want just one of your main points to center on a question of fact, while the speech as a whole may be one of policy or value.

In a speech on questions of fact, you'd want to emphasize logical proof. Facts are your best support. The more facts you have, the more persuasive you'll be in dealing with questions of fact. For example, the more evidence you can find that women earn less than men, the more convincing you will be in proving that women do in fact earn less and, ultimately, that women are discriminated against.

Use the most recent materials possible. The more recent your materials, the more relevant they will be to the present time and the more persuasive they're likely to be. Notice in our example, if you said that in 1980 women earned on average $13,000 less than men, it would be meaningless in proving that the company discriminates against women *now*.

## Organization

Speeches on questions of fact probably fit most clearly into a topical organizational pattern, in which each reason for your thesis is given approximately equal weight. Notice, for example, that the outline under "Main Points" (above) uses a topical order: All three reasons pointing to discrimination are treated as equal main points.

*"The object of oratory alone is not truth, but persuasion."*
—Thomas Babington Macaulay

## Skill Development Experience

### Developing Persuasive Speeches

Select one of the thesis statements below and: (1) Identify the type of persuasive speech it is—fact, value, or policy. (2) From this thesis, generate two, three, or four main points for a persuasive speech. (3) Identify a few forms of supporting material that might prove useful. And (4) select a suitable organizational pattern.

1. Condoms should be distributed to students in junior and senior high school.
2. Sports involving cruelty to animals, such as bullfighting, cockfighting, and foxhunting, should be universally condemned and declared illegal.
3. The United States should follow the lead of Belgium and the Netherlands in recognizing gay and lesbian marriage.
4. Affirmative action is morally warranted.

# Persuasive Speeches on Questions of Value

*Questions of value* concern what people consider good or bad, moral or immoral, just or unjust. In the *New York Times* of June 4, 2006, there are a lot of questions of value debated. For example, Is the Federal Marriage Act good for the country or does it just write discrimination into the U.S. Constitution? Is the new immigration policy beneficial to the U.S. economy? What is the value of physical punishment in Kenyan schools? What are the advantages and disadvantages of applying auction laws to eBay sellers? Are spelling bees helpful to the general elementary and high school population?

Speeches on questions of value will usually seek to strengthen audiences' existing attitudes, beliefs, or values. This is true of much religious and political speaking; for example, people who listen to religious speeches usually are already believers and are willing to listen; these speeches strive to strengthen the beliefs and values the people already hold. Speeches that seek to change audience values are much more difficult to construct. Most people resist change. When you try to get people to change their values or beliefs, you're fighting an uphill (though not necessarily impossible) battle.

Be sure that you define clearly the specific value on which you're focusing. For example, let's say that you're developing a speech to persuade high school students to attend college. You want to stress that college is of value, but what type of value do you focus on? The financial value (college graduates earn more money than nongraduates)? The social value (college is a lot of fun and a great place to make friends)? The intellectual value (college will broaden your view of the world and make you a more critical and creative thinker)? Once you clarify the type of value on which you'll focus, you'll find it easier to develop the relevant points. You'll also find it easier to locate appropriate supporting materials.

## Thesis and Main Points

Theses devoted to questions of value might look something like: "The death penalty is unjustifiable," "Bullfighting is inhumane," "Discrimination on the basis of affectional orientation is wrong," or "College athletics minimize the importance of academics."

As with speeches on questions of fact, you can generate the main points for a speech on a question of value by asking a strategic question of your thesis, such as

"Why is this good?" or "Why is this immoral?" For example, you can take the first thesis given above and ask, "Why is the death penalty unjustifiable?" The answers to this question will give you the speech's main points. The body of your speech might then look something like this:

General purpose: _____ *To persuade.* _____

Specific purpose: *To persuade my listeners that the death penalty is unjustifiable.*

Thesis: _____ *The death penalty is unjustifiable. (Why is the death penalty unjustifiable?)* _____

   I. _____ *The criminal justice system can make mistakes.* _____

   II. _____ *The death penalty constitutes cruel and unusual punishment.* _____

   III. _____ *No one has the moral right to take another's life.* _____

## Support

To support your main points, search for relevant evidence. For example, to show that mistakes have been made, you might itemize three or four high-profile cases in which people were put to death and later, through DNA, found to have been innocent.

At times, and with certain topics, it may be useful to identify the standards you would use to judge something moral or justified or fair or good. For example, in the "bullfighting is inhumane" speech, you might devote your first main point to defining when an action can be considered inhumane. In this case, the body of your speech might look like this:

   I. An inhumane act has two qualities.

      A. It is cruel and painful.

      B. It serves no human necessity.

   II. Bullfighting is inhumane.

      A. It is cruel and painful.

      B. It serves no necessary function.

Notice that in the example of capital punishment, the speaker aims to strengthen or change the listeners' beliefs about the death penalty. The speaker is not asking the audience to do anything about capital punishment, but merely to believe that it's not justified. However, you might also use a question of value as a first step toward persuading your audience to take some action. For example, once you got your listeners to see the death penalty as unjustified, you might then ask them to take certain actions—perhaps in your next speech—to support an anti-death-penalty politician, to vote for or against a particular proposition, or to join an organization fighting against the death penalty.

## Organization

Like speeches on questions of fact, speeches on questions of value often lend themselves to topical organization. For example, the speech on capital punishment cited earlier uses a topical order. But within this topical order there is another level of organization, an organization that begins with those items on which there is least disagreement or opposition and moves on to the items on

*"The most important persuasion tool you have in your entire arsenal is integrity."*

—Zig Ziglar

which your listeners are likely to see very differently. It's likely that even those in favor of the death penalty would agree that mistakes can be made; and they probably would be willing to accept evidence that mistakes have in fact been made, especially if you cite reliable statistical evidence and expert testimony. By starting with this issue, you secure initial agreement and can use that as a basis for approaching areas where you and the audience are more likely to disagree.

# Persuasive Speeches on Questions of Policy

When you move beyond a focus on value to urging your audience to do something about an issue, you're then into a *question of policy*. For example, in a speech designed to convince your listeners that bullfighting is inhumane, you'd be focusing on a question of value. If you were to urge that bullfighting should therefore be declared illegal, you'd be urging the adoption of a particular policy. Items that focused on questions of policy in the June 4, 2006, *New York Times* included, for example, these issues: Should the Federal Marriage Act be approved? Should New Jersey approve a needle exchange program (to help curb AIDS)? What should the U.S. policy be toward Iran's nuclear program? Should California voters approve Proposition 82, creating a universal school program for four-year-olds? What type of memorial should be established at Ground Zero? What punishment should Kenneth Lay receive for his role in Enron's collapse? Should the prison at Guantanamo Bay be closed? Should auction laws be applied to those selling on eBay? What policy should corporations follow regarding workers' access to company computers for their personal use?

Questions of policy concern what should be done, what procedures should be adopted, what laws should be changed; in short, what policy should be followed. In some speeches you may want to defend a specific policy; in others you may wish to argue that a current policy should be discontinued.

## Thesis and Main Points

Persuasive speeches frequently revolve around questions of policy and may use theses such as the following:

- Hate speech should be banned in colleges.
- Our community should adopt a zero tolerance policy for guns in schools.
- Abortion should be available on demand.
- Music CDs should be rated for violence and profanity.
- Medical marijuana should be legalized.
- Smoking should be banned from all public buildings and parks.

As you can tell from these examples, questions of policy almost invariably involve questions of values. To argue, for example, that hate speech should be banned in colleges is based on the value judgment that hate speech is wrong. To argue for a zero tolerance policy on guns in schools implies that you think it's wrong for students or faculty to carry guns to school.

You can develop your speech on a question of policy by asking a strategic question of your thesis. With policy issues the question will be "Why should the policy be adopted?" or "Why should this policy be discontinued?" or "Why is this policy better than what we now have?" Taking our first example, we might ask, "Why should hate speech be banned on campus?" From the answers to this question, you would develop your main points, which might look something like this:

 I. Hate speech teaches hate instead of tolerance.

▼ **E-TALK**

**Blogs**
Visit a few blogs and analyze them in terms of the principles of persuasion discussed in this chapter. How are blogs like persuasive speeches? How are they different?

II. Hate speech denigrates women and minorities.

III. Hate speech encourages violence against women and minorities.

## Support

You would then support each main point with a variety of supporting materials that would convince your audience that hate speech should be banned from college campuses. For example, you might cite the websites put up by certain groups that advocate violence against women and minority members, or quote from the lyrics of performers who came to campus. Or you might cite examples of actual violence that had been accompanied by hate speech or hate literature.

In some speeches on questions of policy, you might simply want your listeners to agree that the policy you're advocating is a good one. In other cases you might want them to do something about the policy—to vote for a particular candidate, to take vitamin C, to go on a diet, to write to their elected officials, to participate in a walkathon, to wear an AIDS awareness ribbon, and so on.

## Organization

Speeches on questions of policy may be organized in a variety of ways. For example, if you're comparing two policies, consider the comparison-and-contrast method. If the existing policy is doing harm, consider using a cause-to-effect pattern. If your proposed policy is designed to solve a problem, consider the problem–solution pattern. For example, a speech advocating zero tolerance for guns in school could be divided into two basic parts:

I. Guns are destroying our high schools. (problem)

II. We must adopt a zero tolerance policy. (solution)

## THE PUBLIC SPEAKING SAMPLE ASSISTANT

**AN EXCELLENT PERSUASIVE SPEECH**

**THE MERCHANTS OF DEATH**

*Andrew Farmer*\*

Khaled Masri was detained in Germany, "beaten, stripped, shackled," then flown to Afghanistan to be interrogated for a crime he never committed. According to the *International Enforcement Law Reporter* of May 2005, Masri was mistaken for a known terrorist with a similar name and, despite this mistake, was detained for over five months. In February 2003 Abu Omar was grabbed off a sidewalk in Milan, maced, then kidnapped by assailants in an unmarked van. Also presumed innocent, with no evidence connecting Omar to terrorism, he remains missing to this day over three years later.

These acts resemble those of an American government willing to make any sacrifice to make gains in a war on

The title of the speech is intriguing and makes you wonder what exactly the speaker is going to talk about.

Using these two dramatic examples clearly gains attention. We've all heard about these kinds of injustices, so we feel we're on familiar ground. But then the topic turns to an issue that many people know little if anything about, the private military forces.

Notice how the speaker wisely gives an authoritative definition—the audience is likely to accept a definition by PBS

terror. But they weren't committed by the U.S. Army, at least not technically. The *PBS Frontline* online of June 21, 2005, defines Private Military Forces, or PMFs, as civilian workers employed by private military companies to guard "supply lines, [run] U.S. military bases and [protect] U.S. diplomats and generals." However, PMFs are also committing torturous atrocities that undermine our relations with other countries and the safety of our soldiers abroad. A December 7, 2005, press release for the new documentary *Shadow Company* states that there are over 20,000 private soldiers currently operating in Iraq alone who cannot be constrained by executive or Congressional mandate. With numbers of these soldiers already in place in Afghanistan, Bosnia, and Colombia, as well as other parts of Africa, and South America, it is crucial that we, first, understand the problems associated with these types of soldiers; second, explore the causes of their increased usage; and finally, determine how we may better regulate companies that the *Ottawa Citizen* of November 16, 2005, states are "a way for mercenaries to gain legitimacy."

The *Edmonton Journal* of November 13, 2005, estimates that the U.S. spends 100 billion dollars annually to employ nearly half a million PMFs in over 50 countries. Outsourcing our military to private soldiers is problematic given their unreliability, the blatant human rights violations they commit, and the corrupting power of money.

The *Defense Daily International* of August 12, 2005, explains that the U.S. military cannot coordinate or control PMFs, "because private security contractors have no direct contractual relationship with the commander." For instance, the *New York Times* of September 10, 2005, states that Global Strategies, a private military company operating out of Iraq, closed and abandoned Baghdad Airport for 48 hours complaining they had not been paid. This reckless strike nearly allowed the airport to fall into the hands of insurgents.

To further complicate the situation, the *Charleston Gazette* of April 11, 2005, notes that PMFs are not accountable to any government oversight and thus do not follow normal rules of combat—which may lead to human rights violations that go unpunished. The *Raleigh News and Observer* of March 23, 2006, states that private military contractors in Iraq "regularly shoot into civilian cars with little accountability." The *Al-Ahram Weekly* of February 16, 2006, reports that military contractors have killed over 1,800 Iraqi civilians since 2003. And when Dyncorp, a private military firm, discovered that 13 of its employees had bought and sold Bosnian women as sex slaves, our government ruled it had no jurisdiction to punish the forces. In fact, the *Vancouver Sun* of November 12, 2005, reveals that the men didn't even receive so much as a slap on the wrist after destroying the lives of women they were supposedly sent to protect.

*Frontline*. These definitions of key terms not only are helpful to those who don't know the topic, or don't know it well, but also help focus the discussion to follow.

The second point made in this introduction is designed to stress the importance of the topic: The topic is important because PMFs' actions undermine our relations with other countries and jeopardize the safety of soldiers.

The third part of this introduction is to orient the audience. Notice that the speaker very clearly indicates the three points he will cover: (1) the problems with PMFs, (2) the causes of their increase, and (3) ways in which they can be regulated.

The speaker doesn't explicitly establish the credibility of the *Edmonton Journal* or other source material. The wealth of cited sources, however, makes you feel that the research was sound and extensive. If you felt your audience might not accept the authority of your sources, you might say something about their authoritativeness or perhaps give some qualifications of the writers of the articles.

The first major point is divided clearly into three parts. There are three reasons why PMFs present problems: (1) They are unreliable; (2) they commit violations; and (3) they are guided by money. Each of these is covered in a separate paragraph in the written speech.

Here the speaker establishes PMFs' unreliability.

Here the speaker identifies in a very dramatic way the violations these PMFs commit.

Additionally, as P. W. Singer writes in his 2005 book *Corporate Warriors*, PMFs have shown themselves to be corruptible. They are businesses for profit, and their loyalty is to the highest bidder—not national interests. The *L.A. Times* of March 4, 2006, explains that since private military companies are reimbursed all operating costs and their profit is a percentage of total money spent, contractors are driven to inflate costs of operation in order to receive greater profit. By hinging our security on those trying to make money off our country rather than defend it, we create an atmosphere of unreliablility and corruption.

While the American Revolution, the War of 1812, two world wars, and other conflicts have all been fought by the American military, PMFs are in charge of defending American democracy today for three reasons: an increased demand for soldiers, the economics of outsourcing, and the ability of PMFs to divert scrutiny placed on military actions.

As American military presence rises internationally, the United States looks to military contractors to compensate for understaffed or undertrained military personnel. An NPR broadcast on January 4, 2006, states that the army missed its recruitment goals by 20 percent in 2005, prompting an increased reliance on private military contractors to perform the duties that were once the responsibility of our men and women in uniform. In fact, as a Government Accountability Office report of July 28, 2005, reveals, the government is forced to subcontract with private security providers because U.S. armed forces lack training in occupation and rebuilding.

Governments that employ PMFs find outsourcing to contractors to be a sound economic practice. The *Liverpool Daily Echo* of June 1, 2005, notes that governments believe private soldiers are more cost effective in the long term because they are not eligible for government retirement or death benefits. Surprisingly, as the *Ottawa Citizen* explains on November 13, 2005, over half of the private military forces currently employed in Iraq are from developing nations because their labor is both cheap and readily available.

PMFs are also useful in diverting attention away from the military. Private forces are being deployed without Congress or the media knowing where PMFs are located. The previously cited *Edmonton Journal* states that since Congress does not currently know the logistics of our use of private soldiers, the United States is open to deny involvement in operations abroad. This practice sounds alarmingly similar to those of countries who finance terrorists to do their will—the very countries we call the "axis of evil."

PMFs need to find ways to provide constructive rather than destructive roles in emergencies. Solutions must be explored to regulate PMFs by the government,

Here the speaker demonstrates PMFs' focus on money and how it leads to corruption.

Here the speaker leads into the second major point, the reasons why the use of these merceneries is growing. Again, there are three clearly identified reasons: (1) increased demand, (2) economics, and (3) PMFs' ability to deflect scrutiny.

Here the speaker establishes why there's a growing demand for PMFs.

Here the speaker illustrates the economic foundation for the practice.

Here the speaker demonstrates that PMFs divert attention from the regular military.

Here the speaker introduces his most important point, and the one that is at the center of the speech: Changes are needed. The speaker's suggestions are three: (1) Enact

encourage PMFs to play positive roles on the home front, and raise public awareness.

This past October, legislators passed the Contractors on the Battlefield Regulatory Act in an attempt to limit the powers of private soldiers. However, an October 20, 2005, *Inside the Pentagon* article asserts the directive "still doesn't answer . . . the fundamental questions of legal status and accountability." Legislators must work to pass detailed legislation that clearly defines PMF accountability to the military chain of command and auditing procedures to safeguard against inflated reimbursements. The *Baltimore Sun* of October 6, 2005, contends that legislators must hold the executive branch accountable to provisions stipulated in the War Powers Act of 1973, which mandates that Congress be consulted before American forces are sent into combat, even if the forces are only paid for by America.

Next, an alternative use of PMFs is needed. The *Christian Science Monitor* of September 19, 2005, suggests that in light of Katrina, PMFs can find a productive role in domestic reconstruction, rather than in dangerous operations abroad. Domestic use of private security forces ensures greater scrutiny and accountability. Using PMFs at home ensures that PMFs are closely monitored and play productive, rather than destructive roles.

Finally, we have to change our attitudes about the way we allow our military to act on our behalf. Visit the websites of human rights and military watchdog organizations such as Amnesty International, the Human Rights and Displacement Consultancy, or the Humatitarian Law Center and educate yourself about ongoing human rights violations. Or better yet, join one of these groups. Military privitization is a public concern, and PMFs need to be held to the same standards as our men and women in uniform.

Machiavelli's *The Prince* warns that "mercenaries and auxiliaries are useless and dangerous, and if anyone supports his state by the arms of mercenaries, he will never stand firm or sure." Heeding his warning, we should act quickly to ensure that we do not let the power of our military fall into the hands of those with dollar signs on the brain. By analyzing atrocities commited by PMFs, and reasons for their widespread use, we can take steps to ensure that private military groups are used ethically. While no steps can be taken to give Khaled Masri five months of his life back, precautions can be made to ensure that no one else ever suffers such a fate.

*Andrew Farmer is a student at the University of Texas at Austin. The speech was delivered at the 2006 American Forensic Association National Individual Events Tournament in Gainesville, Florida, and was accompanied by a complete list of works cited. It is reprinted by permission of the speaker.

legislation to regulate PMF; (2) encourage PMFs' playing a more positive role, and (3) increase public awareness. This section most clearly identifies the address as a speech on a question of policy.

Here the speaker calls for legislation to define PMF's accountability.

Here the speaker shows that there are more positive roles for PMFs to play.

Here the speaker argues that we have to change our attitudes about PMFs.

Notice that in the last part of this third point, the speaker asks the audience to do something—in this case, increase their awareness of the problem. And he's very helpful in directing this call for increased awareness by offering listeners different options; one simple suggestion is to visit a variety of websites, whereas a more extensive commitment would be to join organizations concerned with PMFs.

The quotation from Machiavelli is particularly apt, because most college students will have heard or read of Machiavelli in political science or history classes.

Here the speaker summarizes his speech, repeating the three major points raised in the speech. He then closes the speech by referring back to an example used in the introduction, thus effectively reestablishing the importance of this topic in human terms.

# Summary of Concepts and Skills

This chapter looked at the persuasive speech, first covering guidelines and types of supporting materials for persuasion and then discussing three main types of persuasive speeches.

1. Persuasion has three main goals: (1) To strengthen or weaken attitudes, beliefs, or values, (2) To change attitudes, beliefs, or values, and (3) To motivate to action.
2. Among the important guidelines for persuasive speaking are: (1) Anticipate selective exposure, (2) Ask for reasonable amounts of change, and (3) Identify with your audience.
3. Three major types of support have special importance in speeches of persuasion: logical appeals, emotional appeals, and credibility appeals.
4. Persuasive speeches on questions of fact focus on what is or is not true.
5. Speeches on questions of value focus on issues of good and bad, justice or injustice.
6. Speeches on questions of policy focus on what should or should not be done, what procedures should or should not be adopted.

To be an effective public speaker, you need to master a variety of persuading skills. Place a check mark next to those skills you want to work on most.

_____ 1. In my persuasive speeches I apply (where relevant) the principles of persuasion: selective exposure, amounts of change, and identification.

_____ 2. In my persuasive speeches I critically analyze reasoning from specific instances to generalizations, causes and effects, and sign.

_____ 3. When listening to persuasive attempts, I detect fallacies such as name calling, transfer, testimonial, plain folks, card stacking, bandwagon, and attack.

_____ 4. To motivate my audience I use motivational appeals—for example, appeals to desires for power, control, and influence; self-esteem and approval; safety; achievement; and financial gain.

_____ 5. In my speeches I seek to establish my credibility by displaying competence, high moral character, and dynamism or charisma.

# Key Word Quiz

## The Language of Persuasive Speaking

Match the terms about the persuasive speech with their definitions. Record the number of the definition next to the appropriate term.

a. _____ attitude
b. _____ credibility
c. _____ principle of selective exposure
d. _____ belief
e. _____ questions of value
f. _____ self-actualization needs
g. _____ charisma
h. _____ reasoning from sign
i. _____ questions of policy
j. _____ questions of fact

1. Drawing conclusions from clues (or symptoms) that often occur together.
2. A motive that influences people only after all other needs are satisfied.
3. Issues that concern what should be done or what procedures should be followed.
4. The tendency to respond in a certain way.
5. Issues that concern what is or is not true or what does or doesn't exist.
6. The degree to which your audience regards you as believable.
7. Principle stating that listeners will actively seek out information that supports their beliefs and will actively avoid information that contradicts their existing beliefs.
8. Conviction of the existence or reality of something or of the truth of some assertion.
9. A quality of personal attractiveness, dynamism, and forcefulness that enhances credibility.
10. Issues that concern what people consider good or bad, just or unjust.

Answer: a. 4 b. 6 c. 7 d. 8 e. 10 f. 2 g. 9 h. 1 i. 3 j. 5

## Five for Discussion

1. Think about the persuasive appeals that have been used on you recently. How would you describe them?
2. Examine one issue of a national newspaper. What questions of fact, value, and policy do the news reports cover? Then read the editorials. What types of questions do the editorials address?
3. Visit the History Channel (**www.historychannel.com/speeches**), History and Politics Out Loud (**www.hpol.org**), or C-Span (**www.c-span.org/classroom/lang/speeches.asp**) and search for speeches you consider persuasive. How would you describe the purposes and theses of the speeches on these websites?
4. Visit **www.lawpublish.com/** or **www.hg.org/advert/html** and examine the laws that govern the advertising industry. In what ways do the laws deal with the motivational appeals used in advertising?
5. In establishing the credibility of a source, you may find it helpful to visit the Biographical Dictionary (**http://s9.com/biograph/**). Browse this site and similar others, making note of the kinds of information they contain and how you might use such information in your speeches.

## Log On! MyCommunicationLab

Several additional insights into the nature of persuasion and into the strategies of persuasive speaking are available at **www.mycommunicationlab.com**: "Principles of Motivation"; "Additional Motivational Appeals"; "How You Form Credibility Impressions"; "General Guidelines for Communicating Credibility"; "Thinking Critically about Persuasive Speaking"; "Evaluating the Adequacy of Reasoning"; "Analyzing Arguments: The Toulmin Model"; "Comparative Credibility Judgments"; and "Gender, Credibility, and the Topics of Public Speaking." An exercise for preparing two-minute persuasive speeches and a self-test on the ethics of persuasion are also presented. An excellent persuasive speech by Upendri Gunasekera, "The Perils of Philanthropy," also appears here along with annotations and questions for analysis.

Explore our research resources at **www.researchnavigator.com**.

Research
Navigator.com

# Glossary of Human Communication Concepts

Listed here are definitions of the technical terms of human communication—the words that are peculiar or unique to this discipline. These definitions should make new or difficult terms a bit easier to understand. All boldface terms within the definitions appear as separate entries in the glossary.

**abstraction.** A general concept derived from a class of objects; a part representation of some whole. Also, the quality of being abstract.

**abstraction process.** The process by which a general concept is derived from specifics; the process by which some (never all) characteristics of an object, person, or event are perceived by the senses or included in some term, phrase, or sentence.

**accent.** The stress or emphasis placed on a syllable when it is pronounced.

**acculturation.** The processes by which a person's culture is modified or changed through contact with or exposure to another culture.

**active listening.** A process of putting together into some meaningful whole an understanding of a speaker's total message—the verbal and the nonverbal, the content and the feelings.

**adaptors.** Nonverbal behaviors that satisfy some personal need and usually occur without awareness, such as scratching to relieve an itch or moistening your lips to relieve dryness. Three types of adaptors are often distinguished: **self-adaptors, alter-adaptors,** and **object-adaptors.**

**adjustment** (principle of). The principle of verbal interaction that claims that communication takes place only to the extent that the parties communicating share the same system of signals.

**affect displays.** Movements of the facial area that convey emotional meaning—for example, anger, fear, or surprise.

**affinity-seeking strategies.** Behaviors designed to increase our interpersonal attractiveness.

**affirmation.** The communication of support and approval.

**ageism.** Discrimination based on age.

**agenda.** A list of the items that a small group must deal with in the order in which they should be covered.

**agenda-setting.** A persuasive technique in which the speaker argues that XYZ is the issue and that all others are unimportant.

**aggressiveness.** *See* **verbal aggressiveness.**

**allness.** The assumption that all can be known or is known about a given person, issue, object, or event.

**alter-adaptors.** Body movements you make in response to your current interactions, such as crossing your arms over your chest when someone unpleasant approaches or moving closer to someone you like.

**altercasting.** Placing the listener in a specific role for a specific purpose and asking that the listener approach the question or problem from the perspective of this specific role.

**ambiguity.** The condition in which a message can be interpreted as having more than one meaning.

**analogy** (reasoning from). A type of reasoning in which you compare similar things and conclude that because they are alike in so many respects, they also must be alike in some other respect.

**amounts of change principle.** A principle of persuasion stating that the greater and more important the change desired by the speaker, the more difficult its achievement will be.

**apology.** A type of excuse in which you acknowledge responsibility for the behavior, generally ask forgiveness, and claim that this will not happen again.

**apprehension.** *See* **communication apprehension.**

**arbitrariness.** A feature of human language; the absence of a real or inherent relationship between the form of a word and its meaning. If we do not know anything of a particular language, we cannot examine the form of a word and thereby discover its meaning.

**argument.** Evidence (for example, facts or statistics) and a conclusion drawn from the evidence.

**argumentativeness.** A willingness to speak your mind, to argue for a point of view. Distinguished from **verbal aggressiveness.**

**articulation.** The physiological movements of the speech organs as they modify and interrupt the air stream emitted from the lungs.

**artifactual messages.** Messages conveyed through the wearing and arrangement of various artifacts—for example, clothing, jewelry, buttons, or the furniture in your house and its arrangement.

**assertiveness.** A willingness to stand up for your rights while maintaining respect for the rights of others.

**assimilation.** A process of distortion in which we reconstruct messages to make them conform to our own attitudes, prejudices, needs, and values.

**attack.** A persuasive technique that involves accusing another person (usually an opponent) of some serious wrongdoing so that the issue under discussion never gets examined.

**attention.** The process of responding to a stimulus or stimuli; usually involves some consciousness of responding.

**attitude.** A predisposition to respond for or against an object, person, or position.

**attraction.** The state or process by which one individual is drawn to another, forming a highly positive evaluation of that other person.

**attraction theory.** A theory holding that we form relationships on the basis of our attraction for another person.

**attractiveness.** The degree to which a person is perceived to be physically attractive and to possess a pleasing personality.

**attribution.** A process through which we attempt to understand the behaviors of others (as well as our own), particularly the reasons or motivations for these behaviors.

**attribution theory.** A theory concerned with the processes involved in attributing causation or motivation to a person's behavior.

**audience participation principle.** A principle of persuasion stating that persuasion is achieved more effectively when the audience participates actively.

**authoritarian leader.** A group leader who determines the group policies or makes decisions without consulting or securing agreement from group members.

**avoidance.** An unproductive conflict strategy in which a person takes mental or physical flight from the actual conflict.

**backchanneling cues.** Listener responses to a speaker that do not ask for the speaking role.

**bandwagon.** A persuasive technique in which the speaker tries to gain compliance by saying that "everyone is doing it" and urging audience members to jump on the bandwagon.

**barriers to communication.** Physical or psychological factors that prevent or hinder effective communication.

**behavioral synchrony.** The similarity in the behavior, usually nonverbal, of two persons; generally taken as an index of mutual liking.

**belief.** Confidence in the existence or truth of something; conviction.

**beltlining.** An unproductive conflict strategy in which one person hits at the emotional level at which the other person cannot withstand the blow.

**blame.** An unproductive conflict strategy in which we attribute the cause of the conflict to the other person or devote our energies to discovering who is the cause and avoid talking about the issues causing the conflict.

**boundary marker.** A marker dividing one person's territory from another's—for example, a fence.

**brainstorming.** A technique for generating ideas either alone or, more usually, in a small group.

**breadth.** The number of topics about which individuals in a relationship communicate.

**card stacking.** A persuasive technique in which the speaker selects only the evidence and arguments that build a case and omits or distorts any contradictory evidence.

**causes and effects** (reasoning from). A form of reasoning in which you conclude that certain effects are due to specific causes or that specific causes produce certain effects.

**censorship.** Legal restriction imposed on the right to produce, distribute, or receive various communications.

**central marker.** An item that is placed in a territory to reserve it for a specific person—for example, a sweater thrown over a library chair to signal that the chair is taken.

**certainty.** An attitude of closed-mindedness that creates a defensiveness among communication participants; opposed to **provisionalism.**

**channel.** The vehicle or medium through which signals are sent.

**character.** One of the qualities of **credibility;** the individual's honesty and basic nature; moral qualities.

**charisma.** One of the qualities of **credibility;** the individual's dynamism or forcefulness.

**cherishing behaviors.** Small behaviors we enjoy receiving from others, especially from our relational partner—for example, a kiss, a smile, or a gift of flowers.

**chronemics.** The study of the communicative nature of time—the way you treat time and use it to communicate. Two general areas of chronemics are **cultural time** and **psychological time.**

**civil inattention.** Polite ignoring of others so as not to invade their privacy.

**cliché.** An overused expression that has lost its novelty and part of its meaning and that calls attention to itself because of its overuse, such as "tall, dark, and handsome" as a description of a man.

**closed-mindedness.** An unwillingness to receive certain communication messages.

**code.** A set of symbols used to translate a message from one form to another.

**coercive power.** Power based on a person's ability to punish or to remove rewards from another person.

**cognitive restructuring.** A process aimed at substituting logical and realistic beliefs for unrealistic ones; used in reducing communication apprehension and in raising self-esteem.

**cohesiveness.** A quality of togetherness; in group communication situations, the mutual attraction among members and the extent to which members work together as a group.

**collective orientation.** A cultural orientation that stresses the group's rather than the individual's goals and preferences. Opposed to **individual orientation.**

**collectivist culture.** A culture that emphasizes the group's rather than the individual's goals; a culture that values, for example, benevolence, tradition, and conformity. Opposed to **individualistic culture.**

**color communication.** The meanings that different cultures communicate via color.

**communication.** (1) The process or act of communicating; (2) the actual message or messages sent and received; (3) the study of the processes involved in the sending and receiving of messages.

**communication accommodation theory.** Theory holding that speakers adjust their speaking style to their listeners to gain social approval and achieve greater communication effectiveness.

**communication apprehension.** Fear or anxiety over communicating; may be "trait apprehension" (fear of communication generally, regardless of the specific situation) or "state apprehension" (fear that is specific to a given communication situation).

**communication competence.** Knowledge of the rules and skills of communication; the qualities that make for effectiveness in communication.

**communication network.** The pathways of messages; the organizational structure through which messages are sent and received.

**competence.** One of the dimensions of **credibility;** consists of a person's perceived levels of ability and knowledge.

**complementarity.** A principle of **attraction** stating that we are attracted by qualities that we do not possess or that we wish to possess and to people who are opposite or different from ourselves; opposed to **similarity.**

**complementary relationship.** A relationship in which the behavior of one person serves as the stimulus for the complementary behavior of the other; in such relationships behavioral differences are maximized.

**compliance-gaining strategies.** Behaviors directed toward gaining the agreement of others; behaviors designed to persuade others to do as we wish.

**compliance-resisting strategies.** Behaviors directed at resisting the persuasive attempts of others.

**confidence.** A quality of interpersonal effectiveness; a comfortable, at-ease feeling in interpersonal communication situations.

**confirmation.** A communication pattern that acknowledges another person's presence and also indicates an acceptance of this person, this person's definition of self, and the relationship as defined or viewed by this other person; opposed to **disconfirmation.**

**conflict.** *See* **interpersonal conflict.**

**congruence.** A condition in which verbal and nonverbal behaviors reinforce each other.

**connotation.** The feeling or emotional aspect of meaning, generally viewed as consisting of evaluative (for example, good/bad), potency (strong/weak), and activity (fast/slow) dimensions; the associations of a term. Opposed to **denotation.**

**consensus.** A process in attribution through which we attempt to establish whether other people react or behave in the same way as the person on whom we are now focusing. If the person is acting in accordance with the general consensus, then we tend to attribute the person's behavior to external causes; if the person is not acting in accordance with the general consensus, then we tend to cite internal causes.

**consistency.** A perceptual process that influences us to maintain balance among our perceptions; a process that makes us tend to see what we expect to see and to be uncomfortable when our perceptions run contrary to our expectations.

**contact.** The first stage of an interpersonal relationship, in which perceptual and interactional contact occurs.

**contamination.** A form of territorial encroachment that renders another's territory impure.

**content and relationship dimensions.** Two simultaneous aspects of any given communication: the aspect that pertains to the world external to both speaker and listener (content) and the aspect having to do with the relationship between the individuals (relationship).

**context of communication.** The physical, psychological, social, and temporal environment in which communication takes place.

**contrast (principle of).** Often-followed rule of perception: messages or people who are very different from each other probably don't belong together, and do not constitute a set or group.

**controllability.** One of the factors we consider in judging whether or not a person is responsible for his or her behavior. If the person was in control, then we judge that he or she was responsible. See also **attribution theory.**

**conversation.** Two-person communication that usually includes an opening, feedforward, a business stage, feedback, and a closing.

**conversational management.** The ways in which a conversation is conducted.

**conversational maxims.** Principles that people follow in conversation to ensure that the goal of the conversation is achieved.

**conversational turns.** The process of exchanging the speaker and listener roles during conversation.

**cooperation.** An interpersonal process by which individuals work together for a common end; the pooling of efforts to produce a mutually desired outcome.

**cooperation (principle of).** Cultural principle stating that speaker and listener will cooperate in trying to communicate effectively and to understand each other.

**credibility.** The believability of a speaker; **competence, character,** and **charisma** (dynamism) are its major dimensions.

**critical thinking.** The process of logically evaluating reasons and evidence and reaching a judgment on the basis of this analysis.

**critical-thinking-hats technique.** A technique developed by Edward deBono in which a problem or issue is viewed from six distinct perspectives.

**criticism.** The reasoned judgment of some work; although often equated with faultfinding, criticism can involve both positive or negative evaluations.

**cultural display.** Signs that communicate cultural identification; for example, group-specific clothing or religious jewelry.

**cultural time.** The meanings given to time communication by a particular culture.

**culture.** The relatively specialized lifestyle of a group of people—consisting of values, beliefs, artifacts, ways of behaving, and ways of communicating—that is passed on from one generation to the next.

**culture shock.** The psychological reaction we experience when we find ourselves in a culture very different from our own or from what we are used to.

**cultural rules.** Rules that are specific to a given cultural group.

**date.** An **extensional device** used to emphasize the notion of constant change and symbolized by a subscript; for example, John Smith$_{1998}$ is not John Smith$_{2005}$.

**deception cues.** Verbal or nonverbal cues that reveal that a person is lying.

**decoder.** Something that takes a message in one form (for example, sound waves) and translates it into another form (for example, nerve impulses) from which meaning can be formulated (for example, in vocal–auditory communication). In human communication the decoder is the auditory mechanism; in electronic communication the decoder is, for example, the telephone earpiece. *See also* **encoder.**

**decoding.** The process of extracting a message from a code—for example, translating speech sounds into nerve impulses. *See also* **encoding.**

**defensiveness.** The self-protective attitude of an individual or an atmosphere in a group characterized by threats, fear, and domination. Messages evidencing evaluation, control, strategy, neutrality, superiority, and certainty are assumed to lead to defensiveness. Opposed to **supportiveness.**

**delayed reactions.** Reactions that a person consciously delays while analyzing a situation.

**Delphi method.** A type of problem-solving group in which questionnaires are used to poll members (who don't interact among themselves) on several occasions so as to arrive at a group decision. For example, this technique might be used to decide what are the most important problems a company faces or what activities a group might undertake.

**democratic leader.** A group leader who stimulates self-direction and self-actualization of the group members.

**denial.** One of the obstacles to the expression of emotion; the process by which we deny our emotions to ourselves or to others.

**denotation.** The objective or descriptive meaning of a word; its referential meaning. Opposed to **connotation.**

**depenetration.** A reversal of penetration; a condition in which the **breadth** and **depth** of a relationship decrease. *See also* **social penetration theory.**

**depth.** The degree to which the inner personality—the inner core of an individual—is penetrated in interpersonal interaction.

**deterioration.** A stage in an interpersonal relationship in which the bonds holding the individuals together are weakened and the partners begin drifting apart.

**determinism (principle of).** The principle of verbal interaction that holds that all verbalizations are to some extent purposeful—that there is a reason for every verbalization.

**dialogue.** A form of **communication** in which each person is both speaker and listener; communication characterized by involvement, concern, and respect for the other person. Opposed to **monologue.**

**direct speech.** Speech in which the speaker's intentions are stated clearly and directly.

**disclaimer.** Statement that asks the listener to receive what the speaker says as intended without its reflecting negatively on the image of the speaker.

**disconfirmation.** Communication pattern in which someone ignores a person or that person's messages, even denying the right of the individual to define himself or herself; opposed to **confirmation.**

**dissolution.** The breaking of the bonds holding an interpersonal relationship together.

**dyadic communication.** Two-person communication.

**dyadic consciousness.** An awareness of an interpersonal relationship between or pairing of two individuals; distinguished from situations in which two individuals are together but do not perceive themselves as being a unit or twosome.

**dyadic effect.** The process by which one person in a dyad, or two-person group, imitates the behavior of the other person. Usually refers to the tendency of one person's self-disclosures to prompt the other to also self-disclose.

**earmarker.** A marker that identifies an item as belonging to a specific person—for example, a nameplate on a desk or initials on an attaché case.

**effect.** The outcome or consequence of an action or behavior; communication is assumed always to have some effect.

**emblems.** Nonverbal behaviors that directly translate words or phrases—for example, the signs for "OK" and "peace."

**emotions.** The feelings we have—for example, feelings of joy, guilt, anger, or sorrow.

**empathy.** The ability to feel what another person feels; feeling or perceiving something from another person's point of view. A key component of interpersonal effectiveness.

**encoder.** Something that takes a message in one form (for example, nerve impulses) and translates it into another form (for example, sound waves). In human communication, the encoder is the speaking mechanism; in electronic communication, the encoder is, for example, the telephone mouthpiece. *See also* **decoder.**

**encoding.** The process of putting a message into a code—for example, translating nerve impulses into speech sounds. *See also* **decoding.**

**enculturation.** The process by which culture is transmitted from one generation to another.

**e-prime.** A form of the language that omits the verb "to be" except as an auxiliary or in statements of existence. E-prime is designed to eliminate the tendency toward **projection.**

**equality.** An attitude that recognizes that each individual in a communication interaction is equal, that no one is superior to any other; encourages supportiveness.

**equilibrium theory.** A theory of **proxemics** holding that intimacy and physical closeness are positively related; as a relationship becomes more intimate, the distances between the individuals will diminish.

**equity theory.** A theory claiming that we experience relational satisfaction when there is an equal distribution of rewards and costs between the two persons in the relationship.

**et cetera or etc.** An **extensional device** used to emphasize the notion of infinite complexity; because one can never know all about anything, any statement about the world or an event must end with an explicit or implicit "etc."

**ethics.** The branch of philosophy that deals with the rightness or wrongness of actions; the study of moral values.

**ethnic identity.** Commitment to the beliefs and customs of your culture.

**ethnocentrism.** The tendency to see others and their behaviors through our own cultural filters, often as distortions of our own behaviors; the tendency to evaluate the values and beliefs of our own culture more positively than those of another culture.

**euphemism.** A polite word or phrase used to substitute for some **taboo** or otherwise offensive term.

**excluding talk.** Talk about a subject or in a vocabulary that only certain people understand, often in the presence of someone who does not belong to this group and therefore does not understand; use of terms unique to a specific culture as if they were universal.

**excuse.** An explanation designed to lessen the negative consequences of something done or said.

**expectancy violations theory.** A theory of **proxemics** holding that people have a certain expectancy for space relationships. If that expectancy is violated (for example, if a stranger stands too close to you or a romantic partner maintains abnormally large distances from you), the relationship comes into clearer focus and you wonder why this "normal distance" is being violated.

**experiential limitation.** The limit of an individual's ability to communicate, as set by the nature and extent of that individual's experiences.

**expert power.** Personal power derived from expertise or knowledge.

**expressiveness.** Genuine involvement in speaking and listening, conveyed verbally and nonverbally; a component of interpersonal effectiveness.

**extemporaneous speech.** A speech that is thoroughly prepared and organized in detail and in which certain aspects of style are predetermined.

**extensional devices.** Linguistic devices proposed by Alfred Korzybski to keep language a more accurate means for talking about the world. The extensional devices include **et cetera, date,** and **index** (the working devices) and the **hyphen** and **quotes** (the safety devices).

**extensional orientation.** A tendency to give primary consideration to the world of experience and only secondary consideration to labels. Opposed to **intensional orientation.**

**face-saving.** Maintaining a positive public self-image in the minds of others.

**facial feedback hypothesis.** The theory that a person's facial expressions can produce physiological and emotional effects in the person.

**facial management techniques.** Techniques used to mask certain emotions and to emphasize others; for example, intensifying your expression of happiness to make a friend feel good about a promotion.

**fact–inference confusion.** A misevaluation in which someone makes an inference, regards it as a fact, and acts upon it as if it were a fact.

**factual statement.** A statement made by the observer after observation and limited to what is observed; opposed to **inferential statement.**

**family.** A group of people who consider themselves related and connected to one another and among whom the actions of one person have consequences for others.

**fear appeal.** An effort to exploit or create fear in an individual or group of individuals in order to persuade them to believe or act in a certain way.

**feedback.** Information that is given back to the source. Feedback may come from the source's own messages (as when we hear what we are saying) or from the receiver(s)—in forms such as applause, yawning, puzzled looks, questions, letters to the editor of a newspaper, increased or decreased subscriptions to a magazine, and so forth. *See also* **negative feedback; positive feedback.**

**feedforward.** Information that is sent before a regular message telling the listener something about what is to follow.

**flexibility.** The ability to adjust communication strategies on the basis of the unique situation.

**focus group.** A group designed to explore the feelings and attitudes of its members; usually follows a question-and-answer format.

**force.** An unproductive conflict strategy in which someone attempts to win an argument by physical force, threats of force, or some type of psychological bullying.

**forum.** A small group format in which members of the group answer questions from the audience; often follows a **symposium.**

**friendship.** An interpersonal relationship between two persons that is mutually productive, established and maintained through perceived mutual free choice, and characterized by mutual positive regard.

**fundamental attribution error.** The tendency to attribute a person's behavior to the kind of person he or she is (to internal factors such as the person's personality) and not to give sufficient importance to the situation the person is in.

**game.** A simulation of some situation with rules governing the behaviors of the participants and with some payoff for winning. In transactional analysis, a "game" is a series of ulterior transactions that lead to a payoff; the term also refers to a basically dishonest kind of transaction in which participants hide their true feelings.

**general semantics.** The study of the relationships among language, thought, and behavior.

**glittering generality.** The opposite of **name calling;** a speaker's effort to gain your acceptance of an idea by associating it with things you value highly.

**gossip.** Communication about someone who is not present, usually about matters that are private to this third party.

**grapevine.** Informal routes by which messages in an organization may travel; these informal lines resemble the physical grapevine, with its unpredictable pattern of branches.

**group.** A collection of individuals who are related to one another by some common purpose and in which some structure exists.

**group norm.** Rules or expectations for appropriate behavior for a member of a group.

**groupthink.** A tendency observed in some groups in which agreement among members becomes more important than the exploration of the issues at hand.

**gunnysacking.** An unproductive conflict strategy of storing up grievances—as if in a gunnysack—and holding them in readiness to dump on the other person in a conflict.

**halo effect.** The tendency to generalize an individual's virtue or expertise from one area to another.

**haptics.** The study of touch communication.

**heterosexist language.** Language that assumes all people are heterosexual and thereby denigrates lesbians and gay men.

**high-context culture.** A culture in which much of the information in communication is in the context or in the person rather than explicitly coded in the verbal messages. **Collectivist cultures** are generally high context. Opposed to **low-context** culture.

**home field advantage.** The increased power that comes from being in your own territory.

**home territories.** Territories about which individuals have a sense of intimacy and over which they exercise control—for example, a person's home.

**hyphen.** An **extensional device** used to illustrate that what may be separated verbally may not be separable on the event level or on the nonverbal level; for example, although we may talk about body and mind as if they were separable, in reality they are better referred to as body–mind.

**idea-generation group.** A group whose purpose is to generate ideas. *See also* **brainstorming.**

**illustrators.** Nonverbal behaviors that accompany and literally illustrate verbal messages—for example, upward hand movements that accompany the verbalization "It's up there."

**I-messages.** Messages in which the speaker accepts responsibility for personal thoughts and behaviors; messages in which the speaker's point of view is stated explicitly. Opposed to **you-messages.**

**immediacy.** A sense of contact and togetherness; a feeling of interest in and liking for the other person in an interchange. A quality of interpersonal effectiveness.

**implicit personality theory.** A theory or set of assumptions about personality, complete with rules or systems, that each individual maintains and through which the individual perceives others.

**impromptu speech.** A speech delivered off-the-cuff, without preparation.

**inclusion principle.** In verbal interaction, principle stating that all members should be a part of (included in) the interaction.

**inclusive talk.** Communication that includes all people; communication that does not exclude certain groups, such as women, lesbians and gays, or members of certain races or nationalities.

**index.** An **extensional device** used to emphasize the notion of nonidentity (no two things are the same) and symbolized by a subscript—for example, politician$_1$ is not politician$_2$.

**indirect speech.** Speech that may hide the speaker's true intentions or that may be used to make requests and observations indirectly.

**indiscrimination.** A misevaluation caused when we categorize people, events, or objects into a particular class and respond to them only as members of the class; a failure to recognize that each individual is unique; a failure to apply the **index.**

**individualistic culture.** A culture that emphasizes the individual's rather than the group's goals and preferences. Opposed to **collectivist culture.**

**individual orientation.** A cultural orientation that stresses the individual's rather than the group's goals and preferences. Opposed to **collective orientation.**

**inevitability.** In communication, the fact that communication cannot be avoided—that all behavior in an interactional setting is communication.

**inferential statement.** A statement that can be made by anyone, is not limited to what is observed, and can be made at any time; opposed to **factual statement.**

**informal time terms.** Expressions that denote approximate rather than exact time intervals, for example, "soon," "early," and "in a while."

**information.** That which reduces uncertainty.

**information overload.** A condition in which the amount of information is too great to be dealt with effectively or the number or complexity of messages is so great that the individual or organization is not able to deal with them.

**information power.** Power derived from the possession of information and the ability to communicate logically and persuasively. Also called "persuasion power."

**informative interview.** A type of **interview** in which the interviewer asks the interviewee, usually a person of some reputation and accomplishment, questions designed to elicit his or her views, predictions, and perspectives on specific topics.

**inoculation principle.** A principle stating that persuasion will be more difficult to achieve when the would-be persuader attacks beliefs and attitudes that have already been challenged previously, because the listener has built up defenses (has been "inoculated") against such attacks.

**insulation.** A reaction to territorial encroachment in which you erect some sort of barrier between yourself and the invaders.

**intensional orientation.** A tendency to give primary consideration to the way things are labeled and only secondary consideration (if any) to the world of experience; opposed to **extensional orientation.**

**interaction management.** The control of interpersonal interaction to the satisfaction of both parties; management of conversational turns, fluency, and message consistency. A component of interpersonal effectiveness.

**interaction process analysis.** A content analysis method that classifies messages into four general categories: social emotional positive, social emotional negative, attempted answers, and questions.

**intercultural communication.** Communication that takes place between persons of different cultures or persons who have different cultural beliefs, values, or ways of behaving.

**interpersonal communication.** Communication between two persons or among a small group of persons, as distinguished from public or mass communication; communication of a personal nature, as distinguished from impersonal communication; communication between or among intimates or those involved in a close relationship; often, intrapersonal, dyadic, and small group communication in general.

**interpersonal conflict.** A conflict or disagreement between two persons.

**interpersonal perception.** The perception of people; the processes through which we interpret and evaluate people and their behavior.

**interviewing.** A particular form of interpersonal communication in which two persons interact largely through questions and answers for the purpose of achieving specific goals.

**intimacy.** The closest interpersonal relationship; usually involves a close primary relationship such as the relationship between spouses or partners.

**intimacy claims.** Obligations that a person incurs by virtue of being in a close and intimate relationship.

**intimate distance.** The closest proxemic distance, ranging from touching to 18 inches. *See also* **proxemics.**

**intrapersonal communication.** Communication with the self.

**invasion.** Unwarranted entrance into another's territory that changes the meaning of the territory; territorial encroachment.

**involvement.** The stage in an interpersonal relationship that normally follows contact, in which the individuals get to know each other better and explore the potential for greater intimacy.

**irreversibility.** The impossibility of reversing communication; principle stating that once something has been communicated, it cannot be uncommunicated.

**jargon.** The technical language of any specialized group, often a professional class, that is unintelligible to individuals not belonging to the group; "shop talk."

**Johari window.** A diagram of the four selves (open, blind, hidden, and unknown) that illustrates the different kinds of information in each self.

**kinesics.** The study of the communicative dimensions of facial and bodily movements.

**laissez-faire leader.** A group leader who allows the group to develop and progress or make mistakes on its own.

**lateral communication.** Communication among equals—for example, manager to manager, worker to worker.

**leadership.** The quality by which one individual directs or influences the thoughts and/or the behaviors of others. *See also* **laissez-faire leader, democratic leader,** and **authoritarian leader.**

**leave-taking cues.** Verbal and nonverbal cues that indicate a desire to terminate a conversation.

**legitimate power.** Power derived from people's belief that a person has a right, by virtue of position, to influence or control others' behavior.

**leveling.** A process of message distortion in which a message is repeated but the number of details is reduced, some details are omitted entirely, and some details lose their complexity.

**level of abstraction.** The relative distance of a term or statement from an actual perception; a low-order abstraction would be a description of the perception, whereas a high-order abstraction would consist of inferences about descriptions of the perception.

**listening.** An active process of receiving messages sent orally; this process consists of five stages: receiving, understanding, remembering, evaluating, and responding.

**logic.** The science of reasoning; the principles governing the analysis of inference making.

**looking-glass self.** The self-concept that results from the image of yourself that others reveal to you.

**loving.** An interpersonal process in which one person feels a closeness, a caring, a warmth, and an excitement in relation to another person.

**low-context culture.** A culture in which most of the information in communication is explicitly stated in the verbal messages. **Individualistic cultures** are usually low-context cultures. Opposed to **high-context culture.**

**maintenance.** A stage of relationship stability at which the relationship does not progress or deteriorate significantly; a continuation as opposed to a dissolution of a relationship.

**maintenance strategies.** Specific behaviors designed to preserve an interpersonal relationship.

**manipulation.** An unproductive conflict strategy in which a person avoids open conflict but attempts to divert the conflict by being especially charming and getting the other person into a noncombative frame of mind.

**manuscript speech.** A speech designed to be read verbatim from a script.

**markers.** Devices that signify that a certain territory belongs to a particular person. *See also* **boundary marker, central marker,** and **earmarker.**

**mass communication.** Communication that is addressed to an extremely large audience, mediated by audio and/or visual transmitters, and processed by gatekeepers before transmission.

**matching hypothesis.** The theory that we tend to date and mate with people who are similar to us—who match us—in physical attractiveness.

**meaningfulness.** As a principle of perception, our assumption that people's behavior is sensible, stems from some logical antecedent, and is consequently meaningful rather than meaningless.

**mentoring.** Guidance and support given by an experienced individual to a less experienced person.

**mere exposure hypothesis.** The theory that repeated or prolonged exposure to a stimulus may result in a change in attitude toward the stimulus object, generally in the direction of increased positiveness.

**message.** Any signal or combination of signals that serves as a stimulus for a receiver.

**metacommunication.** Communication about communication.

**metalanguage.** Language used to talk about language.

**metamessage.** A message that makes reference to another message; for example, remarks such as "Did I make myself clear?" or "That's a lie."

**metaskills.** Skills for regulating more specific skills. For example, skills of interpersonal communication such as openness and empathy must be regulated by the metaskills of flexibility, mindfulness, and metacommunication.

**mindfulness and mindlessness.** States of relative awareness. In a mindful state, we are aware of the logic and rationality of our behaviors and the logical connections existing among elements. In a mindless state, we are unaware of this logic and rationality.

**mixed message.** A message that contradicts itself; a message that asks for two different (often incompatible) responses.

**model.** A representation of an object or process.

**monochronic time orientation.** A view of time in which things are done sequentially; one thing is scheduled at a time. Opposed to **polychronic time orientation.**

**monologue.** A form of communication in which one person speaks and the other listens; there is no real interaction among participants. Opposed to **dialogue.**

**motivated sequence.** An organizational pattern in which a speaker arranges the information in a discourse to motivate an audience to respond positively to the speaker's purpose.

**name calling.** A persuasive technique in which the speaker gives an idea or a person a derogatory name.

**negative feedback.** Feedback that serves a corrective function by informing the source that his or her message is not being received in the way intended; serves to redirect the source's behavior. Examples include looks of boredom, shouts of dis-

agreement, letters critical of newspaper policy, or a teacher's instructions on how better to approach a problem. Opposed to **positive feedback.**

**neutrality.** A response pattern lacking in personal involvement; encourages defensiveness; opposed to **empathy.**

**noise.** Anything that interferes with a person's receiving a message as the source intended the message to be received. Noise is present in a communication system to the extent that the message received is not the message sent.

**nominal group.** A collection of individuals who record their thoughts and opinions, which are then distributed to others. Without direct interaction, the thoughts and opinions are gradually pared down until a manageable list of solutions or decisions is produced. When this occurs, the nominal group (a group in name only) may restructure itself into a problem-solving group that analyzes the final list.

**nonallness.** An attitude or point of view that recognizes that we can never know all about anything; that what we know, say, or hear is only a part of what there is to know, say, or hear.

**nondirective language.** Language that does not direct or focus our attention on certain aspects of a topic; neutral language.

**nonnegotiation.** An unproductive conflict strategy in which an individual refuses to discuss the conflict or to listen to the other person in the encounter.

**nonverbal communication.** Communication without words; for example, communication by means of space, gestures, facial expressions, touching, vocal variation, or silence.

**nonverbal dominance.** Nonverbal behavior through which one person psychologically dominates another.

**norm.** *See* **group norm.**

**object-adaptors.** Movements that involve manipulation of some object, such as punching holes in or drawing on a Styrofoam coffee cup, clicking a ballpoint pen, or chewing on a pencil.

**object language.** Language used to communicate about objects, events, and relations in the world; the structure of the object language is described in a metalanguage; the display of physical objects—for example, flower arranging and the colors of the clothes we wear.

**olfactics.** The study of communication by smell.

**openness.** A quality of interpersonal effectiveness encompassing (1) a willingness to interact openly with others, to self-disclose as appropriate; (2) a willingness to react honestly to incoming stimuli; and (3) a willingness to own your feelings and thoughts.

**oral style.** The style of spoken discourse that, when compared with written style, consists of shorter, simpler, and more familiar words; more qualification, self-reference terms, allness terms, verbs and adverbs; and more concrete terms and terms indicative of consciousness of projection, such as "as I see it."

**other-orientation.** A quality of interpersonal effectiveness involving attentiveness, interest, and concern for the other person.

**other talk.** Talk about the listener or about some third party.

**overattribution.** The tendency to attribute a great deal of what a person does or believes to one or two obvious characteristics of the person.

**panel.** A small group format in which "experts" meet to discuss a topic or solve a problem; participants often speak without any set pattern.

**paralanguage.** The vocal but nonverbal aspect of speech. Paralanguage consists of voice qualities (for example, pitch range, resonance, tempo), vocal characterizers (laughing or crying, yelling or whispering), vocal qualifiers (intensity, pitch height), and vocal segregates ("uh-uh" meaning "no," or "sh" meaning "silence").

**parasocial relationship.** Relationship between a person and an imagined or fictional character; usually refers to a relationship between a viewer and a fictional character in a television show.

**pauses.** Silent periods in the normally fluent stream of speech. Pauses are of two major types: filled pauses (interruptions in speech that are filled with such vocalizations as "er" or "um") and unfilled pauses (silences of unusually long duration).

**perception.** The process of becoming aware of objects and events via the senses. *See also* **interpersonal perception.**

**perception checking.** The process of verifying your understanding of some message or situation or feeling to reduce uncertainty.

**perceptual accentuation.** A process that leads you to see what you expect to see and what you want to see—for example, to see people you like as better looking and smarter than people you do not like.

**personal distance.** The second closest **proxemic distance,** ranging from 18 inches to four feet. *See also* **proxemics.**

**personal rejection.** An unproductive conflict strategy in which one person withholds love and affection and seeks to win the argument by getting the other person to break down under this withdrawal.

**persuasion.** The process of influencing attitudes, beliefs, values, and/or behavior.

**phatic communication.** Communication that is primarily social; "small talk" designed to open the channels of communication rather than to communicate something about the external world. "Hello" and "How are you?" in everyday interaction are examples.

**pitch.** The highness or lowness of the vocal tone.

**plain folks.** A persuasive strategy that identifies the speaker and his or her proposal with the audience.

**polarization.** A form of fallacious reasoning by which only two extremes are considered; also referred to as "black-and-white" or "either/or" thinking or as a two-valued orientation.

**politeness.** Good communication manners; a way of interacting considered cultured and refined.

**polychronic time orientation.** A view of time in which several things may be scheduled or engaged in at the same time. Opposed to **monochronic time orientation.**

**positive feedback.** Feedback that supports or reinforces the continuation of behavior along the same lines in which it is already proceeding—for example, applause during a speech. Opposed to **negative feedback.**

**positiveness.** A characteristic of effective communication involving positive attitudes toward the self and toward the interpersonal interaction. Also refers to complimenting another and expressing acceptance and approval.

**power.** The ability to control the behaviors of others.

**power play.** A consistent pattern of behavior in which one person tries to control the behavior of another.

**pragmatic implication.** An assumption that seems logical but is not necessarily true.

**premature self-disclosures.** Disclosures that are made before a relationship has developed sufficiently.

**primacy effect.** The condition by which what comes first exerts greater influence than what comes later. Opposed to **recency effect.**

**primacy–recency.** Principle of **perception** stating that we generally use early information to get a general impression of a person and use later information to add specificity to this impression.

**primary relationship.** The relationship between two people that they consider their most (or one of their most) important; for example, the relationship between spouses or domestic partners.

**primary territory.** An area that you can consider your exclusive preserve—for example, your room or office.

**problem-solving group.** A group whose primary task is to solve a problem, or, more often, to reach a decision.

**problem-solving sequence.** A logical step-by-step process for solving a problem that is frequently used by groups; consists of defining and analyzing the problem, establishing criteria for evaluating solutions, identifying possible solutions, evaluating solutions, selecting the best solution, and testing the selected solutions.

**process.** Ongoing activity; communication is referred to as a process to emphasize that it is always changing, always in motion.

**projection.** A psychological process whereby we attribute characteristics or feelings of our own to others; often refers to the process whereby we attribute our own faults to others.

**pronunciation.** The production of syllables or words according to some accepted standard; for example, as presented in a dictionary.

**protection theory.** A theory of proxemics referring to the fact that people establish a body-buffer zone to protect themselves from unwanted closeness, touching, or attack.

**provisionalism.** An attitude of open-mindedness that leads to the creation of supportiveness; opposed to **certainty.**

**proxemic distances.** The spatial distances that people maintain in communication and social interaction.

**proxemics.** The study of the communicative function of space and of how people unconsciously structure their space—the distances between people in their interactions, the organization of space in homes and offices, and even the design of cities.

**proximity.** As a principle of **perception,** the tendency to perceive people or events that are physically close as belonging together or representing some kind of a unit. Also, physical closeness; one of the factors influencing interpersonal attraction.

**psychological time.** The importance you place on past, present, or future time.

**public communication.** Communication in which the source is one person and the receiver is an audience of many persons.

**public distance.** The longest **proxemic distance,** ranging from 12 to more than 25 feet.

**public territory.** Area that is open to all people—for example, a restaurant or park.

**punctuation of communication.** The breaking up of continuous communication sequences into short sequences with identifiable beginnings and endings or stimuli and responses.

**punishment.** Noxious or aversive stimulation.

**pupillometrics.** The study of communication through changes in the size of the pupils of the eyes.

**purr words.** Highly positive words that express the speaker's feelings rather than any objective reality. Opposed to **snarl words.**

**Pygmalion effect.** Condition in which we make a prediction of success, act as if it were true, and thereby make it come true; a type of **self-fulfilling prophecy.**

**quality circles.** Groups of workers (usually 6 to 12) whose task it is to investigate and make recommendations for improving the quality of some organizational function.

**quotes.** An **extensional device** to emphasize that a word or phrase is being used in a special sense and should therefore be given special attention.

**racist language.** Language that denigrates or is derogatory toward members of a particular race.

**rate.** The speed with which you speak, generally measured in words per minute.

**receiver.** Any person or thing that takes in messages. Receivers may be individuals listening to or reading a message, a group of persons hearing a speech, a scattered television audience, or machines that store information.

**recency effect.** The condition in which what comes last (that is, most recently) exerts greater influence than what comes first. Opposed to **primacy effect.**

**redundancy.** The quality of a message that makes it totally predictable and therefore lacking in information. A message of zero redundancy would be completely unpredictable; a message of 100 percent redundancy would be completely predictable. All human languages contain some degree of built-in redundancy, generally estimated to be about 50 percent.

**referent power.** Personal power derived from others' desire to identify with or be like the individual.

**reflexiveness.** The feature of human language that makes it possible for that language to be used to refer to itself; that is, reflexiveness lets us talk about our talk and create a **metalanguage**—a language for talking about language.

**regulators.** Nonverbal behaviors that regulate, monitor, or control the communications of another person.

**rejection.** A response to an individual that disagrees with or denies the validity of something the individual says or does.

**relational communication.** Communication between or among intimates or people in close relationships; used by some theorists as synonymous with **interpersonal communication.**

**relationship development.** The stages of relationships during which you move closer to intimacy; in the model of relationships presented here, relationship development includes the **contact** and **involvement** stages.

**relationship dialectics theory.** A theory that describes relationships as defined by competing opposite desires or motivations, such as the desire for autonomy and the desire to belong to someone, desires for novelty and predictability, and desires for closedness and openness.

**relationship maintenance.** The processes by which you attempt to keep a relationship stable.

**relationship messages.** Messages that comment on the relationship between the speakers rather than on matters external to them.

**repair.** Attempts to reverse the process of relationship **deterioration.**

**response.** Any overt or covert behavior.

**reward power.** Power based on a person's ability to reward another person.

**rigid complementarity.** Inability to break away from a complementary type of relationship that was once appropriate but is no longer.

**role.** The part an individual plays in a group; an individual's function or expected behavior.

**roundtable.** A small group format in which group members arrange themselves in a circular or semicircular pattern; participants meet to share information or solve problems without any set pattern as to who speaks when.

**rules theory.** A theory that describes relationships as interactions governed by a series of rules that a couple agrees to follow. When the rules are followed, the relationship is maintained; when they are broken, the relationship experiences difficulty.

**schemata.** Mental templates or structures that help us organize items of sensory information and information in memory. (Singular: *schema.*)

**script.** A template or organizational structure describing the sequence of events in a given action, procedure, or occurrence.

**secondary territory.** Area that does not belong to a particular person but that has been occupied by that person and is therefore associated with her or him—for example, the seat a person normally takes in class.

**selective exposure.** Tendency of listeners to actively seek out information that supports their existing opinions, beliefs, attitudes, and values and to actively avoid information that contradicts them.

**self-acceptance.** Satisfaction with ourselves, our virtues and vices, and our abilities and limitations.

**self-adaptors.** Movements that usually satisfy a physical need, especially to make you more comfortable; for example, scratching your head to relieve an itch, moistening your lips because they feel dry, or pushing your hair out of your eyes.

**self-attribution.** A process through which we seek to account for and understand the reasons and motivations for our own behaviors.

**self-awareness.** The degree to which a person knows himself or herself.

**self-concept.** An individual's self-evaluation or self-appraisal.

**self-disclosure.** The process of revealing something about ourselves to another. Usually refers to information that would normally be kept hidden.

**self-esteem.** The value you place on yourself; your self-evaluation. Usually refers to a positive self-evaluation.

**self-fulfilling prophecy.** The situation in which we make a prediction or prophecy that comes true because we act on it as if it were true.

**self-monitoring.** The manipulation of the image we present to others in interpersonal interactions so as to create a favorable impression.

**self-serving bias.** A bias in the self-attribution process that leads us to take credit for positive consequences and to deny responsibility for negative outcomes of our behaviors.

**self-talk.** Talk about the self.

**semantics.** The area of language study concerned with meaning.

**sexist language.** Language derogatory to one gender, usually women.

**sexual harassment.** Unsolicited and unwanted sexual messages.

**shyness.** The condition of discomfort and uneasiness in interpersonal situations.

**sign** (reasoning from). A form of reasoning in which the presence of certain signs (clues) is interpreted as leading to a particular conclusion.

**signal-to-noise ratio.** In verbal interaction, the relationship between what is signal (meaningful) and what is noise (interference). This ratio also is relative to the communication analyst, the participants, and the context.

**signal reaction.** A conditioned response to a signal; a response to some signal that is immediate rather than delayed.

**silence.** The absence of vocal communication; often misunderstood to refer to the absence of any and all communication. Silence often communicates feelings or prevents communication about certain topics.

**similarity.** As a principle of **perception,** the tendency to see things that are physically similar as belonging together and/or constituting a unit. As a principle of **attraction,** our tendency to be attracted to people with qualities similar to our own and to people who are similar to us; opposed to **complementarity.**

**slang.** Language used by special groups that is not considered proper by the general society; language made up of the **argot, cant,** and **jargon** of various groups and known by the general public.

**small group communication.** Communication among a collection of individuals, small enough in number that all members may interact with relative ease as both senders and receivers, the members being related to one another by some common purpose and with some degree of organization or structure.

**snarl words.** Highly negative words that express the feelings of the speaker rather than any objective reality. Opposed to **purr words.**

**social comparison.** The processes by which you compare aspects of yourself (for example, your abilities, opinions, and values) with those of others and then assess and evaluate yourself; one of the sources of **self-concept.**

**social distance.** The third **proxemic distance,** ranging from 4 to 12 feet; the distance at which business is usually conducted.

**social exchange theory.** A theory hypothesizing that we develop relationships in which our rewards or profits will be greater than our costs and that we avoid or terminate relationships in which the costs exceed the rewards.

**social penetration theory.** A theory describing how relationships develop from the superficial to the intimate levels and from few to many areas of interpersonal interaction.

**source.** Any person or thing that creates messages. A source may be an individual speaking, writing, or gesturing or a computer sending an error message.

**specific instances** (reasoning from). A form of reasoning in which a speaker examines several specific instances and forms a conclusion about the whole on the basis of those instances.

**speech.** Messages utilizing a vocal–auditory channel.

**spontaneity.** The communication pattern in which a person verbalizes what he or she is thinking without attempting to develop strategies for control; encourages **supportiveness.** Opposed to strategy.

**stability.** As a principle of perception, the idea that our perceptions of things and of people are relatively consistent with our previous perceptions.

**static evaluation.** An orientation that fails to recognize that the world is characterized by constant change; an attitude that sees people and events as fixed rather than as constantly changing.

**status.** The relative level a person occupies in a hierarchy; status always involves a comparison, and thus one person's status is only relative to the status of another.

**stereotype.** In communication, a fixed impression of a group of people through which we then perceive specific individuals; stereotypes are most often negative but may also be positive.

**stimulus.** Any external or internal change that impinges on or arouses an organism.

**subjectivity.** As a principle of perception, the idea that our perceptions are not objective but are influenced by our wants and needs and our expectations and predictions.

**supportiveness.** An attitude of an individual or an atmosphere in a group that is characterized by openness, absence of fear, and a genuine feeling of equality.

**symmetrical relationship.** A relation between two or more persons in which one person's behavior serves as a stimulus for the same type of behavior in the other person(s). Examples of such relationships include those in which anger in one person encourages or serves as a stimulus for anger in another person or in which a critical comment by the person leads the other person to respond in like manner.

**symposium.** A small group format in which each member of the group delivers a relatively prepared talk on some aspect of the topic. Often combined with a **forum.**

**systematic desensitization.** A theory and technique for dealing with a variety of fears (such as communication apprehension) in which you gradually expose yourself to an anxiety-producing stimulus so as to become hardened to it.

**taboo.** Forbidden; culturally censored. Taboo language is language that is frowned upon by "polite society." Topics and specific words may be considered taboo—for example, death, sex, certain forms of illness, and various words denoting sexual activities and excretory functions.

**temporal communication.** The messages communicated by a person's time orientation and treatment of time.

**territoriality.** A possessive or ownership reaction to an area of space or to particular objects.

**testimonial.** A persuasive technique in which the speaker uses the authority or image of some positively evaluated person to gain an audience's approval or of some negatively evaluated person to gain listeners' rejection.

**theory.** A general statement or principle applicable to related phenomena.

**thesis.** The main assertion of a message—for example, the theme of a public speech.

**touch avoidance.** The tendency to avoid touching and being touched by others.

**touch communication.** Communication through tactile means.

**transactional.** Characterized by mutual influence and interdependence; communication is a transactional process because no element is independent of any other element.

**transfer.** A persuasive technique in which a speaker associates an idea with something the audience respects in order to gain approval or with something the audience dislikes in order to gain rejection.

**uncertainty reduction strategies.** Passive, active, and interactive ways of increasing accuracy in interpersonal perception.

**uncertainty reduction theory.** Theory holding that as relationships develop, uncertainty is reduced; relationship development is seen as a process of reducing uncertainty about one another.

**universal of interpersonal communication.** A feature of communication common to all interpersonal communication acts.

**unknown self.** A part of our self containing information about the self that is unknown to us as well as to others, but that is inferred to exist on the basis of various projective tests, slips of the tongue, dream analyses, and the like.

**upward communication.** Communication in which the messages are sent from lower levels to upper levels of an organization or hierarchy—for example, from line worker to management.

**value.** Relative worth of an object; a quality that makes something desirable or undesirable; an ideal or custom about which we have emotional responses, whether positive or negative.

**verbal aggressiveness.** A method of winning an argument by attacking the other person's **self-concept.** Often considered opposed to **argumentativeness.**

**violation.** Unwarranted use of another's territory.

**visual dominance.** The use of your eyes to maintain a superior or dominant position; for example, when making an especially important point, you might look intently at the other person.

**voice qualities.** Aspects of **paralanguage**—specifically, pitch range, vocal lip control, glottis control, pitch control, articulation control, rhythm control, resonance, and tempo.

**volume.** The relative loudness of the voice.

**withdrawal.** (1) A reaction to territorial encroachment in which we leave the territory. (2) A tendency to close ourself off from conflicts rather than confront the issues.

**you-messages.** Messages in which the speaker denies responsibility for his or her own thoughts and behaviors; messages that attribute the speaker's perception to another person; messages of blame. Opposed to **I-messages.**

# Glossary of Human Communication Skills

-------------------------------------------------------------------------------

**abstractions.** Use both abstract and specific terms when describing or explaining.

**accommodation.** Accommodate to the speaking style of your listener in moderation. Too much mirroring of the other person's manner of communicating may appear too obvious and even manipulative.

**active and inactive listening.** If you wish to listen actively, paraphrase the speaker's meaning, express understanding of the speaker's feelings, and ask questions when you need something clarified.

**active interpersonal conflict.** Engage in interpersonal conflict actively; generally, don't rely on silence as a way of avoiding the issues.

**advantages and disadvantages of relationships.** In evaluating your own relationship choices, consider both the advantages and the disadvantages of relationships generally and of your specific relationships.

**allness.** Avoid allness statements (for example, statements containing such words as *all*, *never*, or *always*); they invariably misstate the reality and will often offend the other person.

**amplifying informative speeches.** Select a variety of amplifying materials: examples, illustrations, and narratives; testimony; definitions; statistics; and visual aids.

**amplifying materials.** Support major propositions with amplifying materials such as examples, statistics, and visual aids and with logical, emotional, and ethical proofs.

**analyze your perceptions.** Increase accuracy in interpersonal perception by (1) identifying the influence of your physical and emotional state; (2) making sure that you're not drawing conclusions from too little information; and (3) identifying any perceptions that may be the result of mind reading.

**anger management.** To manage your anger, calm down as best you can, reflect on the fact that communication is irreversible, and review your available communication options and the relevant communication skills.

**appreciating cultural differences.** Look at cultural differences not as deviations from the norm or as deficiencies but simply as the differences they are. Remember, however, that recognizing differences and considering them as you communicate does not necessarily mean that you accept or adopt them.

**appropriateness of self-disclosure.** Consider the legitimacy of your motives for disclosing, the appropriateness of the disclosure, the listener's responses (is the dyadic effect operating?), and the potential burdens self-disclosures might impose.

**argumentativeness.** In conflict, avoid attacking the other person's self-concept. Instead, focus logically on the issues, emphasize finding solutions, and work to ensure that what is said will result in positive self-feelings for both individuals.

**articulation and pronunciation.** Avoid the articulation and pronunciation errors of omission, substitution, addition, accent, and pronouncing sounds that should be silent.

**artifactual communication.** Use artifacts (for example, color, clothing, body adornment, space decoration) to communicate your desired messages. But check to find out whether others are in fact receiving the messages you think you are communicating.

**audience analysis.** Analyze the audience in terms of its sociological and psychological characteristics and adapt your speech based on these findings.

**before and after the conflict.** Prepare for a conflict by arranging to fight in private, knowing what you're fighting about, and fighting about problems that can be solved. After the conflict, profit from it by learning what worked and what didn't, by keeping the conflict in perspective, and by increasing the exchange of rewards.

**body movements.** Use your body and hand gestures to reinforce your communication purposes.

**brainstorming.** Follow these general rules: Avoid negative criticism, strive for quantity, combine and extend the contributions of others, and contribute as wild ideas as possible.

**channel.** Assess your channel options (for example, speaking face-to-face, sending e-mail, or leaving a voicemail message when you know the person won't be home) before communicating important messages.

**checking perceptions.** Increase accuracy in perception by (1) describing what you see or hear and the meaning you assign to it and (2) asking the other person if your perceptions and meanings are accurate.

**communicating assertively.** Describe the problem, say how the problem affects you, propose solutions, confirm your understanding, and reflect on your own assertiveness.

**communicating power.** Communicate power by avoiding such powerless message forms as hesitations, too many intensifiers, disqualifiers, tag questions, one-word answers, self-critical statements, overly polite statements, and vulgar and slang expressions.

**communicating with the grief-stricken.** Use confirming messages, give the person permission to grieve, avoid directing the person, encourage the expression of feelings, and communicate empathy and support.

**communication apprehension management.** Acquire communication skills and experiences, focus on your prior successes, reduce unpredictability, and put apprehension in perspective.

**communication options.** Assess your communication options before communicating, especially in light of the fact that communication is inevitable, irreversible, and unrepeatable.

**conclusions.** Construct conclusions that summarize the major ideas of the speech and bring the speech to a crisp close.

**confirmation.** When you wish to be confirming, acknowledge (verbally and/or nonverbally) others in your group and their contributions.

**conflict, culture, and gender.** Approach conflict with an understanding of the cultural and gender differences in ideas about what constitutes conflict and how it should be pursued.

**conflict styles.** Adjust your conflict style to the specific conflict in which you find yourself.

**connotative meanings.** As a speaker, clarify your connotative meanings if you have any doubts that your listeners might misunderstand you; as a listener, ask questions if you have doubts about the speaker's connotations.

**content and relationship.** Listen to both the content and the relationship aspects of messages, distinguish between them, and respond to both.

**content and relationship conflicts.** Analyze conflict messages in terms of content and relationship dimensions and respond to each accordingly.

**context adjustment.** Adjust your messages to the unique communication context, taking into consideration its physical, cultural, social–psychological, and temporal aspects.

**conversational maxims.** Follow (generally) the basic maxims of conversation, such as the maxims of quantity, quality, relations, manner, and politeness.

**conversational rules.** Observe the general rules for conversation (for example, using relatively short speaking turns and avoiding interruptions), but break them when there seems logical reason to do so.

**conversational turns.** Maintain relatively short conversational turns and then pass the speaker's turn to another person nonverbally or verbally.

**credibility appeals.** Seek to establish credibility by displaying competence, high moral character, and dynamism or charisma.

**critical analysis.** Critically analyze reasoning from specific instances to generalizations and reasoning from analogy, causes and effects, and sign.

**critical thinking hats.** Using the critical thinking hats technique evaluate problems in terms of facts, feelings, negative arguments, positive benefits, creative ideas, and overall analysis.

**cultural differences in listening.** When listening in multicultural settings, realize that people from different cultures give very different listening cues and may operate with different rules for listening.

**cultural identifiers.** Use cultural identifiers that are sensitive to the desires of others; when appropriate, make clear the cultural identifiers you prefer.

**cultural influences.** Communicate with an understanding that culture influences communication in all its forms.

**cultural sensitivity.** Increase your cultural sensitivity by learning about different cultures, recognizing and facing your own fears of intercultural interaction, recognizing differences between yourself and others, and becoming conscious of the cultural rules and customs of other cultures.

**culture and groups.** Recognize and appreciate cultural differences in ideas about group membership and leadership.

**culture and perception.** Increase accuracy in perception by learning as much as you can about the cultures of those with whom you interact.

**dating statements.** Mentally date your statements to avoid thinking and communicating that the world is static and unchanging. In your messages, reflect the inevitability of change.

**deciding to self-disclose.** In deciding to self-disclose, consider the potential benefits (for example, self-knowledge) as well as the potential personal, relationship, and professional risks.

**delivery method.** In general, use the extemporaneous method of delivery.

**delivery.** During the speech presentation, maintain eye contact with the entire audience, allow facial expressions to convey feelings, gesture naturally, and incorporate purposeful body movements.

**Delphi method.** Use the Delphi method to solve problems when group members are separated geographically.

**dialogic conversation.** Treat conversation as a dialogue rather than a monologue; show concern for the other person, and for the relationship between you, with other-orientation.

**disclaimers.** Preface your comments with disclaimers if you feel you might be misunderstood. But avoid disclaimers when they aren't necessary; too many disclaimers can make you appear unprepared or unwilling to state an opinion.

**disconfirming language.** Avoid sexist, heterosexist, racist, and ageist language; such language is disconfirming and insulting and invariably contributes to communication barriers.

**emotional communication.** To communicate emotions effectively, (1) describe feelings, (2) identify the reasons for the feelings, (3) anchor feelings to the present, and (4) own your feelings and messages.

**emotional display.** Express your emotions and interpret the emotions of others in light of the cultural rules dictating what is and what isn't "appropriate" emotional expression.

**emotionality in interpersonal communication.** Include the inevitable emotionality in your thoughts and feelings in your interpersonal communication, both verbally and nonverbally.

**emotional understanding.** Be able to identify and describe emotions (both positive and negative) clearly and specifically. Learn the vocabulary of emotional expression.

**empathic and objective listening.** To listen empathically, punctuate the interaction from the speaker's point of view, engage in dialogue, and understand the speaker's thoughts and feelings. In listening objectively be careful that you don't hear what you want to hear.

**empathic conflict.** Engage in interpersonal conflict with empathy rather than blame. Also, express this empathy, as in "I can understand how you must have felt."

**empathy.** Communicate empathy when appropriate: Resist evaluating the person's behaviors, focus concentration on the person, express active involvement through facial expressions and gestures, reflect back the feelings you think are being expressed, self-disclose, and address any mixed messages.

**ethnocentric thinking.** Recognize your own ethnocentric thinking and how it influences your verbal and nonverbal messages.

**evaluating.** In evaluating messages, try first to understand fully what the speaker means. In addition, try to identify any biases or self-interests that might lead the speaker to give an unfair presentation of the material.

**expressiveness.** Communicate active involvement in the interaction: Use active listening, address mixed messages, use I-messages, and use appropriate variations in paralanguage and gestures.

**eye movements.** Use eye movements to seek feedback, exchange conversational turns, signal the nature of your relationship with others, and compensate for increased physical distance. At the same time, look for such meanings in the eye movements of others.

**face-saving strategies.** In conflict use strategies that allow your opponent to save face; avoid beltlining, or hitting your opponent with attacks that he or she will have difficulty absorbing and will resent.

**facial messages.** Use facial expressions to communicate that you're involved in the interaction. As a listener, look to the emotional facial expressions of others as additional cues to their meaning.

**facts and inferences.** Distinguish facts (verifiably true past events) from inferences (guesses, hypotheses, hunches), and act on inferences with tentativeness.

**fallacy identification.** Detect such fallacies as name calling, transfer, testimonial, plain folks, card stacking, bandwagon, and attack.

**feedback.** Listen to both verbal and nonverbal feedback—from yourself and from others—and use these cues to help you adjust your messages for greatest effectiveness.

**feedforward.** Preface your messages with some kind of feedforward when you feel your listener needs some background or when you want to ease into a particular topic, such as bad news.

**flexibility.** Because no two communication situations are identical, because everything is in a state of flux, and because everyone is different, cultivate flexibility and adjust your communication to the unique situation.

**friendships.** Establish friendships to help serve such needs as utility, ego support, stimulation, and security. At the same time, seek to serve similar needs that your friends have.

**fundamental attribution error.** Avoid the fundamental attribution error (whereby you attribute someone's behavior solely to internal factors) by focusing on the possible influence of situational forces.

**gaining perspective on problems and solutions.** View problems and solutions from the perspective of facts, feelings, negative arguments, positive benefits, creative new ideas, and control of thinking.

**gender differences in listening.** Speak to men and women with an understanding that women give more cues that they're listening and appear more supportive in their listening than men.

**giving space.** Give others the space they need, which varies on the basis of culture, gender, and emotional state. Look to the other person for any signs of spatial discomfort.

**group norms.** Actively seek to discover the norms of a group, and take these norms into consideration when interacting in the group.

**group participation.** Be group oriented rather than individually oriented, center debates on issues rather than on personalities, be critically open-minded, and make sure that meanings are clearly understood.

**groupthink.** Recognize and actively counter any groupthink tendencies evidenced in a group.

**High- and low-context cultures.** Adjust your messages and your listening in light of the differences between high- and low-context cultures.

**I-messages.** Use I-messages when communicating your feelings; take responsibility for your own feelings (as in "I get angry when you . . .") rather than attributing them to others (as in "you make me angry").

**immediacy.** Maintain nonverbal immediacy through close physical distances, eye contact, and smiling; maintain verbal immediacy by using the other person's name and focusing on the other's remarks.

**implicit personality theory.** In order to subject your perceptions and conclusions about people to logical analysis, bring to your mindful state your implicit personality theory.

**increasing assertiveness.** Increase your own assertiveness by analyzing the assertive messages of others, rehearsing assertive messages, and communicating assertively.

**indirect messages.** Make judicious use of indirect messages when a more direct style might prove insulting or offensive. But be aware that indirect messages can create communication problems, because they are easier to misunderstand than direct messages.

**indiscrimination.** Avoid indiscrimination; treat each situation and each person as unique (when possible) even when they're covered by the same label or name. Index your key concepts.

**individualistic and collectivist cultures.** Adjust your messages and your listening on the basis of differences between individualistic and collectivist cultures.

**individual roles.** In a group avoid playing the popular but dysfunctional individual roles—those of the aggressor, blocker, recognition seeker, self-confessor, or dominator.

**informative speaking.** Follow the principles of informative speaking: Stress the information's usefulness, relate new information to information the audience already knows, present information through several senses, adjust the level of complexity, vary the levels of abstraction, avoid information overload, and recognize cultural variations.

**initial impressions.** Guard against drawing impressions too quickly or on the basis of too little information; be aware that initial impressions can function as filters that prevent you from forming more accurate perceptions on the basis of more information.

**intensional orientation.** Avoid intensional orientation. Respond to things first and to labels second; for example, the way a person is talked about is not the best measure of who that person really is.

**interaction management.** Speak in relatively short conversational turns, avoid long and frequent pauses, and use verbal and nonverbal messages that are consistent.

**intercultural communication.** When communicating interculturally, become mindful of (1) the differences between yourself and culturally different individuals, (2) the differences within the other cultural group, (3) cultural differences in meanings for both verbal and nonverbal signals, and (4) different cultural rules and customs. Communicate interculturally with appropriate openness, empathy, positiveness, immediacy, interaction management, expressiveness, and other-orientation.

**introductions.** Construct introductions that gain attention and preview what is to follow.

**leadership style.** Adjust leadership style to the task at hand and to the needs of group members.

**leading a group.** Start group interaction, maintain effective interaction throughout the discussion, keep members on track, ensure member satisfaction, encourage ongoing evaluation and improvement, and prepare members for the discussion as necessary.

**listening to the feelings of others.** In listening to the feelings of others, avoid the tendency to try to solve their problems; instead, listen, empathize, focus on the other person, and encourage the person to explore his or her feelings.

**making excuses.** Repair conversational problems by offering excuses that (1) demonstrate that you understand the problem, (2) acknowledge your responsibility, (3) acknowledge your regret for what you did, (4) request forgiveness, and (5) make it clear that this will never happen again.

**managing relationship deterioration.** To cope with the ending of a relationship, break the loneliness–depression cycle, take time out, bolster your self-esteem, seek the support of nourishing others, and avoid repeating negative patterns.

**markers.** Become sensitive to the markers (central, boundary, and ear) of others, and learn to use these markers to define your own territories and to communicate the desired impression.

**masculine and feminine cultures.** Adjust your messages and your listening to differences in cultural masculinity and femininity.

**meanings depend on context.** When deciphering messages, look at the context for cues as to how you should interpret the meanings.

**meanings in people.** When deciphering meaning, the best source is the person; meanings are in people. So when in doubt, find out—from the source.

**message overload.** Combat message overload by using and disposing of messages as they come to you, organizing your messages, getting rid of extra copies, and distinguishing between messages you should save and messages you should throw away.

**metacommunication.** Metacommunicate when you want to clarify the way you're talking or what you're talking about; for example, give clear feedforward and paraphrase your own complex messages.

**mindfulness.** Increase your mindfulness by creating and recreating categories, being open to new information and points of view, and avoiding excessive reliance on first impressions.

**mixed messages.** Avoid emitting mixed messages by focusing clearly on your purposes when communicating and by increasing conscious control over your verbal and nonverbal behaviors.

**motivational appeals.** Use motivational appeals (appeals to motives such as fear; power, control, and influence; safety; achievement; or financial gain) as appropriate to the speech and audience.

**negatives and positives of conflict.** Approach conflict to minimize the negative and maximize the positive benefits of conflict and its resolution.

**networking.** Establish a network of relationships to provide insights into issues relevant to your personal and professional life, and be willing to lend your expertise to the networks of others.

**noise management.** Reduce the influence of physical, physiological, psychological, and semantic noise to the extent that you can; use repetition and restatement and, when in doubt, ask if you're being clear.

**nominal group.** Use the nominal group technique to solve problems when anonymity in suggesting ideas may be desirable.

**nonjudgmental and critical listening.** When listening nonjudgmentally, keep an open mind, avoid filtering out difficult messages, and recognize your own biases. When listening to evaluate, listen extra carefully, ask questions when in doubt, and check your perceptions before offering criticism.

**nonverbal communication and culture.** Interpret the nonverbal cues of others not in light of the meanings assigned by your culture but (insofar as you can) in light of the meanings assigned by the speaker's culture.

**online conflicts.** Avoid the common causes of online conflicts—such as sending out unsolicited commercial messages, spamming, and flaming.

**open expression in conflict.** Try to facilitate open expression of your combatant.

**openness.** When appropriate, increase openness by self-disclosing, responding to those with whom you're interacting spontaneously and honestly, and owning your own feelings and thoughts.

**organizing a speech.** To organize the major propositions of a speech, select a thought pattern appropriate to the subject matter, purpose, and audience.

**organizing learning discussions.** Use an organizational structure in educational or learning groups—a chronological or spatial structure, for example—to give order to the discussion.

**other-orientation.** Acknowledge the importance of the other person; use focused eye contact and appropriate facial expressions; smile, nod, and lean toward the other person; express agreement when appropriate.

**overattribution.** Avoid overattribution; rarely is any one factor an accurate explanation of complex human behavior.

**packaging.** Make your verbal and nonverbal messages consistent; inconsistencies between, say, spoken words and body language, often create uncertainty and misunderstanding.

**paralanguage.** Vary paralinguistic features such as rate, pausing, pitch, and volume to communicate your meanings and to add interest and color to your messages.

**pausing.** Use pauses to signal transitions, to allow listeners time to think, and to signal the approach of a significant idea.

**perceptual shortcuts.** Be mindful of your perceptual shortcuts (for example, rules, schemata, and scripts) so that they don't mislead you and result in inaccurate perceptions.

**persuasive speaking.** Apply (where relevant) the principles of persuasion: selective exposure, audience participation, identification, and amounts of change.

**polarization.** Avoid thinking and talking in extremes by using middle terms and qualifiers. At the same time, remember that too many qualifiers may make you appear unsure of yourself.

**positiveness.** Communicate positiveness: Express your own satisfaction with the interaction, and compliment others by expressing your positive thoughts and feelings about and to the other person.

**power communication.** Communicate power through forceful speech; avoidance of weak modifiers and excessive body movement; and demonstration of your knowledge, preparation, and organization in the matters at hand.

**power distance.** Adjust your messages and listening based on the power distance orientation of the culture in which you find yourself.

**power plays.** Use cooperative strategies to deal with power plays: (1) Express your feelings, (2) describe the behavior to which you object, and (3) state a cooperative response.

**present-focus conflict.** Focus your conflict resolution messages on the present; avoid dredging up old grievances and unloading these on the other person (gunnysacking).

**problem solving in groups.** Deal with interpersonal conflicts systematically. For example, (1) define the problem, (2) examine possible solutions, (3) test the solution, (4) evaluate the solution, and (5) accept or reject the solution.

**quality circles.** Use the quality circle technique to improve organizational functions.

**receiving.** In receiving messages, focus attention on both verbal and the nonverbal signals, because both communicate meaning.

**reducing uncertainty.** Increase accuracy in perception by reducing your uncertainty, using passive, active, and interactive strategies.

**rehearsal.** Rehearse your speech often, perfect your delivery, rehearse the speech as a whole, time the speech at each rehearsal, approximate the specific speech situation as much as possible, see and think of yourself as a public speaker, and incorporate any delivery notes that may be of value during the actual speech presentation.

**relationship messages.** Formulate messages that are appropriate to the stage of the relationship. And listen to messages from relationship partners that may reveal differences in perception about your relationship stage.

**relationship repair.** Recognize the problem, engage in productive conflict resolution, pose possible solutions, affirm each other, integrate solutions into normal behavior, and take risks as appropriate.

**relationship rules.** Follow the rules for maintaining relationships when you do in fact wish to maintain and even strengthen them.

**remembering.** In remembering messages, identify the central ideas, summarize the message in an easy-to-retain form, and repeat (aloud or to yourself) key terms and names.

**research.** Research topics effectively and efficiently, and critically evaluate the reliability of the research material.

**responding.** In responding to messages, express support for the speaker using I-messages ("I didn't understand the point about . . .") instead of you-messages ("You didn't clarify what you meant about . . .").

**responding to others' disclosures.** Respond appropriately to the disclosures of another person by listening actively, supporting the discloser, and keeping the disclosures confidential.

**restimulating brainstorming.** Appropriately restimulate a brainstorming group that has lost its steam by asking for additional contributions or for further extensions of previously contributed ideas.

**romantic workplace relationships.** Establish romantic relationships at work only with a clear understanding of the potential problems.

**selecting main points.** After generating the possible main points for a speech, eliminate those that seem least important to the thesis, combine those that have a common focus, and select those most relevant to the purpose of the speech and the audience.

**self-awareness.** Increase self-awareness: Listen to others, increase your open self as appropriate, and seek out information (discreetly) to reduce any blind spots.

**self-concept.** Learn who you are: See yourself through the eyes of others; compare yourself to similar (and admired) others; examine the influences of culture; and observe, interpret, and evaluate your own message behaviors.

**self-esteem.** Raise your self-esteem: Challenge self-destructive beliefs, seek out nourishing people with whom to interact, work on projects that will result in success, and engage in self-affirmation.

**self-fulfilling prophecy.** Take a second look at your perceptions when they correspond very closely to your initial expectations; the self-fulfilling prophecy may be at work.

**self-serving bias.** Become mindful of any self-serving bias; that is, of giving too much weight to internal factors (when explaining your positives) and too little weight to external factors (when explaining your negatives).

**sentence style.** Construct sentences that are short, direct, active, and positive, and vary the type and length of sentences.

**silence.** Silence can communicate lots of different meanings (e.g., your anger or your need for time to think), so examine silence for meanings just as you would eye movements or body gestures.

**spatial distance.** Use spatial distance to signal the type of relationship you are in: intimate, personal, social, or public. Let your spatial relationships reflect your interpersonal relationships. Maintain spatial distances that are comfortable (neither too close nor too far apart) and that are appropriate to the situation and to your relationship with the other person.

**speech of definition.** Consider using a variety of definitions, citing credible sources, and proceeding from the known to the unknown.

**speech of demonstration.** Consider using a temporal pattern, employing transitions to connect the steps, presenting a broad overview and then the specific steps, and providing visual aids.

**speech of description.** Consider using a spatial, topic, or "5 W" organizational pattern; a variety of descriptive categories; and visual aids.

**speech rate.** Use variations in rate to increase communication efficiency and persuasiveness as appropriate.

**stereotypes.** Be careful of thinking and talking in stereotypes; recognize that members of all groups are different, and focus on the individual rather than on the individual's membership in one group or another.

**supportive conflict.** Engage in conflict in ways that will encourage supportiveness rather than defensiveness—avoid messages that evaluate or control, that are strategic or neutral, or that express superiority or certainty.

**surface and depth listening.** To listen in depth, focus on both verbal and nonverbal messages and on both content and relationship messages, and make special note of statements that refer back to the speaker. At the same time, do not avoid the surface or literal meaning.

**talk, not force.** Talk about your problems rather than trying to use physical or emotional force.

**thesis and main ideas.** Expand the thesis or main assertion of a speech by asking strategic questions to develop the main ideas or propositions.

**time cues.** Interpret time cues from the perspective of the other person with whom you're interacting. Be especially sensitive to leave-taking cues; for example, notice if the person comments that "It's getting late" or glances at his or her watch.

**topic and purpose.** Select speech topics and purposes that are appropriate to speaker, audience, and occasion, and narrow them to manageable proportions.

**touch and touch avoidance.** Respect the touch-avoidance tendencies of others; pay special attention to cultural and gender differences in touch preferences and in touch avoidance.

**transitions.** Use transitions and internal summaries to connect the parts of a speech and to help listeners remember the speech.

**turn-taking cues.** Respond to both the verbal and the nonverbal conversational turn-taking cues given you by others, and make your own cues clear to others.

**understanding.** To understand messages, relate new information to what you already know, ask questions, and paraphrase what you think the speaker said to make sure you understand.

**vocal variation.** Vary vocal volume and rate to best convey verbal messages; avoid a volume that is difficult to understand or a rate that is monotonous, too slow, or too fast.

**win–win solutions.** In interpersonal conflict, focus on win–win solutions rather than solutions in which one person wins and the other loses.

**word style.** Word a speech so it's clear, vivid, appropriate, and personal.

# Bibliography

Abel, G. G., & Harlow, N. (2001). *The stop child molestation book.* Xlibris. www.stopchildmolestation.org/pdfs/study.pdf.

Acor, A. A. (2001). Employers' perceptions of persons with body art and an experimental test regarding eyebrow piercing. *Dissertation Abstracts International: Section B. The Sciences and Engineering, 61,* 3885.

Adrianson, L. (2001). Gender and computer-mediated communication: Group processes in problem solving. *Computers in Human Behavior, 17,* 71–94.

Akinnaso, F. N. (1982). On the differences between spoken and written language. *Language and Speech, 25 (Part 2),* 97–125.

Alessandra, T. (1986). How to listen effectively. *Speaking of success* [Videotape Series]. San Diego, CA: Levitz Sommer Productions.

Altman, I. (1975). *The environment and social behavior.* Monterey, CA: Brooks/Cole.

Altman, I., & Taylor, D. (1973). *Social penetration: The development of interpersonal relationships.* New York: Holt, Rinehart & Winston.

Amato, P. R. (1994). The impact of divorce on men and women in India and the United States. *Journal of Comparative Family Studies, 25,* 207–221.

Andersen, J. F., Andersen, P. A., & Lustig, M. W. (1987, Summer). Opposite sex touch avoidance: A national replication and extension. *Journal of Nonverbal Behavior, 11,* 89–109.

Andersen, P. A. (1991). Explaining intercultural differences in nonverbal communication. In L. A. Samovar & R. E. Porter (Eds.), *Intercultural communication: A reader* (6th ed., pp. 286–296). Belmont, CA: Wadsworth.

Andersen, P. A., & Leibowitz, K. (1978). The development and nature of the construct of touch avoidance. *Environmental Psychology and Nonverbal Behavior, 3,* 89–106.

Anderson, C. J., & Fisher, C. (1991, August). Male–female relationships in the workplace: Perceived motivations in office romance. *Sex Roles, 25,* 163–180.

Angier, N. (1995a, February 14). Powerhouse of senses: Smell, at last, gets its due. *New York Times,* pp. C1, C6.

Angier, N. (1995b, May 9). Scientists mull role of empathy in man and beast. *The New York Times,* pp. C1, C6.

Argyle, M. (1988). *Bodily communication* (2nd ed.). New York: Methuen.

Argyle, M., & Henderson, M. (1984). *The anatomy of relationships: And the rules and skills needed to manage them successfully.* London: Heinemann.

Argyle, M., & Ingham, R. (1972). Gaze, mutual gaze and distance. *Semiotica, 1,* 32–49.

Aronson, E., Wilson, T. D., & Akert, R. M. (2002). *Social psychology: The heart and the mind* (4th ed.). New York: Longman.

Aronson, J., Cohen, J., & Nail, P. (1998). Self-affirmation theory: An update and appraisal. In E. Harmon-Jones & J. S. Mills (Eds.), *Cognitive dissonance theory: Revival with revisions and controversies* (pp. 127–147). Washington, DC: American Psychological Association.

Asch, S. (1946). Forming impressions of personality. *Journal of Abnormal and Social Psychology, 41,* 258–290.

Aune, R. K., & Kikuchi, T. (1993). Effects of language intensity similarity on perceptions of credibility, relational attribu-

tions, and persuasion. *Journal of Language and Social Psychology, 12,* 224–238.

Axtell, R. E. (1990). *Do's and taboos of hosting international visitors.* New York: Wiley.

Axtell, R. E. (1991). *Do's and taboos of public speaking: How to get those butterflies flying in formation.* New York: Wiley.

Axtell, R. E. (1993). *Do's and taboos around the world* (3rd ed.). New York: Wiley.

Ayres, J. (1986). Perceptions of speaking ability: An explanation for stage fright. *Communication Education, 35,* 275–287.

Bach, G. R., & Wyden, P. (1968). *The intimate enemy.* New York: Avon.

Banerjee, N. (2005, January 23). Few but organized, Iraq veterans turn war critics. *The New York Times,* National Report, P. 16.

Baringer, D. K., & McCroskey, J. C. (2000). Immediacy in the classroom: Student immediacy. *Communication Education, 49,* 178–186.

Barker, L. L. (1990). *Communication* (5th ed.). Englewood Cliffs, NJ: PrenticeHall.

Barker, L., Edwards, R., Gaines, C., Gladney, K., & Holley, F. (1980). An investigation of proportional time spent in various communication activities by college students. *Journal of Applied Communication Research, 8,* 101–109.

Barna, L. M. (1988). Stumbling blocks in intercultural communication. In L. A. Samovar & R. E. Porter (Eds.), *Intercultural communication: A reader* (5th ed., pp. 322–330). Belmont, CA: Wadsworth.

Barnlund, D. C. (1970). A transactional model of communication. In J. Akin, A. Goldberg, G. Myers, & J. Stewart (Eds.), *Language behavior: A book of readings in communication.* The Hague: Mouton.

Barnlund, D. C. (1975). Communicative styles in two cultures: Japan and the United States. In A. Kendon, R. M. Harris, & M. R. Key (Eds.), *Organization of behavior in face-to-face interaction.* The Hague: Mouton.

Barnlund, D. C. (1989). *Communicative styles of Japanese and Americans: Images and realities.* Belmont, CA: Wadsworth.

Barrett, L., & Godfrey, T. (1988, November). Listening. *Person Centered Review, 3,* 410–425.

Barry, D. T. (2003, June). Cultural and demographic correlates of self-reported guardedness among East Asian immigrants in the U.S. *International Journal of Psychology, 38,* 150–159.

Basso, K. H. (1972). To give up on words: Silence in Apache culture. In P. P. Giglioli (Ed.), *Language and social context.* New York: Penguin.

Baumeister, R. F., Bushman, B. J., & Campbell, W. K. (2000). Self-esteem, narcissism, and aggression: Does violence result from low self-esteem or from threatened egotism? *Current Directions in Psychological Science, 9,* Issue 1.

Bavelas, J. B. (1990). Can one not communicate? Behaving and communicating: A reply to Motley. *Western Journal of Speech Communication, 54,* 593–602.

Baxter, L. A. (1983). Relationship disengagement: An examination of the reversal hypothesis. *Western Journal of Speech Communication, 47,* 85–98.

Baxter, L. A. (1984). An investigation of compliance-gaining as politeness. *Human Communication Research, 10,* 427–456.

Beatty, M. J. (1988). Situational and predispositional correlates of public speaking anxiety. *Communication Education, 37,* 28–39.

Beatty, M. J., Rudd, J. E., & Valencic, K. M. (1999). A re-evaluation of the verbal aggressiveness scale: One factor or two? *Communication Research Reports, 16,* 10–17.

Beck, A. T. (1988). *Love is never enough.* New York: Harper & Row.

Beebe, S. A., & Masterson, J. T. (2006). *Communicating in small groups: Principles and practices* (8th ed.). Glenview, IL: Scott, Foresman.

Bell, R. A., & Daly, J. A. (1984). The affinity-seeking function of communication. *Communication Monographs, 51,* 91–115.

Bellafiore, D. (2005). Interpersonal conflict and effective communication. www.drbalternatives.com/articles/cc2.html (accessed May 7, 2006).

Benne, K. D., & Sheats, P. (1948). Functional roles of group members. *Journal of Social Issues, 4,* 41–49.

Bennis, W., & Nanus, B. (1985). *Leaders: The strategies for taking charge.* New York: Harper & Row.

Benson, S. G., & Dundis, S. P. (2003, September). Understanding and motivating health care employees: Integrating Maslow's hierarchy of needs, training and technology. *Journal of Nursing Management, 11,* 315–320.

Ben-Ze'ev, A. (2003, July). Primacy, emotional closeness, and openness in cyberspace. *Computers in Human Behavior, 19,* 451–467.

Berg, J. H., & Archer, R. L. (1983). The disclosure–liking relationship. *Human Communication Research, 10,* 269–281.

Berger, C. R., & Bradac, J. J. (1982). *Language and social knowledge: Uncertainty in interpersonal relations.* London: Edward Arnold.

Bernstein, W. M., Stephan, W. G., & Davis, M. H. (1979). Explaining attributions for achievement: A path analytic approach. *Journal of Personality and Social Psychology, 37,* 1810–1821.

Blake, R. R., & Mouton, J. S. (1984). *The managerial grid III* (3rd ed.) Houston, TX: Gulf Publishing.

Blieszner, R., & Adams, R. G. (1992). *Adult friendship.* Newbury Park, CA: Sage.

Blumstein, P., & Schwartz, P. (1983). *American couples: Money, work, sex.* New York: Morrow.

Boase, J., Horrigan, J. B., Wellman, B., & Rainie, L. (2006). The strength of Internet ties. Washington, D. C.: Pew Internet & American Life Project (www.pewinternet.org/).

Bochner, A. (1984). The functions of human communication in interpersonal bonding. In C. C. Arnold & J. W. Bowers (Eds.), *Handbook of rhetorical and communication theory.* Boston: Allyn & Bacon.

Bochner, A., & Kelly, C. (1974). Interpersonal competence: Rationale, philosophy, and implementation of a conceptual framework. *Communication Education, 23,* 279–301.

Bochner, S., & Hesketh, B. (1994). Power distance, individualism/collectivism, and job-related attitudes in a culturally diverse work group. *Journal of Cross-Cultural Psychology, 25,* 233–257.

Bodon, J., Powell, L., & Hickson III, M. (1999). Critiques of gatekeeping in scholarly journals: An analysis of perceptions and data. *Journal of the association for communication administration, 28,* 60–70.

Bok, S. (1978). *Lying: Moral choice in public and private life.* New York: Pantheon.

Bok, S. (1983). *Secrets.* New York: Vintage.

Borden, G. A. (1991). *Cultural orientation: An approach to understanding intercultural communication.* Englewood Cliffs, NJ: Prentice-Hall.

Bourland, D. D., Jr. (1965–66). A linguistic note: Writing in E-prime. *General Semantics Bulletin, 32–33,* 111–114.

Bourland, D. D., Jr., & Johnston, P. D. (Eds.). (1998). *E-prime III! A third anthology.* Concord, CA: International Society for General Semantics.

Bower, B. (2001). Self-illusions come back to bite students. *Science News, 159,* 148.

Brandt, A. (2004, August). Does your online profile say something you wouldn't? *PC World, 22,* August 1.

Brauer, M., Judd, C. M., & Gliner, M. D. (1995, June). The effects of repeated expressions on attitude polarization during group discussions. *Journal of Personality and Social Psychology, 68,* 1014–1029.

Bravo, E., & Cassedy, E. (1992). *The 9 to 5 guide to combating sexual harassment.* New York: Wiley.

Bridges, C. R. (1996). The characteristics of career achievement perceived by African American college administrators. *Journal of Black Studies, 26,* 748–767.

Brilhart, J., & Galanes, G. (1992). *Effective group discussion* (7th ed.). Dubuque, IA: Brown & Benchmark.

Brody, J. E. (1991, April 28). How to foster self-esteem. *The New York Times Magazine, 15,* 26–27.

Brody, J. E. (1994, March 21). Notions of beauty transcend culture, new study suggests. *The New York Times,* p. A14.

Brody, J. E. (2000, April 25). Memories of things that never were. *The New York Times,* p. F8.

Brown, C. T., & Keller, P. W. (1979). *Monologue to dialogue: An exploration of interpersonal communication* (2nd ed.). Englewood Cliffs, NJ: Prentice-Hall.

Brown, P. (1980). How and why are women more polite: Some evidence from a Mayan community. In S. McConnell-Ginet, R. Borker, & M. Furman (Eds.), *Women and language in literature and society* (pp. 111–136). New York: Praeger.

Brown, P., & Levinson, S. C. (1987). *Politeness: Some universals of language usage.* Cambridge, England: Cambridge University Press.

Brownell, J. (1987). Listening: The toughest management skill. *Cornell Hotel and Restaurant Administration Quarterly, 27,* 64–71.

Brownell, J. (2006). *Listening: Attitudes, principles, and skills* (3rd ed.). Boston: Allyn & Bacon.

Bruneau, T. (1985). The time dimension in intercultural communication. In L. A. Samovar & R. E. Porter (Eds.), *Intercultural communication: A reader* (4th ed., pp. 280–289). Belmont, CA: Wadsworth.

Bruneau, T. (1990). Chronemics: The study of time in human interaction. In J. A. DeVito & M. L. Hecht (Eds.), *The nonverbal communication reader* (pp. 301–311). Prospect Heights, IL: Waveland Press.

Buber, M. (1958). *I and thou* (2nd ed.). New York: Scribners.

Bull, R., & Rumsey, N. (1988). *The social psychology of facial appearance.* New York: Springer.

Buller, D. B., & Aune, R. K. (1992). The effects of speech rate similarity on compliance: Application of communication accommodation theory. *Western Journal of Communication, 56,* 37–53.

Buller, D. B., LePoire, B. A., Aune, K., & Eloy, S. (1992). Social perceptions as mediators of the effect of speech rate similarity on compliance. *Human Communication Research, 19,* 286–311.

Bullock, C., McCluskey, M., Stamm, K., Tanaka, K., Torres, M. & Scott, C. (2002). Group affiliations, opinion polarization, and global organization: Views of the World Trade Organization before and after Seattle. *Mass Communication & Society*, 5(4), 433–450.

Burgoon, J. K., & Bacue, A. E. (2003). Nonverbal communication skills. In J. O. Greene & B. R. Burleson (Eds.), *Handbook of communication and social interaction skills* (pp. 179–220). Mahwah, NJ: Erlbaum.

Burgoon, J. K., Berger, C. R., & Waldron, V. R. (2000). Mindfulness and interpersonal communication. *Journal of Social Issues*, 56, 105–127.

Burgoon, J. K., Buller, D. B., & Woodall, W. G. (1996). *Nonverbal communication: The unspoken dialogue* (2nd ed.). New York: McGraw-Hill.

Burgoon, J. K., & Hale, J. L. (1988). Nonverbal expectancy violations: Model elaboration and application to immediacy behaviors. *Communication Monographs*, 55, 58–79.

Burgoon, J. K., & Hoobler, G. D. (2002). Nonverbal signals. In M. L. Knapp & J. A. Daly (Eds.), *Handbook of interpersonal communication* (3rd ed., pp. 240–299). Thousand Oaks, CA: Sage.

Burleson, B. R., Holmstrom, A. J., & Gilstrap, C. M. (2005, December). 'Guys can't say *that* to guys': Four experiments assessing the normative motivation account for deficiencies in the emotional support provided by men. *Communication Monographs*, 72, 468–501.

Burnard, P. (2003, December). Ordinary chat and therapeutic conversation: Phatic communication and mental health nursing. *Journal of Psychiatric and Mental Health Nursing*, 10, 678–682.

Bushman, B. J., & Baumeister, R. F. (1998). Threatened egotism, narcissism, self-esteem, and direct and displaced aggression: Does self-love or self-hate lead to violence? *Journal of Personality and Social Psychology*, 75, 219–229.

Butler, J., Pryor, B., & Grieder, M. (1998, February). Impression formation as a function of male baldness. *Perceptual and Motor Skills*, 86, 347–350.

Butler, P. E. (1981). *Talking to yourself: Learning the language of self-support.* New York: Harper & Row.

Byers, E. S., & Demmons, S. (1999). Sexual satisfaction and sexual self-disclosure within dating relationships. *Journal of Sex Research*, 36, 180–189.

Cai, D. A., & Fink, E. L. (2002, March). Conflict style differences between individualists and collectivists. *Communication Monographs*, 69, 67–87.

Campbell, S. W., & Neer, M. R. (2001). The relationship of communication apprehension and interaction involvement to perceptions of computer-mediated communication. *Communication Research Reports*, 18, 391–398.

Canary, D. J. (2003). Managing interpersonal conflict: A model of events related to strategic choices. In J. O. Greene & B. R. Burleson (Eds.), *Handbook of communication and social interaction skills* (pp. 515–550). Mahwah, NJ: Erlbaum.

Canary, D. J., Cody, M. J., & Manusov, V. L. (2000). *Interpersonal communication: A goals-based approach* (2nd ed.). Boston: St. Bedford/St. Martins.

Cappella, J. N. (1993). The facial feedback hypothesis in human interaction: Review and speculation. *Journal of Language and Social Psychology*, 12, 13–29.

Castleberry, S. B., & Shepherd, C. D. (1993). Effective interpersonal listening and personal selling. *Journal of Personal Selling and Sales Management*, 13, 35–49.

Cate, R. J., Henton, J., Koval, R., Christopher, & Lloyd, S. (1982). Premarital abuse: A social psychological perspective. *Journal of Family Issues*, 3, 79–90.

Cawthon, S. W. (2001). Teaching strategies in inclusive classrooms with deaf students. *Journal of Deaf Studies and Deaf Education*, 6, 212–225.

Chang, H., & Holt, G. R. (1996). The changing Chinese interpersonal world: Popular themes in interpersonal communication books in modern Taiwan. *Communication Quarterly*, 44, 85–106.

Chanowitz, B., & Langer, E. (1981). Premature cognitive commitment. *Journal of Personality and Social Psychology*, 41, 1051–1063.

Childress, H. (2004, May). Teenagers, territory and the appropriation of space. *Childhood: A Global Journal of Child Research*, 11, 195–205.

Chung, L. C., & Ting-Toomey, S. (1999, Spring). Ethnic identity and relational expectations among Asian Americans. *Communication Research Reports*, 16, 157–166.

Clark, H. (1974). The power of positive speaking. *Psychology Today*, 8, 102, 108–111.

Coates, J., & Cameron, D. (1989). *Women, men, and language: Studies in language and linguistics.* London: Longman.

Cohen, J. (2002, May 9). An e-mail affliction: The long goodbye. *The New York Times*, p. G6.

Coleman, P. (2002). *How to say it for couples: Communicating with tenderness, openness, and honesty.* Paramus, NJ: Prentice-Hall.

Colley, A., Todd, Z., Bland, M., Holmes, M., Khanom, N., & Pike, H. (2004, September). Style and content in e-mails and letters to male and female friends. *Journal of Language and Social Psychology*, 23, 369–378.

Collier, M. J. (1991). Conflict competence within African, Mexican, and Anglo American friendships. In S. Ting-Toomey & F. Korzenny (Eds.), *Cross-cultural interpersonal communication* (pp. 132–154). Newbury Park, CA: Sage.

Collins, J. E., & Clark, L. F. (1989). Responsibility and rumination: The trouble with understanding the dissolution of a relationship. *Social Cognition*, 7, 152–173.

Comadena, M. E. (1984). Brainstorming groups: Ambiguity tolerance, communication apprehension, task attraction, and individual productivity. *Small Group Behavior*, 15, 251–254.

Comer, L. B., & Drollinger, T. (1999). Active emphatic listening and selling success: A conceptual framework. *Journal of Personal Selling and Sales Management*, 19, 15–29.

Cook, M. (1971). *Interpersonal perception.* Baltimore: Penguin.

Cooley, C. Horton. (1922). *Human nature and the social order* (Rev. ed.). New York: Scribners.

Coombes, A. (2003, June 30). E-termination: Employees are getting fired for e-mail infractions. Retrieved July 14, 2003, from CBS.MarketWatch.com.

Cooper, A., & Sportolari, L. (1997). Romance in cyberspace: Understanding online attraction. *Journal of Sex Education and Therapy*, 22, 7–14.

Coover, G. E., & Murphy, S. T. (2000). The communicated self: Exploring the interaction between self and social context. *Human Communication Research*, 26, 125–147.

Cornwell, B., & Lundgren, D. C. (2001). Love on the Internet: Involvement and misrepresentation in romantic relationships in cyberspace vs. realspace. *Computers in Human Behavior*, 17, 197–211.

Cragan, J. F., & Wright, D. W. (1990). Small group communication research of the 1980s: A synthesis and critique. *Communication Studies, 41*, 212–236.

Crawford, M. (1994, October). Rethinking the romance: Teaching the content and function of gender stereotypes in the Psychology of Women course. *Teaching of Psychology, 21*, 151–153.

Crohn, J. (1995). *Mixed matches.* New York: Fawcett.

Crowley, A. (1999, August 30). Project leaders wanted. *PC Week,* 76.

Davis, M. S. (1973). *Intimate relations.* New York: Free Press.

Davison, W. P. (1983). The third-person effects and the differential impact in negative political advertising. *Journalism Quarterly, 68*, 680–688.

Davitz, J. R. (Ed.). (1964). *The communication of emotional meaning.* New York: McGraw-Hill.

Deal, J. E., & Wampler, K. S. (1986). Dating violence: The primacy of previous experience. *Journal of Social and Personal Relationships, 3*, 457–471.

deBono, E. (1976). *Teaching thinking.* New York: Penguin.

deBono, E. (1987). *The six thinking hats.* New York: Penguin.

Derlega, V. J., Winstead, B. A., & Wong, P. T. P., & Greenspan, M. (1987). Self-disclosure and relationship development: An attributional analysis. In M. E. Roloff & G. R. Miller (Eds.), *Interpersonal processes: New directions in communication research* (pp. 172–187). Thousand Oaks, CA: Sage.

Derlega, V. J., Winstead, B., Wong, P. T. P., & Hunter, S. (1985). Gender effects in an initial encounter: A case where men exceed women in disclosure. *Journal of Social and Personal Relationships, 2*, 25–44.

DeStephen, R., & Hirokawa, R. (1988). Small group consensus: Stability of group support of the decision, task process, and group relationships. *Small Group Behavior, 19*, 227–239.

DeTurck, M. A. (1987). When communication fails: Physical aggression as a compliance-gaining strategy. *Communication Monographs, 54*, 106–112.

DeVito, J. A. (1965). Comprehension factors in oral and written discourse of skilled communicators. *Communication Monographs, 32*, 124–128.

DeVito, J. A. (1981). *The psychology of speech and language: An introduction to psycholinguistics.* Washington, DC: University Press of America.

DeVito, J. A. (1989). *The nonverbal communication workbook.* Prospect Heights, IL: Waveland Press.

DeVito, J. A. (1996). *Brainstorms: How to think more creatively about communication (or about anything else).* New York: Longman.

DeVito, J. A. (2008). *Interpersonal messages: Communication and relationship skills.* Boston: Allyn & Bacon.

DeVito, J. A., & Hecht, M. L. (Eds.). (1990). *The nonverbal communication reader.* Prospect Heights, IL: Waveland Press.

Dillard, J. P., & Marshall, L. J. (2003). Persuasion as a social skill. In J. O. Greene & B. R. Burleson (Eds.), *Handbook of communication and social interaction skills* (pp. 479–514). Mahwah, NJ: Erlbaum.

Dindia, K., & Fitzpatrick, M. A. (1985). Marital communication: Three approaches compared. In S. Duck & D. Perlman (Eds.), *Understanding personal relationships: An interdisciplinary approach* (pp. 137–158). Newbury Park, CA: Sage.

Dion, K., Berscheid, E., & Walster, E. (1972). What is beautiful is good. *Journal of Personality and Social Psychology, 24*, 285–290.

Dodd, C. H. (1995). *Dynamics of intercultural communication.* Dubuque, IA: William C. Brown.

Dolgin, K. G., Meyer, L., & Schwartz, J. (1991). Effects of gender, target's gender, topic, and self-esteem on disclosure to best and middling friends. *Sex Roles, 25*, 311–329.

Donahue, W. A., with Kolt, R. (1992). *Managing interpersonal conflict.* Thousand Oaks, CA: Sage.

Dorland, J. M., & Fisher, A. R. (2001, July). Gay, lesbian, and bisexual individuals' perception: An analogue study. *Counseling Psychologis, 29*, 532–547.

Dosey, M., & Meisels, M. (1969). Personal space and self-protection. *Journal of Personality and Social Psychology, 38*, 959–965.

Dovidio, J. F., Gaertner, S. E., Kawakami, K., & Hodson, G. (2002). Why can't we just get along? Interpersonal biases and interracial distrust. *Cultural Diversity and Ethnic Minority Psychology, 8*, 88–102.

Dresser, N. (1996). *Multicultural manners: New rules of etiquette for a changing society.* New York: Wiley.

Drews, D. R., Allison, C. K., & Probst, J. R. (2000). Behavioral and self-concept differences in tattooed and nontattooed college students. *Psychological Reports, 86*, 475–481.

Dreyfuss, H. (1971). *Symbol sourcebook.* New York: McGraw-Hill.

Driskell, J., Olmstead, B., & Salas, E. (1993). Task cues, dominance cues, and influence in task groups. *Journal of Applied Psychology, 78*, 51–60.

Dsilva, M., & Whyte, L. O. (1998). Cultural differences in conflict styles: Vietnamese refugees and established residents. *The Howard Journal of Communication, 9*, 57–68.

Duval, T. S., & Silva, P. J. (2002). Self-awareness, probability of improvement, and the self-serving bias. *Journal of Personality and Social Psychology, 82*, 49–61.

Eden, D. (1992). Leadership and expectations: Pygmalion effects and other self-fulfilling prophecies in organizations. *Leadership Quarterly, 3*, 271–305.

Ehrenhaus, P. (1988). Silence and symbolic expression. *Communication Monographs, 55*, 41–57.

Einhorn, L. (2006, April). Using e-prime and English minus absolutisms to provide self-empathy. *Etc.: A Review of General Semantics, 63*, 180–186.

Einstein, E. (1995). Success or sabotage: Which self-fulfilling prophecy will the stepfamily create? In D. K. Huntley (Ed.), *Understanding stepfamilies: Implications for assessment and treatment.* Alexandria, VA: American Counseling Association.

Ekman, P. (1985). *Telling lies: Clues to deceit in the marketplace, politics, and marriage.* New York: Norton.

Ekman, P., & Friesen, W. V. (1969). The repertoire of nonverbal behavior: Categories, origins, usage, and coding. *Semiotica, 1*, 49–98.

Ekman, P., Friesen, W. V., & Ellsworth, P. (1972). *Emotion in the human face: Guidelines for research and an integration of findings.* New York: Pergamon Press.

Elfenbein, H. A., & Ambady, N. (2002). Is there an in-group advantage in emotion recognition? *Psychological Bulletin, 128*, 243–249.

Exline, R. V., Ellyson, S. L., & Long, B. (1975). Visual behavior as an aspect of power role relationships. In P. Pliner, L. Krames, & T. Alloway (Eds.), *Nonverbal communication of aggression.* New York: Plenum Press.

Fengler, A. P. (1974). Romantic love in courtship: Divergent paths of male and female students. *Journal of Comparative Family Studies,* 134–139.

Festinger, L. (1954). A theory of social comparison processes. *Human Relations, 7*, 117–140.

Fielder, F. E. (1967). *A theory of leadership effectiveness.* New York: McGraw-Hill.

Fisher, D. R. (1998). Rumoring theory and the Internet: A framework for analyzing the grass roots. *Social Science Computer Review, 16,* 158–168.

Fitzpatrick, M. A., Jandt, F. E., Myrick, F. L., & Edgar, T. (1994). Gay and lesbian couple relationships. In Ringer, R. J. (Ed.), *Queer words, queer images: Communication and the construction of homosexuality* (pp. 265–285). New York: New York University Press.

Folger, J. P., Poole, M. S., & Stutman, R. K. (1997). *Working through conflict: A communication perspective* (3rd ed.). New York: Longman.

Forbes, G. B. (2001). College students with tattoos and piercings: Motives, family experiences, personality factors, and perception by others. *Psychological Reports, 89,* 774–786.

Fraser, B. (1990). Perspectives on politeness. *Journal of Pragmatics, 14,* 219–236.

French, J. R. P., Jr., & Raven, B. (1968). The bases of social power. In D. Cartwright & A. Zander (Eds.), *Group dynamics: Research and theory* (3rd ed., pp. 259–269). New York: Harper & Row.

Frey, K. J., & Eagly, A. H. (1993, July). Vividness can undermine the persuasiveness of messages. *Journal of Personality and Social Psychology, 65,* 32–44.

Friedkin, N. E. (1999, December). Choice shift and group polarization. *American Sociological Review, 64,* 856–875.

Furlow, F. B. (1996). The smell of love. *Psychology Today,* 38–45.

Galvin, K., Bylund, C., & Brommel, B. J. (2004). *Family communication: Cohesion and change* (6th ed.). New York: Longman.

Gamble, T.K., & Gamble, M. W. (2003). *The gender communication connection.* Boston: Houghton Mifflin.

Gao, G., & Gudykunst, W. B. (1995). Attributional confidence, perceived similarity, and network involvement in Chinese and American romantic relationships. *Communication Quarterly, 43,* 431–445.

Gelfand, M. J., Nishii, L. H., Holcombe, K. M., Dyer, N., Ohbuchi, K., & Fukuno, M. (2001). Cultural influences on cognitive representations of conflict: Interpretations of conflict episodes in the United States and Japan. *Journal of Applied Psychology, 86,* 1059–1074.

Gelles, R., & Cornell, C. (1985). *Intimate violence in families.* Newbury Park, CA: Sage.

Giles, H., Mulac, A., Bradac, J. J., & Johnson, P. (1987). Speech accommodation theory: The first decade and beyond. In M. L. McLaughlin (Ed.), *Communication yearbook 10* (pp. 13–48). Thousand Oaks, CA: Sage.

Gladstone, G. L., & Parker, G. B. (2002, June). When you're smiling, does the whole world smile for you? *Australasian Psychiatry, 10,* 144–146.

Glucksberg, S., & Danks, J. H. (1975). *Experimental psycholinguistics: An introduction.* Hillsdale, NJ: Erlbaum.

Goffman, E. (1967). *Interaction ritual: Essays on face-to-face behavior.* New York: Pantheon.

Goffman, E. (1971). *Relations in public: Microstudies of the public order.* New York: HarperCollins.

Goldin-Meadow, S., Nusbaum, H., Kelly, S. D., & Wagner, S. (2001). Gesture—psychological aspects. *Psychological Science, 12,* 516–522.

Goldsmith, D. J., & Fulfs, P. A. (1999). "You just don't have the evidence": An analysis of claims and evidence. In M. E. Roloff (Ed.), *Communication yearbook 22* (pp. 1–49). Thousand Oaks, CA: Sage.

Goleman, D. (1995a). *Emotional intelligence.* New York: Bantam.

Goleman, D. (1995b). For man and beast, language of love shares many traits. *The New York Times,* pp. C1, C9.

Gonzalez, A., & Zimbardo, P. G. (1985). Time in perspective. *Psychology Today, 19,* 20–26.

Goode, E. (2000, August 8). How culture molds habits of thought. *The New York Times,* pp. F1, F8.

Goodwin, R., & Lee, I. (1994). Taboo topics among Chinese and English friends: A cross-cultural comparison. *Journal of Cross-Cultural Psychology, 25,* 325–338.

Gorden, W. I., & Nevins, R. J. (1993). *We mean business: Building communication competence in business and professions.* New York: HarperCollins.

Gordon, T. (1975). *P.E.T.: Parent effectiveness training.* New York: New American Library.

Gosling, S. D., Ko, S. J., Mannarelli, T., & Morris, M. E. (2002, March). A room with a cue: Personality judgments based on offices and bedrooms. *Journal of Personality and Social Psychology, 82,* 379–398.

Gottman, J. (2004). 12-year study of gay & lesbian couples. www.gottman.com/research/projects/gaylesbian, (accessed March 25, 2006).

Graham, E. E. (1994). Interpersonal communication motives scale. In R. B. Rubin, P. Palmgreen, & H. E. Sypher (Eds.), *Communication research measures: A sourcebook* (pp. 211– 216). New York, Guilford.

Graham, E. E. (1997). Turning points and commitment in post-divorce relationships. *Communication Monographs, 64,* 350–368.

Graham, E. E., Barbato, C. A., & Perse, E. M. (1993). The interpersonal communication motives model. *Communication Quarterly, 41,* 172–186.

Graham, J. A., & Argyle, M. (1975). The effects of different patterns of gaze combined with different facial expressions on impression formation. *Journal of Movement Studies, 1,* 178–182.

Graham, J. A., Bitti, P. R., & Argyle, M. (1975). A cross-cultural study of the communication of emotion by facial and gestural cues. *Journal of Human Movement Studies, 1,* 68–77.

Greene, J. O., & Burleson, B. R. (Eds.). (2003). *Handbook of communication and social interaction skills.* Mahwah, NJ: Erlbaum.

Grice, G. L., & Skinner, J. F. (2004). *Mastering public speaking* (5th ed.). Boston: Allyn & Bacon.

Griffin, E., & Sparks, G. G. (1990). Friends forever: A longitudinal exploration of intimacy in same-sex friends and platonic pairs. *Journal of Social and Personal Relationships, 7,* 29–46.

Gross, L. (1991). The contested closet: The ethics and politics of outing. *Critical Studies in Mass Communication, 8,* 352–388.

Gross, T., Turner, E., & Cederholm, L. (1987, June). Building teams for global operation. *Management Review,* 32–36.

Gu, Y. (1997). Polite phenomena in modern Chinese. *Journal of Pragmatics, 14,* 237–257.

Gudykunst, W. B. (Ed.). (1983). *Intercultural communication theory: Current perspectives.* Newbury Park, CA: Sage.

Gudykunst, W. B. (1991). *Bridging differences: Effective intergroup communication.* Newbury Park, CA: Sage.

Gudykunst, W. B. (1994). *Bridging differences: Effective intergroup communication* (2nd ed.). Newbury Park, CA: Sage.

Gudykunst, W. B., & Kim, Y. Y. (1984). *Communicating with strangers: An approach to intercultural communication.* New York: Random House.

Gudykunst, W. B., & Kim, Y. Y. (Eds.). (1992). *Readings on communication with strangers: An approach to intercultural communication.* New York: McGraw-Hill.

Gudykunst, W. B., & Nishida, T. (1984). Individual and cultural influence on uncertainty reduction. *Communication Monographs, 51,* 23–36.

Gudykunst, W. B., Nishida, T., & Chua, E. (1987). Perceptions of social penetration in Japanese–North American dyads. *International Journal of Intercultural Relations, 11,* 171–189.

Gudykunst, W. B., Yang, S., & Nishida, T. (1985). A cross-cultural test of uncertainty reduction theory: Comparisons of acquaintant, friend, and dating relationships in Japan, Korea, and the United States. *Human Communication Research, 11,* 407–454.

Gueguen, N. (2003, Summer). Help on the Web: The effect of the same first name between the sender and the receptor in a request made by e-mail. *Psychological Record, 53,* 459–466.

Guerrero, L. K., & Andersen, P. A. (1991). The waxing and waning of relational intimacy: Touch as a function of relational stage, gender and touch avoidance. *Journal of Social and Personal Relationships, 8,* 147–165.

Guerrero, L. K., & Andersen, P. A. (1994). Patterns of matching and initiation: Touch behavior and touch avoidance across romantic relationship stages. *Journal of Nonverbal Behavior 18,* 137–153.

Guerrero, L. K., DeVito, J. A., & Hecht, M. L. (Eds.). (1999). *The nonverbal communication reader: Class and contemporary readings* (2nd ed.). Prospect Heights, IL: Waveland Press.

Haar, B. F., & Krabe, B. (1999). Strategies for resolving interpersonal conflicts in adolescence: A German–Indonesian comparison. *Journal of Cross-Cultural Psychology, 30,* 667–683.

Hackman, M. Z., & Johnson, C. E. (1991). *Leadership: A communication perspective.* Prospect Heights, IL: Waveland Press.

Haga, Y. (1988). Traits de langage et caractère Japonais. *Cahiers de Sociologie Economique et Culturelle, 9,* 105–109.

Hall, E. T. (1959). *The silent language.* Garden City, NY: Doubleday.

Hall, E. T. (1963). A system for the notation of proxemic behavior. *American Anthropologist, 65,* 1003–1026.

Hall, E. T. (1966). *The hidden dimension.* Garden City, NY: Doubleday.

Hall, E. T. (1976). *Beyond culture.* Garden City, NY: Doubleday.

Hall, E. T., & Hall, M. R. (1987). *Hidden differences: Doing business with the Japanese.* Garden City, NY: Doubleday.

Hall, J. A. (1984). *Nonverbal sex differences.* Baltimore: Johns Hopkins University Press.

Hall, J. A. (1998). How big are nonverbal sex differences? The case of smiling and sensitivity to nonverbal cues. In D. J. Canary & K. Dindia (Eds.), *Sex differences and similarities in communication: Critical essays and empirical investigations of sex and gender in interaction* (pp. 155–178). Mahwah, NJ: Erlbaum.

Haney, W. (1973). *Communication and organizational behavior: Text and cases* (3rd ed.). Homewood, IL: Irwin.

Hanley, S. J., & Abell, S. C. (2002, Fall). Maslow and relatedness: Creating an interpersonal model of self-actualization. *Journal of Humanistic Psychology, 42,* 37–56.

Hart, F. (1990). The construction of masculinity in men's friendships: Misogyny, heterosexuality, and homophobia. *Resources for Feminist Research, 19,* 60–67.

Hart, R. P., Carlson, R. E., & Eadie, W. F. (1980). Attitudes toward communication and the assessment of rhetorical sensitivity. *Communication Monographs, 47,* 1–22.

Hastings, S. O. (2000). "Egocasting" in the avoidance of disclosure: An intercultural perspective. In S. Petronio (Ed.), *Balancing the secrets of private disclosures.* (pp. 235–248). Mahwah, NJ: Erlbaum.

Hatfield, E., & Rapson, R. L. (1992). Similarity and attraction in close relationships. *Communication Monographs, 59,* 209–212.

Hatfield, E., & Rapson, R. L. (1996). *Love and sex: Cross-cultural perspectives.* Boston: Allyn & Bacon.

Hatfield, E., & Traupman, J. (1981). Intimate relationships: A perspective from equity theory. In S. Duck & R. Gilmour (Eds.), *Personal relationships: Vol. 1. Studying personal relationships* (pp. 165–178). New York: Academic Press.

Hayakawa, S. I., & Hayakawa, A. R. (1989). *Language in thought and action* (5th ed.). New York: Harcourt Brace Jovanovich.

Hays, R. B. (1989). The day-to-day functioning of close versus casual friendships. *Journal of Social and Personal Relationships, 6,* 21–37.

Hecht, M. L. (1978). The conceptualization and measurement of interpersonal communication satisfaction. *Human Communication Research, 4,* 253–264.

Hecht, M. L., Collier, M. J., & Ribeau, S. (1993). *African American communication: Ethnic identity and cultural interpretation.* Thousand Oaks, CA: Sage.

Heenehan, M. (1997). *Networking.* New York: Random House.

Hendrick, C., & Hendrick, S. (1990). A relationship-specific version of the love attitudes scale. In J. W. Heulip (Ed.), Handbook of replication research in the behavioral and social sciences [Special issue]. *Journal of Social Behavior and Personality, 5,* 239–254.

Hendrick, C., Hendrick, S., Foote, F. H., & Slapion-Foote, M. J. (1984). Do men and women love differently? *Journal of Social and Personal Relationships, 1,* 177–195.

Henley, N. M. (1977). *Body politics: Power, sex, and nonverbal communication.* Englewood Cliffs, NJ: Prentice-Hall.

Herrick, J. A. (2004). *Argumentation: Understanding and shaping arguments.* State College, PA: Strata.

Hersey, P., Blanchard, K. H., & Johnson, D. E. (2001). *Management of organizational behavior: Leading human resources* (8th ed.). Upper Saddle River, NJ: Prentice-Hall.

Hess, E. H. (1975). *The tell-tale eye.* New York: Van Nostrand Reinhold.

Hewitt, J. P. (1998). *The myth of self-esteem: Finding happiness and solving problems in America.* New York: St. Martin's Press.

Hewitt, J., & Stokes, Randall. (1975). Disclaimers. *American Sociological Review, 40,* 1–11.

Hickson, M. L., & Stacks, D. W. (1989). *NVC: Nonverbal communication: Studies and applications* (2nd ed.). Dubuque, IA: William C. Brown.

Hill, S. E. K. (1997). Team leadership theory. In P. G. Northouse (Ed.), *Leadership: Theory and practice* (pp. 159–183). Thousand Oaks, CA: Sage.

Himle, J. A., Abelson, J. L., & Haghightgou, H. (1999, August). Effect of alcohol on social phobic anxiety. *American Journal of Psychiatry, 156,* 1237–1243.

Hocker, J. L., & Wilmot, W. W. (1985). *Interpersonal conflict* (2nd ed.). Dubuque, IA: William C. Brown.

Hoffner, C., et al. (2001, June). The third-person effect in perceptions of the influence of television violence. *Journal of Communication, 51,* 283–299.

Hofstede, G. (1997). *Cultures and organizations: Software of the mind.* New York: McGraw-Hill.

Hoft, N. L. (1995). *International technical communication: How to export information about high technology.* New York: Wiley.

Holmes, J. (1995). *Women, men and politeness.* New York: Longman.

Horenstein, V. D., & Downey, J. L. (2003). A cross-cultural investigation of self-disclosure. *North American Journal of Psychology, 5,* 373–386.

Huston, M., & Schwartz, P. (1995). The relationships of lesbians and gay men. In J. T. Wood & S. Duck (Eds.), *Under-studied relationships: Off the beaten track* (pp. 89–121). Thousand Oaks, CA: Sage.

Infante, D. A. (1988). *Arguing constructively.* Prospect Heights, IL: Waveland Press.

Infante, D. A., & Rancer, A. (1982). A conceptualization and measure of argumentativeness. *Journal of Personality Assessment, 46,* 72–80.

Infante, D. A., Rancer, A.S., & Womack, D. F. (2002) Building communication theory (4th ed.). Prospect Heights, IL: Waveland Press.

Infante, D. A., & Wigley, C. J. (1986). Verbal aggressiveness: An interpersonal model and measure. *Communication Monographs, 53,* 61–69.

Insel, P. M., & Jacobson, L. F. (Eds.). (1975). *What do you expect? An inquiry into self-fulfilling prophecies.* Menlo Park, CA: Cummings.

Jablin, F. M. (1981). Cultivating imagination: Factors that enhance and inhibit creativity in brainstorming groups. *Human Communication Research, 7,* 245–258.

Jacobson, D. (1999). Impression formation in cyberspace: Online expectations and offline experiences in text-based virtual communities. *Journal of Computer Mediated Communication, 5.*

Jaksa, J. A., & Pritchard, M. S. (1994). *Communication ethics: Methods of analysis* (2nd ed.). Belmont, CA: Wadsworth.

Jambor, E., & Elliott, M. (2005, Winter). Self-esteem and coping strategies among deaf students. *Journal of Deaf Studies and Deaf Education, 10,* 63–81.

James, D. L. (1995). *The executive guide to Asia-Pacific communications.* New York: Kodansha International.

Jamieson, K. H., & Campbell, K. K. (2001). *The interplay of influence* (5th ed.). Belmont, CA: Wadsworth.

Jandt, F. E. (2003). *Intercultural communication.* Thousand Oaks, CA: Sage.

Janis, I. (1983). *Victims of group thinking: A psychological study of foreign policy decisions and fiascoes* (2nd Rev. ed.). Boston: Houghton Mifflin.

Janus, S. S., & Janus, C. L. (1993). *The Janus report on sexual behavior.* New York: Wiley.

Jaworski, A. (1993). *The power of silence: Social and pragmatic perspectives.* Newbury Park, CA: Sage.

Jessmer, S. L., & Anderson, D. (2001). The effect of politeness and grammar on user perceptions of electronic mail. *North American Journal of Psychology, 3,* 331–346.

Johannesen, R. L. (1990). *Ethics in human communication* (3rd ed.). Prospect Heights, IL: Waveland Press.

Johansson, W., & Percy, W. A. (1994). *Outing: Shattering the conspiracy of silence.* New York: Harrington Park Press.

Johnson, C. E. (1987). An introduction to powerful and powerless talk in the classroom. *Communication Education, 36,* 167–172.

Johnson, S. D., & Bechler, C. (1998). Examining the relationship between listening effectiveness and leadership emergence: Perceptions, behaviors, and recall. *Small Group Research, 29,* 452–471.

Johnson, S. M., & O'Connor, E. (2002). *The gay baby boom: The psychology of gay parenthood.* New York: New York University Press.

Joinson, A. N. (2001). Self-disclosure in computer-mediated communication: The role of self-awareness and visual anonymity. *European Journal of Social Psychology, 31,* 177–192.

Joinson, A. N. (2004, August). Self-esteem, interpersonal risk, and preference for e-mail to face-to-face communication. *CyberPsychology and Behavior, 7,* 472–478.

Jones, E. E. (1990). *Interpersonal perception.* New York: W. H. Freeman.

Jones, Q., Ravid, G., & Rafaeli, S. (2004, June). Information overload and the message dynamics of online interaction spaces: A theoretical model and empirical exploration. *Information Systems Research, 15,* 194–210.

Jones, S., & Yarbrough, A. E. (1985). A naturalistic study of the meanings of touch. *Communication Monographs, 52,* 19–56.

Jourard, S. M. (1968). *Disclosing man to himself.* New York: Van Nostrand Reinhold.

Jourard, S. M. (1971a). *Self-disclosure.* New York: Wiley.

Jourard, S. M. (1971b). *The transparent self* (Rev. ed.). New York: Van Nostrand Reinhold.

Judge, T. A., & Cable, D. M. (2004). The effect of physical height on workplace success and income. *Journal of Applied Psychology, 89,* 428–441.

Kanner, B. (1989, April 3). Color schemes. *New York Magazine,* pp. 22–23.

Kelley, H. H., & Thibaut, J. W. (1978). *Interpersonal relations: A theory of interdependence.* New York: Wiley/Interscience.

Kelly, P. K. (1994). *Team decision-making techniques.* Irvine, CA: Richard Chang Associates.

Kennedy, C. W., & Camden, C. T. (1988). A new look at interruptions. *Western Journal of Speech Communication, 47,* 45–58.

Keshavarz, M. H. (1988). Forms of address in post-revolutionary Iranian Persian: A sociolinguistic analysis. *Language in Society, 17,* 565–575.

Kesselman-Turkel, J., & Peterson, F. (1982). *Note-taking made easy.* Chicago: Contemporary Books.

Ketcham, H. (1958). *Color planning for business and industry.* New York: Harper.

Keyes, R. (1980). *The height of your life.* New York: Warner.

Kiel, J. M. (1999). Reshaping Maslow's hierarchy of needs to reflect today's education and managerial philosophies. *Journal of Instructional Psychology, 26,* 167–168.

Kim, H. J. (1991). Influence of language and similarity on initial intercultural attraction. In S. Ting-Toomey & F. Korzenny (Eds.), *Cross-cultural interpersonal communication* (pp. 213–229). Newbury Park, CA: Sage.

Kim, M., & Sharkey, W. F. (1995). Independent and interdependent construals of self: Explaining cultural patterns of interpersonal communication in multi-cultural organizational settings. *Communication Quarterly, 43,* 20–38.

Kindler, H. S. (1996). *Managing disagreement constructively* (Rev. ed.). Menlo Park, CA: Crisp Publications.

Kindred, J., & Roper, S. L. (2004). Making connections via instant messenger (IM): Student use of IM to maintain personal relationships. *Qualitative Research Reports in Communication, 5,* 48–54.

Kirkpatrick, C., & Caplow, T. (1945). Courtship in a group of Minnesota students. *American Journal of Sociology, 51,* 114–125.

Kleinfeld, N. R. (1992, October 25). The smell of money. *The New York Times,* Section 9, pp. 1, 8.

Kleinke, C. L. (1986). *Meeting and understanding people*. New York: W. H. Freeman.

Knapp, M. L. (1984). *Interpersonal communication and human relationships*. Boston: Allyn & Bacon.

Knapp, M. L., & Hall, J. (2005). *Nonverbal communication in human interaction* (6th ed.). Fort Worth, TX: Harcourt Brace Jovanovich.

Knapp, M. L., Hart, R. P., Friedrich, G. W., & Shulman, G. M. (1973). The rhetoric of goodbye: Verbal and nonverbal correlates of human leave-taking. *Communication Monographs, 40*, 182–198.

Knapp, M. L., & Vangelisti, A. (2000). *Interpersonal communication and human relationships* (4th ed.). Boston: Allyn & Bacon.

Knobloch, L. K., & Solomon, D. H. (1999, Winter). Measuring the sources and content of relational uncertainty. *Communication Studies, 50*, 261–278.

Kochman, T. (1981). *Black and white: Styles in conflict*. Chicago: University of Chicago Press.

Koerner, A. F., & Fitzpatrick, M. A. (2002, Fall). You never leave your family in a fight: The impact of family of origin of conflict behavior in romantic relationships. *Communication Studies, 53*, 234–252.

Kollock, P., & Smith, M. (1996). Managing the virtual commons: Cooperation and conflict in computer communities. In S. Herring (Ed.), *Computer-mediated communication: Linguistic, social, and cross-cultural perspectives* (pp. 109–128). Amsterdam: John Benjamins.

Komarovsky, M. (1964). *Blue collar marriage*. New York: Random House.

Koppelman, K. L., with Goodhart, R. L. (2005). *Understanding human differences: Multicultural education for a diverse America*. Boston: Allyn & Bacon.

Korda, M. (1975). *Power! How to get it, how to use it*. New York: Ballantine.

Korzybski, A. (1933). *Science and sanity*. Lakeville, CT: International Non-Aristotelian Library.

Kramarae, C. (1999). The language and nature of the Internet: The meaning of Global English. *New Media & Society, 1*, 47–53.

Kramer, R. (1997). Leading by listening: An empirical test of Carl Rogers's theory of human relationship using interpersonal assessments of leaders by followers. *Dissertation Abstracts International: Section A. Humanities and Social Sciences, 58*, 514.

Krivonos, P. D., & Knapp, M. L. (1975). Initiating communication: What do you say when you say hello? *Central States Speech Journal, 26*, 115–125.

Krolokke, C., & Sorensen, A. S. (2006). *Gender communication theories and analyses: From silence to performance*. Thousand Oaks, CA: Sage.

Kurdek, L. A. (1994). Areas of conflict for gay, lesbian, and heterosexual couples: What couples argue about influences relationship satisfaction. *Journal of Marriage and the Family, 56*, 923–934.

Kurdek, L. A. (1995). Developmental changes in relationship quality in gay and lesbian cohabiting couples. *Developmental Psychology, 31*, 86–93.

Kurdek, L. A. (2003, August). Differences between gay and lesbian cohabiting couples. *Journal of Social and Personal Relationships, 20*, 411–436.

Kurdek, L. A. (2004, November). Are gay and lesbian cohabitating couples really different from heterosexual married couples? *Journal of Marriage and Family, 66*, 880–900.

Laing, R. D., Phillipson, H., & Lee, A. R. (1966). *Interpersonal perception*. New York: Springer.

Lakoff, R. (1975). *Language and women's place*. New York: Harper & Row.

Lamb, G. M. (2005). Product placement pushes into print. www.csmonitor.com (accessed March 20, 2006).

Lamm, K., & Lamm, K. (1999). *10,000 ideas for term papers, projects, reports, and speeches* (5th ed.). New York: Arco.

Langer, E. J. (1989). *Mindfulness*. Reading, MA: Addison-Wesley.

Lantz, A. (2001). Meetings in a distributed group of experts: Comparing face-to-face, chat and collaborative virtual environments. *Behaviour and Information Technology, 20*, 111–117.

Lanzetta, J. T., Cartwright-Smith, J., & Kleck, R. E. (1976). Effects of nonverbal dissimulations on emotional experience and autonomic arousal. *Journal of Personality and Social Psychology, 33*, 354–370.

Larsen, R. J., Kasimatis, M., & Frey, K. (1992). Facilitating the furrowed brow: An unobtrusive test of the facial feedback hypothesis applied to unpleasant affect. *Cognition and Emotion, 6*, 321–338.

Lauer, C. S. (2003, February, 10). Listen to this. *Modern Healthcare, 33*, 34.

Lawson, W. (2005, November–December). Blips on the gaydar. *Psychology Today, 38*, 30.

Lea, M., & Spears, R. (1995). Love at first byte? Building personal relationships over computer networks. In J. T. Wood & S. Duck (Eds.), *Under-studied relationships: Off the beaten track* (pp. 197–233). Thousand Oaks, CA: Sage.

Leathers, D. G. (1997). *Successful nonverbal communication: Principles and applications* (3rd ed.). Boston, MA: Allyn & Bacon.

Lederer, W. J. (1984). *Creating a good relationship*. New York: Norton.

Lederman, L. (1990). Assessing educational effectiveness: The focus group interview as a technique for data collection. *Communication Education, 39*, 117–127.

Lee, A. M., & Lee, E. B. (1972). *The fine art of propaganda*. San Francisco: International Society for General Semantics.

Lee, A. M., & Lee, E. B. (1995). The iconography of propaganda analysis. *Etc.: A Review of General Semantics, 52*, 13–17.

Lee, C. M., & Gudykunst, W. B. (2001). Attraction in initial interethnic interactions. *Journal of Intercultural Relations, 25*, 373–387.

Lee, F. (1993). Being polite and keeping MUM: How bad news is communicated in organizational hierarchies. *Journal of Applied Social Psychology, 23*, 1124–1149.

Lee, H. O., & Boster, F. J. (1992). Collectivism–individualism in perceptions of speech rate: A cross-cultural comparison. *Journal of Cross-Cultural Psychology, 23*, 377–388.

Lee, J. A. (1976). *The colors of love*. New York: Bantam.

Lee, K. (2000, November 1). Information overload threatens employee productivity. *Employee Benefit News*, Securities Data Publishing, p. 1.

Leung, K. (1988, March). Some determinants of conflict avoidance. *Journal of Cross-Cultural Psychology, 19*, 125–136.

Leung, S. A. (2001). Editor's introduction. *Asian Journal of Counseling, 8*, 107–109.

Lever, J. (1995). The 1995 Advocate survey of sexuality and relationships: The women, lesbian sex survey. *The Advocate, 687/688*, 22–30.

Levine, D. (2000). Virtual attraction: What rocks your boat. *CyberPsychology and Behavior, 3*, 565–573.

Levine, M. (2004, June 1). Tell the doctor all your problems, but keep it to less than a minute. *The New York Times*, P. F6.

LeVine, R., & Bartlett, K. (1984). Pace of life, punctuality, and coronary heart disease in six countries. *Journal of Cross-Cultural Psychology, 15*, 233–255.

Lewin, K. (1947). *Human relations*. New York: Harper and Row.

Lewis, D. (1989). *The secret language of success*. New York: Carroll & Graf.

Lewis, P. H. (1995, November 13). The new Internet gatekeepers. *New York Times*, D1, D6.

Lin, Y. W., & Rusbult, C. E. (1995). Commitment to dating relationships and cross-sex friendships in America and China. *Journal of Social and Personal Relationships, 12*, 7–26.

Lloyd, S. R. (1995). *Developing positive assertiveness* (Rev. ed.). Menlo Park, CA: Crisp Publications.

Lucas, S. (2004). *The art of public speaking* (8th ed.). New York: McGraw-Hill.

Luft, J. (1984). *Group process: An introduction of group dynamics* (3rd ed.). Palo Alto, CA: Mayfield.

Lukens, J. (1978). Ethnocentric speech. *Ethnic Groups, 2*, 35–53.

Lumsden, G., & Lumsden, D. (1993). *Communicating in groups and teams*. Belmont, CA: Wadsworth.

Lustig, M. W., & Koester, J. (2003). *Intercultural competence: Interpersonal communication across cultures* (4th ed.). New York: HarperCollins.

Lynch, L. (2000, April 6). Feeling powerless can be health hazard. *Healthscout.* www.healthscout.com/cgi-bin/WebObjects/Af?ap=43&id=93729.

Ma, K. (1996). *The modern Madame Butterfly: Fantasy and reality in Japanese cross-cultural relationships*. Rutland, VT: Charles E. Tuttle.

Mackey, R. A., Diemer, M. A., & O'Brien, B. A. (2000). Psychological intimacy in the lasting relationships of heterosexual and same-gender couples. *Sex Roles, 43*, 201–227.

MacLachlan, J. (1979). What people really think of fast talkers. *Psychology Today, 13*, 113–117.

Mahaffey, A. L., Bryan, A., & Hutchison, K. E. (2005, March). Using startle eye blink to measure the affective component of antigay bias. *Basic and Applied Social Psychology, 27*, 37–45.

Malandro, L. A., Barker, L., & Barker, D. A. (1989). *Nonverbal communication* (2nd ed.). New York: Random House.

Mallen, M. J., Day, S. X., & Green, M. A. (2003). Online versus face-to-face conversation: An examination of relational and discourse variables. *Psychotherapy: Theory, Research, Practice, Training, 40*, 155–163.

Mandese, J. (2006). When product placement goes too far. www.broadcastingcable.com (accessed March 30, 2006).

Manes, J., & Wolfson, N. (1981). The compliment formula. In F. Coulmas (Ed.), *Conversational routine* (pp. 115–132). The Hague: Mouton.

Mao, L. R. (1994). Beyond politeness theory: "Face" revisited and renewed. *Journal of Pragmatics, 21*, 451–486.

Marien, M. (1992, March 15). *Vital Speeches of the Day*, 340–344.

Marsh, P. (1988). *Eye to eye: How people interact*. Topside, MA: Salem House.

Marshall, E. (1983). *Eye language: Understanding the eloquent eye*. New York: New Trend.

Marshall, L. L., & Rose, P. (1987). Gender, stress and violence in the adult relationships of a sample of college students. *Journal of Social and Personal Relationships, 4*, 299–316.

Martin, G. N. (1998). Human electroencephalographic (EEG) response to olfactory stimulation: Two experiments using the aroma of food. *International Journal of Psychophysiology, 30*, 287–302.

Martin, M. M., & Anderson, C. M. (1993, December). Psychological and biological differences in touch avoidance. *Communication Research Reports, 10*, 141–147.

Martin, M. M., & Anderson, C. M. (1995). Roommate similarity: Are roommates who are similar in their communication traits more satisfied? *Communication Research Reports, 12*, 46–52.

Marwell, G., & Schmitt, D. R. (1967). Dimensions of compliance-gaining behavior: An empirical analysis. *Sociometry, 39*, 350–364.

Maslow, A. (1970). *Motivation and personality*. New York: HarperCollins.

Matsumoto, D. (1991). Cultural influences on facial expressions of emotion. *Southern Communication Journal, 56*, 128–137.

Matsumoto, D., & Kudoh, T. (1993). American–Japanese cultural differences in attributions of personality based on smiles. *Journal of Nonverbal Behavior, 17*, 231–243.

Maynard, H. E. (1963). How to become a better premise detective. *Public Relations Journal, 19*, 20–22.

McCarthy, M. (2003, January). Talking back: "Small" interactional response tokens in everyday conversation. *Research on Language and Social Interaction, 36*, 33–63.

McCroskey, J. C. (1970). Measures of communication-bound anxiety. *Communication Monographs, 37*, 269–273.

McCroskey, J. C. (1997). *An introduction to rhetorical communication* (7th ed.). Englewood Cliffs, NJ: Prentice-Hall.

McCroskey, J. C., & Wheeless, L. (1976). *Introduction to human communication*. Boston: Allyn & Bacon.

McDonald, E. J., McCabe, K., Yeh, M., Lau, A., Garland, A., & Hough, R. L. (2005, February). Cultural affiliation and self-esteem as predictors of internalizing symptoms among Mexican American adolescents. *Journal of Clinical Child and Adolescent Psychology, 34*, 163–171.

McGill, M. E. (1985). *The McGill report on male intimacy*. New York: Harper & Row.

McKerrow, R. E., Gronbeck, B. E., Ehninger, D., & Monroe, A. H. (2000). *Principles and Types of Speech Communication* (14th ed.). Boston: Allyn & Bacon.

McLaughlin, M. L. (1984). *Conversation: How talk is organized*. Newbury Park, CA: Sage.

McNamee, S., & Gergen, K. J. (Eds.). (1999). *Relational responsibility: Resources for sustainable dialogue*. Thousand Oaks, CA: Sage.

McNatt, D. B. (2001). Ancient Pygmalion joins contemporary management: A meta-analysis of the result. *Journal of Applied Psychology, 85*, 314–322.

Media Education Foundation (2006a). 20 ways to be a media activist. www.mediaed.org (accessed June 23, 2006).

Media Education Foundation (2006b). 10 reasons why media education matters. www.mediaed.org (accessed June 23, 2006).

Merton, R. K. (1957). *Social theory and social structure*. New York: Free Press.

Metts, S., & Planalp, S. (2002). Emotional communication. In M. L. Knapp & J. A. Daly (Eds.), *Handbook of Interpersonal Communication* (3rd ed., pp. 339–373). Thousand Oaks, CA: Sage.

Meyer, J. R. (1994). Effect of situational features on the likelihood of addressing face needs in requests. *Southern Communication Journal, 59*, 240–254.

Midooka, K. (1990). Characteristics of Japanese style communication. *Media Culture and Society, 12*, 47–49.

Miller, G. R., & Parks, M. R. (1982). Communication in dissolving relationships. In S. Duck (Ed.), *Personal relationships: Vol. 4. Dissolving personal relationships*. New York: Academic Press.

Miller, J. G. (1984). Culture and the development of everyday social explanation. *Journal of Personality and Social Psychology, 46*, 961–978.

Moghaddam, F. M., Taylor, D. M., & Wright, S. C. (1993). *Social psychology in cross-cultural perspective*. New York: W. H. Freeman.

Molloy, J. (1981). *Molloy's live for success*. New York: Bantam.

Monk, A., Fellas, E., & Ley, E. (2004, September–October). Rapport-building activities in corner shop interactions. *Behaviour & Information Technology, 23*, 301–305.

Montagu, A. (1971). *Touching: The human significance of the skin*. New York: Harper & Row.

Moon, D. G. (1966). Concepts of "culture": Implications for intercultural communication research. *Communication Quarterly, 44*, 70–84.

Moore, A., Masterson, J. T., Christophel, D. M., & Shea, K. A. (1996). College teacher immediacy and student ratings of instruction. *Communication Education, 45*, 29–39.

Morahan-Martin, J. & Schumacher, P. (2003, November). Loneliness and social uses of the Internet. *Computers in Human Behavior, 19*, 659–671.

Morris, D. (1977). *Manwatching: A field guide to human behavior*. New York: Abrams.

Motley, M. T. (1990a). On whether one can(not) not communicate: An examination via traditional communication postulates. *Western Journal of Speech Communication, 54*, 1–20.

Motley, M. T. (1990b). Communication as interaction: A reply to Beach and Bavelas. *Western Journal of Speech Communication, 54*, 613–623.

Mullen, B., Salas, E., & Driskell, J. (1989). Salience, motivation, and artifact as contributions to the relation between participation rate and leadership. *Journal of Experimental Social Psychology, 25*, 545–559.

Mullen, B., Tara, A., Salas, E., & Driskell, J. E. (1994). Group cohesiveness and quality of decision making: An interaction of tests of the groupthink hypothesis. *Small Group Research, 25*, 189–204.

Myers, S. A., & Johnson, A. D. (2003). Verbal aggression and liking in interpersonal relationships. *Communication Research Reports, 20*, 90–96.

Naifeh, S., & Smith, G. W. (1984). *Why can't men open up? Overcoming men's fear of intimacy*. New York: Clarkson N. Potter.

Napier, R. W., & Gershenfeld, M. K. (1989). *Groups: Theory and experience* (4th ed.). Boston: Houghton Mifflin.

Neff, K. D. & Harter, S. (2002, November). The authenticity of conflict resolutions among adult couples: Does women's other-oriented behavior reflect their true selves? *Sex Roles, 47*, 403–417.

Neimeyer, R. A., & Mitchell, K. A. (1988). Similarity and attraction: A longitudinal study. *Journal of Social and Personal Relationships, 5*, 131–148.

Nelson, P., & Pearson, J. (1996). *Confidence in public speaking* (6th ed.). Dubuque, IA: Brown & Benchmark.

Neugarten, B. (1979). Time, age, and the life cycle. *American Journal of Psychiatry, 136*, 887–894.

Neuliep, J. W., & Grohskopf, E. L. (2000). Uncertainty reduction and communication satisfaction during initial interaction: An initial test and replication of a new axiom. *Communication Reports, 13*, 67–77.

Neuliep, J. W., Chaudoir, M., & McCroskey, J. C. (2001). A cross-cultural comparison of ethnocentrism among Japanese and United States college students. *Communication Research Reports, 18*, 137–146.

Ng, S. H., & Bradac, J. J. (1993). *Power in language: Verbal communication and social influence*. Newbury Park, CA: Sage.

Nicholas, C. L. (2004, Winter). Gaydar: Eye-gaze as identity recognition among gay men and lesbians. *Sexuality and Culture: An Interdisciplinary Quarterly, 8*, 60–86.

Noble, B. P. (1994, August 14). The gender wars: Talking peace. *The New York Times*, p. 21.

Noller, P. (1993). Gender and emotional communication in marriage: Different cultures or differential social power? [Special issue: Emotional Communication, Culture, and Power.] *Journal of Language and Social Psychology, 12*, 132–152.

Northouse, P. G. (1997). *Leadership: Theory and practice*. Thousand Oaks, CA: Sage.

Nowak, K. L. (2003). Sex categorization in computer mediated communication (CMC): Exploring the Utopian promise. *Media Psychology, 5*, 83–103.

Ober, C., Weitkamp, L. R., Cox, N., Dytch, H., Kostyu, D., & Elias, S. (1997). *American Journal of Human Genetics, 61*, 494–496.

Oberg, K. (1960). Cultural shock: Adjustment to new cultural environments. *Practical Anthropology, 7*, 177–182.

Oetzel, J., Ting-Toomey, S., Masumoto, T., Yokochi, Y., Pan, X., Takai, J., & Wilcox, R. (2001). Face and facework in conflict: A cross-cultural comparison of China, Germany, Japan, and the United States. *Communication Monographs, 68*, 235–258.

Olson, E. (2006, April 6). Better not miss the buss. *The New York Times*, pp. G1–2.

Osborn, A. (1957). *Applied imagination* (Rev. ed.). New York: Scribners.

O'Sullivan, P. B., & Flanagin, A. J. (2003, March). Reconceptualizing 'flaming' and other problematic messages. *New Media and Society, 5*, 69–94.

O'Sullivan, P. B., Hunt, S. K., & Lippert, L. R. (2004, December). Mediated immediacy: A language of affiliation in a technological age. *Journal of Language and Social Psychology, 23*, 464–490.

Park, H. S., Levine, T. R., McCornack, S. A., Morrison, K., & Ferrara, M. (2002, June). How people really detect lies. *Communication Monographs, 69*, 144–157.

Park, W. W. (1990). A review of research on groupthink. *Journal of Behavioral Decision Making, 3*, 229–245.

Parks, M. R. (1995). Webs of influence in interpersonal relationships. In C. R. Berger & M. E. Burgoon (Eds.), *Communication and social influence processes* (pp. 155–178). East Lansing: Michigan State University Press.

Parks, M. R., & Floyd, K. (1996). Making friends in cyberspace. *Journal of Communication, 46*, 80–97.

Parks, M. R., & Roberts, L. D. (1998). "Making MOOsic": The development of personal relationships on line and a comparison to their off-line counterparts. *Journal of Social and Personal Relationships, 15*, 517–537.

Patton, B. R., Giffin, K., & Patton, E. N. (1989). *Decision-making group interaction* (3rd ed.). New York: HarperCollins.

Paul, A. M. (2001). Self-help: Shattering the myths. *Psychology Today, 34*, 60ff.

Pearson, J. C. (1993). *Communication in the family* (2nd ed.). New York: Harper & Row.

Pearson, J. C., & Spitzberg, B. H. (1990). *Interpersonal communication: Concepts, components, and contexts* (2nd ed.). Dubuque, IA: William C. Brown.

Pearson, J. C., West, R., & Turner, L. H. (1995). *Gender and communication* (3rd ed.). Dubuque, IA: William C. Brown.

Penfield, J. (Ed.). (1987). *Women and language in transition.* Albany, NY: State University of New York Press.

Pennebaker, J. W. (1991). *Opening up: The healing power of confiding in others.* New York: Morrow.

Petrocelli, W., & Repa, B. (1992). *Sexual harassment on the job.* Berkeley, CA: Nolo Press.

Petty, R. E., & Wegener, D. T. (1998). Attitude change: Multiple roles for persuasion variables. In D. T. Gilbert, S. T. Fiske, & G. Lindzey (Eds.), *The handbook of social psychology* (4th ed., Vol. 1, pp. 323–390). New York: McGraw-Hill.

Pittenger, R. E., Hockett, C. F., & Danehy, J. J. (1960). *The first five minutes.* Ithaca, NY: Paul Martineau.

Placencia, M. E. (2004, May). The online disinhibition effect. *Journal of Sociolinguistics, 8,* 215–245.

Porter, R. H., & Moore, J. D. (1981). Human kin recognition by olfactory cues. *Physiology and Behavior, 27,* 493–495.

Porter, S., Brit, A. R., Yuille, J. C., & Lehman, D. R. (2000, November). Negotiating false memories: Interviewer and rememberer characteristics relate to memory distortion. *Psychological Science, 11,* 507–510.

Postman, N., & Powers, S. (1992). *How to watch TV news.* New York: Penguin.

Pratkanis, A., & Aronson, E. (1991). *Age of propaganda: The everyday use and abuse of persuasion.* New York: W. H. Freeman.

Rainie, L., & Horrigan, J. (2005). A decade of adoption: How the Internet has woven itself into American life. Pew Internet & American Life Project. www.pewinternet.org/PPF/R/148/report_display.asp (accessed February 20, 2006).

Rainie, L., & Madden, M. (2006). Not looking for love: The state of romance in America. Pew Internet & American Life Project. www.pewinternet.org (accessed February 20, 2006).

Ramsey, S. J. (1981). The kinesics of femininity in Japanese women. *Language Sciences, 3,* 104–123.

Rancer, A. S., & Avtgis, T. A. (2006). *Argumentative and aggressive communication: Theory, research, and application.* Thousand Oaks, CA: Sage.

Rankin, P. (1929). *Listening ability.* Proceedings of the Ohio State Educational Conference's Ninth Annual Session.

Raven, R., Centers, C., & Rodrigues, A. (1975). The bases of conjugal power. In R. E. Cromwell & D. H. Olson (Eds.), *Power in families* (pp. 217–234). New York: Halsted Press.

Rich, A. L. (1974). *Interracial communication.* New York: Harper & Row.

Richards, I. A. (1951). Communication between men: The meaning of language. In Heinz von Foerster (Ed.), *Cybernetics: Transactions of the Eighth Conference.*

Richmond, V. P., Davis, L. M., Saylor, K., & McCroskey, J. C. (1984). Power strategies in organizations: Communication techniques and messages. *Human Communication Research, 11,* 85–108.

Richmond, V. P., & McCroskey, J. C. (1998). *Communication: Apprehension, avoidance, and effectiveness* (5th ed.). Needham Heights, MA: Allyn & Bacon.

Ridge, R. D., & Reber, J. S. (2002). "I think she's attracted to me": The effect of men's beliefs on women's behavior in a job interview scenario. *Basic and Applied Social Psychology, 24,* 1–14.

Riggio, R. E. (1987). *The charisma quotient.* New York: Dodd, Mead.

Roberts, W. (1987). *Leadership secrets of Attila the Hun.* New York: Warner.

Robinson, W. P. (1993). Lying in the public domain. *American Behavioral Scientist, 36,* 359–382.

Rockwell, S. C., & Singleton, L. (2002). The effects of computer anxiety and communication apprehension on the adoption and utilization of the Internet. *Electronic Journal of Communication, 12.* http://shadow/cios.org7979/journal\EJ\012\1\01212.html.

Rodman, G. (2001). *Making sense of media: An introduction to mass communication.* Boston: Allyn & Bacon.

Rogers, C. (1970). *Carl Rogers on encounter groups.* New York: Harrow Books.

Rogers, C., & Farson, R. (1981). Active listening. In J. DeVito (Ed.), *Communication: Concepts and processes* (3rd ed., pp. 137–147). Upper Saddle River, NJ: Prentice-Hall.

Rollman, J. B., Krug, K., & Parente, F. (2000). The chat room phenomenon: Reciprocal communication in cyberspace. *CyberPsychology and Behavior, 3,* 161–166.

Ronfeldt, H. M., Kimerling, R., & Arias, I. (1998, February). Satisfaction with relationship power and the perpetration of dating violence. *Journal of Marriage & Family, 60,* 70–78.

Rosen, E. (1998, October). Think like a shrink. *Psychology Today,* 54–69.

Rosenbaum, M. E. (1986). The repulsion hypothesis: On the non-development of relationships. *Journal of Personality and Social Psychology, 51,* 1156–1166.

Rosenthal, R., & Jacobson, L. (1968). *Pygmalion in the classroom.* New York: Holt, Rinehart & Winston.

Roth, P. L., Schleifer, L. L. F., & Switzer, F. S. (1995, May). Nominal group technique—an aid in implementing TQM. *The CPA Journal, 65,* 68–69.

Rubenstein, C. (1993, June 10). Fighting sexual harassment in schools. *The New York Times,* p. C8.

Rubin, R. B. (1985). The validity of the communication competency assessment instrument. *Communication Monographs, 52,* 173–185.

Rubin, R. B., & Martin, M. M. (1994). Development of a measure of interpersonal communication competence. *Communication Research Reports, 11,* 33–44.

Rubin, R. B., & Martin, M. M. (1998). Interpersonal communication motives. In J. C. McCroskey, J. A. Daly, M. M. Martin, & M. J. Beatty (Eds.), *Communication and Personality: Trait Perspectives* (pp. 287–307). Cresskill, NJ: Hampton Press.

Rubin, R. B., Fernandez-Collado, C., & Hernandez-Sampieri, R. (1992). A cross-cultural examination of interpersonal communication motives in Mexico and the United States. *International Journal of Intercultural Relations, 16,* 145–157.

Rubin, R. B., Pearse, E. M., & Barbato, C. A. (1988). Conceptualization and measurement of interpersonal communication motives. *Human Communication Research, 14,* 602–628.

Rubin, Z. (1973). *Liking and loving: An invitation to social psychology.* New York: Holt, Rinehart & Winston.

Rundquist, S. (1992). Indirectness: A gender study of Fluting Grice's Maxims. *Journal of Pragmatics, 18,* 431–449.

Ruscher, J. B. (2001). *Prejudiced communication: A social psychological perspective.* NE: Guilford Press.

Samovar, L. A., & Porter, R. E. (Eds.). (1991). *Communication between cultures.* Belmont, CA: Wadsworth.

Sanders, J. A., Wiseman, R. L., & Matz, S. I. (1991). Uncertainty reduction in acquaintance relationships in Ghana and the United States. In S. Ting-Toomey & F. Korzenny (Eds.), *Cross-cultural interpersonal communication* (pp. 79–98). Thousand Oaks, CA: Sage.

Scandura, T. (1992). Mentorship and career mobility: An empirical investigation. *Journal of Organizational Behavior, 13,* 169–174.

Schafer, M., & Crichlow, S. (1996, September). Antecedents of groupthink. *Journal of Conflict Resolution, 40,* 415–435.

Scherer, K. R. (1986). Vocal affect expression. *Psychological Bulletin, 99,* 143–165.

Schiller, G. (2006). In risky move, newscasts adopt product placements. http://mediachannel.org/blog/book/print/3705 (accessed March 30, 2006).

Schnoor, L. G. (Ed.). (1997). *Winning orations of the interstate oratorical association.* Mankato, MN: Interstate Oratorical Association.

Schnoor, L. G. (Ed.). (1999). *Winning orations of the interstate oratorical association.* Mankato, MN: Interstate Oratorical Association.

Schnoor, L. G. (Ed.). (2000). *Winning orations of the interstate oratorical association.* Mankato, MN: Interstate Oratorical Association.

Schultz, B. G. (1996). *Communicating in the small group: Theory and practice* (2nd ed.). New York: HarperCollins.

Schwartz, M., and the Task Force on Bias-Free Language of the Association of American University Presses. (1995). *Guidelines for bias-free writing.* Bloomington: Indiana University Press.

Scott, C. R., & Timmerman, C. E. (2005, December). Relating computer, communication, and computer-mediated communication apprehensions to new communication technology in the workplace. *Communication Research, 32,* 683–725.

Seiter, J. S. & Sandry, A. (2003, Fall). Pierced for success?: The effects of ear and nose piercing on perceptions of job candidates' credibility, attractiveness, and hirability. *Communication Research Reports, 20,* 287–298.

Sethna, B., Barnes, C. C., Brust, M., & Kay, L. (1999, July–August). E-mail communications in colleges and universities: Are they private? *Journal of Education for Business, 74,* 347–350.

Shannon, J. (1987). Don't smile when you say that. *Executive Female, 10,* 33, 43.

Sharkey, W. F., & Stafford, L. (1990). Turn-taking resources employed by congenitally blind conversers. *Communication Studies, 41,* 161–182.

Shechtman, Z., Hiradin, A., & Zina, S. (2003, Spring). The impact of culture on group behavior: A comparison of three ethnic groups. *Journal of Counseling and Development, 81,* 208–216.

Shiu, E., & Lenhart, A. (2004). Pew Internet and American life project report: Instant Messaging. www.pewinternet.org/PPF/r/133/report_display.asp (accessed July 29, 2005).

Shuter, R. (1990). The centrality of culture. *Southern Communication Journal, 55,* 237–249.

Siavelis, R. L., & Lamke, L. K. (1992). Instrumentalness and expressiveness: Predictors of heterosexual relationship satisfaction. *Sex Roles, 26,* 149–159.

Siegert, J. R., & Stamp, G. H. (1994). "Our First Big Fight" as a milestone in the development of close relationships. *Communication Monographs, 61,* 345–360.

Signorile, M. (1993). *Queer in America: Sex, the media, and the closets of power.* New York: Random House.

Silverman, T. (2001). Expanding community: The Internet and relational theory. *Community, Work and Family, 4,* 231–237.

Simpson, J. A. (1987). The dissolution of romantic relationships: Factors involved in relationship stability and emotional distress. *Journal of Personality and Social Psychology, 53,* 683–692.

Singelis, T. M. (1994). The measurement of independent and interdependent self-construals. *Personality and Social Psychology Bulletin, 20,* 580–591.

Singh, N., & Pereira, A. (2005). *The culturally customized web site.* Oxford, UK., Elsevier Butterworth-Heinemann.

Slade, M. (1995, February 19). We forgot to write a headline. But it's not our fault. *The New York Times,* p. 5.

Smith, M. H. (2003, February). Body adornment: Know the limits. *Nursing Management, 34,* 22–23.

Smoreda, Z., & Licoppe, C. (2000). Gender-specific use of the domestic telephone. *Social Psychology Quarterly, 63,* 238–252.

Snyder, M. (1992, February). A gender-informed model of couple and family therapy: Relationship enhancement therapy. *Contemporary Family Therapy: An International Journal, 14,* 15–31.

Solomon, G. B., Striegel, D. A., Eliot, J. F., Heon, S. N., et al. (1996). The self-fulfilling prophecy in college basketball: Implications for effective coaching. *Journal of Applied Sport Psychology, 8,* 44–59.

Song, I., LaRose, R., Eastin, M. S., & Lin, C. A. (2004, August). Internet gratifications, Internet addiction: On the uses and abuses of new media. *CyberPsychology & Behavior, 7,* 384–394.

Spitzberg, B. H. (1991). Intercultural communication competence. In Larry A. Samovar & R. E. Porter (Eds.), *Intercultural communication: A reader* (pp. 353–365). Belmont, CA: Wadsworth.

Spitzberg, B. H., & Cupach, W. R. (1984). *Interpersonal communication competence.* Beverly Hills, CA: Sage.

Spitzberg, B. H., & Cupach, W. R. (1989). *Handbook of interpersonal competence research.* New York: Springer.

Spitzberg, B. H., & Cupach, W. R. (2002). Interpersonal skills. In M. L. Knapp & J. A. Daly (Eds.), *Handbook of interpersonal communication* (3rd ed., pp. 564–611). Thousand Oaks, CA: Sage.

Spitzberg, B. H., & Hecht, M. L. (1984). A component model of relational competence. *Human Communication Research, 10,* 575–599.

Sprecher, S. (1987). The effects of self-disclosure given and received on affection for an intimate partner and stability of the relationship. *Journal of Social and Personal Relationships, 4,* 115–127.

Sprecher, S., & Metts, S. (1989). Development of the "romantic beliefs scale" and examination of the effects of gender and gender-role orientation. *Journal of Social and Personal Relationships, 6,* 387–411.

Starkey, J. A. (1996). *Multicultural communication strategies.* Chicago, IL: JAMS Publishing.

Steil, L. K., Barker, L. L., & Watson, K. W. (1983). *Effective listening: Key to your success.* Reading, MA: Addison-Wesley.

Stein, M. M. & Bowen, M. (2003, Summer). Building a customer satisfaction system: Effective listening when the customer speaks. *Journal of Organizational Excellence, 22,* 23–34.

Steiner, C. (1981). *The other side of power.* New York: Grove.

Stephan, W. G., & Stephan, C. W. (1992). *Improving intergroup relations.* Thousand Oaks, CA: Sage.

Stephan, W. G., & Stephan, C. W. (1996). *Intergroup relations.* Dubuque, IA: Brown & Benchmark.

Stern, L. (2007). *What every student should know about avoiding plagiarism.* Boston: Pearson Education.

Stewart, L. P., Cooper, P. J., Stewart, A. D., with Friedley, S. A. (2003). *Communication and gender* (4th ed.). Boston: Allyn & Bacon.

Stewart, S. (1996). Stop searching and start finding. *The Net, 2,* 34–40.

Strassberg, D. S., & Holty, S. (2003, June). An experimental study of women's Internet personal ads. *Archives of Sexual Behavior, 32,* 253–260.

Strecker, I. (1993). Cultural variations in the concept of "face." *Multilingua, 12,* 119–141.

Strom, D. (2006, April 5). I.M. generation is changing the way business talks. *The New York Times,* P. D4.

Suler, J. (2004, June). The online disinhibition effect. *CyberPsychology and Behavior, 7,* 321–326.

Tang, T. L., & Butler, E. A. (1997, Summer). Attributions of quality circles' problem-solving failure: Differences among management, supporting staff, and quality circle members. *Public Personnel Management, 26,* 203–225.

Tannen, D. (1990). *You just don't understand: Women and men in conversation.* New York: Morrow.

Tannen, D. (1994a). *Gender and discourse.* New York: Oxford University Press.

Tannen, D. (1994b). *Talking from 9 to 5: How women's and men's conversational styles affect who gets heard, who gets credit, and what gets done at work.* New York: Morrow.

Tannen, D. (2006). *You're wearing that? Understanding mothers and daughters in conversation.* New York: Random House.

Tardiff, T. (2001). Learning to say "no" in Chinese. *Early Education and Development, 12,* 303–323.

Tersine, R. J., & Riggs, W. E. (1980). The Delphi technique: A long-range planning tool. In S. Ferguson & S. D. Ferguson (Eds.), *Intercom: Readings in organizational communication* (pp. 366–373). Rochelle Park, NJ: Hayden Book.

Thibaut, J. W., & Kelley, H. H. (1959). *The social psychology of groups.* New York: Wiley.

Thomlison, D. (1982). *Toward interpersonal dialogue.* New York: Longman.

Thorne, B., Kramarae, C., & Henley, N. (Eds.). (1983). *Language, gender and society.* Rowley, MA: Newbury House.

Timmerman, L. J. (2002). Comparing the production of power in language on the basis of sex. In M. Allen & R. W. Preiss (Eds.), *Interpersonal communication research: Advances through meta-analysis* (pp. 73–88). Mahwah, NJ: Erlbaum.

Ting-Toomey, S. (1981). Ethnic identity and close friendship in Chinese-American college students. *International Journal of Intercultural Relations, 5,* 383–406.

Ting-Toomey, S. (1985). Toward a theory of conflict and culture. *International and Intercultural Communication Annual, 9,* 71–86.

Tinsley, C. H., & Brett, J. M. (2001). Managing workplace conflict in the United States and Hong Kong. *Organizational Behavior and Human Decision Processes, 85,* 360–381.

Tolhuizen, J. H. (1989). Communication strategies for intensifying dating relationships: Identification, use, and structure. *Journal of Social and Personal Relationships, 6,* 413–434.

Trager, G. L. (1958). Paralanguage: A first approximation. *Studies in Linguistics, 13,* 1–12.

Trager, G. L. (1961). The typology of paralanguage. *Anthropological Linguistics, 3,* 17–21.

Traxler, A. J. (1980). *Let's get gerontologized: Developing a sensitivity to aging.* Springfield, IL: Illinois Department of Aging.

Vainiomaki, T. (2004). Silence as a cultural sign. *Semiotica, 150,* 347–361.

Veenendall, T. L., & Feinstein, M. C. (1995). *Let's talk about relationships: Cases in study* (2nd ed.). Prospect Heights, IL: Waveland Press.

Victor, D. (1992). *International business communication.* New York: HarperCollins.

Wade, N. (2002, January 22). Scent of a man is linked to a woman's selection. *The New York Times,* p. F2.

Wallace, K. (1955). An ethical basis of communication. *Communication Education, 4,* 1–9.

Watzlawick, P. (1977). *How real is real? Confusion, disinformation, communication: An anecdotal introduction to communications theory.* New York: Vintage.

Watzlawick, P. (1978). *The language of change: Elements of therapeutic communication.* New York: Basic Books.

Watzlawick, P., Beavin, J., & Jackson, D. D. (1967). *Pragmatics of human communication: A study of interactional patterns, pathologies, and paradoxes.* New York: Norton.

Weathers, M. D., Frank, E. M., & Spell, L. A. (2002). Differences in the communication of affect: Members of the same race versus members of a different race. *Journal of Black Psychology, 28,* 66–77.

Weinberg, H. L. (1959). *Levels of knowing and existence.* New York: Harper & Row.

Weinstein, E. A., & Deutschberger, P. (1963). Some dimensions of altercasting. *Sociometry, 26,* 454–466.

Weitzman, P. F. (2001). Young adult women resolving interpersonal conflicts. *Journal of Adult Development, 8,* 61–67.

Weitzman, P. F., & Weitzman, E. A. (2000). Interpersonal negotiation strategies in a sample of older women. *Journal of Clinical Geropsychology, 6,* 41–51.

Wennerstrom, A., & Siegel, A. F. (2003, September). Keeping the floor in multiparty conversation: Intonation, syntax, and pause. *Discourse Processes, 36,* 77–107.

Westwood, R. I., Tang, F. F., & Kirkbride, P. S. (1992). Chinese conflict behavior: Cultural antecedents and behavioral consequences. *Organizational Development Journal, 10,* 13–19.

Wetzel, P. J. (1988). Are "powerless" communication strategies the Japanese norm? *Language in Society, 17,* 555–564.

Wheeless, L. R., & Grotz, J. (1977). The measurement of trust and its relationship to self-disclosure. *Human Communication Research, 3,* 250–257.

Whitty, M., & Gavin, J. (2001). Age/sex/location: Uncovering the social cues in the development of online relationships. *Cyber-Psychology and Behavior, 4,* 623–630.

Wiemann, J. M. (1977). Explication and test of a model of communicative competence. *Human Communication Research, 3,* 195–213.

Wiemann, J. M., & Backlund, P. (1980). Current theory and research in communicative competence. *Review of Educational Research, 50,* 185–199.

Williamson, K., Wright, S., Schauder, D., & Bow, A. (2001, October). The Internet for the blind and visually impaired. *Journal of Computer Mediated Communication, 7* (1).

Wilson, J. H., & Taylor, K. W. (2001). Professor immediacy as behaviors associated with liking students. *Teaching of Psychology, 28,* 136–138.

Winquist, L. A., Mohr, C. D., & Kenny, D. A. (1998). The female positivity effect in the perception of others. *Journal of Research in Personality, 32,* 370–388.

Witcher, S. K. (1999, August 9–15). Chief executives in Asia find listening difficult. *Asian Wall Street Journal Weekly,* 11.

Witt, P. L., & Wheeless, L. R. (2001). An experimental study of teachers' verbal and nonverbal immediacy and students' affective and cognitive learning. *Communication Education, 50,* 327–342.

Wolfson, N. (1988). The bulge: A theory of speech behaviour and social distance. In J. Fine (Ed.), *Second language discourse: A textbook of current research* (pp. 21–38). Norwood, NJ: Ablex.

Wolpe, J. (1957). *Psychotherapy by reciprocal inhibition.* Stanford, CA: Stanford University Press.

Wolvin, A. D., & Coakley, C. G. (1996). *Listening.* Dubuque, IA: Wm. C. Brown.

Won-Doornink, M. (1985). Self-disclosure and reciprocity in conversation: A cross-national study. *Social Psychology Quarterly, 48*, 97–107.

Won-Doornink, M. (1991). Self-disclosure and reciprocity in South Korean and U.S. male dyads. In Stella Ting-Toomey & Felipe Korzenny (Eds.), *Cross-cultural interpersonal communication* (pp. 116–131). Newbury Park, CA: Sage.

Wood, J. T. (1994). *Gendered lives: Communication, gender, and culture.* Belmont, CA: Wadsworth.

Wrench, J. S., & McCroskey, J. C. (2003). A communibiological examination of ethnocentrism and homophobia. *Communication Research Reports, 20*, 24–33.

Yau-fair Ho, D., Chan, S. F., Peng, S., & Ng, A. K. (2001). The dialogical self: Converging East–West constructions. *Culture and Psychology, 7*, 393–408.

Zaleski, Z., Cycon, A., & Kurc, A. (2001). Future time perspective and subjective well-being in adolescent samples. In P. Schmuck & K. M. Sheldon (Eds.), *Life goals and well-being: Towards a positive psychology of human striving* (pp. 58–67). Cambridge, MA: Hogrefe & Huber.

Zimmer, T. A. (1986). Premarital anxieties. *Journal of Social and Personal Relationships, 3*, 149–159.

Zornoza, A., Ripoll, P., & Peiró, J. M. (2002, October). Conflict management in groups that work in two different communication contexts: Face-to-face and computer-mediated communication. *Small Group Research, 33*, 481–508.

Zuckerman, M., Klorman, R., Larrance, D. T., & Spiegel, N. H. (1981). Facial, autonomic, and subjective components of emotion: The facial feedback hypothesis versus the externalizer–internalizer distinction. *Journal of Personality and Social Psychology, 41*, 929–944.

Zunin, L. M., & Zunin, N. B. (1972). *Contact: The first four minutes.* Los Angeles, CA: Nash.

# Index

*Note:* Italicized letters *f* and *t* following page numbers indicate figures and tables, respectively

Conflict (*continued*)
collectivist cultures and, 163
content, 161
control and, 169
culture and, 162–163, 170
defensiveness in, 168
empathy during, 171
ethics and, 173
evaluation and, 169
face-detracting strategy in, 170–171
face-enhancing strategy in, 170–171
force in, 168
gender and, 162–163
gunnysacking and, 172
individualist cultures and, 163
listening to messages in, 172
lose-lose situations in, 164–165
management of, 166–177
manipulation and, 169
negative aspects of, 162
neutrality and, 169
nonnegotiation and, 168
online, 160–161
open expression in, 171
positive aspects of, 162
positiveness and, 169
present focus and, 172
principles of, 161–166, 164*f*
provisionalism and, 170
relationship, 161
resolution of, 170
silencers in, 171
in small groups, 202, 210–211
spontaneity and, 169
steamrolling and, 168
strategy and, 169
styles of, 164–166, 164*f*
superiority and, 169
supportiveness in, 168
verbal aggressiveness and, 172–174, 176–177
violence in, 168
win-lose situations in, 164–165
win-win situations in, 165, 166
Connotation, 78
Consensus, 194
Contact stage of interpersonal relationships, 138–139, 139*f*
Content conflict, 161
Content dimension of communication, 18, 19
Content messages, 70
Context of communication, 6–7, 6*f*, 12*t*
Contrast rule of organization, 46
Control
conflict and, 169
of thinking hat, 193
Conversation, 131–138, 133*t*, 136*f*. *See also* Language; Listening; Verbal messages
business stage of, 132–133
closing stage of, 133–134
feedback stage of, 133
feedforward stage of, 132
immediacy in, 137–138
listener cues in, 135–136
metacommunication and, 135
negativeness in, 145, 147

opening stage of, 132, 134
positiveness in, 145
principles of, 134–138, 136*f*
speaker cues in, 135
speech disorders and, 133*t*
turn-taking in, 135–136, 135*f*
Cooperation, 80
Corrective self-disclosure, 42
Creative new idea hat, 193
Credentialling, 63
Credibility
appeals to, 327–330, 328*t*
culture and, 327
Critical listening, 68–69
Critical thinking, 14, 15*f*
avoiding fallacies, 95–97, 202–204, 235, 275, 321, 328
distinguishing facts from inferences, 94–95
logical appeals, 321–323
new perspectives, 52, 202–203, 288
problem solving, 192–196
Critical-thinking-hats technique, 193
Criticism, 115
culture and, 278–279, 281
ethics of, 278
listening to, 276
of public speaking, 273–279, 275*t*
Cues
backchanneling, 66, 136
to emotion, 114
listening, 72, 135–136
speaker, 135
turn-denying, 136, 136*f*
turn-maintaining, 135, 136*f*
turn-requesting, 136, 136*f*
turn-taking, 135–136, 135*f*
turn-yielding, 135, 136*f*
Cultivation theory of media, 167
Culture. *See* Intercultural communication
Culture. *See also* Intercultural communication
and audience analysis, 227
and conflict, 162–163, 164, 171
defined, 22
dimensions of, 23–24
and emblems, 104, 121–122
and ethnic identity, 25–26
and ethnocentrism, 25–28
and facial movement, 122
and feedback, 72
and gestures, 121–11
high- and low-context, 186–187, 221–222, 330–331
identifiers, 90–92
importance of, 22–23
and individual vs. collective orientations, 212–213, 330
and influence on communication, 80–82
and listening, 71–72
and meaning of colors, 122–123
and membership and leadership, 212
and nonverbal behaviors, 72
and persuasion, 330
and power distances, 213–214
and public speaking, 221–222, 223–224
and relationships, 151
and self disclosure, 38

Motivations for self-disclosure, 42
Movement
    facial, 105–108
    nonverbal messages of, 103–104, 105t
    in public speaking, 272–273, 273t
Multiple definition pattern organization, 247

Name calling fallacy, 321t, 328t
Narratives in informative speech, 288–289
Needs
    hierarchy of, 324–327, 326f
    motivated sequence speeches and, 244
Negation, defining by, 292–293
Negative argument hat, 193
Negativity
    computer-mediated communication and, 194
    conflict and, 162
    in conversation, 145, 147
    in relationships, 141
Neutrality in conflict, 169
News items, 224
News sources, 231–232
Noise
    in communication, 6f, 11, 13
    in computer-mediated communication, 73
Nominal group, 194–195
Nonallness orientation, 94
Nonjudgmental listening, 68–69
Nonnegotiation in conflict, 168
Nonverbal communication, 70, 101–125
    adaptors as, 104, 105t
    affect displays as, 104, 105t
    age and, 114
    artifactual, 110–113
    body adornment and, 111–112
    body appearance and, 105
    body movements and, 103–104, 105t
    channels of, 103–120, 105t, 106t, 109t
    clothing and, 111, 112
    color and, 111, 122, 123t
    culture and, 72, 120–125, 121f, 123t, 125t
    deception and, 103
    emblems as, 104, 105t
    emotion and, 103, 104, 105t
    eye communication and, 107–108
    facial movements and, 105–108, 122
    forming impressions based on, 102
    functions of, 101–103
    gender and, 114, 121
    illustrators as, 104, 105t
    influence and, 103
    integration of with verbal messages, 101–102
    listening and, 120
    messages of, 8, 13t
    olfactory, 112–113
    paralanguage and, 114–116, 123–124
    praise and criticism and, 115
    regulators as, 104, 105t
    relationships and, 102–103
    silence and, 116–117
    space decoration and, 112, 113
    spatial distance and, 108–110, 109t
    territoriality and, 109–110
    time and, 117–120, 124–125, 125t
    touch and, 113–114, 122–123
Nonverbal messages, 8, 13t
Norms, small group, 182, 185–186
Notes in public speaking, 273
Nourishing people, 36
Noxious people, 36

Object-adaptors, 104
Objective listening, 68
Objective view of ethics, 16
Offensive listening, 68
Olfactics, 112–113
Open expression in conflict, 171
Opening stage
    of conversation, 132, 134
    of small groups, 182–183, 183f
Open-mindedness in small groups, 202–203
Open self, 34–35, 34f
Operations, defining by, 293
Opinion seekers, 200
Organization
    charts for, 297f
    of perception, 45–47, 45f
    of speeches, 241–248, 307, 308–309, 310–311, 332–337
Outlines for speeches, 261–267
Overattribution, 53
Overload, information, 8–9

Panel, 183–184, 184f
Paralanguage, 114–116, 123–124
Paraphrasing, 63
    active listening and, 71
Parasocial relationships, 147
Participating style of leadership, 206f, 207
Pauses in public speaking, 271–272
Peaceful relations, 81
People in informative speech, 295
Perception, 44–56, 45f
    accuracy of, 49
    analysis of, 54
    attribution and, 52–54
    checking of, 54–55
    contrast rule of organization and, 46
    culture and, 50, 55–56
    defined, 44
    evaluation of, 45f, 47
    fundamental attribution error and, 53–54
    implicit personality theory and, 49–50
    increasing accuracy of, 54–56
    interpretation of, 45f, 47
    listening to others', 53
    memory in, 45f, 47–48
    mind reading and, 54–55
    organization of, 45–47, 45f
    overattribution and, 53
    primacy-recency and, 51
    processes of, 49–54
    proximity rule of organization and, 45
    recall of, 45f, 48
    reducing uncertainty of, 55–56

# Credits

**Text Credits**

Pages 26–27: Ethnocentrism test: This test was taken from James W. Neuliep, Michelle Chadoir, and James McCroskey (2001). A cross-cultural comparison of ethnocentrism among Japanese and United States college students. *Communication Research Reports 18* (Spring): 137–146. Used by permission of Eastern Communication Association.

Page 34: From Joseph Luft, *Group Processes: An Introduction to Group Dynamics*, 3/e. Copyright © 1984 by The McGraw Hill Companies, Inc. Reprinted with permission of the publisher.

Pages 143–145: Test Yourself: What Kind of Lover Are You? From "A Relationship-Specific Version of the Love Attitudes Scale" by C. Hendrick and S. Hendrick. Copyright © 1990 Select Press, *Journal of Social Behavior and Personality*, 5, 1990. Reprinted by permission.

Pages 173–174: Verbal Aggressiveness Test. Reprinted with permission from "How Verbally Aggressive Are You?" by Dominic Infante & C. J. Wigley, *Communication Monographs*, *53* (1986). Copyright © 1986 by Taylor & Francis Ltd. http://www.tandf.co.uk/journals.

Pages 174–176: Argumentative Scale. This scale was developed by Dominic Infante and Andrew Rancer and appears in Dominic Infante and Andrew Rancer, "A Conceptualization and Measure of Argumentativeness" in *Journal of Personality Assessment 46* (1982), pp. 72–80. Reprinted with permission of Lawrence Erlbaum and the authors.

Page 188: Test Yourself: How Apprehensive Are You in Group Discussions? From *An Introduction to Rhetorical Communication*, 7th ed., by James C. McCroskey. Copyright © 1997 by Allyn & Bacon. Reprinted by permission.

Pages 219: Test Yourself: How Apprehensive Are You About Public Speaking? Adapted from *An Introduction to Rhetorical Communication*, 7th ed., by James McCroskey. Copyright © 1997 by Allyn & Bacon. Reprinted by permission.

Pages 285–286: Adapted from Michael Hecht (1978), "The Conceptualization and Measurement of Interpersonal Communication Satisfaction," *Human Communication Research*, 4, 253–264, and is used by permission of the author and International Communication Association.

Pages 312–315: "Controlling the Weather: Moshe Alamaro's Plan for Hurricane Mitigation." Reprinted with permission of Jillian Collum.

Pages 326: From Abraham Maslow, *Motivation and Personality*. Copyright © 1970. Reprinted by permission of Prentice-Hall, Inc., Upper Saddle River, NJ.

Pages 337–340: "The Merchants of Death." Reprinted with permission of Andrew Farmer.

**Photo Credits**

Page 1: AP/Wide World Photos; 21, © Bill Bachman/The Image Works; 22, © Royalty-Free/CORBIS; 23, © Craig Lovell/CORBIS; 24, © Robert Harding World Imagery/CORBIS; 31, © Dinodia/The Image Work; 35, © Gary Conner/PhotoEdit; 41, © Mark Antman/The Image Works; 46, © Bob Daemmrich/The Image Works; 60, © Stuart Cohen/Getty Images; 61, © Steven Rubin/The Image Works; 68, © Paul Barton/CORBIS; 71, © Esbin-Anderson/The Image Works; 77, © Doug Menuez/Getty Images; 80, © Lara Jo Regan/Getty Images; 84, © Lucienne Pashley/Getty Images; 95, © Ajax/zefa/CORBIS; 100, © Peter Correz/Getty Images; 104, © Royalty-Free/CORBIS; 108, © Kevin Radford/Superstock; 122, © Davie Simson/Stock Boston; 124, © Tom Stewart/CORBIS; 129, © Esbin-Anderson/The Image Works; 135, © Artiga Photo/CORBIS; 137, © Christopher Bissel/Getty Images; 143, Bruce Ayers/Getty Images; 152, © Grace/zefa/CORBIS; 159, © Ryan McVay/Getty Images; 161, © Myrleen Ferguson Cate/PhotoEdit; 169, AP/Wide World Photos; 172, © Bob Daemmrich/The Image Works; 175, © Richard Lord/The Image Works; 180, © PhotoAlto/SuperStock; 181, © Heinz-Peter Bader/Reuters/CORBIS; 186, © Spencer Grant/PhotoEdit; 189, © Bill Lai/The Image Works; 194, © Charles Gupton/Getty Images; 199, © Purestock/SuperStock; 202, © Dan Bosler/Getty Images; 208, © Frank Herholdt/Getty Images; 209, © Bob Daemmrich/Stock Boston; 212, © Mark Richards/PhotoEdit; 217, © Michael Newman/PhotoEdit; 230, © Image Source/SuperStock; 232, © Bob Daemmrich/The Image Works; 244, © Blend Images/SuperStock; 251, © Dana White/PhotoEdit; 255, © Jonathan Nourok/PhotoEdit; 272, © Charles Gupton/CORBIS; 277, © Tom Stewart/zefa/CORBIS; 284, © Royalty-Free/CORBIS; 288, © Joseph Nettis/Stock Boston; 292, 294, © David Young-Wolff/PhotoEdit; 317, © Jose Luis Pelaez, Inc./CORBIS; 320, © BananaStock/SuperStock; 333, © Colin Young-Wolff/PhotoEdit; 335, © Bill E. Barnes/Stock Boston.